FROM STATE TO MARKETS

FROM STATE TO MARKETS

Journey of the Jamaican Economy

Cezley I. Sampson

Foreword by
The Most Honourable P.J. Patterson

IAN RANDLE PUBLISHERS
Kingston • Miami

First published in Jamaica, 2023 by
Ian Randle Publishers
16 Herb McKenley Drive
Box 686
Kingston 6
www.ianrandlepublishers.com

National Library of Jamaica Cataloguing-In-Publication Data

Name: Sampson, Cezley I., author.
Title: From state to markets : journey of the Jamaican economy / Cezley I. Sampson; foreword by The Most Honourable P. J. Patterson.
Description: Kingston, Jamaica : Ian Randle Publishers, 2023. | Includes bibliographical references and index.
Identifier: ISBN 9789768286871 (pbk). ISBN 9789768286901 (hbk).
Subjects: LCSH: Jamaica – Economic conditions – 20th century. | Jamaica – Economic conditions – 21st century. | Jamaica – Economic policy. | Economic development – Jamaica. | Free trade – Jamaica. | Structural adjustment (Economic policy).
Classification: DDC 338.97292 -- dc23.

Cover and Book Design by Ian Randle Publishers
Printed and Bound in the United States of America

Contents

PART 3. Preparing Jamaica for a Market Economy

PART 4. Industry Liberalisation: Six Case Studies of Sector Privatisation

List of Figures

List of Boxes & Tables

Foreword

The Most Hon. P. J. Patterson, ON, OCC, OE, KC
former Prime Minister of Jamaica

The task of writing an account of the development and current status of the Jamaican Public Service and its interrelationship with the management of the country's economy over a 350-year span is both a monumental and courageous undertaking. Cezley Sampson's magisterial work titled ***From State to Markets: Journey of the Jamaican Economy*** aptly describes such an undertaking.

It is monumental because of the scope, historical span, and complexity of the project, and courageous because, to my certain knowledge, this has never been previously attempted by one person in a single body of work.

And who better to take on this assignment than Cezley Sampson? I write with some knowledge and authority, having had a personal and professional relationship with the author for close to forty years and particularly during the period from 1985 to 2007, when in holding various government ministerial portfolios (1991–2007) and later as prime minister, I had the benefit of his expertise as special advisor, during which he was conceptualiser and administrator of some of the most innovative and far-reaching institutions of Jamaica's public sector and public enterprises.

The period 1991–2007 saw major institution-building, one of the most comprehensive ever undertaken by a Jamaican administration since Sir John Peter Grant, colonial governor from 1866 to 1874. During this period, I had the honour first as deputy prime minister and then as prime minister for four consecutive terms. In this period, the public sector's role in facilitating economic development was radically redefined, and a set of new institutions: the Executive Agency, the Office of the Cabinet Secretary, The Fair Competition Commission, The Financial Services Commission the National Planning Council, etc., were introduced **(From the author's Introduction).** The author was not only front and centre in all the above, but he was also a key player in several of the privatisation transactions, such as the electricity sector/JPSCo; urban public passenger transport/JOS, the two international airports: Norman Manley and Sangster, and the telecommunication industry/TOJ.

Dr Sampson has brought to this project a background and qualifications second to none – one who was the first Jamaican to receive formal training in management from the UK when this was not even considered a subject for academic pursuit. He then completed his doctorate in public affairs economics and has since authored several academic papers and management consultancy reports for international organisations, such as the World Bank, IADB, and DFID.

Like the quintessential technocrat/public servant/manager he was on the job, Sampson has displayed his vast knowledge and practical experience in producing an even-handed descriptive and unbiased account of the transition of the Jamaican economy *From State to Markets*. If that was not enough, what is most impressive about this work is the fact that he has not asked the reader to take his word as gospel but has backed up virtually every assertion with references, quotations, statistics, tables, and charts from official, as well as authoritative sources gleaned from impeccable research and broad consultation with experts as identified in the acknowledgements section of the work. Moreover, he has added insights gained from over forty years in the design and implementation of public sector and public enterprise policies, utility and financial sector regulations, and institution-building, as well as the privatisation of key sectors of the national economy.

The author is to be commended for what can only be described as a labour of love. He has joined a small and elite group of former public servants and retired executives in the private sector and the professions and political leaders who have taken the time and made the effort to compile their experiences and knowledge for later generations. This should guide important processes and positions that form the basis of economic development policies and governance and organisational structures on which the Jamaican society can move forward.

For example, the in-depth case studies the of six core sectors of the national economy go beyond a mere focus on their privatisation to provide potted histories of the evolution of those sectors, not readily available or accessible from any single source.

In that regard, ***From State to Markets: Journey of the Jamaican Economy*** is to be welcomed and endorsed for use as an indispensable reference source by Jamaican governments present and in the future. The book will assist their advisors and our vast army of public servants in formulating policies and crafting regulations for their implementation. It is equally important for private sector leaders and their companies, especially those in sectors that have been the beneficiaries of privatisation and the creation of a competitive environment, to use this medium to educate themselves on the economic policy changes that account for where they are today. It is also an encyclopaedic reference point for teachers, young scholars pursuing future graduate work, and an authoritative source of material for students.

May 2023

Preface

Jamaicans need to understand the history of our society and where we are coming from to determine the future direction of our country. Unfortunately, Jamaican history has, until recently, been largely written by outsiders and/or by a small elite establishment that considered most Africans and Black Jamaicans as naturally inferior.

This book has been written and is being published in Jamaica's sixty-first year of nationhood for all Jamaicans at home and in its far-flung diaspora. It provides an account of Jamaica's early economic history, from Spanish and British colonisation through the period of enslavement up to its abolition. It then traces the development of the peasant community and the smallholder economy which, for almost 150 years after 1838, formed the backbone of the domestic economy and the role of the middle class of predominantly Black and Brown Jamaicans in pushing for political representation and self-government after the Second World War and finally for independence in 1962.

It also traces the development of the public sector and public enterprises and examines how the legacy of a rigid class structure hindered the development of Black Jamaicans by designating 'Blackness' and cultural norms associated with Africa as being undesirable, while establishing 'Whiteness' and European behaviour patterns and ideas as desirable cultural values to be emulated. It was not until the advent of Black nationalist Marcus Mosiah Garvey with his message of Black pride, radical movements like Rastafarianism, and the cultural influence of the Hon Louise Bennett, along with the popular global music of Bob Marley that Jamaicans shook off that legacy and created national institutions that reflect their dominant culture. And with the rise of increasing numbers of Black people receiving higher education since 1980, Black Jamaican society can now be said to be truly multicultural, with Blackness a desirable feature at long last.

It is against this socio-cultural background that the economic development of the country, the establishment and evolution of its public sector and public enterprises, and the economic and public policies instituted throughout the various stages of the history are described and analysed. While there has been much discussion, debate, and published material on the performance of the Jamaican economy since 1962, there has been little focus on the economic management experiences of the two competing political administrations, the Jamaica Labour Party (JLP) and the People's National Party (PNP), particularly in relation to institutional, regulatory, and industrial structural changes of the economy in each political period. In that regard, I have set out to describe objectively and dispassionately, what I consider to be the pivotal economic and developmental policies that have been instituted over the period, culminating in the creation of a market economy in the 1980s, with the attendant and requisite institutions and regulatory regimes.

Both political parties while in government have had to contend with external economic shocks, ranging from the oil crisis of the 1970s, frequent natural disasters, structural adjustment, and economic stabilisation policies of the 1980 and 1990s; dictates of the so-called Washington Consensus Group, led by the International Monetary Fund (IMF) and the World Bank. Like all other periods throughout the country's history, it is the majority of the Black Jamaican people who have had to bear the brunt of bitter IMF prescription, experienced in the ruination of the agrarian sector and destruction of the rural economy and its peasant smallholder communities.

No comparable single body of work exists that describes the development of Jamaica's public sector institutions, the regulatory framework within which they were developed and operate and the functions they have been designed to perform within an economy that has evolved from state control to a private sector–led market economy. Consequently, liberalising the Jamaican economy and privatising its core economic and service sectors require an understanding of how the public sector and public enterprises operate, as well as details of the forces that influenced major sector liberalisation.

After four decades of structural adjustment and especially since 2015, there have been steep changes in the level of inflation and unemployment, both declining to below single-digit numbers, decline in debt to GDP to under 100 per cent, and a semblance of growth has returned. The IMF would want us to believe that the required structural changes have at last taken place and that Jamaica is on its way to another period of sustained growth. I believe, however, that the jury is still out.

April 2023

Acknowledgements

This book would simply not have been written were it not for the encouragement of the late vice-chancellor of The University of the West Indies (UWI), Professor Rex Nettleford. When I became the executive director and head of the Mona Institute of Business, I was informed that although I had been appointed with the full professor in the Faculty of Social Sciences, I was not allowed to use the title 'professor,' as I needed to have a PhD and improve my publication record. I gained my doctorate from the UWI in public affairs economics under the supervision of Professors Edwin Jones and Nettleford in 2002, both of whom have since regrettably passed away.

More recently, the COVID-19 pandemic gave me a considerable amount of free time to complete this work. I was encouraged to continue writing through the response to the draft chapter on Jamaica's economic development and policies, which I received from the Hon P.J. Patterson, former prime minister of Jamaica. He felt that my practical experience in government policymaking and implementation and the first-hand information on an important phase of Jamaica's development would provide a major addition to our knowledge of Jamaica's modern economic and institutional development.

The book itself could be said to have been in the making since 1975, when I was a post-graduate research scholar at the Department of Civil Design, University of Liverpool, under the supervision of Professor John Proudlove. Several aspects of the chapters on population and road transport were taken from early research work carried out on transport and economic development in Jamaica. I could draw on first-hand information from the late Hon Horace Clarke, who served as portfolio minister variously in public utilities and transport in the 1970s and in agriculture and energy in the 1990s.

Several academic colleagues and associates from the public sector have contributed to the individual chapters by providing research material, reviewing chapters, suggesting changes, and other valuable inputs. Several chapters also drew on earlier published articles or consultancy assignments, such as the chapter on telecommunications, which drew on an earlier work on *Telecommunication Regulation in Jamaica* that I co-authored with Professor Pablo Spiller, an economics professor at the University of California, Berkeley. That work was published for the World Bank in 1996 by Cambridge University Press, US, under the title *Regulations, Institutions and Commitment, Comparative Studies of Telecommunications*. More specifically, I am immensely grateful to my colleagues and public sector associates who provided invaluable input, without whose contribution the material would not be as rich.

Chapters 2, 3, and 8 on the development of the public sector and public enterprises benefited from the insightful and invaluable inputs from Dr Carlton Davis, former cabinet secretary, government of Jamaica, and Professor Lindsay Stirton, professor of public law, University of Sussex, England.

Part 2: chapters 4, 5, 6, and 7. The Jamaican people and its population benefited from scholarly inputs and preparation of tabular data by Dr Julian Devenish and Romario Cameron, lecturers in the Department of Sociology, UWI, Mona. Romario is now with the Bank of Jamaica.

Chapters 6 and 7: the socialist experiment of the 1970s and structural adjustment regime of the 1980s onwards benefited from invaluable inputs from the Hon, P.J. Patterson; Professor Claremont Kirton, Department of Economics, UWI, Mona, and Clinical Professor Ambassador Richard Bernal, formerly pro-vice chancellor for Global Affairs, UWI, who sadly passed away during the final stages of preparation of this book in January 2023.

Several individuals made valuable contributions to the preparation of part 3 on market reform. Chapter 8, on political economy and competition law, policy, and institution, benefited from the input of Faye Sampson, my wife and former general counsel, Financial Services Commission, Jamaica; Taimoon Stewart, lecturer in competition law, Faculty of Law, UWI Cave Hill, and Phillippe Brusick, formerly head of Competition and Consumer Protection, UNCTAD. For chapter 9:

development of regulatory institutions in Jamaica, Ansord Hewitt, director general, Office of Utilities Regulation, was extremely helpful in his detailed review and suggestions, while for chapter 10, on Jamaica's privatisation experience, Professor Peter Williamson, Judge Business School, Cambridge University; Denise Arana, general manager, Public Private Partnership, Development Bank of Jamaica, and her team were very helpful in providing various suggestions and reading material, which helped to improve the quality of the chapter. Chapter 11 covers the 'Conclusion and Key Lessons Learnt.'

For part 4, chapter 12: 'Aviation Sector: Privatisation of Air Jamaica and the International Airports' owe much to the analytical insights of Mark Call, aviation consultant, UK, and a colleague in aviation consultancy in the 1990s who presented some valuable analytical insights. For chapter 13: 'Agrarian Sector Privatisation and Industry: Liberalisation – Sugar and Banana,' Mrs Marjorie Stair, consultant on the banana industry in Jamaica; Dr Donovan Stanbury, former permanent secretary, Ministry of Agriculture, Jamaica; and Dr Marshall Hall, former professor of management, head of the Department of Management, UWI, and former chairman of Jamaica Banana Producers Group Limited together provided detailed guiding hands. Chapter 14: I am grateful for the invaluable input of Ansord Hewitt in the fine tuning of chapter 14: 'Telecommunications Industry, Liberalisation, and Privatisation' and grateful Dr Peter John Gordon, senior lecturer in the Department of Economics, UWI, and former director general of the Planning Institute of Jamaica, for his contribution to chapter 15, 'Financial Sector: Liberalisation and Privatisation.' I must also thank Mrs Sonia Atkinson, who served as a research assistant in the preparation of an earlier draft. In chapter 16, 'Privatisation of the Electricity Sector: Liberalisation and Regulation of the Industry,' Norman Davies, asset manager, New Fortress Energy, provided much new maternal information, especially information on the current energy situation in Jamaica. Again, Ansord Hewitt provided me with information on the latest developments in the sector. For chapter 17, 'Privatisation of Public Passenger Transport and the Public/Private Partnership in the Road Sector,' Kingsley Thomas, formerly managing director, Jamaica Development Bank, and Brian Samuel, formerly of the Caribbean Development Bank and the Inter-American Development Bank, willingly afforded me the benefit of their first-hand experience to fill in the many missing gaps.

While the contributions of all those mentioned above have helped to expand and enrich the overall quality of the work, I take ultimate responsibility for its contents and any omissions or inaccuracies are entirely mine.

Berl Francis, who has been my able editor, took my terribly typed manuscript and reoriented the material into a readable document. She also provided ideas on several themes that helped to make the document more complete. I also would like to thank Ian Randle, whose general editorial direction – and suggestions for restructuring the initial draft of the manuscript – changed the material from a series of uncoordinated chapters, into an interrelated and readable document.

Finally, I wish to say how much I owe my family: my wife Faye Sampson, son Kavin, daughter Melanie, and grandsons Zachery and Tristan Oderman, who have had to live with me during the last eighteen months as I worked on this book. Living together during the global pandemic also made things worse. Family friends like Trudy and Derek Lovell kindly put up with me as I sequestered myself in my office during their regular visits, with welcome interjections about what should be included in the book. This edition is dedicated to the memory of my father Walter and mother Teresa, who provided a solid foundation in my early life in the little village of Epsom at the edge of the Gray's Inn and Iter Boreale sugar estates in St Mary, Jamaica.

While the contributions of all those mentioned above have helped to expand and enrich the overall quality of the work, I take ultimate responsibility for its contents, and any omissions or inaccuracies are entirely mine.

Adopt and Sponsor

The publishers are grateful to the following organizations that have accepted our invitation to adopt and sponsor a chapter in this important legacy publication. Their support for the book is evidence of a commitment to provide policy makers in both the public and private sectors and Jamaicans in general, with an accurate record of past policy initiatives and the ways in which they have either advanced or hindered Jamaica's economic development.

IMPORTANT NOTE

By their adoption and sponsorship of a particular chapter the entities listed below do not necessarily agree with, or support any sentiments expressed or conclusions drawn by the author. However, it is their hope that the information about past experiences provided will be useful in enabling current and future generations to forge a successful development path for Jamaica.

- The Private Sector Organization of Jamaica
- The Office of Utilities Regulation
- Lasco Group
- Mona School of Business and Management
- Cable & Wireless Jamaica
- Future Energy Source Company
- Trans Jamaica Highway
- Betting Gaming and Lotteries Commission

We also record a special acknowledgement of the contribution by Mr Baron Stewart and the Hon Kingsley Thomas to the successful publication of this book.

The Private Sector Organisation of Jamaica (PSOJ) was established in 1976. It is a national organisation of private sector associations, companies and individuals working together to promote a competitive and productive private sector.

The organisation seeks to influence issues of national policy of a political, social, or economic nature. The Executive Committee, with guidance from the Council, leads the process by engaging in discussions with the government, political directorate, and opposition. The organisation also maintains close contact with major multi-lateral and bi-lateral agencies. One of the PSOJ's primary mandates is advocacy. Members participate proactively through various committees that directly impact the private sector's development. The PSOJ provides meaningful representation on behalf of the private sector to ensure that its presence and strong voice are always maintained.

The Office of Utilities Regulation (OUR) was established by an Act of Parliament in 1995 to regulate the operations of utility companies. Our mandate is to provide an Avenue of Appeal for consumers who have grievances with the utility companies. OUR contributes to national development by effective regulation of utility services that enables consumer access to modern, reliable, affordable and quality utility services; while ensuring that service providers have the opportunity to make a reasonable return on their investment. The OUR is ISO 9001:2015 certified and has also been recognized internationally for the pioneering role it has played in the regional development of independent utility regulation and the liberalization of the telecommunications sector.

LASCO Distributors Limited is a leading Jamaican consumer goods and pharmaceutical distribution company whose purpose is to enhance Everyday Family Values through nutrition, hygiene and healthcare. We operate through focused Consumer and Pharmaceutical divisions, serving customers and meeting consumers' evolving demands for food, beverage, nutrition, home care, personal care, pet care and health care solutions. We are part of the LASCO affiliated group of companies that comprise LASCO Manufacturing Limited and LASCO Financial Services Limited. LASCO Distributors Limited was founded in September 1988, by Hon. Lascelles Chin, our Executive Chairman and was listed on the Jamaica Stock Exchange in October 2010. We are driven by the values established from inception: innovation, entrepreneurship and a passion for excellence, as we continue to demonstrate and live our purpose.

Mona School of Business and Management (MSBM) is the premier Business School in the region and produces graduates that are ready to make an impactful contribution to Caribbean development.

MSBM offers a diverse suite of globally competitive professional development, undergraduate and graduate degree programmes which include the Master in Business Administration (MBA) which is internationally accredited by the Association of MBAs (AMBA).

MSBM complements its unique academic programmes with cutting edge consultancy services and public policy research, the principal business objective being to provide decision makers with expert advice for handling their most critical strategic issues.

FLOW

Cable & Wireless Jamaica (CWJ), through its consumer brand Flow Jamaica, is the leading full-service communications provider in Jamaica delivering connected entertainment through mobile, TV, broadband, and fixed lines. We have been at the forefront of innovating infrastructure and services - from historic telegraph poles and cables, to innovative cutting-edge services and products. Today, our services are underpinned by over 50,000 kilometres of the most modern subsea and terrestrial fibre networks in this part of the world. By connecting communities to our network, products and services, we're transforming lives – using technology to provide the building blocks of connection and growth for Jamaica's economic development. And as a business with purpose, we're positively contributing to the fabric of the communities where we operate, empowering Jamaicans and enabling their progress by leading digital inclusion efforts across the country.

FESCO

Fesco's core business is the marketing and distribution of petroleum products such as E10 87 octane, E10 90 octane, automotive diesel oil, ultra low sulphur diesel and lubricants to both retail and commercial customers.

We distribute to our retail customers through our growing network of service stations across the length and breadth of Jamaica. On the commercial side, we provide efficient, reliable bulk fuel to the manufacturing, construction and transportation industries.

We are a Jamaican owned business and we strongly believe that Jamaicans, given the opportunity, are resilient, industrious, highly productive, and second to none!

We appreciate our customers, and truly believe that respect begets respect, love begets love and success begets success. Buy Jamaican, buy Fesco.

TRANSJAMAICAN HIGHWAY LTD

TransJamaican Highway Limited (TJH) was formed in 2001. Our main business activity is the development, operation and maintenance of a tolled road network in Jamaica known as the "Highway 2000 East-West". Highway 2000 East-West is a 49.9km tolled motorway with two distinct corridors: T1 – 43.45km between Kingston and May Pen, and T2 – 6.5km between Portmore and Kingston. The company operates four toll plazas: May Pen, Vineyards (at Old Harbour), Spanish town and Portmore.

BGLC BETTING GAMING & LOTTERIES COMMISSION

The Betting, Gaming and Lotteries Commission is an independent statutory body established in 1975 under the provisions of the Betting, Gaming and Lotteries Act (BGLA) of 1965.

The Commission licenses, regulates and monitors the local gaming industry, facilitates its growth and development, and protects the public from unfair, unscrupulous and illegal activities.

In addition to regulating and controlling the operation of betting, gaming and the conduct of lotteries in Jamaica and granting permits, licences and approvals to persons or entities considered fit and proper to conduct betting, gaming and lottery activities, the BGLC also provide information and advice to the Minister of Finance and the Public Service in accordance with the Minister's function under the Betting, Gaming, and Lotteries Act (BGLA), and recommends legislative amendments to the Act, Regulations, and Orders to ensure the industry's orderly development.

Introduction

In this work, the different junctures in which the Jamaican economy underwent various stages of development and change, dating back to the colonial period are illustrated. However, the focus is on the post-Second World War period and in particular, the period 1980 onwards, characterised by a policy of a free-market economy, trade liberalisation, privatisation of key production and service sectors, and attendant regulatory laws and institutions.

Three distinct junctures are identified, beginning with the European colonial period, during which the economy was based on agriculture, firstly the export of sugar and in the 1870s banana, also grown primarily for export and produced on large plantations. Following the abolition of slavery in 1838, mono-culture plantation sugar cane production, though still dominant, was supplemented by a rural smallholder/peasant economy that produced bananas for export and staple food crops, mainly for the domestic market and which was responsible for the development of a vibrant internal marketing system. This latter system which had its origins in the provision ground and Sunday market activities of enslaved Africans prior to Emancipation gathered pace and momentum after 1838 with the coming of full freedom, triggering flight from the plantation by the freed Africans who established themselves in Free Villages, with the support of the Protestant missionaries, in which smallholdings and small-scale farming became the main economic activity of interior rural Jamaica.

There was little change in the country's economic and social structure and activities during the colonial years up to 1962 when Jamaica became an independent nation, except that in the aftermath of the Second World War deliberate attempts were made to develop an indigenous industrial economy, based on the Puerto Rican model of 'Industrialisation by Invitation.' Up to that point, several factors had combined to ensure a sustained period of economic growth, among which were high levels of foreign direct investment, triggered by the development of the bauxite and alumina industry, expansion of the manufacturing sector, embryonic growth of the tourism industry, and stability for the country's primary exports through negotiated quotas and prices with our main trading partners, the UK and to a lesser extent, the US.

Warning clouds, barely discernible in the 1960s, however, emerged on the horizon in the 1970s, as the export agricultural sector by then had experienced signs of decline because of failing to modernise its farming and manufacturing operations, even as new competitors for the banana market appeared in Central America, and in the case of sugar by the gradual loss of imperial preferences. With Britain entering the European Economic Community (EEC) and later the European Union (EU), these trade preferences were carried over to the 1990s but with the emergence of the World Trade Organization (WTO) economic system of trade liberalisation in the 1990s, Jamaican export agricultural products lost their trade preferences. As the main destination for Jamaica's agricultural exports, the UK had provided a guaranteed market and stable negotiated prices, since 1901, buffeted by the Commonwealth non-reciprocal trade preference of the 1930s so that the sector had little or no incentive to modernise, or diversify.

The beginnings of these changes in economic structure and activity coincided with, or resulted in, an urban drift from the rural areas mainly to the capital, Kingston, for which the city was ill-prepared, lacking as it was in adequate housing and essential social amenities. The result was the creation of urban ghettos, high unemployment, increasing levels of crime, and a slew of other socio-economic problems, which though centred in Kingston, became an endemic national issue with major economic consequences.

Enter the decade of the 1970s, Jamaica experienced a major shift in economic policy under a Democratic Socialist political regime, as the country moved from a policy of private sector development to Statism in which the 'commanding heights' of the economy came under government/public sector control, while the private sector retreated into resistance mode.

The final phase covered by this work is the movement towards the free market system, structural adjustment of the economy, a programme of trade and financial sector liberalisation and privatisation, and transformation of the economy from Statism to one operated as a free-market system.

STRUCTURE OF THE BOOK

This work is divided into four parts, comprising seventeen chapters.

Part 1: *Jamaica's Economic Development in Historical Perspective* comprises chapters 1–3, encompassing a sweeping survey of the country's economic development over the three-hundred-plus years of British colonialism and explains how the policies imposed on Jamaica were guided by prevailing economic theories that prevailed in Britain at various times over the period leading up to Independence. The creation of a public sector and public enterprises did not become a feature of the country's development until late into the nineteenth century, and well after the abolition of African enslavement that was the centrepiece of the economy up to the end of the 1830s. It took the Morant Bay Rebellion of 1865, a Royal Commission of Inquiry in its aftermath, and the arrival of Governor John Peter Grant to institute policies that effectively created public services that were geared to benefit the general population at large. These and succeeding policies and public sector reforms form the basis of chapters 2 and 3.

Part 2: *Economic Policies and Economic Development* takes up the story from independence in 1962 and the imperative to create new institutions for a young nation. One of its main features, as outlined in chapter 5 was the accelerated creation of a public sector through which government assumed the responsibility for providing and managing essential services for the social and economic welfare of the country. Chapters 6 and 7 then describe the differing economic policies that were implemented and the effects of these policies following the decade of the 1970s, first by the adoption of a Democratic Socialist approach that placed government in control of the commanding heights of the economy and a resulting uncontrolled and unsustainable expansion of the public service at the expense of private sector development. That policy was to be reversed in the decade of the 1980s, when Jamaica came under the dictates of the multilateral financial institutions led by the World Bank and the International Monetary Fund, and imposing what came to be known as Structural Adjustment.

Part 3: *Preparing Jamaica For the Market Economy* is the subject of chapters 8, 9, and 10, which trace the transition from state control and the direction of the economy influenced by neoliberalist theories, including privatisation of previously government-owned institutions and acknowledgement of the private sector as the driver of the economy. Liberalisation and privatisation were not instituted in a vacuum, nor did they involve the unregulated pursuit of private sector economic interests. New laws and regulations that were meant to introduce competition and to break up existing monopolies became necessary as well as the creation of new institutions to regulate the practices of private institutions for the benefit of the public, even as the government expanded the reform process within public sector institutions. Chapter 11 presents a summary of the lessons learned from Jamaica's experience of privatisation.

Part 4: *Industry Liberalisation: Six Case Studies of Sector Privatisation* provides further in-depth studies of the experience of privatisation of several core sectors of the economy. Chapter 12 covers the aviation industry, with a focus on the privatisation of the two international airports, while chapter 13 describes how government divested ownership of the major producing sugar and banana operations across the country that had come under its ownership during the 1970s. Telecommunications privatisation and opening up of that sector is the subject of chapter 14, while the financial sector, which experienced major difficulties and dislocations in the 1990s comes in for scrutiny in chapter 15. The final two studies focus on the energy sector privatisation in chapter 16, and the section is capped off, appropriately, by a case study, chapter 17 of public/private partnership in the road sector.

ON A PERSONAL NOTE ...

The seventeen chapters making up this work have been written from the perspective of one who was at the front and centre of the major economic policy changes that occurred from 1974 and into the first decade of the twenty-first century, initially in an advisory capacity, in the Ministry of Public Utilities and Transport (MPUT), under then portfolio Minister Eric Bell, and the then young Horace Clarke. Later, my role was expanded to encompass policymaking and operational duties (I became the chairman of Jamaica Omnibus Services Limited, the Kingston urban public transportation company.) and finally in the implementation of the policies described in the succeeding chapters. It meant that I worked under four different prime ministers and no fewer than five portfolio ministers from both PNP and JLP administrations, including JLP stalwarts, such as Alva Ross and Cliff Stone.

I later had the privilege of working as an economic advisor to the People's National Party (PNP) administration between 1989 and 1998 and 2003 and 2007, providing my professional managerial skills in the service of the government and the nation. In these periods, I was intimately involved in several of the key developments which took place in post-independence Jamaica. The periods of my involvement with the political system in Jamaica can be categorised as follows:

- The period following 1974, a period in which the government of Jamaica used state enterprises to foster economic and social development.
- The period from 1990 to 1998 when the PNP reversed statism for private sector–led economic development and market economy policies.
- The period of 2003–7: continuation with PNP Prime Minister, P.J. Patterson, on market liberalisation and telecommunications and energy sector reform.

In the period 1990–2000, I also served the University of the West Indies, Mona Campus, in setting up the USAID-funded programme for the introduction and development of the master's degree in business administration, working closely with such Caribbean stalwarts as Professor Rex Nettleford and Vice-Chancellor Alistair McIntyre.

It is a matter of some irony that I have played an active role in both the introduction of a state-controlled economic policy and the reverse policy of market liberalisation and privatisation of state assets, and in the development of a private sector–led, market-driven economy. When I was first invited in 1976 to join the MPUT on secondment from Alcan Jamaica Limited, which I had joined in 1968 from the UK, my political views were rather nuanced, with no allegiance to any political persuasion or party.

My education at Cranfield College of Aeronautics and Lancaster University made me one of the first in England to qualify at the graduate level in the management field in the mid-1960s. Experiences in the field, both at Lever Brothers & Associated Limited in the UK and as a senior executive in a multinational Alcan Jamaica (president and chairman of Alcan Products and Sprostons Limited), operating in one of the largest economic sectors in Jamaica, adequately prepared me for carrying out this exercise of writing this book. I have also had the opportunity to provide my expertise at the international level, first serving President Mkapa of Tanzania, for just over three years (1998–2001), on secondment from UWI, then to President Olusegun Obasanjo in the period after 2007 and to President Bingu wa Mutharika of Malawi in 2010. Unquestionably, these experiences qualified me to provide professional managerial services in most economic sectors and at various levels.

In my international economic consultancy activities, I have had the opportunity of working with some of the leading international infrastructure consultancy firms, including Adam Smith International Limited of London, CPCS Transcom Limited of Canada, Oxford Policy Management Limited of Oxford, and London Economics Limited of London. I have had the benefit of consulting on infrastructure development and privatisation in some twenty countries, working in Africa, Asia, and Europe. The professional mindset and attitude that have guided me throughout my years of service in the Jamaican public sector have played a significant role in shaping the perspective from which this book has been written.

Abbreviations and Acronymns

AA	Airport Authority
AAJ	Airports Authority of Jamaica
AAJH	Airports Authority Jamaica Holdings
ABB	Accelerated Book Building
ACB	Agricultural Credit Bank
ACP	African Caribbean and Pacific Countries
AERA	Airports (Economic Regulation) Act
AFD	Agence Française de Développement
Agro 21	Agro 21 Corporation
AIBGA	All Island Banana Growers Association
AIC	Advance Investment Council Limited
AIF	Airport Improvement Fee
AIJCFA	All Island Jamaica Sugar Cane Farmers Association
AJ	Air Jamaica
AJAG	Air Jamaica Acquisition Group
AMC	Agricultural Marketing Corporation
AMU	Advisory and Monitoring Unit
ARP	Administrative Reform Programme
AT&T	American Telephone & Telegraph
ATC	Air Traffic Control
ATLB	Air Transport Licensing Board
ATM	Automated Teller Machine
BA	British Airways
BAFO	Best and Final Offer
BC	Broadcasting Commission
BC	Broadcasting Commission of Jamaica
BECO	Banana Export Company
BET	British Electric Traction

BNS	Bank of Nova Scotia Limited
BNSG	Bank of Nova Scotia Group
BOAC	British Overseas Airways Corporation
BOJ	Bank of Jamaica
BOO	Build, Own, Operate
BOOT	Build-Own-Operate-Transfer
BOT	Build-Own-Transfer
bps	basis points
BRRA	Broadcasting and Radio Diffusion Act
BSP	Banana Support Programmes
BT	British Telecom
BWIA	British West Indian Airways
C&W	Cable & Wireless Limited
C&WJ	Cable and Wireless Jamaica
C&WL	Cable & Wireless of London
CAA	Civil Aviation Authority
CAC	Cotation Assistée en Continu (French stock exchange)
CAC	Competition Appeal Court
CAC	Consumer Affairs Commission
CAD	Civil Aviation Department
CANTO	Caribbean Association of National Telecommunications Organization
CAP	Common Agricultural Policy
CARICOM	Caribbean Community
CC	Contractor General
CCC	Caribbean Cement Company
CDB	China Development Bank
CDC	Commonwealth Development Corporation
CDL	Clarendon Distillers Limited
CEA	Cambridge Economic Associate
CECL	Carib Engineering Company Limited
CEL	Columbia Electric Company
CET	Common External Tariff
CFSA	CARICOM Financial Services Agreement
CHEC	China Harbour Engineering Company Ltd
CHL	Continental Holdings Limited of Montreal, Canada
CIA	Central Intelligence Agency
CIDA	Canadian International Development Agency
CMO	Commonwealth Sugar Organization
CRNM	Caribbean Regional Negotiating Machinery
CSA	Commonwealth Sugar Agreement

CSME	CARICOM Common Single Market
CTL	Caymanas Track Ltd
CTL	Continental Telephone Company of Canada
CTU	Caribbean Telecommunications Union
DBFO	Design, Build, Finance, Operate
DBJ	Development Bank of Jamaica
DCO	Dominion, Colonial and Overseas
DFID	Department for International Development
DG	Director General
EBTA	Earnings plus interest, taxes, and amortization
EC	European Commission
ECTEL	Eastern Caribbean Telecommunications Authority
EEC	European Economic Community
EEF	Extended Fund Facility
EIB	European Investment Bank
EOI	Expression of Interest
EPA	European Partnership Agreement
EPA	Economic Partnership Agreement
EPC	Economic and Production Council
ESOP	Employee Share Option Scheme
ESOS	Employees Share Option Scheme
EU	European Union
FAA	Federal Aviation Administration
FCA	Fair Competition Act
FCA	Fair Trading Commission Act
FCC	Federal Communication Commission
FDI	Foreign Direct Investment
FEREC	Federal Energy Regulatory Commission
FIA	Financial Institutions Act
FINASC	Financial Sector Adjustment Company
FIS	Financial Institutions Services
FMLCo	Frome Monymusk Land Company Limited
FPC	Federal Power Commission
FRI	Factory Recovery Index
FSC	Financial Services Commission
FSSC	Financial System Stability Committee
FTAA	Free Trade Area of the Americas
FTC	Fair Trading Commission
GAP	Grupo Aeroportuario del Pacifico S.A.B. De C.V
GATS	General Agreement in Trade and Services
GATT	General Agreement on Trade and Tariff

GDP	Gross Domestic Product
GG	Governor General
GGSC	Golden Grove Sugar Company Limited
GLN	Gide Loyrette Nouel A.A.R.P.I
GSM	Global System for Communication
HIPC	Heavily Indebted Poor Countries
IADB	Inter-American Development Bank
IATA	International Air Transport Association
IBA	International Bauxite Association
IBRD	International Bank for Reconstruction (World Bank)
ICAO	International Civil Aviation Organization
ICIs	Informal Commercial Importers
ICWI	Insurance Company of the West Indies Limited
IDB	InterAmerican Development Bank
IFC	International Finance Corporation
IFIA	Ian Fleming International Airport
IFIs	International Financial Investors
IMF	International Monetary Fund
IP	Intellectual Property
IPO	Initial Public Offer
IPP	Independent Power Producers
ISP	Independent Service Provider
ITA	Island Traffic Authority
ITU	International Telecommunication Union
JAMINTEL	Jamaica International Telecommunications Ltd
JAMVAC	Jamaica Vacation Ltd
JAS	Jamaican Agricultural Society
Jasco	Jamaica Public Service Company
JBI	Jamaica Bauxite Institute
JBPA	Jamaica Banana Producers Association
JCPC	Judicial Committee of the Privy Council
JCPS	Jamaica Cane Products Sales Limited
JCTC	Jamaica Commodity Trading Company Limited
JDB	Jamaica Development Bank
JDIC	Jamaica Deposit Insurance Corporation
JEL&P	Jamaica Light & Power Company (Canada) Limited
JELC	Jamaica Electric Light Company Limited
JEP	Jamaica Energy Partners
JHNSHC	Jamaica North-South Highway Construction Company
JIDC	Jamaica Industrial Development Corporation
JIO	Jamaica Infrastructure Operator

JLP	Jamaica Labour Party
JMA	Jamaica Minibus Association
JNIC	Jamaica National Investment Corporation
JNIP	Jamaica National Investment Promotions
JOI	Jamaican Infrastructure Operator
JOS	Jamaica Omnibus Services Company
JPG	Jamaica Producers Group
JPPL	Jamaica Private Power Limited
JPSCo	Jamaica Public Service Company
JRC	Jamaica Railway Corporation
JSE	Jamaica Stock Exchange
JSH	Jamaica Sugar Holding Company Limited
JSM	Jamaica Stock Market
JSTC	Jamaica Streetcar Company Limited
JTC	Jamaica Telephone Company
JUTC	Jamaica Union of Transport Cooperative Limited
JUTC	Jamaica Urban Transit Company
KA	Kenya Airways
KFAED	Kuwait Fund for Arab Economic Development
KMA	Kingston Metropolitan Area
KMTR	Kingston Metropolitan Transport Region
KPMG	Klynveld Peat Marwick Goerdeler
KSAC	Kingston and St Andrew Corporation
KWh	Kilowatt hours
LCEP	Least Cost Expansion Plan
LIBOR	London Inter-Bank Offer
LRMC	Long Run Marginal Cost
MNI	Mutual and National Investment
MBJ	Montego Bay Jamaica Airport
MCPH	Marubeni Caribbean Power Holdings
MCR	Merger Control Regulation
MCST	Ministry of Commerce Science and Technology
MEBO	Management Employee Buy-out
MFIs	Multilateral Financial Institutions
MFJ	Mutual Final Judgment
MFN	Most Favoured Nation
MIND	Management Institute for National Development
MMTH	Metropolitan Management Transport Holdings Limited
MOA	Ministry of Agriculture
MOF	Ministry of Finance

MOU	Memorandum of Understanding
MPM	Metropolitan Parks and Markets Limited
MPUT	Ministry of Public Utilities and Transport
MSB	Mutual Security Bank
MT	Metric Tonne
MTBE	Methyl tertiary-butyl-ether
NBFI	Non-Bank Financial Institutions
NCB	National Commercial Bank Jamaica Limited
NCBG	National Commercial Bank Group
NCC	National Contracts Committee
NEPA	National Environment and Planning Agency
NERA	National Resources Conservation Authority
NGO	Non-Governmental Organisation
NHP	National Hotels and Properties Limited
NIBJ	`National Investment Bank of Jamaica Limited
NIEO	New International Economic Order
NMIA	Norman Manley International Airport
NPL	Non-performing loans over gross loans
NRCA	National Resource Conservation Authority
NRJ	National Rums of Jamaica Limited
NROCC	National Road Operating and Construction Company Limited
NSC	National Sugar Company
NTCS	National Transport Cooperative Society
NWA	National Works Agency
NWC	National Water Commission
OACPS	Organisation of African, Caribbean and Pacific State
OCG	Office of the Contractor General
OECD	Organisation For Economic Cooperation and Development
OFT	Office of Fair Trading
OPEC	Organization of Petroleum Exporting Countries
OPIC	Overseas Private Investment Corporation
OPM	Office of the Prime Minister
OUR	Office of Utilities Regulation
PAJ	Port Authority of Jamaica
PCBs	People's Cooperative Banks
PCJ	Petroleum Corporation of Jamaica
PCSC	Pan Caribbean Sugar Company
PDA	Protection of Depositors Act
PDI	Policy Drafting Instrument

PFC	Passenger Facility Fee
PFI	Private Finance Initiative
PIOJ	Planning Institute of Jamaica
PNP	People's National Party
PPA	Power Purchase Agreement
PPP	Public Private Partnership
PPTB	Public Passenger Transport Board
PPTD	Public Passenger Transport (Corporate Area) Board
PRF	Parochial Revenue Fun
PSDAL	Private Sector Development Adjustment Loan
PSOJ	Private Sector Organisation of Jamaica
PUC	Public Utility Commission
PWC	Price Waterhouse Coopers (Coopers and Lybrand merged with Price
QRs	Quantitative Restrictions
RBTT	Royal Bank of Trinidad and Tobago
REOI	Request for Expression of Interest
REP	Rural Electrification Programme Company Ltd
RFP	Requests for Proposal
ROA	Pre-tax Profit over Total Asset
ROE	Pre-tax Profit over Equity
ROR	Rate of Return
ROSCA	Rotating Savings and Credit Associations
RPI	Retail Price Index
RPI-X	Retail Price Index (as consumer price index) and X an effeminacy factor
RPM	Resale Price Maintenance
SAC	Social Action Centre
SALs	Structural Adjustment Loans
SCJ	Sugar Company of Jamaica limited
SEC	Securities and Exchange Commission
SECALs	Sector Adjustment Loans
SES	Social and Economic Studies
SHA	Shareholders Agreement
SIA	Sugar Industry Authority
SMA	Spectrum Management Authority
SOE	State Owned Enterprises
SPA	Spirits Pool Association
SPA	Share Purchase Agreement
SPS	Special Preference Sugar Programme
T&GT	Telephone & Trust General

TA	Toll Authority
TAQA	Dhabi National Energy Company
TJH	Trans Jamaican Highway Limited
TOJ	Telecommunications of Jamaica Limited
TPD	Town Planning Department
TRIPS	Trade Related Aspects of Intellectual Property Rights
TSC	Trelawny Sugar Company Ltd
UCI/AG	United Infrastructure Company/Airport Group International
UDC	Urban Development Corporation
UNCTAD	United Nation Conference on Trade and Development
USAID	United State Agency for International Development
UTOL	United Transport (Overseas) Limited
VADS	Voice Activation Detection Services
VANS	Value Added Network Services
VOIP	Voice over the Internet Protocol
VSAT	Very Small Aperture Technology
WICE	West India and Columbia Electric Company
WIEC	West India Electric Company
WIIC	West India Improvement Company
WISCo	West Indies Sugar Company
WITEC	West Indies Telegraph and Telephone Company
WITP	West India and Panama Telegraph Company
WSLB	Workers Saving and Loan Bank
WTO	World Trade Organization

PART 1
Jamaica's Economic Development in Historical Perspective

CHAPTER ONE

British Colonial Policies and the Shaping of Jamaica's Economic Development

BRITISH COLONIAL ECONOMIC POLICIES

Chapter 1 outlines that the English established the plantation system, which emphasised monoculture export sugar, large landholdings, chattel slavery, and later the indenture system after emancipation. Each plantation became a self-contained unit, catering to cane cultivation, sugar works, and residence (slave village and great house). The plantation system was an instrument of English political colonialism. It brought capital, enterprise, and management to create economic structures based on cheap or chattel labour. The planter class was eventually replaced by companies, both locally based and multinational, sometimes with local participation and integrated export marketing. Often the products were directly used by the same company (vertical integration from production to final sale to consumers) in the export market.

Metropolitan Britain and colonial Jamaica shaped the development of the plantation economic policies on the island during the different historical junctures, reflecting changing economic thought in England up to independence in 1962. Economic policy in Jamaica and the West Indies in the early colonial period of the sixteenth and seventeenth centuries centred on mercantilist doctrine[1] focused on commodity trade, mainly sugar and coffee, and later bananas from Jamaica and other West Indian colonies, exporting British manufactured goods to the colonies, creating a favourable British balance of trade.[2]

Production of foodstuff was discouraged, as resources were focused mainly on sugar and coffee for export, while sustenance needs were met mainly through importation of agricultural products from the temperate regions of the metropole.[3]

Despite a call made to the British Parliament as early as 1698, advocating for diversified domestic agricultural production and a proposal to limit the importation of foodstuff to promote local production in Jamaica and the colonies, this idea was dismissed due to concerns over the reduction of land allocated for sugar production.[4] For most of the period, even after emancipation, smallholders were denied land, forcing many of the newly freed Black Jamaicans to work on the plantations for the benefit of the plantocracy.

Britain began its overseas possessions and trading posts between the sixteenth and eighteenth centuries. At its peak, it was the largest empire in history and, for the period 1689–1815, 126 years described as 'the long sixteenth century,' during which Britain rose to world power status. As a prosperous country, it had a well-developed and functioning agriculture sector, and the Jamaican sugar industry was just an extension of this sector. Jamaica, in this period, was England's prized possession, and its economic development policies were extended to the island as a part of the colonies.

Economic Theories and Theorists

Mercantilism

Britain's economy initially operated under a mercantile system, a term popularised by Adam Smith to describe the system of political economy based on restricting imports into Britain and the colonies and encouraging exports to the colonies and the rest of the world.[5] The system assumed that the global supply of wealth was finite, and it was in a nation's interest to accumulate as much as possible, with wealth measured in gold and silver. Many aspects of the system were about generating and dividing up economic rents among a relatively closed elite, 'the establishment,' which included royalty, baronets, landed gentry, the absentee Jamaican sugar plantation owners in Britain, and the colonial administrators. Under the system, the British economy was operated against the interest of the masses and certainly against the interest of the Black Jamaican population, which, by the middle of the seventeenth century, was in the majority on the island.

The mercantilist system of political economy dominated western European economic thought from the sixteenth to the late eighteenth century. It was introduced in England through a series of Navigation Acts, starting in 1651 and refined in 1663, 1673, and 1696. These acts promoted self-sufficiency of the English empire by restricting imports of foreign goods to England and the empire. The 1651 English Navigation Act was upgraded into a Commonwealth Navigation Act of 1661, requiring all foreign goods to be shipped to the colonies through English ports; in return, colonial commodities were given a monopoly of the English market at preferential treatment. In 1733 Britain passed the Sugar and Molasses Act, intended to protect its sugar market in the UK and revised in 1776, enabling Britain to maintain control over the British sugar market until 1884. Britain then was a more commercial economy, as it was after 1850 that industrialisation became its dominant feature. Money was in widespread use and the essence of capitalism: private ownership of property and the need for most workers to sell their labour for cash took root. Researcher Weldon Duncan argued that capitalism could be traced back to this time and that the take-off and transition from the commercial economy of the 1880s to an industrial one started after 1900, although this is debatable.[6] Industrialisation in nineteenth-century Britain created the need for access to foreign markets and the mercantilist economic policies protected the British and colonial markets.

Adam Smith: Free Trade

Adam Smith rejected the mercantilist framework and advocated the removal of trade restrictions and tariffs in favour of more open free trade. Smith believed that freer trade, especially international trade, enriched all nations and consumers. His other successful contribution to economic policymaking was the notion of the 'invisible hand,' the idea that each individual acting in his own self-interest could contribute to a better outcome for society. For Smith, it was not only international trade which needed freeing up, but markets in general. A free market would not just result in lower prices for consumers, but it would also lead to more efficient firms and reward them with higher profits, allowing them to expand production to meet increasing consumer demand and hire more workers, often at higher wages, and with better working conditions. To make a country's economy grow, he argued, the state should refrain from interfering too much in the market, reflecting the 'laissez-faire' approach to market regulation. Smith's ideas took hold with the new industrial and commercial groups that came to influence the British government and commercial interests over rural rivals after 1832. The result was the repealing of the Navigation Acts in 1849. The repeal of the acts was accompanied by a repeal of the Corn Law in 1846, a protectionist measure adopted in 1815 to protect British agriculture. The trade in enslaved Africans and plantation slavery in Jamaica and the rest of the Caribbean played a key role in financing the transition. When Britain abandoned mercantilist market protection in favour of free trade and repealed the protectionist duties on sugar from Jamaica and other West Indian islands, the industry entered a crisis that reached a critical point in the 1890s.[7] The British economy under free trade had been at the forefront of promoting globalisation.

It was around the 1850s that globalisation was born, involving increasing international economic integration and cross-border movements of goods, services, and capital. Britain's advocacy of free trade after 1840, especially after the repeal of the Corn Laws, opened the UK to the world. Although tariff levels are key factors of globalisation, they are not the whole story; tariff levels rose in Britain in the decade of the 1880–90, yet global trade flourished, even as tariff levels rose. The new technologies of the industrial revolution made it much easier and speedier to move goods and people. The global network of transatlantic cable, which was installed after 1866, reduced the time taken to send messages from London to New York from under one week to just minutes. Advances in shipping significantly reduced the time required to cross the Atlantic.

Ricardo's Theory of Comparative Advantages

Smith's battle against the farmers and landed elite was joined by David Ricardo, a historian of Portuguese ancestry, through his theory of 'comparative advantages.'[8] Ricardo challenged the idea that the purpose of trade was to accumulate bullion, favouring industrial specialisation and free trade. He further argued that it suited countries to specialise in goods and services in which they excelled most, illustrating his ideas on trade in cloth and wine, by showing that Portugal could produce wine cheaper than cloth, while England could produce cloth cheaper than wine. It therefore suited Portugal to concentrate on wine and England on cloth, so both countries would be better off. In other words, Ricardo attributed the cause and benefit of international trade to the differences in their relative opportunity cost. It was a period in which the new industrialists, financiers, and commercial interests had gained increasing representation in Britain's Parliament, allowing Prime Minister Robert Peel's Conservative government to obtain the majority to repeal the Corn Laws in 1846.

Globalisation, which became popular in the 1980s, was not new. Globalisation as Maynard Keynes puts it, results from technological changes.[9] Some of the technological changes which advanced globalisation in the early twentieth century were the telephone and developments in shipping. Alongside faster travel by sea, there was expansion on land by the railways after 1850 and the motor vehicle of the 1920s, further accelerating the movement of people, goods, and services. Introducing refrigerated shipping in the 1870s advanced the range of goods, such as bananas, which could be shipped in large quantities in under eleven days from Jamaica to London. This technological change had an immense economic impact on international trade, drastically slashing the cost of moving goods and people. Technology also reduced price differentials in regional markets, converting the market for some goods into an international market.

Malthus on Population

Another important economic theory which guided politics and economics in the pre-industrial world was that which was orchestrated by Reverend Thomas R. Malthus[10] who argued that the growing population rate contributed to the rising supply of labour, and this inevitably lowered wages; continued population growth was a recipe for poverty. Malthus posited that population was increasing exponentially, while food supply reflected arithmetic growth rate, resulting in a disequilibrium. The growth of food supply from agriculture was not enough to effect an equilibrium, hence positive checks: famine, pestilence, starvation, poverty, epidemics and wars; or negative checks: limits on reproduction, such as birth control, or couples marrying later would be needed to reduce the population and bring about equilibrium. The agricultural revolution seemed to have postponed the Malthusian trap.

Support in Britain for free trade ran into problems after 1890. The continued implementation of free trade created a crisis for the British West Indian sugar industry, whereby competition from Cuba and

Brazil and beet sugar production in Europe caused sugar prices to collapse.[11] Competition, especially from the US and Germany, resulted in significant loss of markets for British industry, which responded to the crisis by establishing a Royal British West Indies Commission in 1897 to assess the needs of the West Indian colonies. The report of the Commission criticised the sugar plantocracy and, for the first time, recommended the establishment of small holder cultivation by a policy of land settlement and the diversification of crops.[12]

As other countries were introducing tariffs, Britain resorted to trade protection for sugar to safeguard its industry in the West Indies with tariffs imposed on German and European beet sugar in 1902. Introducing protection was a response to the precipitous drop in global sugar prices. Most of the other Royal Commission's recommendations were largely ignored, save for the establishment of botanical gardens with extension agents to spread new farming methods to smallholders in Jamaica and the other West Indian islands. Once again, although crisis had created the opportunity to diversify agriculture, it was squandered, and structural dominance of the plantation economy remained intact, with the end of the nineteenth century highly dependent on a declining sugar industry and imported food items.

Economic Policies in the Inter-war Years

The 1930s saw an end to the consensus in British politics which had prevailed over the years, favouring global free trade with the introduction of Imperial Preferences in the 1930s. The British dominions had been enacting imperial trade preferences as early as 1897 when Canada, the first of the dominions to do so, was followed by New Zealand in 1903. Britain, however, had not reciprocated because of its commitment to global free trade. In 1932, Britain and the British colonies and dominions introduced Imperial Preference, or empire trade free zones, which provided trade protection to imperial Britain and her colonies.[13] There were twelve bilateral trade agreements, providing for mutual consensus and certain other commitments. With the gold standard having failed, the US ditched it in 1933, and most other countries followed suit. This non-reciprocal trade preference of the 1930s, with Jamaica and the other Caribbean colonies, led to the revival of the sugar industry and gave a new impetus to banana exports from Jamaica. This protection was carried over into the European Union in the 1970s, when Britain joined the Common Market. The period was also notable for the adoption of several of Maynard Keynes's ideas, such as expanding government spending, lowering interest rates, and increasing money supply. Keynes, unlike Smith, focused on demand and was an ardent exponent of expanding government spending to revive a faltering British economy.

Introducing import tariffs in 1932 brought an end to the free trade debate, which had been the cornerstone of British economic policy since 1845. Free trade had replaced mercantilism and protectionism in Britain in 1845 but not in the dominions. With introducing imperial preferences in the 1930s, Britain experienced a significant rise in imperial trade after the 1930s, rising from 30 per cent in 1932 to 40 per cent in 1935. The US and Europe also responded with higher levels of tariffs in the 1930s. Globalisation, which took off in the 1870s and which was temporarily halted during the First World War, was put into reverse in the 1930s.[14]

Maynard Keynes: General Theory of Employment, Interest, and Money

Maynard Keynes was, by now, one of the most influential economists in the UK. Keynesian economics came to influence British economic policies from the 1940s to the 1980s. Maynard Keynes[15] had developed his ideas into the general theory of employment, interest and money, replacing much of the classical views of Smith and Ricardo. He invented the concept of macro-economics, the study of the economy and became the twentieth century's most influential economist. The general theory provided a theoretical economic basis for government intervention and full employment after the Second World War.

Keynes believed that unemployment resulted from insufficient demand, hence his focus on the demand side, in contrast to the classical economics of Smith, who focused on the supply side. Investments, which responded to variation in interest rates and to expectation about the future, was considered the key factor in determining the level of economic activity. The government could therefore directly influence demand through public expenditure and altering tax policies. Keynes rejected the idea that the pool of investments was finite, which was also the British Treasury's view. If there were idle resources available – the unemployed – then it suited a country to put them to work, he argued, and this was expected to expand overall economic activity. Keynes felt that the UK's interwar period monetary policy was inappropriately tight and unhelpful. The result was that Keynes's ideas became popular, and Keynesian macro-economic theories gained official acceptance with the British authorities. As a result, these ideas were put into practice, with Keynes as the government's key economic advisor and a director of the Bank of England. Keynesian economics became central to British economic management in the period after 1945, heralding a greater role for government in the economy, even by the conservative prime ministers. The conservative coalition government, with other parties, had been in place after 1940. Clement Atlee of the Labour Party was deputy prime minister in the 1945 coalition government, with Churchill as prime minister. Coalition governments prevailed between 1940 and 1945 and, in 1944, produced a white paper which was heavily influenced by Keynes and William Beveridge, a member of Parliament, and this explicitly made full employment for the first time a central goal of the government.

Beveridge was a social economist who, like Keynes, believed in state intervention to address social and economic problems such as unemployment, and was the architect of the British National Insurance System and the welfare state. Under Keynes's influence, the British annual budget exercise ceased to be a simple instrument of raising taxes and dividing the cash between departments of government; instead, it came to represent an active tool of macro-economic management. According to Keynes, if the economy were getting overheated, government could reduce demand and cool inflation; conversely, if recession were on the horizon, government could boost demand by public works and generate employment. For Keynes, macro-economic policy could be adjusted to take into consideration the economic temperature. The trade union movement fully supported Keynesian economic policy of full employment; the unions therefore became early disciples of Keynesianism.[16]

An important economic development in 1956 was also the work of William Phillips,[17] an economist who published a paper on the relationship between wages and unemployment which became known as the 'Phillips Curve.'[18] Empirically, Phillips showed that there was an inverse relationship between the level of employment and the rate of inflation. If unemployment were low, then wage growth would quicken as firms compete to obtain an additional workforce, and this faster growth in wages would push up prices. On the other hand, if unemployment was high, then wage growth would be slower, and prices would rise less rapidly.

EXAMINATION OF THE HISTORICAL DEVELOPMENT OF THE JAMAICAN ECONOMY

The concept of economic development was used by European policymakers for the first time in the nineteenth century to describe solutions intended to ameliorate social and economic problem of post-industrial societies.[19] Specifically for the nineteenth century, with British imperialists the concept of development carried a set of state-centred interventions designed to generate social and economic transformation to secure transitions of British colonies from traditional to a more modern structure. From an analysis of the historical development of the Jamaican economy, Imperial British economic policies benefited Britain and not Jamaica.

In the examination of the development of the Jamaican economy, the following periods have been adopted: 1650–1830s, the slave plantation economy and White domination; the period 1830–1930, the rise of the smallholder economy; the period 1930–50, when Jamaicans agitated for self-government and increased influence in shaping the political, economic, and social agenda of the island. This was followed by the period 1950–75, a short period of bauxite mining and north American colonisation. Since 1975, the Washington Consensus Group of the IMF, World Bank and USAID, under the guise of structural and sectoral adjustment, has largely shaped economic development. Jamaica now seems to add another layer of external control, involving Chinese infrastructure-based colonisation. The one big difference with the relationship with the Chinese as Minister Christopher Tufton of Jamaica said during a BBC 4 broadcast in November 2022 is that, with the Chinese, Jamaicans can decline Chinese participation in the economy and that the Chinese intentions differ from the Europeans, in that they have not had a history of colonising other people, implying that the Chinese may be more altruistic in their relations with Jamaica.

An attempt has also been made to differentiate the stewardship periods of the PNP and JLP administrations in managing Jamaican economic policies and development and their effects on transforming the country. These periods have been broken down as follows: 1962–72, 1972–80, 1980–89, 1989–2007, and 2007–22. This division by the stewardship of each prime minister, especially after independence in 1962, is more one of historical convenience. Various economic historians and analysts have adopted different break periods. Notably, certain economic policies were carried over succeeding period, hence certain trends overlap the different prime ministerial stewardship periods. Table 1.1 shows the different stewardship periods of the two parties, especially since universal adult suffrage in 1944 and the period when local Jamaicans have been able to exercise greater influence over economic and social policies.

Donald Harris, a leading Jamaican economist, conducted an empirical analysis of the Jamaican economy and based his analysis on two broad periods: 1940–73 and 1973–89. The main features of these periods are summarised in the three works of Harris.[20] During the period 1973–89, there were not only dramatic changes in economic performances but also in the economic policies pursued by the different administrations. Harris showed that, in the period 1974–80, there was a sharp reversal of trends compared to the years preceding 1973, while in the period 1981–85, there was a virtual stagnation of the economy, with the situation picking up again in the period 1986–89. Harris also showed that, in the two decades during 1969–89, the economy grew by an annual average of 0.24 per cent. Using comparative data for 1950–965, he also showed that there was a major change in the underlying structure of the economy over the period 1969–89.

In this period, the primary production (agriculture, mining, manufacturing) began a decline, accompanied by a rise in the services sector. It was also in this period, Harris argued, that Jamaica became a debt-propelled economy. Both external and domestic debt expanded to alarming proportions; the servicing of this debt since has been the major constraint to Jamaica's economic growth. Economic policies since the 1970s have also mainly centred on reducing the debt and addressing the debt problem.

Harris's last paper was written in 1992, so we could add another period: 1990–2021, the age of the services economy. This period has shown anaemic growth for much of the three decades, some years negative and some years positive. During this period, real gross domestic growth has been boosted by infrastructural developments in telecommunications, bauxite/alumina mining, tourism, transport, and construction.

Table 1.1: The Stewardship Periods of Jamaica's Political Parties and Prime Minsters 1944-2021

Period	Party	Head of Government
December 12, 1944–54	JLP	Alexander Bustamante, Chief Minister
1954–62	PNP	Norman Manley, Premier
April 10, 1962–72	JLP	Alex Bustamante 1962–February 1967, Prime Minister Donald Sangster, Prime Minister, February 23, 1967–April 11, 1967 Hugh Shearer, Prime Minister, April 11, 1967– March 2, 1972
February 29, 1972–80	PNP	Michael Manley, Prime Minister
October 30, 1980–89	JLP	Edward Seaga, Prime Minister and Finance Minister
February 19,1989–92	PNP	Michael Manley, Prime Minister/P.J. Patterson-Deputy, Re-elected in December of 1997 and in October of 2002
March 30, 1992–March 30, 2006	PNP	P.J. Patterson: resigned from Parliament and office
March 30, 2006–September 11, 2007	PNP	Portia Simpson: called election and was defeated
Sept 11, 2007–October 23, 2011	JLP	Bruce Golding: called election and was defeated
January 5, 2012–March 3, 2016	PNP	Portia Simpson, Prime Minister
March 3, 2016, to date (2022)	JLP	Andrew Holness, Prime Minister

Note: In December 1983, the JLP did not complete its five-year term and instead called a snap election. The PNP did not contest elections; the party won with a majority of 89 per cent, and voter turnout was 30 per cent. Shortly after Manley took office in 1989, he became ill, and Patterson succeeded him March 30, 1992, as prime minister. Between October 1989 and March 30, 1992, Patterson first served as deputy prime minister and minister of production, development and planning, and later minister of finance, development and planning and thereafter as prime minister. Patterson called early elections in March 1993 to seek his own mandate and so served for four consecutive terms.

As a result of the IMF Structural Adjustment policies which came into force in the early 1980s emphasis was placed on expansion of export but after the financial crisis of 1997, the Jamaican economy continued to be plagued by worsening debt problem, high interest rate, and high unemployment. High unemployment levels, which remained a persistent and entrenched feature of the Jamaican economy over the years, have been falling since 2004, when the rate reached 11.4 per cent, falling from the previous levels of between 20 per cent and 25 per cent.[21] The unemployment rate has continued to fall and, in 2015, was under 10 per cent. The debt stock has also been falling from US$21.6 billion in 2012, or 143.9 per cent of GDP to US$14.02 billion in 2021 or 100.2 per cent[22] and IMF Country Data.[23] Inflation has also been brought down to single digit, under 8 per cent in 2021. Agriculture now forms less than 8 per cent of GDP and mining less than 3 per cent in 2021, with services forming 74 per cent of the economy, in terms of share of GDP.[24]

Although economic growth since 2015 has been weak, there is an argument that Jamaica has achieved structural adjustment after four decades of implementing IMF structural adjustment programmes and that, with the debt stock falling below 100 per cent, this augurs well for the growth of the economy, barring major external shocks, like COVID-19, wars, and global economic downturn.

Jamaica's Pre-Emancipation Economic Development

In the mid-seventeenth century, sugar was brought to Jamaica and the rest of the West Indies and quickly displaced cotton and tobacco. As part of the economic development, there was the introduction of European agricultural capitalism, based on sugar cane cultivation. Jamaica and Caribbean sugar became popular in Britain and, by the eighteenth century, it replaced piracy as the main source of income, with Jamaica becoming the largest exporter of sugar in the world. The Jamaican and Caribbean sugar industry was very labour intensive, needing large quantities of cheap labour, and this was supplied by the trade in enslaved Africans and through chattel labour. The sugar monoculture and plantation system spread throughout Jamaica, with the number of sugar estates increasing from 57 in 1673 to 430 in 1739.[25] Jamaica eventually became Britain's most valuable colony during the eighteenth century. The Price family, who came to hold a patent for 840 acres at Worthy Park in St Catharine, was led by one of the richest men. Another notable rich plantation owner was the Beckford family. Peter Beckford was acting governor of Jamaica in 1702 and became a prominent slave owner and businessman, accumulating some twenty estates in the island.[26]

The decline in sugar can be traced back to the abolition of the trade in enslaved Africans in 1807 and accelerated after 1934. Following a slave rebellion in 1831, the British held two enquiries, and the reports from these revealed the appalling conditions under which African Jamaicans worked on the sugar plantations. By 1820, Jamaican sugar had become less competitive compared with that of high-volume producers, such as Cuba and Brazil, so production declined drastically after 1830. The sugar industry also suffered a crushing blow from the abolition of the Sugar Duties Act in 1846, which equalised imports of sugar from British colonies.

Eric Williams has argued that the abolition of the slave trade in 1807 and of slavery just over thirty years later was not a humanitarian gesture by the British, but that plantation sugar had by then become an economically unviable institution.[27] In addition, Jamaica had to contend with the rise of European beet sugar after 1870, especially from Germany, worsening the economic and social conditions on the island.

When Britain was persuaded to emancipate African Jamaicans, sugar was already in decline. By 1832 sugar output was less than 50 per cent of the level achieved in 1828.[28] Unable to convert the formerly enslaved population into a wage-earning class, the colonial administration resorted to recruiting a contingent of cheap labour for sugar estates, this time mainly from Sierra Leone, India, and China. After 1850 Jamaica displayed an interplay of small-scale agriculture and peasantry, alongside the plantation structure.

Growth of Jamaica's Domestic Agriculture and Development of the Rural Smallholder (Peasant) Community

The development of the smallholder or 'peasant' community in Jamaica in the post- emancipation years had its roots in two indigenous institutions: 'provision grounds' and the 'internal marketing system.' Both institutions have been rooted in the island's slavery and plantation system, under which the enslaved people were required to cultivate and provide the largest portions of food needs for their family on plots of land (provision ground), bordering the estates and which were allotted to them by the planters. They could sell or trade the excess at a market in the nearby towns. In this way, the enslaved could accumulate cash through their independent marketing activities.[29] The provision of ground and internal marketing systems must be seen within the framework of the island's agricultural structure, dominated by the estate production of sugar on plantations for exports since the seventeenth century.[30]

Provision Grounds

During slavery, the convention developed concerning the right of the enslaved Afro-Jamaicans to own their produce and the financial rewards of the sale of this produce. This convention not only came to be respected by planters, but the colonial administrators also incorporated its main features in a series of Consolidated Slave Acts (1788,1792 and 1816). The provision grounds were essential to the operation of plantation sugar, and their operations were outside the management of the estate supervisors. The first Slave Act, updated in 1735, empowered the enslaved to produce and sell many provisions, fruits, fresh fish, milk, poultry, and small stocks of all kinds, making their role virtually indispensable in the development of the post-emancipation economy. The acts legislated how to treat and punish the enslaved people; in addition, these acts made it mandatory for every slave owner to allot small plots of land, sufficient for provisioning ground.[31] The planters were required to allow the enslaved people one day per fortnight to work on their provision grounds; however, many planters allowed one day per week. In fact, the system extended to produce domestic foodstuff for the white planters and supervisors; the result was that the plantations needed only to import certain foodstuff, such as salt fish, salted meat, flour, cornmeal, and tinned food, which were not readily available in Jamaica and were imported mainly from Canada after the 1770 American War of Independence. The provision ground system and the experiences from farming and market higglering came to form the backbone of Jamaica's domestic agriculture after 1860.

Once the plantation slavery system was established, planters faced the cost of feeding their enslaved workers. The choice was to import the food at significant cost or to provide the incentives for the enslaved to feed themselves. They chose the latter and, largely, food production by the enslaved grew during slavery in the absence of compulsion and under conditions which implicitly acknowledged their responsiveness to the incentives after emancipation, which operated for the free African Jamaicans. It was in addition to their labour on the plantation that the enslaved found time to produce a variety of foods such as fruit trees, vegetables, edible herbs, and roots, as well as craft materials.[32] The freed Black Jamaican population, after the abolition of slavery in 1838, fled to the interior hillsides to form smallholder farming communities, carrying out cash crop production or ground provision agriculture. The system of provision grounds eventually was extended to the entire island and grew to form the foundation for domestic production. During the First World War, with the temporary suspension of international shipping, Jamaica's domestic agricultural production grew to challenge export agriculture; however, the colonial administrators never acted on the opportunity to expand domestic food production permanently and become self-sufficient in food supply.

In 1838, the smallholder rural communities (landholdings of under forty acres) were reported to number 2,014 and, in the space of two years, had increased to 7,340.[33] By 1880, the number of smallholdings had increased to 49,995, of which 38,000 were under five acres and 13,189 between five acres and forty-nine acres. The policy of public land distribution which was introduced after 1865 to support the African Jamaican rural communities, accelerated the increase in smallholdings and, by 1890, the number under fifty acres had increased to 111,957 of which 95,941were under five acres. In 1930, the number of smallholdings under fifty acres increased further to 184,440, of which 153,406 were under five acres. The number of smallholdings under fifty acres continued to grow up to 1943, then amounting to 209,834, with 179,788 forming smallholdings under five acres.[34]

Sunday Markets and Growth of an Internal Marketing System

The internal market system forms the second connected institution developed by the freed African Jamaicans after emancipation in 1838. The first markets were customarily operated on Sundays, so as not to interfere with estate operation and soon, markets developed outside the slave villages, in the port towns of Kingston; Montego Bay, Lucea, Falmouth, Black River, Savanna-la-Mar, Annotto Bay, Port Antonio and Ocho Rio, as well as inland towns of Spanish Town, Mandeville, Brown's Town, and Chapelton. The previous experiences in developing provision ground agriculture and village marketing provision served as a critical apprenticeship for smallholders and higglers in domestic trade which later required them to travel extensively on foot to other properties to deliver fresh meat, vegetables, and other commodities for their owners. Some of the African women had arrived in Jamaica with a background which facilitated their role as higglers, since the vast majority of African Jamaicans came from West Africa where markets were highly developed and where women were predominantly the marketers.[35]

The economic importance of the higglers to the viability of the estates was not lost on the colonial administration, and, as a result, as early as 1711 the traders were given legal rights to market specific commodities. The rapid growth of the internal market system by enslaved persons was not the result of purely economic factors; it socialised, in that market day, providing a welcome relief from estate life. The markets became cultural centres where news and items of material culture were distributed and popularised.[36]

The plantation system and the smallholder peasant economy led to an insular social structure in which there was a sharply differentiated access to land, wealth, and political power, resulting in a hierarchy of classes and social relations (upper, middle, and lower) based on a criterion of colour, ethnicity, occupation and wealth, with Whites at the top, Browns, or coloureds in the middle and Blacks at the bottom. This replaced the binary structure of Whites at the top and non-Europeans at the bottom, which prevailed during plantation slavery. The socio-economic structure of Jamaica since then has developed to reflect a legacy of this socio-economic structure – a society that has a legacy of categorising its citizens into social groups based on physical characteristics (colour of skin, physical features, and straightness of hair). It became a norm to describe someone using their skin colour as a major descriptor. Through hybridisation (intermarrying or miscegenation), members of society gained social mobility. For an extended discussion of Jamaica's ethno-race structure, see chapter 4 'The Population Dynamics of the Jamaican Economy.'

Eventually, the responsibility for markets fell to local government authorities. In the 1990s, there were ninety-three government supervised parochial market places.[37] In 1960, the government established the Agricultural Marketing Corporation as a wholesale produce distributor, becoming an important link in the national distribution system. Initially, open markets were held in the larger villages and port towns. One of the first open markets to be established was in Spanish Town, providing an outlet for the provision grounds of Sligoville, one of the first free villages to be created in Jamaica just after 1838. After emancipation, market days were held on Wednesdays and Saturdays. In Kingston, several markets were established and some of these, like the Coronation Market, opened daily, although the great market day was always held on Saturday when people from the nearby hill villages would send or take their produce, stocks, and craft items for the weekend trading.[38] Markets after emancipation typically occupied a fixed enclosure, often enclosed to provide some security, instead of being open as in the days of slavery. Some provided covered booths, especially for meat and fish stalls. The facility was owned by the parochial boards, which would then rent it out to private individuals for a fixed sum per annum rent.[39] The authorities then administered its operation, looked after its security and, in return, collected an administration fee from the vendors.

Sellers and buyers sometimes travelled a long distance to visit the market. In the initial days, the goods were transported by donkeys or horse-drawn vehicles; however, after the First World War animal-drawn vehicles were replaced by trucks and country buses. The Kingston electric tram introduced a special market higgler service shortly after its inauguration. The country buses carried the loads on top of the vehicles. Minibuses have largely replaced trucks and country buses since the 1990s. Items of produce available in the markets included vegetables, root plants, fruits in season, spices, ackee, bananas (ripe and green) brown sugar; those higglers who deal in meat and fish require special certification, as well as those dealing in craft items, such as jewellery and handicraft items and jackass rope (tobacco). Cooked food was provided, such as bammy, patties, fried fish, ackee and salt fish, along with drinks such as ginger beer. Articles for household use were also traded, such as crockery, water carriers, tinware, mats, brooms, and dry goods.[40]

Higglers then and now were usually of two types: those who grew their own produce on their provision ground lots and those who bought from the rural smallholder farmer and took supplies to the market to sell. Many Jamaicans, especially poor women, turned to the tradition of higglering in response to deteriorating economic conditions of the island. However, as the informal economy expanded, the formal business community and city residents became concerned about higglers on the streets of Kingston, and tensions build among these groups. However, Higglers have been admired for their ability to survive in the face of great adversity; they are believed to exemplify the strength and resilience of African Jamaican women. On the other hand, a section of society has frowned on higglers for their indiscipline. Such perceptions have long plagued higglers throughout Jamaica's history. There are many examples from Jamaica's colonial past to today of higglers described and treated as nuisances, calling on the government of the day to remove higglers from the streets.

The Jamaican higgler developed in the 1990s to form a new entrepreneurial category of traders: Informal Commercial Importers (ICIs). The ICIs travel overseas to export their wares and on the return journey import a vast array of consumer items which are then traded locally, not only in the designated market places but on the streets as well, trying to make a living under arduous conditions.[41]

Despite the growth of the domestic economy, many African Jamaicans were unemployed or underemployed in the 1860s. It was in this period that many turned to market higglering on a large scale and to domestic service as household helpers and gardeners.[42] The economic conditions were deplorable and wretched, and it was the wretched conditions that triggered the Morant Bay Rebellion of 1865. The rebellion was not only against dire economic and social conditions but the disenfranchisement of Black Jamaicans. In fact, just before the uprising occurred, a group of African Jamaicans, in April 1865, petitioned Queen Victoria who, in a heartless and unsympathetic response, dismissed their plea for help, in effect scolding the people for not wanting to continue under the atrocious working conditions. The punishment, however, which was inflicted on the African Jamaicans by Governor Eyre, was excessive, resulting in him being replaced by the more enlightened Sir John Peter Grant.

One of the early initiatives of the new governor was that for the first-time crown lands were provided on favourable terms to rural farming communities, allowing smallholders to purchase plots of land of up to five acres. The land settlement programme launched over the 1890–1929 period was one of the first steps taken by the colonial government to address the concerns of rural smallholders and the emerging Black working class. The programme of land settlement and improvement scheme, which was initially contemplated to involve a sale of plots after roads, water supply and other village facilities at the time of establishing the schemes, did not occur, resulting in land acquisition being on unimproved land.[43] The number of smallholdings however tripled between 1865 and 1930.[44]

The price of sugar fell sharply in the 1880s–90s and did not recover until after the First World War. Sugar cultivation and sugar works were largely labour intensive, with very little change in terms of new technology up to 1930. However, it was the rise of the banana industry after 1870 that brought some prosperity to rural small farmers, consolidating the growth of the Jamaican economy. By 1890, banana had replaced sugar as the principal export, with production rising from five million stems, or 32 per cent of exports in 1897 to average over twenty million stems a year during the period of the 1920s and 1930s. Banana increased its share to over 50 per cent of domestic exports.[45] Banana export was boosted by the entry of the American multinational United Fruit Company, to the island. At this point, Britain became more interested in the banana industry. Banana could be grown on marginal lands and did not require high levels of capital expenditure or sophisticated agronomy but demanded less labour than sugar and therefore provided fewer jobs.

The main economic problem in the period 1830–1930 was the shortage of gainful employment.[46] In the period 1870–1920, population growth averaged 1.2 per cent per annum; although not rapid, growth outpaced growth in the supply of suitable land. This triggered the first mass migration, mainly to Central America and Cuba.[47] While the British government applied free trade and laissez-faire economic policies at home, enterprises domiciled in Britain had the advantage of exploiting the market of the colonies on favourable terms. The laissez-faire capitalism which prevailed in Britain allowed its firms to exclude rival firms from countries outside the empire from the British market. It was also much more difficult for local Jamaicans to start an enterprise in Jamaica than for a British citizen to do so, a prime example of the imperial system of capitalism.[48]

Jamaica's Economic Situation after 1930

There was a paradigm shift in economic management in Britain, with Keynesian economic ideas replacing liberal capitalism, dominating economic policy after the 1940s and up to 1980. The British government which had been the main promoter of free trade up to 1930, and with a uniquely free economy, made a U-turn during the de-globalisation period after the First World War. Even the US in the period expanded the role of the state, with US presidents after 1940 increasing the government's role in the economy. Protectionism, through imperial preferences of the 1930s, took over in British international free trade policies. However, international trade contracted at the beginning of the First World War, and its effect on the Jamaican economy was harsh. In 1913, sugar production fell to its lowest level since 1710.[49] Economic conditions in the 1920s were mixed, with global export trade reviving; however, demand for Jamaican products remained weak. Agriculture remained the largest sector of the economy in the 1920s, still accounting for 45 per cent of the labour force.[50] The period of the 1930s experienced consolidation of sugar estates, with the entry of British multinational firm Tate and Lyle into the Jamaican sugar industry.

In addition to persistent shortages of gainful jobs for the masses during the period up to the 1920s, Jamaica was a place of poverty, poor housing, inadequate sanitary and social services, poor dietary practises, poor educational facilities, and widespread tropical diseases. Outside of Kingston, there was little suitable housing; what was available were mostly modest huts, the sidings, or outsides constructed from wattle and daub with marl. The *Daily Gleane*r reported these conditions in a series of articles between 1898 and1920.

The 1911 census showed that 81 per cent of dwellings contained only one or two rooms, with an average of 4.5 residents per dwelling, compared to 4.8 per dwelling in 1891. Most of the houses in rural areas lacked piped water, electricity, and sanitary facilities, using mainly pit latrines. Between 1911 and 1921, more houses added floorings and replaced thatched roofs with shingle or metal roofs; however, in 1921, 17 per cent of the houses still lacked any flooring.[51] During the period, Jamaica also suffered from high infant mortality. After a lengthy period without growth, personal consumption expanded in 1910, but slowly and from a low level. Economic data on distribution of income up to 1930 were never provided; however, all indications are that the small rural smallholders improved their economic position after the 1880s. Government spending was minimal prior to 1880, accounting for only 4.5 per cent of GDP in 1910, increasing to 6.5 per cent.[52]

According to the 1921 census, 52.1 per cent of adults could read and write. In the period up to 1890, it was left to missionary societies to provide free schooling (age six to fifteen), with the colonial government offering grants for teachers' salaries. School fees were discarded in 1892, which widely expanded elementary education. By 1920, there were 693 elementary schools (government and denominational), accommodating 92,176 registered students, accompanied by four teacher training colleges. The curriculum, however, was modelled on the system in England. Students were required to learn British history, geography, and politics, with nothing about West Indian conditions. The first public elementary school was established in 1885. By 1940, 60 per cent of children were enrolled in schools; therefore, there were gains in literacy during this period, with regular attendance at 63.2 per cent.[53]

A good health system incorporating district medical officers was introduced in the 1860s, covering forty districts in the island. District medical officers were professionally trained in Britain. In 1884–85, there were eighty-eight hundred people per licensed doctor; by 1900, the situation had improved to sixty-one hundred and by 1920 to fifty-four hundred.[54] Improvements in health and life expectancy began in the 1920s with sanitary improvements in Kingston and a few of the rural towns, especially through the system of dispersed medical care, which expanded after the 1920s; this helped to eradicate certain common diseases, leading to improved health care, and improvements to life expectancy.

Structure of the Economy and Economic Performance: Post-Emancipation 1830–1930

Jamaica's economic policies before 1930, a period of complete colonisation, were inextricably linked to the UK. With the UK's early economic policy initially founded on mercantilism, Jamaica's economic policymaking came to be shaped by UK economic policymaking from the mid-1600s. It was not until the 1940s that the island's economic policymaking could shed policies that were, in the main, externally driven. Free trade, which replaced mercantilism in the 1780s was never extended to Jamaica and the colonies, as Britain continued to protect her colonial market for British products.

Gisela Eisner provides a path-breaking analysis of the Jamaican economy, post-emancipation to 1930.[55] Table 1.2 shows the structure of the economy in 1832 with sugar (includes export sugar) bananas and domestic agriculture, accounting for the major share of GDP, at over 61.1 per cent, falling to 51.8 per cent in 1930.

Table 1.2: Gross Domestic Product at 1910 Constant Prices, 1832–1930, Percentage Share

Sector	1832	1850	1870	1890	1910	1930
Agriculture: export	31.7	15.8	15.5	16.1	21.4	20.6
Agriculture: local food production	28.6	37.4	39.4	36.7	33.3	31.2
Building /Construction	4.8	6.7	4.9	4.5	4.3	5.0
Manufacturing for local consumption	6.5	9.4	12.9	13.3	12.4	13.4
Transportation/communication	-	-	0.5	1.2	1.3	2.0
Distribution	4.8	6.5	4.1	5.4	4.5	4.2
Public administration	6.0	4.7	3.9	4.1	3.8	5.3
Ownership of houses	8.7	10.6	11.3	11.2	10.7	10,5
Domestic services	5.0	5.7	4.8	4.8	5.5	5.3
Professional services	3.9	4.2	2.7	3.5	2.6	3.0
Total	100	100	100	100	100	100

Source: Gisela Eisner, *Jamaican Economy,1830–1930: A Study of Economic Growth* (Manchester: Manchester University Press, 1961).

Export agriculture fell from 31.7 per cent of GDP in 1832 to 15.5 per cent in 1870. Between 1870 and 1890, export agriculture declined in relative terms; domestic agriculture expanded after 1850 from 28.6 per cent to reach its highest point in the 1870, at 39.4 per cent, before falling to 31.2 per cent in 1930.

Up to 1930, the contribution of agriculture to GDP was consistently over 50 per cent.[56] Thorne further notes that there was no important sector of the Jamaican population which was completely outside the price and money economy. Phyllis Deane notes that, for the year 1938, the subsistence production which characterised most colonial activities was a subsidiary form of economic activity.[57] Agricultural products in 1943 accounted for 77 per cent of the value of exports, mainly to the UK.[58]

The public administration's share of GDP in 1832 was 6 per cent; however, its share of GDP fell to 3.9 per cent in 1870, partly the result of a weakening economy. Between 1890 and 1930, the public administration's share of GDP varied between 4.1 per cent and 5.3 per cent. The increased share in 1930 reflected the increased participation of the colonial government after Governor Sir John Peter Grant's initiatives in education, health services, and public works.

Economic, Social, and Political Situation: 1930–50

The economic and social situation in Jamaica took a sharp turn for the worse during the Great Depression of the 1930s, with export prices falling and the opportunity to export labour to Latin America having disappeared. There were, however, marginal improvements in housing, education, and health care. Between 1921 and 1943, the average number of persons per house and per room declined so that houses were slightly less crowded. In 1943, the typical poor household of five persons lived in one room measuring 10ft x 12ft.[59] In constant value, public sector expenditure as a share of GDP increased by 20 per cent between 1925 and 1940 and by 57.0 per cent between 1925 and 1950.[60]

The number of people per medical doctors hovered around six thousand until 1910 when it declined progressively up to 1950s. In the period 1930–40, the supply of Jamaican doctors also increased. By 1940, an extensive network of health clinics had emerged all over the island. More hospitals were also built, including a tuberculosis sanatorium. Jamaicans had better access to health facilities in 1940 than in 1910.[61] Between 1929 and 1940, the duration of the British Colonial Development Act, the British government increased expenditure for welfare and development.

Up to 1890, the upper class, comprising British plantation owners, still controlled the political system, most of the wealth, and held most of the local leadership roles in political, social, and cultural affairs. This position was undermined in the 1890s, resulting from the sharp decline in sugar exports and the declining profitability of the sugar industry. Unable to compete with Cuba and Brazil, many planters sold out and left the island, to be replaced by British and North American transnational corporations. Although the British government had restored some representative government, allowing nine elected legislators in 1884 and fourteen in 1895, one for each parish, it was not enough to meet the demands of the growing middle class who, by 1938, comprised increased numbers of professionals, in addition to the expanding numbers of teachers, nurses, and clerks forming the Jamaica bourgeoisie. Beckford and Witter described the period 1938–62 as an era of the 'mulatto petit-bourgeois.'[62] From the 1920s, this group became increasingly dissatisfied with the Crown Colony government and began an agitation for a more representative system which would satisfy their demands for self-determination.

May 1938 marked another major turning point in Jamaica's social and political history, involving another rioting by disgruntled job seekers who had converged at the new British- owned sugar factory that had just opened in Frome, Westmoreland. Violence broke out among the job seekers, and the agitation quickly spread to dock workers and public employees in Kingston, and then to banana and sugar plantations island-wide. Out of the widespread rioting in 1938 labour unions emerged, associated with the two major political parties which had also been formed coming out of the labour disturbances. The Jamaica Labour Party (JLP), led by labour leader Alexander Bustamante, reflected a contradiction, being composed of a new Black agro-proletariat, joining with the White plantocracy, reflecting the philosophy of conservatism. In the 1944 election, the main planks of Bustamante's JLP platform were workmen compensation and minimum wage law for all workers, eight-hour day for all workers, old age pension, state aid for expectant mothers, and a more extensive land settlement scheme. The People's National Party (PNP), led by the intellectually oriented Norman Manley, a leading Jamaican lawyer, reflected the urbanised middle-class professionals, espousing radical change and threating traditional.[63] In the period up to 1940, there was, however, a consensus between both parties on economic policies, both favouring free trade and private sector–led economic development. Both were in favour of mixed social democratic ideas for community development and high public spending on health, education, and infrastructure, with individuals taking responsibility for the exploitation of economic opportunities that presented themselves. The policy of both parties emphasised self-reliance and community engagement.

The response of the British to the riots of 1938 was another Royal Commission of Inquiry[64] with Lord Moyne as the chairman. The report recommended among other changes, legalisation of the unions to allow labour to bargain collectively, minimum wages, and economic reorientation towards a smallholder's economy and crop diversification. The Moyne Report suggested that the economic future of the Caribbean was based on its natural comparative advantage to produce agricultural products in their primary state, downplayed any possibility for tourism, and definitely ruled out industrialisation through manufacturing.

While the British were preoccupied with voting rights and participation in government, local Jamaicans were more concerned about jobs, community, and social development, and political organisation, including political parties and education. In the 1940s, the British government noted the concerns of Jamaicans and recommended adjustments to the political system. In the period 1940–46, major changes were made to the system, including the introduction of Universal Adult Suffrage. The changes saw a vast expansion of the electorate from sixty-three thousand in 1937 to over six hundred thousand in 1944.[65] The adoption of universal adult suffrage consolidated the hold of the middle class, largely coloured professionals and merchants.

Post-War Economic Policy and Planning

The need for industrialisation of the Jamaican economy was first brought to public attention in September 1929, when the manifesto of the People's Political Party, led by Marcus Garvey, called for a law to facilitate the promotion of native industries.[66] The call for industrialisation became more widespread in the 1930s, with the PNP's economic policy of 1939, also advocating the encouragement of local industries.[67] The PNP followed up with a call for an industrial development board in 1945 and, in 1949, proposed that as part of a comprehensive plan for industrial development, it was necessary to provide incentives to encourage investment and to impose import duties to protect local industries from foreign competition.[68] The period of the 1940s was significant in that it marked a time when a decision had been taken by the British government to move towards political independence for the colonies, giving Jamaicans and the West Indies more say in their own economic policymaking. Although plans for political independence were being considered, no such plans were considered for economic independence. The Westminster ideas on economic development were profoundly suspicious of state involvement in economic ownership.[69] The PNP, in 1947, made the first local attempt to intervene in the economy strategically through introducing the first Ten-Year Plan of Development,[70] which drew on the Colonial Development Acts of 1940. These acts made available around £5 million annually for grants to Jamaica and other West Indian colonies for five years to promote the development of resources and the welfare of their people for social and economic projects. The Jamaican project implementation began in 1940.[71] The Colonial Development 1945 Act increased the amount to £12 million and extended the period to 1956.[72]

Industrialisation was relegated to a secondary position in the first Ten-year Plan. In addition to emphasis on agriculture, including land settlement schemes and encouragement of mixed farming, emphasis was to be placed on improvements to education, health, housing, and water supply. The 1951 revision of the plan, however, emphasised elevation of industrial development to a position of priority, to be implemented through the Pioneer Encouragement Acts, the first of which was passed in 1949. Firms operating under these acts benefited from tax relief or were granted infant industries status, which provided protection. The Industrial Development Corporation was created in 1951 to lead the programme of industrialisation. The 1957 Plan reflected a major departure from previous policy, identifying export production for greater emphasis than production for the domestic market.

Characteristic features of the Jamaican plantation economy were its small size and lack of intersectoral linkages. The sectors did not use enough of each other's resource outputs as inputs and, most importantly, the economy did not have an internal dynamic; it was essentially producing export material for metropolitan UK. The island's economy characteristically has been very open; international trade being large in relation to total economic activity and, as a result, there was a serious disjuncture between aggregate consumption and aggregate production.[73]

The Great Depression of the 1930s and the Second World War had resulted in a prolonged stagnation of Caribbean economies. As there was an urgent need to revive the Jamaican economy, in 1944, the British government engaged Frederick Benham, a distinguished English economist of the post-war years, to advise on the economic policy to be pursued by Jamaica. In 1945, Benham submitted his report, advising against tax incentives, loans, tariff protection, as well as against any form of government investment in industry. He cited the high cost of locally manufactured goods, relative to imported goods and limited employment potential, with the policy recommending continuation of the development of agriculture and improving social services. Benham strongly discouraged industrialisation, as there was the concern that it would damage the interest of British exporters.[74] Benham outrightly dismissed the idea of small islands like Jamaica being industrialised, reflecting the thinking of Britain. The British government supported the position taken by the British economist and did everything to discourage Jamaica from developing its manufacturing capacity and the embryonic tourism industry, arguing that the island was better served by importing manufactured goods from the UK at much lower prices. The development path for Jamaica and other small Caribbean islands, Benham argued, was the continuation of their agricultural sectors.

W.A. Lewis's Theory of Caribbean Economic Development

The period after the Second World War saw the emergence of new theories of economic development orchestrated within the Caribbean with the development theories of the notable St Lucia–born economist Sir Arthur Lewis. In the period 1945–55, the ideas of Lewis came to dominate Caribbean economic thought. The historical context of his views on industrialisation was the Caribbean Post-War expansion of international capital economies, dominated by the US in the era of decolonisation. Lewis sought to develop a meaningful Caribbean approach to economic policy in response to externally directed policies, such as the Report of the Moyne West India Royal Commission Report of 1945 and Benham's Economic Policy Committee Report on Jamaica. Lewis began writing from 1936 and his main interests were the theory of growth, economic development planning and, in particular, economic development in the Commonwealth Caribbean. Bernal et al. are of the view that Lewis's views on economic development of the West Indies shifted between 1936 and 1945.[75] In his two famous articles,[76] he articulated the case for industrialisation of the Caribbean.

In the first article, he reviewed the experiences in establishing manufacturing and the role of an Industrial Development Corporation in the development process. He concluded that the Industrial Development Corporation was an indispensable institution for development, that manufacturing activities should not be limited to processing local material and that, where necessary and profitable, the processing of imported inputs for exports should be encouraged. In the second paper, 'Industrialisation of the British West Indies,' he argued that industrial production should be oriented for the export market because the domestic market was too small.

It was in the second article that the case for industrialisation was fully set out. Lewis argued that, given the threat of overpopulation, Caribbean islands like Jamaica had to expand manufacturing because agriculture did not absorb the surplus labour and relieve the population pressure on agriculture. By relieving the population, pressure on agriculture, productivity, and income would grow. The new industries and the revitalised agriculture would increase the size of the domestic market, and, in his view, the level of output had to be greater than the domestic market could consume. He also argued that the pioneers of industrialisation would have to be foreign investors with their capital, know-how, and market connections. They were to be induced by industrial incentives provided by the state. The role of the state was to be confined to facilitation and not direct involvement in the productive process.

Lewis believed that the rapidly increasing population of the Caribbean and developing economies had exceeded the capacity to provide agricultural employment; the result was increased unemployment and poverty. On top of this, Jamaica had experienced political upheaval in 1938, further aggravating social conditions. The situation was compounded by the seasonality of employment in the sugar industry, the main employer.

For Lewis, Jamaica, and the West Indies displayed a dual economic structure comprising the many subsistence sector small capitalists. The subsistence sector was unproductive as its marginal productivity was near zero, because of excessive amount of labour working on small plots of land, essentially with manual tools and the absence of mechanisation. He argued that labour could leave the subsistence sector without decreasing production or increasing marginal wages. Simultaneously, the capitalist sector could increase profits through paying the low marginal wages determined by the subsistence sector.[77] The large size of the subsistence sector created a condition of a virtually unlimited supply of cheap labour, which could contribute to capital accumulation and reinvestment in the productive sectors.[78] It was at his 1955 presentation on 'Economic Development with Unlimited Supply of Labour' as well as through *The Theory of Economic Growth* where the theoretical base for his thesis was demonstrated.

According to Lewis, Jamaica, and the West Indies could use the unlimited supply of cheap labour as a comparative advantage in attracting industries, initially focusing on manufacturing for export, as it was the only sector capable of expanding without necessitating an expansion of domestic demand, particularly because of the small size of the domestic market and the initial low wages. In relation to the lack of local capital and know-how, he presumed investment would come from foreign sources, although he preferred local capital, if available, and felt it would eventually accumulate and be available for reinvestment. Meanwhile, the subsistence sector would shrink as agriculture modernised and became more productive through such investment.

Bernal et al. maintain that, in focusing on the problem of underdevelopment, Lewis chose Ricardian assumptions, and that Keynesianism is also clear in Lewis's strategy for growth, relying on state intervention, despite his own disclaimer.[79] Lewis was also full of admiration for the small farmer peasant community. He felt small farmer agriculture offered more stability, where it was based on the domestic market, not having to rely on fluctuating export market prices and that the distributional benefit was significant.[80]

Lewis's inclusion of domestic agriculture in his development theories is often overlooked or misunderstood, as several economists focus only on the 'industrialisation by invitation' model of development.[81] Lewis's full prescriptions on economics were not implemented correctly, particularly the need to increase agricultural production for the domestic market, as the policymakers became engrossed with development though industrialisation-by-invitation and by the focus on agriculture for export, partly because of the entrenched position of the plantocracy.[82]

W.A. Lewis was also critical of the Benham Report.[83] His thinking followed that of Prebisch, Raoul who had argued for industrialisation of the Caribbean.[84] Lewis's ideas strongly influenced the colonial administration's formulation of a raft of pioneering industrial encouragement laws.

Despite the position taken by the British government, the PNP in 1951, in its revised 1947 Ten-Year Plan, included the objective of transforming the plantation economy into an industrialised one; however, the state's role was to provide basic infrastructure, social services, and incentives for the private sector to carry out the production of goods and services.[85] Lewis and Benham had opposing poles of thought about economic policy and became engaged in a bitter clash in respect of their differing views as to the most appropriate route to expand Caribbean islands. Benham arrogantly dismissed Lewis's criticisms by stating that his commentary lacked specifics about feasible industries.[86] This clash of views was reminiscent of the earlier Hayek and Keynes clash about the most appropriate route that Britain should take for economic policymaking. Failing to introduce industrialisation earlier in Jamaica was therefore the result of a deliberate policy of the British government in its attempt to continue its traditional mercantilist policies in the colonies, in order to keep the market for its own goods.

The period after the 1950s saw locally elected Black politicians coming into their own. One of the most notable of these parliamentarians was a Jamaican entrepreneur, Robert Lightbourne, who had returned from England where he had established himself as an industrialist in Birmingham. Lightbourne was appointed minister of industry in the Bustamante JLP administration of the 1950s. He helped to establish the Jamaica Industrial Development Corporation (JIDC), which took on the responsibility of leading Jamaica's industrialisation programme. Lewis's view was central to the shift of approach by the colonial government in establishing JIDC. It was a period when native Jamaicans showed greater self-confidence and the middle-class urban merchants took on the challenge of shifting from being merely commission agents, or foreign manufacturing representatives, to creating the local manufacturing sector.[87]

The policy reform formula of introducing industrialisation-by-invitation and industrial incentives, and regulating the private sector through an extensive network of regulatory bodies, was also fully supported by the International Bank for Reconstruction in 1952.[88] In the 1950 report, the IBRD states that: 'Income tax concession has been and will continue to be of some value in attracting capital and stimulating inventiveness and we, accordingly, recommend that the Pioneer Industry Law be renewed at the end of 1952.'

In the period after 1944, a whole suite of industrial incentive laws was enacted to support Lewis's private sector–led approach to economic development. Jamaica introduced several new laws between 1950 and 1960 designed to promote industrial activities. These covered generous fiscal incentives such as ten-year tax holidays, accelerated depreciation, duty-free importation of raw materials, tariff protection, and subsidised factory space. The initiatives emphasised manufacturing, mining, and services (tourism) over agriculture. The relevant pieces of legislations which were enacted comprised the Hotel Aids Law of 1944, the Motion Picture Industry (Encouragement) Law of 1948, the Textile Industry (Encouragement) Law of 1947, the Cement Industry (Encouragement) Law of 1948, the Pioneer Industries (Encouragement) Law of 1949, the Bauxite and Alumina Encouragement Law of 1950, the Industrial Incentives Law of 1956, the Export Industries (Encouragement) Law of 1956, the International Business Companies Law of 1956, the Industrial Incentives (Factory Construction) Law of 1961, and the Export Industry Encouragement Act. Legislation aimed at creating protected monopolies in Jamaica went back as early as the Safeguarding of Local Industries Law of 1935. Under this law, the condensery, Jamaica Milk Products Limited, was given an exclusive production licence in 1940; the cement manufacturing plant, the Caribbean Cement Company Limited, was also given an exclusive production licence in 1949. Besides being a licensed monopoly, the cement plant could fix its price not on its production cost, but on a formula relating to a hypothetical landed price of imported cement. The Jamaica Match Industry Limited, one of the earliest factories outside of the sugar industry to be established in Jamaica, was awarded its production licence by the Privy Council in 1939, coupled with a profit guarantee. The company was protected with the benefit of a massive tariff on imported matches, with a return on capital of 8 per cent, later increased to 10 per cent, after tax. When the company failed to earn its guaranteed profit in any year, it received an appropriate amount out of public revenues in order to meet the established target return.[89] This state of affairs led Paul Chen Young to sharply criticise the monopolies and quasi-monopolies, arguing that, outside of the natural monopolies of the public utilities, they were not in the interest of the Jamaican consumer.[90]

In the National Plan of 1957–67, factors that made planning in Jamaica was the small size of government participation in the economic life of the country; public enterprises were few, and that Jamaica was a country where private companies operated most of economic life, so government planning was confined to providing incentives to private investors.[91] Although Jamaica became independent in 1962, returning the JLP to power and ousting the PNP, no major changes were made to economic policies until the end of 1972. Besides the PNP's Ten-year Plan of 1947, revised in 1951, the post-war period saw two more development plans: the National Plan for Development 1957–67, replaced by the Five-Year Independence Plan, 1963–68.

Economic Performance of the Jamaican Economy 1930–62

Table 1.3 below shows the structural changes in the economy over the period 1938–60. Agriculture, which was 36.2 per cent of GDP in 1938, declined to 16.4 per cent in 1956, with a further decline to 11.1 per cent by 1960. Mining, which did not exist as an industrial sector in 1938, came to contribute of 0.4 per cent in 1950, expanding to 5.5 per cent by 1956, and further expanding to 11.7 per cent by 1960.

Developments in space and aviation technology and the rise in demand for aluminium building products and beverage cans in the US created the expansion and growth in the global demand for bauxite and alumina, the source material for aluminium. Public administration, which was relatively small at 5.4 per cent in the 1938, by 1956 had increased to 7.9 per cent, stabilising at a level of 7.19 per cent in 1960. The manufacturing sector, because of the industrialisation policy, grew from 6.5 per cent in 1938 to 13.2 per cent in 1956, stabilising at slightly below this level at 12.0 per cent in 1960. Between 1955 and 1965, manufacturing endeavours mushroomed in the areas of furniture, metal products, chemicals, food processing, garments, footwear, and beverages, alongside developments in tourism, bauxite, and alumina. The distribution and transport sectors, combined to be treated as one sector (Distribution) in 1938, accounted for 24.4 per cent of GDP in 1938, increasing to 32.7 per cent in 1943, before declining to 22.3 per cent in 1950. Thereafter, distribution declined to 18.2 per cent by 1960.

The International Bank for Reconstruction and Development (IBRD-World Bank), in one of its first advisory missions in a developing country, reported that between 1943 and 1950 Jamaica's real output grew at an annual rate of 4 per cent per annum. However, the high rate of growth did not reduce the proportion of the unemployed to the gainfully employed population. Unemployment in the period varied between 18 per cent and 20 per cent. The gainfully employed in 1943 was reported at four hundred and sixty thousand, with fifty thousand seeking work. The IBRD noted that 75 per cent of economic activity was related to agriculture in 1950, inclusive of primary agriculture and agricultural processing.[92] Owen Jefferson reports that Jamaica's GDP at factor cost, by industrial origin at current prices in 1950 amounted to J$137.0 million, increasing to J$756.9 million by 1968, representing an overall growth of 452 per cent over the eighteen-year period, or an annual growth of 10 per cent.[93] Taking GDP at constant cost (1956) prices, the increase reflected 221 per cent, or an annual average of 6.7 per cent. The growth then, formed one of the highest growth performances in the world. In some years, growth exceeded 11 per cent. Table 1.4 shows the economic growth performances of the Jamaican economy between 1950 and 1962.

Table 1.3: Percentage Contribution by Industrial Origin to GDP at Factor Cost 1938–1960

Sector	1938	1943	1950	1953	1956	1960
Agriculture / Forestry/ Fishing	36.2	27.3	30.8	21.3	16.4	11.2
Mining /Quarrying /Refining			0.4	2.4	5.5	11.7
Manufacturing	6.5	6.5	11.3	13.9	13.2	12.1
Construction/ Installation	3.5	2.2	7.2	9.6	12.7	14.2
Electricity/Gas//Water / Sewerage	0.8	1.0	1.1	0.7	0.8	0.8
Transportation/ Communications			7.1	6.6	6.6	5.4
Distribution	24.4	32.7	15.2	17.0	15.7	18.2
Ownership of dwellings	9.9	9.1	5.9	4.9	4.2	3.7
Government Services / Defense	5.4	5.7	6.1	6.5	7.9	7.1
Miscellaneous Services	12.3	15.6	15.0	17.1	17.1	15.6
Total	100	100	100	100	100	100

Source: STATIN National Income and Product Reports

Table 1.4: Growth Rate of GDP at Factor Cost at Constant (1956): 1950-1962.

Year	Growth %	Year	Growth %
1950–51	7.9	1956–57	14.1
1951–52	8.1	1957–58	1.2
1952–53	12.4	1958–59	4.4
1953–54	11.5	1959–60	6.3
1954–55	10.6	1960–61	2.8
1955–56	9.8	1961–62	1.2

Source: Owen Jefferson, *Post-War Economic Development of Jamaica* (Kingston: ISER, 1972).

The period between 1950 and 1968 was one of exceptional economic growth for the Jamaican economy. During 1950–55, GDP grew at a rate of 10 per cent per annum; during the subsequent five-year period, 1955–60, the rate of growth fell to 7.1 per cent per annum. In 1960–1965, the rate was 4 per cent, even slower. One of the main contributors to the decline in the rate of growth was the reduction in the rate of growth of capital formation which coincided with the drastic reduction in the level of investment in the mining sector, as construction projects had reached completion. The absolute level of capital formation showed little change between 1957 and 1963.[94]

JLP's Economic Performance: 1962–72

As shown in table 1.5, growth was slow in the years 1961–63, ranging between 1.6 per cent and 2.7 per cent, but accelerated in 1964 and 1965, ranging between 7.8 per cent and 8.8 per cent. Growth declined for the years 1966 and 1967, varying between 2.5 per cent and 3.9 per cent but recovered between 1968 to 1970, varying between 6.5 per cent and 7.7 per cent. Despite the strong growth in the 1960s, unemployment remained high, invariably above 22 per cent. During the period 1930–62, a large number of foreign corporations, mainly from the US and Canada, were attracted to Jamaica in the fields of insurance, banking, mining, tourism, and manufacturing. Investments and the earnings from the export trade financed the demand for capital goods and raw materials for the import substituting consumer goods industries.

Table 1.5: Annual Growth in GDP, 1961–1970

Year	Growth %	Year	Growth %
1961	2.8	**1966**	3.9
1962	1.2	**1967**	2.5
1963	2.7	**1968**	6.1
1964	8.6	**1969**	6.5
1965	7.8	**1970**	7.7

Source: STATIN and Owen Jefferson, *Post-War Economic Development of Jamaica.*

There is little doubt that it was the foreign direct investment flows into the bauxite, alumina, and tourism sectors which fuelled the rapid economic expansion in the period 1950–62. The industrialisation by invitation economic policy remained in place between 1955 and 1974. The period also experienced a massive migration of skills, with the health and education sectors starved of funds. More importantly, the disparity between the 'haves' and the 'have nots' widened glaringly.

Despite the strong economic growth performance, towards the end of the 1960s the JLP became increasing unpopular, from excesses of infringements on people's democratic rights, failure to meet the needs of the rural small holders, and rumours of widespread corruption. It was in this period that the passports of several Jamaican citizens were withdrawn by the state.

The JLP in the 1960s had insisted that its economic policy was one of localisation of ownership. However, the policy concentrated ownership in the hands of an exceedingly small elite in the 1960s. Professor Stan Reid's research findings showed that economic power during the 1960s was concentrated in a small group with Chinese and White family lineage. Of the forty-two top companies in Jamaica listed in the Jamaica Stock Exchange Report 1969–73, and of 129 directorships, only two were Black.[95] It was a period in which this Jamaican middle class, thinking largely in harmony with imperial masters, preferred conservative economic policies and gradual movement towards development.

Edward Seaga, as minister of finance in the Hugh Shearer JLP administration of the 1960s, was reported in the *Daily Gleaner*,[96] stating:

> Government's programme of Jamaicanisation of business operations in the country is moving ahead, and soon every Canadian Bank operating on the island will have gone Jamaican ... Lack of Jamaican ownership meant the decision-making power remained outside of the island. The Jamaican Government's policy of Jamaicanisation ... in order that talents and resources of Jamaican might be utilised for the benefit of Jamaican ownership and control.

The various administrations up to 1973 continued with the development strategies, which involved the private sector anchoring responsibility for economic production, as reflected in the Economic Development Plan up to 1967. Government attention focused on providing social and community services to respond to the needs of rural smallholders. Toward the end of this growth period, the overall economic growth slowed, a period in which the cycle of foreign direct investment in the bauxite and alumina sector was on the wane. Tourism, which was initially a luxury business, shifted to a mass market industry in the 1960s. The financial sector, comparatively, was small but grew from 2.8 per cent in 1950 to reach 5.0 per cent in 1960. It was a period in which the Brown elite local merchants replaced the White planters and the sugar barons. By the 1960s, plantation agriculture was well into its decline because of preferential market displacement, with the owners of the plantations no longer monopolising the halls of power in Jamaica.

Exports and imports in the value of foreign trade expanded in nominal terms. The period after 1955 was a time when prices were relatively stable and inflation was low, a general condition experienced internationally. By 1960, Jamaica was the largest producer of bauxite in the world, with some twelve million dry long tonnes annually. Bauxite and alumina exports went from zero in 1950 to J$70.6 million in 1965.[97] It was a classic period of mineral-led export growth in which the American aluminium transnational firms served as the engine of growth.

Over the period, however, the industrialisation by invitation programme generated few manufacturing jobs. Chen Young reported that there were only 1,285 manufacturing jobs generated per annum.[98] In his economic evaluation of Jamaica's incentive programme, Chen-Young concluded that, although manufacturing expanded from 13.5 per cent of GDP to 15.5 per cent over two decades, the cost outweighed the benefits. Often the quality of goods produced was shoddy; the range of goods offered to consumers narrow, and the administratively created monopoly prices were invariably high. Consumers eventually responded by purchasing illegal goods imported from the US. As most of the local manufacturing companies were not competitive, they could not survive and, once the incentive licence period expired, several renewed operations under a different name, while most eventually closed. The result was that the strategy of industrialisation, which was expected to create jobs failed to produce the desired effect.[99] One outcome of the industrialisation policy was an increasing trade deficit.

The Jamaican mining industry during the 1960s maintained its competitive advantages because of its proximity to the US aluminium market, low cost, and high profitability, coupled with Jamaica's liberal policy towards foreign direct investment and economic management, reflected in low mineral taxation and limited government regulation over the industry. The developments in the mineral sector also unleashed expansion in the construction industry. The capital-intensive mining and manufacturing industries, however, could not absorb the fallout of labour from agriculture during the period. Foreign trade was highly concentrated, largely with the US, UK, and Canada, with bauxite/alumina accounting for about two-thirds of exports. Mining, tourism, and small sale manufacturing grew to account for over 35 per cent of GDP by 1968. The investments and earnings from the export trade came to finance the demand for capital goods and raw materials for the import-substituting consumer goods industries.

Bauxite mining companies operating on the island were Kaiser Aluminium and Alcoa Aluminium and Reynolds Metal of the US and for alumina refining, Alcan Aluminium of Canada. In 1957, Jamaica had become the largest producer of bauxite in the world.[100] Alcoa's former Canadian subsidiary, Alcan Aluminium, was the first to establish operations in Jamaica, in 1943, as Jamaica Bauxite Limited. When Alcoa was broken up by the US government, Alcan became a wholly owned Canadian company, and the Jamaican offshoot, Alcan Jamaica Limited, built the first alumina refinery, Kirkvine Works, near Mandeville, in 1953 and in the 1960s built Ewarton Works. In 1944, Reynolds Metals from the US began bauxite mining and drying operations in Jamaica. Alcoa Aluminium in the late 1960s built the Alcoa Alumina plant in Clarendon. Alumina Partners (ALPART), joint ventured with Anaconda of the US with 27.0 per cent, Kaiser with 36.5 per cent, Reynolds 36.5 per cent to build an alumina plant in St Elizabeth in the early 1970s. Revere Copper and Brass of the US also started construction of an alumina plant, but it never went into production. The bauxite/alumina industry was entirely foreign owned, which meant the loss of repatriated profits and lack of control over investments and development, and virtually no forward integration. Alcan, a Canadian company, was the first company to convert bauxite to alumina. Alcan did this because it supplied a more diverse market for the refined alumina, and this was over longer distances. The American companies mined the bauxite ore and shipped dried ore to the US Gulf Coast, where they had alumina refinery plants, with little value added. One ton of bauxite processed into alumina had the prospect of yielding three times more national income contribution. This led to pressure on the companies in the 1960s to increase the level of local alumina refining, so, in 1967, the American companies, Reynolds, Kaiser, and Anaconda, built a refinery at Nain, St Elizabeth, with the capacity to produce about one million tons of alumina, but even then, 57 per cent of the bauxite mined in Jamaica was exported to the US in the raw dried form.

The initial agreement for the price of the exported bauxite was virtually a gift to the companies. In this agreement, the bauxite companies then operating in Jamaica were required to pay only two shillings and eight pence per ton of bauxite mined, covering royalty and taxes. Norman Manley in 1957 renegotiated an increase to the government's take, resulting in an increase to 14 shillings; the result was that gross payment by the companies operating in Jamaica then increased from £314,532 in 1955/56 to £2,937,273.

Outside of the construction period, the bauxite industry had little or no effect on employment, with direct employment peaking at 1 per cent of the labour force in 1970, a point when it contributed 14 per cent of GDP.[101] The industry, however, arrived in the rural landscape and, with its high wages, not only hastened the demise of the agricultural sector but it also aggravated the socio-economic structure in the rural areas where the production plants were located. Almost everything for the industry was imported, not just capital equipment but raw material, caustic soda, heavy fuel oil, maintenance materials, and flour as a flocculant. It was the capital inflows from the bauxite companies that allowed Jamaica to manufacture through industrialisation-by-invitation, with several large North American companies like Johnson and Johnson joining the bauxite companies in establishing manufacturing operations in Jamaica.

The bauxite and alumina refining industries, tourism, and manufacturing, however, paid better than farming, resulting in sharper differentiation among the wage-earning sectors of the economy.[102] Tourism, which grew to be a mass market industry, was also dominated by foreign ownership. Most of the hotel capacity was wholly foreign owned, with visitorship concentrated on North America. The tourism industry also began expansion with expenditure increasing from J$6.6 million in 1950 to J$46.4 million in 1965 (current values).[103]

The period of the 1960s is sometimes described as the halcyon days in Jamaica, a period when the spirit of nation building inspired many young Jamaicans to become involved in entrepreneurial ventures.[104] The period was also one of general buoyancy in the global economy with Japan, Germany, and the US growing at 4-5 per cent on average per year. In 1967, there were two significant developments: first the government started borrowing from commercial banks with completion of negotiations with the Bank of Nova Scotia and the first World Bank loan began disbursement. Government external borrowing, that is the national debt, dominated commercial loans, which from 1946 to the mid-1970s accounted for 80 per cent of debt, with commercial loans predominating up to 1978. Jamaica's gross external debt was small, even up to 1970, reaching US$100 million, with debt payment accounting for only 4 per cent of export earnings, and public debt charges requiring 2 per cent of government expenditure. Richard Bernal points out that Jamaica's debt problem began in the 1960s, a period in which the external debt more than doubled between 1962 and 1971.[105]

Foreign control of the economy during the period of the 1950s and 1960s expanded rapidly. Unemployment doubled during the period, despite a slow labour supply growth rate of 0.9 per cent; unemployment and ghetto slums grew, alongside the luxurious residences and American-style shopping malls that mushroomed in upper St Andrew. One striking feature of this period was the widening of income distribution. This led Seaga, who was minister of finance for most of the 1960s, to coin the famous phrase the 'haves,' meaning the burgeoning middle class, and the 'have nots,' defined as the 'sufferers' from the ghettos of Kingston and in declining rural Jamaica.[106]

Although a rosy picture was being presented there were several storm clouds on the horizon. Agriculture was characterised by structural dualism, with over 50 per cent of farms devoted to export crops owned by 1 per cent of farmers, and with large number of small farmers cultivating on small, poor interior hillside lands, mostly growing domestic crops, and carrying on manually driven farming. Sugar production peaked in 1965 and began a decline thereafter. Manufacture which developed under import substitution devolved into screwdriver, footloose industries, dependent heavily on tariff protection and quantitative restrictions (QRs).

Post-war Social Conditions

By all standards, after the Second World War, Jamaica was one of the better performing developing economies, especially during the 1950s and 1960s. Government expenditure, as a share of GDP in 1950, was 13.5 per cent, remaining at that level through the period up to 1957 and increasing to 21.0 per cent in 1972. The period from the 1950s to the

1960s saw was rising levels of government expenditure on such items as education and public health as a proportion of overall government expenditure, while there was a decline in spending power of the lower income group. However, government's higher expenditure on health and education provided free compensated for the loss in their spending power; in other words, the government was providing these services free instead of the poor having to purchase them. The period from 1970 saw spending on health services quadrupling, with the number of physicians in government service rising to 307, accompanied by several new health clinics and dispensaries. By 1955, nearly every household in Kingston had piped water, while for the rural areas, it was only at a level of 40 per cent.[107]

Between 1943 and 1960, literacy levels improved for both females and males, with emphasis in the period being on primary education. By 1960, 70.7 per cent of the 20–24 age group had completed at least four years of elementary schooling, with 8.8 per cent completing secondary education but only 0.1 per cent completing university education.[108] Attendance fluctuated between 60 per cent and 70 per cent. Errol Miller maintains that the period 1953–78 was an era of educational expansion and development, especially in creating secondary and vocational schools, with the University of the West Indies opening its first campus in 1948 at Mona, Kingston.[109] Primary school enrolment rose from one hundred and fifty thousand in 1950 to four hundred thousand in 1973 and secondary school to twenty thousand in 1968. Still four hundred thousand people were functionally illiterate.[110]

In 1948, E. Ahiram conducted the first income distribution studies for Jamaica, drawing on the Labour Force Surveys of 1957 and 1958.[111] Ahiram's Gini index[112] for the period showed inequality of 0.53 for household income and of individual income at 0.57, compared to 0.33 in Britain in 1951–52. Jamaican households ranking in the top 20 per cent in income accounted for 61.5 per cent of national income, while those in the bottom 20 per cent accounted for 2.2 per cent. Income distribution widened during this period, being more skewed. The top 20 per cent did exceptionally well, while the bottom 20 per cent fared no better than in earlier years. Higher levels of public spending, however, compensated for the worsening level of income for the lower 20 per cent but did not prevent incremental gains in life expectancy. Behind the appearance of economic growth lay the reality of uneven distribution of income and wealth and the alarming and expanding ghettos of Kingston. At the same time, the end of the 1960s was an era in which extravagant weekend and beach parties for the new middle-class elite, especially in Kingston, proliferated.

New Caribbean School of Economic Thought of the 1960s

Despite the rapid economic growth, the external account had been a cause for concern, showing persistent current account deficits, offset by foreign direct investments (FDI) in the capital-intensive mining sector. Most of the manufacturing activities was also highly import-dependent for both capital goods and raw material, hence the term screwdriver industries, benefitting from a low wage economy. Despite the investment inflows from FDI, the period was accompanied by high levels of out-migration, especially to the UK.[113]

There was little change at the end of 1960s, in terms of import dependence and production based on consumer goods, mostly processing local foodstuff and light assembling, unlike some Latin America countries, which transitioned from totally import substitution industrialisation to export of manufactured goods or export industrialisation.[114] As a result of the high level of economic dependency, a group of newly emerging radical Caribbean economists in the 1960s attacked Lewis's industrialisation-by-invitation model of economic development that was blamed for the growing foreign dependence that was antithetical to the struggle for greater economic autonomy in Jamaica and the Caribbean. The group, who was called the Plantation School because of their analysis of the plantation economy, defined as a situation where internal and external dimensions of the plantation system dominate the country's economic, social, and political structure and its relations with the rest of the world system.[115] The Caribbean's economic dependence had emerged out of the legacy of the plantation economy and its dependence on export agriculture, being an appendage of the British economy. The group focused their analysis on the plantation legacy, essentially on monoculture, created out of the exploitation of African chattel labour and its dependency on foreign capital. They argued that the region's continued foreign dependence resulted from Lewis's influence on post–Second World War industrialisation. In their criticism, they claimed the model came from an alien historical context of classical theories of Western Europe. This resulted in a failure to consider the structural obstacles imposed on the Caribbean that disallowed an internalisation of economic growth and reinforced dependency on the developed capitalist economies. For the adherents of the Plantation School, it was necessary to delink the Caribbean economies from global capitalism as a way of modifying the disadvantageous and exploitative relationship with developed capitalist countries. Delinking from this ossified international division of labour was viewed as a necessary foundation for a reorientation of economic development strategy in the Caribbean.

For the Plantation School, the small farmer sector development was critical for achieving the goal of agricultural production for the domestic market, as they were more productive than the plantations because of the utilisation of larger percentage of their land in diversified production.[116] The group argued for distribution of good quality land from the plantations to small farmers in order to increase production for the domestic market, spreading technical knowledge, providing capital for investment and tariff support in order to lessen dependency on volatile agricultural export. Expanding the small farmer sector would provide livelihood opportunities for the surplus labour which was not being drawn into manufacturing as readily as Lewis had hoped.[117] The Caribbean Development Bank was established in 1969 to provide capital for investment in agricultural development.[118]

Clive Thomas, one of the foundation members of this group, stated that the fundamental strategy of the new economic path had to be one aimed at severing the traditional and newer links with international capitalism.[119] Changing the nature and extent of the linkages with Western economies was of fundamental importance to the Dependence/Plantation School, as well as to the Marxist School.[120]

Rodney, one of the leading proponents of the School was a young Guyanese Economic History lecturer, based at Mona in the 1960 and preached revolutionary communist policies of Russia and Cuba, imploring students and the young to look at their idols from Jomo Kenyatta, Nelson Mandela, and other Black leaders and to take up Black Power philosophy of Angela Davis and the teachings of Marcus Garvey and the Rastafarians. Rodney's ideas gained widespread support from young Jamaicans, leading to one of the most destructive mass riots in Jamaica. The matter became a serious concern to Prime Minister Shearer and Rodney's visa was withdrawn. He was banned from entering Jamaica. The Rodney Affair, as the matter was called, marked the beginning of the end of the post-colonial era.[121]

For the plantation school, an important requirement for the development of Caribbean economies was the delinking from the capitalist economies and to change the international trading relations of developing countries. One way of doing this was to develop alternative trading relations with socialist countries, such as the Soviet Union and China, as well as member states of COMECON (Council for Mutual Economic Assistance). For them, economic activity in the Caribbean was geared towards exporting raw sugar for the refineries in Liverpool and London; in return, Jamaica absorbed British manufactured goods. For the Plantation/Dependency School, the Caribbean economies had been captured by foreign capitalists whose agenda was not the same as that of the newly aspiring independent nations. Bernal et al. comment that the Plantation/Dependency School did identity some of the critical problems of the Jamaican and Caribbean economies, such as foreign domination and failure to modernise the domestic agricultural sector.[122] However, the writings of the group demonstrated several weaknesses, including idealism: expecting that change in society would result from a change in people's minds, and that social change could come by the formulation and dissemination of ideas. Another weakness was the tendency to romanticise the peasantry. The group was narrowly technocratic, rather than political-economic, asking that the existing neocolonial state act for the benefit of the entire nation.

Michael Manley agreed with the view that imperialism had created a world economy biased in favour of the imperial powers, which were also the industrial powers, leaving other world regions to play the role of producers of raw material and basic goods. For example, Manley noted that, when Jamaica became independent in 1962, a tractor could be financed with the proceeds of eighteen tons of sugar; by 1980, it would take sixty tons of sugar to finance the same tractor.[123]

Box 1.1 below summaries the key policy prescriptions introduced by the JLP when in power from 1962 to 1972.[124]

Interestingly, for a political party that professed to believe in conservative economic policies, the JLP administration was responsible for the introduction of the National Insurance Scheme, state ownership of electricity and telephone service providers, Kingston urban bus company and of idle lands for allocation to small farmers, sure evidence of a more radical approach to state management.

Box 1.1: JLP Administration's Policies of 1962–72.

1. Promoted local ownership of the domestic financial system; introduced the local Stock Market;
2. Introduced the machinery for price control;
3. Initiated state ownership of electricity, telephone, and Kingston urban bus company: initial nationalisation was initiated by the JLP;
4. Initiated state ownership of idle lands for allocation to small farmers;
5. Established Sugar Industry Authority (SIA) as a state agency to control the sugar industry;
6. Continued lease of Government lands to small farmers;
7. Established Agricultural Marketing Corporation (AMC);
8. Introduced National Festival, promoting local music and folk culture;
9. Initiated large-scale low-income housing;
10. Continued Rent Control;
11. Expanded scholarships for high school and expanded secondary education;
12. Introduced National Insurance Scheme.

Michael Manley and Democratic Socialism: 1970–80

The PNP's Michael Manley, who took over the management of the economy on February 29, 1972, with a majority of thirty-seven of the fifty-three seats in Parliament, had up to then espoused Fabian socialism, which advanced the principles of a democratic framework to achieve gradual reform of society, rather than by revolutionary means. The characteristics of Fabian socialism are:

- Socialism proceeds step by step with people participation and extension of democratic rights.
- It sees the necessity of 'State' as an ultimate arbiter of all disputes. Though power shall be rested in the hands of the state, there shall be no opportunity to exercise it arbitrarily.
- It advocates nationalisation of key industries in the economic structure of the society but does not support management of the entire economy by the state.
- The state has to improve social conditions without curbing public freedom.

- It includes parliamentary processes like universal adult franchise, periodic elections; enacting laws by representatives for the functioning of society.
- It is against complete revolution or armed intervention as it believes that it can ensure only temporary relief but in the long run may cause disastrous results.
- Emphasis on the possibility of reasonable reconstruction of government and society on what they perceived as a scientific basis.[125]

Famous Fabian socialists in history include Indian Prime Minister Jawaharlal Nehru and George Bernard Shaw. The British Labour Party was believed to be completely Fabian in ideology. In the mid-1950s, Michael Manley's father, Norman Manley in 1955, had openly aired the need for Jamaica to gain economic power. The party, however, maintained its Fabian approach to economic management. Based on this philosophy, Norman Manley could extract higher revenues from the North American bauxite producers in the island.[126]

In the 1972 elections, the PNP campaigned on a platform emphasising the high levels of unemployment: 20–25 per cent for most of the 1960s, widening disparities in income, and rising crime rate, calling for the restructuring of the economy with greater local participation in the bauxite industry. The campaign made significant use of communication channels to promote the concept of building a new Jamaica where pride in being Jamaican would take precedence over race, class, and material wealth. Although Michael Manley had to face the consequences of growing unemployment, worsening income distribution, growing foreign control of the economy, and energy dependency, no one had seen the coming rapid increases in oil prices, which reared its head in the energy-dependent economy soon after the PNP took control of the administration.

However, on taking control of the country's economic affairs the oil price increase of 1973 torpedoed the expected revitalisation of the economy which Manley and the public had expected. In 1973, the Arab members of the Organization of Petroleum Exporting Countries (OPEC) put pressure on Western nations by restricting output of oil because of the West's support for Israel during the Yom Kippur War.[127] Oil price more than quadrupled, jumping from just under US$2 per barrel to US$11 per barrel. In 1973, Jamaica imported 19.74 million barrels of oil at US$3.77 per barrel, for a total cost of US$73.7 million, but by 1975 imports of oil, while down to 16.99 million barrels, with the higher price of US$11.29, the oil bill increased to US$215.1 million.[128] The global increase in oil price triggered an unprecedented balance of payments crisis for the non-oil-producing countries and contributed to a global recession. This made the PNP period of administration after 1972 one of the most traumatic in the history of Jamaica.

Notes

1. Scotland, ruled from London since 1603, formally was joined with England and Wales in 1707 to form the United Kingdom of Great Britain.
2. E. St. Cyr, 'Theory of Caribbean-Type Economy,' *in Caribbean Economic Development: First Generation*, eds. S. Lalta and M. Franklinton (Kingston: Ian Randle Publishers, 1993).
3. Benjamin Timms, 'Development Theory and Domestic Agriculture in the Caribbean: Recurring Crisis and Missed Opportunities,' *Caribbean Geography* 15, no. 2 (2008) 101–17.
4. Eric Williams, *From Columbus to Castro: The History of The Caribbean 1492–1969* (New York: Random House, 1970).
5. Adam Smith, *An Inquiry into the Nature and Causes of the Wealth of Nations* (London: W. Strahan and T. Cadel, 1776).
6. Duncan Weldon, *Two Hundred Years of Muddling Through: The Surprising Story of British Economy from Boom to Bust and Back Again* (London: Little Brown Book Group, 2021).
7. Jose Andres Fernandez Mentes des Oca, 'Jamaica in the Age of Development, Petition: Small Farming and Agricultural Planning 1895–1972,' PhD Dissertation, University of Pittsburgh, 2021.
8. David Ricardo, *On the Principles of Political Economy and Taxation* (London: J.M. Dent, 1817).
9. Maynard Keynes, *General Theory of Employment, Interest and Money* (London: Palgrave Macmillan, 1936).
10. R. Thomas, *Principles of Population* (London: J. Johnson, 1798).
11. B. Richardson, *The Importance of the 1897 Royal Commission in Caribbean Land and Development Revisited*, ed., J. Benson and J. Momsen (New York: Palgrave Macmillan, 2007).
12. Hartley Neita, *Hugh Shearer: A Voice For the People* (Kingston: Ian Randle Publishers, 2005).
13. J.E. Latimer, 'The Ottawa Agreement,' 1934.
14. Ibid.
15. Keynes, *General Theory of Employment, Interest and Money.*
16. Ibid.
17. Phillip William, 'The Relationship Between Unemployment and the Rate of Change of Money Wage Rate in the United Kingdom, 1861–1957,' *Journal of Economics* (1958).

18. The Phillips curve is like a balance between people having jobs and prices going up. When more people have jobs, prices tend to go up, and when fewer people have jobs, prices tend to go down.
19. H. W. Arndt, 'Economic Development A Semantic History,' *Economic Development and Social Change* 29, no. 3 (1981).
20. Donald Harris, 'Savings and Foreign Trade as Constraints To Economic Growth: A Study of Jamaica,' *Social and Economic Studies* 19, no. 2 (June 1970), 147–77.

    Donald Harris, 'Capital Accumulation and Resource Allocation in an Import Constrained Economy: A Framework for Economic Analysis of Recent Experiences and Current Trends in the Jamaican Economy,' presented to the PSOJ Symposium on the Jamaican Economy, Kingston, Jamaica, 1970.

    Donald Harris, 'The Jamaican Economy in the Twenty First Century: Challenges to Development and Requirements of a Response,' in *Jamaica Preparing for the 21st Century*, ed. Patsy Lewis (Kingston: Ian Randle Publishers, 1992).
21. Brian Meeks, *Envisioning Caribbean Future: Jamaican Perspective* (Kingston: UWI Press, 2007).
22. Statistical Institute of Jamaica (STATIN), *2021 Annual Report.*
23. IMF Country Data.
24. STATIN, *2021 Annual Report.*
25. Clinton Black, *History of Jamaica* (London and Glasgow: Collins Clear-Review Press, 1961).
26. Nuala Zaheddieh, 'Trade, Plunder and Economic Development in Early English Jamaica, 1655–1689,' *Economic History Review* 39, no. 2 (1986), 205–22.
27. Eric Williams, *Capitalism and Slavery* (Chapel Hill: University of North Carolina Press,1987).
28. Rex A. Hudson and Daniel J. Seyler, 'Jamaica an Island of the Commonwealth Caribbean: A Regional Study,' in *Jamaica*, ed. Sandra Mendez and Dennis M. Hanratty.
29. W. Sidney Mintz, *The Jamaican Marketing System, Some Notes and Hypothesis* (Kingston: Social and Economic Studies, 1953).
30. W. Sidney Mintz and Douglas Hall, *The Origins of the Jamaican Marketing System* (New Haven: Yale University Press, 1960).
31. Lynsey Ann Bates, 'Surplus and Access: Provisioning and Market Participation by Enslaved Labourers on Jamaican Sugar Estates,' PhD Dissertation, University of Pennsylvania, 2015.
32. Lorna Simmonds, 'The Afro-Jamaican and Internal Marketing System of Kingston 1780-1834,' in *Slavery, Freedom, History and Culture*, ed. Kathleen Monteith and Glen Roberts (Kingston: UWI Press, 2002).
33. Padraic X. Scanlan, 'Slave and Peasants in the Era of Emancipation,' *Journal of British Studies* 59, no. 3 (2020), 495–520.

34. Ann Norton and Richard Szymanski, 'The Internal Marketing System of Jamaica,' *Geographical Review*, Taylor and Francis Limited, 1975.
35. Brian Edwards, *The History, Civil and Commercial of the British Colonies in the West Indies with a Continuation to the Present Time*, vols. 1 and 2 (Dublin: Luke White, 1793).
36. Lydia M. Pulsipher, 'They Have Saturdays and Sundays to Feed Themselves,' Caribbean Expedition 32, no. 2 (1990), 24–33
37. Mintz and Hall, *The Origins of the Jamaican Marketing System*.
38. James Phillippo, *Jamaica Past and Present State* (London: Dawsons of Pall Mall, 1969).
39. Jose Andres, 'Jamaica in the Age of Development, Petition: Small Farming and Agricultural Planning 1895–1972.'
40. Mintz, *The Jamaican Marketing System, Some Notes and Hypothesis*.
41. Don Robotham, 'Agrarian Relations in Jamaica,' in *Essays on Power and Change in Jamaica*, ed. Carl Stone and Aggrey Brown (Kingston: Jamaica Publishing House, 1977).
42. Norton and Szymanski, 'The Internal Marketing System of Jamaica.'
43. Phillippo, *Jamaica Past and Present State*.
44. Trevor Burnard, 'Grand Market of the Island: The Economic Functions of Kingston Jamaica in the Middle Eighteen Century,' in *Slavery and Freedom: History, Heritage and Culture*, ed. Kathleen A. Monteith and Glen Richards (Kingston: UWI Press, 2002).
45. Margaret Warren Beckwith, *Black Roadways: A Study of Jamaican Folklife* (New York: Negro University Press, 1929).
46. Ibid.
47. Gina A. Ulysse, *Downtown Ladies: Informal Commercial Importers: A Haitian Anthropologist and Self Making in Jamaica* (Chicago: University of Chicago Press, 2007).
48. Barry W. Higman, 'Domestic Service in Jamaica Since 1770,' in *Trade, Government and Society in Caribbean History 1700–1920* (Kingston: UWI, 1983).
49. Shirley J. Smith, 'Industrial Growth, Economic Opportunities, and Migration Within Jamaica 1943–1970' (PhD Dissertation, University of Pennsylvania, 1975).
50. Hudson and Seyler, 'Jamaica an Island of the Commonwealth Caribbean: A Regional Study.'
51. Ibid.
52. Owen Jefferson, *Post-war Economic Development of Jamaica* (Kingston: ISER, 1972).
53. Barry W. Higman, 'Domestic Service in Jamaica since 1770,' in *Trade, Government and Society in Caribbean History 1700-1920* (Mona: UWI, 1983).
54. James C. Riley, *Poverty and Life Expectancy: The Jamaican Paradox* (Cambridge: Cambridge University Press, 2005).

55. Michelle Harrison, *King Sugar: Jamaica, The Caribbean and the World Sugar Industry* (New York: New York University Press, 2001).
56. Eisner Gisela, *Jamaica 1830–1930: A Study in Economic Growth* (Manchester and New York: University of Manchester Press, 1961).
57. *Colonial Reports for Jamaica 1921* (London: The Colonial Office, 1921).
58. Eisner Gisela, *Jamaica 1830–1930: A Study in Economic Growth.*
59. Riley, *Poverty and Life Expectancy: The Jamaican Paradox.*
60. Ibid
61. Eisner Gisela, *Jamaica 1830–1930: A Study in Economic Growth.*
62. A. P. Thorne, 'Size, Structure and Growth of the Economy,' *Supplement Social and Economic Studies* 4, no. 4 (1955), 1–115.
63. J. R. Hicks and U.K., *Report on Finance in Jamaica* (Kingston: Government Printer, 1955).
64. Phyllis Deane, *The Measurement of the Colonial National Income* (Cambridge: Cambridge University Press, 1948).
65. Norman Girvan, *Foreign Capital and Economic Development in Jamaica* (Kingston: Institute of Social and Economic Research, UWI, 1971).
66. George E. Cumper, 'The Social Structure of Jamaica,' *Caribbean Affairs* 4, (1949), 1–90.
67. Riley, *Poverty and Life Expectancy: The Jamaican Paradox.*
68. Ibid.
69. George Beckford and Michael Witter, *Small Garden ... Bitter Weed: The Political Economy of Struggle and Change in Jamaica* (Morant Bay, Jamaica: N.P., 1982).
70. George Eaton, *Alexander Bustamante and Modern Jamaica* (Kingston: Kingston Publishers, 1975).
71. Lord Moyne, *The West India Commission of Inquiry: Statement of Action Taken on Recommendations* (London: The Commission, 1945).
72. Trevor Monroe, *The Politics of Constitutional Decolonization: Jamaica 1944–1962* (Mona: ISER, 1972).
73. Amy Jacques Garvey, *Garvey Garveyism* (Kingston: Publisher Black Classic Press, 1963).
74. Stacy H. Widdicombe Jr., *The Performance of Industrial Development Corporations: The Case of Jamaica* (New York: Praeger, 1972).
75. Ibid.
76. Edwin Jones and Gladstone Mills, 'The Institutional Framework of Government,' in *Jamaica in Independence: Essays on the Early Years*, ed. Rex Nettleford (Kingston: Heinemann, 1989).
77. Library of Congress Country Study, *Jamaica 10-year Development Plan* (Kingston: Government of Jamaica, 1951).
78. Beckford and Michael Witter, *Small Garden.*
79. Jefferson, *Post-war Economic Development of Jamaica.*
80. Richard Bernal, 'The Struggle for the Old International Economic Order: The Caribbean Basin Plan and Jamaica,' Department of Statistics,

UWI, Paper Presented at a Conference on Geo-political Change in the Caribbean in the 1980s, Mexico City, 1982.

81. F.C. Benham, *Report of the Economic Policy Committee, Kingston, Jamaica (1945).*
82. Richard Bernal, Mark Figueroa, and Michael Witter, 'Caribbean Economic Thought: The Critical Tradition,' Department of Economics, UWI, for the 21st Anniversary Conference of the Faculty of Social Sciences, 1983.
83. W. A. Lewis, 'Industrial Development in Puerto Rico,' *Caribbean Economic Review* 1, no. 1 (1949),153–76.
84. W. A. Lewis, 'Industrialization of the British West Indies,' *Caribbean Economic Review*. 2, no. 1 (1950), 1–51.
85. Lewis, 'Economic Development with Unlimited Supply of Labour,' *The Manchester School of Economic and Social Studies*, 22, no 2 (1954), 139–91.
86. Lewis, *The Theory of Economic Growth* (London: George Allen and Unwin Limited, 1955).
87. Bernal, Figueroa, and Witter, 'Caribbean Economic Thought.'
88. W. A. Lewis, 'The Evolution of the Peasantry in the West Indies,' C*olonial Office Pamphlet* 15, no. 856 (1938).
89. E. Carrington, 'Industrialisation by Invitation in Trinidad and Tobago Since 1950,' *New World Quarterly* 4, no. 2, reprinted in Reading in *Political Economy of the Caribbean*, ed. Norman Girvan and Owen Jefferson (Kingston).
90. Michael Witter, 'Prospect for Jamaica's Economic Development in the Era of the FTAA,' in *The Caribbean Economics in an Era of Free Trade*, ed. N. Karagiannis and M. Witter (Aldershot, UK: Ashgate, 2004).
91. W. A. Lewis, 'An Economic Plan for Jamaica,' *Agenda* 3 (1945).
92. Raul Prebysch, *The Economic Development of Latin America and its Principal Problems* (New York: Economic Commission of Latin America, Department of Economic Affairs, 1950).
93. HMSO, *Commonwealth Development and its Financing Jamaica* (London: HMSO, 1964).
94. Fredrich C. Benham, *An Economic Plan for Jamaica: A Reply to Dr. Lewis* (Kingston: Government Printer, 1946).
95. Carl Stone, 'Power Policy and Politics in Independent Jamaica,' in *Jamaica in Independence: The Early Years*, ed. Rex Nettleford (Kingston: Heinemann Publishers [Caribbean] Limited, 1989).
96. World Bank, *Report on the Economic Development of Jamaica* (Baltimore: Johns Hopkins Press, 1952).
97. Gerald E. Mills, *Issues of Public Policy and Public Administration in Commonwealth Caribbean* (Kingston: Institute of Social and Economic Studies, 1974).
98. Paul Chen Young, 'An Economic Evaluation of the Incentive Programme in Jamaica' (PhD Dissertation, University of Pittsburgh, 1966).
99. National Plan for Jamaica, Kingston, 1957.
100. World Bank, *Report on the Economic Development of Jamaica.*

101. Jefferson, *Post-war Economic Development of Jamaica.*
102. Ibid.
103. Stan Reid, 'An introductory Approach to Concentration of Power in Jamaican Corporate Economy and Notes on Its Origin,' in *Essays on Power and Change in Jamaica, ed. Carl Stone and Aggrey Brown (Kingston: Jamaica Publishing House, 1971).*
104. Edward Seaga, Minister of Finance, Address on the Occasion of Jamaicanisation of Maritime Life Insurance of Canada, reported in the *Daily Gleaner*, December 19, 1970 (Jamaica).
105. Frank Fonda Taylor, 'The Tourist Industry in Jamaica 1919–1939,' *Social and Economic Studies* (1973).
106. Paul Chen Young, 'With All the Good Intentions – The Collapse of the Jamaica's Domestic Financial Sector,' *Policy Papers in the Americas* 1X, Study 12, (1998).
107. Edward Seaga, *My Life and Leadership: Hard Road to Travel 1980–2008*, vol. 11 (Oxford: Macmillan Publishers, 2010).
108. Rex Nettleford, *Manley and the New Jamaica: Selected Speeches and Writings 1938–1968* (London: Longman Caribbean, 1971).
109. Evelyne Stephen and John D. Stephen, 'Democratic Socialism in Jamaica: The Political Movement of Social Transformation in Dependent Capitalism,' *Foreign Affairs* (1986): 191.
110. Elsie Le Franc, 'The Bauxite Labour Force in Jamaica: A High Wage Sector in a Dual Economy,' *Social and Economic Studies* 36, no. 1 (1987), 217–88
111. Taylor, 'The Tourist Industry in Jamaica 1919–1939.'
112. Paul Chen-Young, *Entrepreneurial Journey in Jamaica: When Policies Derail* (Tucson, Arizona: Hats Off Books Publishing, 2006).
113. Richard Bernal, 'Resolving the International Debt Crisis,' in *The Debt Problem in Jamaica*, ed. Omar Davies (Mona, UWI: Department of Economics, 1986).
114. Ibid.
115. James C. Riley, *Poverty and Life Expectancy: The Jamaican Paradox* (New York: Cambridge University Press, 2005).
116. Kalman Tekse, 'Population and Vital Statistics 1832–1964: A Historical Perspective,' Kingston.
117. Errol Miller, 'Educational Development in Independent Jamaica,' in Jamaica in *Independence: Essays on the Early Years*, ed. Rex Nettleford (Kingston: Heinemann Publishers, 1989).
118. UNESCO, *Jamaica National Literacy Programme: Project Findings and Recommendations* (Paris: UNESCO, 1976).
119. E. Ahiram, *Income Distribution in Jamaica* (Mona, UWI: Social and Economic Studies, 1958).
120. The Gini index, or Gini coefficient, measures income distribution across a population. Developed by the Italian statistician Corrado Gini in 1912, it often serves as a gauge of economic inequality, measuring income distribution or, less commonly, wealth distribution among a population.

121. https://www.investopedia.com › Economy
122. Omar Davies, 'Jamaican Economy Since Independence: Agenda for the Future,' in *Jamaica Preparing for the 21st Century*, ed. Patsy Lewis (Kingston: Ian Randle Publishers, 1991).
123. Richard Bernal, 'The Great Depression, Colonial and Industrialization in Jamaica,' *Social and Economic Studies* 37, nos. 1 & 2 (1988), 33–60.
124. George L. Beckford, *Persistent Poverty: Underdevelopment in Plantation Economies of the Third World* (London and New York: Oxford University Press, 1972).
125. George Beckford, *Toward an Appropriate Theoretical Framework for Agricultural Development Planning and Policy* (UWI, Mona: Social and Economic Studies, 1968).
126. 127 W.K. Marshall, 'Peasant Development in the West Indies Since 1938,' in *Rural Development in the Caribbean*, ed. P. I. Gomes (London: Heinemann Educational Books, 1985).
127. V.R. McDonald, 'The Caribbean: Issues of Emergence,' in *The Caribbean Issues of Emergence: Socio-Economic and Political Perspectives* (Seattle: Washington University Press of America, 1980).
128. W.A. Axline, 'Agricultural Cooperation in Caricom,' in *Dependency Under Challenge: The Political Economy of the Commonwealth Caribbean* (Manchester: Manchester University Press, 1984).
129. Clive Thomas, *Dependence and Transformation: The Economics of the Transition to Socialism* (New York: Monthly Review Press, 1974).
130. Lloyd Best, 'Outlines of a Model of Pure Plantation Economy,' *Social and Economic Studies* 17, no. 3 (March–December 1968), 283–326.
131. George Beckford, *Persistent Poverty: Underdevelopment in Plantation Economies of the Third World* (Oxford: Oxford University Press, 1973).
132. Norman Girvan, *Corporate Imperialism: Conflict and Expropriation* (White Plains, New York: M. E. Sharpe, 1976).
133. Walter Rodney, *How Europe Underdeveloped Africa* (London: Bogle-L'Ouverture Publications/Dar es Salaam: Tanzania Publishing House, 1972).
134. Clive Thomas, *Dependence and Transformation: The Economics of the Transition to Socialism* (New York: Monthly Review Press, 1974).
135. Courtney Blackman, 'An Eclectic Approach to the Problem of Black Economic Development,' *The Review of Black Political Economy* 2, no. 1 (1971).
136. Kari Polanyi Levitt, *Reclaiming Development: Independent Thought and Caribbean Community* (Kingston: Ian Randle Publishers, 1969).
137. Anthony Payne, *Politics in Jamaica* (London: Palgrave Macmillan, 1995).
138. Bernal, Figueroa, and Witter, 'Caribbean Economic Thought.'
139. Michael Manley, *Up and Down the Escalator: Development and International Economy: A Jamaican Case Study* (Washington, DC, Howard University Press, 1987).

140. Stone, 'Power Policy and Politics in Independent Jamaica.'
141. https://tlp.iasbaba.com/2019/06/day-5-q-2-what-is-fabian-socialism.
142. Trevor Monroe, *The Politics of Constitutional Decolonization 1944–1962* (Kingston, ISER, 1972).
143. The Yom Kippur War, also known as the 1973 Arab Israeli War, was fought from October 6–25 1973. It was a coordinated assault launched by Egypt, Syria, and their allies against Israel on the holiest day of the Jewish Calendar. The war, which eventually drew both the US and the Soviet Union into indirect confrontation in defence of their respective allies, was launched with the diplomatic aim of persuading Israel to negotiate on terms more favourable to the Arab countries in defence of their traditional land.
144. Bank of Jamaica, *Balance of Payments of Jamaica* (Kingston: BOJ, 1982).

CHAPTER TWO

The Jamaican Public Sector: A Historical Overview

There are no accepted definitions or legal definitions of the Jamaican public sector and public service. When the term public sector is used, it differentiates the private sector from the various branches of government, which form the overall public service. Often, the public service is defined as public sector agencies, comprising the executive arm of government, directly referring to the civil service and departments, together with statutory bodies whose functions and responsibilities are akin to those of civil service departments, especially in delivering services at a national level or at the individual customer level. The Jamaican public service broadly comprises the public bodies, the civil service, and the military, the latter including the Coast Guard and army. In Jamaica, the civil service is taken to comprise the central ministries and their departments. In the definition used for this work, in addition to central and local government and statutory bodies, the public sector is defined to include commercial enterprises, incorporated as limited liability companies.

The limited liability state-owned enterprises (SOEs) and commercial statutory bodies form the category often referred to as public enterprises. The SOEs, comprise the statutory corporations, created by acts of Parliament; limited liability companies, formed under the Companies Act, and departmental enterprises, such as the Post.[1] The SOEs have been the sector that experienced most expansion over recent years. The core civil service refers to the officials performing the administrative functions of government and who assist ministers of government in policymaking, being responsible for policy implementation and supervision of the wider delivery of public services. The civil service is independent of the political bureaucracy and, historically, is expected to be neutral, a colonial legacy and, unlike the US, the senior officials do not change after an election. The supposed neutrality of the civil service came under attack during the Manley era of the 1970s. Manley once commented that civil service neutrality is like a car stuck in neutral.

Until 1865, the public sector in Jamaica at the national level played a minor role in governance and economic affairs. Most public services were delivered by vestries and parochial government. Jamaica under the English had governance, embodying a limited form of representative government. The first major change which witnessed the expansion of the role of central government came after 1865, following the Morant Bay Rebellion. Between 1865 and 1962, Jamaica moved from Crown Colony form of government to being an independent state within the Commonwealth. During this period, the major changes surrounded the process in which Jamaicans increasingly took responsibility for administering their own affairs. Many of the reforms in the machinery of government have occurred since the 1970s, and these reforms have focused on the core civil service, local government, along with the health and educational sectors, the judiciary, the army, and the SOEs. The local government system, which incorporates the parishes, is the administrative unit of which there are thirteen councils, along with the Kingston and St Andrew Municipal Corporation. The local government system has seen major reforms in recent times.

The focus of this chapter is on the overall growth and performance of the public sector, especially the SOEs, since independence in 1962, and the reforms carried out under the Administrative Reform Programmes (ARP 1 and ARP 11) in the 1980s and Public Sector Management Reform Programme (PSMRP) since the 1990s.

THE EARLY YEARS OF GOVERNANCE BY THE ENGLISH

The origins of Jamaica's administrative organisation date back to the latter years of the seventeenth century following the capture of the island from the Spanish by British forces and the subsequent complete overhaul of the governing structure that was to morph into the Westminster system. Until 1655 when Jamaica passed to English control, the island had remained essentially a Spanish fiefdom of Columbus's heirs who were more concerned with their rights rather than the development of Jamaica. As a result, the governors had free control over administrative affairs. Sometimes, the governors never visited or resided in Jamaica.[2]

Beginning with the Stuart monarch's appointing a civil governor to Jamaica, Governor Windsor brought with him in 1662 the system of government, giving Jamaica's non-slave populace the rights of English citizenship, including the right to make their own laws. The first general election was held in December 1663, eight years after Jamaica became an English colony. The three hundred men who voted in the first election amounted to only three per cent of the colony's White population.

The system comprised a governor, representing the Crown, a commander-in-chief for the armed forces, and a vice admiral for the navy. The Council, which is similar to the House of Lords or the Privy Council in England, was appointed by the sovereign, at the recommendation of the governor, through the secretary of state for the colonies. The initial Assembly, comprised forty-seven representatives (two for each parish and, in addition, one to Spanish Town, Kingston, and Port Royal), chosen by the White population, mostly the estate owners. The governor, chief justice, the attorney general, the Anglican bishop, and the commander of the local forces formed the ex-officio members, with the others selected from prominent citizens by the governor, usually twelve.[3] To be qualified as a potential representative, the candidate had to possess freehold land of a certain size on an estate in the parish in which he had a right to vote, or a certain value of rentage recorded in the Island Secretary's Office for twelve calendar months, must be twenty-one years of age, and must be paying taxes to a certain amount per annum. The tiny number of the population enfranchised to vote remained a part of the electoral scene up to 1816.

The chief justice was nominated by the Imperial government while expenditure for the ecclesiastical establishment, being the Church of England was funded by public purse. All legislation passed were subject to confirmation or disallowance by the sovereign of the realm. While the common laws prevailed in Jamaica, the Westminster statute laws were not given such authority. Simultaneously, Slave Acts passed in the colonies had no jurisdiction in Britain.

In the ensuing years, the planter-dominated Jamaica House of Assembly was in continual conflict with the various governors and the Stuart kings; there were also contentious factions within the Assembly itself. For much of the 1670s and 1680s, the Sovereign and Assembly feuded over such matters as the purchase of slaves from ships which were not run by the Royal English Trading Company. In 1689, the planters, however, confirmed local control of the Jamaican Assembly. With the expansion of the sugar estates slave importation expanded resulting in the enslaved population outnumbered the Whites by six to one.[3] With increased numbers of Black slaves and frequent unrest among the slave population the planters were often ruthless in suppressing any rumours of rebellion; punishment for minor transgression was ruthless and severe. It was not until after emancipation the enslaved population was freed, theoretically with the right to vote; however, the stringent property rules severely limited the numbers who secured such a right.[4]

The first White British immigrants were soldiers, followed by a few criminals from Ireland and Scotland as indentured labourers to work the sugar estates; they were accompanied by a few English colonial administrators. Some wealthy planters also migrated from Barbados to Jamaica. Several early settlers also came from Germany, Portugal, and Spain. The early White population was largely men, resulting in concubinage with Black house enslaved women. The outcome was the birth of the coloured or mulatto population, children of White men and African enslaved women.

The period after emancipation in 1834 was initially marked by a conflict between the plantocracy and elements in the Colonial Office over the extent to which individual freedom should be coupled with political participation for Blacks. Towards the end of the eighteenth century and into the early years of the nineteenth century, Britain allowed some leeway for participation by coloured persons in the political system, resulting in the first Black Jamaican to elected to the Legislative Council in 1899. After 1925, the non-Whites represented an increasing number elected to the Legislative Council and by the 1930s, African Jamaicans came to constitute the majority on the Legislative Council, and the Council making it more representative of the population.

In 1863, in the last general election before the Assembly was abolished, the total electorate with the right to vote remained at a minute 1,467 persons. At the same time, the 1861 census recorded a population of 441,264. Consequently, neither emancipation nor the change in voting qualifications resulted in a meaningful change in the political system. In 1866, a new Legislative Council and the Executive Privy Council replaced both chambers of representation: Assembly and Legislative

Council. However, the Colonial Office continued to exercise effective power through a presiding British-appointed governor. The Legislative Council included a few handpicked prominent Jamaicans.

The Morant Bay Rebellion of 1865 provided the first catalyst for change. Its brutal suppression of Black protestors by the local colonial militia drawn from the White population resulted in 439 Black Jamaicans being killed directly by soldiers, and later 354 more were rounded up and slain. Other punishments included flogging for over six hundred men and women (including some pregnant women), and long prison sentences. Thousands of homes belonging to Black Jamaicans were burned.

The brutal response of the local authorities raised some constitutional issues in Britain, where concerns emerged about whether British dependencies should be ruled under the government of law, or through the military. This resulted in the establishment in December 1865 of a Royal Commission of Inquiry to investigate the disturbances. Following the Commission's report and in the rebellion's aftermath, the secretary for the colonies in London persuaded the centuries-old, limited representative Jamaican Assembly to vote to abolish itself, providing for direct British rule from London. This move heralded the end of the dominant influence of the White sugar plantocracy and White establishment in Jamaican elective politics.

The plantation system was self-sufficient, and until 1885 the public service in Jamaica consisted essentially of the militia, the small judiciary, prisons, and the small cadre of administrators dealing with the imports and exports, in addition to local government, responsible for roads, community service, and paupers.

The newly appointed governor, Sir John Peter Grant, wielded the only real executive or legislative power, allowing him for the first time to introduce a wider system of public services for the benefit of the Black Jamaican community. He restructured the colony by creating a police force, reforming the judicial system, introducing public medical services, establishing the Public Works Department, and the Government Savings Bank. He also appointed local magistrates, introduced public education for the masses, and irrigated the fertile but drought-stricken plains between Spanish Town and Kingston. For the first time, provision was made by the government to educate Black Jamaicans, who until this point were mainly educated by church missionaries.

DEVELOPMENT OF JAMAICA'S LABOUR UNIONS AND POLITICAL PARTIES

The rise of nationalism, as distinct from the island identification or desire for self-determination, is dated to the 1938 labour riots that occurred in Jamaica and the islands of the Eastern Caribbean. William Alexander Bustamante, a moneylender in the capital city of Kingston who had formed the Jamaica Trade Workers and Tradesmen Union (JTWTU) three years earlier, captured the imagination of the Black masses with his messianic personality. He was light-skinned, affluent, and aristocratic. Bustamante emerged from the 1938 strikes and other disturbances as a populist leader and the principal spokesperson for the militant urban working class. In that year, using the JTWTU as a stepping stone, he founded the Bustamante Industrial Trade Union (BITU), which inaugurated Jamaica's workers' movement.

A distant cousin of Bustamante, Norman W. Manley, concluded because of the 1938 riots that the basis for national unity in Jamaica lay in the masses. Unlike the union-oriented Bustamante, however, Manley was more interested in access to control over state power and political rights for the masses. On September 18, 1938, he inaugurated the People's National Party (PNP). It began as a nationalist movement supported by the mixed-race middle class and the liberal sector of the business community; its leaders were mainly educated members of the upper middle class. The 1938 riots spurred the PNP to unionise, although it would be several years before the PNP formed a major labour union: the National Workers Union (NWU). The party concentrated its earliest efforts on establishing a network, both in urban areas and in the banana-growing rural parishes, later working on building support among small farmers and in areas of bauxite mining.

In 1940, the PNP adopted a socialist ideology and later it joined the Socialist International, allying formally with the social democratic parties of Western Europe. Guided by socialist principles, Norman Manley was not a doctrinaire socialist. PNP socialism during the 1940s was similar to British Labour Party ideas on state control of the factors of production, equality of opportunity, and a welfare state. The left-wing element in the PNP held more orthodox Marxist views and worked for the internationalisation of the trade union movement through the Caribbean Labour Congress. In those formative years of

Jamaican political and union activity, relations between Manley and Bustamante were cordial. Manley defended Bustamante in court against charges brought by the British for his labour activism in the 1938 riots and looked after the BITU during Bustamante's imprisonment.

Bustamante had political ambitions of his own. In 1942, while still incarcerated, he founded a political party to rival the PNP, called the Jamaica Labour Party (JLP). The new party, whose leaders were of a lower class than those of the PNP, was supported by conservative businessmen and dues paying BITU members. They encompassed dock and sugar plantation workers and other unskilled urban labourers. On his release in 1943, Bustamante began building up the JLP. Meanwhile, several PNP leaders organised the leftist-oriented Trade Union Congress (TUC). Thus, from an early stage in modern Jamaica, unionised labour was an integral part of organised political life.

For the next quarter century, Bustamante and Manley vied for centre stage in Jamaican political affairs, the former espousing the cause of the 'barefoot man'; the latter, 'democratic socialism,' a loosely defined political and economic ideology aimed at achieving a classless system of government. Jamaica's two founding fathers projected quite different popular images. Bustamante, lacking even a high school diploma, was an autocratic, charismatic, and highly adept politician; Manley was an athletic, Oxford-trained lawyer, Rhodes scholar, humanist, and liberal intellectual. Although considerably more reserved than Bustamante, Manley was well liked and widely respected. He was also a visionary nationalist who became the driving force behind the Crown Colony's quest for independence.

As a result of disturbances in Jamaica and other West Indian islands, the Colonial Office appointed the West India Royal Commission, known as the Moyne Commission. The Moyne Report exposed the poor living conditions of the majority in Jamaica and the rest of Britain's Caribbean colonies.[5] The Commission's investigation was a turning point in colonial attitudes toward the rural small settlers and Black community. For the first time, the uprisings were not seen as unprovoked violence by Black people but as justified opposition to the depressing living conditions and absence of justice. The report revealed that, for most of the population, mere subsistence was increasingly problematic and that conditions resulted from institutional barriers that sought to maintain the historical colonial power structure of White planter supremacy and the economic foundations of slavery, with most land holdings in Jamaica continuing to be in the control of a small planter class elite.

The Commission's report explicitly stated that, for the labouring population, mere subsistence was not sufficient. With the intervention of the Commission, the British government passed the Colonial and Development Welfare Act to organise and allocate funds to the British West Indian islands for long-term economic reconstruction.

Arising from these disturbances and the Commission's report more control was given to Jamaicans through a new constitution issued on November 20,1944. The Constitution changed the Crown Colony system and inaugurated limited self-government based on the Westminster model of government and universal adult suffrage. It also embodied the island's principles of ministerial responsibility and the rule of law. Jamaica became the only country within the British empire other than Great Britain to introduce universal adult suffrage. It also provided for a bicameral legislature incorporating a nominated Legislative Council as an upper house (with limited powers) and an Executive Council. The new system of government later incorporated the principle of ministerial responsibility in government.

Thirty-one per cent of the population participated in the 1944 elections. The Jamaica Labour Party – helped by its promises to create jobs, its practice of dispensing public funds in pro-JLP parishes, and the PNP's relatively radical platform – won an 18 per cent majority of the votes over the PNP, as well as twenty-two seats in the thirty-two-member House of Representatives. The PNP won five seats and five were gained by other, short-lived parties. In 1945, Bustamante took office as Jamaica's first premier (the pre-independence title for head of government).

Under the new charter, the British governor, assisted by the six-member Privy Council and ten-member Executive Council, remained responsible solely to the Crown. The Jamaican Legislative Council became the Upper House, or Senate, of the bicameral Parliament. House members were elected by adult suffrage from single-member electoral districts called constituencies. Despite these changes, ultimate power remained concentrated in the hands of the governor and other high officials.

By June 1953, there was further modification to the constitution, providing for the appointment of a chief minister and seven other ministers from the elected House of Representatives. Day-to day-administration devolved to permanent secretaries. For the first time, Black and Brown Jamaican ministers of government could now exercise wide responsibilities in the management of the internal affairs of the island. The only limits placed on the ministers' powers pertained to public security, public prosecutions, and matters affecting members of the civil service, which remained under the control of the colonial secretary. On August 6, 1962, Jamaica became independent, with full dominion status within the Commonwealth, under a constitution that kept the British monarch as head of state.

COLONIAL ADMINISTRATION

The Jamaican public administration system had emerged in the 1950s with rules and culture from the colonial era. To understand how Jamaica arrived at this juncture, with the need for reforms in the 1980s, a historical perspective is provided. Among the pioneering studies and reports on Jamaica's public sector has been the study[6] by which reviewed the existing organisations, emoluments, and other conditions of employment of the public service in Jamaica. The Hodge Report was preceded by the report of the Committee on the Public Service in 1939, which followed the publication of the executive summary of the Moyne Report on economic and social conditions in Jamaica. This Moyne summary, published in 1939, highlighted the deplorable conditions of the people and criticised how local people were excluded from government.

There was then the report of G. Mills[7] followed by the UN Report by M.C. Argus, W.P. Barret and E. Holstein,[8] and the report by Margaret Priestley.[9] The latter report provided one of the best summaries of the various measures taken by successive Jamaican governments: colonial, internal self-governing and politically independent, to improve the performance of public services up to the 1980s. Then there are the notes on managing the public sector.[10]

The British administrative legacy had a long and enduring influence on post-colonial administrative development. Colonial administration represented a notion of 'trusteeship' based on an institutional arrangement that sought to insulate the public service from local political players in Jamaica and the Caribbean. This legacy of insulation shaped the relationship between administration and post-independence political movements and has been a source of criticism, especially by early West Indian advocates of independence, like Norman

Manley, on the lack of responsiveness of the colonial administration to the needs of the Jamaican people.[11]

Between 1944 and 1962, Jamaica transitioned from Crown Colony rule, with a minority of elected representatives in the Legislative Council to a fully independent Commonwealth state, with a Westminster-style constitution. The 1944 constitution was overlaid onto a set of administrative structures and doctrines which date back to the colonial past. Jamaica surrendered its ancient constitution following the Morant Bay Rebellion of 1865 replacing it by Crown Colony rule in 1886 which introduced a measure of representation. Even the Imperial government was outraged at the time at the heavy-handed reaction by the planters and local colonial administrators to the Morant Bay Rebellion.[12]

An Executive Privy Council (commonly referred to as the Executive Council, which had real power, comprised the governor as president, the colonial secretary, the financial secretary, and the attorney general, as well as two nominated officials appointed by Britain on the recommendation of the governor. It was possible for an unofficial (i.e., nominated or elected) member of the Legislative Council to serve on the Executive Council and, according to Hamilton, this was the high privilege of the unofficial member, as it enabled him to participate in the business of policy making. In most instances, the appointment of unofficial members was restricted to the employer planter class.[13]

According to the Moyne Report,[14] the economic conditions of Jamaica at the end of the Second World War were worse than on the eve of the Morant Bay Rebellion. The depressed conditions were part of a global depression which began in 1929 in the US. However, whereas the US rebounded after the war, the depressed conditions in Jamaica continued into the 1940s.[15] These conditions resulted in the first wave of Jamaicans and other West Indians to travel to 'Mother England,' starting with passage on the *Ormonde*, March 1947 bound for Liverpool; the *Almanzora* in 1947 to Southampton, and the *Empire Windrush* which docked in the River Thames in Tilbury, London June 21, 1948, with 1,027 passengers.

The Colonial Form of Government

The form of government and the machinery of public administration Jamaica inherited from Britain was never managerial in the classical sense. It suffered from technical and managerial incapacity and some self-doubt and manifested many irrational practices and structures. The form of trusteeship administration handed down ran counter to post-independence aspirations of a responsive public sector. Following the war, the predilection of the derivative middle-class bureaucracy was reinforced by the JLP's nationalist/pragmatic approach and the PNPs ideological/forced pragmatic impulses. These explain the rise of a large public enterprise in post-colonial Jamaica.[16]

On gaining independence, Jamaica adopted the Westminster parliamentary system of government, which confers on the political party that commands the majority in the lower house, or House of Representatives, the right to name the prime minister and to form the governing administration. The prime minister appoints the cabinet ministers. The legislature is a bi-cameral Parliament, made up of elected members of the House of Representatives and a Senate, comprising several appointed members. The party with the second highest representatives has the right to appoint a leader of the opposition.

The main constraining influence on government is an independent judiciary, which has the responsibility of safeguarding the constitution and the authority to interpret the law and the actions or decisions of the government. The life of each administration is a maximum of five years, and regular elections have been held under universal adult suffrage since 1944.

The head of government, the British king, is represented in Jamaica by the governor general. In the exercise of executive authority, the governor general acts with the advice of the Cabinet. Jamaica is one of fourteen former British colonies where the British king is still the head of state.[17] The last Commonwealth country to abandon the British sovereign as head of state was Barbados in 2021. Jamaica has been debating a move to replace the British sovereign as head of government since the 1990s but has failed to reach a consensus on key governance matters such as the final court of justice and the form and power to be given on the head of government.

Jamaica developed a strong two-party system during the post-war years, with the PNP historically reflecting Fabian socialism,[18] and the JLP, reflecting a more conservative orientation and the interest of the private sector and the rural sugar workers. The institutional system of ministries and permanent secretaries, with the latter imposed between the minister as head of the political directorate and the permanent secretary as the head of the administrative directorate, has created frictions first introduced in 1953. The result is that much of the activities of administrative modernisation in the decade of the 1950s focused on integration of ministries and departments, first started at the Ministry of Agriculture and Lands and the Ministry of Housing in the 1950s. On introduction, the system of ministerial government and Cabinet, as the top executive arm of government, provided for ministers to have control over functions of specialised departments.

The ministerial system of government is also entrenched in the Constitution, with the responsible minister being required to exercise general direction and control over activities related to subject, or departments assigned to him or her, by the prime minister, and with the permanent secretary as the head of the administrative arm, being responsible for implementation of policies and accounting for disbursement of funds. The ministerial system and the fully responsible minister, as an institutional form involved a transfer of power and responsibility from the Colonial Office and colonial governor to locally elected political heads of departments. It continued to create friction, tension, and mutual suspicion between ministers and career civil servants.[19]

Many of these relationships between ministers and civil servants emerged out of the UK and were guided by several Westminster precedents. However, in Jamaica these relationships and precedents were not well developed to guide the relationship. In the UK, the Nolan Report[20] set new principles in keeping with the twentieth century. The tradition emerged where, under the old colonial system of administration, emphasis focused on accounting for inputs and on personnel matters, at the expense of leadership, entrepreneurship, and accounting for outputs which, increasingly, became a requirement of modern forms of government after the 1980s.

As indicated earlier, permanent professionals and other officials were expected to be neutral, exercising control through a hierarchal structure, with no allegiance to any political party. This followed the principle which separated policy formulation responsibility of the Cabinet ministers and policy implementation responsibility to the permanent secretary and the civil service. In carrying out its functions, the civil service traditionally followed a complex and archaic set of rules and procedures involving reams of paperwork. Some of these rules and procedures were outdated and time consuming, not suited for a dynamic economic environment. The independence of the civil service antecedent goes back to 1855[21] and established a centralised bureaucracy in the UK, based on the principle that the state bureaucracy must be neutral, exercising probity, and a sense of public duty and Christian morality. This quasi-judicial governance philosophy, however, was never designed to cope with the rapid expansion of the public sector, which demanded a more managerial, entrepreneurial, and commercial ethos, concerned with efficiency, financial responsibility, and the delivery of quality customer service and good personnel management practices. Further the informal understandings which underpinned relations in the operations of government were never transferred from Westminster to Jamaica and the colonies.

With introducing Democratic Socialism in Jamaica in 1974, the neutrality principle came to be questioned and civil servants came under considerable pressure, with some regarded with suspicion. Gladstone E Mills and Paul Robertson[22] claimed that activist ministers often usurped the role of the permanent secretary. These government officials however did not always do the job required of permanent secretaries, so rather than usurping their role, ministers were unavoidably drawn into administration.[23]

During the 1970s and 80s, the political consensus that had characterised public administration up to the 1960 collapsed. Under the Michael Manley administration, the view also emerged that senior public officials were expected to share the philosophy of the prevailing administration. It was felt that there was a need to have a common philosophical outlook. The Manley administration was frustrated that the civil servants regarded themselves as the defenders of (their understanding of) the public interest against (what civil servants saw as) the whims of politicians. They pursued several parallel strategies to address this, of which the 'common philosophical outlook' was only one. Manley was quite prepared, mostly, to accept civil servants who adhered to traditional notions of neutrality but were willing to serve the political agenda.

The ideological differences between the civil service and the political directorate, some of which were long-standing but could be ignored so long as the distance between political and civil service views was modest, often led to conflict, and resulted increasingly in employment of a larger number of 'special advisors' by ministers. The practice of drafting in outside technical experts had emerged in the UK under the Harold Wilson administration in the 1960s. Special advisors were seen to encroach on the administrative space of the professional civil servant, further increasing the tension.[24]

It was some of these institutional weaknesses that created the need for an administrative transformation of the public service. Unlike the UK metropolitan counterpart, the colonial civil service structure had persisted up to the 1960s, without adapting to new and changing circumstances. It was not prepared for the new role required for a market-led economy. Its rigidity limited its adaptability to respond to a whole set of new developments occurring in society, continuing to operate according to rules and procedures of the colonial times. There was widespread waste from overlapping and duplication of functions among the several public sector organisations, mismanagement of human and financial resources, accompanied by the use of outdated and cumbersome regulations. The public service had developed to be production-oriented, with little regard for markets and consideration of customer service.

Whereas the UK public administration experienced several changes after the Second World War years, the Jamaican civil service remained steeped in pre-war values and structures. This may have worked well towards the end of the colonial period and immediately after independence, but it was no longer appropriate for an independent nation, especially because of the imperative to contend with the technological and economic changes which were being ushered into society in the 1980s. In fact, in the immediate post-war years some of the principal administrators were seconded from Westminster London, being familiar with the ethos of the old British system.

Public Services Commissions

Besides inheriting the system of ministries and permanent secretaries, a feature of political institutions common to the newly independent Caribbean countries was the institution of independent services commissions for the civil, police, and judicial services. Most important of these was the Public Services Commission (PSC). In Jamaica, the PSC system was introduced in 1951 and the system came to form an important arm of public administration with monopoly responsibility for personnel matters, and this was entrenched in the Constitution. The

Services Commission in Jamaica are the Public Services Commission, the Judicial Services Commission, the Police Services Commission, the Local Government Services Commission, and the Parish Council Services Commission.

The PSCs in the Caribbean came about after the British government, in keeping with post-war colonial policy, prepared all its territories for eventual independence within the Commonwealth. The Colonial Office White Paper in 1946 recommended that, in governors' duties of selecting and appointing candidates to the territorial government service for each territory, the colonial government should be advised in these matters by a PSC, composed as to command the confidence of the service and the public. According to the paper, the establishing this institution was necessary because granting political independence to the colonies could potentially pose risks to the integrity of the public service. The public was only to be assured of civil service neutrality by entrusting the control of careers to a body non-political as the judiciary.[25]

The Public Service Commission Law of 1952 placed matters of recruitment and promotion in the hands of a statuary board, the Public Service Commission, the sole objective being to limit political patronage, as against creating a responsible government. The historical legacy and the Public Service Commission Law placed civil servants in an elevated position vis-a-vis elected representatives. However, by the 1940s, politicians had exercised their new authority. This led Eric Mills in 1949 to observe that, in expressing their views to politicians, civil servants 'may put at risk the career of any public servant.'[26]

B.A.N. Collins[27] states that the Imperial British Government had, in keeping with post-war colonial policy, prepared all the territories for eventual independence within the Commonwealth. The Colonial Office White Paper on Organization of Colonial Services[28] recommended that:

> In discharging his duties of selecting and appointing candidates for the respective local services of the territories each colonial government should be advised in these matters by a PSC, so composed as to command the confidence of the Service and the public.
>
> Accordingly –
>
> It was felt necessary to introduce the institution because it was the official view that political independence for the colonies might

> prove dangerous for the integrity of the public service. The public was only to be assured of civil service neutrality by entrusting the control of their careers to a body as non-political and in as high public regard as the judiciary.

It was born out of mistrust of politicians and their friends and the paradox of Whitewall agreeing to give the colonies political independence while revealing continued distrust for the politicians of the territories. English governors could be trusted but not so elected local ministers. It was felt necessary therefore to shield the civil servants from manipulating politicians and the effect of party patronage.[29] In the period of Crown Colony rule, the concept of trusteeship saw local control over administration as an impediment to consistency, prudence, and leadership.

Lindsay Stirton, Lindsay and Martin Lodge have, however, suggested that this was not the real reason but that civil servants were demanding compensation for loss of position on independence, a demand the British government was unwilling to pay and instead bought them off with the services commissions.[30]

The entrenchment of the Services Commissions in the constitution in 1962 made its powers over the civil service virtually unalterable, save for constitutional amendments. Shortcomings had developed as early as in the 1960s as the Commissions, for practical purposes, operated like judicial bodies with little regard for modern management practices. The need to move away from a philosophy focused on integrity and probity and to one focusing on efficiency and administrative performance became overwhelming.

The Jamaican civil service had grown to be one of the major areas of extreme inefficiencies, representing a drain on public resources. Senior civil servants were expected to perform the inter-related functions of policy advisor to ministers, programme formulator, executer of public policy, including management of programmes and projects. The political directorate was expected to determine policy, while the technical directorate was expected to implement policy.

Pressures had developed in the 1970s to reduce the stranglehold of the Services Commissions over a full range of personnel and administrative practices, including conditions of service and to restrict them more to areas of disciplinary matters, and for the administrative functions to be incorporated into a central personnel office, staffed with professionals, delegating more of the personnel matters to line ministries.

Local Government

Another important component of a government in Jamaica is that of the local government system. Local government goes back to the vestry system patterned off the sixteenth century vestry system in England, introduced by Sir Thomas Modyford between 1662 and 1663, soon after the English took the island from the Spanish in 1655. The name derived from the fact that local authorities were governed by a body known as 'vestry,' composed of lay magistrates and the crown clergy of that parish. The main functions of the vestries were to support the clergy, maintain the churches, offer relief to the poor, maintain the few roads which then existed, and ensure public order. It was usually made up of ten men and two church wardens who were elected from the lay magistrates and clergy of that parish. The vestry system lasted for two hundred years until it was abolished in 1886, shortly after Crown Colony government was introduced and was replaced by Municipal and Road Boards.

The major change which occurred during the two hundred years was the number of parishes in that, when the system was first introduced, there were twenty-two parishes. However, this was subsequently reduced to fourteen in 1867. Instead of elected representation, after 1867 members were nominated by the governor, in keeping with the Crown Colony system of government. The system, over the years, operated in the interest of the planter class. Some measure of elected representation was restored after 1886 with the creation of Parochial Boards, which combined the functions of the Municipal and Road Boards. The twenty-one-year period between the abolition of the vestry system and its replacement by the Parochial Boards had seen the responsibilities of local government widen immensely to include public health, public markets, fire services, water supplies, and later, abattoirs, building regulation, public beaches, sanitation, and public cleansing, and street lighting.

The system remained much the same until the 1980s, when the Seaga administration transferred several functions from local government, or parish councils, to central ministries and departments under the pretext that the councils wasted funds and centralisation would bring economies of scale and efficiencies. The Kingston and St Andrew

Corporation (KSAC), for example, saw its responsibility in 1984 for roads and works transferred to the Ministry of Construction and Works; public health to Ministry of Health; water to National Water Commission, and poor relief to Ministry of Social Security.

The remaining twelve parishes kept responsibility for these services; however, they were starved of finances to effectively provide the services. Contracting out of public cleansing and sanitation services, parks, gardens and playing field maintenance to a new entity (Metropolitan Parks and Markets Limited) further reduced the ability of the councils to discharge their functions. The 1993 Local Government Reform programme under the PNP administration provided for a return of local services to the parishes. First there was legal reform, modernising the existing colonial local government laws and regulations to ensure the councils had the required authority to discharge their responsibilities.

Of special significance was the amendments to the Parochial Rates and Finance Act, Kingston and St Andrew Act, the Property Tax Act, and the Road Traffic Act, specifically introduced to facilitate the enactment and creation of the Parochial Revenue Fund, the vehicle introduced to ensure that local councils had independent and dedicated sources of funding provided through property taxes and motor vehicle licensing. Second, policy changes and legislation provided for restoration of functions previously removed from the councils' jurisdiction. Third, organisational and institutional strengthening was implemented to ensure the councils had the administrative capacity to deliver the services delegated to them. The reforms were justified based on restoration of local democracy, giving local representatives more say in meeting local needs, and providing for fair distribution of power between central and local government. Some of these changes were facilitated by the Municipalities Act of 2003.[31] Edris Dawn Schoburgh's thesis overall is that local government was part of the (albeit underpowered) engine of democratic development in pre-independence Jamaica. This also corresponds to English experience.[32] When the UK had a genuine separation of powers, central executive government, in fact, did little, but the local government was a vibrant site of democracy and development.

Notes

1. Gladstone Mills, 'Public Enterprises in Commonwealth Caribbean, with Special Reference to Jamaica and Trinidad and Tobago,' Department

of Government University of the West Indies (unpublished 1976). A revised version was reproduced in a seminar presentation, 'The Role of Management of Public Enterprise,' October 1976.

2. A. Garcia, *History of the West Indies* (London: George W Harrop & Company Limited, 1965).
3. F.R. Augier and S.E. Gordon (1962), *Sources of West Indian History* (London: Longman, 1962).
4. Electoral Commission, *History of the Electoral Commission in Jamaica* (Kingston: Electoral Commission Office, 2014).
5. *The Moyne Report: The Report of the West India Royal Commission*, 1945.
6. A. Hodge, *The Report by the Committee on Public Service in 1939* (Kingston: Government Printer, 1942).
7. G. Mills, 'Working Paper on Staffing and Salary Gradings of the Public Service,' Department of Government, UWI, 1950.
8. M.C. Argus, W.P. Barreth, and E. Holstein, *UN Report on Public Administration in Jamaica* (New York: UN, 1965).
9. Margaret Priestley, 'Administrative Reform Enquiries in Jamaica, 1942–1980,' Administrative Staff College, Ministry of Public Service and Labour, 1983
10. Beryl Miller, 'Notes on Managing the Public Sector: Financial Problems and Possible Solutions,' Ministry of Finance, Kingston, 1985.
11. Rex Nettleford, *Manley & the New Jamaica: Selected Speeches and Writings 1938–1968* (Kingston: Longman Caribbean, 1971).
12. Martin Lodge, Lindsay Lodge, and Kim Moloney, 'Whitehall in the Caribbean? The Legacy of Colonial Administration for Post-colonial Democracy Development,' *Commonwealth and Comparative Politics* 53, no. 1 (2015): 8–28.
13. Eric Mills, *Report of the Commission on Public Service in Jamaica* (Kingston: Government Printer, 1949).
14. *Moyne Report* Cmd 6607, London, HMSO.
15. Richard Bernal, Mark Figueroa, and Michael Witter, 'Caribbean Economic Thought: The Critical Tradition,' Paper delivered for the 21st Anniversary Conference of the Faculty of Social Sciences, UWI, 1983.
16. Rex Nettleford, 'Notes on Privatization in Jamaica,' unpublished manuscript, UWI, 1995.
17. There are fourteen Commonwealth realms outside of the United Kingdom: Antigua and Barbuda, Australia, The Bahamas, Belize, Canada, Grenada, Jamaica, New Zealand, Papua New Guinea, Saint Kitts and Nevis, Saint Lucia, Saint Vincent and the Grenadines, the Solomon Islands, Tuvalu.
18. Fabian socialism, founded in Britain in 1884, is a form of socialism that advances the principles of democratic framework to achieve gradual conversion to socialism rather than by revolutionary overthrow. This originated from the movement for the Utopian socialism

19. G.E. Mills, 'Public Administration in Commonwealth Caribbean: Evolution, Conflicts and Challenges,' in *Social and Economic Studies* 19, no.1 (March 1970): 5–22.
20. Lord Nolan, *Report of the Committee on Standards in Public Life* (London: HMSO, 1994).
21. Charles Trevelyan, *The Organization of the Permanent Civil Service* (London: British Civil Service, 1854)
22. G.E. Mills and Paul Robertson, 'The Attitudes and Behaviour of Senior Civil Servants in Jamaica,' *Social and Economic Studies* 39, no. I (1974): 311–43.
23. United Nations, *Technical Department Report on Jamaica* (Geneva: UN, 1960)
24. Edwin Jones, *Contending with Administrivia: Competition for Source Benefits and Power* (Kingston: Arawak Publication, 2015).
25. HMSO, *Organization of the Colonial Service* (London: HMSO, 1946).
26. Eric Mills, *Report of the Commission on Public Service in Jamaica* (Kingston: Government Printer, 1949).
27. B.A.N. Collins, 'Some Notes on Public Services Commissions in Commonwealth Caribbean,' *Social and Economic Studies* 16, no. 1 (1967): 1–16.
28. HMSO, 'The Colonial Office White Paper on Organization of Colonial Services,' London, 1946.
29. B.A.N. Collins, 'Some Notes on Public Services Commissions in Commonwealth Caribbean.'
30. Lindsay Stirton and Martin Lodge, 'Constitutional Legacy of Politics and Administration in Jamaica Incomplete Settlement,' *Northern Ireland Legal Quarterly* 71, no. 2 (2020): 239–60.
31. Edris Dawn Schoburgh, 'Local Government Reform in Jamaica and Trinidad: A Policy Dilemma,' Online by Wiley Interscience, 2007, http://www.interscience.com.
32. Eris Dawn Schoburgh, 'Local Government Reform: The Prospect for Community Empowerment in Jamaica,' Sir Arthur Lewis Institute of Social and Economic Research, UWI, 2006.

CHAPTER THREE

The Case for Reforming the Public Sector and Public Enterprises

INTRODUCTION

Following independence, Jamaica immediately updated its administrative structure and government institutions to reflect the people's aspirations. Seven major initiatives can be identified in reforming the public sector in Jamaica:

1. The first major reform involved the introduction of the Ministry of Public Service in 1972.
2. The second initiative involved the introduction of the Administrative Reform Programme (ARP) in 1984.
3. The third initiative involved the 1991 ARP11, which provided for the Financial and Programme Management Improvement Project (FPMIP), the Financial Management System (FMIS), and the Human Resources Management Information System (HRMS) subprojects.
4. The fourth major initiatives involved the introduction of the Tax Administrative Reform Project in 1994, which was a World Bank–supported initiative.
5. The fifth major initiative involved introduction of a new set of institutions, including the Citizens Charter by Prime Minister Patterson, which required public bodies to treat users of the public service as customers, with rights to good quality services.
6. The sixth major initiative was the introduction of the Public Sector Modernisation Programme (PSMP1).
7. The seventh involved PSMP 2, started in September 2002 through Ministry Paper Number 56.

REFORMS OF 1973: INTRODUCTION OF MINISTRY OF THE PUBLIC SERVICE

The first initiative saw the creation of the Ministry of the Public Service (MPS) in 1973. The new ministry was charged with the responsibility to introduce and sustain a programme of self-reforming measures aimed at modernising management practices throughout the public sector.[1] But the experiment failed, mainly because of excessive centralisation.[2] The MPS Reforms had been expected to reduce the stranglehold of the Public Services Commissions on civil service personnel administration, from the creation of a single ministry responsible exclusively for public sector management. The ministry was also charged with institutionalising a programme of internal reforms, reflecting the introduction of modern business management and personnel management practices, such as organisation and methods and office studies, based on work study principles as practised by the Institute of Work Study in the UK.

The new ministry was charged with two key responsibilities: personnel management of all functions of the public sector and the institutionalisation of a programme for self-reforms within the public sector, through utilisation of modern management techniques.[3] Accompanying the creation of the MPS, the reform provided to expand in-service training programmes in management and supervision by the Administrative Staff College, and finance and accounting by the Finance and Accounting College. There was also a new and open performance evaluation system, replacing the old system, which was based on confidential reporting on staff by their immediate supervisors, a colonial heritage.

There were several problems which MPS inherited. There were widespread disparities in emoluments within the public sector, whereby the statutory bodies and the public enterprises offered substantially higher salaries, as both bodies felt they had to match salaries in the private sector. Second, there was an overlapping of functions, especially between MPS and the Public Services Commission, leading to wasteful duplication. Third, the new MPS, along with the other two core agencies involved in personnel management, Ministry of Finance, and the Public Services Commission, were not only reluctant to delegate decision-making authority to line ministries but continued to monopolise policy and decision making in the areas of finance, planning, budgeting and personnel deployment in the rest of the central service.[4] There was even a general failure by senior civil service managers to delegate to middle managers and junior staff.[5]

In order to address these problems, two reform initiatives were introduced: reform of the public service compensation system, and measures to facilitate delegation of decision-making in the areas of recruitment, promotions, and exercise of discipline. The government had, since the 1980s, attempted to improve the compensation structure. Between 1983 and 1986, a special effort was made to improve compensation for top civil servants, government lawyers, and other senior civil service officials. This involved benchmarking several civil service positions with similar positions in the private sector. Because of this initiative, there was some progress in that, by 1986, improvements in compensation for civil service managers and professionals had reached a level of between 70 per cent and 80 per cent of their counterparts in statutory bodies and public enterprises. However, this improvement benefited only about 5.5 per cent of civil servants, while at the lower levels of the establishment the compensation gap remained as wide as it was in 1983. The outcome was that numerous positions remained unfilled6 A World Bank Report[7] revealed that there were thirty-two hundred vacancies in the central establishment in 1993, of which 725 were key or senior positions. The government then resorted to a system of acting or temporary appointments to address the problem, so positions were being staffed by personnel without the experience or qualification.

The ministry was expected to work with the Office of the Public Services Commission and the Ministry of Finance, not only to decentralise several of their personnel functions, but they were also expected to restructure their organisations to perform mainly policymaking, regulatory, and appellate functions and provide common services, besides assisting line agencies to build their capacity to conduct decentralised personnel functions. The line ministries were required to implement Performance Improvement Programmes, which involved staff identifying specific problems in their respective ministries and to suggest ways to resolve them. New operations divisions were created at MPS, which focused on facilitating and expediting the transfer of personnel and human resources support services to line agencies. A Standards and Policy Division was created, and proposals were introduced to provide for the delegation of some disciplinary functions to permanent secretaries.

The Ministry Paper of 1973, that initiated reforms relating to the creation of the MPS, stated that the objective was to introduce a service, which could employ up-to-date techniques and procedures in efficiently undertaking public business, a service sensitive and responsive to the needs of the community.[8]

The first permanent secretary was Professor George Eaton, an academic. The ministry was given cabinet status and the MPS's permanent secretary became the head of the civil service, a position formerly held by the financial secretary in the Ministry of Finance, or the permanent secretary in the Office of the Prime Minister. MPS also assumed responsibility for the establishment function from the Ministry of Finance. The Organisation and Methods function was expanded into a Management Services Department, and a cadre of personnel was developed to handle the personnel management function. The new ministry was to be a change agent to facilitate innovation; however, it centralised several of the non-commissions' functions such as pay negotiations, management services, and career development.

The MPS project did, however, lead to increased training and capacity building; introducing a new budgeting model; introduction of a computerised human resources system; reclassification of job positions; and introduction of performance management linking objectives, expenditure, and output, accompanied by increased remuneration. A more frequent performance evaluation system was introduced, emphasising merit, rather than seniority. The personnel function, however, was divided between the Ministry of Finance, the services commissions, and the new Ministry of the Public Service, leading to delays, duplication, and inefficiencies.

The MPS, together with the Ministry of Finance and the Public Services Commission showed little interest in delegating decision-making authority to line ministries and agencies and, instead, continued to monopolise policy and decision making on finance, planning, budgeting, and personnel management in the rest of the public service.[9] The senior civil servants also failed to delegate to middle and junior staff.[10] Resentment developed towards the all-powerful role acquired by MPS, and especially the Permanent Secretary. As the MPS never fulfilled the objectives laid out in 1973 and, as its introduction coincided with the period of rapid expansion of the public service, it was discontinued in 1995. Many of its establishment functions were returned to the Ministry of Finance (responsibility for public service) with the management development functions transferred to the newly created Cabinet Office.

THE ADMINISTRATIVE REFORM PROGRAMME (ARP)

The administrative reform initiatives of 1984 involved a more substantive reform programme. Jamaica's prolonged economic deterioration seemed to have bottomed out towards the middle of the 1980s, reflecting favourable external developments such as the decline in international oil prices, the rise in tourism and an end to the deterioration of the bauxite/alumina industry, accompanied by a reduction in the deficit, both in the central government and in the SOEs. It was in this context that ARP was introduced.

The IMF had encountered difficulties in implementing some aspects of the 1980/82 agreements, and the first World Bank-supported structural adjustment programme, because of shortages of qualified staff to perform the needed policy reforms and the absence of a well-functioning budget, expenditure control, and cash management system. These shortcomings manifested themselves in the poor execution of several development programmes and projects. The problems of the public service had been the subject of the 1980 UN Report on Jamaican public administration. Additionally, local consultants and members of Jamaica's academia had also reported on the failings of the services, such as G.E. Mills and Paul Robertson,[11] Phyllis Green and Marie Slyfield,[12] and Phyllis Green, Derick S. Gordon, and Edwin Jones.[13] These studies cited the major problem of being over centralisation of decision making with excessive reliance on Cabinet decisions; lack of delegation by senior civil service managers; overlapping of functions and the inability of agencies to work together consistently for policy implementation; over-concern with petty details, rules, and regulations at the expense of broader issues, and the need for public service efficiency. There were problems with the Ministry of the Public Service, responsible for compensation policy and administration and staff training and the PSC, which had become overly centralised and bureaucratic.[14] The ARP sought to improve capacity building and human resources development within the public service based on merit principles started by MPS. The ARP was introduced to correct some of these problems MPS reforms had failed to correct and the reforms involved three main strands[15]:

a. rationalisation of government structures (otherwise known as administrative reform), involving strategic mechanisms and processes for policy making, policy coordination, resource mobilisation, and service delivery.

b. human resources management, concerned with personnel issues, covering appointments and capacity building, and involving training and career development, and

c. improvements to morale through compensation and other related incentives.

In addition, there have been reforms centred on public enterprises, involving rationalisation, privatisation, and contracting out of services. After 1984, the Jamaican government came under sustained pressure from the IMF, the World Bank, USAID, and the British Overseas Development Administration (now Department for International Development) and the Private Sector Organisation of Jamaica (PSOJ) to reduce the size of the public bureaucracy and to withdraw from productive activities.

The 1980 ARP reform sought to shift the emphasis of the ongoing reforms towards effective delivery of services, requiring a reorientation towards a smaller public sector. Economy and efficiency were to supersede the traditional civil service values of equity, fairness, and probity. The government established an Inter-Ministerial Committee on Administrative Reform (IMCAR), with a secretariat based at the Office of the Prime Minister and with the prime minister as chairperson. The committee comprised several ministers, permanent secretaries, and technical advisors. ARP had three objectives: to improve efficiency of human resources management; improve effectiveness of financial administration and undertake a fundamental restructuring of the role and mission of line ministries and agencies. The programme sought to optimise the structure of the public service, improve core public service management systems: financial, personnel, and central programme management; simplification of procedures; improvements to service delivery by departments and agencies; administrative reorganisation, and reduction of the state's field of activities.

ARP I

ARP I of 1984–91 specifically had the following objectives:

- Improvements to human resource management.
- Improvements to financial resources management.
- Restructuring of the role, mission, and functions of line ministries.

ARP II of 1990–95 objectives were as follows:

- Establishing optimum size and structures for public services.
- Improvements to core public service management systems, vis: financial, personnel and general programme management, including computerisation of information system, and
- Simplification of procedures and improvements to customer service delivery by departments and agencies.

The ARP objectives sought to bring about radical changes and secure an integrative public sector framework, with the objective of improving operational effectiveness. The IMF's structural adjustment agenda was the driving force for the reforms which sought to stem the decline in the quality of service. The ARP, involving a reduction in the numbers employed, came to be the IMF's key strategy in the reform agenda, and sought to bring about a reduction in numbers to a more manageable size. Finally, as part of ARP I and especially during 1984–88 the government training institutions: the Administrative Staff College, the Finance and Accounts College of Training, the Secretarial and Clerical College, and the Mandeville Training Centre laid on a suite of comprehensive training courses covering human resources management, project management, performance budgeting and accounting, and organisational behaviour and management to support the reform initiative. The ARP I also involved transfer of the responsibilities of Municipal and Parish Councils (local government) to central agencies, or to the Ministry of Local Government. Attempts were made to decentralise more functions from the central Ministries of Finance and the Public Service to the line ministries; for example, the Central Department of Supply was eliminated. Classification of positions was delegated from MPS to the line ministries.

During this period, the government introduced the concept of user fees in selected areas; for example, university students were required to meet 15 per cent of their economic costs. Hospital patients and secondary school children were also required to participate in cost sharing, with patients and students required to pay a portion of the cost for health and educational services, respectively. Major internal reorganisation occurred in several ministries, reflecting downsizing and reallocation of portfolio responsibilities. The human resource side of management addressed further improvements to compensation levels, which started in the 1970s, decentralisation of personnel function, and the removal of archaic rules and regulations.

The following areas were covered: upgrading and reclassification of pay of senior civil servants; initiation of an integrated training service with the establishment of one organisation responsible for civil service training; strengthening of manpower planning in MPS; updating and issuance of new staff orders; introduction of project cycle management; introduction of performance management techniques and strengthening of the permanent secretary's board.

Administrative reform was not only being introduced in Jamaica, but the Caribbean Heads of Government also established a Working Group on Administrative Reform.[16] The Working Group reported in 1995 and encouraged other Caribbean states to embrace the reform agenda.

The ARP I was facilitated by a World Bank loan of US$4.5 million, and projects were implemented under its direction. With this ARP II, the loan contained several discrete components, covering financial management, programme management, computerised management and a personnel and training component. A cell unit was established at the Ministry of Finance with responsibility for the Financial and Programme Management Improvement Programme (FPIM). The ARP's introduction witnessed the second major post-independence effort to reform the public sector in Jamaica.[17]

ARP II

A major initiative of ARP II was the World Bank-assisted Financial and Programme Management Improvement project (FPMIP) of the 1991/92 financial year, which was housed at the Ministry of Finance and Planning, focusing on corporate planning and programme budgeting.[18] The ARP II specifically addressed occupational classification, computerisation of personnel information, human resources management, and fiscal and financial management.

The occupational classification system described the kinds and levels of work, job specification and prescribed the qualification (job requirements) and performance standards to be used in the personnel procedures, covering recruitment, selection, appointment, pay determination, training, career development, and employee evaluation. Computerisation of personnel information provided for development of a computerised data base to ensure accurate employment records, updating information on pensioners and to develop the capability of identifying and channelling personnel to high priority programmes.

In ARP II, the Fiscal and Financial Management initiative focused on restructuring the Ministry of Finance and Planning, with the objective of improving institutional capacity and financial management. In this regard, the Financial Secretary's Office was strengthened by upgrading it to the highest level in the public service, creating two deputy financial secretaries at the grade level of permanent secretary and an executive assistant to the financial secretary.

Several senior appointments were also made, which provided for heads of the following divisions: economics, budget, and public enterprise. In addition, a new position was created, that of controller general charged with two broad responsibilities: to monitor government expenditures and to ensure prompt presentation of financial statements for the various levels of financial management. This was accompanied by a new system of performance budgeting, aimed at increasing productivity among public sector managers by relating expenditures to work done and to objectives. The system was also intended to set targets, keeping up to date with work progress and developing performance data required for decision making and allocation of resources.

Several new permanent appointments were made to the Accountant General's Department in order to facilitate restructuring to secure improved cash management. A computerised debt management system was introduced to improve the efficiency of debt management.

Other objectives of ARP II were:

- Introducing a corporate strategic planning and reporting system for improved programme management.
- Improving financial management systems and standards by strengthening the budgeting and accounting processes for central government, together with computerisation of FMIS.
- Improving personnel management standards and procedures, together with computerisation of HRMS.

- Improving the delivery of customer services by government departments and agencies which interface directly with the public, and
- Providing hands-on training to support implementation and strengthening of the capacity of related public service training institutions.

Following ARP I and ARP II a Tax Administration Reform Programme (TARP) was started in July 1994, with the latter having objective of raising tax revenues without increasing taxes, by broadening the tax base, improving efficiency and effectiveness of tax administration and encouraging voluntary compliance. Under this initiative, the Taxpayer Registration Number (TRN) system was introduced. Second, several taxpayer registration centres were established, with online access to the TRN data base, enabling numbers to be allocated straightaway upon completion of the application form. Problems in areas of tax administration had arisen from duplication of effort and inefficient use of scarce human resources and fragmentation of the enforcement system. The tax administration headed by a director general was restructured along function lines; incentives for improved performance were introduced; better working conditions were provided, accompanied by improved on-the-job training and improved career advancement opportunities.

By the mid-1990s, the government budget deficit was brought down to 3 per cent. It had hovered around 17 per cent of the GDP in the1980s. This was achieved largely by major cutbacks in capital and social services expenditure, and reduction in subsidies to public bodies. It was during this period that most of the government hotels and publicly owned banks were privatised and municipal services, such as public cleansing and minor health services were contracted out. Private management (management contracts) was tested unsuccessfully in the banana and sugar estates and at NWC. Major portions of government-owned lands were leased on long-term arrangements (forty-nine years) to private farmers, and monopoly rights to export trade removed from the marketing boards.

By 1995, the number of ministries had been reduced to thirteen. Both the Ministry of Finance and the Office of the Prime Minister underwent restructuring, delegating more responsibilities away from the financial secretary and the OPM's permanent secretary to the line ministry department heads. It was in this period that the Office of the Cabinet Secretary was created with the appointment of a cabinet secretary. And for the first time, a non-Jamaican was appointed governor of the Bank of Jamaica.

Failure of ARP I and ARP II

At the end of ARP I and ARP II the major impact of the changes was the downsizing of the service; increased pay awards provided to senior civil servants; decentralisation of services, and rapid expansion of training through the Administrative Staff College, subsequently named Management Institute for National Development (MIND). On the negative side there were several major strikes and public demonstrations during the period of reforms. Between the government and the World Bank the programme was, however, rated as unsatisfactory. More specifically, the following reasons have been given for the failure of ARP[19]:

a. Much of the reform initiatives was considered to have focused on the longer-term at the expense of short-term results, which was a demonstration of lack of a clear vision and articulation of objectives.
b. Consultants under the project often worked separately, rather than as a team, and often in the absence of counterparts from within the government; once the consultancies were terminated, reform efforts waned.
c. There was a lack of continued commitment by the government and the World Bank with very little equipment budgeted to cover project requirements (US$100,000), yet the project had called for the development of large-scale management information systems, demonstrating a lack of flexibility and vision by the reform design.
d. There was an absence of a suitably articulated master plan, virtually permitting consultants to assume too much of the leadership role and left little room for independent monitoring of activities. Sometimes, consultants attempted to dictate the conduct of work and, most times, the agencies or persons concerned were unprepared for them. They were not provided with counterparts to carry on in their absence, thus impeding continuity of effort and skills transfer.

e. Targets set for the project were considered too ambitious and were not prepared in collaboration with ministry personnel expected to lead key areas, implying a lack of diagnosis of the reform design involving all shareholders, as well as lack of reform focus.

A major problem of donor-initiated projects like ARP was the lack of ownership and sustained commitment by the government. There was however the creation of useful new institutions during the ARP implementation phase: the Cabinet Office, the National Planning Council, the National Environmental Planning Agency, the Contractor General's Office, the Office of the Ombudsman, the Fair-Trading Commission, and the Consumer Affairs Commission, along with a new set of regulatory agencies, inclusive of the Office of Utilities Regulation and the Financial Services Commission. It was during this period that major changes were also made to the transportation regulatory institutions.

THE NEED FOR PUBLIC SECTOR MANAGEMENT REFORM IN JAMAICA

Privatisation of SOEs was on such a scale in the UK that public enterprises and the Nationalised Industries almost ceased to exist. Besides large-scale privatisation in the 1980s, the UK introduced quasi-markets in the delivery of public services, whereby line managed organisations were disaggregated into service delivery entities, with relations between the parties governed by contracts, rather than traditional hierarchy. New forms of regulation emerged following privatisation, compensating for the retreat of the state. The social functions which remained in the UK public sector sphere were subjected to the process of managerialism and marketisation.

Within the central government, several quasi-independent service delivery entities (Next Step Agencies) were introduced. The financing of these agencies remained public, but they could charge user fees and compete for contracts. Other public functions were also subjected to market testing. 'Maintenance management' was replaced by management of change, with the emphasis on doing more with less.[20]

ARP had failed to reduce the high levels of centralisation; hence, further management reform was necessary. There was continued over centralisation of decision-making by central agencies and the continued use of outdated and cumbersome regulations and procedures, causing inordinate delays in decision-making and in responding to the needs of citizens.

Towards the end of the 1980s New Public Management (NPM) emerged in the UK as a new paradigm informing public sector reform and public enterprise management.[21] NMP represented a distinct break from traditional forms of public sector administration and has been grounded in New Right thinking. It is characterised by the principle that managers are free to manage public sector disaggregated units, with concern for efficiency, outcome, and quality of service delivery, individualism rather than collectivism, and consideration of the public sector users as customers.[22]

NPM's emergence coincided with the development of the New Right economic thinking which actively promoted reform by the World Bank and the Commonwealth Secretariat. The defining feature of NPM was the acceptance that the market was potentially more efficient in delivering public goods than bureaucratic planning and cumbersome administrative procedures. The public sector manager under NPM was expected to be more entrepreneurial, more like the private sector. This involved fundamental changes and radical departure from how the civil service had traditionally operated.

At the international level, towards the end of the 1970s, neoclassical economic thinking, espoused by Milton Friedman and the Chicago School with respect to the role of government in the development process, had taken root.[23] A central theme of neoclassical economics was reduction in the size and role of the state. The key values which underpinned this thinking were individualism, personal freedom, and private property rights. New Right thinking prefers markets over politics, both as a means of production and in distributing goods and services, as well as an institutional arrangement for providing social organisation and social control. Keynesian economics and Morrisonian principles, which had dominated most aspects of the public sector, welfare economics, and socialist thought in the post-war years, came with critical commentaries and were often rejected. The thinking of the New Right, popularly referred to as Thatcherism and Reganism, drew its intellectual respectability not only from the writings of M. Friedman but also A.E. Kahn, [24] F.A. Hayek and Paul Kegan,[25] and Dennis Swan.[26]

But there is an element of paradox to all of this, in that the shift to the neoliberal order required for its accomplishment of ongoing maintenance and massive mobilisation of state resources. Andrew Gamble presented a different view of neoliberalism from that which is described in the works of Friedman and Hayek et al.[27] The view was that the role of the state was to create a free economic environment in which market forces could efficiently allocate resources, and that any deliberate attempt by the state to introduce selective policies to promote certain sectors was to be discouraged, on the premise that this would lead to protectionism. Market failure and the existence of market imperfections were said to result from misconstrued inward-looking domestic policies. Structural imbalances could be corrected through free trade policies and trade liberalisation.-

BUILDING INSTITUTIONAL ARRANGEMENTS IN THE 1990S TO ACCOMMODATE MARKET ECONOMY

Among the institutions to receive government attention in the decade of the 1990s was the Office of the Prime Minister, which had undergone little change since 1962. Several studies had been conducted on the structure of government, including the reports of Kenneth Stowe and Geoffrey Morgan,[28] Rex Nettleford,[29] and Freddie Zenny and Cezley Sampson.[30] Few of the recommendations from the various reports were ever acted upon. Specifically, the Nettleford and Stowe and Morgan reports called for the creation of a unit within the Prime Minister's Office, responsible for the coordination of policy implementation, effectively a Cabinet Office. The IMF believed previous administrations had too large of a cabinet. They expected a new administration to propose a smaller one.

The outgoing administration of Prime Minister Seaga had operated the Office of the Prime Minister with a top-down style of management, working closely with Don Brice, the OPM permanent secretary, and a cadre of six women as the central force of the administration. He had a herculean task in that Mr Seaga was also minister of finance and minister of defence and with the Office of the Prime Minister at Jamaica House, and the Ministry of Finance, with the financial secretary and the secretary to the Cabinet was at National Heroes Circle, a good half an hour's drive in Kingston's congested traffic the effective administration became more difficult. As he was very much a micro-manager, most decisions had to receive his seal of approval, so there was a long back log of matters which required immediate attention.

Prior to the appointment of the cabinet secretary, servicing of the cabinet was handled by the secretary to the cabinet. This position was separate from the position as permanent secretary in the Office of the Prime Minister, When the cabinet system was introduced, the responsibilities as secretary to the cabinet included operation of the Cabinet Office, organising cabinet meetings, setting the cabinet agenda in consultation with the prime minister, recording the minutes of the cabinet meetings, and ensuring that cabinet decisions were distributed to the parties.

The Cabinet Office during Seaga's tenure as prime minister was small and, besides the secretary, comprised a group of steno typists who attended the Cabinet meetings and made verbatim recordings of the proceedings. Prime Minister Seaga would then use these meeting notes to prepare what essentially was the Cabinet decisions notes for circulation by the Cabinet Secretary to members of the Cabinet in the famous red boxes. There was therefore an urgent need to restructure the Office of the Prime Minister, especially to deal with the separate matters relating to the administration of the Cabinet affairs from the rest of OPM's administrative responsibilities.

Although there was an organisational structure on paper, operationally it was dysfunctional, with the deputy permanent secretary responsible for finance and administration, and the secretary to the Cabinet reporting directly to the prime minister. The deputy permanent secretary explained that, under Prime Minister Seaga, there was no requirement for her to report through the permanent secretary. in fact, the practice had developed of several officials reporting directly to the prime minister, rather than through the permanent secretary, so virtually no one reported in practice directly to Seaga's permanent secretary, other than his secretary.[31]

Several organisational models were considered for the re-structuring of the OPM. The eventual structure was based on a report produced by an Australian public sector management consultant, Dr Gilbert Roy.[32] He recommended two broad divisions, with the head of each reporting directly to the prime minister. The divisions were as follows:

a. a Cabinet Office headed by a cabinet secretary, who would also serve as head of the Civil Service and would be the most senior permanent secretary in Government, and

b. an Administration and Government Affairs Office, headed by a permanent secretary reporting directly to the prime minister.

The Cabinet Office Division was to be responsible for:

a. Coordinating economic and social policy matters across ministries, starting new policies, and conducting an analysis of policies and, importantly, servicing the Cabinet.
b. Communicating agendas and Cabinet decisions to the relevant parties for action;
c. Carrying responsibility for the staff college, the Management Institute for National Development (MIND); supervision of the Office of Utilities Regulation (OUR). The Director General of OUR was to report through the Cabinet Office to the prime minister;
d. Serve as head of the entire civil service and the Permanent Secretary Board. Manage a small secretariat to service the functioning of Cabinet and to work in close coordination with the Planning Institute of Jamaica. There was to be a separate director, responsible for the machinery of the government and to have close coordination with the Planning Institute of Jamaica;
e. Assume responsibility for the machinery of government, including the ongoing Administrative Reform Programme, and the Public Sector Management Improvement Programme.

An Administration and Operating Division, headed by a Permanent Secretary for Administration and Government Affairs and with responsibility for the following:

a. The overall administrative functions of the prime minister's portfolio and provide shared services with the Cabinet Office (financial, personnel and office administrations). The sharing of central administrative functions also formed one of the new initiatives, such as personnel administration, financial management and computing services between two government portfolios which formed a part of the new policy direction.
b. Supervise departmental functions and agencies, including functions and enterprises which the prime minister deemed strategic, and which fell under the prime minister, covering information technology, broadcasting, housing, community amenities and scientific and technical services and the

related public bodies. The agencies at the time were the Urban Development Corporation, National Housing Cooperation, Scientific Research Council, Jamaica Information Services, and the Broadcasting Commission.

c. Provide leadership and strategic planning to these agencies.

The new structure was established for the Cabinet Office in 1993.[33] Following approval of the new structure the next step was to find someone from the civil service to fill the post. Following the administrative procedure in July 1993, Dr Carlton Davis, of the Jamaica Bauxite Institute, a long-standing public servant was appointed as the first cabinet secretary. Ambassador Hill was then appointed executive director of NIBJ, and Mrs Charmaine Constantine, who was already a permanent secretary in the Office of the Prime Minister, became permanent secretary responsible for administration of the Office of the Prime Minister.

Economic and Production Committee

One of the early decisions taken by the Cabinet in the second quarter of 1989 was to resurrect the Economic and Production Committee (EPC), a subcommittee of the cabinet. The EPC comprised the principal economic ministers of government, and the senior advisers: Financial secretary, governor of the Bank of Jamaica, director general of the Planning Institute of Jamaica (PIOJ), and the permanent secretary to the prime minister, and was chaired by P.J. Patterson, as deputy prime minister and minister of development planning and production.

The EPC coordinated economic policies and major project initiatives. Most economic and financial matters, as well as major new projects were taken at EPC before going on to Cabinet for a final decision. When a matter related to a particular ministry was being taken, then the permanent secretary for that ministry was invited to participate in the EPC meeting.

National Planning Council

A decision was also taken by Cabinet in June 1989 to create a National Planning Council (NPC), which was to be a separate body from the Planning Institute of Jamaica. The PIOJ had grown out of the National Planning Agency, created in 1984, and was itself created out of the

Central Planning Unit which was formed in 1955. The PIOJ handled the preparation of national and sectoral plans, and the various Five-Year Economic Plans, along with production of the annual report, the Economic and Social Survey of Jamaica. The head of PIOJ serves as the government's chief economic advisor. The NPC was created through Ministry Paper No. 18/89.[34] Patterson's rationale for NPC was to establish a body which could bring all the key political players together to facilitate dialogue, contribute to the subject at hand and, where possible, reach common understanding. Its economic sphere should serve as a consultative body in the formulation of economic policies, to assess economic performances, and to identify measures designed to achieve broad-based development and growth. Like the Economic and Production Council, it was part of Patterson's style of public management, seeking to secure wide inputs and consensus, especially in economic policymaking. The structure took some of its antecedents from the French system of political collaboration and, in fact, a French consultant was engaged by the French Embassy in Jamaica to provide technical, institutional support in the structuring of NPC.

The Council comprised twenty-two members: seven ministers with responsibility for economic and infrastructure portfolios, including the deputy prime minister and minister of development, planning and production, as its chairman, the governor of the Bank of Jamaica, seven members from the private sector, invariably heads of private sector organisations: Jamaica Bankers Association; Jamaica Manufacturers Association; Jamaica Exporters Association; Private Sector Organisation of Jamaica; Jamaica Chamber of Commerce; Jamaica Agricultural Society; Jamaica Employers Federation, and the Jamaica Hotel and Tourist Association; six members from the trades unions: the Joint Trade Unions Research Council, the Bustamante Industrial Trade Union, the Trades Union Congress, the National Workers' Union and the Union of Public Officers and Public Employees; one member from the Professional Association, along with the following representatives from civil society serving as observers: the Consumer's League, and the Institute of Social and Economic Research at UWI. In addition, the following senior government officials: the director general of PIOJ, the financial secretary, the governor of the Bank of Jamaica, and the executive director of the National Planning Council served as technical advisors to the Council.

The Contractor General

The Contractor General's Office had earlier been established as an independent, anti-corruption agency of Parliament, following the enactment of the Contractor General Act of 1983. The main objectives of the Office were to ensure that the public procurement process deliver value for money to the taxpayer, free from corruptions and is conducted transparently. The Office was expected to bring transparency and accountability to the public procurement process which was plagued with allegation of corruptions. The office needed the capacity to monitor and investigate the award of public contracts, licences, and permits.

The contractor general was appointed by the governor general, after consultation with the prime minister and the leader of the opposition and, in the exercise of his or her duty, was not subject to the direction of any other person, or authority. In the initial years, however, it was never provided with the institutional capacity or a meaningful budget, and this limited the amount of work it could carry out. Again, through the initiative of Prime Minister Patterson, major financial and administrative support was provided after 1992 to allow the office to fully discharge its obligations under the act. The office later benefited from the Public Sector Management Reform Programme, directed at addressing deficiencies in the procurement and contracting processes, in order to enhance transparency and accountability in the public sector. The reforms were implemented in three ways:

1. Establishment of a procurement implementation unit within the Inspectorate division of the Ministry of Finance, which was made responsible for developing and updating procurement standards and procedures for the whole public sector.

2. Creation of an independent National Contracts Commission, in order to strengthen the Office of the contractor general; and

3. Strengthening procurement/contracting units and committees in ministries and departments through training, equipment and consulting services. The act was amended in 1999, providing for the creation of the National Contacts Commission, chaired by the Contractor General and assisted by a small secretariat.

Ombudsman/Public Defender

In 1978, two offices were also established: a parliamentary ombudsman, designed to give citizens the opportunity to seek redress against alleged infringement by the government bureaucracy of their rights and to address complaints made by consumers against the utilities. The parliamentary ombudsman was renamed the public defender by the Public Defenders Act of Act 2000 and was given additional jurisdiction to investigate alleged violations of citizens' constitutional rights.

The Consumer Affairs Commission (CAC)

The CAC is an outgrowth of the Prices Commission, which fixed prices between 1960–1980. Prior to the Consumer Protection Act the CAC operated under the Trade Act, 1955. The CAC was established because of the Consumer Protection Act of 2004. The Commission itself is not a regulatory body but plays an important role in correcting market failure because it acts as a consumer advocacy agency.

It champions the causes of the consumers and provides information to citizens about their rights as consumers; investigates complaints of dishonest practices; acts as a mediator from time to time and starts court actions if necessary. The act provides for an advocacy role in the sale, purchase, or provision of goods and services, establishing the rights of protection and duties of consumers and providers. It deals with misleading information, deceptive conduct, false representations, unfair and unsafe practices and ensures that contracts made between consumers and providers contain provisions that satisfy the test of reasonableness.

The problem with the CAC is that its functions came to overlap with many of the functions of the FTC and the industry regulators. There were no provisions in the legislation outlining how the distribution of responsibilities and the interfaces were to be handled. These matters are left to voluntary arrangements. There was also a non-governmental body, the Consumers League, which already served as a consumer advocacy body. The question arose whether consumer advocacy was better handled by a non-governmental organisation, possibly with some support from the government, particularly in an environment where the government itself a major player in is delivering services.

The CAC is supervised by a board of commissioners. It did not appear to have any real powers to determine breaches of the act, enforcement of remedies, and the enforcement of the substantive provisions of the act, requiring remedies through the formal court system. It was only provided with investigative powers in respect to complaints brought by consumers on the conduct of providers. In order to seek redress outside mediation between consumers and providers, it must use the courts for redress. The commission also was required to advise the relevant minister on matters of concern arising from a customer complaint.

ESTABLISHING NEW REGULATORY INFRASTRUCTURE

A whole suite of new institutions was also established, covering the establishing of Office of Utilities Regulation, The Fair-Trading Commission, the Financial Services Commission, strengthening of the Bank of Jamaica regulatory division, and changes to the transport regulation. The detailed changes related to the regulatory arrangements are covered in later sections of this chapter.

Citizens Charter

The Citizens Charter, which was introduced in 1994 was not an organisation and was not part of the organised World Bank reform programmes. It came about following the visit I made to the Cabinet Office in London in the early 1990s. During the visit, I was presented with the UK Citizens Charter document and, upon my return to Jamaica Prime Minister Patterson immediately took hold of the document and, after careful perusing, requested the cabinet secretary, Dr Carlton Davis, and myself to develop a similar Citizens Charter document for Jamaica. This was presented to Parliament in December 1994, requiring public entities delivering services directly to the public to treat users as customers, in much the same way users of services are treated in the private sector. The Citizens Charter's objective was to improve public service delivery by making agencies accountable and user-focused and providing information to the public in an open and easy-to-understand format. The concept was first introduced by John Major, the prime minister of the UK in 1991.

The Citizens Charter, however, came to be incorporated into the MPSM reform in 1996, in that all government agencies, especially executive agencies, were required to develop and operate a Citizens Charter as an essential part of their *raison d'être*. A typical Citizens

Charter addresses issues related to the standard of services offered by the organisation and allows for access to information regarding the response time for citizens' requests. The charter also allows for citizens to make an input into the agency's policymaking through the comments they offer to improve services. It also outlines citizens' rights and informs them how to register complaints when these rights are infringed.

Reducing the Size of the Cabinet

The Jamaican Constitution provides for a prime minister and not less than eleven other ministers to form the Cabinet.[35] Following the 1970s and the expansion of the public sector, several new ministries were created, and, at one point, there were over twenty ministries. In addition, there were several ministers of state and parliamentary secretaries. At one point, almost everyone from the governing party formed a part of the political administration. With privatisation, contracting out of services, and with the reduction in the number of central and local government workers, the IMF saw the need for a smaller Cabinet, especially to send the signal that the new government was serious about reducing the size of the administration. In early March 1993, I was asked by Patterson to consider a reduced Cabinet structure and I proposed the following arrangement:

1. Prime Minister and Minister of Defence
2. The Ministry of Finance and Planning
3. The Ministry of Foreign Affairs, Foreign Trade and Tourism
4. The Ministry of Agriculture and Lands
5. The Ministry of Education Youth and Culture
6. Ministry of Local Government and Community Development
7. Ministry of Health
8. Ministry of Labour, Pension and Welfare
9. Ministry of Security and Justice
10. The Ministry of Production, Mining and Commerce
11. Attorney General
12. The Ministry of Works, Housing, Transport, and the Environment
13. The Ministry of Energy, Water and Communication

Prime Minister Manley, however, felt the recommended reduction to thirteen was too drastic politically, and it did not give him room to reward some key personnel, however the Cabinet was made smaller than in previous years and was much less than twenty.

PUBLIC SECTOR MANAGEMENT PROGRAMME (PSMP): MID-1990S REFORMS

The ARP was replaced by the Public Sector Modernisation Project (PSMP), and the first tranche operated between 1996 and 2001. This was pursued with substantial external support and should succeed where the ARP had failed. The PSMP incorporates NPM principles in the management and operations of the state's business. These principles included:

- A shift in emphasis from command and control at the centre to delegation of authority, based on the theory that those nearest the area of operation are best able to manage it effectively and efficiently.
- Disaggregation of public bureaucracies into managerially autonomous units.
- Placing a much greater focus on quality services and satisfaction of consumers and users of the services.
- A division of labour with the central ministries focusing more on policy, advisory, monitoring, and evaluation functions, and the agencies on the delivery of efficient service functions.
- Providing an appropriate ethical framework to ensure the valuesand characteristic of much of the old public service were not undermined.
- Strengthening the Cabinet Office, shifting it from being merely an administrative secretariat to an Executive Office.
- Introducing and expanding a new form of service delivery institution, that of Executive Agency borrowed from the UK Next Steps Agency.
- Improving the ability of government to undertake regulatory functions effectively and independently, where regulations, as with the utilities, were still necessary.
- Incorporating user fees as a pricing principle whereby users of services of government departments and executive agencies

were required to pay for such services, as against the reliance on budgetary support.

- Introduction of accrual accounting in the new agencies.
- Inculcating a culture of customer service with departments and agencies issuing Citizens' Charters showing the standards of service that the public could expect from them.
- Wider use of computer-based information in financial and human resource management and in the operation of executive agencies and other public bodies.
- Changing the values and attitudes of the public sector in achieving efficiency, cost effectiveness, transparency, responsiveness, and accountability. This meant reorienting organisational culture, such as focusing on the use of inputs to effectively achieve the desired outputs and outcome, i.e., a focus on performance management.

PSMP I was funded by the World Bank, with the Jamaican government being required to provide a contribution, and with the Jamaica Performance Improvement Programme funded by the UK Department for International Development (DFID). Its main initiatives which were pursued included:

a. A permanent secretary's accountability framework.
b. Strengthening of the corporate planning function.
c. Strengthening and deepening of the audit system.
d. Review of public service regulations and staff orders.
e. Reform of social policy development, implementation, and evaluation.
f. Reform of secondary education.
g. Development of a financial management information system.
h. Development of a human resources information system.
i. Pensions and tax administration reform.

PSMP I was structured into stages. In the first stage, a handful of high priority public agencies were identified as pilot for the modernisation programme. The initial public entities identified were converted into executive agencies. Second, government ministries were involved in the formulation, monitoring, and coordination of policies.

A fundamental aspect of the reform of PSMP I was the removal of tenure from many administrative and management positions and introducing a contractual relationship (normally lasting between three to five years) for output performances structured within the framework of a performance agreement. The performance agreement constituted the basic contract between the entity's management and its superior authority and would inform all areas of the entity's operations. The performance agreement signified the formal relationship agreement between the responsible minister and the chief executive officer for achieving the agreed targets in the performance agreement.

In human resources management, the project sought to decentralise and delegate more responsibility in ministries and departments to lower levels in the organisation. To each permanent secretary of the various ministries the focus was on removing responsibility for the personnel function from the Civil Services Commissions to the operating units while, simultaneously, the traditional accounting officer's role of the Permanent Secretary being delegated to the chief executive officer of service delivery agencies.

The project total cost of the first phase (PSMP I) was US$33.04 million, facilitated by a loan of US$28.12 million (73 per cent) from the World Bank, which was used to facilitate activities under the Modernisation of Public Sector Entities component of the project. An additional US$3.1 million, or 9 per cent was used to finance the MIS component. The remaining project funds were allocated towards improvement to the procurement, contracting, and auditing components. The World Bank provided US$27.2 million while GOJ allocated US$5.9 million. Parallel financing of approximately US$3 million came from DFID to finance improvement to services in the Registrar General's Department (RGD), Auditor General's Department (ADP) the Management Institute for National Development (MIND) and the Office of the Registrar of Companies (ORC). The European Union also provided US$7 million, initially allocated for the privatisation component which was, in part, re-allocated to the other components.[36] The initial project objectives were as follows:

1. Bring about major improvement in the quality of services provided by selected public agencies.
2. Improve the ability of selected ministries to

a. formulate sound sector policies, technical standards, and operational norms.

b. effectively monitor and evaluate downstream agencies to ensure that desired policy objectives were achieved, and

c. efficiently perform corporate management functions.

3. Continue the rationalisation of the public sector through

a. private participation of water and sewerage sectors.

b. privatisation and contracting out of other facilities or services, where the government had no comparative advantages.

4. Improve efficiency, value for money, and transparency in government procurement and contracting

5. Enhance public sector accountability by strengthening internal control

6. Improve the quality of financial and personnel management in the public sector through computerised information

7. Prepare the next stage of the modernisation process by

a. extending the reform started in pilot agencies and ministries to the rest of the public sector.

b. introducing other systematic improvements in public sector management.

The privatisation of the water sector component was removed in 2000, as the government pursued this component using its own resources; therefore, the revised components in 2002 were:

c. modernisation of public sector entities.

d. improvement of procurement contracting.

e. internal control and auditing.

f. introduction of management information systems.

g. improvement of project implementation.

h. development of Stage MPSM II.

MPSM required not only changes in values and culture, but in the attitudes of the public sector personnel in order to achieve efficiency, cost effectiveness, transparency, customer responsiveness and accountability. Organisations were to become output-focused, taking on a customer service orientation, which included meeting the demands of clients and customers, simplifying procedures and information for citizens, and using the Citizens Charters. The main features distinguishing the EA from a traditional department or ministry under the old civil service structure were that they were expected to adopt accrual accounting principles and to meet their operating costs.

MPSM I also involved the strengthening of government procurement procedures and involved the following institutional changes:

- Establishment of a procurement unit in the Ministry of Finance, responsible for developing and updating procurement standards and procedures.
- Creation of an independent National Contracts Commission, chaired by the contractor general and assisted by a small professional secretariat.
- Strengthening procurement/contract units and committees in line ministries through training and consultancy services.

To strengthen internal financial control throughout the public services an Internal Audit Division was created at the Ministry of Finance, within the Financial Management Division, with the objective of establishing uniform operating standards and systems for controlling internal audits, conducting internal reviews, coordinating training and professional development of internal auditors, and setting ethical standards.

Establishing the Executive Agency as a Service Delivery Institution

New public management and the Executive Agency institutional concept were probably the most exciting new developments in reinventing government in Jamaica and in the 1980s. In the past, reforms in Jamaican Government entities, especially those through ARP, had centred heavily on financial, personnel and administrative procedures. Little attention was paid to institutional reform and efficient delivery of government services, and few improvements had been seen by the public after ten years of ARP and government reform efforts.

The UK, at the time, was at the forefront of advancing the executive agency form of public management; the Next Steps Agency, as the UK termed the innovation, was part of creating a more efficient and consumer-responsive public service. Departments of government which provided fee-based tradable services should deliver such services by operating like private managers under an incentive framework. New Public Management, which emerged in the late 1980s, adopted a set of new principles from private management to improve decision making and efficiency within the public sector. Rather than treating the recipients of public services as citizens, public managers were to treat users of public services as consumers. Second, accrual accounting was to be introduced, so that public managers would be provided with financial information to assist them in accounting for the assets under their portfolio.

Instead of tenured appointments which prevailed under the civil service personnel practice, managers under executive agency operation were to be given short-term contracts (five years), with no legal requirement for continuation of service. Within the five-year contract period, managers were to be provided with goals and annual objectives, which they were expected to achieve; success carried rewards and failure penalties. With private entrepreneurs and managers, failure could mean loss of capital, or the company could be taken over and the managers removed; with the civil service form of administration, there is no such risk. Often, it was difficult to identify failure, as decisions were often made by committees. Committees can be disbanded, but the officers often remain in their post. Executive Agency form corrects some failures of civil service-type of public administration and, in addition, incentivises managers to perform efficiently, as with their private counterpart.

Introducing Executive Agency institutional form based on a report in March 1994 outlining the requirements to move ahead to introducing Executive Agency form of management.[37] The final set of principles was laid out in in a paper I prepared for the Task Force Organisation.[38] Responsibility for introducing the new institution was delegated to Dr Carlton Davis, the new cabinet secretary.

The most important institutional change which came out of PSMP was the enactment of the Executive Agencies Act which came into being in 2001 and which was operationalised in 2002, providing for several civil service departments to be vertically separated from, but connected to their parent ministry, not through the traditional hierarchy, but through a new reporting system involving contractual arrangements. A key component of the Executive Agency concept was that public entities delivering services were required to charge user fees for the services provided, and to operate in such a manner as to reduce direct funding support. The EAs were required to implement public policies emerging from the central ministries and were to be self-financing from user fees. They were to have the authority to decide on operational matters and to implement accrual accounting procedures.

They were required to operate in such a manner as to reduce funding support directly from the Ministry of Finance. The Jamaican model of EA was borrowed predominantly from the British and New Zealand models and, as a result, has retained certain essential elements of the models of both countries, including the method of holding the chief executive officer accountable through the practice of ministerial responsibility. Funding for the implementation was provided by the Canadian International Development Agency (CIDA).

The first set of agencies identified for conversion to the Executive Agency form of management in 1999 by Dr Davis were: the Registrar General Department and Island Record Office (RGD); the Management Institute for National Development (MIND); the Administrator General Department (AGD), and the Office of the Registrar General (ORG). They were followed by a second group in 2001 comprising: National Works Agency (MWA); National Land Agency (NLA); National Environment and Planning Agency (NEPA), and the Jamaica Information Service (JIS). There were a third set of agencies inclusive of the Child Development Agency, which were to be converted to an executive agency form of operation. The government spent J$41.56 billion on the PSMP I project and, of this, J$619 million was spent to create Executive Agencies. There is no doubt this has been one of the most successful administrations of Jamaica reform initiatives over the years.[39]

Some agencies which were not suitable for EA institutional form were also modernised. They included: the Planning Institute of Jamaica (PIOJ); Jamaica Promotions (JAMPRO), and the Customs Department. Some J$446.6 million was spent on modernising JAMPRO and the Customs Department.[40] The policy of introducing the executive agency institutional form was not part of the IMF, or World Bank agenda and was solely an initiative of Prime Minister Patterson.

Outcome of MPSM I

The performances of the first four Executive Agencies resulted in the achievement of customer satisfaction moving from 83 per cent in

1999/2000 to 95 per cent in 2000/03. Earnings from user fees increased from J$247.7 million in 1999/2000 financial year to J$479 million in 2001/02, an increase of 50 per cent; further increase to J$685.7 million in 2002/03, contributing S$1.2 billion to the Treasury from cumulative earnings of J$2.43 billion in 2002/03. The MPSM also streamlined the Office of the Prime Minister, which was charged with managing MPSM, in collaboration with IMCAR, NIBJ and the Office of the Services Commission.

There were improvements in all areas of the agencies associated with the project, covering the introduction of user fees; accrual accounting; better management of accounts receivables and payables, and the application of computer-based information systems, especially the Financial Management Information System.

MPSM II

The 2002 Ministry Paper No. 56 was issued, setting out the long-term vision and strategy for future public sector operation for the period 2002–12. The MPSM II emphasised eight thematic areas[41]: sustainable national development; governance; values and principles; customer service; resources management; managing people; performance management, and technology, particularly use of information technology.

The project was financed by CIDA, DFID and the IDB, along with contributions from the government and MPSM III covering the period 2008–14, followed by MPSM IV. These later MPSM projects have largely focused on the creation of new Executive Agencies, extension of the principles of new public management, and improvement in policy formulation and execution in other ministries and agencies of government. The Chinese have also participated in the financing of the MPSM project.

Undoubtedly, the MPSM has been successful in the transformation of the Jamaican government service to a more user friendly, customer responsive and efficient operation. There has been a reduction in the numbers employed, while a volume of work delivered has increased.

THE STATE-OWNED ENTERPRISE (SOE) SECTOR

The state-owned enterprise sector has played a key role in the Jamaica's development process and economic reform. Jamaica was no exception among developing countries as, in post-independence Africa, public enterprise also played a key role in controlling key sectors such as agriculture, the mineral sector, transport, communications, and energy.[42] The public enterprise sector was determined not so much by the principle of laisses faire, which prevailed at the time as an important philosophy with regard to economic arrangement, but more so on the relationship of the colony with imperial Britain. The structure of government and especially the civil service was such that most efforts to make substantial changes failed. There was rapid expansion of SOEs in Jamaica and their failure not only led to public criticism, but the level of annual exposure of the Treasury became unsustainable. Except for a few enterprises, they were all loss makers. The SOEs are described as productive entities that are owned and/or controlled by the state and the bulk of whose output is sold in the marketplace. Ahmed Galal[43] and Daintith C. Terrence[44] observe that, in the UK, SOEs took various forms and there was difficulty in arriving at a definitive description. They are wholly state owned.

SOEs in Jamaica operate in a wide range of industries, with little in common other than that they are owned by the state, and there is a tendency for SOEs in Jamaica to operate nationally. They can be divided into groups that operate in competitive markets and others that operate in monopoly markets; these are essentially the water and sewerage, electricity, and telecommunications industries. The latter group provides essential services, with connections to a wide network. Utilities benefit from economies of scale and scope, possess high fixed sunk costs, supply politically sensitive services in that, if supplies are interrupted, there is great inconvenience to the public. This group has, over the years, been subjected to either self-regulation through the sector ministry, or industry-specific regulation through an independent agency, outside the ministerial departmental structure.

In Jamaica and the Caribbean, public passenger transport has been classified as a utility, yet it can be subjected to competition; however, the state from time to time provided the operating company with an exclusive franchise restricting competition. Transport faces competition from related or competing services. Competition comes from operators other than the government or the concessioned operator.

FORMS OF PUBLIC ENTERPRISES AND PRINCIPLES OF GOVERNANCE

The statutory corporation instrument, when it was introduced in the UK as the vehicle to operate public enterprise, should provide the Corporation with the authority of government and the independence of the joint stock company. Under the English legal system, parliamentary approval was needed for the creation of a statutory corporation. Incorporation affects three key areas: private rights and duties; expenditure of funds, and legal personality. When the UK began nationalisation after the War, the public corporation form was adopted.

In Canada, these enterprises are referred to as crown corporations. In creating SOEs and public bodies, Jamaica resorted to departmental enterprise, like the original post office organisation, Statutory Corporation, like Jamaica Railway Corporation, and limited liability companies like Air Jamaica Limited or National Commercial Bank Limited. In addition, the government has created public bodies to discharge many traditional civil service functions, which are clearly planning and administrative, or regulatory, and are not commercial, with no tradable services to offer the market and therefore should never have been created as commercial limited liability companies. Many of these SOEs have no commercial income generation potential or do not provide services directly to the public. An example is the Project Analysis and Monitoring Company Limited, which was a monitoring instrument of government with no tradable services.

The philosophy upon which the supervision of public enterprises is based in Jamaica and the Caribbean follows the principles laid down by Lord Morrison in the 1930s.[45] These principles were imported from the UK in the immediate post-war years. Most of the UK's nationalised industries were taken over by the Labour Government of Clement Attlee in the period over 1945–51, reflecting the party's ideology of common ownership of the means of production. There was also a sense that private ownership had failed, was inefficient, disjointed, and ineffectual. Nationalisation would allow for rational management.[46] The basic principles were that public corporations were to operate separately and at '*arm's length*' from the government in their day-to-day affairs. Their financial obligations required them to be run on commercial lines and to break even, and they were expected to serve the public interest by providing economical and efficient services.

Their boards of directors were to regard themselves as custodians of the public interest.

The problem with the Westminster model which Jamaica adopted was that there was a conflict between public interest and commercial judgment, and there was no guideline provided how this conflict should be resolved. The ill-defined concept of public service obligation and the notion of public interest have created problems over the years, resulting in the need for a special system of controls and accountability to be developed to ensure that the public interest is served in the most efficient way. The public interest itself is not an economic concept.

The UK's policy response in the 1960s and '70s was a series of attempts to give management of public corporation's objectives that were more specific than those provided for in their founding legislation. The call for efficient management of public enterprises surfaced forcefully in the UK in the seventies, when public ownership was extended beyond utilities and infrastructure to involve takeover of sick and dying manufacturing firms, such as Rolls Royce and British Leyland, in order to save jobs. The principle that publicly owned industries should operate independently from the political directorate had already received a setback in 1961, with the publication of a British government white paper on nationalised industries.[47]

The paper attempted to provide a framework for greater control over the state-owned enterprises, particularly in the areas of financial targets, investments, and pricing. The requirement for establishing financial targets by each enterprise was introduced, and they were to be determined by each industry's needs, typically reflecting a rate of return on capital employed. The target rate varied according to the extent to which the enterprise was required to operate unprofitable social services. One concern was that there was a large measure of discretion given to the managers in setting targets. The British government then tightened rules which provided for setting of detailed pricing and investment policy guidelines.[48]

These controls were based on long-run marginal cost pricing principles. Investment was to occur when the expected rate of return exceeded a prescribed test discount rate intended to reflect yields in low-risk private sector projects and was initially set at the real rate of 8 per cent, later increased to 10 per cent. Non-commercial activities were to be accounted for separately by each corporation, and cross-subsidisation avoided. These policies followed the notion that public enterprises were expected to maximise economic efficiency. The changes, however, did not resolve the UK's problems. The policies were not mandatory, leaving the field clear for economic efficiency goals to be displaced by short-run political and managerial objectives.

There was a further set of policy measures outlined in the white paper on nationalised industries of 1978.[49] This went some way to reducing managerial discretion by prescribing the strengthening of financial controls exerted by the Treasury over the SOEs. The test discount rate for individual investment projects was replaced by a required rate of return for investment programmes, which was then set at 5 per cent real response from falling yields in the private sector. In addition, each SOE was required to set a series of performance targets, hence heralding performance management in the public sector for the first time in Britain, as a matter of public policy. Further external financing limits were also prescribed for each corporation. There was criticism, however, to the effect that the measures followed from a view that the enterprises were being run to promote the government's macro-economic objectives, and this stemmed particularly from the fact that enterprises' borrowing capacity came to form part of the overall public sector borrowing requirements.

The UK the model public ownership when dealing with market failure in the monopoly utilities contrasted with the US, which involved a private investor-owned utility, accompanied by public or government regulation. Public ownership, however, creates the need for effective governance control if efficient outputs is to be achieved. With public ownership, the UK faced a major problem of effective governance control of the nationalised industries in the sixties and seventies, often leading to this enterprise chalking up massive losses. They came to be seen by the general public as a failure requiring massive budgetary support to keep many of them alive.

In Jamaica, the public enterprise sector was the area of most concern to the IMF and the World Bank, because of the huge budgetary support needed. The growth of statutory bodies, public corporations and public limited liability companies reflected the competing demands of the political and economic process.[50] Because SOEs are not structured in the traditional administrative framework of the civil service, they have provided their political managers with high flexibility. There is a general assumption that the orientation and skills required for running SOEs and development agencies are not normally found in the central civil service. Thus, the public corporation, or public company, provided a framework where the managers of these institutions would be left relatively free from political interference in the day-to-day management of their operations, and free from the rigidly applied and unimaginative controls of civil service procedures.

Existing legislation in Jamaica did not provide a clear legal definition of a state-owned enterprise. De facto definition of public enterprise is wide. It is sometimes extended to include entities even with 1 per cent public sector ownership. The legislative instrument adopted to establish public enterprises also varied from one department to another, even within the same ministry. In some departments, the statutory corporation arrangement was more common, while in another the joint stock company registered under the Companies Act was favoured. Each instrument provides significantly different levels of autonomy and accountability. The adoption of each, to some extent, was dictated by historical circumstances. Each instrument provides for variation in relationship and accountability of the enterprises to Parliament and to their portfolio ministries.

Up to 1985, the shares of the SOEs were held by forty-four different organisations, and twenty-four of these were subsidiaries. Sometimes, more than one ministry held the shares in one enterprise, and, in other instances, the parent company reported to one ministry and the subsidiary reported to another, leading to uncertainty, which was the controlling ministry. Except for the Ministry of Public Utilities and Transport, there was no attempt at any time to clearly define a system of oversight, so there were often acquisitions of contingent liabilities outside the public sector capital budgeting framework.

The auditing requirements, appointment of board members and the constitution of the boards often differed. The variety of instruments which were adopted, not only led to inconsistencies how the sector ministries, or the government dealt with the enterprises, but it also led to poor coordination.[51] The MPUT had established an Advisory and Monitoring Unit in 1974 to overcome this problem; however, it was disbanded when the MPUT was abolished.in the 1980s.

The poor performance of the SOEs up to the end of the 1970s partly stemmed from large size and wide scope, as well as the inadequate arrangements for their reporting and coordination. The enterprises were plagued with weak management. There was also a failure to adjust prices in a timely manner by the government, most times. Managers often lacked autonomy and independence in areas of investment procurement, pricing, and employment.

Further, the sharp decline in the performance of the economy over the 1970s led to a state of crisis in the public enterprise sector. Most of the services provided by the major utilities (telephone, water, and electricity), deteriorated, resulting in regular periods of water shortages, long periods of power outages, and long waiting time to obtain a telephone line (at one time over two years). The government's policy, which provided limited freedom to the enterprises to fix prices, led to a situation where most enterprises became loss-makers, imposing serious financial pressures on the government's fiscal budget. Several of the enterprises were not only over-manned, but the unions had extracted wage increases, which were not supported by increases in productivity. In some areas, public sector wages fell far behind that of the private sector, so serious skills shortages developed, as technical and management cadres left for higher-paying jobs in the private sector or overseas.

Irrespective of the administration, there was a serious failure by successive administrations to provide clear decisions with respect to the operation of the SOEs, as of the UK regarding the main policy objectives of the SOEs. Often there were conflicts between stated objectives, in that the enterprises were called on to make profits, while some were required to take on excess labour and provide subsidised services. The problem was wrestled with on several fronts.

With Jamaica, in meeting social objectives the rates of the utilities were kept unchanged for several years. JRC fares remained at the same level for over twenty years prior to 1980. Political interference in the day-to-day operations was endemic. Managers often lacked autonomy and independence in areas of investment, procurement, pricing, and employment. No wonder the corporation eventually collapsed. Despite the experiences of poor service standards, it was the very unhealthy state of the financial affairs of public enterprises, the escalating impact on the central budget, and the inability of the government to sustain the SOEs' loss-making operations, like Air Jamaica and the sugar industry, and their ever-expanding foreign debt obligations, which finally resulted in the government resorting to the policy of privatisation in 1981.

The Institutional Form for the Management of the SOEs

The three institutional forms which Jamaica adopted to create SOEs were departmental enterprise, statutory corporation, and public limited liability company. Most times the choice of instrument adopted was dictated more by historical circumstances than any logical arrangements. Each instrument provided various levels of autonomy and accountability. There was variation in terms of accountability to Parliament, accountability to the sector minister, the system of auditing and reporting, appointment of personnel, the composition of the boards, and the rights of workers and consumers. These assorted instruments of as practised in Jamaica, provided for a weak governance structure.

Not only was there widespread political interference in the day-to-day operations of the SOEs, but managers also lacked the autonomy and independence in areas of investments, procurement, pricing, and employment. The auditing requirements and conditions of appointment of board members of the several bodies invariably were different. The variety of instruments not only led to inconsistencies in how the sector ministry or government dealt with the enterprises, but also led to poor coordination. There were often acquisitions of contingent liabilities, outside the public sector capital budgeting framework, unknown to the Ministry of Finance. The basic problem was that the different institutional forms and the several differing legislative instruments did not provide for an effective governance framework.

Irrespective of the administration, until recently there was a serious failure by successive administrations to provide clear directions regarding the main policy objectives of public enterprises and to outline an appropriate governance structure. There was no attempt in Jamaica to outline a clear and sustained financial guidelines, as in the UK in the 1970s. In order to provide for a common framework of oversight, eventually there was the creation of the Public Enterprise Division in the Ministry of Finance, and the World Bank imposed a requirement for regular reporting of the largest twenty-one public enterprises, and inclusion in the government's general budgetary programme. This was followed up with the amendment to the Financial Administrative Act, providing for an improved governance framework.

The sharp decline in the macro-economic performance of the economy by the early 1980s eventually led to a state of crisis in the public enterprise sector. Most of the services provided by the major utilities had deteriorated sharply, resulting in regular periods where the entity failed to provide services. Several of the enterprises were not only over-manned, but they were also not supported by increases in productivity.

While the stated position of both administrations was to appoint qualified members to the boards of the SOEs, most appointments were based on party affiliation. Most of the chairmen were well-known party supporters. The public enterprises were notorious for not reporting financial results and many SOEs persistently failed to meet their PAYE, NIS, and National Housing Trust obligations. There was gross laxity and inefficiency in most of the enterprises in financial reporting and planning.

The Departmental Enterprise form of Public Organisation

Unlike New Zealand, where the system of departmental enterprise was widely adopted, Jamaica rarely used this institutional form. Here, the state conducted business activities through a civil service department, or a ministry, as with the postal and telegraph department, or the railway department. These enterprises did not have a legal personality of their own and hence were not separate from the state. The enterprise benefited from sovereign immunity of the state, was subject directly to the public budget and followed government's accounting practices of income and expenditure, with no accrual accounting. It lacked financial discipline, a basic requirement of commercial operations. The rigid framework of the civil service under which it operated served as a serious inhibiting factor to entrepreneurship. The bureaucracy of central government also presented serious constraints to individual initiative. Besides raising insurmountable delays in which to carry out commercial endeavours, it did not lend itself to financing from the financial market. The administrative autonomy was only partial. The few departmental enterprises which operated in Jamaica were mostly created before 1960 and have been phased out.

Statutory Corporations

The statutory corporation created by a distinct statute of Parliament was not only widely used to create SOEs this institutional form was widely used to create regulatory, development, and judicial bodies.

They had a separate legal personality from the state and could sue and be sued, separately from the state. Immediately after the Second World War, this institutional form became the vogue in Jamaica to carry out public functions. They initially emerged out of what was previously a government department, as in the conversion of the Railway Department to a statutory corporation (Jamaica Railway Corporation in 1960, and in creating the Port Authority out of the Marine and Harbours Department). This should provide the authority of the government with the independence of a joint stock company. In the UK, it drew its antecedent from the post-war Labour government; the difference was that in the UK the statutory corporations were initially, in the main, created to take over businesses that were being nationalised.

The relative independence of the statutory vehicle made them adaptable as instruments of social and economic development, freed from the bureaucracy of the civil service. As a result, the statutory vehicle was used to establish several development and regulatory boards and came to be referred to as statutory boards. E. Jones states that the original decision to use statutory boards in the politico-administrative process of Jamaica did not evolve from the Jamaican society.[52] The statutory corporation structure was an imported institutional form which had gained popularity, through the 'responsible' sponsorship of British political parties. The interesting thing is that statutory boards in the UK served the purpose of insulating commercial decision-making from political processes (or at least were supposed to – it never worked). In Jamaica, with its unresponsive core civil service, statutory boards were being more responsive to policy demands and objectives of the government.

The rationale for selecting the public corporation form was based on the notion that such an institution would function more in line with private business culture, offering greater autonomy from the civil servants, more flexibility, more scope for speedy decision-making than that which obtained under departmental enterprise structure and the restrictive arm of the central civil service.

The basic characteristic of the statutory corporation or statutory body is that its functions, purposes and reporting relationships and immunities are typically set out in an act of Parliament. An important doctrine of law applies to statutory bodies, and that is the principle of *ultra vires*; its legal personality only exists when it is performing the functions which Parliament conferred upon it in the founding legislation. Legislative incorporation sought to ensure democratic control over the extent of the functions of the entity so constituted.

The statutory corporation institutional form provides for accrual accounting, separate budgeting and auditing; entities obtain revenues from the sale of goods and services, as well as receiving financing from the government, especially for capital expenditures. It may take on loans independently, subject to approval of the government. Financial institutions, however, typically request government cross-guarantee for such loans. Its governance is performed by a board and its management by executive management group headed by a chief executive or director general, or a managing director, and more recently a president, typically appointed by the portfolio minister. Employees are normally recruited under terms and conditions set by the corporation's bylaws, rules, and regulations.

There are many instances, however, where statutory corporations create subsidiaries, with the subsidiaries being incorporated as limited liability companies registered under the Jamaican Companies Act. Many of these statutory corporations have developed extensive portfolios of subsidiaries. Examples of this type of operation have been exemplified by the Urban Development Corporation, the Petroleum Corporation of Jamaica, and the Port Authority.

There are problems associated with the statutory corporation institutional form in that, sometimes, the founding legislation is often too detailed, while in others they are too general. In several instances, the objectives of the funding legislation are no longer relevant. It does not provide for capital sharing and easy adoption of public/private partnership. When the government finds it difficult to fund all the capital requirements of the public sector, this can be a severe limitation. However, the founding legislation may be designed, it cannot exhaustively and conclusively deal with all substantive matters and often is inadequate in addressing pricing, investment, accountability, and accommodation of technological developments. Entities may also be created as chartered corporations. Here, legislation may not be necessary to allow the carrying out of functions. A chartered corporation's undertaking is acquired from an agreement granted by the Crown in the exercise of the royal prerogative. The University of the West Indies is an example of an entity created by royal charter.

The Public Company or Limited Liability Company

The limited liability company (joint stock company) institutional form is a state-owned business which is subject to ordinary company law. It is required to register with the Registrar of Companies who operates under statutory powers. The state may be the sole or majority shareholder. Since 1970, this has been the most popular instrument used in Jamaica for the creation of SOEs. The flexibility which these institutions have, because of not being a part of the traditional civil service structure led Jamaican politicians to see the joint stock company as a route to gain control of public administration and to speed up implementation of projects and programmes.

Unlike statutory corporations, it can be created without reference to Parliament, and here lies one of its major weaknesses. The instrument of incorporation which determines its legal capacity is not a specific statute but the company's memorandum of association (now an instrument of incorporation under the 2004 Companies Act). The memorandum may be varied from time to time by a majority vote of the shareholder, the state itself. The power and relationship of the portfolio minister to the enterprise is simply that of a capitalist shareholder in any joint stock company and, most times, the minister is not the holder of the shares. The accountant general historically holds the shares for the state, acting as trustee. This form provides for the greatest independence and for capital sharing through joint ownership in majority or minority relationships. Its basic weakness is that it provides for poor parliamentary control over expenditure and is a diminution of parliamentary control of public expenditure. The government, the trustee of the public, often finds that it has less control in various areas over the firm's operation than it has over privately owned enterprises. Ministers can vary their proportion of ownership established new companies, or divest ownership, without reference to Parliament, or even the Ministry of Finance. There are also several companies where the state or statutory corporation is a minority shareholder. Over the years, the government has not been unable to keep track of several of these holdings.

There was much expansion of SOE's in the 1960s and beyond. Noteworthy among these were Air Jamaica established in 1968 out of national pride, and a joint venture with Cable and Wireless UK to establish the external telecommunication company JAMINTEL (51 per cent state owned). The state also acquired majority holding in the American bauxite/alumina firms; in one case, Kaiser, a 51 per cent majority holding and increased its 6 per cent equity interest to 50 per cent in the Jamalco joint venture with Alcoa Minerals. The rationale for the acquisition was to protect the national interest and to give Jamaica an equal voice in the operation of the bauxite industry. The Shell oil refinery was also acquired, and large sums invested in hotel construction and ownership as was Agro 21 and the Spring Plain high-tech agriculture project. The State Trading Corporation had its name changed to Jamaica Commodity Trading Company and operated with a wider remit on imports and trading.[53]

The Growth and Performance of the SOE Sector

Despite the experiences of poor service standards, it was the very unhealthy state of the financial affairs of SOEs, the escalating impact on the central budget, and the inability of the government to sustain the loss-making SOEs' operations and their foreign debt obligations, which finally resulted in the government resorting to the policy of privatisation in 1981.

Tyndale reported that there were 315 public sector entities by the 1980s. His figure included entities with separate legal SOE personalities, either fully or partially owned and with commercial sets of accounts.[54]Helen McBain, from a detailed census, reported 315 public sector entities.[55] The World Bank reported that, in 1982, the public sector comprised 530 public bodies and that two hundred of these were public enterprises.[56] The number seems to vary according to the definition used. There is no doubt that the number was large and had significantly increased since 1960.

In 1984, public enterprises, as a percentage of GDP for developing countries were 10.8 per cent, and 9.1 per cent for the Caribbean. It is only in the African developing countries that the public enterprise sector has loomed larger than in Jamaica.[57] These sets of data clearly showed that, in the 1970s and '80s, the public sector and public enterprises, in particular, loomed large in the Jamaican economy, with major problematic implications for fiscal matters. Table 3.1 below shows the extent to which the size of the SOE sector had grown in Jamaica by 1991.

The importance of improved SOE performance was therefore critical to addressing the fiscal problems of the central budget, as several of these enterprises relied heavily on the government for operational subsidies, repayment of their debt, coverage of losses and financing of their investments. In 1984, the public enterprise share of GDP was 21 per cent.[58] The external debt of the SOEs as a percentage of GDP averaged 9.2 per cent, with SOE average share of investment as a percentage of GDP at 5. 0 per cent between 1978 and 1991.

Table 3.1: Size of SOEs in Jamaica for Selected Years (1978–91)

	1978	1980	1982	1984	1986	1988	1991	1978–91 Avg.
Share of SOE investment in GDP investments	29.2	20.9	27.7	35.6	25.5	28.8		24.1
SOEs investment as a per cent of GDP	4.4	3.3	5.8	8.2	4.8	6.5		5.0
Share of SOEs / Gross Domestic credit	5.9	6.3	6.6	5.0	1.6	2.6	1.3	4.4
Share of SOE in total external debt per cent	14.3	11.7	7.2	7.2	7.2	7.5	7.4	8.8
External debt of SOEs as a per cent of GDP	8.2	7.2	5.1	10.4	11.7	10.8	9.2	9.2

Source: A. Galal, M. Shirley, and P. Keifer, *Bureaucrats in Business: The Economics and Politics of Government Ownership,' Statistical Appendix, World Bank Policy Research* (Oxford: Oxford University Press, 1995. Note: SOE is described as a state-owned or controlled economic entity that generates the bulk of its revenues from selling goods and services. Country data vary what is considered as a SOE.

The SOE sector was performing badly, suffering from political interference, minimum accountability, absence of monitoring from the unavailability of audited reports, many of which were outstanding for years and were not submitted to Parliament. Coincidentally, the period 1974–80 experienced successive years of negative economic growth.

Because of the pressing need to reduce the financial deficit, SOE reform became central to the IMF and the World Bank, with a major objective being to reduce the size and impact of public enterprises on the central budget. The share of SOE investment as a percentage of GDP first declined from 29.9 per cent in 1978, fell to 20 per cent, increased to 35.6 per cent in 1984, then fell to 28.8 per cent in 1988, with an average of 24.1 per cent over the fourteen-year period. The SOE sector had grown to be larger than the central civil service, hence the importance the IMF attached to improved performance of the sector. Several of the enterprises relied heavily on central government loan guarantees.

With the constraints of the budget, many of these enterprises were restrained from expanding to meet domestic demand in crucial areas. The shortage of capital also prevented SOEs from introducing new technologies which were central to ensuring higher levels of productivity. Initially, the reforms took the form of adjustment to tariffs and prices to increase general revenues. This was followed by efforts directed at improvements to the management of public firms in order to contain costs. These efforts are sometimes referred to as commercialisation policies whereby the state continued to keep ownership but imported private sector techniques into the public managerial field. Table 3.2 shows the financial picture for the individual enterprises (of the selected twenty-one SOEs) in current prices for the periods 1979/80 to 1985/86.

The improvements did not come so much from improved management measures but more from restructuring measures such as liquidation of the unprofitable holdings by SIA, leasing out of properties by NHP, benefits from devaluation by PCJ and AJ and price increases by the monopoly utilities.

Of the enterprises, JPSCo, JTC, AJ and PCJ accounted for 62 per cent of the improvements. Except for the Broadcasting Corporation, all the enterprises had eliminated their deficit position by 1985/86. Because of their monopoly position, many of the enterprises could use the quick-fix solution of price increases and cutbacks in capital expenditure to reduce the deficit.

The ones that continued to be loss-makers during the period were Air Jamaica, Jamaica Broadcasting Corporation, Jamaica Merchant Marine, and Jamaica Sugar Holdings. Although several of them could generate surpluses, their domestic, and international borrowing requirements had to be guaranteed by government and, in this respect, continued to be a financial liability. These enterprises were major recipients of international loans.[59]

Table 3.2: Operating Surplus of the Selected Twenty-one SOEs 1979/80 to 1985/86 J$ million, Fiscal Years

Selected SOEs	1979/80	80/81	81/82	82/83	83/84	84/85	85/86
AS	-3.5	-20.0	-23.8	-20.5	-32.9	28.3	27.7
AAJ	-0.1	0.7	-2.0	1.3	3.0	8.5	11.3
BC	Nil	nil	Nil	-27.3	-19.2	-16.2	-4.2
JBC	-2.3	-2.6	-2.4	-3.1	-2.0	1.4	8.6
JCTC	Nil	nil	Nil	30.7	1.8	-2.7	8.6
JAMINTEL	7.5	8.8	9.6	15.0	17.5	9.5	18.1
JMM	2.6	1.5	8.0	2.2	0.2	-2.1	3.4
JPSCO	27.9	34.6	8.8	2.5	48.3	46.8	202.5
JRC	Nil	nil	Nil	-9.9	-5.5	4.4	5.8
JIC	23.6	38.2	25.6	42.5	34.3	72.4	124.4
NHC	-0.5	-0.8	-0.9	-3.0	-0.3	0.5	0.2
NHP	-9.5	-10.0	-41.9	-23.1	-14.3	7.2	11.4
NSC	-17.1	-4.1	Nil	-40.1	-83.1	nil	nil-
NWC	-15.3	-22.5	-41.2	1.8	1.1	17.6	29.2
PCJ	Nil	nil	Nil	-1.0	31.3	28.9	77.9
PA	6.6	6.0	5.0	6.2	8.9	20.8	21.3
SIA	Nil	nil	Nil	-44.5	37.6	1.2	nil
UDC	-28.8	-22.0	-37.9	0.7	6.3	7.7	5.5
SOS	-12.4	-10.3	Nil	-15.5	nil	nil	nil
MBC	1.6	2.4	2.8	Nil	nil	nil	nil
WC	2.0	1.3	13.2	Nil	nil	nil	nil

Note: The data are taken from different sources and contain actual and estimates, which may have been revised later. Source; M. Somasundram, L. Stanley, and A. Vahcic, *External Governance of Public Enterprise* (Kingston: Ministry of Finance, 1986).

There was an overall improvement in the deficit position of the major enterprises over the five-year accounting period ending 1988/89. The solutions which were implemented were essentially political and were not available on an ongoing basis. The reforms concentrated on financial performance rather than improvements in operational efficiencies. In the 1980/81 fiscal year, there were no contributions from the group to finance capital expenditure and investment. By 1985/86 fiscal year, internally generated funds enabled the 21 SOEs to finance 56.4 per cent of their capital needs, increasing to 97.8 per cent by 1987/88 fiscal year.

Tyndale has also shown that the income of the twenty-one SOEs specially selected for monitoring amounted to J$7.5 billion in 1991.[60] The budget support needed for the 1990/91 financial years amounted to J$539.0 million. These figures showed that the profitable entities generated a surplus of J$711.3 million, while the loss-makers showed a deficit of J$975.7 million.

Gladstone A. Hutcheson reported that, in 1980/81, the selected 21 SOEs recorded a negative operating balance (a loss) and thus could not cover their operating capital and investment expenditures.[61] By1985, from being subjected to closer monitoring and control, they improved their financial performance and their ability to finance capital expenditures and investments internally, rather than through the Treasury. In 1985/86, the internally generated surplus accounted for 56.4 per cent of their capital expenditures and investments. By 1989/90, that ratio had increased to 103.8 per cent and remained well above 100 per cent until the departure of the IMF from Jamaica in 1995.

Following the IMF's departure, in 1996 SOE capital expenditure and investments increased to US$115.3 million (71 per cent) with internally generated surplus falling from by US$81 million (41 per cent) covering a mere 43 per cent of capital expenditure and investments. The bulk (94 per cent) of this expenditure was accounted for by two SOEs: NHT and the PAJ. There was a significant decrease in the operating balance of NWC. The situation reversed itself in the post-1994/95 fiscal year, again impacting on the debt burden. There was a sustained rise in the debt after the IMF's departure, and the years following the severing of ties with the IMF saw a continuation of transfers from the government to the SOEs, albeit at a lower rate than the period up to 1980. The aggregate outcome for the fiscal period 1981/82–1988/89 is shown in table 3.3. Current operating balance moved from -1.0 per cent in 1987/88 to 6.9 per cent, then falling back to 4.0 per cent of GDP, reflecting both revenue-raising measures and expenditure control.

Net transfers from the central government moved from 4.5 per cent to 1.3 per cent of GDP, an improvement of 21 per cent of GDP. The debt situation, however, deteriorated, moving from 10.2 per cent of GDP to 15 per cent in 1987/88, before falling to 13.3 per cent in 1988/89. Air Jamaica, Jamaica Broadcasting Corporation, Jamaica Railway Corporation, Jamaica Sugar Holdings, National Hotels, and Properties and the National Water Commission had been very unprofitable.

Table 3.3: Summary of SOEs Performance: 1980/81–1988/89

	1980/81	1985/86	1986/87	1987/88	1988/89
Operating balance / GDP %	-1.0	6.4	5.8	6.9	4.0
Government guaranteed debt / GDP US$	306.6	330.8	289.2	443.4	444.8
Transfer From Central Govt /GDP %	4.5	-0.5	-1.1	-1.3	1.1
Government guaranteed debt/ GDP %	10.2	14.5	11.0	15.0	13.3

Source: World Bank (1998a) Bank of Jamaica Statistical Bulletin Note: List of twenty-one companies: Air Jamaica Limited, Airports Authority of Jamaica, Jamaica Broadcasting Corporation), Jamaica Merchant Marine Limited, Jamaica Mortgage Bank Limited, Jamaica Public Service Company Limited, Jamaica Railway Corporation, Jamaica Sugar Holdings Limited, Jamaica Telephone Company Limited, Jamaica International Telecommunications Limited, National Hotels & Properties Limited, National Housing Corporation, National Investment Bank of Jamaica Limited, National Water Commission, Petrojam Limited, Petroleum Corporation of Jamaica, Port Authority of Jamaica, Sugar Industry Authority, and Urban Development Corporation.

Except for the NWC, all the other five had been privatised since 2000, or their operations suspended. HEART, JPSCo NHP, National Housing Corporation, National Insurance Fund, Port Authority of Jamaica Petrojam and SIA were net contributors to the consolidated fund. The UDC and NWC have been the chief beneficiary of government transfers. Over the period 1998/89–1997/96 NWC received US$178 million while amortising US$9.0 million in foreign loan guarantees, net of disbursement; of this, US$103 was provided as equity in 1995/96. Over the same period, the UDC received US$162 million while amortising US$4 million in foreign guaranteed loans. PAJ, in contrast, received funding support mainly as loan guarantees.[62]

Table 3.4 shows the performance of the selected SOEs over the period 1980/81 to 1988/89. Operating balance for the twenty-one selected SOEs moved from J$-37.7 million in fiscal year 1980/81 to J$752.6 million in 1988/89, with capital revenues increasing from JS$127.5 million to J$256.7 million and the overall revenue balance increasing from J$89.9 million to J$1.009 billion.

Table 3.4: Group Performance of the Twenty-one Selected SOEs Fiscal Years 1980/81–1988/89 J$m

	1980/81	1985/6	1986/7	1987/8	1988/9
Operating balance	-37.7	694.3	778.7	589.3	752.6
Capital revenue	127.5	138.3	246.9	566.9	256.7
Balance	89.9	832.6	1025.7	1156.2	1009.3
Less Amort. (Exclusive GOJ)	105.9	376.8	448.3	422.4	205.3
Surplus available for capital expenditure and investment	nil	455.8	577.4	733.8	804.0
Capital expenditure and investment	239.7	807.7	930.4	750.7	933.1
Amount financed by surplus	nil	455.8	577.4	733.8	804.0
% Financed by surplus	nil	56.4	62.1	97.8	86.1
Balance after capital expenditure/investment	-255.8	-351.9	-353.1	-17.0	-129.1
Financed by foreign loans	116.6	357.5	233.8	242.1	131.9
Financed by domestic loans	32.9	2.6	131.1	157.4	-124.8
GOJ loans	91.3	55.9	293,5	109.5	67.2
-Equity	19.9	99.7	118.9	42.5	3.7
-Other	nil	Nil	85.5	11.1	78.7
Total	260,6	515.7	863.9	562.6	156.7
Balance	4.8	163.8	510.9	545.7	27.6
Transfer to GOJ	12.9	11.7	108.7	57.1	338.0
Working capital (exclude cash)	-8.1	152.1	402.2	488.6	-310.3
Number of entities	21	21	21	19	19

Source: Ute Schumacher and Gladstone Hutchinson (1991) Privatisation in Developing Economies: The Case of Jamaica Countries in Privatisation and Economic Efficiency: A Comparative Analysis of Developed and Developing Countries, ed. Attiat F. Ott and Keith Hartley (Cheltenham, UK: Edward Elgar, 1991), 241.

As a group, they could not finance their operating expenditures, pay taxes and dividends and service their debt, let alone generate a surplus that could go toward capital expenditure. The surplus available for capital expenditure increased from nil in 1980/81 to J$804.0 million in 1988/89. The net effect was that the improvements resulted in the

SOEs financing 86.1 per cent of their capital expenditure. In the period, the number went down from twenty-one to nineteen, reflecting the divestment of two enterprises in 1987.

Hutchinson also found that there was an upward increase in employee compensation as a percentage of total compensation in respect of the specially selected SOEs.[63] In 1988/89, compensation accounted for 17.6 per cent; by 1999/2000 this had risen to 26.4 per cent over the period 1988/89 to 1999/2000.

RATIONALISING PUBLIC BODIES

The final programme of public sector reform has been the programme to rationalise public bodies. In the introduction of the rationalisation programme, C. Davis commented that an important aspect was that, notwithstanding the need to resort to multilateral funding agencies for financing the programme of reforms, it was critical that the reforms be adapted as closely as possible to the domestic agenda and not just be accepted from external institutions, as part of the standard 'structural adjustment reform package.'[64] This rationalisation programme provided the systematic basis for the rationalisation of public entities and covered all areas of government. A Committee for Restructuring Public Sector Entities coordinated the programme. Its Report on Restructuring was submitted to the Cabinet in June 1999 and the Cabinet directed implementation of most of the Committee's recommendations.

Consultancy assignments to determine the efficiency and effectiveness of the operations of public sector entities were carried out by seven accounting consultancy firms. This was to eliminate waste and duplication of functions, as well as to effect cost reduction. A project manager, Judith Robinson, was engaged by the Cabinet Office to manage the programme, and the writer later took over the responsibility for the execution of the project from Ms Robinson. She played a key role in the programme's design, facilitating the examination of some 128 public entities by external consultants.

The objectives of the rationalisation programme were to determine the necessity for continued operation of entities, the efficiency, and effectiveness of their operations; to restructure marginal operations (eliminating waste and duplication of functions, as well as to ensure cost reduction); to identify entities suitable for conversion to executive agencies and/or effect mergers, divestment, or liquidation, with a view to ultimately reducing the number of entities and the cost of public sector operations.

In addition to mergers of entities and departments the exercise involved elimination of duplicated entities, removal of entities, sharing of services such as accounting, information technology, personnel management, and office administration, and eventual removal of redundant entities from the Public Sector Registry of Entities. The programme also called for public sector entities to be transformed into performance-based and output-oriented bodies. All public bodies were required to introduce realistic user charges, where practicable, to enable them to become self-financing, depending on charges for services delivered and less on subsidies and annual subventions from the central budget.

Most times, the purpose for which many of the entities were created no longer applied. The entitles with large numbers of redundant subsidiaries were the UDC, the Port Authority and Sugar Holdings Corporation of Jamaica. Some of these subsidiaries were created, in many instances, without approval of Parliament. Sometimes the Ministry of Finance was not aware of the creation and existence of the entity. The Cabinet Office placed much effort on rationalisation; however, it was difficult to obtain the sustained involvement of several of the SOEs operating with large numbers of subsidiaries, or as conglomerates, such as UDC and the Port Authority.

A list of the entities which were being considered in 2005 for winding up, liquidation, or merger with other organisations is shown in table 3.5, the list covers enterprises in transport, agriculture, energy, industry, and commerce, tourism hosing, and the Office of the Prime Minister. Interestingly, the Office of the Prime Minister, mainly through NHP, UDC, and the Agriculture Ministry, had the most public entities and some of these were the most suitable cases for winding up, having ceased operation but continued to appoint board members, with the consequent cost of their operations.

Table 3.5: Government Companies for Consolidation or Winding Up as of 2000

Transport

Sangster International Terminal
National Vehicle Corporation Limited
National Development Agency
Metropolitan Management Transport Holdings Limited
Jamaica Omnibus Services Limited
Jamaica Merchant Marine Limited

Agriculture

Clarendon Sugar Company Limited
Coffee Industry Development Company Limited
Eagle Farms Company Limited
Forest Industry Development Company Limited (FIDCo)
Builders Mart Limited
Waterwell Construction and Engineering Company Limited
Jamaica Sugar Manufacturing Co National Sugar Farms Limited
National Sugar Company Limited
Agricultural Reconstruction Company Limited
Clarendon Sugar Company Limited
Duckenfield Sugar Company Limited
Long Pond Estates Limited
Long Pond Sugar Company Limited
Monymusk Land Company Limited
Trelawny Sugar Company Limited

Energy

Electricity Authority
Font Hill Farms Limited

Industry and Commerce

Cotton Polyester Textile Company Limited
Millennium Textiles Limited
Jamaica State Trading Corporation Limited
National Tool and Die Company
Paradise Garment Factory Limited
Jamaica Marketing Company Limited

Office of the Prime Minister

Jamaica Broadcasting Corporation
Jampress Limited
Hellshire Bay Development Company Limited
Hellshire Bay Marble Limited
Hotel Corporation of Jamaica Limited
National Hotels & Properties Limited
Mallards Resort Hotel Limited
Negril Jamaica Estates Limited
Point Hotel Limited
Rose Hall Hotel Limited
Rose Hall (HI) Limited
Sea Castle Resorts Limited
Turtle Beach Towers Management Limited
Portmore New Town Development Co.

Tourism

Jamaica Attractions Development Company Limited
Things Jamaica Limited
Jamaica Reservation Service (JRS) Limited - Jamaica Vacations (JamVac) Limited
Central Parks and Markets Limited

Housing

Caribbean Finance Housing Corporation Limited
National Housing Corporation Limited
Estates Development Limited
Sugar Industry Housing Limited

Source: Compiled from the Public Bodies Registry in the Cabinet Office.

Table 3.6 provides another list which was developed in 2000 and intended to serve as a basis for further rationalisation. Again, the Ministry of Agriculture, the Office of the Prime Minister, and the Ministry of Finance had the most entities on their books. Most times, the entities listed had ceased to operate, making them candidates for immediate liquidation.

Table 3.6: List of SOEs to be Considered for Rationalisation in 2000

Public Enterprise-Trading and Commercial
Office of the Prime Minister
Ackendown New Town Development Co. Limited
Creative Production Training Centre (CPTC)
National Housing Trust (NHT) (1979)
Public Broadcasting Corporation of Jamaica
Sports Development Foundation
Urban Development Corporation (UDC) (1968)
Independence Park Limited
International Centre for Environmental and Nuclear Sciences (ICENS) Limited
Jamaica Information Service (JIS)
Mining
Bauxite & Alumina Trading Company Limited (1997)
Clarendon Alumina Production Limited (1985))
Jamaica Bauxite Mining (JBM) Limited (1975)
Tourism
Bath Fountain of St. Thomas the Apostle
Devon House Development Company Limited.
Jamaica Business Development Centre Limited
Jamaica National Heritage Trust
Milk River Bath
Tourism Product Development Company Limited (TPDCo)
Tourism Enhancement Fund
The Ministry of Finance
Betting Gaming & Lotteries Commission (1975)
Caymanas Track Limited (1990)
Container Services Limited

Public Enterprise-Trading and Commercial
Development Bank of Jamaica Limited (2000)
Financial Institutions Services Limited
Financial Sector Adjustment Company Limited (1997)
Fiscal Services (E.D.P) Limited
Jamaica Deposit Insurance Company Limited (1998)
Jamaica Social Investment Fund Limited
Air Jamaica Limited (1966) divested 1994
Bank of Jamaica
National Ex-Im Bank Limited (1986)

Education
Human Employment and Resource Training/HEART Trust/NTA (1982)
Nutrition Products Limited

Health
Health Corporation of Jamaica Limited (1994)

Agriculture
Agricultural Development Corporation (1952)
Agricultural Credit Board
Agricultural Development Corporation (1976)
Agricultural Marketing Corporation
Agricultural Support Services and Productive Projects Fund Limited
Banana Insurance Fund
National Irrigation Commission Limited
Rural Agricultural Development Authority (RADA)
St Thomas Sugar Company Limited.
Sugar Industry Authority (including SIRI)
Trelawny Sugar Company Limited.
Wallenford Coffee Company Limited. (2004)
Sugar Company of Jamaica Limited. (1993) return (1998)
Trelawny Sugar Company Limited.
National Rum company

Industry, Energy and Commerce
Central Information Technology Office Limited
Factories Corporation of Jamaica Limited (1987)
Jamaica Business Development Centre Limited.
Kingston Free zone Sone Company Limited (1982)

Public Enterprise-Trading and Commercial
Micro Investment Development Agency (1991)
Montego Bay Free zone Company (1985)
Self-Start Fund (1983)
Trade Board Limited

Energy and Telecommunications
Electricity Authority
Petrojam Limited
Petrojam/Ethanol Company Limited (1983)
Petroleum Company of Jamaica (1982)
Petroleum Corporation of Jamaica (1979)
Postal Corporation of Jamaica Limited (1995)
Rural Electrification Programme (1978)
Spectrum Management Authority Limited (2000)
Universal Access Fund Company Limited (2005)

Ministry of Housing, Transport, Water & Works
Aeronautical Telecommunications Limited (1978)
Airports Authority (1974)
Jamaica Railway Corporation (1960) – (1992)
Jamaica Urban Transport Company Limited (1998)
National Road Operating & Constructing Company (NROC) (1995)
Port Authority (1972)
Jamaica Urban Transport Company
The Ports Security Corps (PSC) 19890
National Water Commission (1980)
Rural Water Supply Company
Jamaica Mortgage Bank
National Housing Development Corporation Limited (1998)
Metropolitan Management Transport Holdings
Trans Jamaica Airlines

Ministry of Local Government & Environment
National Solid Waste Management Authority Limited (parks, markets & regional waste companies)

Source: Ministry of Finance Public Bodies Registry

The last list, table 3.7, covers the many regulatory and development agencies established over the period 1940–2008. Some of them were created during the days of colonial rule. Several of the regulatory bodies were without a clear policy framework and the result was that new regulatory institutions have been added to the older ones, creating a disjointed affair. Sometimes, where regulation is still needed, a reduced number of institutions would be sufficient. These entities for example include: the Banana Board – Regulatory/promotion (1953), Pimento Board – Regulatory promotion, Cocoa Industry Board – Regulatory/promotion (1957), Coffee Industry Board – Regulatory/promotion (1948), Coconut Industry Board – Regulatory/promotion (1945), Veterinary Board – Regulatory, Tobacco Industry Control Authority – Regulatory/promotion and Sugar Industry Authority (including SIRI – Regulatory/promotion).

Table 3.7: Development and Regulatory Public Bodies 2007/08

Development and Regulatory Public Bodies	Funding	Category
Office of the Prime Minister		
Broadcasting Commission (BC) (1986)	SF	Statutory
Cinematograph Authority	PF	Statutory
Office of Utilities Regulation (OUR) (1997)	SF	Statutory
Jamaica Bauxite Institute (JBI) Limited -Regulatory/ Development (1975)	SF	Limited
Tourism		
River Rafting Authority	FF	Statutory
Ministry of Finance		
Financial Services Commission (2001)	SF	Statutory
Jamaica Racing Commission (1972)	SF	Statutory
Public Accountancy Board (PAB)	SF	Statutory
Ministry of National Security		
Firearm Licensing Authority	PF	Statutory
Private Security Regulation Authority	PF	Statutory

Development and Regulatory Public Bodies	Funding	Category
Ministry of Labour		
National Insurance Fund	SF	Statutory
Ministry of Health		
Beach Control Authority	SF	Statutory
Ministry of Agriculture		
Banana Board - Regulatory / promotion (1953)	PF	Statutory
Pimento Board -Regulatory promotion	SF	Statutory
Cocoa Industry Board -Regulatory/promotion (1957)	SF	Statutory
Coffee Industry Board-Regulatory/promotion (1948)	SF	Statutory
Coconut Industry Board -Regulatory/promotion (1945)	SF	Statutory
Veterinary Board -Regulatory	SF	Statutory
Tobacco Industry Control Authority- Regulatory/ promotion	PF	Statutory
Sugar Industry Authority (including SIRI)- Reg/ promotion.	PF	Statutory
MITEC		
Anti-Dumping and Subsidies Commission	SF	Statutory
Bureau of Standards (1968)	SF	Statutory
Consumer Affairs Commission	FF	Statutory
Companies Office of Jamaica (Office of the Registrar of Companies)	PF	Statutory
Fair Trading Commission	FF	Statutory
Registrar/Department of Co-operatives and Friendly Societies	PF	Statutory
Public Accountancy Board (1970)	F	Statutory
Ministry of Housing, Transport, Water & Works		
Toll Authority of Jamaica Limited (1987)	SF	Limited
Air Transport Licensing Board	SF	Statutory
Civil Aviation Authority (1995)	PF	Statutory
Island Traffic Authority	SF	Statutory

Development and Regulatory Public Bodies	Funding	Category
Transport Authority/Urban and Rural Transport Boards	PF	Statutory
Rent Assessment Board	SF	Statutory
Water Resource Authority	PF	Statutory

Ministry of Local Government & Environment		
Beach Control Authority	PF	Statutory
Real Estate Board	PF	Statutory
National Environmental and Planning Agency (**NEPA**) (includes National Resource and Conservation Authority, Town Planning Department, Town & Country Planning Authority, Negril & Green Island Planning Authority and Land Development & Utilisation / Negril and Green Island Development)	PF	Executive Agency

Source: Compiled from Data provided to the Cabinet Office in 2006 Notes: SF= Self-Funded, PF= Partially Funded FF =Fully funded.

GENERAL COMMENT

The public sector, after 1865, progressively developed to be a major aspect of the Jamaican economy. In the period 1965–1960, the service was less concerned with efficiency with very little regard for costumer need. Under the development administration following 1960, the public sector including public enterprise extended rapidly in all aspects of the economy without regard to the quality and efficiency of services provided. The extensive reliance on the public sector, especially between 1970 and 1980, as key to drive economic development not only failed to expand the economy, but it also failed to achieve some of its other stated objectives of increased employment and redistribution of income. By 1980, it had become clear that the public sector-led approach was not working. While there has been a definite shift in the balance from public sector to the private sector since 1985 and a reduction in the number of public entities, as well a reduction in their operations, the public sector and public enterprises in Jamaica remained large and complex.

Undoubtedly, some activities, especially in the infrastructure and development areas, will probably continue to see active public sector participation. One of the critical issues for the future will therefore be continued improvement in financial performance and rationalisation of the number of existing entities, several of which are virtually inactive; there is no valid case which can be advanced for their continued existence.

Ute Schumacher and Gladstone Hutchinson concluded that the poor performance of the Jamaican economy since the 1970s is because of the overburdened public sector which operated at a level well beyond the size necessary to ensure sustained economic growth.[65] Jamaica's public sector in the 1980s operated at over 45 per cent of GDP and this is compared to the US at 33 per cent; the UK below 44 per cent; Australia below 38 per cent, and in Canada below 49 per cent. If this hypothesis holds true that large public sector exceeding 40 per cent produces a drag on the economy, then the reduction of the public sector through privatisation, contracting out concessions and rationalisation should see continued improvements in the economy over the future. What is important however is not just the size of the public sector but its effective management and control by the authorities.

The independence of the civil service antecedent goes back to 1855, when a centralised bureaucracy in the UK, based on the principle that the state bureaucracy must be neutral, exercising probity, and a sense of public duty and Christian morality was established. This quasi-judicial governance philosophy, however, was never designed to cope with the rapid expansion of the public sector, which demanded a more managerial, entrepreneurial, and commercial ethos, concerned with efficiency, financial responsibility, and the delivery of quality customer service and good personnel management practices. Further the informal understandings that underpinned relations in the operations of government were never transferred from Westminster to Jamaica and the colonies.

Notes

1. G.E. Mills, 'Some Notes on Public Services Commissions in the Commonwealth Caribbean,' *ISES* 16, no. 1 (March 1967).
2. Ibid.
3. G.E. Mills and M. Slyfield, 'Public Services Reform in Jamaica: Human Resources Management,' *Institutional Review of Administrative Sciences* 53, no. 3 (1987).
4. Government of Jamaica, Ministry Paper, No. 21, The New Ministry of Public Service, April 17, 1973.

5. Edwin Jones and Charles Mills, 'The Institutional Framework of Government in Jamaica,' in *Independence: Essays on the Early Years*, ed. Rex Nettleford (Kingston: Heinemann Caribbean, 1989).
6. Phillip Glaessner, *Genesis of Administrative Reform Programme in Jamaica, in Issues and Problem of in the Caribbean Public Administration*, ed., Selwyn Ryan and Deryck Brown, (St. Augustine, Trinidad: ISER, 1992).
7. Ibid.
8. World Bank, *Staff Appraisal Jamaica: Public Sector Modernisation Project* (Washington, DC: World Bank, 1996).
9. Mills and Slyfield, 'Public Services Reform in Jamaica: Human Resources Management.'
10. Jones and Mills, 'The Institutional Framework of Government in Jamaica.'
11. Glaessner, *Genesis of Administrative Reform Programme in Jamaica.*
12. G. E. Mills and Paul Robertson, 'Attitude and Behaviour of Senior Civil Servants in Jamaica,' *Social and Economic Studies* 23, no. 2 (1974): 311–43.
13. Phyllis Green and Marie Slyfield, *Some Problems in Strengthening of Administrative Capability of Small States* (Kingston: Administrative Staff College, 1983).
14. Phyllis Green, Derick S. Gordon, and Edwin Jones, *Report on Employee Morale in the Jamaican Civil Service* (Kingston: Administrative Staff College, 1983).
15. Phillip Glaessner, *Review of the Approaches and Prospects of the Administrative Reform Programme in Jamaica* (Geneva: UNDPP, 1987).
16. Sobhan Rahman, *Public Enterprise and the Nature of the State; Development and Change* (Sage, London: sage, 1979).
17. P. Sutton, 'Public Sector Reform in the Caribbean: A Review of Recent Experience,' *Centre for International Governance Innovation*, Paper, no. 6, 2008.
18. Ryan Selwyn and Deryck Brown, 'Genesis of Administrative Reform Programme in Jamaica,' in *Issues and Problems in Caribbean Public Administration Institutions* (St Augustine, Trinidad: ISER, 1992).
19. Marie Slyfield and Paulette Morgan, 'Downsising: Jamaica's Experience 1992–1993,' World Bank Conference on Civil Service Reform in Latin America and the Caribbean, Washington, DC, May 20–21, 1993.
20. World Bank, *Project Completion Report: Jamaica Administrative Reform, Report No. 12595-Jm* (Washington, D.C: World Bank, 1995).
21. E. Ferlie, 'The Creation and Development of Quasi Markets in the Public Sector; A Problem of Strategic Management,' *Strategic Management Journal* 13.
22. Kate Mclaughlin, Stephen Osborne, and Evan Ferlie, *New Public Management: Current Trends* (London: Routledge, 2002).
23. Christopher Hood, 'Public Administration and Public Policy: Intellectual Challenges for the 1990s,' *Australian Journal of Public Management* 48, no. 4 (1989): 346–358.

24. Milton Friedman, *Capitalism and Freedom* (Chicago: University of Chicago Press, 1962).
25. A.E. Kahn, *Economics of Regulation* (New York: Wiley Press, 1970).
26. F.A. Hayek and Paul Kegan, *Law, Legislation and Liberty* (London: Rutledge, 1976).
27. Dennis Swan, *The Retreat of the State* (Ann Arbor, Michigan: University of Michigan Press, 1988).
28. Andrew Gamble, Andrew, *The Free Economy and the Strong State: The Politics of Thatcherism* (London, Palgrave Macmillan, 1988).
29. Kenneth Stowe and Geoffrey Morgan, 'Report of the UNDP Management Development Programme Mission to Jamaica,' UNDP (1991).
30. Rex Nettleford, *Report of the Committee of Advisers on Government Structure* (Kingston: Bank of Jamaica Printers, 1992).
31. Freddie Senny and Cesley Sampson, 'Accountability: The Advisory and Monitoring Unit – An Experiment in Monitoring Performance Appraisal,' Presentation at the MPUT Seminar on Public Administration of Public Utility Enterprises, Kingston, 1976.
32. Cezley Sampson, Edwin Jones, Andrea Blackwood-Harriet, and Anne Crick 'Organisation Study of the Office of Prime Minister.' For the Office of the Prime Minster, Institute of Business, Mona (1991).
33. Roy Gilbert, *Options on the Role and Structure of the Office of Prime Minister Internal Report* (Kingston: Jamaica House, 1992).
34. Cabinet Office, 'Strategic Review of the Cabinet Office: Public Sector Modernisation Project,' Kingston, July 2005.
35. Ministry Paper No18/89 (1989), 'The Establishment of the National Planning Council,' Government of Jamaica, Kingston.
36. HMSO, *Report of The Jamaican Independence Conference 1962* (London: HMSO, 1962).
37. World Bank, *Implementation Completion Report on Loan to the Jamaican Government for Public Sector Modernisation Project* (Washington, DC: World Bank, 2003).
38. Kate Jenkins and Cesley Sampson, 'Implementing Better Government: Improvement in Service Delivery,' Jamaica House, 1994.
39. Cezley Sampson, 'Executive Agency in Jamaica: Organisational Framework for Service Delivery,' Office of the Prime Minister, Kingston, 1997.
40. Carlton Davis, 'Executive Agency in Jamaica: The Story So Far and the Central Management Mechanism,' Presentation at UWI/MIND Conference on Executive Agency in Action, 2001.
41. P. Osei, (2001), 'Executive Agency: Intellectual Background to the Search for Appropriate Initial Forms,' *Caribbean Journal of Public Sector Management* 3, no. 1 (2001): 73–83.
42. Jimmy Kasaara Tindigarukayo, 'An Assessment of Public Service Reforms in Jamaica,' *Social and Economic Studies* 53, no. 3 (2004).

43. Barbara Grosh, *Public Enterprise in Kenya* (London and Boulder, Colorado: Lynne Rienner Publishers, 1991).
44. Ahmed Galal, Mary Shirley, and Phillip Keefer, 'World Bank, Washington, DC, Research Report' (Oxford University Press, 1995).
45. Daintith C. Terrence, *The United Kingdom in Public and Private Enterprise in Mixed Economies*, ed., Wolfgang Friedmann (London: Stevens & Sons, 1976).
46. H. Morrison, *Socialisation of Transport* (London: Constable, 1993).
47. Christopher Foster, *Privatisation, Public Ownership, and the Regulation of Natural Monopoly* (London: Blackwell, 1992).
48. H.M. Treasury, 'Financial and Economic Obligations of Nationalised Industries, Cmnd. 1337 London, HMSO, 1961.
49. H.M. Treasury, Nationalised Industries: A Review of Economic and Financial Objectives, Cmnd. 3437, London: HMSO, 1967.
50. H.M. Treasury, 'The Nationalised Industries,' Cmnd. 7131, London, HMSO, 1966.
51. London Economics, 'Exchange Control Liberalisation in Jamaica: A Study for the Private Sector Organisation of Jamaica,' Kingston, March 1991.
52. Freddie Senny and Cesley Sampson, 'Accountability: The Advisory and Monitoring Unit – An Experiment in Monitoring Performance Appraisal.'
53. E. Jones, 'The Role of Statutory Boards in the Political Process in Jamaica,' in *Public Administrative Change in Commonwealth Caribbean*, eds., G.E. Mills (UWI: ISER, 1970).
54. G.E. Mills, 'Privatisation in Jamaica, Trinidad, and Tobago,' in Privatisation in Developing Countries, ed. V.V. Ramanadham (London: Routledge 1989).
55. C. Tyndale, *Survey of Public Enterprises* (Kingston: Bank of Jamaica, 1991).
56. Helen McBain, *Policy Management and Implementation Strategies of Privatisation in the Caribbean* (UWI: ISER, 1995).
57. A. Akin-Karasapan, 'Report and Recommendations of the President of the World Bank on a Proposed Loan for Private Sector Development Adjustment', World Bank, Washington, DC, 1993.
58. Barbara Grosh, *Public Enterprise in Kenya* (Boulder and London: Lynne Rienner Publisher, 1991).
59. A. Galal, M. Shirley, and P. Keifer, 'Bureaucrats in Business: Economics and Politics of Government Ownership.'
60. In Jamaica the most of the SOEs, as limited liability companies were required to resort to conventional accounting practices involving accrual accounting, as against the peculiarities of public sector accounting (in particular no distinction between investment and expenditure, or between loans to enterprises v government).
61. Tyndale, *Survey of Public Enterprises.*
62. Gladstone A. Hutcheson, 'The Challenge of Fiscal Sustainability: Evidence from Financial Relationship between Government and State-Owned Enterprise Sector in Jamaica,' Lafayette College, US, 2000.

63. Ibid.
64. Ibid.
65. C. Davis, 'Public Sector Reform in Jamaica: A Question of Balance,' in *Business Government and Society: Caribbean Writings on Caribbean Issues*, ed. Anydeke-Danes (St Augustine: Centre for Management Development, 1995).
66. Ute Schumacher and Gladstone Hutchinson, 'Privatisation in Developing Countries' Economies: The Case of Jamaica,' in *Privatisation and Economic Efficiency: A Comparative Analysis of Developing Countries*, ed., Ott Attiat and Keith Hartley, (London: Edward Elgar, 1991).

CHAPTER FOUR

The Population Dynamics of the Jamaican Economy

INTRODUCTION

In this chapter population dynamics is presented over the pre-emancipation and post-emancipation periods; especially size, growth, age, fertility, ethnicity, and in addition, employment by industrial sectors. The size of Jamaica's population imposes serious economic pressures, because of the limited land space and high dependency ratio. Over 20 per cent of the population lived on lands that were environmentally fragile and unsuitable for residential purposes.[1]

Table 4.1 shows the recorded population, as well as the population by different racial/ethnic groups, from 1658 to just after emancipation. The recorded population increased from 5,900 in 1658 to 371,070 by emancipation in 1834.

Table 4.1: Historical Review of Jamaica's Early Population by Ethnic Groups, 1673–1871

Years	Whites	Free Coloured	Free Blacks	Slaves	Indians	Chinese	Maroons	Total
1658	4,500			1,400				5,900
1673	7,768			9,504				17,272
1754	12,000			130,000				132,000
1775	12,737	4,093		192,787				209,617
1791	30,000	And free blacks 10,000		250,000			1,400	291,400
1824	34,000			335,000				569,000

Years	Whites	Free Coloured	Free Blacks	Slaves	Indians	Chinese	Maroons	Total
1834 Emancipation	15,000	40,000 coloured	5,000	311,070				371,070
1844	15,729	68,576 coloured	293,128 blacks					377,433
1871	13,101	100,346	392,707					506,154
1881	14,432	109,946	444,186		11,016	99	1,125	580,804

Source: S. Musson and T.L. Roxborough, *Handbook of Jamaica* (Kingston: Jamaica Government, 1893) and R.M. Martin, *History of the Colonies of the British Empire* (London: N.P., 1843).

The early statistics are based on records the planters had to keep on their enslaved stock. Freed Blacks numbered five thousand in 1834, the first time they were recorded separately. Initially, the White population, at forty-five hundreds, outnumbered the slave population, which stood at fourteen hundred. With the expansion of the sugar and coffee estates, by 1775, the enslaved population had increased to 192,787, with the White population at 12,737.

In 1775, the records for the coloureds were shown at 4,093, while in 1791 the Maroons were shown to have a population of 1,440. This group was never large in numbers. When the first census was taken in 1844, more reliable data on population totals were provided, showing a population of 377,433: 15,000 Whites, 68,576 coloureds, and 293,128 Blacks. The White population peaked around 1824, numbering thirty-four thousand or 6 per cent of the total.

With the termination of the slave trade in 1807, inflows from Africa were severely curtailed, triggering a decline in the population up to the 1820s. The locally born African population grew to account for approximately 25 per cent of the overall population by emancipation.[2] Over the period 1655 and 1807, about nine hundred and twenty-seven thousand Africans disembarked on the island. In 1808, the year following the abolition of the slave trade the slave population numbered three hundred and fifty-four thousand, and by 1838 the slave population had increased to three hundred and eleven thousand.[3] In the period up the termination of the slave trade, the social and economic environment in Jamaica was not conducive to reproduction. The reproduction process meant loss of labour and an additional cost, so it suited the planter to replace rather than to permit reproduction. Following termination of the slave trade there was an incentive to encourage reproduction.

The key population statistics over the period 1944–70; the first 126 years showed that an increase from 377,433 to 1,848,510. The intercensal annual increase varied from 0.32 per cent in 1921 intercensal period to 1.67 per cent in the 1943 intercensal period. Up to 1921, the natural increase varied from 14 per 1,000 to 18 per 1,000, except for two periods: 1850–55 and 1915–20, with the crude birth rate exceeding 30 per 1,000 and with crude death rate ranging between 37 and 40 per 1,000.[4] The two exceptional periods were marked by major epidemics: cholera 1850, smallpox 1852 and influenza in 1918. In the latter period, the death rate reached its highest, 33 per 1,000. In the second phase, 1921–43, natural increase remained at around the same level of 13 per 1,000; however, both birth and death rates declined, with the former declining from 36 per 1,000 to 32 per 1,000 and the latter from 27 per 1,000 to 15 per 1,000.

The fall in birth rate, to some extent, was caused by increases in the number of marriages. In this period, the death rate declined because of improvements in health standards arising from the 1926 Public Health Act. Fertility rates also returned to the level of the previous period, with gross reproduction rates reaching 2.77 female births per woman.

The period towards the end of the nineteenth century experienced a significant increase in population size but levelled off between 1911 and 1921. In this period immigration which had become a feature of the economy after 1860s slowed somewhat, accompanied by an acceleration in population growth after 1921, Department of Statistics 1973, and 1974, and National Planning Agency 1975.[5] Between 1970 and 2011, intercensal period the population growth, increased from 1,848,512 in 1970 to 2,697,983. Most significantly, the annual rate of increase since 1970 has been falling, declining from 1.39 per cent in the 1970 intercensal period to 0.36 per cent in the 2011 intercensal period, Statistical Institute of Jamaica (SIJ) 2011.[6]

The crude birth rate fell from 39.1 per 1,000 in 1970 to 17.4 per 1,000 in 2011, a level comparable to many developed countries. Death rates have also been falling from 8.2 per 1,000 in 1970 to 6.4 per 1,000 in 2001 but increased to 7.1 in 2011. Changes in these two rates resulted in a young population, with approximately 45 per cent of the population being under age twenty-five. However, the Jamaican population in the twentieth century now reflects an aging population.[7]

With an aging population Jamaica has been experiencing a high dependency ratio: the dependency ratio expresses the relationship of the age groups zero to fourteen and sixty-five-plus and fourteen and sixty-four and is a product of changes in age structure of the population. High dependency ratio means a greater portion of the population not economically active, depending on a smaller base working-age population. Jamaica's age dependency ratio peaked at 107.34 per cent in 1970 and in 2011 had fallen to 54.82 per cent, United Nations Statistics 2017.[8]

Between 1943 and 1970, there were important changes in the age structure of the population, with the population fourteen years and under increasing its share from 36.6 per cent in 1943 to 45.9 per cent in 1970, which is almost twice as high as Britain was in 1971. In the period 1960–70, the rate of increase for the young population was over 2.3 per cent per annum, while for the period 1970–90 the increase was relatively stable.

In 2020, life expectancy of Jamaicans was 74.88 years, with infant mortality at 10.7 per 1,000 and the death rate at 13.6 per 1,000. Death rate recently has been on the upward trend. Net migration has also been declining, from minus 18,000 in 2000 to 11,000 in 2020, with the annual population growth rate falling from 0.94 per cent in 2000 to 0.44 per cent in 2021. Net migration, which peaked at 29,387 in 1960, has been declining steadily since 1990 and is expected to slow to around 11,500 per annum in future years. In 2011, the younger working age population (15–44 years old) represented 1.3 million or 49 per cent of the population with the older working population age group (45–64) accounting for 18 per cent and this has been increasing, reflecting the aging of the survivors of the high fertility period of the 1940–60, STATIN 2012.[9] There has been a narrowing of the base of the population pyramid, reflecting the changing structure of the population. The forecast by STATIN is that population up to 2050 will continue to age slightly, with a median age of 41.5 years, as Jamaica progressively moves over the intercensal periods. This pattern is also reflected in most of the advanced European economies.

OUT-MIGRATION

Jamaica's has been exporting its working age population, which, on the face, is a negative feature. However, this exported population, through remittances, has been supporting the resident population, especially Jamaicans who are not gainfully employed. Some 50 per cent of the population now receives remittances regularly. A third important feature of the Jamaican population is that since 1943 the rural population has been falling. In 1943, it was 1.043 million (82 per cent) of the 1.24 million overall population. By 2011, the rural population accounted for less than 45 per cent of the populace and this has been falling in absolute numbers. Many Jamaicans, especially from the rural areas have sought to make their livelihood overseas since the 1880s, and this history of out-migration has mainly followed available employment opportunities in the Americas region during the late nineteenth and twentieth centuries.

There have been about four major flows of out-migration to the Americas, first to Panama as construction workers on the railways in 1853 and later to Navy Bay the Atlantic terminus of the Panama railway.[10] This was followed by a major outflow again to Panama during the 1880s, as labourers to build the Panama Canal. Migration to Panama continued up to 1888; however, when the French company developing project ran into financial problems, there was large-scale return to Jamaica. Many Jamaicans, however, returned to Panama to complete the project, re-started by an American company after 1904. There was also small-scale migration to the US during the period.

The second major outflow occurred between 1881 and 1890, with an outflow to Costa Rica, also for railway construction. Small numbers also departed to other Latin American countries. There was a third outflow between 1904 and 1914 to Costa Rica to work on banana plantations, followed by another outflow to Cuba in 1917 for a variety of agricultural and service jobs. In 1917–18, 7,351 persons left Jamaica for Cuba and 3,699 returned.[11] Work on the sugar estates reached a peak 1919, when twenty thousand Jamaicans left to work in Cuba. All these outflows were marked by heavy returns and, by 1935, most of the Jamaican immigrants had returned. Migration to Panama ceased after 1913, on completion of the canal project. During this period, over thirty-five thousand Jamaican workers went to Panama.

In the fourth outflow, migration to the US began around 1910. Between 1911 and 1921, some thirty thousand Jamaicans travelled to the US, mostly for labouring work. The depression of the 1930s, however, saw massive repatriation and, in this period, 1930–35 there was an inward net balance of 20,500.

The net outward movement between 1881 and 1991 and 1911 and 1921 amounted to one hundred and forty-six thousand.[12] Although many Jamaicans returned after a period overseas, several remained, especially in the US and Panama, so large groups of Jamaicans were found living in Panama, Cuba, Costa Rica, and the US in the 1930s. Restrictive legislation in the 1930s by Latin American countries, favouring White European migrants soon put an end to flows of Jamaican and other West Indian migration to Latin America. Migration to the US, however, resumed after 1943 and, later, to Canada, involving agricultural, industrial, and domestic workers.

Migration to the UK after 1945 heralded a new phase for Jamaicans. Travelling to the UK first started as munitions workers during the Second World War to serve the British Royal Air Force, predating 417 Jamaicans who travelled to England on the *Empire Windrush* in 1948 with 1,027 immigrants[13] and the one hundred Jamaicans who arrived on the *Ormonde* in March 1947 from Jamaica for Liverpool, followed by the *Almanzora* later that year which set sail for Southampton.[14] The modern phase of settler immigration started in 1953 when the outflow to the UK increased from twenty-one hundred to a peak of 39,200 in 1965, being mainly poor working-class people, mostly from the rural areas of the island. By 1951, some seventeen thousand Jamaicans had travelled to the UK to find employment and take up permanent residence. The need for labour for reconstruction and to work in the transport sector in the Britain post-war years was so great that it triggered intense recruitment of labour from Jamaica and Barbados. Between 1948 and 1970, about half a million West Indians travelled to Britain for work.[15] By 1961, Great Britain recorded a population of some two hundred thousand West Indians, of which half were from Jamaica. It was in this period that my siblings and several other relatives trekked to England, starting with my eldest brother who settled in Midland in 1955 and who bought his first house in Wolverhampton, two up two down, for £500.

The influx into Britain eventually went sour and elicited negative responses among the White resident population in the 1960s and 1970s, and this evoked a major change in British government migration policies. Restrictive immigration laws were introduced, severely limiting the flows from the West Indies to the UK after the 1970s. This coincided with passaging legislation in the US and Canada that made education and skills more important determinants for entry than nationality and race.

It was also during this period that many dissatisfied Jamaicans abandoned Jamaica following the famous statement made by Prime Minister Manley that there were several flights available from Jamaica to Miami. Many, especially from the middle-class community, not only departed for Miami, but Atlanta and New York, and Toronto in Canada.

Table 4.2 below shows that during the 1990s the outflow declined to 212,832 and, over the period 2000–2006, it amounted to 135,493, making a total out-migration of 915,371 over the period 1970–2006. Over the entire three and a half decades the US accounted for 82.4 per cent of the overall recorded emigration, with Canada accounting for 15 per cent and to the UK only 2.6 per cent. In 2008, approximately 637,000 foreign-born Jamaicans lived in the US, with approximately 123,500 in Canada and 150,000 in the UK in 2006.[16]

Out-migration in recent years has slowed because of tighter immigration controls in North America. Quantitatively, out-migration has had a major impact on Jamaica's demographics, affecting the population growth rate and the structure of the population.[17] Since the 1990s, there has been a reverse flow of returning Jamaicans from the UK, accompanied by in-migration of Commonwealth citizens and aliens, and the return of deportees from the US and the UK.

Table 4.2: Flows: Data on Primary Destinations of Jamaican Emigrants, 1970–2006

Decade	Number of Migrants	USA	Canada	United Kingdom
1970s	327,779	256,984	56,965	13,831
1980s	239,207	201,177	33,973	4,057
1990s	212,892	170,291	39,443	3.158
2000–2006	135,493	107 205	15,374	2,914
Total	915,371	745,657	145,754	23,960
per cent	100	82.4	15.0	2.6

Source: Thomas-Hope (2004, updated 2008), Compiled from Data in the Jamaican Economic and Social Survey.

DEVELOPMENT OF THE SMALLHOLDER RURAL COMMUNITY (THE PEASANTRY)

An important aspect of the Jamaican economy has been the development of the rural smallholder community following emancipation. In the period 1865–1930, the number of smallholdings in rural Jamaica tripled, with the rural area accounting for the larger portion of the population. The rural areas however failed to maintain its dynamism because of the inadequate settler policies pursued by the colonial government. Until the 1890s, little public sector support services were provided to the rural smallholder communities. It was not until 1895 that colonial government introduced a scheme for the acquisition of lands through the leasing of Crown lands in small parcels to the rural smallholders and not until in the 1930s that a meaningful land settlement scheme was introduced providing small settlers with titles to the land. However, most of the distribution involved forested lands in the interior hills and mountains. My father received two lots of about twenty acres of this land in places called Gordon Hall and Dover Wood in St Mary, which no one in the family has visited since 1960.

Despite numerous efforts to restrict the flow of people from the rural areas into urban centres, mainly Kingston and St Andrew the flow continued unabated after the 1970s. Measures introduced to stem the flow, such as various land settlement schemes, between 1938 and 1965, as well as the various programmes of the Jamaica Agricultural Society and Social Development Commission have all failed to have a measurable impact on rural out-migration. The problem with these programmes is that they were agriculture-driven, when the rural needs have become more non-agricultural including the need for community and welfare services, like health clinics.[18]

Small settlers came to play an important role in the economy's development. In 1850, their share of export crops was 10.4 per cent, and this increased to 39.0 per cent by 1890, then to 41.4 per cent by 1930. Small settlers' share of total agricultural output also increased from 50 per cent in 1850 to 75 per cent in 1890. However, its share failed to keep pace over the next forty years due to relatively greater growth of estate production, especially banana cultivation, and by 1930 the small settlers' share of agricultural output had fallen back to 68 per cent. The increasing prosperity of the small settler community up to the 1930s was because of diversification into export crops; first in coffee cultivation and later, bananas in the 1890s. In 1870, sugar and rum accounted for 73.6 per cent of exports, with banana at 0.1 per cent and coffee at 18.4 per cent. By 1910, sugar and rum's share had declined to 14.1 per cent and banana had increased to 52 per cent of exports. Sugar had received a devastating commercial blow in 1847 with economic policies shifting away from mercantilism. The 1901 Brussels Convention provided for the elimination of European beet sugar bounties, and this reduced European bounty-fed imports to the UK, resulted in West Indian sugar improving its competitive position. Beet sugar again rebounded after the First World War and it took the International Sugar Agreement of 1937, which introduced quotas for exports, to rein in beet sugar and Cuban sugar exports to the UK.[19]

After 1940, there was a major retreat from the interior dispersed settlements. A typical village of this type is Penlyne Castle in the Yallahs Valley where, despite heroic attempts to deal with the ecological environmental problems, the population all but vanished by 1970. Tony Weis, (2006) provides a powerful exposé of the decline of rural communities around Annotto Bay area in St Mary, once a leading sugar production centre and latterly the leading banana parish.[20] This decline epitomises the malaise of rural Jamaica. Young rural folks have largely abandoned farming, as they now associate small farming with underdevelopment and colonialism, with their expectations firmly set on migration to the industrialised US or Canada, or on receiving remittances from relatives overseas.

RACIAL MIX OF THE POPULATION

The portion of the of the population of African descent varied between 75.8 per cent and 78.1 per cent, remaining relatively stable throughout the period. Census statistics show that Jamaica's overall population grew from 377,433 in 1834 to 1,609,814 in 1960 and further to 1,848,510 in 1970. In the post-emancipation period 1844–60, population growth never exceeded 1.7 per cent, which was comparatively low by developing world standards.

The share of the population by Whites, or Europeans declined from 2.5 per cent in 1981 to 0.8 per cent, in 1990, while for Browns, or Jamaicans of mixed White and Black origin, the share ranged between 17.5 per cent and 19.6 per cent between 1881 and 1943 but declined to 15.1 per cent in 1960. The Chinese and Afro-Chinese increased their share from

0.1 per cent in 1891 to 1.2 per cent in 1960, while the Indians and Afro-Indians increased their share from 1.9 per cent in 1881 to 3.2. per cent in 1960. People of Syrian and Lebanese descent made up the rest and, in 1960, accounted for 3.2 per cent of the population.[21] The Chinese also concentrated in Kingston, although they were found in almost every village in the period up to 1950. In 1943 the Brown or coloured group in Kingston accounted for 30 per cent of the population, compared to 17.5 per cent for the rest of the island, whilst the Whites accounted for 2.6 per cent in Kingston. The Syrians, Jews, and Lebanese, invariably lived in Kingston and St Andrew. The mixed, or Brown population which once accounted for 15 per cent in earlier years by 2011 was reported to be just over 6 per cent.[22]

The percentage share of the population accounted for by the Black population came to be the majority by the end of the seventeenth century. By the 2001 census, Black Jamaicans represented 76.3 per cent of the population and this percentage share remained for several decades at between 70 and 76 per cent. Since the 1970s, more Jamaicans who once would describe themselves as coloured or mixed now clearly identify themselves with Africa and describe themselves as Black. In the 2011 census count, people were asked to record their racial groups and 91 per cent of the population described themselves as Black.

Out of the legacy of the plantation economy emerged the rigid and structured form of racism, based on colour discrimination, and which divided Jamaica into three hierarchical cultural, social, and racial classes of White, Brown, and Black. These three groups are accepted as correlating with socio-economic categories of upper class, middle class and working class. Out of this history was the view that the White race was physically, morally, intellectually, and culturally superior to the Black race. The racism which emerged was used by the Europeans to justify the internal structure of economic exploitation. It was used to justify the colonial domination of Black Jamaicans and to subjugate them on the sugar plantations.

Orlando Patterson, however, states that the hierarchically organised Jamaican society, once dominated by the White Europeans and 'Whiteness,' and whose relationship is structured mainly on race, ethnicity, and class, has been a melting pot, post-1990.[23] While in post-independence Jamaica colour continues to be of importance, political power has been taken over by Black and Brown leaders, originating mainly from the more prosperous small farm holders and professional middle class who, beginning in the late 1980s, have pushed hard to penetrate the commercial sector. Since the Manley administration of the 1970s, and more so the Patterson administration after 1993, there is no doubt the social structure of Jamaica has seen dramatic changes. Black Jamaicans have largely taken over political power, having taken control of political administration, business management, sports, and musical expression. The structure is now more fluid and one's racial background arguably, is no longer the marker of one's future.

URBANISATION

Urbanisation is a recent phenomenon in Jamaica. Urbanisation refers to the population shift from rural settlements to urban settlements, the gradual increase in the proportion of people living in urban areas, and how each society adopts to change. It is the process by which towns and cities develop and grow into larger areas and is the dominant human ecological trend of the late twentieth century.

It took Jamaica over two hundred years, from 1770 to 1970, for its level of urbanisation to increase from 10 per cent to 40 per cent. In contrast, over the period 1970–2018, urbanisation increased to 55.7 per cent. Figure 4.1 showed that the urban population had grown to 55.7 per cent with the rural population, which at one stage was 80 per cent declining to 44.3 per cent.

Figure 4.1: Urban-rural Balance

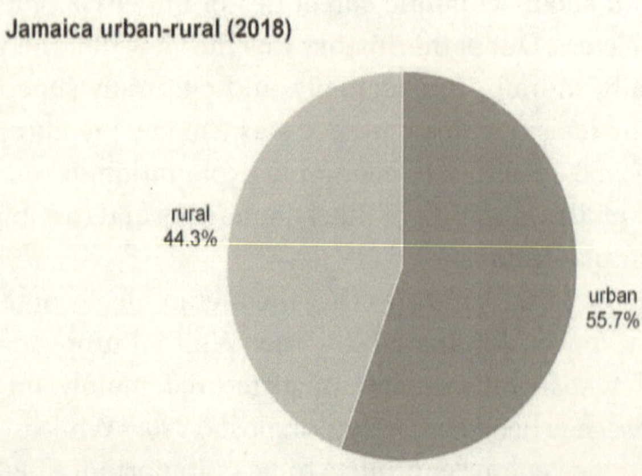

Growth of Urbanisation by Parishes

Table 4.3 below shows recorded and estimated population and distribution by parishes for the intercensal periods, 1921–2021. The number of parishes was reduced from twenty to fourteen for administrative purposes in 1867. In 1778, the population recorded in each of the twenty parishes was fairly well distributed, with Kingston the only parish with a large urban population, then 26,478. Kingston did not begin urbanisation expansion until 1800.[24] Jamaica's urbanisation occurs through rural urban migration, returning residents from overseas to the urban areas and high birth rate, typical of urban settlements.

Table 4.3: Distribution of Recorded Population of the Fourteen Parishes, 1921–2011

Parishes	1921	1943	1960	1970	2011	Estimate 2021
Kingston	63.700	110,000	123,400	109,800	89,057	90,544
St Andrew	54,600	128,100	296,000	421,700	573,369	571,947
St Thomas	42,500	60,700	68,700	71,200	93,902	94,391
Portland	49,000	60,700	64,500	69,000	81,744	80.921
St Mary	71,400	90,900	94,200	100,400	113,737	115,090
St Ann	70,900	96,200	114,400	122,700	172,362	177.054
Trelawny	34,600	47,500	56,100	61,900	75,164	78,487
St James	41,900	63,500	83,000	103,100	183,811	191,737
Hanover	38,200	51,700	53,900	59,400	69,533	72,519
Westmoreland	68,900	90,100	109,600	115,800	144,103	149,857
St Elizabeth	79,300	100,200	116,700	127,800	150,205	151,911
Manchester	63,900	92,700	111,800	122,900	189,797	191,720
Clarendon	83,000	123,500	164,000	178,300	245,105	247,122
St Catherine	96,000	121,100	153,500	184,200	511,756	520,804
Total	**858,500**	**1,237.000**	**1,809.800**	**1,848,500**	**2,686,105**	**2,734,093**

Source: Linda Hewitt, Linda, 'Internal Migration and Urban Growth,' in *Recent Population Movements in Jamaica*, ed. George Roberts (Geneva and Kingston: United Nations Statistics and Statistical Institute of Jamaica, 1974).

Kingston, as a parish by 1970, was fully urbanised and has remained so to date. The parish of Kingston began urbanisation in 1891 and by 1950 the parish was fully urbanised. With restricted capacity to absorb further increase in population, the adjoining parishes of St Andrew and St Catherine have absorbed the increases in the urban population. Kingston's population increased from 63,700 in 1921 to 123,400 in 1960, after which decline set in and by 2011 was 89,057. By 1970, Kingston's share of the population had declined to 5.94 per cent. The forecast is for Kingston to remain at much the same level of just over ninety thousand. The urban areas of Kingston expanded into the parish of St Andrew after 1921 because of internal migration. In the same period, St Andrew increased its population from 54,600 in 1921 to reach 573,369 by 2011. St Andrew went from one of the smallest parishes in terms of population size in 1921 to the largest in 2021. The population is estimated to decline in 1921 to 571,947 a small decrease over 2011.

St Catherine increased its population relatively slowly, from 96,000 in 1921 to 184,200 in 1970, and thereafter accelerated to 511,756 in 2011, the second largest in population size. St Catherine has accelerated its growth to second position in population size in 2011 and expanded through the growth of Portmore as a new town, as well as from light manufacturing in the Spanish Town area and as dormitory. The estimate is for the St Catherine population to grow to 520,804 in 2021, reflecting a slowing down in its growth. The major growth occurred between 1991 and 2011, increasing from 381,972 to 511,756, three times the growth rate observed for all of Jamaica. The expansion of St Catharine reflects the most significant population shift in modern times on the island. In 1960, St Catherine accounted for 9 per cent of the population by 2011 St Catherine accounted for 19 per cent of the island population, St Catherine increase has occurred simultaneously with a declining share of the population by St Andrew. The increased urbanisation of St Catherine after independence resulted from the urban growth of the towns of Portmore, Spanish Town, Hillshire, and Old Harbour. Growth resulted from both planned and unplanned development, but largely unplanned.

Clarendon also displayed significant population expansion over the period, increasing from eighty-three thousand in 1921, then the second largest parish by population to 245,655 in 2011 and is estimated to reach 247,122 by 2021. The growth of Clarendon since 1970 has been influenced by the development of the bauxite and alumina refining.

This is followed by the parish of St Elizabeth, which increased its population from 70,300 in 1921 to 150,205 in 2011 and is estimated to reach 151,911 in 2021, a small increase.

Hanover over the years remained the smallest parish, increasing from 38,200 in 1921 to 69,684 in 2011 and is estimated to reach 72,519 by 2021. The slowest growing parishes were St Thomas and Portland and they saw their population grew by only 2 per cent in the intercensal period.

A new settlement feature of Jamaica increased urbanisation outside of Kingston the primate city. Urbanisation of Kingston which took hold after 1921 has declined since 1970. Portmore was a fishing village up to 1891, with a population of only fifty-one hundred in 1970 and hardly existed as town saw it population increasing to one hundred and eighty-two thousand in 2011, the second largest town in Jamaica. Portmore is now much larger than Spanish Town, the parish capital. Spanish Town also grew from a small town of about five thousand 1881 to 39,204 in 1970, and by 1991 Spanish Town had grown to 114,677, increasing further to one hundred and forty-seven thousand in 2011.[25]

Similarly, Montego Bay increased from 4,651 in 1881, to 43,251 in 1870, reaching 110,115 in 2001. Most parish capitals now have a population exceeding ten thousand. In 2011, 39 per cent of the population lived in parish capitals. The total population of the Kingston Metropolitan Region (KMA) and all the parish capitals was 1,041,084 in 2011, compared to 993,581 in 2001.

A recent development has been the growth of towns outside of parish capitals. This started after 1970 and the main towns in this category, other than Portmore are Old Harbour, Linstead, Bog Walk, Ewarton, Ocho Rios, Runaway Bay, Santa Cruz, Duncans, Spalding and Negril. The fast-growing urban centres since 1990 are Old Harbour in St Catherine, Ocho Rios in St Ann. Old Harbour's population was projected to reach 55,543 in 2030 using 1991–2001 growth rate,[26] making Old Harbour one of the fastest growing urban centres in Jamaica. Ocho Rios before 1891 was a sleepy fishing village, growing from 5,851 in 1970 and reaching twenty-five thousand in 2011. Between 1991 and 2001, Ocho Rios grew by 5.72 per cent compared to 89.42 per cent, between 2001 and 2011. Highway 2000 is already impacting development in the area and land speculation has already started where the Highway 2000 hits Mammee Bay.

Census 2011 shows that Jamaica's level of urbanisation reached almost 56 per cent, representing an increase of 1.9 per cent over 2001. Urbanisation can either be 'push' or 'pull.' Push factors drive citizens from the countryside; lack of land to make a good living from agricultural pursuits and absence of community service. Pull factors attract people to the urban areas, educational and health facilities and employment opportunities. A further development of urbanisation has been sub-urbanisation involving a shift of residences outwards to the edges of the inner city, resulting in urban sprawl. Sub-urbanisation is associated with more affluent groups moving to the suburbs, taking advantage of improvements in transportation. Like most other developing countries and the rest of the world, Jamaica in recent years has been urbanising at an unprecedented pace, presenting many new environmental, economic, and settlement challenges. This growth has been the result largely of unplanned development. Small towns become larger towns, large towns become cities, and several urban areas became an agglomeration, or metropolis.

Relationship of Urbanisation and Economic Development

Since 1950, the proportion of economic activity in primary sectors (agriculture, manufacturing, and mining) has been decreasing, whilst the share of the services sector (financial, tourism and telecommunications) has been increasing. By 1970, services sector accounted for over 65 per cent of economic activities. Table 4.4 below shows that increases in the level of urbanisation is associated with a decline in the primary sector and especially the agricultural sector.

Table 4.4: Urbanisation and Decrease Primary Sector in the Level of Economic Activity

	Urbanisation	Industrial Sector	Primary Sector
1850		6 %	51 %
1870	6 %	6 %	52 %
1890	10 %	6 %	52 %
1900	10 %	6 %	52 %
1910	1 %	6 %	53 %
1930	10 %	6 %	50 %
1950	14 %	14 %	25 %
1960	21 %	21 %	20 %
1970	32 %	23 %	18 %

Source: Computed from Handbook of Jamaica and STATIN – Sundry Years.

Figure 4.2 graphically presents this relationship, showing that as urbanisation increases the proportion of economic activities in the primary sector decreases, whilst the share of the services sector increases. The service sector increases because more service activities become monetised as society urbanises. In rural society, because of familial and related connected relationship and fewer activities are monetised. In urban society, with increasing distant relationship there is an increase in monetised services. Arguable then as society urbanises the share of activities in the service sector increases, measured in GDP and the share of the primary sector decreases.

Figure 4.2: Movements in Urbanisation and Changes in the Primary Sector

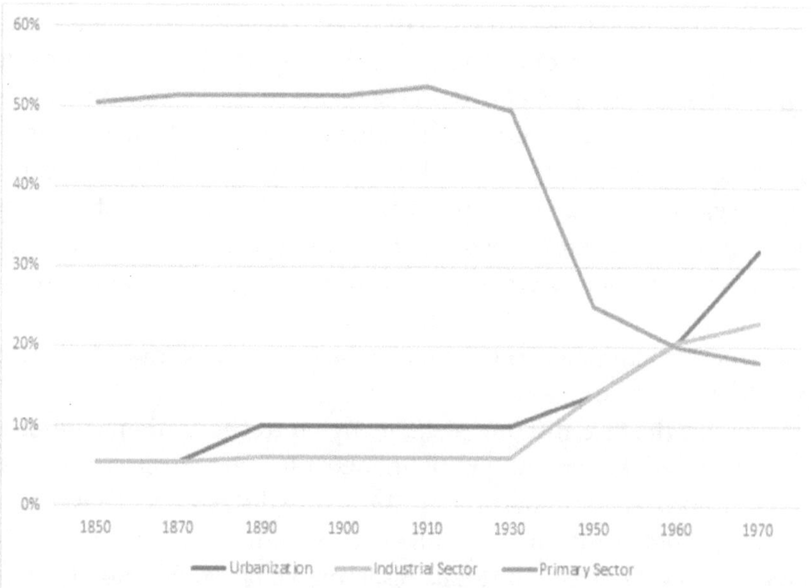

Sources: Generated from levels of urbanisation and changes in the size of the primary sector over the period 1850–1970, *Handbook of Jamaica* and STATIN data.

ACCOMMODATING JAMAICA'S FUTURE POPULATION GROWTH

Between 1991 and 2023, the number of larger urban settlements has dramatically increased. Kingston and St Andrew in population 2023 is estimated to reach one million. Three other cities: Montego Bay, Spanish

Town, and Portmore will have a population of exceeding one hundred thousand. In addition, there will be nine towns with a population of over twenty thousand. There are now seventy-eight urban population centres in Jamaica with population sizes of over twenty-five hundred, a steep change from when only eight urban population settlements in 1943 exceeded one thousand.[27]

This development towards urbanisation in larger urban centres presents the Jamaican government with immense challenges to provide the public services, such as housing, social amenities, infrastructure, and jobs, hence there will be a need for a greater degree of urban planning, requiring greater consideration to be given to the environment and more professional approach to municipal public management.

Future settlement and township development in Jamaica will need to be centred around economic growth spots, where the geography of the area supports urban development without encroaching on valuable agricultural lands. The Ocho Rios area seems to be one area that meets these characteristics and was identified by former Prime Minister Seaga as far back as 1960. The idea of development in the area came to Mr Seaga during a leisure weekend trip to the north coast, entirely unplanned.[28] Ocho Rios area presents a strong economic resource base for further development to become a Tourist and Entertainment Tech-City. It may even be possible to persuade the American companies to construct an alumina plant to reduce the shipment of low value dried bauxite from St Ann.

Similarly, the St Catherine plain, going on to Old Harbour presents another economic growth point. This area has over twelve thousand acres of land, largely underutilised. Agro 21 in the 1980s had developed a project that would have involved a five hundred acres reservoir, several times the size of the Mona reservoir which would trap the flood waters of the Rio Cobre, 80 per cent of which now flows to the sea in times of heavy rainfall. The reservoir could be gravity fed from river to storages and storage to farm, generating electricity as a pumped storage facility, Seaga.[29] The Old Harbour Bay area could be planned as another High-Tech City: high-tech agriculture and Big Data. This Old Harbour area should be planned to take a significant proportion of the urban population growth associated with Kingston, St Andrew, Portmore, and the Spanish Town. Steps should be taken to ensure that distinct boundaries are drawn for the metropolitan area of Kingston and St Andrew, and the towns of Portmore and Spanish Town through green belts (if this is not too late) to avoid morphing the areas into one urban mega metropolis. Thes two new cities could each develop to accommodate between one hundred and fifty thousand and two hundred and fifty thousand over the next three decades and this should lessen the population pressures associated with Kingston and St Andrew.

THE NEED FOR PLANNED NEW TOWNS

Caribbean towns historically developed largely port settlements, established in locations that had natural harbours, sheltered by embayment, or peninsulas, serving as gateways for the trade of the islands, mainly agricultural products in return for more expensive manufactured goods from the mother country. There has been a legacy of 'dependent urbanisation'; the main purpose of the city historically was to create wealth for the metropolitan colonisers. This early population settlements served as a deterrent to the development of a modern industrialised self-sufficient towns.[30] While European cities passed through the industrial revolution, Caribbean cities remained dependent on agriculture and commerce for much of their economic well-being.[31] When the urban population growth in the several urban towns outside of Kingston was small, it was possible to accommodate development by unplanned growth, without too much environmental harm, and this was although the percentage growth was large. This will not be the case, going into the future. Jamaica will need to abandon its past of unplanned settlement and township development.

In accommodating urbanisation, Jamaica has recently resorted to a policy of infilling. Whereas prior to 2010, residential and commercial developments, hardly involved buildings beyond four to six levels, today with infilling, developments regularly exceed ten levels, a recipe for further environmental degradation, congestion, and reduction in the quality of life especially in Kingston and St Andrew. Jamaica and other Caribbean cites of the future will need to address these historical problems.

In designing prosperous urban cities of the future, Jamaican planners will need to take into consideration critical issues like social connectivity, public health, and community space, good air quality, and the friendly environment. Future cities should be a place that values walkability and a mix of uses involving. mixed-use spaces, human-powered and intermodal transit systems, and green spaces. Special consideration will also need to be given to issues, like public health and community services. Cities need to be designed around the idea that a community should be authentic, highly curated, easily accessible, and green. This kind of cityscape encourages walking and biking, as well as micro-communities where people live, work, and play in the same vicinity. This vision for new Jamaican towns and cities of the future should be to move away from the colonial legacy, which shaped the growth of towns. It should be a place that is scaled to people, providing safe pedestrian environments and open spaces for public life. Most importantly, it should be a place that is well-grounded in the unique culture and values of the Jamaican people, while embracing modern technologies and the global community. Jamaican cities of the future will need innovative technologies to enhance liveability more connected public space and new levels of sustainability. There will be the need for better connectivity between modes and hubs. Day-to-day activities increasingly will be tied with digital interconnectivity and interfaces. The changes however should be evolutionary.

JAMAICA'S LABOUR FORCE

The Jamaican labour force and employment data have, over the years, been problematic statistics. Estimates of unemployment up to 1970 varied from 12 per cent to 25 per cent. There is a major conceptual definition of the labour force itself and this makes it more difficult to determine unemployment levels or make international comparisons.

It is to be expected that, for countries with high proportion of own account workers and seasonal agricultural workers, employment data would become difficult. In Jamaica, however, the labour force, not only includes persons who were working, or seeking work but also could accept work. Table 4.6 shows information abstracted from the census data on labour force and the Labour Force Sample Surveys of 1968 and 1974. G.E. Cumper shows that there were significant differences and inconsistencies observed in the statistics and even in the census data, because of the problem of definition. Certain important features can, however, be observed, starting with the school age.[32] In fact, Cumper also stated that, strictly speaking, the census data and the labour force data are not comparable and adjustments had to be made to the data to make them more consistent.[33]

In the period 1891–1943, the Jamaican labour force increased from 373,500 to 484,300. During this period, the population increased by nearly 30 per cent, but the labour force remained relatively stable. In the period up to 1943–46, the agricultural sector accounted for 47.21 per cent of the employed labour force, with domestic workers, the next largest category, accounting for 12.49 per cent. Accounting for the number of domestic workers has been a major data collection problem.

In 1970, four hundred and sixty-six thousand students were at school, or 25 per cent of the population and, of this total, eighty-three thousand, or 4.5 per cent were in higher education, mainly in the urban areas. The labour force participation in the period was between 68 per cent and 70 per cent, and this, more or less, stabilised over the years.[34] Although there was almost constant high economic growth in the period up to 1974, unemployment remained between 20 per cent and 25 per cent. With out-migration of 434,300 over the period 1960–85 the unemployment rate would have been much higher.[35] Unemployment first declined from 26.7 per cent in 1983 to 15.7 per cent 1991, falling to 13 per cent in 2011 and 7.1 per cent in 2021. Unemployment levels in Jamaica have fallen to the standards of industrialised countries.

Jamaica has been exporting its working population, and this has accelerated the fall in the rate of unemployment. It is not a case of the economy generating sufficient jobs to meet a rising population. Jamaica's industrialisation, as the economic theory would expect, did not increase employment, and this questions the theory of forced employment as being an appropriate avenue for economic development for developing countries like Jamaica.

SECTORAL DISTRIBUTION OF THE LABOUR FORCE BY INDUSTRY GROUP

The earliest national income data in Jamaica is that of Gisela Eisner.[36] In the period 1834–1930, agriculture dominated industrial activity, accounting for 71.5 per cent of labour by classified industry, with domestic servants at 12.8 per cent, and manufacturing and construction at 11.4 per cent. By 1921, agriculture's share of employment had fallen to 55.5 per cent, manufacturing had increased to 17.6 per cent and domestic servants to 17.9 per cent. Manufacturing was mainly production of tobacco, tanning, beer, and ale, mineral water, soap, copra, sisal, and rope. Manufacturing began its rise towards the end of the 1880s. The rapid fall in agricultural employment occurred after 1881. Emancipation made very little difference to labour distribution, except that there was a shift from the plantation to smallholdings/independent farming. The labour requirement for banana which expanded after 1870, however, was much lower than the labour requirement for sugar.

Tables 4.5 and 4.6 show the sectoral distribution of the classified labour force by industry groups for the period, 1968–82 and 1992–2020.[37]

Table 4.5: Sectoral Distribution of Classified Labour Force by Industry Group

Industry Group	1968	1972	1982
Agriculture (included Mining for 68 and 72)	35.2	30.6	30.6
Mining /Refining and Quarrying			1.0
Manufacturing	11.2	12.7	11.9
Construction/Installation	7.4	7.2	4.9
Commerce/Distribution	11.3	12.4	12.9
Public Utilities			
Transport/Communication	4.1	4.0	4.2
Public Administration		10.3	14.6
Other Services	21.3	23.0	19.4
Unspecified	-	-	0.9
Total classifiable labour force	100.0.	100.0	100.0

Source: STATIN

From as early as 1943, agriculture's share of the employed labour experienced a sharp decline. Mining, although having grown from less than 1 per cent contribution to GDP in 1950 to 8.1 per cent in 1960, employed less than 1 per cent of labour force in 1960.[38] The share of agriculture employed in the labour force in 1941 was 45.1 per cent however agriculture's share of the labour force has progressively dwindled and, in 2020, accounted for less than 15 per cent of the labour force. The recent declines in agricultural labour coincides with the EU's removal of a trade preference, which resulted in the sharp declines in export banana and sugar.

Table 4.6: Sectoral Distribution of Classified Labour Force by Industry Group

Industry group	1992	2002	2012	2020
Agriculture/Forestry/Fisheries	24.5	17.6	16.7	14.3
Mining /Quarrying/Refining	0.5	0.4	0.5	0.4
Manufacture	10.6	7.7	7.0	5.6
Construction/Installation	6.0	10.2	8.7	8.9
Commerce/distribution/ hotel /restaurant	18.9	23.2	28.0	30.1
Public Utilities/electricity/water	0.6	0.6	0.7	0.6
Transport/communication	3.7	6.4	6.4	6.0
Public Administration	4.6	7.7	5.2	5.0
Financing/Real Estate	4.3	6.3	7.2	10.0
Community/social/ Personal service	24.5	27.1	5.1	5.4
Education/health/Private household			8.5	8.3
Private households with employed persons			5.7	5.2
Not Classified	1.8	0.5	0.3	0.2
Total classifiable labour force	100.0	100.0	100.0	100.0

Source: STATIN. Note: The classification of industrial groups has repeatedly been changed over the years. Since 2000, several new classification groups have been introduced. Interestingly, a new category was introduced in 2012; private household with employed person (mainly house helpers and gardeners) employing between sixty-nine thousand and seventy-two thousand. Hotel and Restaurant group is now reported separately and accounts for 8 per cent to 9 per cent of employed labour force.

THE FUTURE POPULATION OF JAMAICA

The census of July 2011 showed a total population of 2,686,105.[39] The Planning Institute's projection was that the Jamaica's population would reach 2,961,000 in 2021. However revised estimates for 2021 now puts the country's population at 2,734,093 (United Nations Statistics and Statistical Institute of Jamaica 2019).[40] This slowing of the Jamaican population growth is expected to continue over the next two decades.

Forecasting Jamaica's population growth is extremely problematic. This is because of high levels of out-migration, which along with the fertility rate has fallen to just under 1.9 child per child bearing female, declining from 2.3 child per child in 2011. Most analysts have found it difficult to predict the level of out-migration. The population density in 1943 was 292 per square mile, by 1982 it was 516 per square mile. The period up to 1982 saw density increasing by 51.6 per cent per person per square mile. The density per square mile increased at the rate of natural increase of fifteen persons per square mile. The population density will have increased from to 436 per square mile in 1970[41] to around 708 in 2021 per square mile, making Jamaica the forty-ninth most densely populated country in the world.

This population growth in Jamaica's urban areas is causing real problems for the development and planning of cities, as well as for municipal public management. With a predominantly urbanising and less bounded socially structured society, there will be many future challenges. Export sugar and banana once provided rural Jamaica with its vitality, all but having disappeared, presenting increasingly new administrative challenges to the national government which has centralised governance, largely in Kingston. Jamaica now has to look to the services industry to drive the economy in the future.

Notes

1. USAID, 'Climate Chane Vulnerability Assessment and Adaption Prioritisation,' August 31, 2011, https://www.climatelinks.org/resources/usaidusfs-climate-change-vulnerability-assessment-and-adaptation-prioritization.
2. John H. Hinton, *Memoir of William Knibb, Missionary in Jamaica* (Kingston: Forgotten Books, 1847).
3. Simon P Newman, Michael Deason, Yanis P. Pitsiladis, Antonio Sales and Vincent Macauley, 'The West African Ethnicity of Enslaved Jamaican' (Routledge, Taylor and Francis Group, 2013).
4. *1974 World Population Year: Recent Population Movements in Jamaica*, CICRRED Series, http://www.cicred.org/Eng/Publications/pdf/c-c28.pdf, and the Department of Statistics Jamaica, 1973.
5. Department of Statistics, 1973; and 1974 'Population and Vital Statistics'; 'Demographic Statistics'; and the National Planning Agency, 1975.
6. Statistical Institute of Jamaica, *Population and Housing Census* (Kingston: STATIN, 2011).
7. Ibid.
8. United Nations, *Population Prospects 2017* (Geneva: UN, 2017).
9. Statistical Institute of Jamaica, *Population and Housing Census* (Kingston: STATIN, 2011).
10. UN, 'Recent Population Movements,' in *Statistical Year Book* (Geneva: UN, 1972).
11. Erna Brodber, 'The Second-Generation Freemen in Jamaica 1907–1944' (unpublished PhD thesis, UWI, 1984).

12. Douglas Manley, 'Migrants Past and Present,' in *The West Indian Comes to London*, ed. S.K. Ruck (London: Routledge & K. Paul, 1960).
13. David Ellis, 'The Product of More than One Country: Race, Identity and Discourse in Post-Windrush Britain,' *Journal of Native Theory* 30, no. 2 (2001): 214–32.
14. Eric Walrond, 'Negro Migration in Britain 1947–1948,' CO876/88.
15. Elizabeth Thomas-Hope, Pauline Knight, and Claudel Noel, *Migration in Jamaica: A Country Profile 2010* (Grand-Saconnex, Switzerland: International Organization for Immigration, 2010).
16. L.A. Eyre, *Geographic Aspects of Population Dynamics in Jamaica* (Gainesville, FL: University of Florida Press, 1972).
17. Elizabeth Thomas-Hope, *The Future of Migration Policies in the Caribbean* (Geneva, International Organisation for Migration, 2019).
18. Carl Peach, 'The Caribbean in Europe, Contrasting Patterns of Migration and Settlement in Britain, France and the Netherlands,' Research Paper on Ethnicity, 2019.
19. Erna Brodber, *Rural-Urban Migration of the Jamaican Child* (Paris: UNESCO, 1986)
20. Ibid.
21. Tony Weis, 'The Rise, Fall and Future of the Jamaica Peasantry,' *Journal of Peasant Studies* 33, no. 1 (2006): 61–88.
22. Adam Kuper, *Changing Jamaica* (Kingston: Kingston Publishers, 1978).
23. Colin G. Clarke, *Kingston, Jamaica: 'Urban Development and Social Change 1692–2002* (Kingston: Ian Randle Publishers, 2002).
24. Ibid.; Census of Jamaica 1943; Table Credit.
25. Orlando Patterson, '*The Confounding Island: Jamaica and Post-colonial Predicament* (Cambridge, Massachusetts and London: The Bellnap Press of Harvard University Press, 2019).
26. Colonial Office Report on 'Jamaica,' 1951.
27. S. Musson and T.L. Roxborough, *Handbook of Jamaica 1893* (Kingston: Government Statistical Institute of Jamaica, 1893).
28. PIOJ, Population Unit, 'Urbanisation in Jamaica,' presentation to high school students, 2005.
29. United Nations, 'World Population Review 2023,' https://worldpopulationreview.com.
30. Seaga Edward, 'Tourism as a Driver of Change in Jamaica Economy,' in A Collection of Speeches, UWI, Mona, 2005.
31. Edward Seaga, 'Vision of Energy in the 21st Century,' address given to the Scientific Research Council, Jamaica Pegasus Hotel, November 2005.
32. Thomas Boswell, 'Characteristic and Processes of Urbanisation in the Caribbean, Benchmark,' Conference of Latin Americanist Geographers Vol. 17/18, University of Miami, 1990.
33. C. Clarke, 'Urbanization in the Caribbean,' *Geography* 59, no. 3 (1974): 223–32.

34. G.E. Cumper, 'Non-Economic Factors Influencing Rural Development Planning,' *Social and Economic Studies* 17, no. 3 (1986): 243–51.
35. G.E. Cumper, 'Comparison of Statistical Data on Jamaican Labour Force from 1943 to 1961,' *Social and Economic Studies* 13, no. 4 (1964): 430–39.
36. Carmen McFarlane, 'Education and Employment: An assessment of Institutional Responses by Jamaica Education on System of the Demands for Skills' (MSc Thesis, Mona, UWI, 1968).
37. Own Jefferson (1972), 'Post War Economic Development in Jamaica' ISER, UWI; Omar Davies and Michael Witter, *The Development of the Jamaican Economy since Independence* (Kingston: Heinemann, 1989); and STATIN, *Sundry Years: Labour Force Statistics* (Kingston: STATIN, 1968, 1972, 1982).
38. Ibid.
39. Gisela Eisner, *Jamaica, 1830 to1930: A Study in Economic Growth* (Manchester: Manchester University Press, 1961).
40. Accurate data on the size and characteristics of Jamaica's labour force in the initial years (and still) has been problematic. Labour force data have been derived from two sources: censuses of 1943, 1953, 1960, and 1970 and Labour Force Sample Survey of 1957 and 1966. The problem arises from the pattern of employment exhibiting high levels of seasonality, and subsistence economy, as is the case with agriculture and construction and high levels of domestic or household workers (domestic and gardeners).
41. Owen Jefferson, *Post War Economic Development of Jamaica* (Kingston: ISER, 1972).
42. Planning Institute of Jamaica, *Vision 2030: Jamaica – Population Sector Plan-Predicting Population Growth* (Kingston: PIOJ, 2010).
43. United Nations Statistics and Statistical Institute of Jamaica 2019.
44. Statistical Yearbook, 1973.

PART 2
Economic Policies and Economic Development

CHAPTER FIVE

Post-independence Development of the Public Sector and Public Enterprise

SPONSORED BY

BGLC
BETTING GAMING & LOTTERIES COMMISSION

RATIONALE FOR INTERVENTION OF THE STATE

The expansion of the public sector is explained by the theory of Wagner's Law also known as the law of increasing state activity, which contends that public expenditure increases as national income rises and will give rise to increasing size of the public sector.[1] To this we can add democratic competition for power, as experienced in Jamaica's post-independence expansion of the public sector.

The major principle informing public sector management in post-independence Jamaica up to 1980 was development administration.[2] R. Rees gives four reasons for wider state intervention: to correct market failure, to alter the structure of payments in the economy, to facilitate centralised long-term planning and coordination, and to change the nature of the economy from a capitalist to a socialist one.[3] There was also the widely held argument for public production of goods and services, which maintained that, where there is market failure, private firms will pursue profit maximisation in the owners' interest at the expense of the consumers. Even where there is no market failure, and it is possible to achieve the most optimal and efficient production, there may still be a case for government intervention.[4]

Oliver MacDonagh believes that public problems are not one-off to be solved by a temporary commission, or an act of Parliament, but are polymorphous, requiring turn-by-turn response to problems, with an active bureaucracy exercising judgment and discretion.[5] The point is not just to see this in qualitative terms, but to see a qualitative shift in administration, which is as important as any quantitative dispensation.

Beyond market failure, the state may intervene where skewed income distribution exists (today we call this levelling up); competitive markets may initiate an unequal distribution of income, which may leave some individuals with insufficient resources to live. We see much of this today as a result of globalisation. Second, individuals may not act in their own best interest and, even if they are fully informed, they may make bad decisions (referred to as the 'nanny state'). The government may also alter the structure of payments – how benefits and risks are distributed among consumers, employers, and employees.

The extension of the state into the production of goods and commercial services is of particular significance with Jamaica, especially in the 1970s. In Jamaica and other English-speaking Caribbean states, participation in the productive sector needs to be set against developments in the UK, from which Caribbean countries took their precedents and from where the political environment came to be shaped by the socialist policies of successive post-war UK Labour governments. Intervention, which may have been tolerated initially on emergency grounds in the UK, later came to be permanent and necessary, even by constituencies previously inclined towards a laissez-faire approach in the immediate post-war years. Public ownership took two distinct forms in the UK: the transfer of existing activities and firms from private owners to the state, or nationalisation, and the creation of new public enterprises to manage completely new activities. A surprising amount (e.g., in energy) of public ownership also arose out of rationalisation of a mis-mash of local government service provision.

The circumstances which fostered state ownership in the UK in the immediate post-war years were, however, differred from those which prevailed in the Jamaican and Caribbean colonial democracies in the 1960s and '70s. During the transition from colonial rule to independence, the demands of the public for the government to assume greater control of what was perceived to be strategic activities in the economy became a pressing force. Trinidad and Tobago was the first Caribbean country where the state first intervened to take over private businesses (nationalise). The development was initiated by the takeover of the public passenger transport industry in 1960 in the first instance. The record of transition from colonialism to independence was, for Trinidad and Tobago, a process where the state came to take formal control of several key aspects of the economy. The Trinidad political leadership justified public ownership based on the principle of national interest, when the government took over the British West Indian International Airways (BWIA) in 1960 because it needed to prevent its liquidation and retrenchment of several hundred workers, as well as to ensure that a vital field of international transport would not fall entirely into foreign hands.[6] In 1960, the Trinidadian government also nationalised the telephone company to ensure continued employment of workers in the industry. Much of the rationale in Trinidad and Tobago reflected increasing levels of economic nationalism, the growing desire to control the national economy, partly inspired by the young academic radicals who had emerged at the University of the West Indies and the University of Guyana, calling for release of the economy from foreign domination and for the nations of the Caribbean to exert sovereignty over the economic sphere, with the objective of gaining economic independence to buttress political independence.[7] By 1970, the major public utilities: transport, water, telephone, and electricity were in the hands of the government of Trinidad and Tobago. Further, in 1970, the Trinidad and Tobago government entered the fields of oil, sugar, and commercial banking, again based on the rationale of enlarging national decision-making area over the economy. The *Nation* newspaper[8] reported that the Trinidad and Tobago government in 1972 gave two important reasons for public ownership: to accelerate the transfer of foreign-owned firms to local hands and to protect the national interest, reflecting both socialist ideology and economic nationalism.

Up to 1970, in Jamaica, the state's role in the productive economy was confined essentially to developmental activities and various forms of regulation. Although there were a few cases of state intervention in the commercial and productive sectors before 1960, this was motivated by pragmatism, as in the case in 1956, when the assets of the Kingston Ice Making Company, which had gone into liquidation, were acquired by the government and re-established as the Jamaica Ice Company Limited. Given Jamaica's tropical climate, ice-making then was seen in the nature of a public utility; salvaging the business was regarded as a value to the community.[9] This was followed by the acquisition of Zero Processing and Storage Limited in 1957, with the objective of providing refrigeration and storage accommodation for surplus supplies of fish and other perishables. Incorporating the railway as a statutory body was a direct outcome of the World Bank's recommendation in 1952.[10]

The unwillingness of the Jamaican private sector to take on new areas of enterprise up to the 1950s also provided successive administrations with the opportunity for state intervention, especially after independence. Pre-independence private sector involvement in the economic activities took the path of assured avenues of commission agents, distribution of imported goods, real-estate development, and the traditional export agriculture. The sector also did not display entrepreneurship and a willingness to invest in major developmental projects that involved high risks and long periods of gestation, yielding moderate returns over the long run.

To fulfil to the development needs of the people after independence, the public sector had to respond to the failures of the private sector to enter several fields of economic activities. The growth of tourism led to the acquisition and exclusive occupation of prime beach land by private owners, denying the general population access to most of the beaches for recreational and fishing purposes. Public concern led to the creation of the Beach Control Authority, with powers to control and regulate use of foreshores and beaches in the interest of the community. The authority was empowered to acquire beaches compulsorily and declare them public. In the 1960s and '70s, the private owners of the utilities (Jamaica Omnibus Service, the Jamaica Telephone Company, and the Jamaica Public Service Company) all failed to provide the needed capital to expand their services to meet the demands of consumers and the economy, requiring government to acquire these companies.[11]

The wider public expectations which came with independence pressured the government to significantly expand its role. Initially, this took the form of creating agricultural, industrial, and financial development corporations. Even then government's direct intervention in the 1950s and '60s was in the manufacturing sector and was limited to building several industrial estates and factory facilities. These were rented to private manufacturers by the Jamaica Industrial Development Corporation (JIDC). Up to 1970, few of the manufacturing enterprises, established under the various incentive laws, were owned by the state. These state-owned development entities were expected to create the environment for private sector development. However, major investments in manufacturing and by the private sector did not come about pre-independence.

The state's role in pre-independence Jamaica in the tourism sector confined itself to providing incentives to mostly foreign investors as capital grants and sovereign guarantees for the construction of hotels. The objective was to shift hotel demand from the limited winter traffic to an all-year business. It was also expected that the tourism sector would provide high levels of employment, including rural employment, an overriding force encouraging the state to take on a wider role in the sector. In the financial and infrastructure sectors, the Jamaica Development Bank of 1969, the Urban Development Corporation of 1968, and the Kingston Waterfront Development Company Limited accelerated the pace of infrastructure and housing development.

The attainment of Independence in 1962 increased pressures and expectations for the state to take on a wider role, including a more direct role in the productive sectors.[12] There was also an increased level of nationalism, thus strengthening the forces calling for localisation of economic entities in the areas of banking, insurance, and the utilities. State intervention initially, therefore, was introduced as a policy, only where the private sector had failed to respond to development needs. Ownership, based on national interest to ensure reasonable utility rates to consumers, to facilitate integration of facilities and to ensure that development of the essential services, matched the wider national development programme. For Edwin Jones, state intervention was informed by pragmatic and nationalistic considerations, as well as the drive for cultural self-sufficiency, if not autonomy.[13]

Jamaica was more cautious, when compared with Trinidad and Tobago and Guyana, in pursuing the policy of public ownership of commerce in the 1960s. Then Finance Minister Edward Seaga was clear in his statement about the role of the state in the productive sector in the 1960s. It was Seaga who prescribed localisation of ownership to Jamaicans in the financial sector, and made it clear he did not mean public ownership, or nationalisation of industries and the means of production. In essence, Finance Minister Seaga's policy replaced foreign ownership with private local ownership. The policy of localisation of certain businesses was a means of consolidating economic independence and increasing national control over the economy. Local ownership in Jamaica did not involve government ownership and enlarging the national decision-making process of the state over the economy and transferring foreign-owned firms to the state, as in Trinidad and Tobago.[14]

Several of the financial institutions were branch operations, and Seaga's requirement was for them to incorporate locally under the

Companies Act, appoint local board members and float a part of their shares on the embryonic Jamaica Stock Exchange (JSE). Seaga also called for a policy of 51 per cent foreign ownership, to allay any concerns of nationalisation by foreign investors.

From this survey, the development and expansion of Jamaica's public sector can be broken down into four distinct periods:

- pre-independence: the first period lasted up to 1962
- the second period between 1962 and 1974
- the third period between 1974 and 1980
- the fourth period, from 1980 to 1990
- the fifth period post-1990s

PRE-INDEPENDENCE DEVELOPMENTS OF THE PUBLIC SECTOR: THE FIRST PERIOD UP TO 1962

During the first period, pre-independence Jamaica, responsibility for the productive sector (mostly sugar and banana) remained with the private sector, including foreign private interests. The colonial administration, however, was an active player in establishing a supportive marketing, financial and regulatory framework to support export agriculture and the private sector. First, there was the Small Business Loan Board in 1956, followed by the Finance Corporation in 1959. In the agricultural sector, the colonial government established several agencies to facilitate export agriculture, among them, the Coconut Control Authority in 1945, the Coffee Industry Board in 1950, the Banana Board 1957, and the Coconut Industry Board (CIB) in 1957. In the tourism sector, the state's role was confined to providing incentives to mostly foreign hoteliers. To implement this policy, the Jamaica Tourist Board was established in 1960, replacing the Tourist Trade and Development Board, a 1922 organisation. Of the 180 private enterprises established under the various incentive laws over the period after 1940s, only ten involved government part-ownership. The government also built several industrial estates and factories, most of which were rented to private manufacturers by the JIDC.

Developments between 1960 and 1972

The period of the 1960s saw the establishment of several development and regulatory agencies in almost all the sectors. The state also acquired an interest in the Seprod Group of Companies, established Jamaica Frozen Foods Limited in 1966 and Caribbean Processing Limited in 1967. To support the export industry, the Jamaica National Export Corporation (JNEC) and Export Trading Company Limited focused on facilitation and direct participation in the export business, especially in relation to non-traditional items. The Agricultural Development Corporation (ADC) was created in 1965 to promote the development of agriculture and, at one stage, owned Amity Hall Farm, Minard, the New River Farm, and a large dairy herd. In addition, the Agricultural Marketing Corporation (AMC) was established in 1963. The motivating force for a wider role in agriculture was to provide for regulation in the un-coordinated distributive system and to minimise the volatility of agricultural prices. Control boards were also created for almost all the export commodities: the Tobacco Industry Control Authority, Coffee Industry Board, Coconut Industry Board, Jamaica Dairy Industry Development Board, and Banana Board.

In the utilities sector, new statutory authorities or corporations were established in the 1960s. The administration established Jamaica International Telecommunications Limited (JAMINTEL) and Trans Jamaican Airlines Ltd in 1971. JAMINTEL was established as an international communications joint venture with Cable and Wireless Limited, with the government owning 51 per cent and Cable and Wireless Limited of the UK, 49 per cent. There was Kingston and St Andrew Water Commission and the rurally focused National Water Authority. The Port Authority, a maritime agency, was established in 1972, responsible for regulation and development of ports and shipping. The Urban Development Corporation of 1968 established National Hotels and Properties Limited (NHP) as a subsidiary to take on a wider role in hotel property and tourism infrastructure development.

New regulatory bodies were created, including the Public Utilities Commission in 1965, and the Passenger Transport Corporation and Rural Area Boards, which were established earlier to regulate the private utilities and public passenger transport system. The Prices Commission was established in 1960 with the power to fix prices on a wide range of commodities.

In the financial sector, the government created the Bank of Jamaica (BOJ) in 1961, followed by a development finance agency, the Jamaica Development Bank (JDB) in 1969.

Some factors that influenced the government to intervene in the utilities sector were the questionable accounting practices of the three foreign owned utilities (electricity, telephone, and urban transport), failure on their part to carry out expansion of the physical facilities to meet national development needs, and the practice of inflating the rate base in their submissions to the Public Utilities Commission for price increases. These developments first led to the purchase of 10 per cent of the Jamaica Telephone Company (JTC) stocks in 1970.

Similarly, it was the refusal of the electricity utility company, Jamaica Public Service Company (JPSCo), to expand production unless it was given an exclusive long-term all-island franchise and a guaranteed rate of return, and also questionable accounting and transfer pricing practices that led the administration of the day to acquire Stone and Webster's 20 per cent equity interest in JPSCo in 1969. Stone and Webster, at the time, was JPSCo's managing partner, and the company was accused of transfer pricing.

With transport, Jamaica Omnibus Service Company (JOS), a British-owned company, was also taken over for failure to expand the services and questionable accounting practice.[15] The government established Air Jamaica in 1968. It was fashionable for newly independent countries to establish a national airline although, with Jamaica, the rationale for establishment of the airline was the necessity to facilitate development of tourism.

A levy was introduced on the bauxite industry in the early 1970s and some proceeds were used to fund the nationalisation programme. Faced with public pressures considering the impending closure of three of the largest sugar manufacturing facilities on the island (Frome, Monymusk, and Bernard Lodge), the government intervened and acquired the three factories in the 1970s. It also established the Sugar Industry Authority in 1970 to coordinate and regulate the industry.

Developments between 1972 and 1980

Even up to 1970s, the rationale for public ownership continued to be based on pragmatic grounds. When the government acquired the Ariguanabo textile mills in 1973, it was seen to be an important commodity providing employment for a considerable workforce. Wider intervention into the productive sector followed Manley's declaration of democratic socialism in 1974 and to acquisition of majority ownership of electricity (97 per cent and telephone (90 per cent) in 1975. A national shipping line was created in 1976, another instance where the rationale was more for prestige; at the time, the feeling was that newly developing countries should also have a shipping line. Jamaica also wanted to break the monopoly that the American aluminium companies held over the shipment of bauxite to North America. In 1978, the government also established the Rural Electrification Programme Limited to fast-track the expansion of electricity to rural areas. Some of these interventions could also be described as tactical, meaning they were more about electoral tactics and strategy.

Although nationalisation of essential services, based on the UK precedent, had been an important aspect of PNP electioneering over the years, it was never taken to the policy implementation stage until 1974. Prior to the 1970s, the only enterprise that was nationalised was the railway service in the 1890s, and this was after the private owners had failed to meet interest costs to its bondholder.[16] The colonial government had intervened to secure the continued operation of the railway, which had become vital to the operation of the sugar and banana industries.

With the rapid expansion of public ownership in the 1970s, the state became almost the dominant player in the mining, hotel, banking, agriculture, and distribution businesses.

In the distribution sector, the government extended its role through the establishment of Jamaica Nutrition Holdings Ltd (JNH) in 1973 to address the global shortage of food supplies, especially basic staples such as grains, soya, and milk solids, needed to serve the country's nutritional requirements. The state Trading Corporation (STC) later replaced JNH in 1977 to implement the government's policy of providing adequate food and nutrition at a low cost. STC integrated backwards and acquired Jamaica Soya Products Ltd and Cornwall Dairy Products Ltd. The entity also extended its responsibilities to cover the importation of drugs, textiles, building products, and motor vehicles among a wide range of items and became one of the largest importing agencies in Jamaica. While STC's activities were limited to the import business, it took on regulating all major items offered in the distributive trade.

The oil price shocks of 1972, and the drastic fall off in demand and depression of the hotel industry which followed, led many of the foreign operators to abandon their tourist businesses in Jamaica. The government, as sovereign guarantor to most of the hotels' loan capital, was forced to intervene to protect the long-term interest of the industry, as well as to cushion the negative impact on employment. By 1978, the state came into possession of eleven hotels and controlled a further six out of ninety-six hotels, giving it control of 48 per cent of room capacity. Through National Hotels and Properties Limited (NHP), the government became a major owner of hotel properties. At the time, UDC as the parent company of NHP came under the portfolio of the Ministry of Finance, while NHP came under the portfolio of the Ministry of Foreign Affairs. Further restructuring of the institutions in the tourism sector was carried out in 1975, resulting in creating Jamaica Vacations Ltd (JAMVAC), with a mandate to develop air charter operations, and the Tourism Product Development Company (TPDCo), to deal with industry standards and product development.

The government's entry into the financial sector in the 1970s began with the Post Office savings activities. A new company, Workers Savings and Loan Bank Limited, was created in 1973, with the government retaining 45 per cent ownership and control. The administration had begun acquisition of equity interest in Barclays Bank's subsidiary at the beginning of the 1970s and its re-establishment as National Commercial Bank Ltd (NCB) and by 1977, NCB was fully state-owned. In a third initiative, the Jamaica Development Bank was vertically separated in the 1970s into two public bodies: the Agricultural Credit Bank (ACB) and the Jamaica Development Bank (JDB), with the former focusing on loans to the agricultural sector and the latter on loans to the industrial sector. In 1973, the Jamaica Mortgage Bank (JMB) was established, followed by the Jamaica National Investment Corporation (JNIC) in 1974. The JNIC also became the holding company for a new institution in the bauxite sector in 1974, the Jamaica Bauxite Institute. An export credit finance agency, Jamaica Export Credit Insurance Corporation, was formed in 1977, as a subsidiary of the Bank of Jamaica.

Public participation in the ownership of bauxite and petroleum in the 1970s was an act of deliberate policy. The Jamaica Bauxite Institute was established as a technical advisory and regulatory arm of government. This was followed by the establishment of the Jamaica Bauxite Mining Company Limited in 1976 to operate as the holding company for the state's interest in the sector. In 1980, the government acquired 51 per cent equity interest in both Kaiser's and Reynolds's operations (both American-owned companies); 7 per cent equity interest in another US company, Alcoa, and 6 per cent interest in Canadian Alcan's operations. In 1977, the Bauxite and Alumina Trading Company Limited (BATCo) was formed as the marketing arm for the state's interest in the industry.

State intervention in the bauxite industry became a most acrimonious issue between the US and Jamaican governments in the 1970s, with the US accusing it of expropriation. The intervention, coupled with imposing the bauxite levy by the Manley administration, led to the North American companies' reduced interest in Jamaica and curtailment of any further major expansion. The other two major mining companies, the Jamaica Cement Company, which later became the Caribbean Cement Company Limited, and Jamaica Gypsum Limited also came under state ownership and control in the 1970s.

In 1976, the National Housing Trust (NHT) was established, along with the National Housing Corporation, with the former having responsibility for financing housing construction and the latter operating as a building and housing construction agency. Two other agencies facilitated economic development in the agricultural sector: the Black River Upper Morass Development Company Limited in 1977 and the Forest Industry Development Company Limited (FIDCo) in 1978. The Port Authority and Airports Authority, both of which were formed in the 1960s, were given wide mandates to own and control the state's interest at the two international airports and the seaports.

Except for the Port Authority, all the utilities and transport enterprises experienced major financial problems, as the subsidised pricing policies meant they could not fund their recurrent costs and contribute to capital formation. In 1978, the government established a new infrastructure investment policy, calling for enterprises to generate finances to meet all their recurrent expenditure and 30 per cent of their capital needs. They were also expected to meet universal service obligations. However, no clear mechanisms were provided to finance these social obligations. With the rapid increase in illegal minibus operations on Jamaica Omnibus Service Limited (JOS) franchise routes, it was not long before the company ran into serious financial problems and, by 1980, had become bankrupt.

Size of the Public Sector in 1980

N.C. Argus, W.P. Barrett, and E. Holstein reported that, in 1965, there 124 public bodies; thirteen classified as advisory (such as the Minimum Wages Advisory Boards); eleven as appellate (such as the National Appeal Tribunal); forty-six as regulatory (such as the Public Utilities Commission – PUC), and fifty-four as commercial or developmental, such as the Jamaica Railway Corporation (JRC) and the Water Commission.[17] There were 249 bodies listed with regulatory, distribution and promotional functions forming the major group. Stone reported that the public sector in Jamaica, in terms of government expenditure as a percentage share of GDP, had increased from 7 per cent in 1960 to 21 per cent in 1980. In the 1940s and '50s, it was near 4 per cent and 6 per cent, respectively.[18]

By the 1980s, the Jamaican public sector, especially the public enterprise sector, had grown significantly from the immediate post-war years. Table 5.1 below lists the sectoral distribution of public entities in 1980. The sector comprised over eighteen to twenty ministers of government, fifty ministry departments, and over four hundred statutory bodies and public corporations, with over one hundred and ten thousand central and local government employees.

Table 5.1: Distribution of Public Sector Entities in 1980

Type of Public Sector Entity	Number
Regulatory, distribution and promotional entities	49
Social and community service	20
Service to agriculture, fisheries and forestry	10
Communications	3
Financial services	18
Agricultural distribution services	25
Sugar industry	18
Mining	7
Manufacturing	43
Utilities and transport	17
Tourism	26
Others	13
Total	**249**

Source: Adlith Brown and Helen McBain, *In Caribbean Public Enterprise* (Kingston: ISER, 1983). Note the 1991 figure includes entities with separate legal personalities, either fully or partially owned and with commercial sets of accounts.

In 1995, the government reduced the number of ministries to thirteen; the separate Ministry of the Public Service (MPS), which was created in 1973, was abolished and its activities distributed between the Ministry of Finance (establishment function) and the Office of the Prime Minister with the machinery of government function.[19] In addition, there was the Public Services Commission, with separate services commissions for the police, the judiciary and for local government.

The World Bank, however, reported that, at its peak in 1982, the public sector comprised 530 public bodies, and that two hundred of these were SOEs, accounting for 21 per cent of GDP and 11 per cent of investment.[20] Although the IMF discontinued it clientelist relation with Jamaica in 1996, the government continued the programme of private sector market-driven economic policies, including the privatisation programme.

1980–90 and Structural Adjustment

In this period, the government's economic policy increasingly came to be dictated by the World Bank and the IMF under a structural adjustment loan programme that mandated a reduction of the state's role, the number of public enterprises, size of the public sector and the number of public employees. When Seaga regained power in 1980, this time as prime minister, although he had declared that he would roll back the PNP's policy of public ownership of the productive sector, he acquired major private sector interests with the takeover of Esso's oil refinery in Kingston in 1983 and increase of government's equity in bauxite companies. The Petroleum Corporation of Jamaica (PCJ), which was established in 1975 under PNP stewardship, was the vehicle used by Seaga to acquire the Esso Oil Refinery. The new subsidiary company was named Petrojam. PCJ owned several subsidiaries; Petcom, a marketing company created in 1973, was only made operational in 1982. The government of the day also expanded the role of the JCTC in the 1980s, a company, which Seaga had earlier criticised as being a source of major inefficiency in the economy.

The JLP administration, in coming to power in 1980, focused its efforts on placing the principal entities which were candidates for divestment in a condition that would make them attractive to private investors. For the first time, in 1981/82, the twenty-one major public enterprises which the IMF had selected for closer monitoring and reform had their consolidated returns tabled annually in Parliament. The reform programme required management changes, improved systems of financial reporting, pricing of the utility service based on long-run marginal cost, and elimination of subsidies and cross-subsidies. Incidentally, the word privatisation did not even exist in Jamaica in the 1980s as, at that time, the word Jamaican authorities used to reflect the sale of government assets was 'divestiture.' The Ted Heath UK government in the 1970 talked of 'denationalisation.'

The government of Jamaica was also required to restructure the financial sector. Financial restructuring allowed an enterprise saddled with accumulated debt to clean up its balance sheet, as of the Cement Company prior to privatisation. Where debt liabilities were large, the state often had no choice but to absorb the debt, as of Air Jamaica. In this instance, the government absorbed over J$2.2 billion prior to the first privatisation action. Jamaica National Investment Corporation, in this period, was converted to a holding company, National Investment Bank of Jamaica (NIBJ). The intention was that the NIBJ would centralise most of the government's equity holdings under the Ministry of Finance.

Restructuring of the agricultural enterprises was also necessary. In the case of the marketing boards, the changes provided for most of their commercial functions covering the provision of credit, extension services, nurseries, warehousing, and sorting stations were to be hived off and divested or contracted out to the private sector. Most of their farming functions were also removed and new organisations created and given the responsibility of marketing of their respective crops. Therefore, export agriculture was deregulated. The Agricultural Marketing Company was restructured to coordinate the various agencies trading in non-traditional crops and, in this respect, equipped itself with high-speed packing lines to facilitate efficient and speedy loading and containerisation, mainly for export. The company's retail outlets were closed down or divested. It was in this period that Agro 21 Corporation piloted high technology production and marketing of winter vegetables and promote the growing of non-traditional crops for export.

As part of these policy changes, the banana boxing plants and farms of the Banana Board were sold to small and medium-sized farmers and a new grower organisation, Banana Export Company (BECO), assumed responsibilities for export marketing and the licensing of growers.

BECO engaged the Jamaica Marketing Company Limited (JAMCO), a state-owned company based in the UK, to handle the shipping and overseas marketing of bananas. The Banana Board was required to relinquish all its responsibilities for supplying planting material, leaf spot control, and extension services to BECO.

With sugar, some of the cane lands were leased to the private sector for growing non-traditional crops. Tate and Lyle, a British sugar company, was also engaged under contract to manage the sugar factories and related cane lands. With coffee and citrus, where farmers had an annual output exceeding a certain volume, they were permitted to export directly. Although the Coffee Industry Board remained operational, it was required to compete with the private growers/exporters.

In the utilities sector, the rural National Water Authority was merged with the Kingston-based Water Commission to form the National Water Commission. Telegraph operations were separated from the post office and merged with the telephone company. In the manufacturing sector, the government of the day embarked on a major factory expansion exercise at the Free Zones to attract 807 American textile manufacturers to the island. The sector grew to employ over forty thousand workers, mainly women, at one stage.

Despite the restructuring efforts and declared support for market economy reforms by the JLP administration, the divestment initiatives up to 1984/85 were disappointing. This slow progress was also due to lack of experience and absence of a clear policy statement on the privatisation objectives, as well as the absence of clear guidelines. During this period (1981–89) the Divestiture Committee, which was established at the NIBJ, stressed divestment of equity in commercial enterprises based on commercial criteria, after considering national interest, as well as the discontinuance of enterprises that were no longer commercially viable, with priority for sale based on budgetary and social impact and employment linkages. Seaga's stated position, as a public policy, was that the utilities, air transport, bauxite mining, the petroleum refinery, and telecommunications were not part of the divestiture programme. The emphasis of divestiture was to be on the financial, manufacturing, tourism, agriculture and selected public transport sectors, firms in more or less competitive markets.

Over the seven years, 1979/80–1985/86, the SOEs that, as a result of re-engineering, contributed most to fiscal improvements were Air Jamaica, Jamaica Public Service Company, Jamaica Telephone

Company, National Hotels and Properties, Petroleum Corporation of Jamaica, Urban Development Corporation, Sugar Industry Authority and National Water Authority. The improvements did not come so much from improved management measures, but more from the restructuring measures, such as liquidation of the unprofitable holdings by SIA, leasing of properties by NHP, benefits from currency devaluation by PCJ and AJ, and price increases by the monopoly utilities. Four of the major enterprises: JPSCo, JTC, AJ, and PCJ, accounted for 62 per cent of the improvements. Except for the Broadcasting Corporation, all the enterprises had eliminated their deficit position by 1985.[21] Because of the monopoly position of most of the enterprises, the government could use the quick fix solution of price increases, as well as cutbacks in capital expenditure to reduce the deficit. These, essentially, were political solutions which were not available going forward. The reform concentrated on financial performances rather than improvements to operational efficiencies.

The Fifth Period Commencing in 1990

There were few new SOEs created in the 1990s. Among these were the Rural Agricultural Development Authority (RADA), created by Minister Horace Clarke to consolidate the Ministry of Agriculture's intervention in rural agriculture in the 1990s, and Wigton Wind Farm Limited, a subsidiary of PCJ, introduced to pilot renewable energy which was incorporated in 2000 and began operation in 2004. Wigton Wind Farm started off as a private project, but when the private investor decided not to proceed with the venture, the government opted to pursue the project as an SOE. In addition, Petrojam Ethanol Company, another renewable energy related initiative, was incorporated in 2000.

After 1990, the World Bank, IMF, and USAID by then fully dictated the agenda through their loan conditionalities, requiring the state to privatise its operation in the productive sector, or contract out a broad range of services, or liquidate insolvent or obsolete entities. Much of the effort in the SOE sector was therefore devoted to rationalisation, privatisation, and reduction in the number of SOEs in the 1990s and onwards.

Table 5.2 below shows the growth of the public sector in Jamaica as percentage of GDP and debt service obligation over the period 1965–90. Government expenditure on public sector entities as a percentage of total expenditure increased from 14.57 per cent in 1965 to 50.20 per cent in 1975, before falling back to 41.69 per cent in 1990. Annual growth rate in public expenditure during the period 1964–70 was 8.47 per cent, increasing to 8.98 per cent for the period 1971–80. For the period 1981–90 there was a decline at minus 1.99 per cent.

Table 5.2: Growth in Government Expenditures, Selected Years (Percentage of GDP), 1965–90

Years	Total Government Expenditure (SOE Percentage)	Debt Service (SOE Percentage
1965	14.57	1.24
1970	22.51	2.15
1975	39.68	5.39
1980	50.20	12.21
1985	41.69	19.18
1990	38.71	15.92
Av. Annual Growth Rates		
1964–90	4.79	12.89
1964–70	8.47	14.83
1971–80	8.98	20.59
1981–90	-1.99	3.84

Source: G. Hutchinson. and Ute Schumacher, 'Public Sector Growth and Economic Performance: Implication for Privatisation Policy, Evidence from Jamaica' (Unpublished manuscript, 1994).

In 1965–85, debt service increased from 1.24 per cent to 19.18 per cent in 1985, before falling back to 15.92 per cent in 1990. The total expenditure of the non-financial public sector climbed from 30 per cent of GDP in 1970 to 60 per cent in the 1980s.[22] M. Somasunderam, L. Stanley, and A. Vance reported that the public sector's share of GDP in 1986 amounted to 34 per cent arising especially from the dramatic expansion of SOEs during the 1970s.[23] Employment's share of the public sector was 24 per cent of which 13 per cent went to administration and 5 per cent to infrastructure. The share in investment was 65 per cent of which 14 per cent was in social infrastructure and public administration, and 37 per cent in economic infrastructure, with 14 per cent directly in productive activities. The share of public sector capital was calculated as a depreciated past investment, on the assumption that the initial capital output ratio in 1972 was 3 per cent, and the annual depreciation was 5 per cent. During the 1980s, external public debt, as a percentage of GDP increased from 70 per cent 1980 to 150 per cent in 1985, before falling to 112.5 per cent in 1989. This was because of extensive build-up of structural and stabilisation loans from the World Bank, IADB, and IMF and bilateral loans from USAID by the Seaga administration of the 1980s.

G. Hutchinson and U. Schumacher found a negative relationship between economic growth and growth in the size of the public sector in Jamaica.[24] This negative growth may have been because of inefficiency in the allocation of scarce resources in the public sector, crowding out any effect of government investments in the private sector and diminishing returns. An important factor also was capacity limitation in decision making and the rigid hierarchal structure of government. All governments have a small group of people who are required to take the major decisions on investments, salaries, and prices, along with macroeconomic decision. The more concentrated the decision-making process the greater the capacity constraint. This was clearly demonstrated in the period of the Seaga administration when decision-making was centralised to a small elite group surrounding the prime minister, The matter was made worse, as Seaga was a centralist minister and, at one time in the 1980s, held the portfolios of minister of finance and prime minister at the same time.

Several economists have argued that there is an optimum size of the state, beyond which negative returns set in.[25] This negative growth was because of inefficiency in the allocation of scarce resources in the public sector and diminishing returns.

In the UK, the total outlay of the public sector as a percentage of GDP in 1978 was 41.4 per cent, increasing to 44.0 per cent in 1985, and falling to 39.9 per cent following the major divestitures in the 1980. The size of the public sector then increased to 43.2 per cent by 1994. The size of the UK's public sector may have lost its economic development role, but its social role has expanded, especially in health, education, criminal justice, and social security. Rising expenditure in Europe in these areas was the hallmark of an advanced post-industrial society. In the US, where the public sector has been comparatively smaller when compared to European countries, in 1978, the public sector's share was

30.0 per cent in 1978, rising to 35.2 per cent in 1985 and stabilising at 33.3 per cent in 1990 and 33.6 per cent in 1994. Countries like France and Italy, however, have had much larger public sectors. In France, the public sector was 44.6 per cent in 1978, rising to 56.0 per cent in 1994, while in Italy the size of the public sector increased from 42.4 per cent in 1978 to 56.0 per cent. Sweden has had one of the largest public sectors in Europe, increasing from 58.6 per cent in 1978 to 67 per cent in 1994.[26]

Just as there are strong arguments for governments to expand public production and the public enterprise sector, there are equally strong arguments to limit government's reach into productive activity. Ahmed Galal, Mary Shirley, and Phillip Keefer posit that with government ownership, there is the risk of government failure.[27] The government is said to have too many constituencies, and lacks a unified chain of command, raising agency problems. Public enterprises rarely face the threat of bankruptcy and mergers and the forces of financial market competition like private firms. Because no one has a clear stake in the public asset's return, no one has a clear responsibility and motivation to set clear performance objectives and to ensure that they are attained. There is no particular individual or group ownership, hence the absence of private property rights. Instead, politicians, public servants, employees, and other special interest groups will interject their own objectives into the public sphere, resulting in multiple and often conflicting goals: profit maximisation, employment maximisation, and universal service obligation. This was certainly the case in Jamaica.

Notes

1. Richard E. Wagner and Warren E. March, 'Wagner Law Fiscal Institutions and Government,' *National Tax Journal*, 30, no. 1 (1977): 59–68.
2. Edwin Jones and Mills Gladstone, 'The Institutional Framework of Government,' in *Jamaica in Independence: Essays on the Early Years*. ed. Rex Nettleford (Kingston: Heinemann Caribbean, 1989).
3. R. Rees, *Public Enterprise Economics* (London: Widenfield and Nicholson, 1984).
4. Joseph Stiglitz, *Economics of the Public Sector* (New York: W. W. Norton & Company, 1988).
5. Oliver MacDonagh, *The 19th Century Revolution in Government: A Reappraisal* (Cambridge: Cambridge University Press, 2009).
6. Eric Williams, *History of the People of the Trinidad and Tobago* (Port of Spain PNM Publication Co. Limited, 1962).

7. Norman Girvan, 'Multinational Corporations and Dependent Underdevelopment in Mineral Export Economies,' *Social and Economic Studies* 19, no. 4 (December 1970): 490–526.
8. Lloyd Best, 'A Model of Pure Plantation Economy,' *Social and Economic Studies* 17, no. 3 (1968): 283–326.
9. The *Nation*, 'Perspectives for the New Society,' August 1970, Port of Spain.
10. Government of Jamaica, 'Ministry Paper,' no. 37, House of Parliament, September 1956.
11. Helen McBain, 'External Financing of the Water Commission of Jamaica,' *Social and Economic Studies* 30, no. 1 (March 1981): 171–96.
12. Gladstone E. Mills, 'Regulation and Control of Private Enterprise in Commonwealth Caribbean: Development of the Private Sector,' Department of Government, UWI, 1977.
13. The level of pressure and expectation from the 1920s onwards is often under-appreciated. A reading of the various commissions from the 1890s Royal Commission onwards shows that this is at most a question of degree and focus rather than anything absolutely fundamental.
14. Edwin Jones, 'The Role of the State in Public Enterprise,' *Social and Economic Studies* 30, no. 1 (March 1981): 17–44.
15. Gladstone E. Mills, 'Public Enterprise in the Commonwealth Caribbean with Particular Reference to Jamaica and Trinidad,' Department of Government, UWI, 1976.
16. Raphael A. Swaby, 'Some Problems of Public Utility Regulation by a Statutory Board in Jamaica: The Jamaica Omnibus Company Case,' *Social and Economic Studies* 23, no. 2 (June 1974): 242–63.
17. Veront Satchell and Cezley Sampson, 'The Rise and Fall of the Railways in Jamacia,1845-1975,' *Journal of Transport History* 24, no. 1 (March 2003): 1–21.
18. N.C. Argus, W. P. Barrett, and E. Holstein, 'Public Administration in Jamaica,' United Nations, No. TAO/JAM/6, April 1965.
19. Carl Stone, 'Putting Enterprise to Work: A Study of Privatisation in Jamaica,' Kingston, National Investment Bank, 1992.
20. International Institute of Administrative Science Administration Modernisation Working Group, Prime Minister Office, 1995.
21. A. Akin-Karasapan, *Report and Recommendations of the President of the World Bank on a Proposed Loan for the Private Sector Development Adjustment (PSDAL)* (Washington, DC: World Bank, 1993).
22. M. Somasunderam, L. Stanley, and A. Vance (1986), 'External Governance over Public Enterprises in Jamaica; Establishing the Relationships but Ensuring Operational Autonomy,' USAID.
23. IADB, *Jamaica Socio-Economic Report* (Washington, DC: Economic and Social Development Department, 1990).
24. M. Somasunderam, L. Stanley, and A. Vance (1986), 'External Governance over Public Enterprises in Jamaica; Establishing the Relationships but Ensuring Operational Autonomy.'

25. G. Hutchinson and U. Schumacher (1994 unpublished).
26. R. Borro, 'A Cross – Country Study of Growth, Savings and Government,' Washington, DC, NBER Working Paper No. 2885, 1989.
27. D. Amery and R. Amery, *The Freedom Revelation: The New Republican House Majority Leader Tells Why Big Government Failed, Why Freedom Worked and How We Will Rebuild America* (Washington, DC, Regnery Publishing Inc., 1995).
28. R. Rahn, and H. Fox (1996), *What is the Optimum Size of Government?* (Worcester, MA: Vernon K. Krieble Foundation, 1996).
29. G. Scully, *Measuring the Burden of High Taxes: Report,* no. 215 (Texas: National Centre for Policy Analysis, 1998).
30. OECD, Paris, 1994.
31. Ahmed Galal, Mary Shirley, and Phillip Keefer, *Bureaucrats in Business: Economics and Politics of Government Ownership* (Washington, DC: World Bank Research Report; Oxford: Oxford University Press, 1995).

CHAPTER SIX

The Socialist Economic Policy Adventure of the 1970s

REPLACEMENT OF SUGAR PLANTATION COLONIALISM WITH BAUXITE COLONIALISM

The administration of the People's National Party (PNP) that took control of the economy on March 2, 1972, had won the election that same year with thirty-seven of the fifty-three seats in Parliament. Although its election campaign platform had promoted a strongly reformist agenda, inclusive of a commitment to providing more opportunities for Black Jamaicans, along with improvements in social services, the party had not outlined a formal agenda. For the first two years of his tenure as prime minister, Michael Manley persisted with the prevailing economic strategies of private sector–led development which had, since the 1940s, enjoyed bi-partisan support. It was two years into the electoral cycle, in 1974, when Manley responded suddenly to the storm clouds by declaring 'democratic socialism,' heralding a period when state intervention was to be taken to unprecedented levels.

Unsettling major new developments were already occurring in the economy. Production in the two main export sectors, bauxite and agriculture sectors, had declined. Major investments in the bauxite/alumina industry had ended because of a decision by the North American companies to shift their investments to Australia, Guinea, and Brazil as part of a strategic move to diversify their supply base and be less dependent on Jamaica. The original bauxite contract negotiated in 1950 by the colonial government carried an important condition that during the tenure of the agreement, no law would be introduced to change the fundamental terms.

Besides bauxite mining and drying and alumina refining, the companies had made major investments in ports and terminal facilities, mining roads and railway operations, and agricultural operations, mainly dairy and tenant farming. With the subsequent expansion of the companies in Jamaica, the US became overly dependent on bauxite and alumina supplies from the island. Strategically, Jamaica's location was advantageous, as the shipping route was short, from Jamaica to the Gulf Port area where the American companies had their alumina refinery operations involving less than two to three days' sailing time. The US government had supported the expansion in Jamaica, providing subsidies from which all the companies benefited. Reynolds, for example, received US$8.5 million, and Alcan, as part of the Marshall Plan loans fund, received US$5 million. The expansion of the bauxite mining and alumina refining by the companies in Jamaica replaced British sugar plantation colonialism with North American bauxite colonialism. Jamaica's trade relations after the 1950s also shifted from the UK to North America. Between Alcan and Alcoa, their annual gross revenues of over US$5.7 billion was greater than Jamaica's GDP.[1] The companies' White expatriate senior managers were joined by the ruling twenty-one major Jamaican families, mostly creole Whites, Jews, Chinese, Syrians, and coloureds, to rule Jamaica between the 1950s and 1960s, with a new brand of colonialism. For example, Alcan practised a form of racial segregation in its housing arrangement at the Ewarton works, where the houses were separated into three distinct areas: Hayfield Housing Estate for the White expatiate managers and engineers; Pleasant Farm Housing Estate for the mostly coloured administrative staff and Jamaican engineers; and Orangefield for the hourly paid operatives, mostly Black Jamaicans. In Mandeville, the Alcan Ingleside housing enclave was the preserve of the senior expatriate managers. In the Mandeville Head Office, the clerical staff was predominantly coloured. It was pressure from the Hugh Shearer government in the 1960s that led Alcan to change its policy to recruit Black Jamaicans for managerial positions in the company and which eventually resulted in Dr Keith Panton becoming president and managing director of Alcan Jamaica in the 1980s. I was recruited in England in 1968 as part of the drive to increase the number of Black graduates in the company.

An important factor in Jamaica's economic structure in the period 1969–74 was the relatively high share of international trade in goods and services as a percentage of GDP, being 80.3 per cent in 1969, declining to 70 per cent in 1970, but increasing to 80.8 per cent in 1974. In the entire period, imports as a percentage of GDP exceeded exports as a percentage of GDP, varying between 4.2 per cent and 9.5 per cent, reflecting an import dependent economy. International trade was also concentrated in a few markets: US, Canada, and the UK, with minimal inter-Caribbean trade varying from 72.0 per cent in 1969 to 53.1 per cent in 1974. There was excessive dependency on these three international markets for the key products: bauxite/alumina, tourism, and sugar and bananas.[2]

An interesting feature of the bauxite industry was that, like sugar, it was in the rural areas and, as the companies' labour rate was several times higher than that of rural agricultural wage earners, a rural-based *nouveau riche* class was established around Mandeville, Ocho Rios, and Ewarton/Linstead. By the 1960s, the industry had generated less than six thousand new permanent jobs, mostly unionised (less than 0.6 per cent of the labour force). In the 1950 bauxite agreement with the government of Jamaica, the bauxite companies only paid US$0.4 per ton of bauxite mined compared to Suriname, where it was US$2.04 per ton. This was subsequently increased over the years with a tax of US$1.85 per ton. This rate remained in force until it was renegotiated by the Michael Manley government in 1974 and increased to US$2.71 per ton. The taxation had been based on a price of US$7.50 per ton of bauxite, while the companies showed a value on US$15 per ton of bauxite to US custom in their books. The Jamaican tax and royalty take was minuscule compared to the overall cost of aluminium and weighed heavily in favour of the companies. There was no easy way to determine the value of bauxite, as it was not a commodity traded in the international market and the Jamaican government was left to take a value literally offered by the companies in assessing the tax take.

The 1973 oil price increase resulted in a quadrupling of Jamaica's oil bill from US$50 million to US$200 million. In order to finance the foreign exchange gap and counter the deflationary impact, the government borrowed from transnational commercial banks, which were the primary means of recycling the so called Petro-dollars. The result was a further deterioration of the economy. Manley then took a series of steps to gain control of the bauxite industry on the domestic front and unexpectedly declared democratic socialism as the political path for Jamaica, reflecting a more leftist socialist path of economic policymaking. As part of the new industry policies, the government in 1974 notified the bauxite companies of its intention to renegotiate the existing agreement. After several months of lengthy negotiations, no agreement was reached and, as a result, Manley announced the government's intention to introduce a bauxite levy on all bauxite, either exported or processed into alumina. This was regarded by the companies as abrogation of the existing agreement by Jamaica. The new rate was set at 7 per cent of the selling price of aluminium ingot, instead of the previous method of computing the tax based on an artificial profit presented by the companies. As a result, the tax rate increased by 480 per cent between 1972 and 1985, from US$2.50 to US$14.51 per ton.

The bauxite companies had also come to own vast tracts of land, amounting to approximately one hundred and forty-two thousand acres of prime Jamaican agricultural properties, alongside a land-starved rural small-holder group. As part of the new measures, the government acquired all the company's land at book value and returned to them the land which was needed for their bauxite operation based on a long-term lease. The government also acquired 51 per cent (majority) interest in the American bauxite mining and drying operating companies and 6 per cent to 7 per cent of the equity in the alumina refining companies. The alumina companies could retain equity majority and manage control of the alumina refining business, control of the technology and control of access to the market. In addition, Manley created the International Bauxite Association (IBA) in 1974, a producers' cartel similar to OPEC, to provide a common front on trade matters with the transnational aluminium companies.[3] The government also established the Jamaica Bauxite Institute (JBI) as a professional entity to manage its interest in the industry.

It was not so much that the increase in the Jamaican companies' operating costs impacted significantly on the costs of the aluminium industry, as the companies could absorb this cost with no real negative impact on their profits. What irked the American managers was the fact that a small, Black Caribbean country could dictate the economic terms under which they were now required to operate. The government's decisions concerning the bauxite companies' compensation to Jamaica brought the country into sharp conflict with the American bauxite companies and the Nixon administration. The result was that introducing the new policy in the mining sector culminated in the cut-back of the companies' operations in Jamaica, followed by a shift of their global industry investments to other countries in the 1970s and 1980s. The result was a long-term decline in Jamaica's share of global bauxite output, as it went from being the top producer in the world to a diminished position. As a result, the Jamaican economy went into a downward slide as international financial reserves dwindled.

Manley was not only seeking more control over the Jamaican natural resource, but he was also at the forefront in promoting the New International Economic Order (NIEO), which argued for more favourable economic conditions for developing economies in global economic affairs.[4] Jamaica was among the leading countries, along with Cuba, pushing for this 'third path' development strategy, which sought to end the dominance of advanced Western capitalist countries. The International Bauxite Association (IBA) headquarters was established in Jamaica on July 28, 1975. Simultaneously, Manley firmly entrenched himself with the group of non-aligned, independent Third World countries.[5] His relationship with Cuba's Fidel Castro, when the US was trying to isolate Cuba, did not go down well in Washington. As a result, Jamaica suffered harsh economic consequences from the Nixon American administration.[6] These changes in the early 1970s came at an inconvenient time for Jamaica, as they coincided with a global recession. Because the operations of the bauxite companies in Jamaica were geared to US Gulf Port plants, the companies were confident that Jamaica could not find alternative sources for bauxite investment. Fortunately, aluminium prices recovered from US$0.25 cent per pound in 1973 to US$0.54 in 1977, a major boost to the economy and to Jamaica's tax intake from the industry.

Percival J. Patterson, a leading member of the PNP in the 1970s, explained that the PNP administration was intent on wresting Jamaica from a repressive system to ensure that the country's economy would not return to total dependence on the capitalist system. Part of reducing dependence on the global capitalist system was to diversify international trading patterns and arrangements. This was to be accomplished by negotiations with multinational corporations and developed countries, such as the European Union and to diversify trade by developing economic relations with socialist countries.

Diplomatic relations between the Soviet Union (USSR) and Jamaica were established on March 12, 1975.[7]

A major achievement was the trading of alumina with the Soviet Union, with payments in US dollars, rather than the rouble, which was not an internationally convertible currency. Part of the deal also was to spend 25 per cent of the proceeds on imported goods from the Soviet Union, including Russian-made Lada motor vehicles through bartering. Ironically, a lucrative deal was negotiated in the 1980s for the sale of bauxite to the Soviet Union by a JLP government not committed to trading with socialist countries. Later UC Rusal invested in the ownership of the bauxite-alumina industry in Jamaica.[8]

The US Nixon Administration was apoplectic of the strong relations Manley had developed with Fidel Castro of Cuba. In December 1975, Henry Kissinger, the powerful US secretary of state holding the position of national security advisor and foreign secretary at the same time, visited Jamaica and invited Manley to a private meeting at a hotel in Ocho Rios,[9] at which he issued an ultimatum to Manley to discontinue his friendly relations with Castro and his espousal of the non-aligned path that Castro was promoting. Manley flatly refused.

Under Manley's democratic socialism, the government attempted to implement some ideas of the Socialist and Plantation Schools; foreign investors were not seen as part of the new economic growth agenda. However, the rising oil prices in 1973 decreased export earnings and the declining economic growth left the economy with an increasing debt burden and social discord. Implementation of the Dependency School economics in Jamaica experienced a short life and was largely abandoned after 1980.

Between 1974 and 1980, Jamaica experienced continuous negative GDP growth, despite the positive cultural and political developments in favour of increasing political and economic power of the Black Jamaican majority. Real Gross Domestic Product (at 1974 constant prices), which was at J$1.720.8 billion in 1980, was 18 per cent below the peak of 1973. Investments declined from 22 per cent to 13 per cent of GDP, while public expenditure and consumption escalated. The manufacturing sector's output fell by 31 per cent. Unemployment over the period 1977–79 ran at 22–24 per cent and peaked at 26.9 per cent by October 1980. Inflation rose from 11.5 per cent in 1977, to 35 per cent in 1978, before falling back to 28.8 per cent in 1979.[10]

By 1980, the budget deficit had expanded to US$1,209 million, or 46 per cent of GDP and, at the same time, the net international reserves moved from a surplus of US$37 million in 1973 to a deficit of US$532 million by 1980. The impact of the PNP administration's re-distributionist policies, sharply rising oil prices and depressed prices in commodity markets, mounting debt service, capital flight, increased crime, and a highly unstable political climate combined to depress the economic prospects by 1980. There was also resistance from various quarters to the cooperatives, community enterprises, and land lease policies that had been introduced as part of the socialist thrust. These initiatives proved to be too overwhelming for rural, agriculture-based Jamaicans, whose understanding of land ownership was deeply rooted in the concepts of private property, freedom, and independence. Together, these factors led to sharp divisions in the society and widespread migration of professionals, managers, and skilled workers to North America. Even within the PNP party itself, there were internal splits. Some of the socialist policies of self-reliance, community councils, sugar cooperatives, worker participation, land lease, voluntary price inspections, and economic ties with Cuba were strongly resisted by the middle class.[11]

In the 1960s, migration primarily consisted of unskilled workers and farm laborers from the rural parishes. However, in the 1970s, the trend shifted, and the migration of workers increasingly included individuals with technical skills and at least a secondary education. This migration trend of Jamaica's skilled workforce has never been reversed. Prime Minister Manley's angry response, urging migrating Jamaicans to take one of the five daily flights to Miami, only exacerbated the situation, and many individuals heeded his suggestion.

THE ECONOMIC PERFORMANCE OF THE ECONOMY DURING THE 1970S

Table 6.1 shows the economic growth rate over the period 1971–80. The economy grew at 4.1 per cent in 1971, 7.9 per cent in 1972, and 2.8 per cent in 1973. It was in 1974 that the decline set in, following the announcement of democratic socialism. The period up to 1980, except for 1978, was a period of negative annual growth each year. In 1980, the economy had fallen by minus 5.7 per cent. The period 1974–80 was undoubtably the worst ever modern-day performance of the Jamaican economy.

Table 6.1: Annual GDP Rate of Growth, 1971–80

Year	Growth %	Year	Growth %
1971	4.4	1976	-6.3
1972	7.9	1977	-2.4
1973	2.8	1978	0.7
1974	-5.4	1979	-1.8
1975	-1.2	1980	-5.7

Source: Damien King, *The Evolution of Structural Adjustment and Stabilization Policy in Jamaica* (Geneva: United Nations/Economic Commission, 2000).

Table 6.2 shows the structural changes in the economy over the period 1970–79.

Table 6.2: Gross Domestic Product by Sector of Origin, Constant (1974) Prices, 1970–79

SECTOR	1970	1971	1972	1973	1974	1975	1976	1977	1978	1979
Primary Sector	7.1	7.8	7.2	6.5	6.5	7.3	7.3	8.3	9.0	8.2
Agriculture/ Forestry/Fishing	7.1	7.8	7.2	6.5	6.5	7.3	7.3	8.3	9.0	8.2
Secondary Sector	38.8	38.7	37.6	37.0	37.0	36.6	36.6	33.3	32.7	32.2
Mining and Refining	7.1	7.3	7.2	8.1	8.1	7.3	7.3	7.5	7.6	7.6
Manufacturing	17.6	17.5	17.9	17.8	17.8	18.4	18.4	17.8	16.9	16.3
Electricity	0.8	0.9	0.9	1.0	1.0	1.1	1.1	1.2	1.2	1.2
Construction	13.3	12.9	11.5	10.0	10.0	9.8	9.8	6.8	7.0	7.1
Tertiary Sector	54.1	53.5	55.2	56.5	56.5	56.2	56.2	58.5	58.3	59.6
Commerce	21.2	21.1	22.6	21.5	21.5	19.3	19.3	15.8	15.5	15.1
Transportation Communication	5.5	5.7	5.5	5.5	5.5	6.7	6.7	6.5	6.6	6.7
Financial Services	11.3	10.7	10.5	10.8	10.8	11.2	11.2	12.7	12.4	13.0
Government Services	9.1	8.9	9.3	11.2	11.2	12.3	12.3	16.7	17.4	18.6
Other Services	6.9	7.0	7.3	7.5	7.5	6.7	6.7	6.7	6.4	6.1
GDP	100	100	100	100	100	100	100	100	100	100

Source: Cezley Sampson, 'Structural Adjustment, Privatisation, Trade deregulation: The Jamaican Experience,' in *Competing Globally: Challenges and Opportunities*, ed. S. Neelamegham (New Delhi: Allied Publishers, 1994.)

Public administration's portion of GDP sharply increased; the agriculture sector's share remained relatively constant, while the distributive trade declined, and the financial services expanded. The public sector doubled its share of GDP from 9.1 per cent in 1972, the year the new administration came to power, to 18.6 per cent in 1979. The overall public sector deficit equalled 16 per cent of GDP, and the external account deficit equalled 14 per cent of GDP.

The most notable structural change in the 1970s was the swift expansion of the government sector. In the five years following October 1972, the number of individuals employed in the public sector increased by 66 per cent, while real non-debt service expenditure of the government witnessed an 88 per cent increase.[12]

The period from 1972 to 1980 marked significant growth in Jamaica's services sector, primarily driven by the expansion of financial services, tourism, telecommunications (including IT), and transportation. Tourism emerged as the dominant economic activity during this period, surpassing agriculture and mining in its importance. Jamaica's economic growth from 1973 to 1980 compared unfavourably with developing countries where the GDP advanced by 80 per cent over the period.[13]

The PNP's administration of the economy in the 1970s should ideally be examined over two distinct periods: 1971–76, the first five-year term when the emphasis was on redistributionist economic and social policies, and 1976–80, the second term which was heavily influenced by attempts of the IMF, World Bank and USAID to implement the IMF's economic stabilisation and the World Bank's economic structural adjustment policies. With this change in economic policy, direct intervention by the state took a sharp turn. Richard Bernal and Winsome Leslie report Manley's statement that 'In the economic sphere, socialism requires social ownership and/or control of the means of production, distribution, and exchange, which must begin with a dominant public sector which owns and/or controls the commanding heights of the economy.'[14]

This signalled a new position in Jamaica's economic management and involved a wide range of trade and fiscal policy measures. These included prices and import controls, restrictions on the operation of the financial market, significant increases in the marginal tax rates, and expansion of public spending on social services. Redistributionist policies were implemented in various ways during this period. First, wages and income of the lowest income group were raised, and minimum wages were established. Generous wage increases were introduced in both the public and private sectors. A special employment programme, often referred to as the 'crash programme,' was initiated. Price controls and rent restrictions were implemented, and subsidies were provided on the prices of essential food items. Land redistribution efforts were undertaken, and public expenditure was expanded in areas such as education, health, and agriculture. Alongside these measures, there was a focus on raising the 'social wage' through various initiatives. An intensive literacy programme was implemented to improve literacy rates. Worker cooperatives were established, providing opportunities for collective ownership and participation. Skills training programmes were introduced to enhance the workforce's capabilities. Community health programmes were developed to improve access to healthcare services. The National Youth Service was created to engage young people in community development activities. Additionally, free secondary education and subsidised university education were provided to increase access to higher education opportunities.

One of the significant developments during the 1970s was the implementation of exchange controls, which became increasingly stringent after 1974. These controls included restrictions on Jamaicans traveling abroad, as they were not allowed to carry more than US$50 with them on overseas trips. Foreign capital was not encouraged under the guise of self-sufficiency; stringent licensing requirement was introduced for the importation of most items and a high tariff regime became the order of the day, especially on luxury goods. Some of these developments had the unintended consequence of restricting international trade and deterring foreign direct investment, thereby impacting the economy. These effects were an inevitable repercussion of the political path pursued by Prime Minister Manley, who believed it was in the best interest of Jamaica's development.

The budget deficit, which stood at 8.6 per cent in 1965, significantly increased to 19 per cent of GDP by 1973. The ratio of government spending as a percentage of GDP, which was 15 per cent in the 1960s, rose to 35 per cent in the latter part of the 1970s and reached 42 per cent in 1978. The contribution of the public sector and public enterprises to the generation of GDP also saw a notable rise, increasing from 13 per cent in 1972 to 25 per cent in 1976.The public sector expanded as the government tried to use public enterprise activities to counteract declining private sector initiatives. On the capital account of the balance of payments, there was a significant decrease in foreign direct investments (FDI) following the completion of the major expansion program by the bauxite companies in 1972. As a result, the usual current account deficit could no longer be offset by inflows of FDI, exacerbating the impact of the oil price increase and import price inflation between 1973 and 1974.

In response, the government sought to replace foreign borrowing with inflows of foreign direct investment (FDI), much of which came in the form of syndicated Eurodollar loans. As a consequence, this type of debt grew significantly, accounting for 61 per cent of the total external debt by the end of 1975, compared to 17 per cent at the end of 1971. The exchange rate gradually became uncompetitive, and real investment experienced negative growth for most of the period. The macro-economic environment imposed significant disincentives for the private sector, particularly foreign investors, to enter the productive and export sectors.

By 1977, the oil bill constituted 30 per cent of the value of imports. Domestically, a lack of confidence and confrontational conflicts emerged between the government led by Manley and the private sector, spearheaded by the Private Sector Organisation of Jamaica, which represented private capital. Omar Davies noted that the government's utilisation of the fiscal budget to tackle socio-economic issues may have been an inappropriate policy response. Measures such as import restrictions, foreign exchange rationing, and price controls were criticized as inward-looking and protectionist in nature.[15] The only sector that seemed to benefit from this policy was the domestic agriculture sector. However, the overall result was a deterioration in the balance of payment situation.

The period following 1976 was one of the most challenging and traumatic for Jamaica in terms of economic performance. Prime Minister Manley, who had initially been elected on a non-IMF platform in 1976, was ultimately compelled to sign Jamaica's first IMF policy loan agreement in 1977 because of the absence of a viable alternative. At one point in 1977, the country's reserves at the Bank of Jamaica dwindled to only US$30 million, a sharp decline from US$120 million in 1975. Despite these difficulties and the negative economic growth, the People's National Party (PNP) administration secured a significant victory in the 1976 general elections, largely based on the expectation of addressing economic and social inequalities within Jamaican society.

The government aimed to reduce reliance on foreign investments and transnational corporations by expanding state ownership in various sectors. This involved compensating the owners of key utilities such as electricity, telephone, and urban transportation. Additionally, the state acquired ownership in certain hotels, the cement company, and several industrial enterprises. Over time, Jamaica transitioned from having only a few major state-owned enterprises (such as railways, posts, and water) before 1960 to the state owning nearly all major infrastructural enterprises in the country by 1975. During this period, the state expanded its role as a significant participant in the productive sector of the economy, including the distributive sector. The government completed the acquisition of major entities such as the British-owned Barclays Bank DCO, several sugar factories, and acquired equity interests in bauxite operations. These endeavours were often financed through deficit spending and the bauxite levy. As a result, limited resources from the bauxite levy remained available for major public capital investment projects.

The World Bank believed that, until 1970, the government in Jamaica had been promoting monopolies rather than fostering competitive enterprises. Although the industrial incentive schemes were on par with international standards, they had a trade-restrictive effect. Combined with restrictive exchange rate policies, they served as significant disincentives for investment. The system primarily favoured protected domestic market-oriented import substitution industries, leading to a situation where industries found it more profitable to produce inefficiently and deliver substandard goods for the domestic market rather than efficiently catering to both domestic and export markets. The World Bank concluded that the industrialisation policy pursued during the 1950s and 1960s had failed and should have been discontinued.

A series of controls which had been introduced to stem capital outflow failed, resulting in creating a parallel foreign exchange market and expansion of the informal economy. In this period, the society was marked by high levels of violence, both of a political and criminal nature. The Washington Consensus group[16] later came to push for free market policies, opening and liberalisation of international trade, smaller government with less involvement in the productive sector, and less indebtedness support,[17] as we shall see in the following chapter. The need for support from the IMF in 1977 grew out of the decline in the country's economy and foreign exchange reserves. The combination of factors such as the significant increase in oil prices in 1973, the downturn in the bauxite sector, capital flight, reduced inflows from tourism, and the global economic recession created substantial pressures on Jamaica's balance of payments. These challenges were further compounded by the experimental fiscal policies implemented by the PNP administration. These circumstances left limited room for the administration to manoeuvre and address the mounting issues within the economy. Fiscal and balance of payments constraints had made the government's social welfare policies almost impossible to maintain, especially since little had been done to boost and deliver the growth of exports in this highly import-dependent country. To maintain its previous spending levels, the government responded with rapid increases in borrowing from the Central Bank, triggering an inflation spiral. Higher taxes, new controls on wages, prices, and imports and larger foreign borrowing in the late 1970s did nothing to stem the erosion of external reserves.

The government was forced to enter into two IMF Extended Fund Facilities (EFF) agreements; the first in June 1977, which was terminated in December 1977 after only one drawdown and the Three-year Standby agreement, signed in May 1978, which ended in December 1979 after less than half of the amount approved had been disbursed.

The objectives of the IMF loan agreements were to address the balance of payment constraints and facilitate the revival of economic growth. The key measures included raising taxes, increasing prices in public enterprises, reducing investments in public enterprises, restraining wages in the public sector, effectively reducing the size of the public sector and public enterprises, enhancing export competitiveness, and providing incentives for private sector investments. Additionally, the IMF agreed to provide supportive loans if the government implemented significant currency devaluation, implemented a wage freeze, and practised fiscal prudence. These measures were aimed at stabilising the economy and promoting economic recovery under the guidance and support of the IMF.

From the inception, IMF monetarist policies were in sharp contrast to the state interventionist policies of successive Jamaican administrations (both PNP and JLP). The result was that, at times, the relationship between the IMF and Jamaican administrations was strained. The new IMF policies also heightened political and social instability within the country.

In the 1978 IMF agreement, it was mandated that the Jamaican currency undergo further devaluation, with a 13.6 per cent devaluation for the basic rate and a 5.2 per cent devaluation for a special rate. Jamaica had been operating a parallel rate of exchange control system, which was unified as a result of this development. A crawling-peg system was then implemented, which involved regular devaluations over the following year. Additionally, new taxes were imposed on consumer goods, increased charges for government services were introduced, and wage and price controls were implemented.

Jamaica's compliance with the IMF's requirements led to an increase in the limit of the Extended Fund Facility (EFF) in June 1979. This increase aimed to cover the costs of recovering from a severe flood that had affected the island and to offset the significant increase in oil prices that had occurred during 1979.

However, relations between the IMF and the Manley administration further deteriorated, leading to the government breaking off negotiations with the IMF in 1979. The IMF took the stance that the People's National Party (PNP) administration was never fully convinced of the necessity of these policies and never implemented them wholeheartedly. Prime Minister Manley, in rejecting the IMF's recommendations, cited the harsh measures demanded by its conditionalities as a reason for his stance.

The hostile reaction by the local capitalist and landed elite to Marxist leanings of factions of the PNP, perceived by them to be the blanket philosophy of the party, led to the PNP falling into disfavour; this was exacerbated by the rising crime rate.[18] For the first time since the end of the Second World War, Jamaica and the trade unions, on both sides of the political spectrum, could not achieve wage increases in line with, or in excess of inflation. In fact, during the 1970s, Manley had to face a considerable number of strikes, and this was despite his background as a labour leader and his pro-working class political ideology. Jamaica, however, entered the decade of the eighties with accelerating inflation, falling output, a severe foreign exchange crisis, and political and social tension.

Social Conditions During the Period of Democratic Socialism During the 1970s

Expenditure on health and education increased considerably during the 1970s, especially in the allocations for secondary and university education. Enrolment in secondary and tertiary education increased from 63 per cent to 74 per cent, resulting in improvements in the levels of literacy. Life expectancy at birth increased from 70.8 per cent to 75.0 per cent, while infant mortality declined.[19] In 1977, there were thirty hospitals with some sixty-seven hundred employees, providing hospital beds amounting to 7,547, of which on average 82 per cent were regularly occupied. The government focused on primary health care and public health, increasing the number of health centres and rural maternity centres. The increases in social expenditure after 1974 were critical elements in Manley's reformist and redistributionist policies. Jamaica had entered the period of the 1970s with a skewed distribution of income towards the elite; it ended in the 1980s with a more equitable distribution in consumption.[20] The PNP continued with the JLP's policies, of rent control, the National Insurance Scheme which Manley had criticised while in Opposition, and promotion of the annual Festival and Jamaican culture.

Other social programmes that were introduced included maternity leave with pay, equal pay for women, the lowering of the voting age to eighteen, the Special Employment Programme (crash programme), family court, home guard, the Suppression of Crime Act and Gun Court, an increase in capital gains and inheritance tax, a self-supporting farmers' development programme, food subsidies, youth training and the National Youth Service, and a public housing programme.

The economic crisis and social unrest were the major reasons for the defeat of the PNP at the 1980 general elections. The Jamaican middle class had responded negatively to tighter economic control, worker participation, community enterprises, and nationalisation.[21]

Despite the poor economic performance in the 1970s, it is important not to overlook the significant and lasting achievements that were made. These include the implementation of a new bauxite policy, land reform initiatives, the establishment of the National Housing Trust, which has had a significant impact on working-class housing, the enactment of labour legislation, and efforts towards social inclusion.

Box 6.1 provides a more detailed catalogue of PNP policies introduced between October 1972 and February 1980. The more notable policies introduced in this period were the bauxite production levy, worker cooperatives, national minimum wage, and free education services.

Box 6.1: Summary of the Economic Policies Pursued by the PNP, 1972–80

1. Set up cooperatives in agriculture and community enterprises, and established the land lease programme;
2. Established state-owned food farms, and promoted food self-sufficiency;
3. Promoted worker participation across industries;
4. Promoted New International Economic Order (NIEO) and developed close ties with several socialist countries, including Cuba, Angola, and Tanzania;
5. Promoted foreign policies which the US perceived to be hostile towards global interests and promoted anti- imperialist policies;
6. Established mechanism to control basic food items established Jamaica Nutrition Holdings in 1973, restricted to handling the nutrition programmes such as school lunch, including assuming responsibility for importing basic food: wheat, corn, soy, rice, and salt fish, and expanded into the State Trading Corporation in 1977 to take over importation and distribution of pharmaceutical items, basic foods and even motor vehicles, much to the opposition of Kingston merchants;
7. Imposed production levy on bauxite and alumina companies and increased major equity holding to 51 per cent in all bauxite companies, and 6–7 per cent of the companies involved in both bauxite mining and alumina refining (Alcan and Alcoa) – seen as nationalisation by the American companies; repatriation of bauxite lands; establishment of the Jamaican Bauxite Institute; formation of an international bauxite industry cartel –The International Bauxite Association (IBA), created the Capital Development Fund (CDF) to receive the proceeds from the bauxite levy;
8. Introduced tight foreign exchange controls at Bank of Jamaica;
9. Established National Housing Trust and national levy to fund the Trust to finance housing development for low and middle-income Jamaicans;
10. Established national wage guidelines;
11. Expanded national literacy drive; National Literacy Board replaced by the Statutory Board for Adult Education (JAMAL);
12. Announced free education in Parliament in 1973;
13. Completed nationalisation of urban bus company, Jamaica Omnibus Service Limited, Jamaica Telephone Company, and Jamaica Public Service Company (electricity) and NCB.

At the international level, the promotion of the New International Economic Order (NIEO) was pursued, and close relationships were developed with several socialist countries, including Cuba, Angola, and Tanzania. The JLP had initiated the nationalisation of the electricity, urban transport, Jamaica Telephone Company, and the National Commercial Bank Limited. The Manley administration then completed the process.

Socialism and Its Influence on the Economic Policies of the 1970s

Besides the Plantation School, the PNP in the 1970s was influenced by the economic ideas of Karl Marx, who emphasised the struggle between the capitalist class and working class,[22] and presented an analytical approach to the class struggle (historical and present), the conflict of capitalism and the capitalist mode of production, rather than a prediction, or a blueprint for communism. For Marx, the relationship between capitalism and the working class was intrinsically exploitative, inevitably leading to class conflicts and the eventual downfall of capitalism.

The history of Marxist influence in Jamaica and the Caribbean dates back to the 1920s when a group of Caribbean intellectuals, George Padmore, Claude McKay, and C.L.R. James was exposed to Marxist ideology.[23] However, it was in the 1960s that Marxism generated substantial interest in the region, particularly in Cuba. In effect, the Cuban economy became fully socialist.[24]

In the period between 1974 and 1989, when the Manley administration showed affinity towards Marxism, Manley himself never embraced revolution as a means of reform. In fact, he found himself in a situation similar to Harold Wilson in 1977 when the British Labour administration had to seek financial assistance from the IMF to stabilise the pound. Within his party, Wilson faced divisions, with one faction led by Anthony Wedgewood Benn, a prominent 'hard leftist' who opposed any agreement with the IMF, and the moderates led by James Callaghan, the finance minister, and Dennis Healey. Manley faced a similar division within his own party, with a faction representing the hard left, advocating for revolutionary measures. This group was led by Dr D.K. Duncan, the minister of mobilisation, and included Anthony Spaulding. On the other hand, there were ministers like David Coore, the minister of housing, and P.J. Patterson, who still adhered to Fabian socialism and advocated for a more gradualist approach to implementing changes. They believed that changes should be evolutionary and policies should demonstrate tangible benefits for a broad cross-section of the Jamaican population.

JLP RETURNED TO POWER IN 1980, EMBRACING SUPPLY-SIDE ECONOMICS

Edward Seaga came to power in 1980 with fifty-one seats of sixty seats in Parliament, having preached free market economy during the elections. The JLP on gaining power in 1980 initially returned to a new variant of the model of dependent capitalism that had been pursued in the 1950s and 1960s. By 1983, it was clear that an attempt to resurrect dependent development would not work. The Jamaican economy faced many challenges entering the 1980s: rising prices for oil and imported products; low export prices; a declining economy and, most importantly, an increasing debt burden.[25] During this period, not only Jamaica and the Caribbean but also several Latin American countries were grappling with economic crises and the possibility of debt default. In response, the IMF and the World Bank devised a set of stringent policies known as Structural Adjustment Programs (SAP). These programmes were designed to accompany new loans aimed at avoiding default by imposing strict conditions, including the reduction of public expenditure and the generation of additional revenues to meet debt obligations. The underlying economic principles guiding these policies came to be known as supply-side economics, which involved measures such as wage controls and currency devaluation to lower export prices in the international market. Theoretically, this was expected to increase demand for exports and stimulate domestic production. The prescriptions not only called for scaling down the size of the government through reduction in the numbers employed in the public sector, but it also required increased user fees for the delivery of public services, especially the tariff of public enterprises, removal of subsidies and raising.[26]

The supply-side economics presented by the IMF and the World Bank to Jamaica in the 1980s, along with the accompanying austerity measures, drew inspiration from the ideas of Milton Friedman and the Chicago School of economics. These policies can also be seen as a restatement of the principles advocated by Friedrich von Hayek and the Austrian School of economists. In the 1930s, there was a bitter clash between Keynes and Hayek. Hayek criticised Keynes's belief in monetary policies that drive down interest rate through increased monetary supply and argued that this would only increase inflation and economic malinvestment.[27] Hayek and Keynes had opposing poles of thought about making economic policy, with Keynes a vigorous flag bearer of government intervention and Hayek a champion of laissez faire and free market economics.

The group consisting of the World Bank, IMF, USAID, and entities like the American Heritage Foundation, collectively became known as The Washington Consensus. This term was used to describe their shared approach, which went beyond the goal of maintaining global economic stability through strict fiscal policies. The Washington Consensus also encompassed conditionalities that promoted laissez-faire economics, including measures such as privatisation, deregulation, and liberalisation.[28] The policies completely ignored the development of domestic agriculture, reversing some programmes Manley had created out of the ideas of the Plantation/Dependency School. The initial effects of the measures were to aggravate the decline which had affected the agricultural sector after 1965.

Margaret Thatcher in the UK and Ronald Reagan in the US emerged as influential political figures in the 1980s, championing the principles of free-market ideology and neoliberal supply-side economics. Reagan's four-pronged economic policy aimed to combat inflation and stimulate economic growth. It involved reducing government spending on domestic programmes, lowering taxes for individuals, businesses, and investments, easing regulatory burdens on businesses, and implementing tighter control over the money supply. The IMF's macro-economic policies shared many similarities with Reagan's supply-side economics, although they had a short-term focus on stabilisation and structural adjustments. The IMF's policies primarily aimed at curb inflation and realign exchange rates.

The World Bank claimed that the Jamaican economy had been stifled by the inefficiencies of protectionism implemented during the period of influence by Arthur Lewis and the Plantation School. As a consequence, domestic agriculture in the Caribbean, including Jamaica and the West Indies, faced significant challenges due to the inability to compete with the highly industrialised agricultural sectors of North America and Europe. Jamaica, in particular, relied on American PL480 food subsidies, which were accompanied by a surge of inexpensive food imports from the US flooding the local market. Instead of locally produced milk, Jamaica became reliant on American milk powder. While the reduction of subsidies and trade barriers was intended to promote competition among producers, domestic agriculture in Jamaica found itself in direct competition with the protected agricultural sectors of the US and Europe, which continued to benefit from the very trade barriers and subsidies that the IMF criticised. Unfortunately, the IMF neglected to address the issue of food security in its policies. In fact, the flooding of the Jamaican domestic market by inexpensive and subsidised milk powder was a short-term strategy which decimated the country's milk industry. Domestic milk production fell from 38.8 million litres in 1992 to 14 million litres in 2007, the latter representing only 10 per cent of the milk consumed in Jamaica. Disregard of the milk industry, brought about by subsidised prices, proved to be short term, as soon thereafter, demand for milk on the global market shot up because of increased demand from China, resulting in the doubling of the price of milk powder on the domestic market.[29] The effect of the IMF policies on agriculture was increasing food trade deficit, partly because of low prices from export commodities and increasing food import bill.

Notes

1. Keith Sherry and Robert Girling, 'Jamaica vs the Transnational Battle over the Bauxite Levy,' 2007, https://www.nacia.org.
2. Michael Witter and D. Ramjeesingh, 'An Analysis of the Internal Structure of the Jamaican Economy 1969–1974,' *SES* 35, no. 1 (1986):1–72.
3. Carlton Davis, 'Jamaica in the World of the Aluminium Industry 1974–1988: Bauxite Levy Negotiation,' Vol II (1985) (Volume I Present Situation and Prospect: 1938–1973 and Volume III; The Partnership and Joint Venture Agreement), Kingston, Jamaica Bauxite Institute.
4. Sherry and Girling, 'Jamaica vs the Transnational Battle over the Bauxite Levy.'
5. Richard Bernal, 'The Struggle for the Old International Order: The Caribbean Basin Plan and Jamaica,' Paper prepared for the Conference of Geo-political Change in the Caribbean in the 1980s, Department of Economic, UWI, Mona and Centro de Estudios Económicos y Sociales del Tercer Mundo (CEESTEM), Mexico City, 1982.

6. Damien King, *The Evolution of Structural Adjustment and Stabilization Policy in Jamaica* (Chile: United Nations/Economic Commission for Latin America Santiago, 2000).
7. Richard L. Bernal, *Dragon in the Caribbean: The Global Re-Dimensioning of China: Opportunities and Challenges for the Caribbean* (Kingston: Ian Randle Publishers, 2016).
8. P.J. Patterson, *My Political Journey: Jamaica's Sixth Prime Minister* (Kingston: University of the West Indies Press, 2018).
9. Colin Palmer, *Inward Yearnings – Jamaica's Journey to Nationhood* (Kingston: The University of the West Indies, 2016).
10. Michael Manley, *Jamaica Struggle in the Periphery* (London: Third World Media Limited, 1982).
11. World Bank, *Jamaica Recent Developments and Economic Prospects Report No. 4905-JM*, (Washington, DC: World Bank,1974).
12. Evelyne Huber Stephens and John, D. Stephens, *Democratic Socialism in Jamaica: The Political Movement of Social Transformation in Dependent Capitalism* (London, Macmillan Educational Press, 1986).
13. King, *The Evolution of Structural Adjustment.*
14. N.A. Owen, *A Study of the Private Sector Organisation of Jamaica, Exchange Control Liberalisation in Jamaica* (London: London Economics Limited, 1991).
15. R. Bernal and W. Leslie, 'Privatization in the English-Speaking Caribbean: An Assessment,' *Policy Papers on the Americas*, volume X, study 7, University of Miami, Miami, 1997.
16. Omar Davies, 'An Analysis of the Management of the Jamaican Economy: 1972–1985,' *Social and Economic Studies* 35, no. 1 (1985): 73–109.
17. Washington Consensus: a set of economic policy recommendations for developing countries, and Latin America in particular, that became popular during the 1980s. The term Washington Consensus usually refers to the level of agreement between the International Monetary Fund (IMF), World Bank, and US Department of the Treasury on those policy recommendations.
18. Bernal L. Richard, 'The IMF and Class Struggle in Jamaica, 1977–1980,' *Latin America Perspective* 11, no. 3 (1984): 53–82.
19. Carl Stone, *Democracy and Socialism in Jamaica 1962–1979* (Kingston: The University of the West Indies, 1981).
20. Kari Polanyi Levitt, 'The Origins and Consequences of Jamaica's Debt Crisis 1870–1990,' Consortium Graduate School of Social Sciences, UWI, Mona, 1991.
21. James Riley, 'Poverty and Life Expectancy: The Jamaican Paradox,' (Cambridge: Cambridge University Press, 2005).
22. Owen, *A Study of the Private Sector Organisation of Jamaica.*
23. Karl Marx, *'Das Kapital' – 'A Critical Analysis of Capitalist Production* (Berlin: Octavo, 1867).

24. Karl Marx and Friedrich Engel, *The Communist Manifesto* (London and Chicago: Pluto Press, 1848).
25. C. L. R. James *Notes on Dialectics, Hegel, Marx, Lenin* (Westport: Lawrence Hill & Company, 1948).
26. Bertram Silverman, *Man and Socialism in Cuba: The Great Debate* (New York: Atheneum, 1973).
27. T. Harker, 'The Caribbean in the Context of the Global Crisis in Development,' in *Suspense: Selected Papers and Proceedings of the First Conference of Caribbean Economists*, ed. George Beckford and Norman Girvan (Kingston: Friedrich Ebert Stiftung in association with the Association of Caribbean Economist, 1989).
28. Dennis J. Gayle, 'Trade Policies and Hemispheric Integration Process,' in *Globalisation and Neoliberalism: The Caribbean Context*, ed. T. Klak (Lanham, MD: Rowman & Littlefield Publishers, 1998).
29. Friedrich Von Hayek, *The Pure Theory of Capital* (Chicago: University of Chicago Press, 1941).
30. Benjamin F. Timms, 'Development Theory and Domestic Agriculture in the Caribbean: Recurring Crisis and Missed Opportunities,' Social Sciences Department, California Polytechnic State University, San Luis Obispo, California, 2008.
31. P. Myers, Jr., '$1 Billion Dairy Rescue Plan – Milk Production at 20-Year Low,' *The Gleaner*, March 7, 2007.

CHAPTER SEVEN

Economic Policymaking Post-1980: Structural Adjustment and the Role of the Multilateral Financial Agencies

HOW JAMAICA'S ECONOMIC POLICIES CAME UNDER THE CONTROL OF THE WASHINGTON CONSENSUS GROUP, 1980–89

Jamaica's recent journey towards economic liberalisation and its endeavour to adopt a market economy strategy must be viewed in light of domestic politics and external international events beyond the country's influence. This progression has unfolded as an evolutionary process, rather than a deliberate outcome of policy decisions, and is closely linked to Jamaica's establishment of a client relationship with the International Monetary Fund (IMF) in 1977, coinciding with the UK's engagement with the IMF, as discussed in the previous chapter.

During the period of 1980–96, the economic management of Jamaica was significantly influenced by four institutions: the World Bank, the Inter-American Development Bank, USAID, and the IMF (commonly referred to as the Washington Consensus). These institutions played a dominant role, essentially relegating the government to the task of implementing various detailed conditionalities imposed through each new programme initiated by the IMF and the structural adjustment loan provided by the World Bank.

The JLP administration led by Edward Seaga, which replaced the Manley's socialist-leaning administration in 1980, was oriented more towards free market economics and, on the face of it, was more in tune with the neoliberal economic thinking of the IMF, the World Bank, and the US administration. Seaga, a Harvard-educated anthropologist, brought his understanding of the importance of the African culture to the political scene. With his deep understanding of Jamaica and his capitalist orientation, it was expected that the new Seaga-led administration could mobilise substantial external resources on concessional terms to revitalise the economy. Seaga, however, offered Jamaica as a client state to the US based on the perceived Cuban threat. Seaga's 1980s economic management of Jamaica can also be viewed over two distinct periods: 1980–85, when few free market economic policies were implemented, and 1985–90 when Seaga was forced to absorb the full IMF medicine of structural adjustment.

Although Seaga espoused support for private enterprise and supply-side economic policy and pledged to ensure private sector initiatives, he was as distrustful of market-oriented economic solutions, in much the same way as socialist Michael Manley was. Government intervention under Seaga in the first five years of the 1980s was directed to bringing foreign direct investments to the competitive sectors of the economy. Shortly after becoming Jamaica's new prime minister, he was invited as the first foreign leader to Washington to meet President Reagan. A strong bond developed between Seaga and Ronald Reagan, who also had just been elected, such that out of the meetings, Reagan appointed one of the US's leading capitalists, David Rockefeller, to head a high-powered foreign investment group to bring foreign capital to Jamaica. It was out of these meetings the Caribbean Basin Initiative (CBI) was developed. Seaga also joined forces with Reagan and Margaret Thatcher, the Conservative prime minister of the UK, in promoting neoliberalism. Seaga was even awarded The Freedom Foundation's American Friendship medal for the stance he had taken.

Seaga's second essential requirement was the institutions to facilitate foreign direct investment. A new entity, Jamaica National Investment Promotion Limited (JNIP), was formed to act as a one-stop shop to spearhead the new drive to lure foreign investors to Jamaica. In 1981, the Export Development Fund was created and the promotional role of the Jamaica National Export Corporation (JNEC) expanded. In 1986, the Jamaica Export Credit Insurance Company was disbanded and replaced by Jamaica Export-Import Bank. Seaga was determined to reverse the Manley socialist bias against exports and the manufacturing industry and sought to focus on third country markets.

Jamaica was the first victim of the third world debt crisis and for the IMF the remedy was structural adjustment during which the country received some six structural adjustment loans from the World Bank up to the end of the 1980s.[1] Of eleven IMF agreements between 1977 and 1996, five were contracted between the Seaga administration and the IMF between 1981 and 1988. There is no doubt the Seaga administration received unprecedented external financing from the multilateral lending agencies and from the US, through USAID. During the early part of his regime, the US government purchased bauxite worth US$120 million for their strategic stockpile, which America need not have taken as part of Reagan's support for Seaga's administration.

The Reagan administration had chosen Jamaica as the country to showcase successful application of supply side free market economics in the Third World and as a model of capitalism for the Caribbean, to counter the Cuban communist model. Part of Reagan's solution was the Caribbean Basin Initiative (CBI), centred on forging direct investment, with a generous aid component, geared to creating a receptive environment for American foreign investors. The CBI should facilitate the development of stable Caribbean Basin economies by providing beneficiary countries with duty-free access to the US market. With Jamaica, the aid was needed to cushion the country until market forces tripped in to generate employment internally.[2] Seaga also believed that, since local private capital had not come to the table in the past, private direct investment was critical. He, however, differed from the Americans, as he saw public investments as indispensable to development, especially for critical infrastructure.[3]

The Caribbean Basin Initiative and CARIBCAN, respectively, provided a one-way free trade with the US and Canada and formed part of the new Caribbean geopolitics. The Seaga government's industrial policies focused on several subsectors, specifically garments and sewn products, food and agro-industry, construction materials, furniture, electronics, and electrical goods, sometimes referred as 'sweat swap' industries. These were areas where the government felt Jamaica with a high level of unemployment possessed comparative advantages as cheap labour and production sharing. World Bank loans were used to build factory space for the Export Free Zones in Kingston, Montego Bay, and Spanish Town. Light manufacturing, especially garments and sewn products, flourished under the 807 programmes, named after the US Tariff Schedule number that allowed these exports preferential access into the US. One of the major benefits of the light manufacturing industries was that they employed mostly women, hence converting large numbers of household domestics into factory workers, with its rigid discipline of mass production lines.

Seaga created a high-profile, high-tech agricultural enterprise, Agro 21 Corporation, which was fully state-owned, headed by an Israeli international businessman ,Eli Tisona. Argo 21 fell directly under the prime minister's control with the objective of bringing high technology development to new agricultural crops for export and to modernise farming methods. Agro 21 corporation expanded floral exports and inland fisheries and embarked on the large-scale Spring Plain high technology winter vegetable project, mainly for export to the US. At the same time, instead of curtailing the Commodity Trading Company, Seaga having previously criticised its role as a sole importer, it was expanded to include a whole range of new items.

Seaga's administration initially bought into the IMF stabilisation loan programmes. Purportedly, these gave some financial breathing space to the administration, reduce the domestic deficit, and create a surplus on the recurrent (primary surplus) account. The arrangement was for the World Bank to support the restructuring of the economy to reduce the external debt through the Structural Adjustment Programme, to improve the capability of the market to increase export earnings through deregulation, removal of price controls, import restrictions, labour rigidities, and other market imperfections.

In March 1981, the government readily received US$40 million from USAID, US$40 million from branches of overseas banks operating in Jamaica, and US$25 million from Venezuela, and opened negotiations with the IMF for support under the Extended Fund Facility.[4] Under the Extended Fund Programme, which was agreed immediately upon taking office, the Seaga government received an initial drawdown of US$40 million under the Compensatory Financing Facility. International commercial banks deferred US$100 million which was due in 1981–82 and 1982–83. The IMF also agreed to provide a further amount of US$698 million, to be disbursed over three years. The World Bank, concurrently, agreed to provide support through three Structural Adjustment Loans (SALs), to be disbursed over the period 1981–85. In addition, the World Bank and the IDB provided a further package of US$450 million, while the total grants from the US government amounted to US$91 million in 1981.[5] World Bank support comprised a Structural Adjustment Loan (SAL 1) for US$76.2 million of February 1982, SAL 11 of US$60.0 million of June 14, 1983, and SAL 111 of US$55 million.

From this US$91 million, some US$10 million was provided to the University of the West Indies, Mona Campus, to create a Harvard University–style graduate business school. At the start, the new Institute of Business which was created was twinned to Penn State University Business School. Some twenty UWI graduates were recruited and sent to US universities to complete, first the master's degree, and then the doctorate in business and to return to UWI to staff the new Institute and the Department of Management Studies. I became executive director of the UWI/USAID Management Education Project and, in 1991, executive director of the Institute of Business and managed most of this programme.

Danielson Anders (1991) notes that Jamaica received some six SALs from the World Bank up to the end of the 1980s.[6] The suite of IMF loans provided to Jamaica over the period 1977–92 is shown in table 7.1 below. The majority was extended between 1980 and 1990.

Table 7.1: IMF Balance of Payment Support for Jamaica, 1977–92

Type of Agreement	Date of Approval	Expiration Date	Amount Approved US$	Amount Drawn US$
EFF *	May 1977		75	
EFF*	June 11,1979	April 13,1981	240	66
EFF	Apr.13,1981	April 12,1984	399	336
Standby	June 22,1984	June 21,1985	62	62
Standby	June 17, 1985	June 16, 1986	111	40
Standby	Mar 02,1987	May 31,1988	66	66
Standby	Sep 19, 1988	Mar 22, 1990	64	32
Standby	Mar 23,1990	May31,1991	63	63
Standby	June 28, 1991	Sep 30,1992	33	33
EFF	Dec 11, 1992	Mar 15,1996	79	63

Note *: The June 11 agreement was cancelled prior to expiration June 10, 1981. The June 11, 1977, loan was suspended to December 1977. Source: Thompson Fontaine, (Undated), 6. Caribbean 'Country Experiences with IMF Stabilisation Programs within the Context of Globalisation,' IMF, Washington, DC.

The first five years of the Seaga administration in the 1980s, as previously stated, saw few market-oriented policies. Initial moves towards trade liberalisation and the granting of 'no funds' licences only fuelled consumer expenditure, as the middle class sought to catch up on luxury goods that they were denied under the PNP's administration of the 1970s.

Domestic investors, instead of channelling funds into export manufacturing, diverted investments into trading and real estate, creating further pressures on the demand for foreign exchange. Although Seaga showed his desire to follow a privatisation path, little privatisation occurred under his watch up to 1985. In fact, when Exxon Corporation exited Jamaica and abandon the sole oil refinery, Seaga felt obliged to purchase the plant, bringing it under state control. Similarly, when Alcoa closed the Halse Hall alumina plant in Clarendon in early 1980s because of a downturn in the demand for aluminium, Seaga again felt obliged to keep the plant going, first by leasing, and then by taking the government's equity stake of 50 per cent.

Jamaica failed the quarterly IMF test in March 1983, and had to seek a waiver, which was reviewed favourably, with no penalties. Harmonisation of the exchange rate was imposed, with the Jamaican dollar depreciating to J$3.15 to US$1.00, a devaluation of 43 per cent. This marked the first major achievement of the IMF objectives with the new administration. Subsequently, the focus shifted towards addressing the public sector deficit, leading the government to implement tax increases of J$138 million in April 1985, followed by an additional J$45 million through the regular budget later that year. Over the years, public sector employment had risen from 67,500 in 1972 to 106,100 in 1983. However, in order to meet the reduction target of 99,800 set by the IMF, the administration was compelled to reduce the workforce. With a depressed domestic market, high interest rates, scarce foreign exchange, and the additional burden of high taxes, the credibility of the touted pro-market administration and as a promoter of private investment was questioned by the Heritage Foundation, the arch-right-wing Washington Think Tank. The relationship of the Seaga administration with the local private sector also came under severe strain and was eventually seriously ruptured. The administration, instead of reducing public expenditure, introduced its own redistribution programmes, expanding the role of the State Trading Corporation and bringing some two hundred thousand indigent people under a US Food Aid Programme.

Furthermore, under the JLP administration, Prime Minister Seaga introduced three micro-enterprise training and loan programmes: HEART, Self-Start Fund, and Solidarity. However, despite these initiatives, Jamaica's GDP growth during the initial five years of the 1980s remained feeble. The significant devaluation of the Jamaican dollar had far-reaching consequences, including reduced government expenditure, increased inflation, declining real wages, diminished purchasing power for consumers, widespread layoffs, and a surge in the country's debt burden. Another IMF loan was granted to the country in June 1984, not only providing much needed balance of payment support but also facilitating the roll-over by the Paris Club* credit of US$135 million, which was due for repayment in 1985. However, once again, the government failed the September 1985 quarterly IMF test. With inflation running at 35 per cent, fuelled by an expansion in credit, the Jamaican dollar continued its downward slide and fell to J$5.00 to US$1.00 by the end of 1985.

Seaga sought to use the World Bank loans to rebuild and expand a selected sector of export manufacturing, capitalising on the duty-free and quota-free conditions of the Caribbean Basin Initiative. In addition, a programme to expand tourism was introduced, along with the high-tech agriculture at Spring Plains. The focus of economic strategy was to grow export, with an emphasis on penetrating the US market and, in this way, encourage the private sector to direct production to hard currency markets. The objective was to shift from the traditional import substitution model of industrialisation-by-invitation that prevailed in the 1960s and 1970s to a much more export-focused approach. Seaga hoped to model his export-led development on the industrialised economies of South East Asia: Singapore, South Korea, and Hong Kong, borrowing heavily from the international institutional financial lenders.

Although relatively small in size, Jamaica's manufacturing sector experienced significant development starting from the 1950s, enabling

* The Paris Club is an informal group of creditor nations whose objective is to find workable solutions to payment problems faced by debtor nations. The Paris Club has twenty-two permanent members, including most of the western European and Scandinavian nations, the US, UK, and Japan. https://www.investopedia.com

the production of a diverse array of goods, including processed foods, garments, chemicals, and electrical equipment. As part of its new policy approach, the government aimed to capitalise on the US 807 and 807A Law, along with the associated incentive programme, which specifically focused on bolstering the textile industry in the US. By leveraging these initiatives, Jamaica sought to derive benefits and opportunities for its manufacturing sector. Specially, the US law pertains to the textile industry and allows fabric to be cut in the US, garments to be assembled in Jamaica and other Latin-American countries, where wages are lower and returned to the US and, instead of paying taxes on the finished product, companies only pay taxes on the added value. Introduced in the mid-1980s, the 807 programme played a pivotal role within the Caribbean Basin Initiative, which aimed to enhance trade between the US and the Caribbean region. Despite its limitations regarding technology transfer, one notable advantage of the programme was its facilitation of extensive employment opportunities for the female labour force. Simultaneously, the government prioritised the Export Industry Encouragement Act (EIEA) over the Industrial Incentive Act (IEA) to support its objectives. Under the EIA, a complex system of quotas and licences was initiated in order to promote substituting production. These included depreciation allowances, duty-free imports of raw material and machinery, tax-free dividends, and certain income tax exemption.[7] Under the IEA, producers selling in the domestic market were eligible to receive certain benefits, whereas producers selling entirely to the extra-regional markets received incentives under the EIEA. The EIFA carried specific criteria.

To facilitate production expansion during the initial five years of the 1980s, approximately one million square feet of new factory space was constructed and operationalised. Additionally, the establishment of the Kingston Free Zone aimed to foster the growth of 807 textile production. Moreover, between 1981 and 1985, there was an increase in the number of eligible firms approved under the Export Industry Encouragement Act (EIEA), compared to the Industrial Incentive Act (EIA) in the period from 1976 to 1980. Specifically, during the 1976–80 period, twenty-seven firms received approval under the EIEA, and thirty-nine under the EIA. However, between 1981 and 1985, fifty-seven firms were approved under the EIEA, whereas only fourteen firms were approved under the EIA.[8]

Seaga on Tax Reform Policies: 1980–90

One of Seaga's early economic policy initiatives was also reform of the tax system. Prior to to 1980, the focus was on indirect taxation as one of the main sources of government revenue. In 1970–71, the indirect component formed 49 per cent of total tax revenue; by 1982, it had increased to 55 per cent, while the direct component fell from 41 per cent to 38 per cent. The tax burden rose from 17.4 per cent of GDP in 1973 to 27.3 per cent in 1981–82, reaching 30 per cent by 1986 making it the highest in Latin America and the Caribbean. Roy Bahl, a Regent Professor of Economics at Georgia State University, shows that in the 1970s Jamaica's taxation levels were 25 per cent above the international average.[9] This burdensome tax level not only discouraged investment, it badly distorted relative prices, and this was compounded by a complex and poorly administered system. The system proved to be unfair by not pursuing those with the ability to avoid or evade the burden of taxes. In addition, there was widespread legal avoidance within the pay-as-you-earn (PAYE) system range of non-taxable perquisites. The high nominal marginal rates of 57.5 per cent personal tax resulted from the wide exemptions that existed and which significantly reduce the tax base. Industry and firm-specific incentives and tax holdings also reduced the corporate tax base. Only 20 per cent of the value of imported goods was subject to import tax and, with this narrow base, the rates on some items exceeded 200 per cent. Only 16 per cent of final consumption of services and 33 per cent of domestic manufactured output were in the tax net. There were five different indirect taxes, and, within the family of sales, excise, and import duties, there were one hundred different rates.

Seaga's first proposal at tax reform came in the period 1980–82 when he sought to improve the efficiency of the administrative system. In June 1985, the administration released a government policy paper, and a new system went into effect in January 1986.[10] The new policy reflected a sharp reversal of the previous policy of progressive taxation and the use of taxation as a tool to stimulate economic activity in a desired direction which prevailed until 1980. The new system introduced the neutrality principle and sought to make the market, and not the tax system, the basis for allocating resources. The system also sought to correct the re-distributional effect and provided for simplification of tax administrative procedures.

All the tax credit systems and the progressive structures were replaced by a standard flat rate of 33.3 per cent, and all fringe benefit allowances, with a few exceptions, were made taxable. The tax base was broadened to include overtime, interest income and allowances. With introducing a corporate tax rate of 33.3 per cent, taxation on wages, dividends, profits, and interest on savings was harmonised. A direct result of the changes to the income tax structure was the rolling of fringe benefits into the taxable base salary, as there were no longer any benefits to be gained from a large fringe benefit base. Over the years, the non-taxable fringe benefit had grown to be larger than the taxable salary base.

JLP Administration's Economic Management 1985–90

The first half of the 1980s was complicated for the government because of the collapse of the world bauxite market. In 1985, net foreign exchange earnings from bauxite and alumina had fallen by 60 per cent, greatly affecting the country's terms of trade. The combination of a depressed domestic market, high interest rates, scarce foreign exchange, and the additional burden of high taxes led to further questioning of the credibility of the supposedly pro-market administration as a promoter of private investment. At a meeting of the IMF in Seoul in October 1986, Seaga complained that the IMF policies were taking a huge toll on the country in terms of human suffering because of their hasty reform measures. His once cordial relationship with the IMF was now ruptured, and he was subjected to constant and sharp criticisms by the arch-conservative US Think Tank Group, the Heritage Foundation, for failure to implement market-oriented economic policies.[11] The relationship of the Seaga administration with the private sector in Jamaica also came under severe pressure and eventually was seriously damaged. With increased pressure from the IMF and the US, the government was forced to accept the IMF staunch medicine, so the years 1985–90 saw a period of extensive privatisation, starting with the privatisation of National Commercial Bank and Jamaica Telephone Company. Privatising the utilities was a central condition of the international financial institutions and the US government.

The government's economic outcome continued to be poor, and as a result, it failed to meet the performance criteria of the 1986 IMF Standby Agreement after only a year, with less than half the funds not drawn down, leading the administration to call for a combined team of the

IMF, World Bank, and USAID, 'to take a fresh look' at the situation. The special mission visited Jamaica for talks which produced a report that essentially insisted on continuation of IMF required policies.[12]

The IMF, as a condition of its loan which was to run to March 1987, not only demanded further reduction in the level of the budget deficit and the size of government, but it also directed the administration to impose a 10 per cent wage freeze on public employees. This resulted in the first general strike in post-independence Jamaica. The IMF programme also required further reductions in the number of public sector employees, to seventy-eight thousand by 1988. Some subsidies on food products were eliminated; the policy of free education was abandoned; public-school fees were increased, and university tuition fees reintroduced.

The IMF abandoned the Standby programme, which was to run until March 1987, in favour of a new three-year programme, this time imposing much harsher conditionalities: mandating a further reduction in the budget deficit; dismantling of import licencing regime; acceleration of the privatisation programme, along with introducing a general 10 per cent wage guideline. Over the period, the administration contained inflation, averaging 8.4 per cent annually. Following the third Structural Adjustment Loan (SAL) and the strained relationship between Seaga's administration and the World Bank, the disbursement of further loans was suspended until 1987. In September 1986, the Jamaican dollar experienced a significant devaluation, reaching a rate of J$6.00 to US$1.00. As a result, the living standards of the large population of low-income earners were severely impacted. However, in the first half of the 1980s, the reduction in global crude oil prices provided some relief and had a positive effect on Jamaica, leading to a decrease in the inflation rate during that period.

After 1986, there was a notable improvement in Jamaica's terms of trade, primarily because of a more favourable external environment. This improvement was driven by the revival of bauxite and banana production, resulting in increased earnings from these industries, as well as a boost in tourism. Additionally, there were increased investments in clothing and apparel manufacturing. Despite the poor economic performance observed between 1980 and 1985, there appeared to be an initial turnaround in the economy during the period from 1986 to 1989. In this period, economic growth averaged approximately 3 per cent, for the first time in over fifteen years.[13]

Changes in Economic Growth Rate, 1980–89

Table 7.2 shows the changes in the economic growth rates during the Seaga stewardship of the economy for the period 1980–89. The economy slipped sharply in 1980, with a decline of minus 5.7 per cent. However, growth returned in the 1981–83, varying between 1.2 per cent and 2.6 per cent. After 1984 and 1985, the economy again slipped, declining by minus 0.9 per cent in 1984 and minus 4.5 per cent in 1985. In 1986, the economy rebounded, with an annual GDP growth rate of 1.6 per cent in 1986, and 6.2 per cent in 1987. The growth rate in 1988 was 1.5 per cent, and in 1989 the growth rate was 4.6 per cent. In the period 1986–89, the average growth was 3 per cent per annum, the five-year performance since the 1960.

Over the period, government deficit progressively declined from minus 17.5 per cent in 1980 to minus 2.9 per cent in 1987, achieving a surplus of 6 per cent in 1988. In the period, foreign investments as a percentage of GDP rose from 15.7 per cent in 1980 to 29.1 per cent in 1989. Jamaica has always attracted high levels of foreign direct investment flows.

Table 7.2: Selected Macro-economic Data, 1980–89

Years	Real GDP Growth- %	External Debt/GDP %	Central Govt. Deficit/GDP %	External Debt US$ Billion	Investments %/GDP
1980	-5.7	70.0	-17.5	1.9	15.7
1981	2.6	77.2	-15.7	2.3	20.4
1982	1.2	81.8	-14.0	2.7	20.9
1983	2.3	82.6	-15.7	3.0	22.3
1984	-0.9	135.6	-6.5	3.2	23.0
1985	-4.6	180.3	-6.2	3.6	25.0
1986	1.8	150.2	-2.4	3.7	18.5
1987	6.2	140.4	-2.9	4.0	22.6
1988	1.5	NA	6.0	4.0	25.9
1989	4.6	112.5		4.3	29.1

Source: Christopher Adam, William Cavendish, and Percy Mistry, 'Adjusting Privatization: Case Studies from Developing Countries,' 1996.

Despite US$320 million in official grants from the US and other friendly governments, external debt rose from US$1.9 billion or 70 per cent of GDP in 1980 to US$3,900 billion, or 180 per cent of GDP in 1985 before declining to I12.5 per cent in 1989. Debt service increased from 18 per cent of GDP in 1980 in 1980 to 48 per cent of GDP by 1988, necessitating further debt reduction measures. Imports during the period averaged a stable US$1.12 billion.[14]

After 1990, the issue of high indebtedness became a major problem for the Jamaican economy, severely limiting the flexibility of economic policies. Over the years, Jamaica faced considerable challenges in reducing its high level of debt, which had a devastating impact on public sector investments. As a result, living standards experienced a significant decline, the transportation system in urban areas deteriorated, and the state of education and health services worsened. Despite the substantial capital inflows in the 1980s, apart from the positive developments in tourism and free zone activities, the overall progress in productive economic sectors remained stagnant, failing to advance beyond the level achieved in the 1970s.

Cheryl Gopaul explains that the impact on the Kingston Metropolitan Area was increased urban decay, increased slums, squatting and non-conforming land use, deterioration of the urban infrastructure, and collapse of the urban transportation system.[15] It was during this period that the public transportation system was phased out as part of the process of reducing the subsidy cost of transportation on the central budget. There was an increase in the proportion of those living below the poverty line, especially in the rural areas and in Kingston's ghettos. In June 1991, it was estimated that seventy thousand Jamaicans were receiving the weekly US$3 (J$50) food stamps. Food stamps from the US replaced government food subsidies. As a percentage of GDP social services expenditure fell from 14.5 per cent in 1979 to 4 per cent in 1986. Recurrent expenditure on health and education was drastically reduced. Investments in social infrastructure such as building of new schools and hospitals contracted, while the necessary maintenance of social facilities was cut to the bone. In 1980, the public sector doctor/population ratio was one doctor to three thousand; by 1985, it had declined to one doctor to fifty-two hundred persons, while nursing personnel per population declined from one nurse to 540 persons in 1975 to one nurse to 1,172 persons in 1985. As a percentage of GDP education expenditure declined from 18 per cent of public expenditure in 1975 to 10.8 per cent in 1984. Capital expenditure on education fell from 10 per cent in 1974 to 1 per cent in 1986. In 1975, seven thousand students took the English language O-level examination, achieving a pass rate of 60 per cent; by 1989 the number taking the English language fell to 5,747, with a pass rate of 34.5 per cent. The price of a one-bedroom house in Kingston in a typical middle-class suburb in 1990 had reached US$30,000 (J$600,000) and for a three-bedroom house, the price was US$150,000 (J$3.0 million).[16]

ASSESSING IMF/WORLD BANK STRUCTURAL ADJUSTMENT POLICIES

The various IMF and World Bank policies came to aggravate the hard times, especially for the Jamaican poor and rural citizens during the 1980s and 1990s.[17] According to the argument of Le Franc and Witter, the IMF and World Bank policies had an overall negative impact. They claim that these policies contributed to a widening income gap that disadvantaged the poor and failed to alleviate high levels of unemployment. Additionally, the implementation of these policies led to reduced spending on education and healthcare, while also increasing reliance on foreign food imports, exacerbating Jamaica's food security concerns.

Derick Boyd, however, contends that the IMF Structural Adjustment policies were not the main cause of Jamaica's 1980/1990 economic problems but were the relics of policies pursued in the 1950s–1960s, which not only left Jamaica dependent on imports but also allowed wealth and income to be concentrated in the hands of a small elite, with widening distribution of income and with the economic growth then doing little for the rural economy and small farmers.[18] For Boyd, failed government policies were the cause rather than IMF structural adjustment.

A further interpretation of Jamaica economic problem is provided by Damien King, who argues that the reforms toward structural adjustment were half-heartedly implemented by Jamaica and other Caribbean countries prior to the 1990s.[19] As a result, these countries were left behind Latin American governments that had reformed earlier. Criticism of neoliberal economic policies came from Joseph Stiglitz,a leading international economist who had spent time at the

World Bank, emphasising that the time frame prescribed by the IMF policies, which tried to force resources to move from less productive sectors to more productive sectors was too short.[20] Critics argue that the IMF's approach to structural adjustment, characterised by a one-size-fits-all mentality, disregarded historical and local realities. This approach failed to consider the unique circumstances and challenges of individual countries. As a consequence of neoliberalism, IMF policies, and the trade platform established by the World Trade Organization (WTO), there has been a noticeable rise in food trade deficits and an escalation in the cost of food imports.

Jamaica should prioritise the introduction of advanced technology in the agricultural sector and move away from the prevalent and dominant 'fork and hoe' methods still used in domestic agriculture. In contrast to the UK, which developed a robust manufacturing sector from the 1870s onward, fuelled by the emergence of new towns during the Industrial Revolution, Jamaica had relatively few significant factories throughout the twentieth century. Aside from a match factory and several sugar processing facilities in rural areas, the country lacked substantial industrial infrastructure. Consequently, the Jamaican economy remained small, reliant on technology and financial support from external sources, and had limited capacity to independently diversify its production capabilities during the 1980s.

The failure to achieve the desired outcomes of the IMF and World Bank programmes can be attributed to several factors, including the lack of comprehensive medium-term planning and inconsistencies between the programmes of the two institutions. For instance, the imposition of unplanned import duties contradicted the objective of import liberalisation. These gaps and inconsistencies hindered the effective implementation of the programmes. For further information on the structural changes in the economy during the 1980–89 period, please refer to table 7.3.

The tertiary sector fluctuated between 1980 and 1990, with 60.3 per cent in 1989, the lowest and to 62.9 per cent in 1982, the highest. The tertiary sector comprised the services industries. Mining fell from 8.3 per cent in 1981 to 5.1 per cent in 1988, before increasing to 6.7 per cent in 1989, whilst manufacturing, owing to the increase in 807 exports, increased from 15.4 per cent to 17.1 per cent. There was also a reduction in the size of the public sector, the main change in this ten-year period, with this sector falling from 19.2 per cent to 15.6 per cent. These developments, however, left a massive foreign debt burden on the economy by 1989. External debt to GDP climbed from 70 per cent in 1980 and to 150.2 per cent in 1986, before falling back to 112.5 per cent in 1989. Unemployment had, by then, grown to 25 per cent, despite massive-out migration to the US and Canada. The external account deficit registered 14 per cent of GDP. Jamaican businesses and households responded to the restrictions by increasing their involvement in informal economic activity.

Table 7.3: GDP by Sector of Origin, Constant Cost at (1974) Prices, 1980–89

	1980	1981	1982	1983	1984	1985	1986	1987	1988	1989
Primary Sector	**8.3**	**8.3**	**7.6**	**7.9**	**8.8**	**8.9**	**8.6**	**8.5**	**8.0**	**7.4**
Agriculture	8.3	8.3	7.6	7.9	8.8	8.9	8.6	8.5	8.0	7.4
Secondary Sector	**31.0**	**30.5**	**29.6**	**29.7**	**28.9**	**28.7**	**29.3**	**29.7**	**30.0**	**32.3**
Mining	8.9	8.8	6.2	6.1	6.2	5.2	5.4	5.4	5.1	6.7
Manufacturing	15.4	15.1	16.1	160	15.5	16.3	16.5	16.4	16.3	17.1
Electricity	1.3	1.3	1.3	1.4	1.4	1.5	1.7	1.7	1.7	1.7
Construction	5.4	5.3	6.0	6.3	5.9	5.7	5.7	6.2	7.0	6.7
Tertiary Sector	**60.7**	**61.2**	**62.9**	**62.3**	**62.3**	**62.4**	**62.1**	**61.8**	**62.0**	**60.3**
Commerce	17.0	17.5	18.6	167.6	17.7	17.2	17.9	18.7	18.3	18.8
Transportation	6.8	6.7	6.7	6.9	7.2	7.7	8.2	8.3	8.3	8.3
Financial Services	13.7	13.9	14.1	14.8	15.0	15.1	14.4	14.1	14.4	13.6
General Government	19.2	19.2	19.4	19.1	18.4	18.2	17.2	16.3	16.6	15.6
Other Services	4.0	4.0	4.0	3.9	4.0	4.3	4.3	4.3	4.3	4.2
GDP	**100**	**100**	**100**	**100**	**100**	**100**	**100**	**100**	**100**	**100**

Source: Cezley Sampson (1994), 'Structural Adjustment, Privatisation, Trade deregulation: The Jamaican Experience,' in *Competing Globally: Challenges and Opportunities*, ed. S. Neelamegham (New Delhi, India: Allied Publishers, 1994).

Box 7.1 below summarises the IMF and World Bank reform policies and which the government largely adopted in the 1980s. The JLP government predominantly adopted the reform policies put forth by the IMF and World Bank during the 1980s, as outlined below. However, despite undergoing thirteen years of structural adjustment programs under the IMF, there were no significant widespread benefits that reached the majority of the Jamaican population by the end of 1989. This lack of tangible improvements had an impact on the popularity of the ruling JLP, which had declined to such an extent that it lost its majority in the Parliament to the PNP in the general elections held in February 1989.

Despite thirteen years of structural adjustment under the IMF, at the end of 1989, there were no increased widespread benefits to be shared by the mass of the Jamaican people. By the time of the February 1989 general elections, the popularity of the Jamaica Labour Party had fallen so low that it lost its majority to the PNP in the Parliament.

Box 7.1: 1980–89 IMF and World Bank Market Reform Policies

IMF Stabilisation Measures

- **Exchange Rate Policies**: liberalisation of exchange rate to provide for market determined rates
- **Fiscal Policies**: increased mobilisation of revenues, reduction in recurrent public expenditure, and reduction in general subsidies
- **Tax Reform**: elimination of progressive taxation, introduction of neutral taxation and promotion of value added tax measures
- **Privatisation:** Requiring privatisation of government assets, supporting PPPs, and contracting out of service through competitive tender
- World Bank Structural Reform Measures
- **Reduction of the public enterprises** through privatisation contracting of services; introduction of cost recovery and user fees designed to improve the financial performances of enterprise
- **Public Sector Management: reduction** in the size of the civil service, increases in pay and pay differentials, decentralisation of the personal and accounting function of government departments, and creating executive agencies
- **Liberalisation of the Financial Sector/Financial Sector Reform** involving market determined interest rate promotion of Stock Exchange improvement to prudential regulations, and encouragement of competition in the banking and financial sectors
- **Trade Liberalisation and Tariff Reform:** removing import controls and opening the domestic market and liberalising the export trade
- **Providing a Safety Net** involving well targeted programmes of transfer to financially vulnerable; granting of training credits or grants and special employment programmes for low-income people.

RETURN OF THE PNP UNDER MANLEY/ PATTERSON ADMINISTRATION, 1989–2007

On return to power in 1989 the PNP continued with the IMF and World Bank programmes. The World Bank Private Sector Adjustment Loan Programme's carried two main conditionalities: reduction of tariff protection under the CET and reform of customs in processing imported goods and reducing the administrative costs of clearing goods from the wharf. Like in the Agricultural Sector Adjustment Loan Programme, the conditions of these loans bore no relation to the title. A Privatisation Structural Adjustment Loan Programme, which was introduced by the World Bank in 1991, provided support to the National Investment Bank of Jamaica for the privatisation of electricity, the sugar industry, the railway, airports, and the airlines.

A major economic problem facing a new administration under the PNP was the financial sector crisis of the mid-1990s, causing major government bailout of some of the faltering industries and financial institutions. The first sign of the financial problem in the economy showed up when two of the local financial institutions ran into liquidity problems. In January 1997, the government realised the extent of the problem and rescued the sector. Absorbing the full cost of the financing of the adjustment burden through the Financial Sector Adjustment Company (FINSAC) necessitated the largest expansion of national domestic debt. Chapter 11 in carries in more detail the forces, which triggered the financial crisis and how the crisis was resolved. It was felt that financial sector liberalisation was introduced when the legal and regulatory framework were not in place.

During 1989–96, the new PNP administration continued the client relationship with the IMF and the World Bank and, although this relationship was discontinued after 1996, the administration continued to pursue private sector market-oriented policies

The administration on coming to power inherited 1989 World Bank Agriculture Sector Structural Adjustment Programme Loan 28, The Trade and Finance Structural Adjustment Loan 26, and The Privatisation Sector Loan. The Agricultural Sector Adjustment Loan (ASAL) required the opening of the agricultural sector and the elimination of licensing requirements for a range of agricultural imports, covering vegetables, peas, roots, oils, and fats and products made from the aforementioned, while mandating lifting of export licensing in relation to fruits, vegetables, plants, and coffee. It also required the removal of quantitative restrictions (QRs) and import licencing on food items, to be replaced with a maximum tariff of 100 per cent. Under pressure from the Inter-American Development Bank (IDB), both the Agricultural Credit Bank and the National Development Bank of Jamaica were compelled to suspend their differential interest rate policies in December 1990. The IDB argued that these policies resulted in the inefficient allocation of investment resources.

Both development banks saw the removal of the monopoly rights of the State Trading Corporation and the Jamaica Commodity Trading Company Limited (JCTC) as a strategic step towards the reintroduction of a competitive domestic market environment. The result was that, from 1991, the government progressively transferred imports to the private sector, replaced the prohibitive regulations on the importation of pharmaceuticals, introduced protection for locally manufactured products, opened government procurement to competitive bidding and divested JCTC of its interest in Jamaica Soya Products and Grains Jamaica Limited.

From as early as 1983, the World Bank had sought also to eliminate the monopoly position of the agricultural marketing boards in fixing the purchase price of exports and as the sole marketing channel for overseas sales. The marketing functions of the Banana Board and the other commodity boards for cocoa, coffee, citrus, and pimento were discontinued over the years. An outcome of these measures has been that larger farmers have been able to enter the export market, directly in competition with the marketing boards. By 1990, private distributors replaced the commodity boards in exporting of bananas and minor export crops.

However, with the elimination of centralised marketing, rural farmers experienced difficulties in accessing the export markets for their produce. Many concentrated on supplying the domestic market, especially supermarkets and informal trading. Gradual elimination of price controls and the generalised subsidy system formed the last major agricultural trade conditionalities of the IMF and World Bank. In 1990, controls on basic food items, flour, rice, milk, and bread were removed. Except for transportation services, price controls ceased to apply in all sectors after 1991.

The trade liberalisation policies was introduced in the early 1990s and required the dismantling of Quantitative Restrictions and reduction of tariff levels after 1990s.[21] One of the most important policy changes introduced involved the reversal of the import substitution measures for domestic and CARICOM markets, to shift to export-led growth. More specifically, the protectionist policies in agriculture shielded the large group of hillside farmers who experienced low yields per acre. Both domestic agriculture and manufacturing were afforded subsidies through the differential interest rate policies of the two development banks and the over-valued currency, which prevailed for much of the period. The State Trading Corporation was seen by the IMF as a monopoly importer and the marketing boards as monopoly purchasers, denying competitive farmers direct access to export markets. The IMF viewed both measures as detrimental to efficient production and the growth of a competitive market economy. The World Bank argued that Jamaican manufacturers, enjoying a protected domestic market, lacked sufficient motivation to engage in exports. The provision of tax and import duty concessions further subsidised capital-intensive industries, despite the relatively high cost of capital in the country. These policies hindered the maximisation of consumer welfare, as consumer choices were often limited and prices of locally produced goods remained high.

Moreover, Jamaican businesses developed a tradition of imposing significant mark-ups on their products, even in competitive environments where price competition should have been encouraged. The firms that emerged under the incentive programmes became reliant on foreign raw materials and intermediate inputs, neglecting potential linkages with domestic resources. This further hindered the development of a self-sustaining and integrated economy.

Firms in the manufacturing sector operated as net users of foreign exchange rather than net savers. Manufacturers were under no pressure to update equipment and introduce new technologies and manufacturing processes, hence low and falling productivity, with most local firms in the 1980s and 1990s finding it difficult to compete in export markets. Often, businessmen went to Florida and acquired discarded equipment, renovated them, and brought them back to Jamaica to benefit from the industrial incentives.

From the Bank's perspective, the trade reform policies were aimed at helping the manufacturing sector in maintaining a competitive real exchange rate. The policies also removed the anti-export bias and expose the domestic market to competition.

The World Bank obtained an agreement for the aggregate rate to be first reduced to a maximum of 60 per cent in 1980, except for a few items, with further reductions to reach a maximum of 30 per cent for consumer items, 20 per cent for capital goods, and 10 per cent for raw materials.[22] In the end, the government and the World Bank settled on the adoption of the CARICOM Common External Rate with a maximum of 45 per cent. In 1985, of a total CIF import value of US$776 million, net of oil imports, only US$237 million or 31 per cent attracted duty.

In order to minimise taxation on exports, a 7.5 per cent duty rebate system was introduced in 1988. This was later replaced with a duty drawback scheme. Under this rebate scheme, the exporter first paid the duty, which was later rebated while under the duty drawback scheme, the exporter deferred payment until the goods were sold in export markets. This had significant benefits in terms of cash flow in an environment of high interest rates.

It has already been shown that exports as a percentage of GDP declined from 1980 to 1990, while imports as a percentage of GDP increased. Exports and imports amounted to 96.1 per cent of GDP in 1980, an example of an open economy. The major manufacturing tradable exports have been textiles and garments, resulting from the development of the free zones in the 1980s. Apparel exports which took off in the second half of the 1980s peaked in 1995 at 19 per cent of mercantile exports, before falling to 13 per cent in 1999. Most of the imports have been consumer goods, rather than capital or intermediate goods for productive activity. Jamaica benefited from the cheaper imports with overall beneficial effects on inflation.[23]

Liberalisation immediately impacts on imports, as the liberalising country needs to build up export capacity to take advantage of the opportunities offered in the export market, and this takes time; the result is that the Jamaica's liberalisation policies seemed to have shifted the trade balance in favour of increased imports, with limited positive impact on exports.

The WTO and Liberalisation of Trade in Agriculture and Services

The IMF trade liberalisation in the 1980s and 1990s followed the advent of the World Trade Organization (WTO) protocol of 1990. The WTO was born out of negotiations that followed the Uruguay Round of 1986–84 and the earlier General Agreement on Tariff and Trade (GATT), which focused on reducing tariff. By 1980, tariffs on industrial goods had been reduced to about 4.5 per cent, and hardly affected agricultural produce. Whereas GATT dealt with trade in goods, WTO also dealt with trade in services, which was becoming an increasing part of global trade. At the time of the establishment of the World Bank and the IMF, there was indeed a vision for a third Bretton Woods institution. This institution was meant to address trade barriers and facilitate negotiations for their reduction. The WTO was established in 1995 to fulfil this role. The WTO served as a forum for trade negotiations and set rules for international trade.

However, as the WTO negotiations progressed, the non-reciprocal trade preferences that Jamaica and other Caribbean countries enjoyed with the UK and the European Union eventually came to an end. These preferences, which provided trade advantages to the Caribbean countries, were phased out as part of the WTO's efforts to promote more equitable and reciprocal trade relationships among its member countries.

Under the European Union/African Caribbean and Pacific (ACP/EU) Lomé convention of 1975, Jamaica and the Caribbean up to 1990s benefited from considerable trade preferences, especially for agricultural products. The World Trade Organisation (WTO) protocol mandated the liberalisation of trade between Europe and the ACP countries in 2000, providing a transition period of eight years starting in 2000.

Soon after the creation of WTO in 1995, Latin American producers of sugar and bananas, supported by the large US multinational agricultural companies and their government challenged, EU Trade practices. The Latin American countries informed the EU that its trade preference was in breach of WTO protocol and had to be discontinued. Jamaica's sugar and bananas and, to a lesser extent, the minor export crops which it had traded with Britain since 1902 first under imperial trade preference, now found itself at the beginning of the completely new set of trade conditions which did not cater for preferential quotas and prices. In effect, Jamaica and the other Caribbean countries faced full competition for the international market for all agricultural products, and this has been a major challenge to successive administrations since 2000.

The trade provisions of the Cotonou Partnership Agreement** have been replaced by the CARIFORUM-EC Partnership Agreement, signed in August 2008. These agreements put an end to the Lomé Convention agreements that had offered a protected market for bananas, sugar, and the other minor export crops: coffee, cocoa, citrus, and pimento, virtually putting an end to sugar and banana as export sectors. Jamaica's trade situation suffered immensely, despite the development assistance which was provided to CARIFORUM countries like Jamaica.[24]

The aim was to transition the ACP countries towards full integration into the global market, a situation where various countries like Jamaica could not accommodate global competition for banana and sugar and the minor export crops. Jamaica's export market for produce has been obliterated since 2010, contracting every year since 2000, reflecting weak performances in both traditional and non-traditional export sectors.

The economic effects of the experiences of the WTO trade liberalisation have been to widen the external current account deficit of Jamaica from 3 per cent of GDP in 1998/1999 to 8.6 per cent of GDP in 2001/2002.[25] The application of liberalisation policies by the IMF and WTO fails to acknowledge the historical reality that industrialised countries achieved their development under the shield of protectionism. These countries only embraced free trade, albeit with selectivity and incompleteness, once their industries had gained a competitive advantage.[26] Table 7.4 shows the average import tariff for the period 1989–98. Import tariff levels fell from 25 per cent in 1989 to 11.8 per cent in 1998.

Since the 1990s, Jamaica has enjoyed three beneficial developments namely, a tradition of high capital formation high levels of remittance flows from exporting labour to the develop world and increase services trade, especially tourism and telecommunications. Jamaica enjoyed one of the highest rates of gross capital formation as a percentage of GDP in the Caribbean during the 1990s. Between 1995 and 2005, the country attracted US$4.7 billion in foreign direct investments, averaging US$450 million per annum, with the average annual rate of investments reaching 27.7 per cent of GDP at its peak year.[27]

** Cotonou Agreement is a partnership agreement between members of the African, Caribbean and Pacific (ACP) Group of States and the European Union and its member states, to promote and expedite the economic, cultural and social development of the ACP states, with a view to contributing to peace and security and to promoting a stable and democratic political environment. (https://home-affairs.ec.europa.eu/pages/glossary/cotonou-agreement)

Table 7.4: Average Import Tariff, 1989–98

Year	Average Import Tariff %	Year	Average Import Tariff %
1989	25.0	1994	15.9
1990	25.0	1995	14.0
1991	22.1	1996	14.0
1992	22.1	1997	14.0
1993	15.9	1998	11.8

Source: Damien King and Sudhanshu Handa, *Balance of Payments, Liberalisation, Poverty and Distribution of Income, Department of Economics*, University of the West Indies, Mineo, 2000, 30.

Remittance flowed in increasing volumes from around the 1960s. Ransford Palmer provides estimates of remittances from the US in the period 1962–72.[28] During the 1960s, Jamaicans migrated to the US, mostly for unskilled and low-wage jobs which paid more than they could earn at home. Migration then composed of two economic groups: domestic workers, labourers, and farmworkers, and the other professional and skilled workers. The new class of skilled workers could afford to send back more as remittances to Jamaica. In the 1970s, private transfers to Jamaica were only 0.17 per cent of GDP; by 1990, the net private transfers totalled 9.1 per cent of GDP.[29] According to official statistics, remittances increased from US$130 million in 1990 to nearly US$470 million in 1994. Remittances certainly reduced the incidence of poverty in the 1990s.[30] Remittances increased further to US$698 million in 2000.

Table 7.5 shows the official between 1984 and 2000.

Table 7.5: Official Remittances in Real Terms (constant 1995 US$), 1984–2000

Year	Remittances US $ million	Year	Remittances US $ million
1984	38	**1993**	197
1985	130	**1994**	470
1986	75	**1995**	582
1987	79	**1996**	618
1988	87	**1997**	609
1989	144	**1998**	618
1990	159	**1999**	627
1991	152	**2000**	698
1992	171		
Annual percentage change 12.7 per cent			

Source: Richard Adams, 'International Migration, Remittances, and the Brain Drain: A Study of 24 Labour Exporting Countries,' World Bank Research Working Paper 3069, Washinton, DC, 2003.

Over the period 1975–2003, remittances amounted to 6.7 per cent of GDP, placing Jamaica in the top ten countries in terms of remittance inflows, with Jordan being the highest at 18.6 per cent.[31] In 2004, remittances was more than double the combined sum from overseas development assistance and foreign direct.[32] By 2005, remittances to Jamaica amounted to 182 per cent of bauxite and alumina export earnings. Between 2000 and 2007, remittance inflows increased at an annual average of 4 per cent, totalling US$1.96 billion, or 15 per cent of GDP in 2007. Remittances increased from US$698 million in 2000 to US$2.2 billion in 2008.[33] By 2020, remittance inflows amounted to 21.4 per cent of GDP.

In the period since the 1990s, remittance has had a favourable impact on the current account deficit, and there has been growing evidence that remittance reduces the incidence of poverty in developing countries like Jamaica. It is a significant income flow to the lower income groups, as many Jamaicans now come to rely on funds sent from overseas to meet their ongoing living expenses. Foreign exchange from remittances improves the creditworthiness of the country. Since 1994, several countries have employed remittances as a securitisation instrument, enabling them to access international financial markets with lower interest rate spreads and longer maturities compared to the international bond market. The influx of remittance income granted the Patterson administration a degree of flexibility in its economic policies that previous administrations had not enjoyed.

Prime Minister Patterson's 1990s Policy Agenda

Because of ill-health, Michael Manley tenure as prime minister only lasted from October 1989 to March 1992 when he was succeeded by P.J. Patterson. Besides conducting several institutional reforms, considerable time was spent on the phasing in of the market reform programme. Patterson, as deputy prime minister, had led the administration in the areas of economic and development policies. In a paper titled 'The Emerging Role of the State,' presented at a Ministerial Roundtable August 12, 1993, in Ocho Rios, Patterson carefully outlined the path the administration would take, one of the state-steering economic and productive activities rather than rowing.[34] The policies and major programmes which he pursued over the period 1989–2006 can be summarised along the following seven platforms:

1. ***Institutional Building:***

- Restructuring the Office of the Prime Minister and creating new ministerial departments, including the Cabinet Office
- Establishing the National Planning Council
- Creating the Office of Utilities Regulation
- Creating the Financial Services Authority to regulate the financial sector and to restructure the Bank of Jamaica to carry out more effective prudential regulation
- Establishing the Fair-Trading Commission and the Consumer Affairs Commission
- Establishing the Financial Sector Adjustment Company (FINSAC) to deal with the mid-1996 financial meltdown
- Establishing the Executive Agency institutional framework and establishing the initial set of executive agencies
- Restructuring the regulatory framework for air and road transport to provide for clearer separation of operation and regulatory responsibilities
- Establishing or strengthening governance agencies: Office of Public Defender, Electoral Advisory Commission, Office of Child Advocate, Police Public Complaint Authority, Political Ombudsman, the Anti-Corruption Commission, and the National Contracts Commission
- Restructuring the tax administration system and its implementing institution

2. ***Implementing the Major Privatisation Transactions***

- Implementing the privatisation of air transport, airports, and telecommunications; restructuring and privatising electricity; privatising National Commercial Bank, the sugar industry, and the banana industry and providing for the private sector to assume responsibility for urban transport in the 1990s
- Establishing Public Partnership Agreements (PPAs), for example, National Road Operating Construction Company (NROCC)

3. ***Building New Infrastructure, Especially Roads Covering the Following:***

- The North Coast Road Development Project from Negril to Montego Bay, to Ocho Rios, and then on to Port Antonio

- The Trans-Jamaica Highway: from Spanish Town to Mammee Bay in St Ann
- The Old Harbour bypass.
- Rebuilding Sangster and Norman Manley Airport Terminals

4. ***Restructuring the Health Sector:***
   - Creating Regional Health Authorities as part of devolving operating responsibility from the Ministry of Health
5. ***Expanding Hotel Capacity in the Tourism Sector:***
   - Facilitating the construction of new hotels: Ritz Carlton, Hotel Riu, Hotel Iberostar, Hedonism III, Bahia Principe, Breathe Whitehouse and Fiesta, as well as building the Montego Bay Convention Centre
6. ***Trade Liberalisation, Especially Dealing with the World Trade Organisation (WTO)***
   - Elimination of imperial trade preference, especially for sugar and banana, which had been in operation since 1902
7. ***Dealing with Land and the Environment***
   - Creation of the Environment Foundation of Jamaica
   - Merging the National Resources Conservation Authority, the Town Planning Department and the Land Utilisation Commission to create the National Environment and Planning Agency.

Patterson/Manley 1990s Tax Reform

The new administration recognised the necessity of addressing the tax system, despite the changes made by the Seaga administration in the 1980s. In October 1991, they embarked on the third phase of the tax reform programme, which involved the introduction of the General Consumption Tax (GCT). This new tax system replaced sales, excise, and consumption taxes with a value-added tax (VAT) model. The new tax started at a standard rate of 10 per cent and included all commodities and services, other than fuel oil and motor vehicles, and carried the same rate, except for selected items, which were to be zero-rated. The result was that the effective rate of taxation fell while revenue yields increased. These changes helped immediately to reduce the budget deficit and had the effect also of facilitating expansion of the stock market.

The tax regime which emerged out of the early 1990s reform comprised the following:

- A value added tax (VAT) referred to in Jamaica as General Consumption Tax (GCT)
- Income tax of 33 1/3 per cent on capital (profits obtained by any business in Jamaica are taxed at a rate of 33 1/3 per cent) and a flat income tax of 25 per cent for individuals, with a minimum exempt level
- Excise taxes and import duties that are equivalent to consumption taxes
- Taxes on labour, or payroll taxes, and
- Property taxes, stamp duties and an increasing number of other levies such as environment levy, and telecommunications access fund

Approximately 40 per cent of total tax receipts came from income and property taxes, with tax revenues amounting to 26.3 per cent of GDP in 2002/3, starting at a standard level of 10 per cent; however, changes were later made to include several tax rates and exemptions that did not fit into a logical framework.[35] The general rate was then set at 15 per cent, but later reduced to 12.5 per cent for some construction items. The zero-tax rate, which is the solution for exports to allow the recovery of tax paid on previous stages of production, was extended to a whole range of other items. The wide differences in rates came to create inefficient allocation of resources and increased administrative cost controls. These changes were a fiscal cost, forcing the government to raise other taxes to comply with its revenue target. Several generous investment incentives were incorporated in the corporation tax regime. The tax system also favoured debt financing over equity financing, as firms could deduct all their payments for interest.

The Jamaican tax system has undergone major reforms since the 1980s to achieve the multiple objectives of simplicity, equity, and effectiveness and to make the system more capable of stimulating investment and economic growth. The marginal rate of income tax moved from 57.5 per cent in 1980 to 25 per cent in the 1990s. The growth of the informal sector has, however, reduced the tax base and has contributed to the decline in GCT as a per cent of GDP. The relatively high levels of taxation meant there was little room to increase taxes to reduce the fiscal deficit during the 1990s. Special effort, with an expensive administrative structure, therefore had to be made to ensure compliance.

Development of the Informal Economy in the 1990s

As a part of the informal economy in the 1990s more people were engaged in petty trade, pirating or informal transport, the ganja trade, with higglering becoming more structured. In the 1980s higglering, through the Informal Commercial Importers (1CIs), expanded to include imported goods from the US and China. The informal economy has always presented a problem when computing Jamaica's GDP. The IMF in 2006 noted this as a problem when computing Jamaica's national accounts because of the high proportion of activities in the services sector (70 per cent) and the fairly large size of the informal sector. When the period 1993–2003 was taken as an example, real GDP growth was shown to vary between minus 1 per cent in the period 1996–97 and 1.5 per cent in the period 1991–2001. In the entire period, the average growth in GDP was 1 per cent, whilst electricity sales growth over the period 1993–2003 varied between 3 per cent and 7 per cent.[36]

The IMF concluded that, since there was a fairly large discrepancy between the growth in electricity consumption and growth in real GDP, real GDP growth may have been understated during the period 1993–2003. A survey conducted by the IDB in 2002,[37] using different methodologies and data collected from the Jamaica Survey of Living Conditions, showed the informal sector to have grown from 12.9 per cent in 1991 to 40 per cent of GDP in 2000. The informal economy in Jamaica in 2001 was not only large, but it also more than doubled over the previous decade of 1991. The rapid growth in the informal sector, however, contributed to the significant decline in poverty and the growth differed in many respects from the formal economy.

The IDB also noted that estimates based on electricity consumption put the informal sector at a fairly large size, some 40 per cent of total GDP in 2002. Both electricity consumption and monetary data showed that the informal sector grew more than the formal sector during the 1990s. In an effort to rectify this underestimation, the IDB conducted an analysis and determined that the average GDP growth during the period 1991–2000 could be estimated as high as 3.7 per cent, which was 2.7 per cent higher than the officially recorded figures. This revised estimate reflects a more accurate assessment of the country's economic performance during that period.

Furthermore, it was revealed that approximately 60 per cent of informal business operators in Jamaica are property owners, and about 33.0 per cent of them hold university degrees. These findings challenge the commonly held perception that workers in the informal economy lack education. It highlights the fact that a significant portion of individuals engaged in informal economic activities possess higher levels of education and are not necessarily uneducated.

Previous studies by Michael Witter and Claremont Kirton during the first two decades after independence showed similar results as to the growth in the size of the informal economy.[38] In their estimation the informal economy increased from 8 per cent of official GDP in 1962, to 15 per cent in 1975, increasing further to 24 per cent in 1985 and 39 per cent in 1989, using the Gutmann's model based on the size of the fiduciary money. The percentage is even higher when the Feige's method is used on the velocity of money in the economy showing an increase in the informal sector from 18 per cent to 63 per cent. Gutmann's model and Feige's method are econometric models used to calculate the size of the informal economy. Feige method is based on the velocity of money, while the Gutmann method is based on the fiduciary of money. These methods are noted in an article used by Witter and Kirton and involve mathematical formulae which are unnecessary in this report by the IMF.[39] Unemployment may have been overstated and the level of economic activity understated.[40]

Performance of the Economy Under Patterson, 1989–2004

Table 7.6 shows selected economic and social data for the period 1990–2005. During this period, Jamaica experienced a financial meltdown, leading to a significant increase in public debt to cover the expenses arising from the banking crisis of 1995/96. From 1996 to 1999, the public debt continued to grow as a result of this crisis.

Table 7.6: Selected Economic and Social Indicators, 1990–2002

	1990	1995	1996	1997	1998	1999	2000	2001	2002 Avg.	1995-2002
Population (million)	2.41	2.46	2.52	2.54	2.56	2.56	2.63	2.60	2.63	2.6
Labour Force (thousand)	1059	1150	1143	1134	1129	1119	1105	1105	1125	1126.1
Unemployment (per cent of total labour force)	15.7	16.2	16.0	16.5	15.5	15.7	15.5	15.0	15.1	15.7
Gross Domestic Product and Prices										
US$ billion, current prices	4.6	6.6	6.5	7.4	7.7	7.7	7.9	8.1	8.4	7.5
Jamaica $ billion, current prices	33.0	230.2	241.5	262.9	282.2	300.9	338.7	372.2	407.7	304.5
per capita, US$, current prices	1,907	2,631	2,582	2,923	3,016	3,010	3,016	3,112	3,203	2,937
per capita, constant J$ (1986 base year)	7,996	8,111	7,938	7,725	7,629	7,542	7,548	7,642	7,688	7,728
GDP growth, annual per cent change, constant J$	5.5	0.5	-1.3	-2.0	-0.5	-0.4	0.7	1.7	1.0	0.0
Gross Domestic Investment (per cent of GDP)	25.9	29.3	29.7	29.8	26.7	25.1	27.6	31.0	34.3	29.2
Gross National Savings (per cent of GDP)	16.0	23.3	24.9	23.2	20.6	20.0	21.1	21.9	17.5	21.6
Consumer Prices, annual change (per cent)	21.9	19.9	26.4	9.7	8.6	6.0	8.2	7.0	7.1	11.6
Exchange Rate, J$ per US$ (period average)	7.18	35.14	37.12	35.40	36.55	39.04	42.70	46.00	48.40	40.00
Real Effective Exchange Rate	100.0	92.4	109.9	126.9	134.2	133.0	130.6	131.8	131.0	123.7
Interest Rate (treasury bill rate, per cent per annum, EOP)	26.21	27.7	38.0	21.1	25.7	20.9	18.2	16.7	15.5	23.0
Total Debt	138.3	85.9	79.1	102.3	115.7	132.7	131.9	130.6	148.5	115.8
Domestic	38.1	26.4	35.4	59.3	73.1	90.0	83.6	78.2	89.8	67.0
External	100.2	59.5	43.7	43	42.6	42.8	48.3	54.2	58.8	49.1
External Sector										

	1990	1995	1996	1997	1998	1999	2000	2001	2002 Avg.	1995-2002
Exports of Goods and Non-factor Services (US$ mn)	2,325	3,541	3,465	3,547	3,540	3,643	3,782	3,573	3,229	3,540
Imports of Goods and Non-factor Services (US$ mn)	2,928	4,246	4,231	4,504	4,502	4,507	4,989	5,248	4,829	4,632
External Current Account Balance (per cent of GDP)	-6.8	-1.7	-2.2	-4.6	-4.4	-2.9	-5.0	-10.1	-13.3	-5.5
Net International Reserves, US$ million	397.3	428.2	692.6	541.0	582.0	450.2	969.5	1840.7	1597.0	887.7
Gross Reserves, US$ million	168.2	681.3	880.0	682.1	709.5	554.5	1053.7	1900.9	1645.4	1013.4

Notes: Includes FINSAC interest payments on a full-year basis
Source: Sanjay Kathuria, Errol Graham, James Hanson, and Rina Obera

Between 1995 and 2002, the country's GDP growth remained stagnant, averaging zero, which was a lacklustre performance. This occurred despite Gross Domestic Investment as a percentage of GDP fluctuating between 25.9 per cent and 24.3 per cent, with an average of 29.2 per cent during the same period. The highest investment percentage reached 34.2 per cent in 2002. Major improvements were made to the net international reserves, increasing from US$397.3 million in 1990 to US$1,840.7 in 2001, before falling back to US$1,597 in 2002, with an average of US$887.7 between 2002 and 2005. The balance of payment (BOP) was positive, except for 1991 when BOP was minus 21.3 per cent, with the best year being 1994 at US$357.7 million. Between 1981 and 1990, the economy recorded GDP growth averaging 2.59 per cent; however, in the period 1991–2000, growth averaged only 0.85 per cent, declining further to 0.65 per cent between 2001 and 2010. In this period, Jamaica's fiscal balance fluctuated between 0.2 per cent of GDP and 4 per cent of GDP. The exchange rate jumped from J$7.14 to US$1.0 in 1990 to J$35.14 in 1995, averaging J$40.0 between 1995 and 2002. After 1995, the exchange rate in Jamaica achieved a degree of stability. However, despite this stabilisation, the country experienced low levels of economic growth. This has been a paradox considering the high levels of investment, including foreign direct investments, in the Jamaican economy.

Changes to the Structure of the Economy, 1990–2004

Table 7.7 below shows the structure of the economy over the period 1990–2004 in which all the major sectors experienced significant changes. Agriculture continued its decline, with its share of GDP falling further from 6.9 per cent in 1990 to 5.2 per cent in 2004. Similarly, the mining sector fell from 8.6 per cent in 1991 to 5.1 per cent in 1999, before a modest rise to 5.4 per cent in 2004. Manufacturing, however, showed the greatest decline, falling from 21.4 per cent in 1990 to 12.9 per cent in 2004. The sectors that grew were transportation and communication, from 8.9 per cent to 20.5 per cent, and real estate from 7.4 per cent to 12.9 per cent in 1999, before falling back to 12.5 per cent in 2004. Government services, which had been falling in the 1980s, stabilised at around 6–7 per cent between 1990 and 1996 but increased to over 9.0 per cent between 1999 and 2002.

Table 7.7: Percentage Contribution to GDP by Industrial Sector in Producers Value at Constant (1986) Price (Percentage), 1990–2004

	1990	1991	1992	1993	1994	1995	1996	1999	2004
Primary Sector	6.9	6.9	7.6	8.1	8.6	8.7	9.2	na	na
Agriculture, Forestry and Fishing	6.9	6.9	7.6	8.1	8.6	8.7	9.2	6.8	5.2
Secondary Sector									
Mining, Quarrying	8.2	8.6	8.2	8.1	8.6	7.9	8.6	5.1	5.4
Manufacturing	20.1	18,5	18.4	17.7	17.6	17.3	16.7	13.3	12.9
Electricity /water	4.0	4.1	4.1	4.1	4.1	4.2	4.4	3.5	3.7
Construction	9.2	9.1	9.1	8.8	8.2	8.7	8.4	8.8	9.2
Tertiary Sector									
Distributive Trade	17.5	18.4	18.4	18.7	18.7	19.3	19.7	21.0	20.5
	8.9	9.5	9.5	10.1	10.6	11.5	12.7	11.2	20.5
Financial Services	8.9	10.5	11.1	10.3	15.0	14.6	14.0	na	na
General Govt. Services	6.8	6.6	6.5	6.3	6.1	6.1	6.2	9.8	9.3
Real Estate/ Business Services	7.4	7.8	8.1	8.2	8.7	8.9	9.2	12.9	12.5
Miscellaneous Services	8.8	8.6	8.9	9.3	9.2	9.4	9.7	7.8	8.3

Note: At the end of 1991 GCT, a VAT tax was introduced and does not form part of Producers Value.

Source: Computed by M. Witter and L. Brown (2005), 'Trade Liberalization: The Jamaica Experience' & STATIN data

P.J. Patterson concluded his tenure as prime minister in 2006, succeeded by Portia Simpson-Miller, who became the first female to hold the position. However, Simpson-Miller faced electoral defeat when she sought her own mandate, as the JLP's Bruce Golding emerged victorious in the polls. Golding's time as prime minister was relatively short-lived, subsequently giving way to Simpson-Miller for a second term.

In 2016, Andrew Holness assumed office, succeeding Simpson-Miller as the prime minister. Holness has maintained his position of power, extending into 2023, ensuring a continuity in the implementation of economic policies inherited from the PNP. His approach emphasises the preservation of stability, avoiding unnecessary changes for the sake of change itself.

SOCIAL AND ECONOMIC CONSEQUENCES OF PNP AND IMF POLICIES AFTER 1990

One consequence of the IMF structural adjustment programme in the decade of the 1990s has been a rising adverse agricultural trade balance. In the period 1991–95, the agricultural trade balance was US$47.9 million; in the period 1996–2000 it had risen to US$144.7 million, and in the period 2001–5 it had worsened to US$249.7 million. This was because of the low prices for export commodities and the increasing food import bill.[41] Inflation in 1990 was 22 per cent, increasing to 35 per cent in 1994, before falling to 8.2 per cent in 2001. The unemployment rate in 1990 was 15.3 per cent and fluctuated around the level of 16 per cent in the mid-1990s, before falling back to 15 per cent in 2001. Life expectancy at birth maintained a level of 72.2 per cent. The foreign debt to GDP ratio averaged 75 per cent in the 1990s.[42]

The proportion of Jamaicans living below the poverty line, which has been estimated annually in the survey of living conditions since 1989, showed 30.9 per cent in 1987. The proportion in 1997 was 16.9 per cent.[43] The Gini coefficient (a coefficient, or statistical measure representing income inequality, or wealth inequality within a country developed by Corrado, a sociologist) showed improvements, with the ratio falling from below 0.45 by 1989; by 1998–2000, the coefficient was between 0.37 and 0.38, slightly more equitable than the US and resembling Australia and the UK. In 1997 it was 0.416.[44] The value is between zero and 1 per cent.

During the 1950s to 1970s, income distribution in Jamaica was heavily skewed in favour of the wealthy elite. The intention behind this skewed distribution was to stimulate the supply side of the economy, encourage higher savings, and increase the availability of capital for investments. However, in Jamaica, these intended outcomes did not materialise.

Instead of using their improved economic situation for productive investments, the wealthy elite in Jamaica indulged in conspicuous consumption, primarily purchasing imported consumer goods. This extravagant spending was evident, as observed by an IMF official during the 1990s, who noted that within the small area of New Kingston, he witnessed more Porsche motor cars than he typically saw in the centre of Washington, D.C. Even prior to the establishment of a Porsche dealership in Jamaica, the island had developed a habit of purchasing expensive foreign cars.

The benefits of a more fair distribution of income would expect to come on the demand side: higher personal spending on housing, education, health, personal services, and reduction of poverty. What helped the poor during the difficult times was higher levels of government spending, remittances from Jamaicans living abroad, and expansion of the informal economy, which have been outlined earlier.

In 1990, the poorest 10 per cent of the population accounted for only 2.5 per cent of total national consumption, while the richest 10 per cent accounted for 29.6 per cent of total national consumption. The top 10 per cent of households in the society consumed more than eleven times the poorest 10 per cent. The gap between the 'haves and the have nots' during the Patterson administration of the 1990s worsened slightly, as the top 10 per cent came to consume several more than the poorest 10 per cent.[45]

The incidence of poverty in the decade of the 1990s showed a fluctuating trend. In 1990, 28.4 per cent of households were living below the poverty line, with the incidence of poverty highest in the rural areas at 37.5 per cent of households. The situation worsened in 1991, with 44.6 per cent of households living below the poverty line, with the rural area households living below the poverty line at 57.2 per cent. The incidence of poverty was 22.8 per cent in 1994; however, it increased to 27.5 per cent in 1995, with the level in the rural areas living below the poverty line at 37 per cent. It improved steadily up to 1998, registering 15.9 per cent of households living below the poverty line, the lowest since 1989. In 2001, the incidence of poverty: those living below the poverty line was 16.9 per cent of households, with the rural areas at 24.1 per cent. The improvements (reduction of poverty) after 1995 were due to lower inflation rates after 1995, combined with the success of the public poverty alleviation programmes, along with significant contributions from overseas remittances. What is surprising is that, in 2001, some 71.2 per cent of households were using pit latrines; 4.5 per cent had no toilet facilities, with 28.5 per cent relying on standpipes for their drinking water.

In terms of the relationship between poverty levels and educational attainment, poor children showed a higher level of absenteeism and poorer educational attainment in 1997/98. Only a small proportion of children from poor households received secondary or university level education. With limited education, most of this group ended up being self-employed, or part of the grey economy. In 2001, 74.3 per cent of the Jamaican labour force had passed no examination; only 15.4 per cent had passes in the Caribbean Examinations Council (CXC) and Cambridge Advanced Level subjects and only 3.5 per cent had a university degree. Partly because of the IMF policies, the living standards of the poor deteriorated.[46] The factor which severely affected the poor was the rising cost of fuel oil and energy. The Jamaican economy has been at a disadvantage from heavy reliance on fuel oil for electricity generation, as well as for almost all its transportation requirements. The effect of energy cost on the economy is captured in chapter 15, 'Electricty Industry reform and Privatisation.' The foreign exchange cost of oil import rose from US$201.0 million in 1988 to US$1,734.4 in 2006.[47]

Jamaica's Debt Problem

As shown earlier in this chapter, the debt problem has become the most intractable economic problem in Jamaica, severely constraining post-independence Jamaican economic growth.

Early History of the Debt

In 1946, Jamaica's external debt amounted to J$9 million (£4.5 million).[48] The external debt ratio to exports was only 2.7 per cent. In this first period up to 1960, Jamaica had a relatively small domestic capital market, hence almost all the debt was externally sourced from commercial banks and bilateral and multilateral institutions such as the World Bank and IDB, the IMF and friendly governments such as the UK, Canada, and the US. Some of the external debt were commercial loans or stocks issued on the London Capital Market and, after 1959, and on the New York Market. The debt to GDP ratio in the 1960s was negligible; however, the practice of external borrowing by the Jamaican government had developed even before there was a local capital market.

The 1970s was the first episode of severe debt build up, the result of external shocks caused by the rise in oil price and contraction in bauxite export earnings. With the oil crises of 1971, Jamaica's total debt had increased to US$233 million, with external debt at US$87.0 million, representing 37.8 per cent, and domestic portion at US$146.0 million representing 62.2 per cent. By 1975, the external debt had increased to US$688 million, with debt service of US$83 million. The external debt service to exports rose to 7.4 per cent and external debt to GDP rose to 31 per cent. In 1980, when the Manley administration left office, the external debt had increased to US$1.9 billion, with a debt service of US$263 million. The external debt service to exports had increased to 24 per cent and the external debt to GDP to 70 per cent.

Some of the economic policies introduced, like imposing exchange controls, diminished the incentives to export and encouraged private hoarding of foreign exchange. The overly ambitious redistributive policy at a time resulted in a shrinking of the economy because of the negative impact of exchange control and import restrictions on production.

In this period, the fiscal deficit grew from J$95 million in 1973/74 to J$515 million in 1978/79. GDP fell by 26 per cent between 1973 and 1980.[49]

Following the 1973 oil price increase, many international commercial banks received sizeable increases in deposits of Petro-dollars, mainly from the Organisation of Petroleum Exporting Countries (OPEC) member states. With this increased level of funds, commercial banks will extend loans to developing countries with limited due diligence and limited conditionalities, having determined that sovereign debt then represented sound credit risk. Concurrently, developing countries, with a worsening balance of payment problems resulting from increases in the price of oil and other commodities, will take out foreign loans, almost on any conditions, including borrowing at variable interest rates.

The situation worsened with the 1980s global recession, when developing countries experienced a sharp reduction in their primary export commodity prices, accompanied by increases in international interest rates, resulting in some countries defaulting on their loans.[50] There is, however, the view that the debt crisis in this period was not only because of external factors, such as the oil price increase, interest rate increase, and declining commodity export, but also to internal factors, such as the use of foreign borrowing to finance non-productive consumption.[51]

The Seaga period of the 1980s formed the second episode of excessive debt build up. In this period the debt accumulation was influenced by geopolitics, as the Reagan administration's efforts to make Seaga's Jamaica more pro-Western, a symbolic demonstration case. During the 1980s, the Seaga government in its attempt to control external debt service payments focused on the payment of principal (but not interest), postponed in 1985, 1987, and 1990. The commercial banks facilitated multi-year rescheduling programmes.[52] In 1987, a debt conversion policy was instituted targeting the reduction of debt to commercial banks. Approximately 50 per cent was converted to equity. The government also gave priority to investments in export-oriented activities, such as the export free zones. A few projects were targeted for the social sector, which involved UNICEF funds, and which facilitated US$4 million in debt repayment to be converted to investments in social programmes, targeting women and children. In addition, a debt for nature swap was instituted whereby funds released were allocated to two national parks.

The share of the debt which formed the domestic portion as percentage of GDP, which was 44.6 per cent in 1980, first rose to 56.3 per cent in 1983, and then progressively declined to 19.5 per cent in 1993. Conversely, the share of the external debt as a percentage of GDP reached its highest in 1984 at 171.8 per cent, falling progressively thereafter to 99.3 per cent in 1989. Increasingly a significant proportion of the stock of domestic debt came to be issued in foreign currency at interest rates that were like those paid on bonds issued in the overseas private voluntary capital market, while the remaining portion was issued in local currency, at interest rate following Treasury Bill rates. External bonds on the New York market and other private financial overseas market, invariably came at rates over 11 per cent. The result was that at the end of Financial Year 1990/91, a year after the Seaga administration demitted office, the total public debt (external and domestic) had increased to US$5.6 billion, an almost 300 per cent increase, made up of domestic debt of US$1.4 billion (25.9 per cent) and external debt US $4.2 billion (74.1 per cent).[53]

The Patterson administration of the 1990s formed the third episode of the debt build-up. The debt level rose in the mid-1990s and the early part of 2000, increasing from US$5.6 billion in 1990 to US$8.49 billion in 2000, or 91.61 per cent of GDP. The impact of earlier measures to reduce the debt was marginal. Jamaica had always been concerned about embarking on debt reduction measure unless supported by the IMF. By 2006, when Patterson left office, the debt had increased to US$14.46 billion, or 117.02 per cent of GDP, a per capita debt of US$7,920. It was at this point the debt was becoming unsustainable.

Table 7.8 shows the debt stock for the financial years 1995/96 end 1996/97. By 2009, Golding had replaced Simpson Miller as prime minister and by then the debt had reached US$17.58 billion, or 141.93 per cent of GDP.[54]

The economy's debt service was equivalent to 15 per cent of GDP. The Caribbean Policy Research Institute-CaPRI noted that, by 2003, Jamaica had become the fourth most indebted country in the world, measured by debt to GDP, or debt per capita, behind Lebanon, Japan, and the Seychelles.[55]

Table 7.8: Total Public Debt Indicators – Million Jamaican Dollars

	1995/96	1996/97
External Debt Stock (US$)	3,402.51	3,170.32
Domestic Debt Stock (J$)	57,675.00	85,180.80
Total Debt Stock (J$)	193,843.45	196,363.92
End of Period Exchange Rate US$	40.02	35.07
Gross Domestic Product (GDP) (J$)	167,274.80	222,747.00
National Debt/ GDP (Per cent)	115.88	88.16

Source: Martin Naranjos and Emilio Osambela, 'Jamaica Financial System: Diagnostic & Recommendations,' Economic Study Series, IDB, Washington, DC, 2003, 20.

Notes *Provisional 1 GDP - at current prices, on a fiscal year basis.

During the period of the 1990s, the World Bank instituted the Structural Adjustment Loans (SAL) and the Sectoral Adjustment Loan (SECALs). In this period, the Jamaican financial sector experienced major transformation. Whereas in the earlier years limits were placed on commercial bank interest rate, these however were lifted between 1990 and 1991 and the existing exchange control, which was introduced in 1974 was discontinued. By 1994, a new set of legislations was introduced to allow primary dealers to buy government securities, further financial deepening of the market. This was followed by the BOJ discontinuing the use of direct controls on the amount and distribution of credit in favour of open market operation as the primary instrument of government's monetary policy. As a result of these liberal policy moves, the number of operators in the financial sector significantly increased and the range of financial instruments available in the market expanded. Savers were offered a broader range of saving instruments and there was more competition from the increased number of financial intermediaries. The government was also afforded a new range of borrowing options. At the same time, there was increased purchase of domestic instruments by international purchasers of government hard-currency instruments, allowing the government to place larger amounts of foreign debt than otherwise would have been the case. With the liberalisation of the financial market at the beginning of the 1990s, a condition of the IMF, the domestic capital market expanded rapidly in both size and sophistication.

The financial sector became one of the fastest growing sectors in the economy in the 1990s, increasing from 6.3 per cent in 1994 to 8.2 per cent. The outcome was the financial market crisis of 1996, where the government voluntarily absorbed the financial cost, as happened in Mexico and Thailand. The bailout had led to an increase in the domestic debt by 37 per cent, accounting for 27 per cent of GDP. In the period of the 1970s and 1980s, primary fiscal shortfalls and external account deficits created the need for external borrowing to provide foreign exchange and support for public expenditure. In the 1990s, CaPRI's analysis of the growth of Jamaica's debt concluded that the entire debt growth in the 1990s was because of the government absorbing the cost of the financial crisis, and this was although it had to take on the contingent liabilities of Air Jamaica and the sugar industry. At the same time, having no access to the IMF and other institutional financial market Jamaica had to resort to the local and international bond markets, beginning in mid-1990s substantially increasing the capacity of government to maintain a large debt overload.

The government became exposed to two types of obligations: explicit for which a contractual arrangement, or budgetary promise was made; or implicit for which moral, social, or political reasons suggest responsibility. In absorbing all the FINSAC debt, the government took the position of implicit obligation, although many argued at the time that only debt of the non-professional investors warranted its support, as the professional investors should have been able to determine the risk involved in their action and should not have been released from their financial obligations. It could be concluded such intervention created a moral hazard.

Not only did the size of the debt change, but its composition also underwent shifts over time, particularly in the 1990s. Table 7.9 illustrates the debt stock, which was heavily skewed towards foreign loans in the early 1990s. However, there was a shift in this composition after 1996. Domestic debt as a proportion of the total debt stock increased from 26 per cent of GDP in 1990/91 to 43.5 per cent in [year].

Jamaica's decision to sever its client relationship in 1996 resulted in the country being largely excluded from the multilateral financial markets of the IMF and the World Bank. As a result, Jamaica had to rely on reduced flows from bilateral financial institutions, such as the IDB, CDB, DFID, Japanese sources, and the New York bond market. This shift in financial sources had implications for the country's debt profile and access to international capital markets.

Table 7.9: Distribution of Debt between Domestic and External, 1990/91–2001/02

	1990/91	1992/93	1994/95	1996/97	1998/99	2000//01	2001/02
Internal debt per cent to total debt	26	20.4	29.4	43.4	52.8	56.5	60.7
External debt to GDP	74.1	79.6	70.6	50.6	46.9	43.5	39.3

Kirton, Claremont and Marjorie Harper (2004) *Jamaica's External Debt Estimation, Policy Implications*, Arawak Publication.

In the period, the government not only widened the market but also its geographic location, and to market-based determined public debt issues. Paper certificates also widened. The government extended the maturity structure, primarily by issuing long registered stock, with maturities ranging between seven and ten years. Under the PNP administration Jamaica's debt strategy was set out in Ministry Paper No. 10 1999/2000 and updated in 2002/03 in Ministry Paper No. 15.[56] In 1999, a Debt Management Unit was established at the Ministry of Finance, responsible for monitoring public debt programmes.

The domestic debt market mix developed to comprise Fixed and Floating Rate Medium to longer term local registered stocks, medium-term debentures, short term Treasury Bills, fixed rate foreign currency, domestic bonds, savings, and development bonds and commercial loans. Long Registered Stock (LRS) came to account for 42 per cent of domestic debt in July 2007. Over 86 per cent of the domestic debt were redeemable in local currency. Approximately 9 per cent was denominated in US and 4.6 per cent in USD, indexed bonds, with 0,007 per cent in Euro Bonds.[57]

Table 7.10 shows the Debt to GDP ratio for the period 1990–2002. The total stock of debt to GDP showed sharp increases from 79.1 per cent in 1996 to 148 per cent in 2002, averaging 115.8 per cent.

Table 7.10: Jamaica's Debt as Per Cent of GDP 1990–2002

Debt	1996	1997	1998	1999	2000	2001	2002	Av 1996/2002
Domestic	35.4	59.3	73.1	90.0	83.6	78.2	89.8	67.0
Total	79.1	102.3	115.7	132.7	131.9	130.6	148.5	115.8

Source: Sanjay Kathuria, Errol Graham, James Hanson, and Rina Obera 'Jamaica's Fiscal Consolidation for Growth and Poverty Reduction.'

The burden of servicing both foreign and domestic debt consumed a significant portion of Jamaica's resources, leaving limited funds available for critical areas such as capital and recurrent expenditure, social services, health, education, and infrastructure development, including roads. As a consequence, countries facing such challenges often experience credit rating downgrades, just as Jamaica did. This downgrade makes it more challenging to access financing from international and domestic private markets, and when successful, it typically comes at a higher interest rate, further straining the country's financial situation.

Countries with large external debt must face high external debt servicing cost. Excessive external debt servicing limits a country's access to further foreign borrowing; leads to increases in domestic interest rate and domestic inflation; capital flight; interest rate uncertainties, as well as limiting capital investment. A higher portfolio of loans in the private market, however, not only meant higher interest rates, but higher fiscal effort (higher primary surplus) was also needed. Loans from the multilateral and bilateral international sources came at a much lower cost, ranging from 4 per cent to 6.5 per cent. In shifting the structure of the debt portfolio from multilateral financing after 1996, especially from the IMF and World Bank to the private bond market and the local financial market, denominated at overseas bond market rates, Jamaica was paying a premium of approximately 5 per cent for the privilege of independence in determining its economic policies. One reason Jamaica dispensed with the clientele relationship with the IMF and also with the World Bank was the multitude of restrictive conditionalities which tied the hands of the government, virtually making it a passenger with respect to the determination of macroeconomic policies.

In the 1990s, numerous sectors of the Jamaican community also became critical of the IMF/World Bank, claiming that the government had abandoned its responsibility and placed the economy in the hands of the private sector and the multinational financiers, and that there was no evidence that the Jamaican private sector was responding to the country's economic challenges. In going to the private financial market, the Jamaican authorities was seeking to avoid the constraints of the multinational financial agencies' conditionalities.[58]

The increasing amount of funds mobilised through the bond issues also had serious implications for debt servicing, as bond obligation must be serviced and cannot be rescheduled. Jamaica's constitution requires the government debt to be serviced before other budgetary allocation. The result of the increasing bond issues was an inflexibility in dealing with the external debt. By the end of the Financial Year 2001/2002, the total debt had increased to US$10.4 billion with domestic debt at US$6.2 billion (60.7 per cent) and external debt at US$4.1 billion (39.3 per cent). In 1995/96, the debt which was issued as Jamaican bonds was recorded zero; by 2001/2002 financial year, the amount issued as Jamaican bonds increased to J$47 billion.[59]

The high cost involved in financing of the public sector increased the cost to the private sector in accessing funds for productive activities and reduced returns to investment. With a sizeable proportion of domestic debt indexed to the US dollar, the debt stock became sensitive to exchange rate movements. From a global perspective, the relative size of the debt was greater than that of Argentina, the Philippines, and Indonesia.

Empirical analysis shows that there is a relationship between the size of the national debt and economic growth. The IMF in a 2006 Cross Country Study of Public Debt and Inflation[60] concluded that movements of public debt do matter for inflation dynamics in Jamaica, with the likelihood of continued rise of the debt-inflation spiral. In this environment, the management of monetary policy is challenging. To reduce the debt service problem, Jamaica needed to export its way out of the problem rather than engage in further borrowing.[61] The debt in 2009 reached 142.0 of GDP, almost the level of the 1996 financial crisis. Table 7.11 shows the debt for the period 2009–20.

Table 7.11: Jamaica's Debt, 2009–20

Year	Jamaica's Debt in Billion US$	Debt as a Percentage of GDP
2009	17.580	141,93
1910	18.960	141,40
2011	20.427	139.47
2012	21.658	143,90
2013	20.135	138.74
2014	19.451	137,89
2015	17.77	121.88
2016	16.266	113.70
2017	15.199	101.23
2018	14.959	94.39
2019	14.976	94.26
2020	15.09	108.07
2021	14.61	92.35

Source: https://countryeconomy.com/national-debt/Jamaica.

The size of the debt became the main preoccupation of government policies in 2009. The government came under extreme financial pressures, beginning in the second half of 2008 because of the spill over of the global financial crisis in 2008. Tourism receipts had declined in 2009; remittances, which had been the recent saviour, showed a decline in 2009. In addition, bauxite/alumina income fell, as some of the local plants had to close because of global market oversupply. The debt, however, was by now mostly owed to domestic creditors and subject to significant exchange rate and/or interest risks. The domestic debt had interest payments on treasury bills first increased to 25 per cent, before settling at approximately 29 per cent. Most of this debt was short, dated instruments, as the government was finding little market uptake for long-dated instruments.

With the Jamaican dollar depreciated by 22 per cent, and the international reserve falling from US$2.4 billion in August 2008 to US$1.6 billion in February 2009, the government faced the problem of economic survival. The current account peaked at 20 per cent of GDP in 2008, as imports fell because of the recession; with the nominal exchange rate depreciating against the US dollar, the current account deficit widened from approximately 7 per cent in 2010. Revenues were coming in below what was projected. Interest payments on debt had increased to an average of 52 per cent of fiscal revenues during 2000/06–2008/09 financial years, giving the government little room to address other needs. In addition, the sharp increase in interest rates raised the financing bill to 60 per cent of revenues. This was to set the conditions the Jamaican government faced at the time of considering the debt exchange. The global financial crisis of 2008 only made the situation worse.

Deficit cutting measures were introduced in 2009 to address some problems, including a freeze in civil service salaries, reduction in capital expenditure, and increase in petrol tax. Although the VAT base had been broadened, its effect was marginal, reducing financing needs by only 1 per cent of the GDP. Government was therefore forced to consider debt exchange.

THE PERIOD AFTER 2009: GOLDING/SIMPSON/ HOLNESS

The JLP's Golding-led administration, which replaced the PNP administration in September 2007, continued the policy of working towards fiscal balance and export-led development. In 2009, under JLP Finance Minister Audley Shaw, the Jamaican government restored its clientele relationship with the IMF and, as a result, the World Bank and its technical services once again became available to Jamaica.

Debt Exchange

Prior to the debt exchange the interest payment on debt was 17 per cent of GDP in fiscal year 2009/10. The general picture was of a tight fiscal space, which formed the background for the IMF offering to provide financial support facilities.[62]

The debt exchange initiative of 2010 was risky and innovative. However, it was a necessary step that the GOJ had to take to obtain the promised twenty-seven-month IMF standby credit arrangement. The IMF promised the government support in 2009 through the Extended Fund Facility, and this was to be followed in 2013 by further financial support and later still in 2016 the Precautionary Standby Arrangement. The IMF, however, imposed one overriding condition: the exchange had benefit from of 100 per cent participation.

The debt exchange which Jamaica carried out occurred in two tranches over the period 2010 and 2013 and involved domestic bondholders voluntarily swapping their existing bonds for new bonds with lower coupons and longer maturities. The government had earlier resisted restructuring proposals by the IMF, which initially involved scenarios requiring substantial principal 'haircuts' on domestic and global bonds. The government was even more reluctant to restructure external debt, as it was concerned about its standing in the financial market. Before implementing the exchange, there were considerable consultations and public communications designed to maximise voluntary participation, similar to the consultation, which occurred in the 1980s with debt rescheduling with the Paris Club. The new debt exchange package was launched on January 14, 2010, to reverse the public debt levels, hovering approximately 140 per cent of the GDP in 2009. The existing bonds targeted for exchange included local currency (fixed, variable and US$ indexed) securities and US$ denominated debt. In total, these bonds amounted to US$7.8 billion, equivalent to 65 per cent of GDP. The domestic debt accounted for over 75 per cent of interest expense with 40 per cent (or 27 per cent of GDP) maturing within two years. The exchange generated interest savings of 3.5 per cent of GDP and reduced the amount of maturing debt over the next three years by 65 per cent. The Jamaican dollar denominated debt carried an average interest rate of 19 per cent, while the US dollar denominated debt carried an average interest rate of 9 per cent. In exchange for existing bonds, investors were given the option of selecting from a menu of fixed, floating and US$ indexed securities, subject to the allocation rules. The initial average yield on the Jamaican dollar denominated replacement bonds was set at 12.5 per cent across all instruments and maturities, while the yield on the new US$ denominated bonds was set at an average of 7 per cent.[63]

The outcome of the first tranche of the debt exchange was a high participation rate of 99.2 per cent, against an expected 80 per cent, resulting in significantly larger fiscal savings (approximately 3.5 per cent of GDP). The average maturity of the Jamaican denominated debt was significantly extended from 4.7 years before exchange. This resulted in a reduction to 8.3 years after the exchange and a reduction of project amortisation from 2010 to 2012 by J$300 billion. A small amount of eligible debt that was not tendered was subsequently called and redeemed for cash at face value in May 2010. The part was executed between January 14 and February 24, 2010. The first debt exchange of 2010 did not fully address the debt overhang, and as a result, a second debt exchange package was launched on February 12, 2013. The second exchange also formed a condition of the of further 2013 IMF financial support. Between 2010 and 2012, there was not only a significant increase in wage cost, deteriorating fiscal performance and leading to stalled negotiations with the IMF and this posed serious challenges for the government to conclude the full IMF support package. Large maturities were also due in 2013.

The second debt exchange achieved fiscal savings of 8.5 per cent of GDP (J$17.0 billion per year) and thereby lowering the debt-to-GPD ratio to 95 per cent by 2020. The programme also required voluntary participation of government of Jamaica securities by accepting new instruments with lower coupon between 75 and 500 bps and extended maturities of three to ten years. The second debt exchange was completed in two offerings with the expected participation rate also of 100 per cent. The first offering of the exchange only included domestically issued and held bonds, while the end offering was a private exchange of a broader set of eligible instruments, including foreign law bonds, with eight large institutional holders of government domestic debt. With the successful implementation the government could reduce it signal rate by over 100 per cent basis points.[64]

Following news of the successful debt exchange in 2010, the IMF approved a twenty-four-month US$$1.27 billion standby arrangement with the Jamaican government. This was followed by approval of a new financing programme by the World Bank of US$450 million, the IDB of US$600 million and funding from the CDB. In all, the pledged assistance amounted to 20 per cent of GDP. The debt service relief, coupled with the international financial support, significantly reduced the short-term liquidity risk.

Although the rating agencies prior to the launch of the first debt exchange had downgraded the domestic debt to selective default, within one week following settlement date, they all upgraded Jamaica's debt above the levels that had existed prior to the exchange; with Standard and Poors moving its long term foreign and local currency sovereign credit ratings on Jamaica to B minus. Moody's rating on Jamaican bonds was upgraded to B3 and Fitch moved its rating to B minus, out of a highly speculative region. There was very little negative fallout from the debt exchange.[65]

THE PERIOD AFTER 2011

The Golding-led administration had replaced the PNP administration at the election held in September 2007. General elections were contested again on December 29, 2011, with the PNP led by Portia Simpson and the JLP Andrew Holness. Porta Simpson–led PNP won by a landslide. General elections we held again on February 25, 2016, and the result a narrow parliamentary victory was achieved by the Holmes led JLP admiration, winning thirty-two of the sixty-three seats. General elections were not due until between February 25, 2021, and June 10, 2021. Holness, however, called an early election in August 2020 and was returned with a much larger majority, defeating the Peter Phillips led PNP and taking forty-nine of the sixty-three seats. Holness has largely continued the policies he inherited in 2016, essentially striving for fiscal balance and export-led development.

STRUCTURAL CHANGES IN THE ECONOMY SINCE 2007

Table 7.12 below shows the changes in the structure of the economy over the period 2006–20. Agriculture, mining, and manufacture (the primary sectors) as a proportion of GDP, have all declined. Agriculture as a percentage of GDP varied between 5.3 per cent and 7.3 per cent.

Similarly, manufacture stabilised between 8 per cent and 8.4 per cent over the period 2006–16. Mining, which had increased to 11 per cent in the 1960s, has fallen to under 3 per cent by 2016.

Table 7.12: Gross Value-added Percentage by Industry at Constant Cost, 2006–16

PRODUCT GROUP	2006	2007	2010	2014	2016
Agriculture, Forestry and Fishing	5.9	5.3	6.0	6.6	7.3
Mining and Quarrying	4.4	4.2	2.1	2.3	2.2
Manufacture	8.9	8.9	8.5	8.4	8.5
Electricity and Water	3.2	3.2	3.3	3.1	3.2
Construction	8.1	8,3	7.3	7.2	7.2
Wholesale/ Retail /Installation	18.5	18.5	18.1	17.6	17.4
Hotel and Restaurant	4.7	4.7	5.4	5.7	5.8
Transport /Storage / Communication	11.7	11.7	11.3	11.0	11.0
Finance & Insurance services a) less financial intermediation	10.0 -5.3	10.3 -5.6	10.2 -5.8	11.1 -6.7	11.6. -7.1
Real Estate /Renting /Business activities	10.2	10.4	11.0	10.8	10.7
Government Services	12.5	12.5	13.3	13,1	12.8
Other Services /household service	6.5	6.5	6.8	7.0	7.0
Total GDP	100.0	100.0	100.0	100.0	100.0

Note: a) Financial services less financial intermediation

Source: PIOJ: Economic and Social Survey.

PERFORMANCE OF THE ECONOMY SINCE 2010

The IMF noted that, with the US$1.66 billion standby arrangements from the IMF, the country is on a path to increased sustained growth, with public debt to GDP falling from 145 per cent of debt-to-GDP in 2010 to 100 per cent 2020, on target to fall to 50 per cent by 2026.[66] The Jamaican economy continued to benefit from high remittance inflows and in 2020 remittance had grown to US$3.4 billion with unemployment at 7.8 per cent, an all-time best.[67]

Between 2008 and 2010, the economy shrank as a result of global downturn but experienced muted recovery of 1.5 per cent in 2011. A major contributor to growth has been construction and other public works, including continuation of the major road programme facilitated by Chinese financing and engineering expertise. Jamaica's external position remained weak in 2011, registering consistent and large current account deficit which translated into sharp increases in Jamaica's net international liabilities for both public and private sector, resulting in debt to GDP rising to 134 per cent in 2010, up from 97 per cent in 2005. The sharp increase in the debt to GDP ratio triggered implementation of the debt exchange programme. Growth in the economy has been positive since 2015, a four-year period of positive growth up to 2019. Contribution to GDP of hotels and restaurants, reflecting tourism activities, was under 5 per cent between 2006 and 2007, increasing to 6.2 per cent in 2019. The sector suffered a decline in 2020 because of the COVID-19 epidemic, falling to 3.2 per cent but showed a robust recovery in 2021 to 4.2 per cent. Government services also stabilised to between 12 per cent and 14 per cent over the period 2006–21. Growth in the economy, however, while positive, except for negative growth in the years 2012, 2017, 2019, was relatively small, typically under 1 per cent, with the best year being 2011 at 3.19 per cent. Growth in 2020 was minus 9.4 per cent due to COVID-19 pandemic but rebounded to positive of 4.6 in 2021.[68] Over the period 2016–20, the economy declined by 1.1 per cent.[69]

With the switch from direct to indirect taxes, Jamaica could resort to tax cuts for the first time in living memory. The macroeconomic landscape has shown improvement, with inflation and unemployment being brought down to the historically low levels of under 8 per cent. Jamaica's economic problems of high unemployment, which peaked at 27.6 per cent in 1981 and higher levels of inflation in consumer prices, increased indebtedness and higher spending on debt service seem to have made a change for the better. The public debt has fallen, helped also by the Petrocaribe buy back, with Jamaica's credit ratings moving up, and with bond spread having fallen.

Figure 7.1 below provides a graphic picture of the structural changes in the economy over the period 1960–2004, during which the country changed from being a goods-producing economy to a service producing economy. Services' share of the economy, which was 52 per cent in 1964, expanded to just under 70 per cent by 2006.

Figure 7.2: Services vs Goods Producing Sector's Share to GDP, 1960–2006

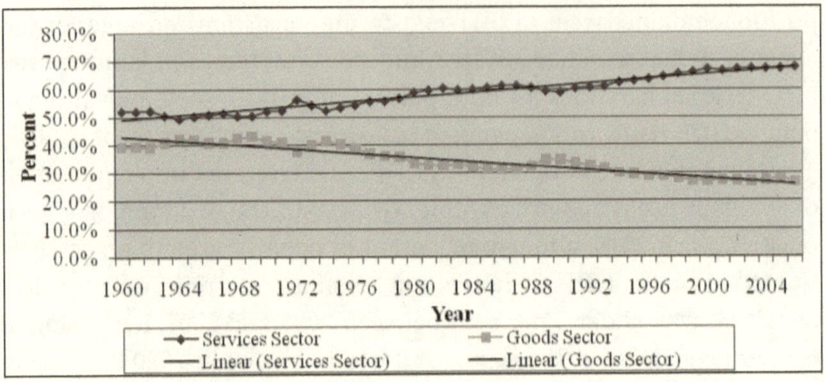

Source: Constituted from STATIN GDP Data.

Significant economic progress seems to have been made at last after four decades of IMF effort to stabilise the economy. Undoubtedly, the return to the IMF after 2009, the debt exchange and the continuation of the economic and financial policies by successive PNP and JLP administrations over the period 2007–20 have contributed immensely to what seems to be the turnaround of the Jamaican economy. After forty years of unsuccessful attempts by the IMF to restructure the Jamaican economy, important changes have at last occurred.

The IMF is now showcasing Jamaica as the example of a country that achieved macro-economic stabilisation without political upheaval. The IMF states that it no longer dictates economic policies to governments and that it waits until the governments present a satisfactory proposal. Gone are the days that a government signed a Fund agreement used to negotiate debt restructuring. Table 7.13 shows changes in Jamaica's currency value over the period 1938–2020.

Table 7.13: Changes in Currency Values Over the Years, 1938–2020

British Pound to the USD			USD to the JMD		
Year	**GBP**	**JMD**	**USD to GBP**	**USD**	**JMD**
1938	1	-	4.89	-	-
1945	1	-	4.03	-	-
1969	1	2.0	2.39	1	0.77
1974	1	2.13	2.34	1	0.91
1980	1	4.15	2.33	1	1.78
2015	1	178.0	1.53	1	125.0
2020	1	207.7	1.28	1	150.0

Source: Leroy Cooke, *Land of My Birth* (Kingston: Negro River Publishers, 2018) and data from BOJ Annual Report

Notes

1. Anders Danielson, 'Economic Reforms in Jamaica,' *Journal of Anti-American Studies and World Affairs* 38, nos. 2/3 (1996): 97–108.
2. Jerry Haar, 'The Caribbean Basin Initiative: An Interim Assessment of the Trade Provision's Impact,' *International Marketing Journal* 7, no. 2 (1990), https://doi.org/10.1108/EUM0000000001529.
3. Edward Seaga, 'Development Strategy for the Next Decade,' Paper presented to the Commonwealth Finance Ministers Meeting, September 1996.
4. Ibid.
5. J. Calene, 'From Manley, To Seaga: The Persistence of Clientelist Politics in Jamaica,' *Social and Economic Studies* 38, no. 1 (March 1989).
6. Danielson, 'Economic Reforms in Jamaica.'
7. M. Ayub, 'Made in Jamaica,' World Bank Occasional Paper, No. 31, Baltimore, John Hopkins, 1981.
8. Girjanauth Boodraj, 'Technological Behaviour Under Structural Adjustment: A Case Study,' Kingston Consortium Graduate School of Social Sciences, UWI, Mona, 1995.
9. Roy Bahl, *Economic and Politics of Jamaica Tax Reform: The Jamaican Tax Reform* (Cambridge: Lincoln Institute of Land Policy, 1990).
10. Government of Jamaica Board of Revenue, *Comprehensive Tax Reform* (Kingston: Government of Jamaica Board of Revenue, 1985).
11. Anthony, J. Payne, 'Politics in Jamaica' (Heinemann Educational Book (Caribbean); C. Hurst & Company, 1988).
12. Nomad Bahram, 'The IMF and Its Critics,' *Princeton Essays in International Finance*, no. 146, Princeton University, 1980.

13. Christopher Adam, William Cavendish, and Percy S. Mistry, *Adjusting Privatisation; Case Studies from Developing Countries* (London: James Curry Limited, 1996).
14. Damien King, 'The Evolution of Structural Adjustment and Stabilization Policies in Jamaica,' Paper prepared for the government of the Netherlands (HOL/97,6034), 2000.
15. Cheryl Gopaul, 'Kingston, Jamaica: Structural Adjustment and Policy,' in *Cites and Structural Adjustment*, ed. Nigel Harris and Ida Fabricius (London: UCL Press, 1996).
16. Claremont Kirton, 2004, op. cit.
17. Elsie Le Franc, ed., *Consequences of Structural Adjustment: A Review of Jamaican Experience* (Kingston: Canoe Press, 1994).
18. Michael Witter and Patricia Anderson, 'The Distribution of the Social Cost of Jamaica's Structural Adjustment 1977–1989,' SALISES, UWI, 1991.
19. Derick Boyd, *Economic Management, Income Distribution and Poverty in Jamaica* (New York: Praeger, 1988).
20. King, 'The Evolution of Structural Adjustment and Stabilization Policies in Jamaica.'
21. Joseph Stiglitz, *Globalisation and Its Discontent* (New York: W.W. Norton & Company, 2003).
22. World Bank, 'Trade and Finance Sector Adjustment Loan,' FSAL, Aide Memoire, 1990.
23. Ibid.
24. David E. Bloom, Ajay Mahal, Damien King, and Philip Castillo, 'Globalisation and Liberalisation and Sustainable Development: Progress and Challenges in Jamaica,' UNCTAD/UNDP, Occasional Paper, 2001.
25. Jessica Byron and Patsy Lewis, 'Formulating Sustainable Development Benchmark for EU-Caribbean EPA: Caribbean Prospective,' Prepared for Trade and Sustainable Development (ICTSD), 2007.
26. Brian M. Francis, 'Trade and Economic Growth in the Caribbean' (PhD Thesis, University of Florida, 2003).
27. Deep J.R. Ford and A. Rawlins, 'Agricultural Trade Policy and Food Security in the Caribbean: Structural Adjustment Issues, Multilateral Negotiations and Competitiveness,' in *Trade Policy, Trade and Food Security in the Caribbean*, ed. Deep J.R. Ford, C. Dell'Aquila and P. Conforti (Rome: FAO, 2007).
28. P. J. Patterson, *My Political Journey: Jamaicas Sixth Prime Minister* (Kingston: University of the West Indies Press, 2018).
29. Ransford Palmer, 'A Decade of West Indian Migration to the USA 1962–1972: An Economic Analysis,' *Social and Economic Studies* 23, no. 4 (1974): 571–87.
30. Elizabeth Thomas-Hope, 'Return Migration to Jamaica and its Development Potential,' *International Migration* 37, no. 1 (1999): 183–207.
31. Andrew Downs and Elsie Le Franc, 'Measuring Human Development in Countries with Invisible Economies: Challenges Posed by the Informal

and Remittances Sectors in Jamaica,' *Social and Economic Studies* 50, no. 1 (2001): 169–98.

32. Roger Asgaral, Asli Demirque-Kunt, and Marie Peria, *Do Remittances Promote Financial Development?* (Washington, DC: World Bank, 2006).
33. World Bank, *World Bank Global Economic Prospects: Implication of Remittances and Migration – 2006* (Washington, DC: World Bank, 2006).
34. George Ramocan, (2010), *Remittances to Jamaica* (Kingston: Bank of Jamaica, 2010).
35. P.J. Patterson, 'The Emerging Role of the State,' Ministerial Roundtable, Ocho Rios, August 12, 1993.
36. Daniel Artana and Fernando Narnjo, *Fiscal Policy Issues in Jamaica: Budgetary Institutions, The Tax System and Debt Management* (Washington, DC: IADB Economic and Sector Study Series, 2003).
37. IMF, 'IMF Country Report, no 06/157,' 2006.
38. Maximo Torrero, Miguel Robles, Manuel Hernandez, Joyce De La Roco, and Maureen Weber, 'The Informal Sector in Jamaica,' Economic and Sector Studies Series, Washington, DC, IDB, 2006.
39. Michael Witter and Claremont Kirton, 'The Informal Economy in Jamaica: Some Empirical Experiences,' ISER Working Paper no. 36, 1990.
40. IMF, *Jamaica Selected Issues*, IMF Country Report, no. 06/157, 2006.
41. Claremont P. Kirton, unpublished (1991).
42. Benjamin Timms, 'Development Theory and Domestic Agriculture I the Caribbean: Recurring Crisis and Missed Opportunities,' *Caribbean Geography* (2008): 101–117
43. Kari Levitt, 'The Origins and Consequences of Jamaica's Debt Crisis 1970–1990,' Consortium Graduate School of Social Science, UWI, Mona, 1991.
44. Elizabeth Susan Emmanuel, 'The Impact of Socioeconomic Factors on Health Status in Jamaica' (Master's Thesis, UWI, Mona, 1997).
45. James Riley, *Poverty and Life Expectancy: The Jamaican Paradox* (Cambridge: Cambridge University Press, 2005).
46. Claremont Kirton and Monique Harper, *Jamaica's External Debt Estimates, Analysis and Policy Implication* (Kingston: Arawak Publication with Oxfam, 2004).
47. Ibid.
48. Information provided by PIOJ from PETROJAM Ltd, the oil marketing companies and the Bauxite and Alumina Companies.
49. HMSO (1964), 'Commonwealth Development and Its Financing Jamaica,' London.
50. Caribbean Policy Research Institute – CaPRI, 'Jamaica's Debt: Exploring the Causes and Strategies,' 2001.
51. Elmar Altvater and Kurt Huber, 'The Causes of the International Debt Crisis,' in *The Poverty of Nations: A Guide to the Debt Crisis – From Argentina to Zaire*, ed. by Elmar Altvater and Kurt Huber, translated by Terry Bond (London: Zed Book, 1991).

52. R. William Cline, 'International Debt and Stability of the World Economy Policy Analysis,' *International Economics* 4, (1983).
53. Kirton and Harper, *Jamaica's External Debt Estimates, Analysis and Policy Implication.*
54. Ibid.
55. https://countryeconomy.com/national-debt/Jamaica.
56. CaPRI, 'Jamaica's Debt: Exploring the Causes and Strategies.'
57. Ministry Paper No. 10 1999/2000 and updated in 2002/03 in Ministry Paper No. 15.
58. Ibid.
59. The conditions which developed became too onerous for the finance minister, Dr Omar Davies. Dr Davies served as finance minister for most of the Patterson stewardship as prime minister. Dr Davies, however, became unpopular with the press and certain PNP insiders and was subjected to daily criticisms, to the point where it made it difficult to for him carry on the job. When Portia Simpson became prime minister in 2006, she eventually replaced Dr Omar Davies with Dr Peter Phillips as finance minister.
60. Kirton and Harper, *Jamaica's External Debt Estimates, Analysis and Policy Implication.*
61. Kwon Goohoon, Lavern McFarlane, and Wayne Robinson, *Public Debt, Money Supply and Inflation: A Cross Country Study and Its Implications for Jamaica* (Washington, DC: IMF, 2006).
62. A. Francis, 'The Dynamics of Debt in Jamaican Economy or Domar vs Omar: The Burden of Debt and National Income,' Dept of Economics, UWI, Mona, 2000.
63. Jake Johnson and Joan Montecino, 'Update on Jamaica,' Center for Economic and Policy Research, 2012.
64. IMF, 'World Economic Outlook Database,' 2012.
65. R. Langrin Brian, 'Policy Lessons from Postmortems of Jamaica's Two Recent Debt Exchanges,' Bank of Jamaica, Kingston, September 2013.
66. Ibid.
67. David Grigorian, Trevor Alleyne, and Alejandro Guerson, 'Jamaica Debt Exchange,' IMF Working Paper, Washington, DC, 2012.
68. IMF, 'Jamaica on a Path to Higher Economic Growth,' 2019.
69. Ibid.
70. World Bank Economic Data Base, Sundry years.
71. PIOJ, 'Economic and Social Survey 2021,' Kingston, Jamaica, 2022.

PART 3

Preparing Jamaica for a Market Economy

CHAPTER EIGHT

Political Economy and Competition Policy, Institution, and Law

SPONSORED BY

Mona School of Business & Management

MSBM The University of the West Indies, Mona

BACKGROUND TO INTRODUCING COMPETITION POLICIES IN JAMAICA

Jamaica was one of the first set of twenty developing and emerging countries to introduce competition policy and law in the 1990s, and one of the first to mandate competition in professions, such as the medical and legal professions. This initiative was entirely home-grown and not part of the conditions dictated by the International Monetary Fund (IMF) in the1980s. Since then, following on Jamaica's initiative and benefiting from the country's experience, several Caribbean countries have introduced competition or anti-trust laws and established a Competition Commission.

Colonial Jamaican economy has been one of cartels and monopolies controlling imports and exports, domestic distribution, and retail trade based on the 1950s economic policy of 'industrialisation-by-invitation.' The idea of competition and a market economy was not only new to Jamaica but viewed with suspicion and hostility by the industrial and professional class who had benefited from protection over the centuries. This then formed the environment in which the competition policy and law was introduced, hence there was strong resistance. Deputy Prime Minister Patterson was, however, determined to shake up the industrial scene, whatever compromises had to be made. For example, merger control regulation was purged from the final legislation because of the strong resistance encountered.

Once the law was introduced, and the Fair-Trading Commission (FTC) was established. The Commission initially faced many legal challenges in executing its mandate, leading to several court cases, some of which were appealed to the Privy Council in London, Jamaica's final Court of Appeal. In addition, the initial institutional structure of the Fair-Trading Commission revealed several deficiencies, which effectively stymied its operations for several years. Although these deficiencies were identified in the early years, agreement could not be reached among the bureaucrats as to the best institutional arrangements to facilitate restructuring of the law and the Commission. In recent times, the Commission has been allowed more leeway from a UK Privy Council's ruling, which concluded that, although there were no specific merger control clauses in the law, the Commission had the authority to regulate mergers; further, the legal mandate of the Commission extended to all sectors of the economy.

The government is now drafting a new competition bill which, hopefully, will resolve the institutional and legal issues. Political economy focuses on the interaction between institutions and human behaviour, how the former shapes choices and how the latter changes institutional frameworks. The development of the competition policy and competition law in Jamaica is a classic example of the reshaping of a market economy by ascribing a wider role for the private sector in the production of goods and services and in the allocation of economic resources. All the major bilateral and multilateral donor agencies since 1990 now acknowledge the central role of the private sector, not only in economic development but also in poverty reduction.

Private sector development and competition are inextricably linked in economic development, and competition plays a major role in improving allocative and productive efficiency. Whether it is a change of ownership from public to private or competition that matters most in improving economic efficiency is still the subject of debate. In fact, economic regulation, in the case of the monopoly utilities, needs to be supported by competition regulation. Despite the centrality of competition in economic theory, ideas of how it works in facilitating economic development differ widely. The concept of perfect competition, freedom of entry and exit, and equilibrium has been the standard theoretical construct for economic analysis, with a profound influence on competition policy and law.

The Genesis of Competition in Economic Thought

The history of competition in economic thought goes back to Adam Smith in 1776[1] and P. Cook et al.[2] According to these authors, Smith saw the concept of competition from the point of view of independent rivalry between two firms acting as a force that would, in the long run, eliminate excessive profits and unsatisfied demand. Participants in the market would adjust prices in response to market conditions, principally through the process of rivalry, reflecting the classical economic approach. Since then, the neoclassical approach has developed, viewing competition as characterised by a state of equilibrium, dependent on the forces of demand and cost structures that determine who survives and who fails; this is formally presented in the concept of perfect competition. The neoclassical approach focuses on the effects of competition, rather than a definition of the underlying behavioural process that characterises competition. The classical economist relates competition to business behaviour, involving organisational and technological development, while the neoclassical is more concerned with market structures.

The two schools of thought have therefore been shaping competition policy; the neoclassical structure, conduct, and performance approach states that market behaviour and performance are related strictly to market power, and that the degree of competition is determined in relation to the notion of perfect competition. The evolutionary approach, on the other hand, does not take the view that, in all situations, market power can be interpreted as harmful to competition. For the Evolutionary School, dynamic efficiency is more important than static efficiency. Static efficiency describes the level of efficiency at a certain point in time. This, therefore, describes both allocative and productive efficiency. A firm is productively efficient if it is at its minimum cost or is producing a level of output that puts that firm at the lowest point of its average cost curve. Allocative efficiency describes when the allocation of resources reflects consumers' wants and needs and is at the point where the price of the good equals the marginal cost.

The implication for small, developing economies is that simple transfer of institutional regimes from industrialised countries that, traditionally have focused on structural remedies, may not provide the most appropriate solution. In small economies, monopolies, and oligopolies may have to be accommodated since such structures may be more efficient, and the focus may well have to be on the removal of government-imposed market restrictions.

One of the important issues which comes up in introducing competition law and policy is the size of the economy. The question is, what constitutes a small developing economy? Michael S. Gal defines a small economy as an independent sovereign state that can support only a few competitors in most industries when catering to demand.[3] This definition is said to reflect certain characteristics: the highly concentrated nature of most industries, particularly manufacturing and mining; high entry barriers and below-efficient scale levels of production or sub-optimal levels of production. In small economies, industries have to be more concentrated to benefit from minimum scale economies. Rajan Dhanjee contends that Gal's definition of size is incomplete, and questions whether all economies meeting Gal's definition have enough in common to benefit from their concentration levels and entry barrier.[4]

The smaller the economy, however, the more likely there will be concentrated industry structures. A small population limits the size of demand and the number of firms that can efficiently service a market. Hence, small economies display monopolistic or oligopolistic tendencies. Balance between productive efficiencies and competitive considerations is the most important feature which distinguishes small from large economies. The presence of concentrated market structures and high entry barriers often requires that competition policies in small economies focus more on conduct rules rather than structural remedies.

The Purpose of Competition Policy

B. Hoekman and Peter Holmes argue that competition policy has an important role to play in developing countries, both in promoting a competitive environment and in building and sustaining public support for pro-competitive policy stance by governments, with liberal trade and investment policies being key elements of good competition policy.[5]

The most common objectives cited for competition policy is the maintenance of the competitive process or protection of effective competition. These are synonymous with removing or preventing unreasonable restraint on trade. For the World Bank, the ultimate objective is the enhancement of consumer welfare, while for the United Nations Conference on Trade and Development (UNCTAD) the ultimate objective is broader, emphasising domestic and international trade and economic development. As a result, implicitly incorporates a wider range of objectives such as consumer welfare, social welfare, economic efficiency, and protection of small businesses.

In the design of the law, the question then arises whether the objective should be pure economics with efficiency and consumer welfare goals, or whether the broader goals of equity and public interest should be included, thereby opening the door for political opportunism. In the Jamaican situation, it was felt that it was more appropriate, at the stage of economic development in the 1990s, to put the emphasis on economic efficiency and precision, following the view of the US policymakers that the markets will correct itself.[6]

The choice between broad and narrow competition policy objectives has implications for the instruments, criteria, and legal and economic standards in administering and enforcing competition law. Broad objectives, which include social and fairness consideration, can be vague and conflicting. Barbara Lee, in a broad survey of twenty-three countries, found enhancement of competition in nineteen cases: elimination of restrictive business practices in eleven instances; economic efficiency in eleven instances; consumer welfare in eight instances, and economic trade freedom in six instances, being the most cited objectives from the surveys.[7]

A History of Jamaican Anti-Competitive Market

The long history of the economic development accompanied by in anti-competitive markets policies and laws encouraged by successive governments meant that by 1980 all areas of the economy: manufacturing, distribution, agriculture, banking, finance, and construction were characterised by anti-competitive markets. Anti-competitive markets in Jamaica have been fostered through general merchandise laws, such as the 1951 Trade Law and specific industry measures, particularly as they relate to agricultural and agro-industrial products. The laws introduced to control agricultural products were of two types: those designed to control the products of specific industries, mainly export crops, and those which covered the marketing of minor crops and domestic farm products. Marketing controls over agricultural products and essential items emerged from the defence regulations, which were introduced during the Second World War and during the emergency period which followed the end of the war. Industry control laws were introduced after 1945 for sugar, coconut, coffee, cocoa, banana, and rice. Minor products have been regulated under the Agricultural Marketing Law and the Produce Law. Under these laws, the government fixes prices, regulates trade, and operates as a monopsony purchaser of produce for export.

Under the Trade Law, the government either fixed the minimum prices for hardware items, drug products, and motor vehicles parts or fixed the percentage margins for wholesalers and retailers. In the 1960s and 1970s, importers of drugs were allowed a mark-up of 10 per cent and pharmacists 25 per cent. Similarly, wholesalers were allowed a mark-up of 10 per cent for hardware items and retailers between 12.55 per cent and 17.5 per cent. Under the Motor Vehicle and Motor Vehicle Parts and Accessories Prices Control Order of 1961, successive governments regulated the mark-up on motor vehicles and motor vehicle parts.

The 1955 Trade Law established the Prices Commission, and, over the years, the Prices Commission carried the responsibility for fixing and monitoring items under price controls. Up to the time of removing price controls in 1992, well over one hundred groups of items were still regulated. Price controls and regulation of distribution were administered by the Agricultural Marketing Corporation (AMC) and the Jamaica Commodity Trading Company (JCTC). Both institutions monopolised the trade for a wide range of goods in the 1970s and 1980s. In the 1970s, JCTC monopolised trade in basic food items such as rice, as well as motor vehicles, pharmaceuticals, and hardware. By 1990, the company's annual losses amounted to J$113M (US$15.61M)[9] and its indebtedness exceeded J$1.5B, evidence of massive subsidies as part of the government's redistributionist policy. In 1990, the exchange rate was J$7.24 to US$1.0.

A second area in which anti-competitive markets prevailed was through the system of capacity licensing and industrial incentive legislation. Capacity licensing was used to balance supply and demand, to regulate entry to markets and bar new entrepreneurs. Between 1948 and 1970, various incentive laws were introduced as part of the country's industrial policy. Important among these incentives were specific laws relating to the textile industry, the motion picture industry, and the cement industry.

The granting of exclusive manufacturing rights, high tariffs, and quantitative restrictions encouraged the development of a manufacturing sector based on monopoly rather than competition. The result was that most firms were never motivated to modernise their plants and processes for higher levels of productivity or developed the marketing skills needed to enter the competitive global marketplace.

The Planning Institute of Jamaica concluded that the effect of the government's industrial incentive and capacity licensing regime was the creation of monopoly enterprises that relied on protection rather than competition for their survival.[9] Accordingly, the incentives rewarded inefficiency through high prices instead of promoting efficiency. The lack of competition allowed firms to ignore the need to introduce modern technology, the result being that Jamaica entered the 1990s with obsolete equipment and processes in its factories. In the 1986 PIOJ study, a sample survey of prices of 48 per cent consumer goods showed that the licensing system had the effect of restricting entry and raising prices on three quarters of the goods in the sample. The report further concluded that the system of protection was not only arbitrary but distortionary and resulted in resource misallocation.

Over the years, the government of Jamaica has imposed entry restrictions with conditions conducive to price-fixing in several other areas of commerce. Permits were needed to operate car rental and taxi services for the hotel industry, as well as to operate petrol stations. The sale of telephone equipment was in the hands of one franchised operator. With the professions (medicine, accounting engineering, and architecture) the system of fee schedules effectively eliminated price competition regarding the marketing of services.

There has been several very strong business associations supporting the cartelisation of trade. In the distributive trade, the several cartels included: The Block Makers Association, the Pharmaceutical Association, the Bakers Association, the Hardware Merchants Association, the Gasoline Retailers Association, to name but a few. In rural Jamaica, retailing groups established cartels and indulged in widespread price-fixing in the local market.

Data collected by the Prices Commission in 1980 on a broad range of food items found that a single price prevailed island-wide in a vast majority of cases. With pasteurised and condensed milk, cornmeal, rice, bread, flour, and chicken, a single price prevailed in at least 85 per cent of the shops surveyed.[10] The Prices Commission report concluded that these findings were typical of the result of the Commission's Price Monitoring Surveys which covered eighty-three supermarkets, grocery shops, and other retail outlets island-wide. After five decades of concerted effort under import substitution policies, local producers and traders, as a matter of general business practice, came together to fix prices, cartelise markets and adopt other trade restraining practices as part of their routine business strategies. Eventually, Jamaicans came to regard variation in price for a given item as socially unjust and against the public interest. Fostering competition culture against this public perception was a challenge.

Introduction of Competition Policy and Law

Because, for decades, the state had fixed prices, fostered monopolies, limited entry to various industries, and encouraged restrictive business practices, one may question why Jamaica introduced a competition policy and law in the early 1990s. In the early 1990s, there were very few developing countries with a competition policy and law. The World Bank at the time was more concerned with the development of regulatory frameworks for utilities which were being considered for privatisation.[11] The bank itself had little expertise in competition and regulatory policies and in the development of regulatory institutions. Derek McKoy pointed out that the law was not reflective of Jamaica's economic history and involved a radical break from the past with the objective of making the Jamaican economy competitive for the twenty-first century.[12] In McKoy's view, it was a deliberate attempt by policymakers to engineer Jamaica's passage into a market-driven economy, rather than to ameliorate deficiencies in existing laws.

In debates on the issue, the government maintained that, by removing controls from the market, it would demonstrate its commitment to protecting the interests of consumers.

The idea of a competition policy and law came out of a Cabinet meeting early in 1990. During the PNP's days in the political wilderness, party chairman, P.J. Patterson, and I had had several discussions on some of the key requirements for a market economy to be addressed on a PNP administration's return to power. When competition policy surfaced in Cabinet shortly after the PNP was returned to power, Patterson then deputy prime minister gave his colleagues a lecture on the topic, whereupon the response to Patterson by Prime Minister Manley, a product of the London School of Economics, was: 'since you seem to be so well versed on the matter you may as well take responsibility and provide us with a policy statement for presentation to Parliament.' Hence Patterson, a lawyer, came to be responsible for the development of the new law and the regulatory reform programme. He regarded competition policy as an important instrument in levelling the playing field and creating opportunities for small entrepreneurs.[13]

Following this development, the Cabinet announced in early 1990 that it had established a subcommittee and a technical task force to design and develop new policies and legislation to provide the country with the legal framework for a competitive and deregulated economy. Jamaica had launched an ambitious programme of market-oriented economic reforms in 1982 involving: removal of price controls; privatisation of state assets and enterprises; liberalisation of financial markets and international trade; and reform of public management. By the early 1990s, however, it had become clear that the full benefits of market reforms would only be realised if enterprises operated under the spur of competition, so that consumer dissatisfaction about services and market sanctions for poor performance were felt; hence, a more assertive competition policy was needed[14] to eliminate distortions in the marketplace, minimise misallocation of resources, and provide for a more competitive economy. The 1990 increase of electricity rates evoked unfavourable public response, requiring government ministers and the senior management of the electricity company, Jamaica Public Service Company (JPSCo), to meet with consumers and the public to allay their concerns.

Jamaica's market structure bore little resemblance to that of the US at the end of the nineteenth century, when abuse by private monopolies and the fear of concentration of economic power by 'trust' companies prevailed, until the government was forced to enact anti-trust, or pro-competition legislation. Rather, Jamaica's business environment had developed under an umbrella of government controls, high levels of state participation and state-supported restrictive business practices that severely restricted competition in the private enterprise sector.

Introducing greater competition to the marketplace required a profound change in attitudes and behaviour among the PNP politicians, consumers, and businesspeople. When the government removed price controls from bread and construction blocks in 1991, bakers and block makers – acting through their respective trade associations – imposed a single price. The producers claimed that fixing a single price was in the interest of consumers. Even consumers accepted fair prices would prevail only if they were set by the government. Following the statement on competition policy, delivered in Parliament, Manley announced in 1990 that the government would establish a Cabinet subcommittee and a technical task force to design and develop new policies and legislation to provide the country with the legal framework for a competitive market and deregulated industries. The new policy measures were to address four related areas of market operations. First, regulatory measures were to be introduced to address fiduciary responsibilities and market imperfection in the financial services sector through the Bank of Jamaica Act and the Money Lenders Act. New legislation to regulate the banking and financial sector was to be introduced as a Banking and Financial Services Act. These new policy measures would address the criteria for entry, capital adequacy, asset diversification, insider, and connected party transactions, as well as establish areas of permissible activity.

Second, new legislation measures were to be introduced to provide for introducing a Securities and Exchange Commission and to strengthen the role of equity investment in the deregulation of the economy. Previously, the system of regulating the Jamaican stock market was through voluntary action. The Council of the Jamaica Stock Exchange (JSE), responsible for its own regulation, was composed of a majority of its members and, over the years. The members had acted to limit entry of new stockbrokers into the market arguing that the market was not large enough to be exposed to competition.

Third, regulatory measures were to be introduced to control market power of the natural monopolies and utilities, to afford consumer protection against injurious acts of the utilities and to provide for more transparency in the establishment of utility prices. It was expected that the new regulatory measures would apply to water, electricity, and telecommunications. The authority to regulate these industries was contained in the existing industry-enabling legislation and the sector minister had effective power to grant licences and approve price increases. The Public Utilities Commission (PUC), which was introduced in 1965 to regulate telephone and electricity services, was disbanded in 1975 when both utility services were nationalised. When the government introduced the privatisation programme for telecommunications in 1989, no provision was made for the reintroduction of a transparent regulatory regime. The conclusion of Spiller, Pablo and Sampson[15] was that the regulatory changes of 1987 in the telecommunications sector seemed to have erred in preserving a tight monopoly over all telecommunications segments and that this represented a missed opportunity in the process of regulatory reform and market liberalisation.

Fourthly, new policies and legislation were to be introduced to encourage market competition, to curtail restrictive business practices and anti-competitive behaviour, provide for consumer protection and to regulate mergers and acquisitions. Up to 1990, like most developing countries, Jamaica had never considered a policy to enhance competition. The Jamaican law, as it then stood, was based entirely on common law. English common law developed around the restraint of trade doctrine. Courts normally would not enforce a contract which provided for unreasonable restraint of trade, as to do so would be contrary to public policy.[16]

In January 1991, a policy paper entitled 'Principles, Purpose and Policy Objectives of the Jamaican Competition,'[17] which I had prepared, was presented to the public by the government and carried in its entirety by the *Daily Gleaner*. The central features of the new competition policy were prohibition of certain types of restrictive business practices; restriction of interlocking directorates; control over horizontal mergers; restriction of unfair consumer practice; liberalisation of the market for professional services, as well as the establishment of a Competition and Monopolies Commission and a Competition Court.

Following the publication of a policy paper, the government secured technical assistance from the United States Agency for International Development (USAID) to review and advance the ideas in the policy paper. As a result of the engagement of a technical team from the Brookings Institute, US, the policy paper was updated and refined.[18]

The team of US specialists, two competition economists and a competition lawyer, visited Jamaica for a week to conduct their fieldwork. Following the consultants' report, the earlier policy recommendations and the views of the technical task force were restructured into a revised policy document and presented to the public for further consultation.

Public debate was extensive; besides papers from the Private Sector Organisation of Jamaica (PSOJ), the Jamaica Chamber of Commerce (JCC), the Cane Farmers Association, the Jamaica Bar Association, as well as Myers, Fletcher, and Gordon, a leading law firm, comments were also received from the University of the West Indies, the UK Overseas Development Agency (later called DFID) through the Office of Fair Trade, the World Bank, and the Inter-American Development Bank. Almost simultaneous with the engagement of the US competition specialists, the government received technical assistance from DFID to look at the wider issues of utilities and financial market regulation and competition policy. Through this initiative, an economist from the UK Treasury, A.J. Meyrick, was engaged in April 1991. In the resulting report,[19] one of the key recommendations was that the government should facilitate encouragement of competition in the utilities industries, especially telecommunications and electricity.

Almost from the beginning the private sector and the Jamaica Bar Association (JBA) took the position that, in a small economy such as Jamaica's, there was no justification for the proposed legislation. Considerable sums were spent to mount a publicity and lobby campaign to quash the bill. Notwithstanding the strong private sector opposition and criticisms, the government completed the competition policy and law. The report from the US consultants was published in late January 1991, supporting the major policy prescriptions outlined in the earlier report on the competition principles. This report was followed by a Green Paper, tabled in Parliament (August 1991)[20] for public discussion. After two years of debate, the Fair Competition Act (FCA)[21] was adopted by Parliament in March 1993. McKoy incorrectly noted that the Green Paper was prepared by a US consultant. However, the Green Paper was prepared by me and the permanent secretary in the Ministry of Industry and Trade. It did, however, draw on the two USAID consultants' report in the development of the policy in the initial phase.[22]

There were some major changes between the early policy paper and the final legislation. The requirement for a Competition Court was removed. The idea of the Competition Court had been adapted from the Japanese system, which combined two stages, the first stage being administrative and the second stage being judicial, through appeals to the courts. The Act eventually provided for a Fair Trading Commission with very wide powers of investigation which authorised its officers to enter business places and to recover relevant documents and summon persons to appear before the Commission under oath. It was provided with powers to prescribe remedies deemed fit for any abuse of dominant positions and other breaches of law. Its orders are enforceable by pecuniary sanctions through the Supreme Court. The law also allows an individual a private right of action to pursue breaches of the Act directly with the Supreme Court.

The FTC Act is of mixed heritage, drawing from the US and UK regarding concepts and principles, and from the UK, Australia, and New Zealand for detailed provisioning. It is an example of legal engineering, and several features were new to the Jamaican legal landscape, such as the pecuniary penalty. The concept of pecuniary civil penalty to enforce public law was not a part of the Jamaican legal milieu prior to the FCA. Its antecedent however is found in other Commonwealth legislation, such as in Australia and New Zealand.[24] It was a deliberate policy also to avoid criminal proceedings, coming from Jamaica's long history of state-supported restrictive business practices. The criminal law is therefore only used to enforce the powers of the Commission.

In most developing countries and member countries of the Organisation for Economic Cooperation and Development (OECD) competition proceedings are not criminal offences in character. Remedial relief is designed towards regulating or prohibiting future conduct, while imposing fines for past violation, except in merger case matters. In the US, however, certain aspects of competition law are criminal and the remedies are extensive. Under the Sherman Act, collusive or cartel-like behaviour can be punished by fines and/or imprisonment.

Issues Emerging from the Public Consultations

The most important issues raised by the commercial sector and the international agencies coming out of the several consultation meetings fall into nine categories:

1. the scope, objectives and reach of law;
2. the relationships between trade policies and competition policies;
3. arguments based on economies-of-scale and the need to exclude measures to regulate mergers and acquisitions;

4. exemption of the professions and inclusion of trade unions;
5. types of restrictive business practices and consumer unfairness practices which should be prohibited;
6. the structure and independence of the Commission and the enforcement procedures which should be adopted;
7. interface of Competition Law with Industry Regulatory Law;
8. that the management cadre in Jamaica was too small and the prohibition of interlocking directorates would harm business;
9. that the criteria established to determine which activities should be exempted were inadequate.

The Purpose and Reach of the Competition Act

The general position taken by the business sector and legal profession was that the legislation contemplated at the time was too broad in scope, too complicated, misguided, and inappropriate for an economy the size of Jamaica and at the country's stage of economic development. The business sector claimed that, if the policies recommended were enacted, they would put Jamaica at a comparative disadvantage vis-a-vis the country's CARICOM trading partners, and weaken its international competitiveness. It called for the legislative effort to be abandoned or that Jamaica should conclude negotiations with its CARICOM partners to ensure harmonised competition policies and legislation. If anything had to be legislated, the measure should be confined to constraints on restrictive business practices such as horizontal price-fixing, restrictive trade agreements, and consumer protection matters.[24] The Jamaican business community claimed that no other developing country had a competition law.

While it is true to have stated that, in the past competition policies had been pursued more aggressively in OECD countries, some eighteen developing countries or emerging market economies had also introduced competition legislation before 1960 and several Central and Eastern European States were introducing new legislation in 1990.[25] Detractors also argued that the new and costly authority which was being recommended was unnecessary, and new legislation as was needed could be enforced by the attorney general and the director of public prosecutions, but it was never the intention of the Green Paper to provide the final wording of the Act, merely to show the broad principles which were to be the subject of more precise legislative formulation by those experienced in drafting bills within the Commonwealth and English system of jurisprudence.

No piece of legislation should be considered as an end in itself. Legislation is the means for securing policy objectives. Whether the legislation is desirable or justifiable at all involves an evaluation of the merits of these objectives. Moreover, legislation related to competition engaged in social and economic engineering rarely engenders the precise result desired by Parliament. Careful consideration must be given to the actual provisions to be adopted in the legislation.

One view of competition policy was that its sole purpose should be to secure efficiency; in this context, efficiency is taken to mean maximisation of consumer welfare. Restrictive business practices should not be permitted if business conduct reduced total output of a particular industry. No other benefits to society should be accommodated; otherwise, conflicts would arise, and their eventual solution would give rise to political decisions, rather than economic decisions. Competition was to be seen to ensure efficiency, and only to this extent should it be protected.

Another view, which is also concerned with efficiency, maintains that efficiency – in the narrow terms of allocative and productive efficiency – should not be regarded as the only goal of competition legislation because other important benefits can also be secured. Competition can also prevent control of economic activities falling into the concentrated hands of a few firms. Where industry is concentrated, monopoly power arises, and the consumer is eventually harmed, as the monopolist seeks to increase prices by reducing supplies. Firms with economic power will acquire political power and leverage to a degree inconsistent with democracy, especially where there is an absence of countervailing power. Concentration of economic and market power may curtail individual choice and liberty and could also lead to the stifling of innovation.

Most times, where one or two firms came to dominate the Jamaican markets under the protective trade regime, they failed to introduce new technology in their products or processes. This behaviour was evidenced in the telecommunications industry in Jamaica in the years prior to 1990.

The FTC has been using the courts similar to a prosecutorial model since the fallout from the Stock Exchange case. Eleanor Fox and Michael J. Trebilcox, in an evaluation of the appropriateness of various types of institutions, found that the prosecutorial, or judicial model was appropriate only in jurisdictions with well-functioning, efficient courts and a well-established rule of law.[26] In the Jamaican situation, the courts played a key role, especially in the telecommunications sector in securing the early gains in competition and in the erosion of JTC's monopoly.

Vigorous domestic competition was expected to enhance the ability of local firms to enter and prosper in competitive overseas markets, through engendering the skills and vigour needed to compete at the global level. A firm facing vigorous competition develops the capability to offer more innovative products and more choices for the consumer. In addition, domestic competition enhances a firm's ability to compete in international markets.[27] The protective regimes and domestic monopolies which emerge therefrom cannot prepare domestic companies to compete globally. In brief, many Jamaican firms could not compete even in CARICOM markets, much less global markets.

In accepting the related principles, Jamaican competition policies were developed to encompass the multiple objectives of ensuring economic efficiency, protecting consumer interest, and to constrain undue concentration of economic power. It was recognised that tension and conflicts would emerge from the multiple objectives. The obvious way to resolve such conflicts in the law is to give priority to the interest of the consumer. Behaviour or practices which increase costs to domestic consumers by protecting firms from competition should be subordinated to the criteria of competition legislation.

Extraterritorial Coverage

The competition policies and laws of a country protect competition within the domestic economy and rarely extend to protecting consumers and producers in other states. Questions concerning jurisdiction over foreign persons and entities and the proper treatment of export-oriented activities by domestic persons and entities are among the most difficult issues facing competition authorities. It is not unusual for governments actively to encourage restraint of trade where such restraint is seen to benefit the national interest. Export cartels may encourage firms to fix the prices of goods in overseas markets and buying pools may be expected to countervail the bargaining power of overseas exporters. Governments sometimes constrain domestic firms from competing with one another in export markets.

Domestic legislation sometimes provides for a country's enterprises to not cooperate with foreign competition authorities. Chapter 6 of the enacted Polish Act blocks Polish domestic firms from providing information to overseas competition authorities. For many years, the US tried to take legal action against the London-based diamond cartel, to no avail.

Conflicts arise in these instances because of the economic transfers, which result from pursuing different industrial policies to promote growth and efficiencies of one nation at the expense of another. If all states were to respect one another's competition laws regarding significant adverse effects, and if all nations were to aid rather than hinder enforcement, major gains would be made in international competitiveness and efficiency. In the absence of such international good-will, the second-best solution is bilateral agreements for each country's competition laws.

In general, there is considerable disagreement on the application of public international law to competition issues. In recent years, the World Trade Organization (WTO) has tried, without success, to produce mutually accepted common rules on international competition. A feature of the WTO during its first ten years (after 1995) has been the impact of the so-called Singapore issues, which refers to four working groups established during the WTO's Ministerial Conference of 1996 in Singapore. These groups were tasked with addressing issues of investment, competition, government procurement, and trade facilitation. The name association arises because the WTO Doha round in 2008 stalled over refusal to compromise over special safeguard mechanisms.

Competition Law and Anti-Dumping Legislation

One recommendation advocated by the Ministry of Industry and Commerce at the time was that the competition law should embrace anti-dumping provisions in order to protect domestic competitors from foreign anti-competitive practices. It is not customary for competition authorities to be responsible for anti-dumping matters because anti-dumping is a trade policy matter and not related to competition policies. Competition policies seek to protect competition. The effect of injury is on local industry rather than domestic consumers. Enforcement of anti-dumping measures involves extra-territorial jurisdiction and may involve major diplomatic initiatives. Where anti-dumping measures are to be included in the mandate of a competition authority, there is the risk of breaching the authority's independence.

The basic issues involved in anti-dumping laws relate to the legitimacy or illegitimacy of various competitive advantages which foreign producers enjoy over domestic producers and the resultant harm the foreign producers may inflict on the domestic industry. Actions are often motivated by the desire to exclude competition. Anti-dumping laws apply to sales in a domestic market at prices below those charged by the exporter in his home market and where such a practice results in material injury to domestic producers. Competition laws encourage price competition, with interventions only when pricing is predatory to eliminate competition. It was felt that firms would also use the changing global political and economic scenario to allege unfair competition and, in so doing, divert a large share of the authority's limited resources. The prevailing thinking was that, should the government consider it necessary, for other reasons, to combine the two areas under one authority, then the anti-dumping laws should specify a minimum level of imports that could justify investigation, and that the Commission should only be required to consider market structure in reaching its decision on dumping. Ultimately, the FTC was only required to account for market structures, with the Anti-Dumping and Subsidies Commission focusing on trade remedies under the rules of international trade agreements.

Competition Law and the State

The doctrine of sovereign immunity is such that the state is normally excluded from competition law. However, members of the private sector argued that the actions of government companies and corporations, particularly those engaged in matters of trade, needed to fall within the jurisdiction of the competition legislation. Jamaica's situation is unique in that, in practice, it has widely adopted the rules under the Company's Law to establish public companies, as against the more established practice of special statutes and the creation of statutory corporations.

As such, state enterprises incorporated as limited liability companies or as statutory corporations were not exempted from the law. With JPSCo, a special exemption was, however, granted by the FTC, without an explanation.

The doctrine of sovereign immunity is very clear when it is cited as a defence for the actions of the government. The matter is less clear when it relates to statutory corporations or public companies, particularly when their actions relate to matters of trade. The Jamaican private sector argued that the actions of government companies and the government itself should also be subjected to the measures of the new competition law. The view which eventually prevailed in the debate was that public companies should be subject to competition law where their anti-competitive actions relate to trade, and that the actions of the government under the doctrine of sovereign immunity would be excluded from the reach of the competition measures. The government was to be encouraged, however, to continue its practice of liberalisation of the economy.

Competition Law and Professional Services

As in many countries, Jamaica's legal profession is extremely powerful in influencing public policy, and the nation's lawyers argued professional services should not be subject to the new law. Self-regulatory bodies such as those regulating a profession (doctors, lawyers, accountants, architects, and engineers) continuously attempt to restrict advertising, limit the institutional relationships with other commercial firms, and seek to control professional fees through fee schedules. These restrictive business practices, which were defended by local lawyers, were judged to be nothing more than measures to prevent price competition and restrict the flow of information to consumers and were more in the interest of the producers (the professionals) than the consumers. The restrictions went well beyond quality considerations.

It was expected that including professional services in the jurisdiction of the new competition law would evoke strong hostility from the powerful legal fraternity. The responses and arguments for exclusion were not only predictable, but they also followed much the same lines as those argued in other countries where competition measures were being extended to professional services. Historically, professions have been free to regulate the means by which professionals compete. Under specific legislation (self-regulation), they were exempted from standard rules of competition and from restrictive business practices, reflecting a belief that competition in professions would not provide socially optimum outcomes or maximise consumer welfare. It was felt that professions were best qualified to regulate themselves and to establish ethical practices. Through the power of self-regulation granted by governments, professions restrict entry to their markets, seriously constrain advertising, fix fees, and charges and prohibit business structures which would enhance efficiency and consumer welfare.

The professions justified these anti-competitive practices because they were necessary to promote and preserve the quality and integrity of their services. In the 1990s, however, the escalating costs of professional services, as well as changes in technology no longer made certain established conditions relevant and prompted a re-examination of the relation of professionals to competition policies.[28] The response of the Jamaica Bar Association was that the canons of the legal profession allowed attorneys to have regard to the Bar Association's scale of fees in assessing reasonableness of fees, also that the canons of the profession prohibited advertising; these acts of history were to remain forever, and the professions excluded from the new law.

Interestingly, the response of a leading law firm in Jamaica was that the restriction limiting legal partnerships to twenty members was a historical relic, long since abandoned in the UK. There was also support for allowing professionals to practise as limited liability companies. The regulation of professional services was still entrapped in English eighteenth-century rules and regulations which had either been abolished in UK and several other countries or were actively being considered for abolition.

The Jamaican Cabinet at the time included between seven and eight lawyers, including P.J. Patterson. These lawyers, like their private sector counterparts, also argued for the professions to be excluded from the new competition legislation. Patterson, however, countered that if the legal fraternity in the Cabinet was not prepared to accept the new legislation and the regulatory constraints being considered, he did not see how the government could sell the bill to other producers in the society. It was indicated that in countries where such restrictions have been removed, there has been no identifiable lowering of standards or injury to the consumer; in fact, competition has led to innovation and lowering of prices in several instances, such as in the market for optical and dental services and equipment in the US. With this intervention Cabinet approved proceeding with including the professions in the new competition law.

Interlocking Directorates

The most vigorously opposed section of the draft bill was the proposal to bar anyone from serving on the board of directors of more than one company, which were not necessarily of common ownership. The intent was to prevent the flow of information that might have anti-competitive effects and reduce the concentration of economic power. However, many businesspeople argued that, in a small economy such as Jamaica's, a general ban on interlocking directorates would be inappropriate because of a scarcity of managerial talent. There were strong views that the mere existence of interlocks should not, in itself, be prohibited unless it could be shown that the behaviour of any person caused or represented a material threat of causing anti-competitive effects. The view was that it should not be the conduct which should be outlawed but the effect of the conduct. The PSOJ considered restrictions against interlocking directorates as being not only misguided but unconstitutional, violating the rights of freedom of association. Some argued, if the policy were implemented, it would inhibit shareholders from being free to elect directors with experience and would create impediments to corporate expansion, with consequent ill-effects on investment.

The law firm Myers, Fletcher and Gordon concluded that, in an economy the size of Jamaica's, a general ban on interlocking directorate was inappropriate because of scarcity of managerial talent.[29] Interlocking directorate, however, provided an opportunity for information to flow between tied organisations with anti-competitive effects. The policy was not intended to restrict interlocking, which was not horizontal, especially in a small country; however, a bank director sitting on the board of a hotel could convey information about a competing hotel's information divulged to that bank, to the detriment of the competing hotelier.

The unconstitutional claim by the PSOJ is a misstatement of the Jamaican law. Section 13 of the Constitution of Jamaica provides for freedom of association, but expressly states that such freedom is subject to respect for the rights and freedoms of others, in the public interest. Section 3 further states that a law which is reasonably required to protect the rights and freedoms of others is not unconstitutional.[30] The prohibition on interlocking directorates was ultimately removed from the draft bill. The Banking Act, however, adopted this approach. Incorporating similar provisions into both the Banking Act and the Competition Act should have a complementary effect.

Exemption of Trade Unions

The PSOJ and the Jamaica Bar Association argued that the blanket exemption of trade unions in the draft bill reflected a failure to recognise the economic power unions exercise in the workplace. Indeed, they argued that collective bargaining itself was a kind of cartelisation of workers and affected competition in some industries. The government's position, however, was that the basic purpose of a trade union is collective bargaining over wages and working conditions, and subjecting unions to the competition legislation would defeat the very purpose of unionisation. Trade unions enjoy broad immunity from competition regulations in almost all countries.

Most countries have excluded trade union activities as they relate to collective bargaining from the scrutiny of competition and anti-trust legislation and, as such, organised labour for collective bargaining enjoys broad immunity. Collective bargaining is cartelisation in labour markets and has significant effects on competition in certain industries.

It was not the intention of competition policies to eliminate trade unions. The general conclusion therefore was that union members and trade unions should be exempted when conducting practices relating to remuneration and conditions of work. In the Albany case[31] brought by a Dutch textile company in 1999 before the European Court of Justice, the Court ruled agreements concluded in collective negotiations between management and labour in pursuit of such objectives must because of their nature and purpose, be regarded as falling outside the European Article 85 (1) of the Treaty, so trade union have largely been an excluded from competition laws. In the UK, trade unions and analogous bodies may be subjected to the test of reasonableness under the doctrine of restraint of trade; hence, sporting associations such as the Test and County Cricket Boards and the Football Association have been challenged under the restraint of trade doctrine.[32]

Exemption Clause

The criticism of the policy advanced concerning exemptions was that it provided examples of activities which might be approved, rather than establishing applicable criteria for exemption. Some argued the continuation of exemptions should be conditional on continued compliance with the criteria established. Almost all jurisdictions provide for exemptions to accommodate economic and political considerations. Exemption weakens competition legislation. The level of exemption provided by a jurisdiction depends on the historical view towards competition. In some European countries, competition has been viewed less favourably as a tool to foster economic efficiency and growth, hence legislation systems are established for sanctioning restrictive activities while, at the same time, allowing for pursuing trade and industrial policies. Cooperative agreements, for example, are exempted in the UK and France, while in the US and Germany cooperative agreements among competing suppliers are often subjected to per se prohibitions.[34]

Cartelisation, which allows suppliers to realise economies of scale or supports sector-specific public benefits such as product quality standards, is an area which is often exempted. Research and development agreements, standardisation of agreement on product quality, and export cartels are other specific areas. Competition law is invoked when there is a direct effect on the domestic economy or consumers. Taimoon Stewart, international consultant in competition law, maintains that cartelisation of conduct on purely export goods or services does not affect the domestic economy and so is exempt. Exemptions are provided as block exemptions or individually. Block exemptions provide desirable certainty for firms and eliminate the need for notification to the authorities. Individual exemptions apply where the firm has to notify the authority of the specific agreement. Where individual exemptions are allowed, it is necessary to state the application criteria for exemption. The FCA also provides for specific exemptions to be granted to other institutions other than the trade unions. Some arrangements which restrict competition may produce economic benefits which would not otherwise be obtained. Where such benefits outweigh the restrictive effects and are widely shared, exemptions may be considered. In this respect, intellectual property rights, and international treaty obligations under the rule of sovereign immunity are usually exempt. It was under the exemption provision that the JPSCo, the monopoly utility, was initially exempted from the reach of the FCA.

It has since been realised that total exemption of conducts by those holding intellectual property (IP) monopoly is short-sighted since abuse of IP monopoly power is prevalent. Indeed, article 40 of the Trade Related Aspect of Intellectual Property Rights (TRIPS) Agreement addresses this issue and suggests that countries adopt competition law as a way of sanctioning such abuse. The Barbados Fair Competition Act s. 16.4(c) provides a more nuanced treatment of exemption of conducts by Intellectual Property (IP) holders.

Merger Control

The business community objected to the proposed provisions in the draft bill calling for scrutiny of mergers and acquisitions because concentration was inevitable in a small economy such as Jamaica's. In addition, some argued restrictions on size could make Jamaican firms less competitive in international markets. The view was that the small size of the economy made a certain concentration of the domestic market inevitable and that efficient market size in a fully competitive market approximated a significant part of the total economy. To eliminate monopoly markets in a small economy such as Jamaica, some argued, could thus make some markets less, not more, efficient.[34] The lobbyist ignored the fact that it was horizontal mergers which were to be restricted. The rationale for subjecting mergers to competition oversight is that they may reduce competition and harm consumers, especially in horizontal markets. Studies carried out in the US and Britain showed that, while most mergers do benefit competition, many were indeed harmful. It was further argued that, in a small economy such as Jamaica's, where international trade plays an important role, restrictions on size would hamper Jamaican firms from competing in international markets. Most importantly, it was contended that the draft competition policies were based on the presumption that the basic unit of production would remain that of the firm. The consequences of growing interdependence in the world economy are that the complicated joint venture structure which has emerged in many industries created what Robert Reiche calls 'The Enterprise Web.'[35] Critics either did not know or ignored the fact that

Merger Control Regulations (MCR) require identifying the relevant market and overlapping products/services between the firms merging, and competition from trade is also counted among rivals in the market. Also, it is only if in these overlapping areas, competition is substantially reduced to the detriment of the consumer.

Although the historical focus of competition policies has been on regulating conduct, structural regulation has been gaining more attention in recent years. In fact, several OECD countries, over the fifteen years prior to 1990, had strengthened their merger control laws. Structural competition policies are concerned with the control of long-run contractual relationships such as mergers, takeovers, asset transfers, and joint ventures. The rationale for subjecting mergers to some level of competition scrutiny is that they may substantially reduce competition and adversely affect consumer welfare and the public interest. In such a case, regulation of market structure is complementary to conduct regulation.

There is no doubt that global economic conditions have become more competitive, supporting the position that merger plans should not be evaluated against the competitive structure of domestic markets, but against wider international markets. However, the monopolistic structure of Jamaican firms that developed over three decades did not help them, either to enter export markets, nor to meet competition from international suppliers. Furthermore, the distribution, insurance, and real estate sectors have not been exposed to any significant international competition. Changes in technology have eliminated the natural monopoly characteristics of many infrastructure industries, allowing for competition to benefit consumers, as with the telecommunications and electric utility industries.

Mergers raise important public issues that involve consideration of the type of merger, whether it is of a horizontal, or vertical or conglomerate nature. Horizontal mergers are those which occur between competitors in the same product field or at the same level of the distribution chain and are considered the greatest threat to competition. Vertical mergers occur between firms at different market levels of a product chain. Conglomerate mergers occur between firms in unrelated markets and may result from product line extensions, geographical market extensions, or simply a pure conglomerate merger with no functional linkage between the merged firms. Vertical mergers can harm competition, but less so than horizontal mergers, and hence present a weaker case for regulation. The rationale for the control of conglomerate mergers is that they may lead to a concentration of economic power and, eventually, the accumulation of more political power than desirable in a democracy. Many mergers in recent years in the US have been motivated by short-term benefits leading to asset-stripping rather than economies-of-scale.

The Jamaican private sector claimed that intervention to prevent a merger was an interference in the free market and in the market for corporate control. Several mergers do in fact benefit economic efficiency. It may be cheaper to take over a distributor than to establish a new distribution system. Hence a merger may provide access to cash and patent rights, allow firms to reach the critical mass needed to fund research and development, or provide access to management skills. The threat of a takeover acts as a major disciplining effect on managers of a firm. Under the principal agent theory, the effectiveness of the takeover mechanism in establishing incentives for good financial performance of a firm is especially important.[36] An interventionist approach could distort the market for corporate control. The conclusion is that, while vast numbers of mergers benefit competition, in various instances they are harmful. US anti-trust regulators have taken a much stricter position on mergers than countries in Europe where the policy towards mergers, up to 1990, was essentially benign and implied the presumption that mergers were in the public interest. The recommendation for the Jamaican situation was to have been that of a benign policy; however, the powerful lobby evoked by the private sector ensured that the merger control clauses were removed from the final act and the emphasis placed on abuse of a dominant market position. The Jamaican Competition Act, therefore, does not delineate any measures to deal with mergers and acquisition. The FTC Act does not explicitly outlaw either the possession of market power, or the pursuit of it; the law merely restrains the abuse of dominant position – a position of strength that allows an enterprise to operate in a market without effective constraint from competitors, one which is also found in the New Zealand law. It was not until 2017, in the legal issue of the *Jamaica Stock Exchange vs the FTC*, that a Privy Council decision provided the FTC with the authority to review certain kinds of mergers.

Market Dominance and Market Power

The position adopted by the authorities is that the mere act of market power or market dominance does not, of itself, violate competition and that it is dominant behaviour and conduct that would be subjected to sanction. Dominant position is defined as being that position which an enterprise holds in the market such that it can operate in that market without effective constraints from competitors. Where dominant position is sanctioned by licence, there is the question of how abuse of such dominance would be dealt with in the legislation.

Market power and market dominance are terms often used interchangeably. Market power is often defined as the ability to vary price without suffering loss of sales volume, owing to the absence of substitutes. In examining market power, consideration must be given to the product market and the geographical market. Merger authorities regulating monopoly power through market power often provide guidelines regarding what constitutes a product market. Countries differ in their construction of anti-competitive markets. In the US, the definition includes competition from potential suppliers if that competition is sufficiently immediate, occurring within one year of a hypothetical price increase. The US policy takes into effect potential entry and, to some extent, the contestability of the market.

The geographical market can vary from small areas, with a retail shop, to the global market. Trade protectionist policies such as tariffs and quotas may further curtail the size of the market. The ability to exercise market power is influenced by the number of competing suppliers or product alternatives available. The US Hirschman-Heritindahl (Index HHI), defined as the squared market shares expressed in percentage, adopts a concentration index, expressed in percentage terms for all suppliers in the market.[37] The index increases as the market becomes more concentrated.

European competition laws, unlike those in the US, are based on the concepts of market dominance and freedom from constraints of competition. However, in Jamaica, market dominance is concerned with the unilateral exercise of market power. Similarly, as in the European case, it is not the existence of dominance that is relevant and prohibited, but the abuse of the firm's market power. If there are no restrictions to entry, a large market share is whittled away. Barriers to entry and factors which deal with product differentiation must be considered. The determination of dominant market and market dominance requires more than legal competence; it requires a sophisticated understanding of how markets work.

With Jamaica, the FTC Act identifies three criteria that must be met for an order to be issued:

1. A firm must be in a dominant position if it can operate in a market without effective constraints from competitors, or potential competitors. A market share of 50 per cent is usually taken as the threshold for a firm to be dominant, but this may vary to meet circumstance.
2. It must be proven that the firm abuses its dominant position and impedes the maintenance or development of effective competition in a market.
3. It must be seen that the abusive conduct has had, is having, or is likely to have the effect of substantially lessening competition in a market.

Competition laws based on market power emphasise economic efficiency and the economic welfare of consumers. On the other hand, the dominance concept, while encompassing the exercise of market power, emphasises the welfare of upstream or downstream trading partners rather than final consumers.[38] Identifying the existence of a dominant position is just the first step, as the more complicated issue is to decide what constitutes dominant behaviour. Behaviour which may be considered perfectly legitimate where a competitive market exists may be condemned when conducted by a dominant firm. Practices which constitute dominant behaviour under various forms of legislation can involve unfair or predatory pricing, limitations on production, price discrimination, refusal to supply, exclusionary deals, and unfair trading conditions. The concept of market dominance will not allow the Jamaican authorities to deal effectively with monopoly power. Experience over the twenty-five-year operation of the FTC Act has confirmed this position.

Consumer Issues

Over the last twenty years, policymakers agree that the single unifying goal of competition policy should be to enhance consumer welfare, and the best way to do this is through competition.[39] Many competition issues involve an overlap between antitrust matters and consumer concerns, such as protecting consumers against fraud or misrepresentation. In these instances, competition authorities can help policymakers find the appropriate balance between protecting consumers and protecting the competition process.

Consumer unfairness practices have been widespread over the years in Jamaica, as hoarding, deceptive information, tie-in sales, and infringement of warranties. More often than not, the principle of Buyer Beware has been standard market practice. Jamaica could not support a strong consumer lobby and, although a Consumer Affairs Commission, a Consumers' League, and a Taxes and Rate Payers Association exist, their impact has been ineffective or sporadic. The presence of a strong consumer lobby group elicits more responsible behaviour from companies operating in the market.

There were no major objections from the business community to the policy measures outlined in the Green Paper to deal with consumer protection, except for the section which called for the posting of prices. It was felt that, for small market traders and service providers, the posting of prices would be impractical and uneconomical. The consumer issues comprised three separate matters: the need for consumer protection related to the disclosure of information; the need for legislation dealing with the sale of goods; and the need for consumer public education on the role of prices and competitive process in a market economy. The question was raised, however, of whether consumer protection legislation should form part of legislation dealing with competition policies and whether the same authority should adjudicate on both matters. Much of what was proposed in the Green Paper could be classified as matters involving transactions in goods, such as fair labelling, product standards, and warranties of sale. It was felt that, as part of a revision, these could readily be incorporated into the Sale of Goods Act and the Hire Purchase Act, possibly in addition, or instead of their inclusion in the Competition Act.[40]

There are advantages in having one government authority enforcing both antitrust matters and consumer protection. Consumer protection issues, however, can evoke strong political interest. Therefore, it is important that the competition authority not allow itself to be overwhelmed by consumer affairs matters or be seen as another consumer lobby group and be distracted from more important issues dealing with market efficiency and the enhancement of the competitive process.

Interestingly, the FTC dealt mainly with consumer protection matters in the first decade of its existence, and this had a public impact, as consumers recognised that there was an institution protecting their interest. This period allowed the FTC to find its feet and become known and appreciated. Competition authorities are also well placed to promote competition policy and to advance the cause of consumers, particularly in the nascent years of operation. There is a need to educate the public about the benefits of competition, especially when one considers that the country is coming from an environment where price fixing and monopolisation of markets were normal business behaviour. The policy therefore provided for the FTC to play a major role in consumer advocacy. The FTC eventually incorporated consumer protection issues with antitrust matters, especially those which dealt with misleading advertising and information relating to warranties and the sale of goods. Tied selling, double ticketing, sale above advertised prices, and bait selling all come under the scrutiny of the FTC.

Restrictive Business Practices

Private sector organisations accepted the need to introduce policies which would restrain anti-competitive market behaviour. Concern, however, was expressed at two levels. First, it was felt that phrases such as 'market dominance,' 'relevant markets,' 'anti-competitive effect,' and 'substantial business justification,' which appeared in many areas of the Green Paper, were too vague. Interpreting and applying these concepts, some argued, would require in-depth economic research and analysis. Second, it was felt that little data existed, and acquisition of such data and the expertise would be a gradual process. American anti-trust laws approach potentially anti-competitive acts using a *per se*, *rule of reason*, or *prima facie* decision rule, depending on the category of restraint. These terms have become widely used in the general vocabulary concerning competition legislation. In interpreting the 1980 Sherman Act, US courts concluded that there were types of contracts which, on the face of it, were plainly in restraint of trade and injurious to the consumer. The judicial task, therefore, was simply to show that the restraint existed.

Other conducts or behaviour could not be treated as *per se* and required weighing the probable benefits of the act against any potential harm. In such instances, US courts applied the *rule-of-reason* approach. This approach, however, is cumbersome and time-consuming. It requires reliable information on industry conditions and involves case-by-case analysis of each situation. With the *rule of reason* approach, the burden of proof falls on the plaintiff. The *prima facie* approach shifts the burden of proof from the plaintiff to the defendant and therefore favours the plaintiff. The distinctions between these approaches are not rigid. US courts, however, regard horizontal price-fixing, bid-rigging and collusive tendering, market allocation, concerted refusal of suppliers to sell, or consumer boycotts as *per se* categories because these actions are directly limiting competition. They are so obviously harmful that once the evidence is found, there is no need to prove the effect.

The recommendation made in the Jamaican competition policy paper was to prohibit horizontal restraints based on the *per se* principle. One advantage of this approach is that it creates certainty for commerce and is less costly to enforce. Horizontal restraints between competing suppliers are considered the most damaging practices affecting competition. Price-fixing between competing suppliers is considered the most anti-competitive behaviour, as it allows firms to create the conditions of a monopoly. Parallel price-fixing occurs where suppliers refrain from using price as a means of competition, as with oligopolistic industries, where price-fixing is an indicator that the market is engaged in anti-competitive practices. It is difficult to adjudicate such questions and hence the *rule of reason* approach is often relied on. Some countries distinguish between vertical and horizontal restraint; however, Jamaica does not make this distinction. Horizontal restraints between competing suppliers are often exempted from competition laws, where such agreements can enhance economic efficiency and produce other beneficial effects. Research and development agreements, joint production, and standardisation agreements are examples of exempted agreements.

Vertical restraint agreements between firms operating at different levels of the market may, on the one hand, damage competition or allow firms to exercise market power, while on the other hand, sometimes such constraints give rise to complex theoretical and analytical economic problems. For this reason, the *rule of reason* approach was advanced for the Jamaican legislation. Examples of vertical restrains are exclusive dealings, selective premium offers, price discrimination, tying agreements, refusal to sell, and territorial restraints. The Resale Price Maintenance (RPM), a vertical restraint, poses a special problem. There is still widespread disagreement between economists as to the rationale for prohibiting RPM. A common view is that it is a retailers' cartel and a form of monopoly. Economists have argued that the relationship of a retailer with a manufacturer is that of an agency relationship and that restrictions on how the agent-retailer should operate do not differ from policies that the manufacturer would use if he owned the outlets. By contrast, surveys have also found that prohibition of RPM was often followed by significant retailing innovation, as exemplified in the UK, Canada, Sweden, and Denmark. Resale price maintenance acts against the interest of low-cost retailers and may lead to prices being higher than they would otherwise be. While RPM keeps the inefficient retailer in the market, retailers should not be deprived of the opportunity to compete. RPM also deprives the consumer of choice.

Vertical price-fixing can trigger undesirable horizontal effects in industries which are oligopolistic. On the other hand, low-cost retailers can act as free-riders, taking advantage of high-cost retailers engaging sufficient staff to display and explain details of the goods or services, when customers then go to low-cost retailers, once they have decided by wasting the time and resources of high-cost retailers. Among the arguments in favour of RPM are that it ensures price stability and orderly marketing; producers will impose restrictions on distributors of their own products only in order to intensify intra-brand competition; it provides small firms with protection against the overwhelming power of the chain stores and supermarket groups. Section 9 (1) (a) of the 1976 United Kingdom Resale Prices Act renders RPM agreements void, and it is unlawful to include such agreements in a contract. Conversely, US laws treat resale price agreements under the *rule of reason* approach. The policy recommendation in the Green Paper argued for RPM to be prohibited in Jamaica, and this was accepted; the Fair Competition Act therefore prohibits resale price maintenance. Because of the higher levels of concentration in many consumer goods markets in Jamaica, intra-brand competition is likely to be weak and RPM could facilitate horizontal price collusion. Except with RPM, the general recommendation was that vertical agreements to restrain trade should receive more lenient treatment than horizontal restraints.

Restrictive business practices have, over the years, been sanctioned by several pieces of legislation in Jamaica. It was, therefore, important to consider the new competition legislation in relation to such existing legislation. The government had, over the years, enacted a range of legislation which led to the creation of exclusive monopolies; the fixing and regulation of prices; creation of capacity licences; self-regulation of professions, and protecting consumer welfare. New legislation such as the Securities Act, the Banking and Financial Services Act, the Office of Utilities Regulation Act, and the Revised Companies Act required examination in this regard, not only as part of developing new competition policy but in the wider context of creating a more liberalised economy. The Rent Restriction Act, Trades Act, various Commodity Boards Acts, and Transport Authority Act provided for the fixing of prices. These acts were introduced before the 1990s, when the government sought to control commercial activities; they became inconsistent with market liberalisation and the creation of a competitive market.

Institutional Arrangements

In order to ensure autonomy and high independence of the commission, the original policy proposal called to appoint a board of commissioners by the governor general on the recommendation of the prime minister, after consultation with the leader of the opposition. The original structure also called for a three-to-five-man commission with a permanent secretariat headed by a director general to be appointed by the chairman of the commission. The private sector was of the expressed view that a high level of independence was necessary in order for the commission to avoid political appointments and damage to the credibility of the agency. This recommendation from the private sector was rejected by the government, and the portfolio minister was provided with extensive powers over the appointment of commissioners.

There are three key parties involved in the administration and enforcement of the FTC Act: the portfolio minister, the FTC and the Jamaican courts. The commission came to comprise two distinct arms: an investigative section composed of full-time professionals and administrators, headed by an executive director appointed by the commissioners to serve for seven years, and a quasi-judicial section, represented by part-time commissioners. The day-to-day operations of the commission are carried out by an executive director, supported by a professional staff, including lawyers and economists. The full-time professional staff is vested with the authority to engage with parties and find resolution to matters prior to formal recommendation to the commission that a complaint has been filed. The administrative section starts complaints based on observations of seemingly uncompetitive practices in any industry.

The stipulations are that there should be a minimum of three commissioners and a maximum of five, one of whom the portfolio minister appoints as chairman. The executive director is an *ex-officio* member of the Commission. The minister determines their compensation package. Tenure of the Commission members is a maximum of three years, with entitlement for further reappointment. The minister has the power to terminate the appointments of a member, other than the executive director, upon cause. If the administrative section cannot arrive at an undertaking with the party being investigated, it may request a hearing by three commissioners, acting as a body. The Commission is a quasi-judicial body established under Section 4 of the FTC Act and is a body corporate to which Section 28 of the Interpretation Act Applies. It is largely funded from the government, accountable through the portfolio minister and is vested with all the rights and powers which accrue to a natural or juridical person – including the right to sue in its corporate name and the right to acquire, hold and dispose of property. The FTC has very wide investigative powers, in that it can summon and examine witnesses, administer oaths, subpoena and examine documents, and can carry out searches.

The Commission may decide that the company's behaviour is sufficiently serious to warrant taking the firm to court to obtain pecuniary damages, and the lawsuit is presented as *FTC vs Company Y* and not *Mr X vs Company Y*; alternatively, it may decide if some other settlement would be appropriate. The Commission's decision may be appealed to a judge of the Supreme Court within fifteen days of the relevant decision. The judge may confirm, modify, or reverse the decision, giving reasons. Other functions of the Commission include carrying out investigations at the request of the minister and advising the minister on sundry matters relating to the operation of the FTC Act. The Commission therefore functions as the investigator, complainant, prosecutor, and adjudicator; and commissioners are treated as adjudicator judges in that there can be no discussion of the matter being adjudicated without the other side being present.[41] It must be noted that the FTC established no clear demarcations between the role of the commissioners and the role of the staff, especially in view of the executive director's status; this has resulted in what the Jamaican Court of Appeal has referred to as the merger of its judicial function with its investigative and prosecutorial functions. The Court also observed that there was no provision for the delegation of the investigative functions of the Commission to the staff or other agencies to be administered independent of the Commission. In those circumstances, the Court found, a determination by the Commission would likely lead to a breach of the rules of natural justice.[42]

The FTC may also order cessation of any breaches of the Act. The law also gives the initial complainant the private right of action to recover damages for actual losses by going directly to the Court. Other powers of the FTC authorise the Court to grant injunctions and it would appear that there is also the right to grant declaration under the general supervisory functions.

The emphasis of the legislation and enforcement rules is that the agreement or practice which unduly affects competition in the relevant market is against the public interest. Competition is to be seen as the means of promoting economic efficiency and is to be protected by legislation. Certain actions and practices, however, are prohibited *per se* because they always restrict competition. These actions are mainly horizontal restraints such as price-fixing, restraint on output, market division, exclusionary practices, restraint on entry, and predation. The act therefore specifically prohibits price-fixing, bid-rigging, collusive tendering, conspiracies to limit production or competition, and agreements designed to lessen competition in a market.

The Commission is also empowered to examine the effects of vertical restraints on competition, except for the case of resale price maintenance. RPM is treated on a *per se* basis. Vertical restraints that lessen competition have to be proven, and these are practices such as tying deals, abuse of negotiating position, price discrimination, premium offers, refusal to deal, exclusive dealing (except in cases of abuse of dominance), and territorial restraints.

Considerable public education and public participation was sought before enactment. It is said that the FCA has been the most widely canvassed piece of legislation to emanate from Jamaica's Parliament.[43] Government policymakers and business leaders in countries weighing changes in their competition policy would do well to consider how Jamaica approached these issues.[44] Predictably, various interest groups brought pressure to bear to amend the draft legislation before it became law and, in many cases, they succeeded. After decades of supporting monopolies and fixing prices, this reversal is among the most remarkable of Jamaica's recent reforms.

Evidently, the provisions of the FTC Act may apply to conduct that is also subject to supervision by the Office of Utilities Regulation (OUR) under the Telecommunications Act. This is now the case for the electricity sector because of the 2015 Electricity Act. Potential conflicts and overlaps may arise, particularly in relation to the restrictions on abuse of dominant position and the restrictions on price discriminations. The FTC Act, initially, did not expressly address either how overlap in substantive law matters, or in the jurisdiction of industry regulators and the FTC to deal with competition. In relation to the Financial Services Commission (FSC), this overlap has given rise to a dispute between the FSC and the FTC over which entity should have primacy in determining competition matters in the financial sector. The same problem has arisen with the professional services. The Privy Council Decision of 2017 confirmed the primacy of the FTC over the regulated sector in competition issues.

The Forms of Remedy

The American consultants with a background in US law introduced the concept of punitive damages. The recommendation was three times the amount of the actual damages proved in determining the penalties to be imposed. An additional feature which was recommended provided for any injured consumer to sue in a Competition Court as representative of a class of all similarly situated consumers seeking damages and injunctive relief for the represented class. Class action and triple damage suits were not features of the Jamaican legal environment and were strongly opposed by the professions and the private sector and were eventually excluded also from the FTC Act.

SECTORAL REGULATOR AND THE COMPETITION COMMISSION AGENCIES AND THEIR INTERFACES

Introducing a competition agency and agencies that regulate specific sectors or industry presents the problem of how the two types of bodies should conduct their principal mandate and who should carry primary responsibility for competition in a given regulated industry. Introducing competition law and competition agency in Jamaica brought into focus this relationship issue. The two types of agencies have some differing characteristics. Industry specific regulators apply an ex-ante prescriptive approach, while competition authorities apply ex post control approach except in merger control matters. Industry regulators also intervene more frequently and require a continual flow of information from the regulated entities, while the competition agencies rely more on complaints and research only, when necessary, in connection with possible enforcement action. Competition agencies typically provide economy-wide coverage, while regulatory agencies typically relate to one industry or sector. As we have seen from experiences in the US, sectorial regulators accept the status quo in imposing needless restraints on market entry and are more subject to intensive pressures from industries they regulate; however, they are closer to the industry. Competition agencies have a better appreciation of social and economic benefits of competition. Where a network or financial sector industry is being opened up to greater competition, there is the need to facilitate competition, where competition is possible and practical. The establishment of regulatory agencies alongside the competition body, especially in network infrastructure and financial services industries, forcefully brings to the forefront the conflict and interface problems.[45]

In the post-war years outside the US, and especially in developing countries, the infrastructure and financial industries have typically been operated as monopoly state enterprises; hence, addressing jurisdictional conflicts has, until recently, typically been less relevant. The global trend of utility and financial privatisation and the proliferation of sectorial regulatory agencies, alongside competition authorities, however, raised these issues with a new urgency in countries like Jamaica undertaking the process of privatisation and market liberalisation for the first time. The new wisdom is of 'competition where feasible and regulation where not' suggests that regulation should be confined to the natural monopoly elements, typically the networks, with network services subject to competition law. The regulatory interface problem is centred on the degree to which these sectors which are being opened up to greater competition should also be subject to general competition laws and how and by whom such laws are to be administered. Goals of competition and regulatory agencies do not exist in isolation and must consider existing political, economic, and social institutions, practices, and customs. Synergies also exist between the two types of bodies. There is no single correct solution to the proper distribution of powers; however, experiences have provided some guiding principles. Interestingly, the FCA does not have stated goals, in contrast to the Barbados Fair Competition Act.

The technological developments, which emerged in the 1980s and which transformed several of the utility industries, have been more pronounced in the telecommunications and electricity sectors, so major segments of these industries, once treated as vertically integrated monopolies, are now being subjected to competition. In the financial services, the global trend has been a move towards liberalisation of financial markets and reduction of public ownership of financial enterprises, with industry regulation focused on fiduciary conduct and systemic risk. In professional services, for instance, regulation has usually been as self-regulation, but professional service associations unnecessarily restrict competition, to the detriment of the consumer (higher prices). With introducing competition into these sectors, new mechanisms are needed to ensure a conflict-free interface between the two regimes. Second, there is the increased need to exploit complementary expertise and perspectives of the two types of regulators. Competition rules relating to the misuse of a dominant position to take on added importance in relation to access to essential facilities for the network utilities. With telecommunications and electricity, the network segments remain natural monopolies, therefore non-discriminatory access to encourage new entrants to the industry is critical, if competition is to develop in the competitive segments. Competition rules prohibiting the misuse of a dominant market position can address this problem. This is the case, for example, in the EU and New Zealand. The critical areas where competition rules interact with industry-specific rules are interconnection or access, monopoly pricing, restrictive business practices, anti-competitive agreements, and merger control.[46]

In telecommunications, electricity, and some transport industries there is a critical need for non-discriminatory access to encourage new entrants to the industry if competition is to develop in the competitive segments. In some regimes, competition rules and judicial precedents on interconnection prohibit misuse of dominant market position, and this may address the problem. Refusal to allow a competitor to a network on non-discriminatory terms could be ruled unlawful. This rule therefore has the potential to overlap or conflict with industry-specific rules addressing network access and interconnection under utility regulation law, especially where exclusive licences are granted by the industry regulator to an incumbent operator.

In an examination of the interface between competition and sectorial regulation institutions and laws, it is instructive to revisit a quotation of David Boies, chief council and staff director of the US Anti-Trust Subcommittee[47]:

> The interface between anti-trust and regulation is a veritable no-man's land for students and practitioners alike. Since the theories of anti-trust and regulation reflect differing assumptions about government intervention into the marketplace, it is often difficult to rationalise their impact on particular industry behaviour. The anti-trust laws, to borrow a phrase, are brooding omnipresence, with pervasive, almost constitutional meaning in our jurisprudence. Direct economic regulation (which is entrusted to agencies rather than the Courts) may supplant the anti-trust laws and specific industries for carefully carved-out purposes. But at the edges these purposes thin out and the anti-trust laws inevitably reappear in the background. At this point, it is no small matter to blend the policies of the two conflicting regimes into an overall regulatory purpose that preserves the values of both.

This comment was echoed at the commencement of the American deregulation movement. The US has had a tradition of anti-trust regulation going back some 130 years. Regulatory institutions go back to 1830 state regulatory commissions and the creation of the Interstate Commerce Commission in 1887 to control interstate rail and other transport, including oil pipelines. In countries where the roles and responsibilities of the utility regulatory agency and competition authority often are ill defined, creating the opportunities for turf-disputes and legal wrangling. Whatever the division of labour between competition agencies and sector regulators, there are very few countries where the problem can be regarded as finally settled, especially since the transition to greater competition is far from complete.[48] For small developing country markets, the issue may well be more one of conduct, because of the small number of players possible and the lessened focus on market threshold. What is often more important for competition in small developing country markets is trade liberalisation.

There have therefore been two conflicting philosophies: the American approach which, until recently, restricted the reach of competition law on regulated industries, and the UK approach which provided for the promotion of competition and the application of general competition laws in once regulated industries. Since the 1990s, several developing countries have followed the UK example. Among the early reformers to have liberalised infrastructures and privatised, their vertically integrated monopoly utilities were Chile, New Zealand, and Jamaica.

Specific sectoral regulatory regimes, in relation to competition, primarily reflect the need to actively inject and promote effective competition into the sector, and to address the risk that businesses in these sectors have inherited; or, because of the characteristics of the markets involved, possess, either alone or with others, power in the markets in which they operate, i.e., the ability to exercise control over the price and/or output in a particular market, and (if not placed under additional controls to other undertakings) possess the opportunity to frustrate competition.

Where the boundaries are not clearly delineated in the legislation, then the matter will be left to the courts to interpret the language of the respective legislation and determine the applications as to the respective legislative provisions, as we have seen in the Jamaican situation. This approach, however, can be costly and time consuming. It is therefore preferable to clearly define the roles of the two classes of regulators in the legislative structure. International experience proves that the interaction between industry and competition regulators can be managed through institutional approaches: by giving primacy to the competition law or the sectorial regulatory law, or giving concurrent jurisdiction, requiring consultation between both regulators. The overlap problem and jurisdictional disputes typically arise in the following areas:

- **Licensing Conditions:** the number of licences and the conditions of the licences will influence the intensity of competition.
- **Market Dominance**: market definition and assessment of dominance by the sector regulator in establishing which operator should offer interconnection services on the one hand, and by the competition authority in establishing an abuse of market power by an operator.
- **Monopoly Pricing**: some competition regimes include rules which restrict excessive or unjust prices. Such rules could also conflict with industry-specific pricing rules established under the utility sector or industry-specific regulation. Alternatively, the industry regulator, in fixing prices, may find that the competition rules against price fixing are so general that they give the competition regulator the mandate to challenge the price fixing decisions of the sectorial regulator. Prices set by sector regulators for interconnection will determine the extent of price competition (or lack of competition).
- **Restrictive Business Practices**: where there is one vertically integrated monopoly firm, there are no competitors, and the monopolist can abuse full market power. When the industry is unbundled or liberalised and opened up to competition, the opportunity to engage in anti-competitive agreements or conducts, which could restrict or lessen competition, is magnified.
- **Merger Control:** restrictions on mergers between utilities and other firms, or restrictions on reintegration, are often provided for under industry or sector-specific regulatory laws. In the new unbundled environment of infrastructure firms, common ownership, for example, of generation firms with transmission or generation with distribution firms, is normally restricted under sector-specific regulation. Merger regulation incorporated in industry-specific laws could conflict with merger control rules embodied in competition laws.

Resolving or Managing the Problem

Experience has shown that the problem can be managed through three broad institutional approaches:

1. Giving primacy to the sectorial regulatory law over competition matters in the regulated industry.
2. Giving primacy to the competition law over sectorial regulatory law in the regulated industry; or
3. Concurrency, both competition law and industry or sectorial regulation law carry equal jurisdiction over competition matters in the regulated industry. This may be accompanied by a requirement for consultation between both competition and sector regulatory authorities.

Within the three institutional approaches, there are in practice five models governing the resolution to the interface problem, which can be adopted; these are as follows:

1. There is no economic regulation in one or more sectors; instead, the competition agency applies general competition law to accomplish some or all of the objectives commonly associated with economic regulation. New Zealand used the competition (anti-trust) agency as the utility regulator. The Competition Act states that actions which lesson competition or abuse of dominant position is prohibited. New Zealand initially had no separate industry legislation.
2. Sector or industry regulators are given primacy to deal with competition issues in the regulated industry. They are the principal enforcers of competition laws, if any, applying to their sectors.
3. The economy-wide competition law enforced through the competition authority takes primacy over industry or sector regulatory law and the sector or industry regulator. Competition agencies are also the principal economic regulators.
4. Sector or industry regulators and competition authorities are given concurrent jurisdiction to enforce competition laws (excluding situations where regulators are merely given a general duty to promote competition, but no specific instruments to carry out that mandate).
5. In general, mandate-driven division of labour competition laws are exclusively applied by the competition agency and regulation exclusively by technical and economic regulators (UNCTAD 2007, Guidebook on Competition Law).

Practical examples of these are illustrated below.

- **Eliminate the Need for Separate Industry or Sector Regulator – 'Light-handed' Regulation**

  New Zealand adopted what is often referred to as 'light-handed regulation.' Competition issues are dealt with under the Commerce Act by the Commerce Commission, the economy-wide competition authority. The generality of the competition rules is such that problems of interpretation and application often arise, with reliance on the courts through judicial precedents to resolve the problem.

- **Use of Competition Authority to Administer Sectorial Regulatory Rules**

  This is a variation of the New Zealand approach and involves the use of the competition authority to administer the sectorial regulatory rules. It is a further alternative for the administration of industry-specific rules; Australia's reforms illustrate this approach. Responsibility for the administration of industry-specific rules on access and related matters has been entrusted to the competition agency, the Australian Competition and Consumer Commission.

- **Concurrent Jurisdiction**

  A concurrent power refers to the application of competition law in a regulated industry by either the industry or sectoral regulator and the competition authorities. The UK system best illustrates this model; from the beginning, the utility regulators shared power with the director general of the Fair Trades Practices Authority to refer to the old Mergers and Monopolies Commission, except for merger matters, where the responsibility was with the secretary of state.

  Following from the provisions of the UK Enterprise Act 2006, the sectorial regulators have all the powers of the Office of Fair Trade (OFT) to deal with competition issues under the Competition Act. Concurrency working arrangements between the OFT and the sectorial regulators are set out in the Competition Act 1998 (Concurrency Regulations), which specifies how the system of concurrency should apply. The OFT has also issued guidance on the arrangements for concurrency. Once it has been decided which UK authority will exercise prescribed functions in relation to a case, the Concurrency Regulations prevent another authority from exercising prescribed functions, unless the case is formally transferred under the Concurrency Regulations. Prescribed functions are defined in the Concurrency Regulations.

There is, however, exclusion of merger remit from the concurrency arrangements and responsibility for dealing with mergers lies with the OFT and the Competition Commission, subject to any intervention by the secretary of state on public interest grounds. However, the regulators are typically consulted by the OFT and the Competition Commission on merger cases relating to their sector. There are other regulated sectors where the regulator does not have concurrent functions: for example, the financial services sector, where the Financial Services Authority has a subsidiary duty to promote effective competition but no concurrent competition powers.

Concurrency, however, creates a problem of consistency between regulators with different views. The experiences in the UK initially have been both types of agencies publishing rules and the emphasis has been different. Sectorial regulators have found that the competition agency norms are not always suitable to address market power issues in network industries. For example, electricity firms with as little as 10 per cent of market share have been found to carry significant influence on prices in the electricity wholesale market in England and Wales. The result is that sectorial regulators have sought to impose licence conditions to control anti-competitive conduct (or market abuse) and often these use different criteria and different market share rules showing that dominance exist. Concurrency can also lead to duplication and provides for less efficient use of scarce resources.

- **Collaborative Approaches**

Mexico has adopted a collaborative approach. Here, the competition agency is entrusted with the responsibility for determining whether the conditions for effective competition exist or are sufficiently absent to justify the continued imposition of price regulation.

Administration of price control rules is then entrusted to the sectorial regulator, if conditions for effective competition exist and such conditions are justified.

- **Primacy of the Sector Regulator**

  The industry or sector regulator (sector law) is given powers over competition matters in the regulated industry over the competition authority and the competition law. It is also possible to give precedence to the industry-specific, anti-competitive, and merger control rules and the industry regulator over the competition rules which have been adopted by some jurisdictions. In this situation, the regulated industry is exempted from the jurisdiction of the competition law and the reach of the competition authority, or the industry-specific rules of the utility regulator are given primacy over the rules of the competition regulator. This is the case in the US and Canada. In these jurisdictions, conduct permitted or decisions of the utility regulator under the industry-specific laws are excluded from the scrutiny of the competition regulator's rules. However, with merger control, some regimes require both regulators to approve merger transactions within the regulated industries.

- **Use of Courts to Interpret the Rules**

  When the government fails to clearly establish regulatory boundaries in legislation, interpreting the language of the legislation and determining respective responsibilities falls upon the courts. This approach, however, can be costly and time consuming. The preferred course is to clearly determine the roles of the two classes of regulators in the new legislative structure. As competition is introduced into what have been traditionally monopolistic utility industries, many of these industries are likely to migrate from utility-specific regulatory regimes to economy-wide competition regimes; some mechanism is therefore required to ensure a smooth and effective interface between the two regimes. The need to manage this transition process efficiently will make imperative establishment of well-defined relationships between historically distinct utility and competition regulators. The Australian system illustrates one such attempt to facilitate the evolutionary process without abandoning the certainty of industry-specific rules for activities, which continue to display substantial market power in hardcore areas of natural monopolies.

Tony Prosser has, however, argued that it is not possible to do without regulatory institutions and leave matters to the market and competition law, as is suggested by the New Zealand approach.[49] Regulation should not be seen as an intrusion in a naturally self-regulating marketplace, but is necessary to limit monopoly power, and to create and police the conditions for effective competition. Regulation for competition will continue to be necessary even after unbundling in such areas as water distribution, rail, electricity, and telecommunications transmission and distribution, gas transportation, and airports. In fact, in New Zealand, the law gives the portfolio minister power to impose price controls in goods and services where competition is limited. If regulatory structures are not created, disputes on interconnection and access will inevitably occur, as well as litigation. Imposing the requirement for consultation on competition matters in regulated industries between industry or sector regulator and the competition authority can only help to improve efficiency and effectiveness of the regulatory process. This conclusion is supported by experiences in Zambia and Kenya. Here there is a statutory requirement to consult with the Competition Commission, and this has led to very constructive communication, so effective regulation is enhanced.[50]

In the telecommunications sector in Jamaica, there was considerable overlap between Competition Law and the Telecommunications Industry Law. These issues are taken up in the section on telecommunications liberalisation and privatisation of the telecommunications sector. Suffice to say that the FTC took the lead in breaking down the telecommunications monopoly market structure. Since introducing the FTA in 1993, the FTC has done a good job to date. In most instances, there has been a general willingness by businesspeople to arrive at a mutual agreement with the FTC, rather than to litigate cases. This course of seeking mutual agreement arose as a result of the Stock Exchange case and the judge's requirement that the institution be reformed to separate the investigative and adjudicative responsibilities. The judge suggested the creation of a tribunal. The commissioners, thereafter, stopped calling witnesses and adjudicating cases, and the FTC focused on consent agreements and where this was not possible, it took cases directly to the court for adjudication. It therefore de facto used the prosecutorial model of the institution by default.

It is quite easy after the fact to criticise the designers of the Act, but it is not fair to state that local lawyers were not involved. Dr Kenneth Rattray, O.J., then solicitor general, was fully involved, along with other officers of his department. When the competition policy and legislation were developed in the early 1990s, the designers had limited experience with the development of competition policy and law and certainly no experience with the application of such a law. There is now a strong case for addressing the deficiencies that have since emerged and to consider developments in competition matters which have arisen because of requirements of the World Trade Organization and the CARICOM Single Market (CSME), and the rise of e-commerce.

D. McKoy summarised several other shortcomings and differences between the Jamaican law and the Sherman Act and other legislation with the FTC Act[51]:

- The power to declare the law is part of the inherent equitable powers of the court, thus the Supreme Court has to declare that the respondent has broken the law. The FTC Act binds the crown, subject to contrary statutory provision, which opens the way for disputes over issues of exemptions from the reach of the FTC Act.
- The use of foreign experts, which he called the 'black box': the practice of using expert consultants, who import provisions from statutes; the draft is then passed on to local legislators/drafters of law, who lack expertise and understanding of the provisions, often producing strange results.
- The Act was a mishmash of provisions from Australia, New Zealand, and Canadian laws, with the legislature inadvertently codifying some inarticulate language, which lost much of their substantive meaning in translation. For instance, he referred to the word 'unduly' limit, 'unduly' prevent, and 'unduly' lessen competition, etc., into the language of the FTC Act being

imported from Canadian law, but there was no legislative history to clarify the meaning of 'unduly.'

Need for Clear Definition of the Objects and Purpose of the Act

According to Richardo Parades, the FTC Act does not adequately define its goal and purpose, and this is essential if we are to reduce legal uncertainties, on competition.[52] More specifically, the objects are found not in the law itself but in explanatory material of the FTC explaining the objects as follows[53]:

- to encourage competition in conduct of trade and business in Jamaica;
- to ensure that all legitimate opportunity exists to participate in the Jamaican economy, and
- to provide consumers with better products and services at a wide range of choices at best possible prices.

The Act and the Commission's document also mention the prohibition of agreements containing provisions having as their purpose the substantial lessening of competition in the market or having or being likely to have the effect of substantially lessening competition in the market. However, when goals are stipulated which are not related to the promotion of economic efficiency, such as ensuring an opportunity to participate in the economy, interpreting the legislation may be such that it prohibits conducts that would cause a less efficient economy.

The Independence of the FTC

Under the FTC Act, the portfolio minster is given blanket powers to grant exemptions without having to give reasons and justifications. It is under these wide powers that the JPSCo and the coffee company came to be exempted in 1993. The JPSCo exemption has since been removed. There should be some guidance as to what factors a minister should take into consideration when granting exemptions or should mandatorily act on the advice of the FTC. Ministerial powers to grant exemptions need to be limited, either by listing categories of reasons for exemptions or by issuing guidelines stating the conditions under which future exemptions would be granted. Alternatively, there should be a requirement that the minister: (i) consult the FTC;

(ii) publishes the FTC response, and (iii) provides reasons for any disagreement with the FTC. This would provide more transparency. The FCA also permits the portfolio minister to request investigation and gives the minister powers to issue general direction, as necessary.[54] In Trinidad and Tobago, however, the competition policy provides for clear separation and operation of the Commission as a quasi-judicial body acting independently from government, to keep competition matters away from the political arena. Specifically on merger control, the merger threshold in Trinidad and Tobago, under section 15.4 of the TTFTA, the minister may, by order, vary the asset limit specified. Regarding Abuse of Dominance, section 22 (2) the Commission should not investigate an enterprise under this section, unless it is satisfied that the enterprise controls 40 per cent of the market or more or such percentage as the minister may by order prescribe.

Currently, the tenure for appointments gives the minister the option of appointment varying between three and seven years. There should be provision for a specific period of a five-year fixed term, with some staggering of the appointments so that they do not fall simultaneously with the electoral system and that all commissioners' terms should not expire simultaneously. This provides for institutional memory and continuity.

There should be a more transparent and objective appointment process. Because of the importance of the FTC to the economy, the appointments should be made by the governor general on the recommendation of the prime minister, after consultation with the leader of the opposition. Dismissal conditions should clearly state that such dismissal can only occur for cause: bankruptcy, by unsound mind, criminal offence, or failure to apply the provision of the Act. Where a member feels that he or she is dismissed unfairly, there should be provision for a senior judge to review the matter and provide findings to the prime minister.

Absence of Provisions to Deal with Structure and Merger Control

Experience has shown that the legislative rules embodied in the FCA are inadequate for managing the issue of mergers and monopolies. In principle, mergers are an important means of achieving a more efficient and productive economy, help to ensure a vigorous market for corporate control and provide a strong incentive for managerial competence. There is, however, an important policy issue, in that some mergers give rise to a concentration of market power, such that society may be worse off from their consumption of goods and services. The Jamaican government is updating the competition law, and the revised Competition Bill includes merger control regulation. FTC has, however, been conducting merger reviews under section 17 of the FTC Act since the Privy Council decision of 2017.

Dominance regulation, which has been substituted for merger control, has proven to be ineffective, and this has meant that this area of anti-competition regulations is virtually absent within the Jamaican jurisdiction. The government had no effective instrument to address the situation when the largest commercial bank in Jamaica acquired the fourth largest and monopolise just under 50 per cent of the deposit-taking financial and foreign exchange market. This was the case for many years in the European Commission itself, which relied on dominance rules before it finally adopted merger regulations: Council regulation EC No 139/2004 of January 20, 2004, on the control of concentrations.

The Jamaican Act has no provision to deal with merger control and deviates somewhat from its Commonwealth counterparts in requiring 'substantially' lessening of competition in a market.[55] The Act also does not define 'substantial' so the FTC has failed to bring a successful charge of abuse of dominance. The Jamaican legislation focusses on conduct of business, unlike the South African legislation which includes clear provisions to deal with structure and merger control.[56] The FTC should also be provided with the powers to prescribe structural remedies and to grant powers requiring changes in ownership, if behavioural consent agreements are not forthcoming.

Clearer Provisions to Deal with Predatory Pricing

In the US, the courts have often taken the view that predatory pricing is selling below marginal cost, and this follows an economic approach. In other jurisdictions, predatory pricing is considered as pricing in another market well below what is charged in its usual market and which the competition in that market could not meet without making a loss. In the Jamaican situation, it is not clear what constitutes predatory pricing, and this need to be clarified.

Horizontal Agreement

There are several provisions concerning horizontal agreements, with duplications and contradictions, rendering law unclear and there are uncertainties and overlaps in the provisions concerning vertical agreements, variously subject to *per-se* prohibitions and 'substantial lessening of competition' tests. These contradictions need to be removed.

Level of Fines

At present, the level of fines which the FTC may prescribe is inadequate. Typical competition jurisdictions have chosen a ceiling based on a percentage of turnover for each year of violation, as against a fixed amount. Without adequate sanctions available to the FTC, the money spent on its administration might be considered largely wasted. In addition, one of the most effective anti-cartel tools should be inclusion of a leniency policy towards whistle-blowers on price fixing.[57] This can only work where there are real sanctions against price fixing. The FTC jurisdiction on competition matters is constrained because the level of fines it can impose is limited. The maximum fine it can impose on an entity is J$5 million (less than US$40,000 at the time of writing) and, for an individual it is J$1 million (approximately US$7,782) for each act or breach. With constant devaluation of the Jamaican dollar against the US dollar the fine no longer serves as a deterrent. Government should not provide for a fixed sum in the Act; instead, it should give the power to the portfolio minister, upon recommendation of the FTC, to revise the fines periodically.

Overlapping Jurisdiction of the FTA and the OUR Act

There is an absence of comprehensive powers for dealing with the interface of competition law and other laws and regulatory institutors, i.e., overlaps with other sector regulators and other bodies. As regards matters relating to terms of access to networks, this should be the domain of the Office of Utilities Regulation (OUR). All other competition matters should fall under the jurisdiction of the FTC. It is therefore important, in the drafting of new legislation, that the roles and jurisdictions of the various bodies are clearly defined to avoid overlap and/or conflict in ways which will cause uncertainty.

There is the need to develop some specialist expertise within FTC in the areas of telecommunications and electricity to enable the Commission to handle referral matters from the OUR. The FTC should also be able to charge the OUR for the handling of referral cases. Notwithstanding any charges, there should be a statutory duty by the different regulated industry agencies and the FTC to consult whenever there is a danger of duplication and/or inconsistency of approach, or the need for specialised expertise.

The boundary issues affecting the FTC need to be resolved, e.g., with the OUR, the Financial Services Commission in the financial sector, the Bank of Jamaica regarding banking regulation and the Consumer Affairs Commission, regarding consumer affairs matters. With the recent merger of the Consumer Affairs Commission and the FTC, the overlap between these two agencies would have been addressed. It is hoped that the revised FTC Bill will have addressed this issue with the other agencies. There are several provisions in the FCA which overlaps with the Consumer Protection Act of 2006. Many of the CPA provisions either repeat or overlap with the provision of the FCA, particularly in dealing with misleading information and deceptive conduct, false representation, misleading advertising, and unfair trading practices.

Multiple Powers of the FTC

The constitutionality of the multiple powers of the Commission was challenged with the *Stock Exchange vs the FTC*.[58] In 1992, Dehring, Bunting, and Golding (DB&G) Limited applied to be admitted as a member of the Jamaica Stock Exchange (JSE). The application by the Supreme Court was not determined until 1993 and, in response, DB&G submitted a complaint to the FTC requesting an investigation, whereupon the FTC carried out an investigation of the rules and procedures concerning the JSE in admitting new members. The FTC, on investigation, concluded that the JSE was in breach of the law, in that it had created a barrier to entry into the market since the JSE had failed to respond to the application for membership within a reasonable time, therefore abusing its dominant position.

The JSE then responded to the FCA to the effect that the FTC had no jurisdiction on the matter, as the FTC Act of 1993 was not applicable to JSE matters, in that it expressly excluded securities from the definition of goods. It was the Securities Act, which was applicable; and further the JSE's constitutional rights to be heard by an independent decision-maker was breached when the FTC conducted the hearing and adjudicated on the matter. In the Jamaican case, the executive director of the FTC participates in both the administrative and investigation phase, as well as when the matter comes to the FTC for adjudication. The JSE sought and obtained leave to take the matter to the Court of Appeal.

The JSE claimed that FTC, in performing the multiple functions of investigation, complainant, and adjudication breached the rules of the natural law of justice. The Court of Appeal in 2001 ruled in the JSE's favour and restricted the FTC from taking the matter further and directed the Commission to address breach of natural justice. The judge also gave his opinion how the matter could be remedied and suggested that the legislative branch of the government should reform the institutional structure in the law to provide for separation of the investigative function to be assigned to the FTC and the adjudicative function to the courts or another appropriate body. The problem was in the law's drafting.

Some of the jurisdictional problems involving the merger of the investigation and adjudicative functions encountered with FTC in Jamaica were also encountered with the Tanzanian Fair Competition Commission (FCC). As a result, there have been successful challenges at the courts, against the multiple powers of the Tanzanian FCC. The Tanzanian FCC, like the Jamaican FTC, carries administrative, investigative, prosecutorial, and adjudicative functions; however, there is a right of appeal from the Tanzanian FCC to a Fair Trades Tribunal and the decision of the tribunal is final.[59] With South Africa, the several functions are separated with the adjudication function coming under a tribunal and further appealable to the High Courts.

CARICOM, the CSME, and Cross-border Issues

With increased globalisation of markets and cross-border flows of goods and services, competition agencies in countries like Jamaica need to address the international dimension of competition law. Extra-territorial effects of competition can arise in a variety of situations. Jamaica is a signatory to the CARICOM Single Market and Economy (CSME). Under Article 176 (1) of the Revised Treaty of Chaguaramas agreement, national competition agencies of the CSME are enjoined to conduct a preliminary examination of conduct of a business within the CSME on the request of the Commission, where the Commission is of the view that business conduct within CSME prejudices trade and prevents, restricts, or distorts competition within CSME. The Jamaican FCA carries no provision for investigation to be conducted at the request of an external body. Section 2 (3) of the FCA states that every reference in the act to a 'market' is reference to a market in Jamaica for goods and services, as well as other goods or services that, as a matter of fact and commercial common sense, are substantially for them. The Jamaican legislation not only needs to address CARICOM cross-border issues, but it also needs to address the wider issues relating to the World Trade Organization. It is not clear how cross-border matters involving companies whose conduct influences a market or a territory of the investigating authority would be treated by the FTC.[60] There are other provisions in the Jamaica FTC Act which would need to be reconciled with legislative changes in competition law in the region.

Institutional Options Available to the Jamaican FTC

Some of the challenging issues with developing competition institutional structures is whether the same institution should handle investigative and prosecutorial matters, as well as adjudicative functions, or whether adjudication should fall under a separate body. It was in this respect the Ministry of Industry, Technology, Energy and Commerce (MITEC), the portfolio Ministry, in 2006 sought to resolve the problem and submitted a proposal to Cabinet seeking amendment to the Fair Competition Act. The Cabinet submission considered three institutional options: administrative judge, institutional commissioner, and Fair Commission Tribunal.

1. Administrative Judge

Employ the services of an independent administrative law judge to act as an adjudicator, while the commissioners would act as investigators and continue their regulatory functions. The commissioners would later ratify the decisions of the administrative law judge. The ministry did not support this option because of the concern that, if the commissioners ratified the decision of the administrative law judge, this may be viewed as a breach of natural justice, the FTC judging its own case.

2. Investigating Commissioner

Adopt the structure of the US Federal Trade Commission to fit the local circumstances. However, in this model there would be no administrative judge to hear matters. Instead, individual commissioners would be appointed for specific periods to supervise the investigation process. The relevant commissioner would be prohibited from participating in the hearing of the said matter and other commissioners would preside at hearings and not be involved in the investigative process. The ministry did not support this option as it felt that this proposal did not adequately separate the investigative and adjudicative functions and may be subject to successful challenge as per the previous case with the JSE.

3. Fair Competition Tribunal

Create a Competition Tribunal and provide for separation of powers, with the FTC to retain the administrative, investigative, and prosecutorial functions and the Fair Competition Tribunal to take on the adjudicative function. The attorney general's chambers also recommended that the FTC retain its investigative and administrative functions and that matters requiring adjudication be overseen by a newly created Fair Competition Tribunal with a right of appeal to the Courts.

Having considered the above options, the ministry believed that the appointment of an independent body (Competition Tribunal), a separate legal entity from the FTC to adjudicate competition matters, was the more prudent course and one that would more readily meet the rules of natural justice. The ministry felt that to safely address the risk of further court challenges, there was a need to separate the FTC's adjudicative functions into an independent Competition Tribunal. The over-riding concern must be to allow effective and fair operation within the Jamaican legal system.

Jamaica legislation dealing with the infrastructure industries and the financial services sector provides for the creation of several tribunals to adjudicate on decisions coming from the OUR, the Financial Services Commission (FSC), and similar regulatory agencies. The creation of ad hoc appeal tribunals is institutionally inefficient, costly, does not provide for institutional memory, and does not augur well for consistency and continuity. There has also been the suggestion of creating a super-tribunal to hear competition matters and appeals from these other regulatory bodies. This approach would provide for economies of scale and for the development of a permanent structure supported by specialised expertise and would address cost efficiency concerns. The South African model could be adopted for Jamaica, providing for several panels of judges. The panel could incorporate a blend of lawyers, economists, and engineers or other appropriate professionals, except that the chairman of the hearing panel should be a judge with experience at the Supreme Court.

Derek McKoy considered three options: retooling of the existing FTC functions by legislation, regulation, through the Commission's own internal rules and procedures to maintain as much of the present structure and keep adjudication separate from the investigation/prosecutorial functions within the same institution; transfer the adjudication out of the Commission to a specialist competition tribunal, leaving the Commission only with investigative/prosecutorial function and transferring the adjudicative function from the FTC to the courts, leaving the administrative/investigative/prosecutorial functions with the FTC[61]. Of the three options, he argued for the third, transferring the adjudicative functions to the courts.

McKoy further pointed out that the merger of the investigative, prosecutorial, and adjudicative functions did not, by itself, mean that there was a breach of the doctrine of separation of powers; in the circumstance being adjudicated meant that there was a breach of the natural rules of justice. McKoy, a lawyer and former lecturer at the University of the West Indies, maintains that the policymakers in Jamaica provided for a law which was difficult to enforce.

His recommended remedy was to amend the law and provide for the FTC to carry out the policy, advocacy, investigative and prosecutorial functions, and for the adjudicative and enforcement functions to be passed to the courts. It was his view also that the FTC could constructively enforce the existing law by referring all disputes to the courts.

Peter John Gordon, an economist at the University of the West Indies, offered two solutions to remedy the problem of the merger of the investigative, prosecutorial, and adjudicative functions[62]:

a. separation of the adjudicative and investigative/prosecutorial functions into two separate institutions (each with separate legal personality) and
b. separation of the adjudicative functions from the investigative/prosecutorial function within a single institution through ring-fencing or a firewall to ensure that the separation did not breach the rules of natural justice.

Gordon's recommendation is for a single institution based on an adaptation of the single legal institutional model drawn from the US, incorporating the principle of ring fencing or firewalls to ensure that the rules of natural justice are preserved. From the experience of the public utility regulation in Jamaica in the 1960s, building on a structure based on US laws is not the appropriate route for Jamaica to adopt. Gordon's rationale for a single institution is based on cost (there would be savings from having one institution) and institutional effectiveness. Having two separate institutions (an independent body for adjudication, separate from FTC with responsibility for investigation and policy) cannot in any reasonable time develop the competence or expertise required to adjudicate effectively on matters as technical as competition. There is the likelihood of delays which will be encountered in adjudicating competition matters through having two institutions, besides the difficulty of finding competent person on competition matters in a small society as Jamaica to staff and effectively address competition or antitrust matters. He also refers to the recommendation of the 2006 Regulatory Impact Study by Cambridge Economic Associates which claimed that separation into two institutions would not be efficient for Jamaica, in that Jamaica would embark on a structure with the potential for overlaps, conflict, and relationship problem.[63]

With a single institution there is the need for suitable procedures to guarantee due process, facilitate the efficient submission and consideration of evidence. Even if Jamaica were to provide the firewall with potentially appropriate safeguards at the FTC to ensure that the requirement for natural justice obtains, under the Jamaican constitution parties could still take matters to the Jamaican courts, hence there is not likely to be any cost savings. The UNCTAD Peer Review Report indicates that combining the functions of investigation and adjudication in a single institution may save cost but may also dampen internal critique and raise concerns about checks and balances.[64] Although the Appeal

Court judge made a suggestion showing that the adjudicative function could be carried out by the courts, his view was only a suggestion how the government could ensure that the institutional structure addressed the problem to ensure that the rules of natural justice were not breached.

In both Tanzania and South Africa, a separate tribunal exists. In fact, in most English and Commonwealth jurisprudence the courts, or a separate judicial tribunal, perform the function of adjudication on anti-competitive practices. With South Africa, on investigation of a matter, the Competition Commission refers the case to the Competition Tribunal if further action is needed. The Competition Tribunal has a panel of judges and at least three judges from this panel sit to hear a case. In addition to the Competition Tribunal, there is a Competition Appeal Court (CAC) with a similar status to that of a High Court and is also composed of three judges of the High Court. The South African determinations are also appealable to the South African Supreme Court or to the Constitutional Court on constitutional matters.

Gordon implies that there is a need to understand competition and anti-trust economics to adjudicate on the problem of the merger of multiple functions in the Jamaica Stock Exchange case.[65] The issue before the courts, however, was not one of competition economics – dealing with markets – but rather of new institutional economics. This field encompasses social, legal, and organisational norms and requires an understanding of institutional economics, law, political science, and organisational behaviour. Institutional economics embraces such matters as organisational arrangements, property rights, transaction cost, commitments, modes of governance, bounded rationality and enforcement mechanism, its proponents are Ronald Course,[66] Douglas North,[67] and Oliver Williamson.[68]

Shyman Khemani states that 104 countries, mostly from developing and transition countries enacted or significantly updated their competition legislation after 1990 and, of this number, 62 per cent were created as independent agencies.[69] He shows that there is a line of argument which states that these countries lack the supporting institutions with public servants who have the expertise to make competition law work effectively. Gordon alludes to this sentiment as well, when he states that the competence does not exist in Jamaica, and it would take a long time to develop the expertise required to adjudicate effectively on matters as technical as competition matters. Khemani, however, points out that undeniably, there are risks but they apply to other areas where a government is introducing new social and economic legislation. With a proper institutional design and capacity building programme it is possible for Jamaica and other developing countries to rise to the tasks. Khemani also highlights the point that, if effective application of competition law deters just 1 per cent of the value of public contracts (preventing bid rigging), it would cause price reduction of 15 per cent on public contracts.[70] The cost saving would amount to 3 per cent in Zambia and 170 per cent in India of the budget of the competition agency. While the application of competition law involves a cost, the savings to the government budget, consumers and the wider economy is immeasurable and more than the cost of administering the law. The Tribunal in South Africa has also developed the competence to address complex competition issues. Cost savings cannot be the determining factor in establishing the institutional mechanism needed for the dispensation of justice. Khemani further maintains that, regardless of the institutional model adopted, certain principles need to be reflected in the design to ensure the creation of an effective agency for competition law; one such important principles is that investigation and prosecutorial function should be separated from the adjudication function to avoid constitutional and legal challenges.[71] He further points out that this was not the case in India's new Competition Act of 2002, and this gave rise to the legal and constitutional challenges leading to the Supreme Court of India's opinion that the Indian Act and the establishment of the Competition Commission did not provide for sufficient separation of powers between investigation and adjudication of cases. This resulted in the Indian government having to introduce legislation to amend the 2002 Act to correct the institutional deficiency. The UNCTAD lists several critical areas in which the existing legislation departed from international best practices. Most importantly, the Act need to state the purpose of the law.[72] The power given to the minister to exempt activities from application of the FCA is wide, does not contain any guidance as to the factors the minister should consider or the process that should be followed to reach a decision. The absence of mere control provision needs to be corrected. Express powers need to be given to the FTC to engage in competition advocacy. There is an absence of comprehensive powers for dealing with the interface of competition law and other laws and regulations. The need for a shift in enforcement priorities of the FTC towards increased enforcement of the anti-competitive practice's provisions of the FCA. There are uncertainties and overlaps in the provisions concerning vertical agreements, variously subject to *per se* prohibitions and 'substantial lessening of competition' tests.[73]

Lessons from Jamaica

The UNCTAD Peer Review Report of 1995 states that, although the FTC is fully funded by the government of Jamaica and that commissioners continue to be appointed by the portfolio minister, there has been no evidence of political interference in the operations of the FTC. This is not to understate the significance of financial independence in the functioning of a competition agency. Jamaica's experience shows that an assertive competition policy fits hand in glove with other measures such as trade liberalisation, financial market liberalisation, and privatisation. Modern competition policy and law is not inimical to but complements other measures aimed at fostering competitiveness. Since the law was enacted in 1993, the globalisation of markets dominates international trade. Jamaica needs to re-examine its legislation considering development in the CSME and cross-border competition policy.

An examination of Jamaica's experience also underscores the old lesson that any policy that attacks entrenched privileges will face strong resistance from the interest groups that stand to lose. Opposition to the fair competition function, as shown earlier was fiercely demonstrated by the business and professional groups. While their efforts failed wholly, political interests helped shape a more lenient law. Other emerging market economies hoping to introduce competition legislation can expect to face opposition from the same quarters. Some changes are already clear in how Jamaica's businesses compete. In most cases, businesses have tried to comply with the new law without resorting to excessive litigation. One example of this pragmatism is the consent decree between The FTC and Telecommunications of Jamaica Limited, which eliminated that company's monopoly over customer equipment in the mid-1900s. It is apparent that Jamaica has a general problem concerning the lack of certainty created by the multiple functions of adjudication and investigation which coexist at the FTC.

One cannot overemphasise the importance of capacity building. Jamaica was a pioneer in developing countries in adopting a competition law, and the FTC has now accumulated a fair amount of experience in investigating cases of alleged abuses. With the range of training and education facilities in Jamaica, it is certainly possible to provide the specialised training and development to the legal and other professionals in the country so that the capacity is built up to ensure effective application of competition policy and law. Just as it is important for lawyers to understand the economic concepts of competition economics, it is equally important for economists to understand complex competition legal concepts.

Notes

1. P. Cook, 'Competition Policy and Its Regulation: Key Issues,' Paper No 2, Centre for Regulation and Competition, Manchester University, 2001.
2. P. Cook, Colin Kirkpatrick, Martin Minogue, and David Parker, 'Competition, Regulation and Regulatory Governance an Overview,' in *Leading Issues in Competition, Regulation and Development*, ed. by Paul Cook, Colin Kirkpatrick, Martin Minogue, and David Parker (Cheltenham,UK: Edward Elgar Publishing, 2004).
3. Michael S. Gal, 'Size Does Matter: The Effects of Market Size on Optimal Competition Policy,' *Southern California Law Review* 74 (2001).
4. Michael Gal, 'Competition Policy for Small Market (Boston: Harvard University Press, 2003).
5. Rajan Dhanjee, 'The Tailoring of Competition Policy to Caribbean Circumstances: Some Suggestions,' Working Paper Series, Centre for Regulation and Competition, Manchester University, 2004.
6. B. Hoekman and Peter Holmes, 'Competition Policy, Developing Countries and the World Trade Organization,' Policy Research Working Paper, No. 2211, World Bank Development and Research Group, World Bank, Washington, DC, 1999.
7. Taimoon Stewart, 'The Quest for Relevant and Inclusive Competition Laws and in Small Vulnerable Economies,' in *Liber Americorum Antitrust Ambassador to the World*, ed. Nicholas Charbit and Sebastien Gachot (New York: Institute of Competition and Law, 2021).
8. Cassey Casety Lee, 'Model Competition Laws: The World Bank and the UNCTAD Approaches Compared,' Working Paper No. 96., Centre for Regulation and Competition, University of Malaysia, 2005.
9. In 1990, it took J$7.24 to the US$1.0.
10. Planning Institute of Jamaica, *Competitive Advantage and Incentive Study: Final Report, February 1986.*

11. Prices Commission, Report Provided by the Prices Commission and by the Technical Sub-committee on the Commerce Sector, established in 1990 to Examine Restrictive Business Practices in Trade, Ministry of Development, Planning, 1990.
12. The bank had approached the writer to calibrate on an empirical research project and the proposal submitted called for research in teleconnection, transport, and energy. Finally, the bank advised that fund only existed to carry out the empirical studies for six countries (Jamaica, UK, Philippines, Chile, and Argentina) in the telecommunication sector.
13. Derek McKoy, 'Antitrust Law in Jamaica: The Fair Competition Act of 1993, Transnational Law,' and Policy (1995/1996).
14. Hon. P.J. Patterson, 'Statement in the House of Parliament on Government's Plans on Monopolies and Competition Policies,' Kingston, Jamaica, 1990.
15. Trade and Development Board, 'The Role of Competition Policy in Economic Reforms in Developing and Other Countries,' UNCTAD, Geneva, September 1995.
16. T. Spiller Pablo and Cezley Sampson, *Regulation, Instruction and Commitment: The Jamaican Telecommunication Sector* (Washington, DC: World Bank).
17. Richard Whish, *Competition Law*, 2nd ed. (London: Butterworth, 1989).
18. Cezley Sampson, *Principles, Purpose and Policy Objectives of the Jamaican Competition Act* (Kingston: Ministry of Planning, Production and Development, Government of Jamaica, 2001).
19. Note: The United States Technical Team consisted of economists Robert Crandoll and Bruce Owen and attorney Robert Skitol. See *Final Report of the Advisory Team, Competition Policy in Jamaica*, USAID, 1991.
20. Anthony J. Meyrick and Cezley Sampson, *Proposal for the Regulation of Public Utilities in Jamaica* (Kingston: Ministry of Finance Planning and Development, 1991).
21. Government of Jamaica, 'Proposal for a Competition Act.' Ministry of Industry, Production and Commerce, Kingston, 1991.
22. Government of Jamaica, 'Fair Competition Act,' Kingston, March 1993.
23. McKoy, 'Antitrust Law in Jamaica.'
24. Derek McKoy, (1996). 'Competition Law and Policy in Jamaica,' in *Business, Government and Society* in the Caribbean, eds. by Anadaiye-Dane.
25. Private Sector Organisation of Jamaica, 'Comments of the POSJ submitted to the Deputy Prime Minster in response to Government Proposal for A Competition Policy Act,' August 30, 1993.
26. UNCTAD, 'The Role of Competition Policies in Economic Reform in Developing Countries and Other Countries,' (TD/B/RBT/96), Geneva, Switzerland, September 1993.
27. Eleanor Fox and Michael J. Trebilcock, 'The Design of Competition Law Institutions and Global Convergence of Process Norms: The GAL Competition Project,' Law and Economic Research Paper Series, Working Paper, No .12–20, 2012.

28. C. Sampson, 'Competition Policy: Jamaica's Experience,' *Economic Reform Today*, no. 1 (Summer 1997).
29. The Bar Association of Jamaica, *Report of the Commercial and Industrial Law Standing Committee on the Proposal of the Competition Act*, June 1991.
30. Myers, Fletcher, and Garden, 'Proposed Notes on the Competition Act,' July 1991
31. T. Spiller and T. Palo Pablo, (June 1993) 'Comments and Recommendations on the Proposal for a Jamaican Competition Act ,' (World Bank, Washington, 2003.
32. http://www.eurofound.europa.eu.
33. Whish, *Competition Law*, 9.
34. Restraints analysed under the *per se* rule are those that are always (or almost always) so inherently anticompetitive and damaging to the market that they warrant condemnation without further inquiry into their effects on the market or the existence of an objective competitive justification. https://www.bonalaw.com/insights/legal-resources/antitrust-standards-of-review-the-per-se-rule-of-reason.
35. IADB, 'Comments on the Legal and Regulatory Framework for Business in Jamaica,' Washington, 1991.
36. Notes on the Competition Law from Sir Alister McIntyre (July 1991), UWI. Kingston, Jamaica, 2888. (personal note submitted to the Deputy Prime Minister responding to the Proposal for A Competition Policy Act).
37. John Vickers and George Yarrow, 'Privatisation and Economic Analysis,' 1987, 16.
38. Roger Bonner and Reginald Krueger, 'The Basics of Anti-Trust Policy: A Review of Ten Nations and European Communities,' no. 160, 1993.
39. Ibid.
40. Todd. J. Zywicki, 'How Should Competition Policy Transform Itself ? Designing the New Competition Policy,' Fair Trade Commission of Japan Inaugural Symposium, Japan, November 2003.
41. IADB 'Comments on the Legal and Regulatory Framework for Business in Jamaica.'
42. Foster, 'The Fair Trading Commission: Role, Structure and Current Interpretation of the FCA,' Paper presented at the Bar Association Seminar, Ocho Rios, Jamaica, April 1966, 11 (32).
43. The Jamaica Stock Exchange vs the Fair-Trading Commission, Supreme Court Civil Appeal No 92/97- Prepared by the Fair Trading Commission October 2004.
44. Phillip Paulwell, 'The Fair Competition Act, 1993,' Ministry of Industry, Tourism and Commerce, Kingston, Jamaica, 1994.
45. Jamaica in the development of the competition policy provided for a whole series of meetings with special interest groups, like the lawyers, organised labour in addition to public forum. Special interest groups were also allowed to submit written briefs for consideration of the policymaker.

46. OECD, *Relationship Between Regulators and Competition Authorities* (Geneva: OECD, 1999).
47. Smith Warrick and R. David Gray, 'Regulatory Institutions for Utilities and Competition, International Experiences' unpublished, World Bank Paper, 1998.
48. David Boies, *Price Control of Business,* (Little, Brown & Co., 1977).
49. DTI Report (May 2006), 'Concurrent Competition Powers in Sectorial Regulation,' URNO6/1244, UK.
50. Tony Prosser, *Law and the Regulators* (Oxford: Oxford University Press, 1997).
51. C. Sampson and Faye Sampson, 'Competition and Sectoral Regulation Interface,' Briefing Paper, Cuts Center for Competition, Investment and Economic Regulation, no. 5/2003.
52. Mckoy, 'Competition Law and Policy in Jamaica.'
53. Richardo Parades, 'Privatisation Regulatory Challenge in Jamaica,' IADB, July 2001.
54. See FTC www.jftc.com
55. Roger Moore, 'Competition Policy and Law in CARICOM.'
56. Geraldine Foster, 'The Treatment of Dominant Companies by the Fair Trading Commission,' FCA, Kingston, Jamaica, 1994.
57. Moore, 'Competition Policy and Law in CARICOM.'
58. In the case of the US and Europe, the Lenience Programme has become much less effective, with far fewer whistle-blowers coming forward. Plus, this sort of procedure may not be suited in Caribbean jurisdictions where underlying conditions that triggers whistleblowing are not present: fear of discovery by the commission, fear of the commission, fear of incarceration, and the fact that in our jurisdiction, personal safety of a whistle-blower is not just guaranteed, but is highly threatened because of the homicide levels and the lack of rule of law.
59. E. Prosper, 'A Critique on the Investigation and Adjudication Powers of the Fair Trades Competition Commission and Finality Clause of the Fair Competition Tribunal of Tanzania: A Reflection on the South African and Jamaica Competition Law,' Research Dissertation in part Fulfillment of the requirements of the Master of Laws in Commercial Law, University of Cape Town, South Africa, 2014, also available at http://pdba.georgetown.edu/Constitutions/Jamaica/jam62.html.
60. Ibid.
61. Delroy Beckford, 'Implementing Effective Competition Policy through Regional Trade Agreements: The Case of CARICOM,' Workshop on Competition Policy and Regional Trade Integration in Developing Countries, Max Planck Institute of Intellectual Property, Competition and Tax Law, Bavaria, Germany, 2010.
62. D. McKoy, The Courts as the Preferred Means of Competition Law Enforcement,' University of the West Indies, Faculty of Law, 2009, page

2, also available at SSRN https://ssm.com/abstract=1913529 Mckoy has served two periods on the FTC.

63. Peter-John Gordon, 'The Case for Maintaining a Single Competition Agency for the Investigation and Adjudication of Anti-Trust Cases,' September 2012, available at www.jftc.gov.jm. Gordon has also served as a commissioner of the FTC.
64. Cambridge Economic Policy Associates in association with University of the West indies, *Final Report: Jamaica Regulatory Impact Study* (Kingston: Cabinet Office: 2006).
65. OECD, *Report on European Commission – Per Review of Competition Law and Policy* (Geneva: OECD, 2005).
66. Gordon op. cit.
67. Ronald Coarse, 'The New Institutional Economic,' *American Economic Review* 88, no. 2 (1998): 72–74.
68. Douglas North, 'The New Institutional Economics and Third World Development,' in *The New Institutional Economics and Third World Development*, ed. J. Harnes, J. Hunter, and C. Lewis, 17–26 (London: Routledge: 1995).
69. Oliver Williamson, 'The New Institution Economic,' *Journal of Economic Literature* 38, no. 3 (2000): 595–613.
70. R.S. Khemani, *Competition Policy and Promotion of Investment, Economic Growth and Poverty Alleviation in Least Developed Countries* (Washington, DC: World Bank, 2007).
71. Ibid.
72. R. Khemani, *Competition Law and Policy: Challenges in South Asia* (Washington D.C: World Bank, 2007).
73. UNCTAD, 'Voluntary Peer Review of Competition Policy: Jamaica,' 2005.
74. Ibid.

CHAPTER NINE

The Development of Regulatory Institutions in Jamaica

SPONSORED BY

REGULATORY DEVELOPMENT IN THE UTILITIES SECTOR

The decision to re-examine Jamaica's regulatory framework, and a resulting report by a technical committee in 1991, was influenced by the need to provide for a structure consistent with the move towards a market economy and an improvement in the efficiency of the country's regulation regime. That report recommended the revamping of the utilities' regulatory framework.[1]

The infrastructure industries, especially electricity and telephones along with urban public passenger transport, historically have been regulated in Jamaica because they were privately owned monopolies. As these three industries were developed under private ownership, they were subjected to public regulation, dating from the 1940s. Their prices were first determined by 'ad hoc' rate boards, appointed by the colonial governor. A fundamental weakness of the rate board's system of regulation was that they lacked institutional memory.

Introducing public regulation through a statutory body marked the second important change to the regulatory institutional structure. Jamaica had established a Public Utilities Commission (PUC) in 1965 to regulate the telephone and electricity companies, and earlier in 1947, a Public Passenger Transport (Corporate Area) Board (PPTB) to regulate the urban public passenger transport company in the Corporate Area. A PPTB was also established for rural Jamaica.[2] The Jamaica Telephone Company's forty-year licence, which was granted by the colonial governor, was also due to end in the period immediately preceding independence in 1962 and just before the PUC was established.

Price Control

The Jamaican economy pre-1960 developed under widespread price controls, cartelisation, and other restrictive and anti-competitive business practices. Over one hundred traded goods were subject to price control by the Prices Commission, which was established in 1955 under the Trade Law (1955). Price control, capacity licensing, and control of the distribution sector were therefore endemic. The anti-competitive market had been encouraged through the general merchandise laws, such as the Trade Law and specific industry and industrial incentive legislation.

In order to support the liberalisation and the development of a market-based economy, the government of Jamaica introduced policies to tackle problems of market distortion and to provide a framework for a more competitive economy. This resulted in introducing the Fair Competition Act (FCA) of 1993 and the Fair Trading Commission (FTC). The Commission ensured that the competition process was being carried out in a fair, honest, and equitable manner. The FTC has the power to conduct investigations in relation to the conduct of business in Jamaica to determine if any enterprise is engaging in practices that contravene the Act. Such investigations may be self-initiated by the FTC or be conducted following a complaint.[3] The central features of Jamaican government policy in the 1990s and, as set out in the law, were the prohibition of certain types of restrictive business practices, restricting unfair consumer practices and liberalisation of the professional services market.[4]

Early Urban Public Transport Regulation

Urban public passenger transport regulation was exercised by the Public Passenger Transport Board (Urban Area) Act, which was substantially amended in 1953; the Public Passenger Transport (Corporate Area) Legislation, which was enacted in 1947 (Law 1947), and substantially amended in 1953 based on a UK municipal type of franchise. Regulatory legislation was introduced because of the chaos that was being experienced on the streets of Kingston from the increase in the number of taxicabs and illegal minibuses (robots), which had partly contributed to the demise of the JPSCo-operated tramway service in 1948. Prior to the entry of the Jamaica Omnibus Service (JOS), semi-exclusive licences were granted to locally owned and operated passenger transport companies. However, they failed to meet their commitments and, as a result, their licences were revoked and an exclusive licence was granted to a new company (JOS), owned by the UK companies United Transport and British Electric Traction (BET), to provide public passenger transport service in Kingston. The PPTB was granted sub-judicial powers to regulate JOS, which began operation in 1953.

The independent sub-judicial boards were considered devices for eliminating direct political interference in the private sector, and their independence and autonomy were emphasised. The PPTB regulated JOS during the period 1953–70. There were frequent applications for fare increases and, during the rate hearings, several concerns were raised by the PTTB. In the 1958 rate application, the company had used the straight-line method of depreciation at 20 per cent per annum and not the income tax assessment procedure of reducing balance method. Second, BET was paid 7.5 per cent of gross operating revenues as a management fee for technical and advisory services, a matter not mentioned in any agreement. During the period 1953–59, the management fees paid to BET amounted to 40.2 per cent of the net revenues of the company. The company resorted to the practice of capitalising profits to increase its capital base and failed to expand its fleet. These developments eventually led to the government offering to acquire the shares of JOS. BET accepted the offer in the early 1970s; thereafter, the company was operated as a state-owned enterprise.

Raphael Swaby complained about the predatory tendencies of foreign-based multinational corporations through transfer pricing, exacting disproportionate tributes from the country through their companies, partly because of the prevalence of ad hoc boards and the lack of in-house legal and accounting personnel, which made it difficult for the boards to regulate the company in the public interest.[5] Gladstone Mills noted that Jamaica's experience with JOS was a classic example of the challenges of effectively regulating public utility activities, where a private operation was substantially foreign owned.[6] This was a period of increasing public complaints about the quality of services provided by the regulated company. Edwin Jones expressed reservation in adopting statutory bodies based on precedents in developed countries with access to expertise and procedures not normally available to the bureaucracy in a developing country like Jamaica.[7]

Early Telephone and Electricity Regulation

As with public urban passenger transport, the Jamaica Telephone Company was initially regulated by an ad hoc system – that of the Rate Board System. During the rate hearings, fundamental disagreements often arose between the company and the rate board over the definition and composition of investment, and the problem of identifying the proper charges to be assigned for services and equipment purchased from the parent company before calculating true profit. Because of the experiences gained from the various difficulties with the rate board, fundamental changes were made regarding the JTC's licence in 1967. An insertion in the licence prohibited any company, firm, or individual from holding more than 20 per cent of the company's stocks. The result was that the overseas parent company was required to dispose of its holding over that percentage. The government encountered several problems in its dealings with JTC, including controversy as to the adequacy of the capital being provided by the company. The rate board form of regulation could not induce the utilities to carry out the needed investments they were contractually obligated to undertake and to improve the services.[8]

The Public Utilities Commission

The Public Utilities Commission was created in 1966 to replace the ad hoc rate board system of regulating the private utilities. It had powers to ensure satisfactory services, fix rates which were reasonable to subscribers, but also rates at levels to enable the operators to secure a reasonable return on their investment. In the new regime, a detailed definition was provided of the rate base and its composition. An interesting development, prior to the expiration of the licence granted by the colonial government to the regulated companies, was that the companies and the government embarked on opportunistic actions to improve the companies' bargaining position in the period immediately prior to renewal or granting of a new licence. The period of uncertainty was heightened further as the method of valuation of company assets was not clearly specified in the licences. The companies resorted to revaluation of their assets in order to increase the asset base on which the rate of return was calculated. With JPSCo, the company increased asset valuation by J$4 million.

With introducing the PUC Act in 1965, the existing system of common law and licence ended. The PUC was given the power to examine the profitability of the electricity and telephone companies, both being monopolies. Its regulatory power extended to the establishment of the fee consumers were required to pay for the services provided by the companies. Jamaica was one of the first countries outside the US to introduce a multi-sector structure to regulate privately operated utilities. The forty-nine states of the US states regulated utilities through independent multi-sector statutory authorities, while, at the federal level, regulation was at the sector or industry level.

A new public policy enshrined in the licences issued by the PUC provided for increased local ownership and management of the companies. The licence called for the Jamaican public to hold a larger portion of the shares, with limits placed on the holdings of any one individual. The minimum rates of return provision provided under the rate board system of rate regulation was replaced with the principle of 'fair rate of return' on the utilities' rate base, a central principle of American-style regulation. Despite these new safeguards and the more professionally constituted PUC, the commissioners experienced difficulties in satisfying themselves about the efficacy of the rate base as computed by the companies, the ingredients included, and their valuation. In the early 1970s, the firms were found to have inflated their rate bases (gold plating) through questionable accounting practices, in order to earn higher profits, the Averch and Johnson effect.[9] There was also concern about compensation for management and technical services, provided in each instance by the parent company, whether these were provided at competitive prices. With JPSCo, Stone and Webster, a US energy company, was a major overseas shareholder also providing management and technical services to JPSCo. In the case of the telephone company, it was Montreal Engineering. With JOS, it was British Electric Traction Limited (BET) of the UK. In all cases, the companies refused to increase investments to meet national development objectives, and this became a critical issue for the newly independent government that was trying to increase the pace of economic development.[10]

Jamaica adopted the US Federal Power Commission model for PUC. While, initially, the relationship between the PUC and the companies was cordial, when the firms applied for rate increases, this ceased with adoption by the PUC of the American-style quasi-judicial procedure involving long drawn-out public hearings and lawyers representing the companies (often US lawyers and investment bankers); the process had now become litigious and adversarial. The Commission was composed of part-time commissioners, with each commissioner serving for three years. They were supported by a small permanent secretariat. The Commission's members held their appointment based on tenure. This facilitated the development of independence, institutional memory, and addressed some problems of information asymmetry.

The twenty-five-year licence awarded by the PUC to the JPSCo in 1967 incorporated a provision for renewal, and this provided a more stable investment environment for the company. Jamaica Telephone Company also received its licence in 1965; however, this was amended in 1966 to accommodate the PUC Act. The PUC, having been created as a statutory authority, had considerable decision-making powers, subject only to judicial review by the Supreme Court. It was given a very wide mandate, and, regarding the electricity industry, both the Act and the licence gave the Commission decision-making powers over the equity structure of the company, the determination of rates, technical standards, and universal services obligation. Additionally, the Commission had to satisfy itself that the ownership structure was in the best interest of Jamaicans. The new licence also made provisions for the regulated utility to carry out development programmes, and additional programmes, as agreed with the PUC within the existing rate structure.

Utility rates set by the PUC were required to achieve a reasonable rate of return on equity, after meeting all expenses, including depreciation and debt charges. The Commission had regulatory powers over construction standards as they related to new facilities, as well as the system of accounts maintained by the utilities. It also had regulatory powers over disputes between the utilities and consumers. Significantly, it carried a statutory requirement to ensure that due regard was given to the country's need for expanded electricity services.

Jamaica had abandoned the policy of a precisely specified operating licence, as was a feature of the rate board system; it was felt that this approach unacceptably constrained the democratic process. In moving over to the US model, the cost-of-service regulation, and the rates set based on a specific rate of return, which prevailed under the colonial administration, were abandoned. These were radical and fundamental new regulatory innovations, especially for a country embarking on self-government for the first time. Raphael A. Swaby opined that the new regulatory structure...

> indicated that the Government wished to attempt to exercise regulatory control over the privately-owned utilities in a manner based on the North American precedents, combining the powers of the Federal Power Commission and the Securities and Exchange Commission in a manner subject to interpretation against a large body of law and practice built up in the USA.[11]

Regulatory systems need to reconcile investors' entitlement to receive reasonable rates of return on investments with concern that the firm with monopoly power can misuse it to the detriment of consumers. In the US, the system involves conferring substantial description to an independent regulatory agency, with legislative guidance on tariffs often defined only as 'fair or just.' Discretion of this breadth on an issue as politically sensitive as tariff is a source of considerable risk to investors, with capital-intensive and immobile assets. However, these risks have been mitigated in the US by a series of Supreme Court decisions, dating back to the 1890s, that have interpreted the American constitution in ways that create effective safeguards for investors in regulated industries. The US process is insulated from the political process, and the Jamaican regulatory endowment lacked the complementary institutional safeguards that developed in the US.

The Jamaican Commission also became politicised. Developing countries need to be wary of transplants from advanced economies.[12] Laws and regulatory systems in advanced economies may appear to offer a convenient way to modernise regulatory systems. Sometimes consultants retained by developing countries may be familiar with the systems in his or her home country, offering such systems as international best practices without taking into consideration the need for adaptation to local circumstances.

Period of State Ownership of the Utilities

The resolution of the problems of regulation of privately owned firms proved intractable and, as a result, the government resorted to nationalisation of all three companies, JTC, JOS, and JPSCo in the early 1970s. With state control of the utilities, in 1975 the Advisory and Monitoring Unit (AMU) in the Ministry of Public Utilities and Transport assumed responsibility for advising the minister on rate determination. This was the third institutional change to the regulatory process involving a twenty-year period of direct ministerial regulation (1975–95).

Ministerial regulation continued, more or less, until the Office of Utilities Regulation (OUR) Act was amended in 2000, transferring regulatory decision-making power from the portfolio minister to the OUR. The PUC Act was rescinded when it was replaced by the OUR Act in 1995; however, in the ensuing five years, regulation continued to be exercised by the minister until the defect in the OUR power was eventually corrected by the OUR Act 2000. Part of the mandate of the AMU was to advise the minister on rate matters and, in this regard, it took into consideration social criteria, external economic cost and benefits, the inflationary potential of the utilities rate increases, the sustainability of the product, possible consumer resistance, and that a controlled utility, especially a government-owned monopoly producing an essential service, was not entitled to speculative profits at the expense of the consumer.[13] During the three-year period, 1997–2000, following the establishment of the OUR, the office functioned more as an advisor to the portfolio minister, as the utilities refused to deal directly with OUR.

Economic Rationale for Regulation

The primary reasons for regulations are natural monopoly (economies of scale and scope), information asymmetry and externality, and public goods. With transportation, destructive competition is advanced as the rationale for regulation. Monopoly arises when a firm (or group of firms) acting in concert (cartelisation) has enough power to raise prices above the competitive levels, thereby extorting higher profits at the expense of consumers and economic efficiency. The threat of entry by new firms, as well as from products that may be effective substitutes in a contestable market may also induce competitive behaviour.[14] Competitive pressure introduced by governments also can address natural or administrative monopoly concerns by removing unjustified regulatory barriers to competition. It is also possible through competition law or, in extreme cases, by regulating prices and quality of goods or services. Sometimes, governments use public ownership as regulation, as with the case of the water sector in Jamaica.

Network industries like telecommunications, electricity, gas pipelines, railways, water, and sewerage typically confer benefits to all its users, and usually the network is subject to scale economies and requires large fixed sunk costs. Historically, network industries were operated as vertically and horizontally integrated industries and regulated as natural monopolies. Since 1980, the structure of these industries has been subject to disintegration; thus, in electricity there is the possibility of independent generation.

Information asymmetry arises when market participants lack the information to make well-informed choices. For example, consumers may lack reliable information about the quality or safety of a product, or qualification of a service provider. In professional services, for instance, there were cases in Jamaica where self-regulation was used to set common fees and to restrict advertising. In banking, concerns were raised about the stability of the system, and systemic regulation, leading to regulators seeking to restrict price competition. Regulation sometimes may become rigid, making it challenging to keep pace with changes in technology, or the way business is conducted.

Another reason for regulation is the product or service being a public good. These are goods and services supplied to one person which does not prevent supply to others. Where a good or service is non-excludable, there will be the tendency for consumers to be 'free riders,' refusing to pay for it. Society may also decide that the free-market outcomes are unacceptable because of the resulting distribution of income, or because the market would produce unacceptable outcomes.[15] Regulation to secure redistribution involves interference with private property rights (wealth redistribution) or interfering with consumers in terms of revenue received from these property rights (income redistribution).[16]

In much the same way that there is market failure, there can also be government failure. Even when a market failure exists, it may make sense to intervene only when the expected benefit for government exceeds the likely cost of the failure. There may be rent-seeking behaviour. Officials may extract bribes in return for favourable consideration or special privileges, and regulated firms have an incentive to work with their regulators through a range of activities.[17]

The rationale for intervention in the delivery of transport services has been the fear of destructive competition. If there was no government intervention, for example in the public passenger transport market, or airline market, there is the argument that there would be excessive competition, resulting in prices being depressed below marginal costs, eventually affecting safety and service standards. Destructive competition would emerge if, in a market, the most efficient production technique implies heavy fixed cost, so that there is a difference between short-term and long-term marginal costs: if demand is variable so that the firm's market must in the average have excess capacity, and if entrance by suppliers from other sources is possible in the period of high demand. Competition may lead to pricing below the levels necessary to ensure replacement of the equipment at optimal levels, and the market alone could not allow efficient techniques to prevail. In many countries, regulation of transport modes, in particular, truck, bus, and airline transportation, was predicated on the negative effects on the structure of the industry which could be induced by destructive competition.[18]

Until recently, the provision of road infrastructure in Jamaica was the sole preserve of national and local government. With the intervention of the private sector in the provision of highway infrastructure facilities since 2000, a separate toll road regulator has been added to the transport regulatory institutional structure. Although delivery of urban public passenger bus transportation can be provided through a competitive market, the Jamaican government, after 1970, chose a publicly owned administrative monopoly to deliver public urban bus passenger transport services. With privately owned public transport, the same argument was put forward for an administratively created monopoly, but subject to public regulation. The arguments have been economies of scale in having one company in the industry. Similarly, in the provision of aviation service (airport infrastructure), this has been the preserve of the state, providing the infrastructure services and acting also as regulator.

There have been different academic reasons for regulation, with arguments such as public interest theory, private interest theory, and the rational contractional school. For the Public Interest School, the purpose is to achieve certain publicly desired goals where ordinarily the market would fail. The problem with this theory is the difficulty in an agreed conception of the public interest and there are doubts concerning the disinterestedness and efficiency that the public interest attributes to a regulator. Capture theory asserts that the regulatory agencies may come to regulate in other interest (powerful industry group) other than the public, captured by such interest group.[19] It may even be used by politicians against the interest of the public. Private interest group theorists stressed the extent to which regulatory development are driven not by the interest of the public but by private interest.[20]

Forms of Regulation for the New Structure in the 1990s

In developing the new regulatory structure, the government had to decide if Jamaica should continue with the US-style regulation or adopt the untested UK model. There were fundamental differences between the US and UK style, or model of regulation, as advanced in the 1990s. Prime Minister Patterson, from experience, did not favour the US model. Historically, the US favoured private ownership and independent regulation, while the UK, up to 1980, favoured public ownership and self-regulation. The US economic reform of the 1980s took the form of structural changes and liberalisation of prices and free entry to markets, while the UK followed privatisation, structural changes, and regulatory reform. The US regulation has, over the years, developed along a quasi-judicial path, with collegiate decision-making bodies, essentially based on profit controls, rate of return/rate base price mechanism and legalistic open hearings. The UK in 1980 rejected the eighteenth-century Railway & Canal Commission model, which the US had adopted and opted for a new institutional form, involving a single decision maker, a director general, price control (RPI-X) pricing mechanism, informal and consultative procedures, and managed competition. There are also several other areas of difference. The US Public Utility Commission's regulatory process is lengthy, expensive, and inefficient. Regulation seeks to balance public interest and the interest of industry owners. The US system goes back to 1830 State Regulatory Commissions and the creation of the Interstate Commerce Commission in 1887 to control interstate rail and other transport, including pipelines, and the eighteenth-century British institution mode, which was exported across the Atlantic to the US.

The Jamaican PUC process followed the court-style procedures, and lawyers were required to represent interested parties. Parties other than consumers and industry participants may seek representation. Parties may appeal a decision to State High Courts, Appeals Court, and US Supreme Court in the case of the US. Cases can take up to seven years. In Trinidad and Tobago, there were instances when a rate determination case went on for over two years.

The rate formula (see below) determines the revenue requirement which, *inter alia*, produces the required rates of return on the utilities' capital.[21] A test year is selected to determine the rate base, and the assets considered relevant to the regulated services. The utilities' capital cost is usually determined by historical method, less depreciation. In setting the RR the firms' operating costs are added to the cost of capital.

Some of the other issues which arose was whether there should be industry-specific regulator, or multi-sector regulator and which section of government should the regulator report to, either through the sector ministry or the Office of the Prime Minister or the attorney general. With the multi-sector approach, on its merit, it was concluded that reporting to the prime minister would be a better option to secure arm's length relationship with the political authorities. One of the most important requirements of a robust regulatory structure is the independence of the regulator from political influence. It was felt that such institutional autonomy would be better secured with the regulator reporting administratively through the Cabinet Office to the prime minister who is more likely to weigh the costs of political opportunism on investments compared to an individual minister.

The argument for a multi-sector agency (as was established in Canada, Brazil, Australia, Panama, and the US at the federal level) is that it allowed scarce resources to be shared. For example, economists, financial analysts, lawyers, and other professionals can work across industries as demand arises, which is of particular advantage where expertise in regulations is scarce; there are also opportunities to realise economies of scale in supporting services. With a multi-sector structure, one avoids the risk of the regulator developing too close a relationship with the sector ministry, with the possibility of the regulator being compromised by the industry being regulated. The multi-sector structure also reduces the risk of political interference, as would be the case with an industry-specific structure.

Industry-specific, however, has the advantage of concentrating on a single industry which, other things being equal, facilitates specialisation and should improve the ability for more appropriate regulatory decisions. This problem, however, can be addressed by industry-specific departments in a multi-sector structure, therefore securing the benefits from specialisation and focus. Some argued putting regulation under one authority is akin to putting all one's eggs in one basket, thereby increasing the risk and impact of regulatory failure. A counter to this argument, however, is that with a multi-sector structure a stronger basket is created. A multi-sector structure enables the institution to better deal with the blurring of boundaries in industries. Deregulation, for example, has witnessed water companies entering telecommunications business and gas companies entering electricity business, resulting in the birth of multi-utilities. The multi-sector structure is better able to accommodate the multi-utilities. Multi-sector agencies are better off to adopt consistent approaches to common issues and thus guard against such distortions as regulatory arbitrage.[22]

No single approach can be considered as unambiguously superior; a balance has to be struck and, with Jamaica taking into consideration its small size and limited resources, it was felt that it was more advantageous to adopt the multi-sector structure. The issue has been revisited several times since, as there has been pressures from the sector minister to change industry specific regulator, giving him more control over the regulatory process. In fact, it has been presented that a single communication regulator, involving communications and telecommunication sectors would be better off to address convergence trend in technology, blurring of the boundaries between broadcasting, telecommunications, internet and information technology, which were previously regulated separately.[23] The call for the unbundling of the OUR came only from the telecommunications sector because converged regulation cannot occur in the multi-sector structure, although no evidence was provided to support this position.

The matter was again revisited in 2014 when Phillip Paulwell, then minister of science technology, energy and mining, engaged a consulting firm to revisit the issue.[24] The consultants' findings were inconclusive, and the Cabinet Office took the matter no further, to the disappointment of the telecommunications sector minister, who argued for unbundling of telecommunications regulation and creating one communications sector regulator.

Some of the other considerations were that the agency should be exempted from civil service conditions of appointment and that there should be criteria to reduce political partisan appointment. The appointment of a director general would be made by the governor general, on the recommendation of the prime minister, and after consultation with the leader of the opposition. The OUR fell under the administrative responsibility of the prime minister, through the Cabinet Office.

It was also felt that, instead of a single decision-making and governance being solely in the hands of the director general (DG), as with the UK, an 'Office' would be created comprising the DG and two deputy directors general. The agency was also provided with a measure of independence in establishing its budget, in that the OUR was provided with earmarked access to funding and did not have to depend on budget allocation from the Ministry of Finance. To further secure its independence, the recommendation was for the appointments to be on fixed terms, with the specification that these officials could only be dismissed for cause.

The Offices of Utilities Regulation

The Office of Utilities Regulation (OUR) was not established until 1997, fully ten years after privatisation of the telecommunications industry. The OUR regulated the telecommunications, electricity, water, and sewerage disposal sectors, and public transportation by road, rail, and ferry. It was felt that establishment of the regulatory framework for the newly privatised firms left little time to evaluate best regulation options.[25]

The Act (2000) establishing the OUR was an enabling legislation, and its purpose was to provide for the legal structure and the institutional arrangements covering functions, processes, and enforcement arrangements, and to denote the industries which were to fall under its purview. Separate legislation was required for each industry, setting out how the OUR should regulate the respective industries. In the immediate period after the passing of the Act, and up to 2000, the portfolio minister was effectively the decision-maker on regulatory matters. Both the telecommunications and electricity utilities refused to accept regulatory decisions of the OUR on its establishment in 1997, on the grounds that the OUR Act did not give the agency any direct decision-making role over the regulated industries.

The OUR Act of 2000 made several modifications to the system. Most importantly, it gave powers to the agency to determine the rates, or fares that may be charged by a utility (unless the manner for fixing a rate was set out in the industry instrument); provide for standards of quality; prescribe the system of accounts and impose fees. In relation to licences, the OUR's remit was to receive and process applications and to make recommendations to the responsible minister in relation to their issue, based on needs of the community, operational efficiency, need to protect the environment, need to provide consumers with economical and reliable service, and provide reasonable returns on utilities' investment.

The OUR was specifically required to undertake measures it considered necessary, or desirable to encourage competition and protect the interests of consumers. The Act did not directly involve the OUR in determining issues relating to competition matters or to structure and operation of the sector, unless specifically provided in the relevant industry laws. However, it was given competition responsibility under certain sector statutes for example, the Telecommunications Act).

The structure of the OUR, at inception, followed closely the UK model of a single director general as the regulatory decision-maker, as against the multi-member, or the collegiate form American-style PUC, which operated between 1965 and 1975. In the Jamaican case, however, an office was established and comprised a director general and two deputy directors general, with tenure for three to seven years and eligible for re-appointment. The structure differed from the UK model in another important area, in that it provided for an across-industry regulatory agency, instead of a separate regulator for each utility industry, as existed in the UK until 1998. The UK promoted the industry-specific regulatory structure and the single director general approach across the Commonwealth; however, it discontinued the single director general institutional arrangements, replacing it with a regulatory supervisory board, beginning in 1998 to reduce the concentration of power in a single individual.

The main institutional issues associated with the OUR can be summarised as follows:

- the definition of regulatory terms for director general (DGs), or deputy directors general as being between three to seven years, rather than for a fixed term, which is more usual internationally;
- the ability of portfolio ministers to issue directions 'of a general nature' to the OUR, without necessarily providing reasons, or making such direction public;
- the arrangement which provided for the director general and the two deputy directors general to form the office or governance

of the authority, in effect, functioning as the board of the OUR while, at the same time, the same three officials served at the senior executive at administration level;

- the Office of Utilities Regulation (Amendment) Act 2015 amended the 2000 Act, correcting some of the major deficiencies in the previous legislation.

The 2015 OUR Act created a part-time non-executive board of six members and included the director general as an ex-officio member to make seven. The prime minister, after consultation with the leader of the opposition, appoints four members. The Private Sector Organisation of Jamaica (PSOJ), or such body as the governor general is satisfied has succeeded the PSOJ in representing the private sector, on the recommendation of the prime minister and after consultation with the leader of the opposition, nominates one more member. A body appearing to the governor general to represent the interest of consumers completes the final membership. Members must have experience or capacity in industry, finance, economics, engineering, accountancy, commerce, or law; and there should be no conflict of interest. Appointments of the chairman and deputy is also made by the governor general on the recommendation of the prime minister, after consultation with the leader of the opposition.

Under the amended Act, tenure has been fixed at five years; eligibility for appointment and dismissal must be for cause. Notably, however, the three-to-seven-year appointment for the DG remains in place. The DG's function is now defined to cover responsibility for the general management and administration of the Office and any other functions assigned under the Act or delegated by the Office. The OUR's mandate, pursuant to the 2000 amendments, specifically covers telecommunications services, supply, and distribution of water, sewerage services and generation, transmission, distribution, and supply of electricity by licences and specified organisation providing utility services and operating prior to October 11, 2000. It receives and processes the applications and makes recommendations to the portfolio minister, except for electricity. The OUR is also no longer required to play a role in transport regulation and in the award of licences.

Electricity Regulation

Up to 1972, the electric utility was fully privately owned and controlled. However, major problems were encountered during the period of private ownership and public regulation involving:

a. transfer pricing;

b. unacceptable accounting (gold plating practices);

c. asymmetric information in favour of the incumbent monopoly operator;

d. costly and lengthy rate hearings, often lasting as long as a year.

In addition, Jamaica lacked constraints on regulatory discretion, and there was no containing body of administrative law, such as provided under the US 1946 Administrative Act. With state ownership, populist policies in the 1970s meant electricity rates were kept well below costs and subsidisation continued into the 1980s. Public ownership led to non-commercial factors dominating pricing, overshadowing efficiency considerations. Pricing was used as a mechanism for income redistribution. The government attempted to privatise the vertically integrated JPSCo in 1995, against the advice of the World Bank, but this attempt was unsuccessful. The JPSCo was not privatised until 2001 when a new twenty-year licence over transmission and electricity distribution was granted to the new owners. There was no vertical unbundling of the industry on privatisation; however, generation was subject to competition for the market.

In 2015, the government passed the Electricity Act 2015, repealing the Electricity Lighting Act which dated from 1890s, the Electricity (Frequency) Act and the Electricity Development Act, consolidating the law relating to electricity generation, transmission, distribution, supply, despatch, and use. The changes to the Electricity Act extended the role of the portfolio minister in regulating the industry, rather than providing for more independence for the OUR and the regulatory framework. The Act introduced a wide range of roles for the minister, without checks and balances, leaving the way open for opportunistic political behaviour. It does not seem that Jamaica has learned from the experiences of the 1990s with telecommunications sector regulation and the ostensible capture of the minister by the company.

Telecommunications Regulation

Telecommunications is the other main industry regulated by the OUR. In 1987, the Jamaican government vertically integrated the international and domestic telephone companies and created a new monopoly, Telecommunications of Jamaica Limited (TOJ), which became Cable & Wireless Jamaica Limited (C&WJ) in 1988. Under the 1988 licence, the company was given twenty-five-year exclusivity for domestic wire line telephone service, with the option to renew for a further twenty-four years. Similar rights were given for external telecommunications.

C&WJ was also given a mobile licence in 1993, without having to pay for the radio spectrum, along with the rights to approve all network interconnections until 1995, in which the law did not define the tariff. The licence would subsequently prove to be a severe restriction on the powers of the OUR as an independent regulator when it eventually assumed such responsibility. The licence regime generated considerable controversy and challenges, especially regarding the wide exclusivity claimed by the company in the 1988 licence: monopoly of telecommunications in, out, or through Jamaica.

Competition, however, was finally permitted in 2000 with the enactment of the Telecommunications Act. The result of this was that competition was introduced regarding domestic calls, internet service, international calls, and data service provision. In fact, there were two licenced fixed-line telephone service providers, besides four mobile operators in Jamaica in 2005.

The Telecommunications Act was last amended in 2012, and the substantive result of that amendment was to allow the OUR to set interim rates and to exercise enforcement forbearance regarding certain aspects of the Act. The minster's power to give general direction remained unchanged. The findings of the Privy Council case were that the direction given was not general, but specific. The provision is found in many other statutes and poses no problem. The problem arises where a minster attempts to use this to give specific directions to the regulator. There is still, however, a need to craft an Information, Communications and Technology Act to reflect the convergence of telecommunications and information technology. The new Act fails to address the rapidly converging technologies and issues such as the interface between ICT and broadcasting and traditional telecommunications and big data analytics, artificial intelligence, and block chain technology.

Regulating Urban Public Passenger Transportation

In 1987, the government restructured the delivery of public passenger transportation, so Metropolitan Management Transport Holdings Limited was created as a public company to own the infrastructure, including the fleet of buses, while Jamaica Urban Transit Limited (JUTC), another publicly owned company was created in 1998 to provide bus services for the Kingston Metropolitan Region, covering Kingston and urban St Andrew, Portmore, and Spanish Town.

Until 1983, public passenger transportation was provided by Jamaica Omnibus Service (JOS) Limited, under a fifty-year franchise. JOS, a foreign-owned company, was nationalised in 1974 because the service should be run in the public interest. However, after a period of poor performance the company ceased operations in 1983, being unable to meet competition from illegally operated minibuses and taxi operators. While under foreign private operation for the years 1954–68, fares were determined by a public regulator and which remained unaltered for fourteen years.

Jamaica liberalised the public passenger transport market and opened the sector to competition, involving minibus operators. The portfolio ministry first introduced a package holder franchise system, with a tenure of six years as sub-franchised operators of JOS. This was followed by a new franchise feature; package holders could further sub-franchise services, giving an individual the right to operate within a designated franchise area. The consequence of this was a one-man-one-bus operation, with the package holders focusing on increasing earnings at the expense of operating the package effectively and efficiently. The package holding system was ended in 1990 and was replaced in 1992 with a co-operative model. This co-operative system was short-lived, and the government returned to public delivery of urban passenger transportation in 1998, following a consultancy report by Wilbur Smith and Associates.[26] Route or shared taxi services were also introduced island-wide, allowing for some competition in the public passenger transport market.

Regulating Broadcasting

The Broadcasting and Radio Re-Diffusion Act (BRRA) governs broadcasting, and the Act was amended in 2004 to allow the portfolio minister to extend the terms of the licence for subscriber television for more than six years. The Act provides for the licensing of certain activities, with the licence to be issued by the minister of information, on advice from the Broadcasting Commission of Jamaica (BCJ).

The BCJ is a statutory body with the responsibility to monitor and regulate commercial broadcasting, subscriber television services, and radio re-diffusion activities. The focus on BCJ regulation is on content and not on economic regulation. It makes recommendations to the portfolio minister on policy, for example, the Television and Sound Broadcasting regulations, which were approved by the minister in May 1996.

Functions of the BCJ are as follows:

- administer the BRRA;
- recommend vetted licence applications to the minister;
- ensure that operations and programming of licences meet set standards;
- advise on content issues;
- carry out research relating to electronic media;
- provide public and media education.

Operators of electronic services typically need a radio spectrum facility, and the award of a broadcasting licence is linked with the award of spectrum. BCJ does not have any statutory role in spectrum management; however, the Commission works closely with the Spectrum Management Authority, which is mandated to regulate the radio spectrum under the Telecommunications Act 2000.

Some concerns on regulation under the BRRA relate to potential overlap in regulating cable companies, which are regulated by the BCJ, while OUR processes the Independent Services Provider (ISP) licences (issued by the minister). The key regulatory issue for the sector is that of convergence between technologies and product delivery, and the ability of the new cable operators to provide voice, data, and television as one package.

The Spectrum Management Authority was incorporated as a limited liability company under the Companies Act of Jamaica, with its shareholders being the postmaster general and the accountant general, each having equal shares. It is mandated by the Telecommunications Act 2000, as the regulatory body charged with the management and regulation of the radio frequency spectrum in Jamaica. The

SMA is governed by a board of directors, appointed by the portfolio minister for telecommunications. Day-to-day management is by a managing director. The Authority is financed through a cost recovery mechanism, whereby licensed spectrum users are required to pay licencing and regulatory fees. Before the BCJ issues a broadcasting licence, an authorisation is usually requested from SMA for the use of the radio frequencies. A representative of the SMA is a member of the BCJ platform that prepares the licence so that the spectrum management issues can be coordinated seamlessly. The SMA provides necessary technical support for preparing the licence. After a licence is issued, the SMA exerts regulatory oversight, particularly on spectrum interference. The problem that arises with this arrangement is that, as the licence and regulatory fees charged to the broadcasting licences are paid to the BCJ, there is no compensation for the work done by the SMA for these regulatory functions.

The SMA currently has no formal enforcement powers. Usually, any transgressions of licence obligations are resolved through the powers of the postmaster general. Changes would need to be made to the legislation from which the postmaster general drives enforcement powers to be transferred to the SMA.

Water Sector and Water Regulation

There have been little regulatory and structural reforms in the water industry in Jamaica, other than in the 1970s, when the Kingston-based Water Commission was merged with the National Water Authority, which covered the rest of Jamaica, to form the National Water Commission (NWC), a statutory utility. Between 1983 and 1986, contract management was tried twice without success on both occasions. In the early 1990s, a twinning arrangement was established between NWC and Thames Water International of the UK. In 1996–97, Price Waterhouse was also contracted to provide certain management support services to NWC. All these initiatives were unsuccessful, in that they did not bring significant improvements in the performance of the NWC.

On matters of water economic regulation, OUR carries the main responsibility for determining tariffs and is required to allow NWC to recover costs, including both capital and operating costs London Economics.[27] As with most countries, in Jamaica's case the major problem encountered with commercial or potable water has been difficulty in providing water and sewage at affordable rates, while ensuring satisfactory returns to the operator. This, to some extent, reflects the social and political concerns surrounding the provision of utility water. At one point, NWC was only recovering approximately 30 per cent of its long-run marginal cost and has had to face large, accumulated deficits. Uncollectable bills have run as high as over 40 per cent, with distribution losses from leaks and theft at about another 50 per cent. Although NWC doubled supply coverage between 1984 and 1998, sales during this period did not reflect the expansion because of high water losses. Across the country, the percentage of households with piped water increased from 61 per cent in 1990 to 71 per cent in 2001, with Kingston at 97 per cent and the rural areas 45 per cent.[28]

In sewerage treatment and disposal, while the vast majority of services are provided by NWC, private operators have been playing an increasing role. Water services are also provided by local authorities and communities. Government policy has been emphasising greater use of build-operate-transfer (BOT) type arrangement for both water and sewage treatment plants. Despite the many changes in the sector, water utility service remains monopolistic, with little competition. Water remains the classic natural monopoly, with significant economies of scale from a one-entity operation. Both water distribution and extraction are driven by externalities. Most rural water in Jamaica, until recently, was un-priced at the point of consumption, with most customers un-metered. These features presented further difficulties for commercial operation. The provision of water and sewerage services is capital intensive and, in order for government to be relieved of the full burden of financing the sector, it has been encouraging private investment in new infrastructure and private operation of water services.[29] Up to 2006, only two private providers could enter the industry in specific urban centres; however, by 2020, there were approximately sixteen private providers of water and sewerage services. According to the National Water Sector Policy, 2019, some 30 per cent of Jamaicans still obtain potable water from standpipes, water trucks, wayside tanks, community catchment tanks, rainwater catchment tanks, and direct access to rivers and streams. The NWC produces over 90 per cent of the total potable water, supplying over two million people with water service daily.

The NWC has always operated at a deficit and its capital is provided directly by the Treasury, mainly through loans from international financial agencies. Most of the water NWC produces is not recovered through revenues, as over 50 per cent leaks away in old, rotted infrastructure or is not paid for by the users. The government has engaged the IMF in looking at the water sector's needs. Arrangements using privatisation or public/private partnership, using a BOT or BOOT, approach are being considered.

There is a 2019 National Water Sector Policy and Implementation Plan; however, unlike with electricity and telecommunications, government has failed to enact the specific water and sewerage sector legislation, which was expected, and which would clarify and delineate the role of the different authorities. A specific law would also provide for specific empowerment, allow for greater clarity on the economic structure of the sector, and address coordination more explicitly.

Financial and Banking Services Regulation

Jamaica has a diverse financial sector comprising the Central Bank (Bank of Jamaica), several commercial and merchant banks, non-banking financial institutions (finance houses, building societies, credit unions, trust companies), development banks, money market traders, and the Jamaica Stock Exchange. Both the financial and banking sectors developed in the pre-1980s period under severe fiscal restrictions. The ownership of the institutions falls into three broad groups: foreign-owned incorporated firms, mostly of American and Canadian origin; locally owned and incorporated businesses, and government institutions, like the development banks. Until 2001, there was also a post office savings network. There is no legislation permitting offshore banking. Until the 1990s, commercial banks dominated the market with their several branches dispersed all over the island. With liberalisation and privatisation in the financial sector after 1987 instituted at the behest of the IMF and World Bank, the concern was market failure because of information asymmetry and externalities and failure to operate prudentially. There is no doubt that deregulation and liberalisation were instituted without due consideration for an appropriate regulatory framework, a response to the requirements of the Washington Consensus[30] to liberalise the Jamaican economy and included in the loan conditionalities.

The financial market operates through intermediaries; the most serious problem affecting financial markets is information asymmetry, or imperfect distribution of information, necessitating prudential regulation. Prudential regulation is also associated with the contagion risk, i.e., the distinct risk of problems spreading from one institution to another. Prudential regulation establishes outer limits and constraints placed on financial institutions to ensure safety and soundness of their operations and the overall financial system.

The regulatory structure which existed prior to the 1990s relied on self-regulation and was inadequate. The principal legislation governing the sector that were introduced over the years have been the BOJ Act of 1960, the Banking Act of 1992, the Financial Institutions Act of 1992, which succeeded the Protection of Depositors Act, the Building Societies Act of 1987, the Bank of Jamaica (Building Society) Regulation of 1995; and the general and life insurance were governed by the provision of the Insurance Act of 1973, with the Office of Superintendent of Insurance carrying responsibility for enforcement of the provision of the Act. Regarding the trading of securities, the matter of regulation came under the Securities Act of 1993. Prior to this, only stocks traded on the JSE were subject to regulation. The Securities Commission enforced the provision of the Securities Commission Act.

In the banking sector, concerns were more about the reduction of systemic risks, given the possibility of contagion and protecting depositors. This concern arose from the prospect of the adverse selection nature of banking contracts and the high level of information asymmetry involved in such transactions.

In the securities and insurance sectors systemic concerns were far less important, as the likelihood of contagion was virtually non-existent. Thus, the objective of regulation in these areas was to provide protection by enhancing disclosure requirements and setting conduct of business rules.[31]

The first move by the government to modernise the financial sector's legal and regulatory framework was not taken until 1991. A special subcommittee was set up, under the chairmanship of the governor of the Bank of Jamaica, which recommended a new policy approach. As a result of accepting these recommendations various amendments were made to the 1960 Bank of Jamaica Act in 1991. The Act was further amended in 1994, 1995, 2001, and 2002. This Act and the respective amendments sought to clarify the multiple responsibilities of BOJ, as well as providing for increased supervision by authorities over commercial banks. Prior to the changes banks and specified non-bank supervisory responsibilities were carried out through the Department of Supervision of Banks and Financial Institutions at the Bank of Jamaica. However, the department was low in the hierarchy of the bank's operations and was not given due attention in terms of resources and skills. There is evidence to support the view that the condition which precipitated these reform efforts was the collapse of the financial sector in 1996.[32]

This first move was followed by introducing the Banking Act 1992 (amended 1997, 2002, and 2004), giving BOJ more regulatory control over commercial banks, and the Financial Institutions Act 1992 (amended 1997, 2002, and 2004) under which merchant banks, finance houses, and trust companies were regulated. Building societies were originally regulated under the Building Societies Act, 1897; however, this Act was amended in 1995 and 2002, bringing building societies under tighter fiduciary regulation. Although credit unions have had a long history of prudent and profitable operations and did not form part of the financial crisis in the 1990s, as a precautionary step, licensed under the Cooperative Societies Act and the Friendly Societies Act, they were made 'specified financial institutions' subject to BOJ's regulation.

The JSE was established in 1968 and, in 1989, it opened a subsidiary, the Jamaica Central Securities Depository to facilitate electronic transfer and settlement of securities. The Securities and Exchange Act followed in 1993, providing for the establishment of the Securities and Exchange Commission to regulate the securities sector. Further legislation was introduced in 2001 as the Financial Services Commission (FSC) Act, widening regulation to cover the rest of the non-banking sector in 2002, replacing the Securities and Exchange Commission.

The problems of the financial sector were mainly problems of the banking and insurance sectors. Prior to 1990 Jamaica went through a period of strong financial repression. The period between 1970 and 1980 was characterised by government's involvement in the operation and development of financial institutions, accompanied by bureaucratic controls on entry and dominance of commercial banks in the financial intermediation market.[33] Firm control over the financial system was part of government's policies, agreed with the IMF under the stabilisation loan programmes, with the objective of achieving a market-determined exchange rate.[34] The system was accompanied by strict credit controls; high reserve requirements were used to constrain demand, focused on limiting money supply.

Liberalisation of the financial industry occurred in two clearly defined stages, between 1986 and 1988, as part of the structural adjustment loan programme; the period starting in 1991 saw an acceleration of the previously agreed changes.[35] Liberalisation involved removal of restrictions on investments, and de facto entry to each market, removing the demarcation that had developed and which had been used to supervise the sector. With liberalisation, several new players entered the financial industry, and the result was that no single firm came to dominate a segment of the market. As market segments were small, firms seeking to expand entered new markets, resulting in individual firms operating in a multiplicity of market segments, and this gave rise to domestic conglomerate financial firms. Competition was therefore not as successful as it appeared from the rise in numbers. Small conglomerates came to operate commercial banking, insurance, building society, and merchant banking activities, as well as to diversify from core banking and finance activities, entering fields outside of traditional commercial banking.

Several new financial instruments were also introduced, many of them for the first time in Jamaica; often they were off-balance sheet and defied traditional classification. There was a proliferation of unregulated party-related transactions among financial and non-financial institutions. The regulatory structure which, relied up to 1990 on self-regulation, proved to be inadequate to address these developments.[36]

The Banking Sector

Following the reform of the financial sector, regulatory measures were introduced to deal with fiduciary responsibilities and market imperfection as changes to the Bank of Jamaica Act and the Money Lenders Act, and new legislation in the form of the Banking Act and Financial Services Act. These acts sought to improve prudential regulation and to address such issues as criteria for entry to the financial market, capital adequacy, asset diversification, insider trading and connected party transaction, as well as establishing areas of punishable activity for regulated financial institutions. For an institution to be classified as a bank in Jamaica, it must be registered under the conditions stipulated by the Banking Act. The Act defines banking business as the business of receiving public money by a bank, and other business of like nature, as determined by the minister of finance. Banks may be commercial or merchant. Commercial banks distinguish their business by accepting interest-free current-account deposits and low interest-bearing saving account deposits and provide shorter credit terms to the market. A few provide longer-term mortgage financing. Merchant banks principally serve the local capital market by providing medium- and long-term loans to individuals and businesses and must be licensed under the Financial Institutions Act.

Regulating the Banking Sector

Prior to 1960 the framework for bank regulation was limited, and what little supervision which was carried out fell to the Ministry of Finance (MOF); however, MOF in 1973 delegated this responsibility to the BOJ, with MOF retaining overall responsibility. Although the Bank of Jamaica now carries responsibility for banking supervision, this responsibility extends back to 1960 with the establishment of the BOJ as the government central bank under the 1960 Banking Law. This law has been transferred to the successor BOJ Act of 1997.[37] Bank regulation in Jamaica is now carried out by the BOJ through the provisions of the Banking Act 1962 (as amended in 1997 and 2015). The Ministry of Finance, however, carries responsibility for the overall fiscal and economic policies and for sound management of the country's financial institutions. The ministry has a Financial and Regulation Unit which operates in close collaboration with the BOJ and the Financial Services Commission.

Until 2015, bank supervision was discharged through the Financial Institutions Supervisory Division of the Bank of Jamaica. The department handled prudential regulation of deposit-taking financial institutions established by several primary and secondary legislation covering commercial banks and merchant's banks. The various statues provided the legal basis for the licensing and supervision of the deposit-taking financial institutions, as well as the various powers available to the BOJ and the Minister of Finance in the event of bank stress, or where failure appears imminent, or threats to the soundness of the financial system. The new Banking Act of 2014, however, repealed the former Banking Act, the Financial Institutions Act and the Bank of Jamaica (Building Societies) Regulations which, up to then, governed regulation and supervision of deposit-taking institutions. An important aspect of the new Act, in order to secure independence in banking regulation, is that certain critical supervisory responsibilities have been transferred from the Ministry of Finance to a Supervisory Committee, comprising five members: three ex-officio and two independent members. The Act designates the governor of the Bank of Jamaica as the banking supervisor, with responsibility for chairing the Supervisory Committee. Another important institution in the sector is the Jamaica Deposit Insurance Corporation (JDIC). Although the JDIC is not a regulatory agency, it plays an integral part in the regulatory process by maintaining deposit insurance for prescribed financial institutions. With the new set of legislation, an important function of the BOJ is the achievement and maintenance of stability of the financial system.

There are two aspects of banking regulation in Jamaica, namely inspection (periodic examination) and monitoring. Inspections are carried out annually on site and involve direct contact with a bank's management regarding its profitability, its operations and internal controls, based on analysis of specific financial information. Monitoring is enforced through analysis of statistical information submitted to BOJ. Prior to 1997, off-site monitoring was mainly concerned with broad-based issues, such as maintaining limited licensing requirements, and assessing capital and liquidity adequacy ratios. Despite the existence of 'fit and proper rules,' in the 1990s only limited attention was made to appraising the quality of management and the culture of risk management.

Regulating Financial Services

The FSC was created as an independent statutory body in 1991 and carries the mandate of prudential regulation of investments, insurance, and the pension industries. It is the successor to the Office of the Superintendent of Insurance, Unit Trusts and the Securities Commission. The FSC began operation in August 2001, as an integrated financial sector regulator with the responsibility to protect users of financial services in the areas of insurance, securities, and pensions. It has powers of investigation, supervision, and sanction over entities falling under its jurisdiction. The FSC derives its power through five statutes:

1. The Financial Services Commission Act which outlines the responsibilities of the FSC as they pertain to the prescribed financial institutions;
2. The Insurance Act, which prescribes provision for regulating insurance business in Jamaica;
3. The Securities Act which prescribes the requirement for licensing, operation and supervision of entities dealing with securities;
4. The Pensions (Superannuation Fund and Retirement Scheme) Act which prescribes requirements for the licensing, operation, and supervision of private pension funds, and
5. The Unit Trust Act which prescribes the requirement for licensing, operation, and supervision of unit trust schemes.

The objectives of the various statues are to protect investors from securities fraud and other abuses, thereby ensuring that there is investor confidence in the market. The FSC looks at unsafe or unsound business practices; ensures directors, or managers are fit and proper persons, and that they observe the FSC licence conditions under the laws or regulations under which the licensee operates, or its memorandum and articles of association. The FSC is provided with a range of remedial actions, such as requiring the institution in question to give specific undertaking to take corrective actions; issuing cease and desist orders; issuing instructions to halt a course of action, or restraining the licensee's business; limiting new business, credit, investment, or limiting dealing in securities; restricting any other activity in which the licensee may be involved and prohibiting the institution from soliciting business or entering any other transaction and removing any director or manager from the management of the business. The FSC may also invoke temporary management of a licensed institution or may revoke its licence. The FSC may impose penalties ranging from J$25,000 to J$2 million.

Financial regulation ensures that owners and managers of financial service institutions are honest and have the skills to carry out their responsibilities in an ethical, prudent, and lawful manner. The FSC came about as a result of Jamaica's financial sector experiencing considerable instability, involving problems of major liquidity and solvency between 1986 and 2000. As a result, the FSC was created and provided with wide-ranging powers to supervise, investigate, and sanction entities falling under its jurisdiction. To a large extent, the factors bearing on an efficient and sound financial sector were prudential regulation, focusing on solvency, quality of internal controls, risk management, and corporate governance within the regulated institution.

The Commission is governed by a Board of Commissioners, made up of a chairman and seven other commissioners, including an executive director, appointed by the minister of finance. The purpose of the FSC's actions is to protect consumers who have limited information, or knowledge of (a) the products, services, and operations of financial institutions, and (b) the integrity, experience, and skills of those who manage these institutions. The FSC is divided into divisions covering insurance, corporate services, pensions, legal, actuarial, and investigation. The Commission licenses securities dealers, investment advisors, and representatives, mutual funds, unit trust, insurance companies, insurance brokers, insurance sales representatives, insurance loss adjusters, insurance consultants, and insurance managing agents.

In 2020, the FSC's scope was expanded to include national and international virtual assets, service providers, and trust services providers. The Commission also stepped up its activities in the fields of anti-money laundering and counter-financing of terrorism, as it relates to non-banking activities.

Rationale for Regulating Banking and Financial Services

Like many countries, Jamaica, experienced significant banking and financial sector problems in the period after 1980. The main causes of these problems in developing countries were poor credit controls, connected lending, and insufficient liquidity and capital; in short, poor internal governance, highlighting the need for external supervision to reinforce internal controls.[38] The failures in Jamaica were aggravated by the move towards early liberalisation of the financial sector, being part of the IMF and World Bank's structural adjustment and stabilisation loan programmes. As R.H. Coase pointed out, liberalised and free markets require considerable internal institutional structure and self-regulation to function efficiently, with minimal transaction costs, while the majority of such market regulations are the outcome of private agreements among those involved.[39] Private agreements, however, need the underlying support of commercial and contract law to provide sanctions and prevent opportunistic and imprudent behaviour.

In fact, there was a public revolution against the financial sector's failures; however, the case for regulation of the sector does not rest solely on public pressure. The case also relies on circumstances that the private sector, left to itself, produces market failure, or at least sub-optimal results, which are arguably worse than public regulation.[40]

The first case for regulation arises where there is private sector monopoly, or oligopoly, not normally found in Jamaica in the financial sector (more the case in the telephone and electricity markets). Although the financial market was very competitive, there were supporting components, like the clearing and payment systems, which incorporate network economies. The second rationale, client protection, arises for two reasons: because the institution where the clients hold their funds may fail or because of the adverse behaviour (unsatisfactory conduct) of a firm with the customer; this may cause systemic instability and cause losses to individual depositors, regarded as incapable of looking after their own interest. Much of this relates to asymmetric information in favour of the financial institution. Systemic stability requires that the authorities have a prudential concern about the liquidity, solvency, riskiness, and general health of the financial institution. In this respect, both systemic regulation and prudential regulation require supervision of the institution, rather than merely the function they perform. Systemic protection is about the risks that the entity poses to the system, in terms of contagion and runs on similar institutions. Regulating conduct, while having a systemic protection objective, is, however, largely about protecting consumers and investors. Notably, systemic protection is more a concern for banking, whereas ensuring prudential operations is more a concern for securities and investments.

The case, therefore, for prudential regulation and supervision (rather than systemic) of financial institutions is that consumers are not in a position to judge the safety and soundness of financial institutions. Prudential regulation is therefore necessary because of information asymmetry (imperfect consumer information) and agency problems associated with, say, life insurance, or life insurance companies, even in the absence of the systemic dimension. Problems arise from inadequate information by the consumer, and hence prudential and systemic regulation is needed to protect not only consumers but also those who finance the safety net, or for compensation schemes, especially when the premiums levied on members of such schemes are not closely related to their relative riskiness.[41]

Conduct of business regulation is usually delegated to the competition authority. In Jamaica, this is carried out largely by the Fair Trading Commission under the Fair Competition Act, but there are elements that are administered by both the BOJ and the FSC; indications are that there is increasing cooperation between the FTC and both regulators. Dimitri Vitas, however, argues that the main rationale for financial regulation is the existence of market failure; market failure arises from externalities, and information asymmetry.[42]

Banks' form of regulation differs significantly from non-banking financial services, where long-term contracts are involved. Systemic issues are central to regulating banks, whereas consumer protection issues are central to the other financial services (pensions, life, and health insurance). Systemic failures are externalities. Other extenuating factors are the achievement of macroeconomic stability and the assurance of an efficient financial system. The rationale for bank regulation can therefore be justified for four reasons: the pivotal position of banks in financial systems; potential systemic risk and run on banks; problems of moral hazard associated with being a lender of last resort; and the nature of bank contracts. At one stage, the argument was for a single banking and financial sector regulation, as in Austria, Denmark, Malta, Norway, and Sweden. In these countries, a multi-sector regulator regulates banking, insurance, and the securities sector. The argument for a single multi-sector financial and banking regulator is that, under a single regulator, the agency would most likely have a complete picture of what is occurring within the entire financial sector, including the conglomerate sector.

In the absence of a single regulator, Jamaica's current financial regulatory framework provides for high coordination and cooperation between the critical regulators and functionaries. The Bank of Jamaica Act 2015 provides for the establishment of a Financial System Stability Committee (FSSC) that assesses financial system stability, make recommendations to the BOJ for carrying out its financial system stability mandate, and help inform the BOJ's use of macro-prudential rules and standards. The fundamental objective of the FSSC would be to review BOJ's macro-prudential risk assessments and make applicable policy recommendations to address any identified risks. The Financial System Stability Committee fulfils its functions through the guidance of quarterly reports on key aspects of BOJ's financial system stability assessments.

The role of the FSSC, more specifically, is to review BOJ's macro-prudential assessments; advise on the macro-prudential tools that may manage and/or mitigate the emergence of systemic risks; and to help monitor the implementation and transmission of macro-prudential tools, and to communicate with the public on the use and impact of tools on the system. Based on the amendment, provision is made for the FSSC to be comprised six ex-officio members, as well as two members appointed by the Minister of Finance, based on the recommendation of the governor of the Bank of Jamaica.

Transport Regulation

Public passenger transport has been subjected to regulation since the 1940s. The regulatory structure for the transport sector is set out in table 9.1. Regulation is split across a range of agencies.

With road transport, the Road Traffic Act 1938 and its subsequent amendments is the primary legislation governing the regulation of road transport and traffic. It provides for the establishment of the Island Traffic Authority, the chief institution for the regulation and control of traffic on the roads, granting certificates of fitness, driver's licences, licensing, and registration of motor vehicles. It also oversees regulations concerning construction and weight of vehicles and licensing of public passenger vehicles.

In addition, separate regulation was provided for urban public passenger transport under the Public Passenger Transport (Corporate Area) Act of 1947 and the Public Passenger Transport (Rural Area) Act. These acts gave power to the portfolio minister to issue exclusive licences for public passenger transport and provided for a Board of Control to regulate and monitor operations and to determine fares and operating conditions for franchised operators.[43]

Table 9.1: Transport Regulatory Structure

Segments	Economic Regulation	Responsibilities	Private Participation
Airports	Civil Aviation Authority (CAA)	• Licensing • Regulation of scheduled airports » pricing » anti-competitive behaviour » Quality issues (shared with NEPA)	There are two airport companies: Norman Manley and Sangster. Sangster is operated under a thirty- year concession by a consortium of four international companies.
Toll Roads	The Toll Authority of Jamaica (TAJ)	Toll Authority • Monitoring and enforcement of the toll road concession • Issuance of future concessions • Pricing issues	Further toll roads are under construction
Bus Transport	Transport Authority	Public Passenger Transport • prices • licensing	Public and private
Rail	No independent regulator		No public rail services are currently offered. The alumina companies operate private rail services on JRC tracks under contract. Reactivation of public railway through Rites of India is under consideration.
Sea Ports	Port Authority	Standard public service port where the vast majority of functions are delivered by the Port Authority	The public port in Jamaica is a landlord port with the Port Authority as the landlord. Several of the service delivery functions are contracted out to private firms, such as Kingston Wharves.

Source: Cambridge Economic Policy Associates Ltd EPA (2006) PPIAF -Jamaica Regulatory Impact Assessment for the Cabinet Office, Government of Jamaica

In 1987, the Jamaican government restructured the public passenger transport industry and introduced the Transport Authority Act, 1987. This provided for a new regulatory body with the responsibility for regulating public passenger transport throughout the island and to take over the duties of the licensing authorities for public passenger transport under the Road Traffic Act, the Public Passenger Transport (Corporate Area) Board of Control Act, and the Public Passenger Transport (Rural Area Board) of Control Act. The inspectors of the Authority are empowered to ensure compliance with the terms of the road licences and relevant road traffic enactments. Similar power was also given to the police.

The composition and procedure displayed in the Road Transport Act for the establishment and operation of the Transport Authority raises concerns about its independence. The Authority comprises ex-officio members, including the relevant permanent secretary, the solicitor general, and the commissioner of police and two additional members appointed by the portfolio minister. No provision is made for appeals from a decision of the Authority, or for cooperation between the Transport Authority and the FTC.

The problem of the transport market in the period after 1990 has been that of multiple agencies to regulate public passenger transport. Taxis have always been regulated and they now come under the Transport Authority. Two types of taxi services are regulated: hackney carriage service and route taxi services. Hackney service is where the operators may offer a service to commuters without restrictions to a specific route or geographic area. Route service is where operators are permitted to provide services on a clearly defined route.

Toll Roads Regulation

The Toll Authority of Jamaica (TAJ) is responsible for the monitoring and enforcement of the highway concession contracts and is the first of the road agencies established with the introduction of the highway programme that emerged after 2000. The second body is the National Road Operating and Constructing Company (NROCC), which issues the concession contracts, provides access to initial funding, and also carries responsibility for delivering the government's obligations under the contract. Much of NROCC's work is done through contracting out; consequently, it operates from a small office.

The Toll Authority has a board appointed by the minister of transport and works, comprising eleven members (one of whom is the chairman) and was established as an economic regulator, with the responsibility for determining the applicable tolls on specified highways. However, the role of the Toll Authority is prescribed by the respective concession agreement. In effect, the Toll Authority is responsible for:

- determining the escalation factor to be applied to the initial toll level; schedule 15 of the concession agreement establishes the initial toll levels and clearly sets out the formula for the escalation factor, which sets the capped toll level for any one period;
- imposing tolls less than the capped level (which requires the payment of compensation). (The conditions under which tolls less than the capped level can be imposed by the TA are not clear. Presumably, this would be in response to government policy decisions; otherwise the TA would be imposing a cost on the government which pays the compensation).

Civil Aviation and Airports Regulation

Prior to the decision in 1992 to liberalise the aviation sector, entities in the sector were entirely under state ownership. The system comprised a domestic air service, Trans-Jamaican Airlines and an international airline, Air Jamaica Limited. In the initial privatisation, the government retained about 25 per cent of the equity in both companies. The airline industry has been subjected to international convention regarding its regulation. Airports came under the ownership and control of the government through the Airports Authority, established under the Airports Authority Act of 1974 to provide for the development and operation of the two international airports: Norman Manley in Kingston and Sangster in Montego Bay, and domestic aerodromes: Tinson Pen in Kington and Negril; Boscobel in St Ann; and Ken Jones in Port Antonio.

Accompanying the AAJ was the Civil Aviation Department (CAD) responsible for civil aviation regulation, along with the Air Transport Licensing Board. The CAD provided air navigational services: air traffic control, communications and regulation of aviation services covering safety, licensing and regulation of airport operations (excluding economic regulation). Another government-owned company, Aerotel Limited, provides for the maintenance of CAD's equipment and facilities. The government decided in 1991 to liberalise the civil aviation market and to privatise the two airports. As a result, AAJ created Sangster International Air Terminal Limited and Norman Manley Air Terminal Limited to own the two international airports. With the decision to introduce private interest into the ownership and operation of the international airports, the Airports (Economic Regulation) Act 2002 was passed, making the Civil Aviation Authority, restructured from CAD, responsible for economic, safety and technical regulation covering licensing, pricing, competition, and quality issues at airports. Air Traffic control and air navigation were incorporated as part of the new Civil Aviation Authority. Price regulation was imposed at the two international airports.

The CAA is required to undertake consultation, provide affected parties with opportunities to be heard and to give written reasons for its decisions, and provide a framework which conforms to best international practices. The Authority is also required to approve airport charges imposed by airlines, although responsibility for fixing of the passenger transport airport improvement fee is retained by the portfolio minister. With price regulation for the determination of landing, parking, and terminal fees, these charges averaged US$6 per passenger in 1991. In the case of the fees for landside services, these were to be liberalised and subjected only to the competition legislation. At the time of the proposed changes, the aviation charges were negotiated between the airlines and Airports Authority, subject to ministerial approval. The government also imposed an airport tax (US$11 per passenger) at the time, and part of this was earmarked as user fee and assigned to AAJ as part of the privatisation package. The portion assigned to AAJ was to be replaced by a passenger facility fee (of US$5) with the income from airports in privatisation going to the concessionaire.[44]

The Airports Authority

The Airports Authority Act 1974 established the Airports Authority of Jamaica with functions to administer, control, and manage the two international airports and the aerodromes and other property vested in it under the Act. The Authority is bound by ministerial directions of a general character as to policy to be followed. With privatisation of the two main international airports, the role of the Airports Authority in the regulatory process has been removed.

Appeals Tribunals

There are multiple appeals tribunals within the regulatory structure regarding the several industries. Appeals tribunals in the utilities and transport sectors up to 2005 were established only on an ad hoc basis when there was a case to be heard. The legislative structure of the different areas provided for several potentially separate appeals tribunals. The tribunals for industries regulated by the OUR are provided for in the respective industry legislation. In addition, provisions exist for similar tribunals to be established for communications under the Broadcasting Act and for the financial sector under the Financial Services Commission (FSC) Act. In practice, they are established on an ad hoc basis, providing for potential proliferation of regulatory appeals tribunals; these are summarised as follows:

- The Telecommunications Appeal Tribunal provided for under the Telecommunications Act;
- The JPSCo electricity licence provides for an Electricity Appeals Tribunal, although not described as such in the licence; the tribunal appears in practice to be ad hoc, and a tribunal was established to hear the dispute between JPSCo and the OUR in relation to Hurricane Ivan;
- The Broadcasting & Radio Re-Diffusion Act provides for a Broadcasting Appeals Tribunal;
- The NEPA Act provides for appeals directly to the minister, whose decision is final;
- The Road Traffic Act (s. 21) provides for an Appeals Tribunal.
- An Appeals Tribunal is provided for under the Financial Services Commission Act, to hear appeals against the FSC, concerning insurance, pensions, and securities
- The Civil Aviation Act (pursuant to a 2004 amendment) provides for appeals related to decisions of the CAA.

A right of further appeal lies with the general law courts. Sometimes, this right is expressly limited to judicial review. Appeals related to decisions of the FTC are handled by the courts. This is not an appeal tribunal but a mechanism for hearing and determining on matters in the first instance directly to the courts. An appeal process before moving to litigation through the courts would seem appropriate. The central issue that has emerged is the need for rationalisation of the structure to address appeals from the decisions of several regulatory bodies, and possibly to create permanent appeal bodies, properly funded with specialised staffing, drawing from a panel of experts, depending on the dispute, so that a body of expertise can be an institutional memory, accompanied by dedicated administrative support. Many of the issues arise from the fact that several of the legislation are outdated, leading them to be inappropriate for the situation which the government needs to address. There is also the need to set limits on the appeals process, the grounds on which appeals may be permitted and the composition of the tribunals.

There is inconsistency in how these tribunals are to be established and funded. With electricity, the tribunal comprises three members appointed by the portfolio minister: one member to be a judge, one to be recommended by the OUR, and one to be recommended by the licensee. With the telecommunications sector, the members, other than the judge are recommended by the Telecommunications Advisory Council, which was established in 2002 to monitor the liberalisation programme, and the Consumer Affairs Commission. Neither the OUR nor the licensee may recommend a member to the telecommunications tribunal. With the Broadcasting Commission, the tribunal is appointed solely by the portfolio minister, with no right of interested parties to make any recommendations as to its membership. Similarly, the Natural Resources Conservation Act provides for the establishment of an appeals tribunal but does not set out any provisions for its composition.

Notes

1. Anthony Meyrick and Cezley Sampson, 'Regulation of Public Utilities in Jamaica,' UK Overseas Development Administration, 1991.
2. The two PPTBs were replaced by the Transport Authority in 1987, operating under the 1987 Transport Act with responsibility for regulating public passenger transportation. Anthony Meyrick, and Cezley Sampson, 'Regulation of Public Utilities in Jamaica,' UK Overseas Development Administration, 1991.
3. https://jftc.gov.jm/about-us/functions-and-powers.
4. Cezley Sampson, *Economic Competition and Restrictive Business Practices: The Development of the Jamaica Competition Legislation* (Geneva: UNCTAD, 1995).
5. Raphael K. Swaby, 'Some Problems of Public Utility Regulation by Statutory Boards in Jamaica: The Case of JOS in Issues of Public Policy and Public Administration in Commonwealth Caribbean,' *SES* 23, no. 2 (1974): 242–63.

6. Gladstone Mills, 'Public Policy and Private Enterprise in the Commonwealth Caribbean in Issues of Public Policy and Public Administration in Commonwealth Caribbean States,' *SES* 23, no. 2 (1974): 216–41, Mona, UWI.
7. Jones Edwin, 'The Role of Statutory Board in the Political Process in Jamaica,' *SES* 19, no. 1 (1970): 114–34, Mona, UWI.
8. Gladstone Mills, 'Regulation and Control of Private Enterprise in Commonwealth Caribbean, Part 1,' Department of Government, UWI, Mona, 1976.
9. Gladstone E. Mill, 'Public Enterprise in Commonwealth Caribbean, with Special Refence to Jamaica and Trinidad & Tobago,' Department of Government, Mona, UWI, 1976.
10. Harvey Averch and Leyland L. Johnson, 'Behaviour of the Firm Under Regulatory Constraint,' *American Economic Review* 52, no. 5 (1962): 1052–69.
11. Swaby, 'Some Problems of Public Utility Regulation by Statutory Boards in Jamaica.'
12. Raphael A. Swaby, 'The Rationale for State Ownership of Public Utilities in Jamaica,' *Social and Economic Studies* 30, no. 1 (1981): 75–107, UWI, Special Issue, Public Sector in the Caribbean.
13. Pablo Spiller and Cezley Sampson, 'Regulating Telecommunications in Jamaica,' in *Regulations, Institutions and Commitment*, ed. Brain Levy and Pablo Spiller (Cambridge, UK: Cambridge University Press, 1996).
14. Cezley Sampson, *Jamaica Public Service Company Limited, in Strategic Marketing: Cases in a Developing Country* (Kingston: Mona Institute of Business, 1993).
15. W.J. Baumol, 'Contestable Markets: An Uprising in the Theory of Market Structure,' *American Economic Review* 72, no. 1 (1982): 1–15.
16. Ronald Dworkin, *Taking Rights Seriously* (Boston: Harvard University Press, 1977).
17. David Parker, 'Economic Regulation: A Preliminary Literature Review and Summary of Research Questions Arising, Centre on Regulation and Competition,' Working Paper Series, No. 6, 2001.
18. Ibid.
19. A.E. Kahn, *The Economics of Regulation*, vol. 11, (New York: Wiley, 1971).
20. George J. Stigler, 'The Theory of Regulation,' *Bell Journal of Economics and Management Science*, 2, no. 1 (1971): 3–21.
21. Robert Baldwin and Martin Cave, *Understanding Regulation, Theory and Practice* (Oxford: Oxford University Press, 1999).
22. RR = OC + DI + T + r (C-D2)

    Where RR = revenue requirement

    OC = operating cost of the firm in the test year

    DI = depreciation

    T = taxes in the test year

    r = per cent ROR

C = total historical investment
D2 = prior year depreciation

23. Warwick Smith, 'Regulating Utilities – Thinking Location Questions,' World bank Summer Workshop on Market Institutions, Washington, DC, 2000.
24. ICT Technical Working Group, 'Recommendations in Relation to a Single Regulator for Communications Industry in Jamaica, Central Information Technology Office (CITO), 2006.
25. Jacobs and Associate Limited, 'Enhancing the Information and Communications Technologies – Creating of Jamaica's Converged Standalone ICT Regulator,' Ministry of Science Technology, Energy and Mining, Jamaica, 2014.
26. Richardo Parades, *Privatisation and Regulatory Challenges* (Washington DC: IADB, 2003).
27. Roy H. Alexander, *History and Background to Public Transportation* (Kingston: Ministry of Transport, 1996).
28. London Economics, *Private Sector Involvement in Water and Sewage: Case Study and Conclusions* (Kingston: Ministry of Water, 1996).
29. Ministry of Water & Housing, *Jamaica Water Sector Policy: Strategies and Action Plan* (Kingston: Ministry of Water & Housing, 2003).
30. Ibid.
31. The Washington Consensus describes a list of policies that had gained support among Latin American policymakers in response to the macroeconomic turbulence and debt crisis of the early to mid-1980s. These policies also had the backing of experts at Washington's international institutions – especially the International Monetary Fund and the World Bank, as well as the US Treasury – to help recovery from the debt crisis. (https://www.piie.com/blogs/realtime-economic-issues-watch/what-washington-consensus)
32. Charles Goodheart, Phillip Hartmann, David Llewellyn, Liliana Rojas-Suarez, and Steven Weisbrod, *Financial Regulation: Why, How, and Where, Now?* (London: Routledge, in Association with Bank of England, 1998).
33. Celia Blake, 'Under One Roof: Integrated Regulator for Non-Deposit Taking Institutions in Jamaica,' *Caribbean Law Bulletin* 6, no. 2 (2001).
34. Kenloy Peart, 'Financial Reform and Financial Sector Development in Jamaica,' *Social and Economic Studies* 44, no. 4 (1995): 1–22.
35. Dennis Morrison, 'Response of the Economic Crisis Situation-The Jamaican Financial Sector,' paper presented to the Life Underwriters Association of Jamaica, September 1997.
36. Colin Kirkpatrick and David Tennant, 'Responding to Financial Crisis: Better Off Without the IMF: The Case of Jamaica,' Finance and Development Working Paper Series, University of Manchester and UWI, 2002.

37. Kamau Chionesu, 'Rehabilitation Jamaica's Financial Sector: Goodbye Crash, Hello Currency – Financial Crash,' *Social and Economic Studies* 50, no. 1 (2001): 39–66.
38. Margaret Mendes, 'Regulating Framework of Banking in Jamaica,' Mona, Department of Management UWI, 1973.
39. M. Goldstein, *The Case for an International Banking Standard* (Washington: Institute for International Economics, 1977).
40. R.H. Coase, *The Firm, The Market and the Law* (Chicago: Chicago University Press, 1988).
41. Charles Goodhart, Phillip Hartmann, David Llewellyn, Liliana Rojas-Suarez, and Steven Weisbrod *Financial Regulation: Why How, and Where Now?* (London: Routledge in Association with Bank of England, 1998).
42. Ibid.
43. Dimitri Vitas, 'The Impact of Regulations on Financial Intermediation,' in *Financial Regulation- Changing the Rules of the Game*, ed. Dimitri Vitas, EDI Development Studies (Washington, DC: World Bank, 1992).
44. Cezley Sampson, 'Institution Building for Transport Development: With Special Reference to Jamaica,' *Third World Planning Review* 2, no. 1 (1980).
45. E. Juan and Cezley Sampson, 'Airport in Jamaica,' in *Airport Infrastructure: The Emerging Role of the Private Sector, Recent Experiences*, ed. E. Juan (Washington, DC: World Bank, 1995).

CHAPTER TEN

Privatisation: The Inside Story

SPONSORED BY

INFLUENCE OF THE PRIVATE SECTOR

A major development of the 1970s was the establishment of the Private Sector Organisation of Jamaica (PSOJ), which came into being partly as a response to the increased state-directed control of the Jamaican economy. The PSOJ whose membership then and up to the present comprised the country's major businesses across all sectors had among its objectives assuming the role of advocate as it sought to influence not only economic but social and political issues of national policy. From its inception, the organisation was consistent, resolute, and strident in its promotion of economic policies, in particular those related to the process of liberalisation, deregulation, and privatisation, including National Commercial Bank, Jamaica Public Service, and the Jamaica Telephone Company, among others. One of its most significant areas of advocacy was for the lifting of exchange controls going as far as to commission a study on Exchange Control Liberalisation by the UK-based London Economics whose report in addition to recommending the removal of exchange controls also advocated an acceleration of the programme of deregulation of the domestic economy, more competition, less public ownership, and the removal of price and wage controls.

Overall, PSOJ advocacy and support for these policy initiatives led to the expansion of the Jamaica Stock Exchange by providing room for more firms to be listed on the JSE and the organisation can be credited with what was to become the official adoption of the market economy as the most appropriate framework for Jamaica's economic development.

PRIVATISATION AS ECONOMIC REFORM MEASURE

Of all the market reform techniques, privatisation has developed to be one of the most widely used economic reform measures adopted globally over the last three decades. During the decade of the 1990s, some eighty countries had privatised at least one of their state-owned enterprises (SOEs).[1] Privatisation can, however, be considered covering a wide range of activities that broaden private sector involvement in an economy, as well as involving an adaptation of private sector culture and incentives. Jamaica is not new to privatisations, as the railway was built by the private sector in 1945. However, in 1878, Governor Sir Anthony Musgrave nationalised the railway. After a decade of public operation, during which the railway ran into financial difficulties, the new governor, Sir John Norman, privatised the railway on January 1, 1890, by trade sale to a syndicate led by Frank Wesson, a New York merchant. This marked one of the earliest privatisation transactions in the English colonies.

What Privatisation Normally Covers

David Newberry notes that privatisation covers a wide range of activities that seek to broaden the scope of private sector involvement in an economy, as well as involving an adaptation of private sector culture and incentives to business operation.[2] It could involve the sale of public assets or share sales to private firms; private development of infrastructure facilities; project-based privatisation for the provision of services to a government, such as health care and operation of environmental facilities by private firms under contract to a public body.

Privatisation of assets and firms can also be separated into two broad categories: firms in competitive or contestable markets, and industries with major market failure characteristics; natural monopolies, or public goods. *Considerable data exist to show that, while ownership is important, it is not ownership which provides for production and allocation efficiencies (lowest cost and lowest prices) but competition.* Ownership, however, does matter. Where firms are in a competitive or contestable market, the need for government involvement in regulation is less, except for the removal of restrictive business practices, removal of barriers to entry and exit, and control over mergers that seek to distort the competitive process – anti-trust or competition legislation.

Theoretical Reasons for Privatisation

Privatisation is based on the fundamental assumption that assets and firms in the hands of private owners will be more efficiently managed, and consumer surplus will be enhanced when compared to public ownership and operation. The prevailing view is that government-owned and controlled firms perform below privately owned firms in competitive markets. Privately owned and managed firms can respond more efficiently to market conditions in competitive markets. Response time of public firms suffers from inflexibility because of the bureaucratic structures of the public sector decision-making process.

Where firms operate under conditions of natural monopoly[3] and competition is not available, that is, the process of supply and demand is not a characteristic feature in determining prices, then industry regulation becomes essential to protect the consumer and minimise inefficiency. There is still no clear evidence to prove that private ownership, however, is more effective in managing and operating firms and industries characterised by natural monopoly. There is, however, a strong case to unbundle the industry and introduce competition where this opportunity presents itself. Jamaica failed to unbundle telecommunications and electricity at privatisation. In fact, domestic and international telecommunications businesses were re-bundled, enhancing the opportunity for monopoly rent by the privatised firm. Sale of firms as monopolies offers higher proceeds to the Treasury; hence there is often pressure from Treasury resisting unbundling. Privatisation provides the opportunity and allows for a new set of conditions to facilitate efficiency-enhancing behaviour. Private ownership and management provide effective shareholder monitoring, and the private investors face the risk of takeover and of bankruptcy. Performance-related reward systems are the standard form.

In the case of public enterprise, the objectives of the public firms are too complex, and often are in conflict and be less measurable. The assumption that the public interest can be represented by a well-defined function which ministers of government seek to maximise as an alternative to the assumption that private firms are profit-maximisers is questionable. The decision-making process is usually captured by powerful interest groups who seek favoured positions in the distribution of resources. Public officials also use public resources to purchase the support of interest groups.

Under a more restricted definition, privatisation is a process providing for a change of ownership and transfer of risks: outright, or partial sale of assets by a government; transfer of assets under leasing arrangements; contracting out of services and contractual arrangements for private management and transfer through concessions, as well as public private partnership (PPP). The governments of developed countries, transition economies of the former socialist states and developing countries, have been widely involved in various privatisation programmes since the 1980s. Private sector involvement in the infrastructure industries, however, is not a new policy tool and goes as far back as the eighteenth century when private firms were called on to build toll roads, turnpikes, canals, waterways, railways, and airports.

Privatisation is a process of selling publicly owned assets, or companies providing for the change of ownership and transfer of risks. Here, it involves a transfer of operational control of an enterprise from government to a private owner, involving outright or partial sale of assets by the state, transfer of assets, contracting out of services and contractual arrangements for private management of services. In the 1980s, the term *divestiture* was more widely used for this type of economic activity, meaning any transaction by which government transferred title in, or sold some, or all its assets, or shares in an enterprise, regardless of any operational restrictions.[4] This form of privatisation is a neutral process, resulting in a change in the composition of the sector's net wealth, and merely involves an adjustment of liquidity status in which the state sector exchanges fixed assets with the private sector, and in return acquires liquid assets.[5] The process itself does not change the net worth or enhance the gross domestic product of a country.

Positive benefits can be derived if the state spends the privatisation proceeds efficiently, that is, if the value of the funds in the hands of governments is enhanced and if the private sector, in acquiring these assets, improves their productive efficiencies. The revenues derived from the sale must be invested in a manner that gives rise to an equivalent stream of revenue, which should be no less than the revenues derived from the sale. Where the private sector increases growth in taxable GDP, then positive benefits may also accrue. The decision about the use of resources, given the competing claims on divestiture proceeds, is one of the most important strategic privatisation decisions which will have to be taken and which must be addressed early in the programme. Political pressures will arise for the use of the proceeds in directions that will not generate efficiency or growth. Competing claims will come from several directions: to finance job creation; to support the development of small business and entrepreneurship; to finance compensation of retrenched workers; or to finance the creation of social safety nets and retire public debt. In Jamaica, the proceeds are placed in the Consolidated Fund, after liquidation of the enterprise debt and payment of enterprise termination costs, with the net proceeds used mainly to reduce the public debt.

Privatisation can, however, produce several non-neutral effects, as in the case where the state is strapped for foreign exchange, or where government is credit-constrained and, in the process of the sale, offers a discount rate reflecting its preference for foreign exchange, or for current revenue. In such a situation, the purchaser will end up paying less than the value of the future profit stream, discounted at the purchaser's rate of discount. In a number of cases where the Jamaican government has had to obtain much-needed foreign exchange to meet IMF conditions, such as the liquid asset test, the government has had to make hasty sale decisions. In such situations, the purchasers were able to exploit their purchasing advantages and acquire the assets at values less than would have been obtainable under competitive bidding. This was certainly the case when the government's 20 per cent equity in Telecommunications of Jamaica (TOJ) was sold to C&W of the UK in 1990.

Privatisation is expected to provide new investment capital, more access to markets, more access to technology, management, and entrepreneurship. This is based on the theory that private sector managerial culture and market incentives are more effective in enhancing efficiency than public bureaucracy. In perfect competition, the market is assumed to comprise numerous private players whose economic decisions are guided by signals from the market in equilibrium and the desire to maximise profit. Some argue that, in pursuing profit maximisation, the private sector also promotes welfare, guided by the invisible hand. Hence, the market is also more efficient in allocating resources and determining prices than the bureaucracy. Analysis of pre-and post-privatisation performance of firms in the 1990s point to a significantly higher profitability and higher turnover, operating efficiencies and capital investment after divestiture.[6]

In the 1980s, several governments across the world needed to introduce policies to reduce the size of and the number of SOEs and reduce the drain on public resources. The main economic framework in which privatisation programmes are undertaken is therefore vital for successful market transition. The importance of macroeconomic factors will depend on the size of the privatisation programmes, relative to the size of the overall economy. In small developing countries like Jamaica, where the public sector was large, and the programme was substantial, privatisation became a crucial part of the macroeconomic reform and structural adjustment process and was undertaken as part of efforts to reduce the balances in external and internal accounts, and in stabilising monetary conditions. The sale of loss-making enterprises was then seen as an important reform measure to reduce the fiscal deficit. Privatisation programmes have as their central focus the elimination of economic distortions caused by public sector growth through realignment of state responsibilities.

Infrastructure enterprises often require large capital investments, particularly as foreign exchange. In such instances, the sale of these enterprises not only reduces public sector borrowing requirements in both local dollars and foreign exchange, but it also releases the enterprise from the limitation placed on its capital expansion, and allows it to attract foreign direct investment, overseas technology, and highly skilled management. This was certainly done in the cases of the telecommunications company, the hotels, and the Caribbean Cement Company. The reduction of the state's need for capital also reduces the 'crowding out effect' and allows the private sector increased access to funds at lower interest rates. Where foreign investment is a source of funds after divestment, it could ease the crowding out effect.

Privatisation objectives are varied; they can reflect economic, social, as well as political factors. In most instances, they reflect a combination of these factors. The reversal of the socialist policies of the Manley administration of the 1970s by the Seaga administration of the 1980s was an important strategic objective of the Jamaica Labour Party. To this end, it was more important to demonstrate success by the sale of 51 per cent of the shares of National Commercial Bank Limited (NCB) in the mid-1980s. In the NCB privatisation, Seaga felt it important to secure success, hence the shares were substantially underpriced. This allowed the 'small man' to benefit from capital gains and helped to generate stronger interest in private ownership and property rights within the economy.

Making the emerging stock market more attractive to both domestic and foreign investors also formed an important macroeconomic objective in Jamaica. The sale of NCB and Caribbean Cement Company shares on the Jamaica Stock Exchange (JSE), not only helped to strengthen the domestic capital market by increasing the quality and range of stocks traded, but it also deepened and widened local share ownership and raise the rate of domestic savings.

Objectives of Privatisation

In the Jamaican case, the major objectives of privatisation were very similar to those identified in the UK exercise, and can be summarised as follows[7]:

- Improving the efficiency of the individual SOE;
- Raising revenues for the national treasury to reduce the debt and reducing public sector borrowing requirements;
- Reducing the government's involvement in enterprise decision-making;
- Easing problems of public sector pay determination;
- Diversifying corporate ownership, widening and deepening private share ownership and expanding the national stock market;
- Encouraging employee share ownership;
- Opening-up markets to competition and improving service delivery;
- Attracting strategic foreign investors, foreign management, and foreign technology;
- Improving economic or sectoral performances; and.
- Gaining political advantage and reversing socialism.

In the more mature markets, the rationale for state ownership is more likely to be the need to remedy market failure and to provide goods and services for which there are no likely private suppliers. Government ownership may also be justified for reasons of health, safety, and education. In emerging markets, the rationale may sometimes be defined more broadly and may relate, for instance, to the SOEs' role in national development strategies, or in the provision of a broader set of public services or safeguarding national interest. In both markets, there is a need for clear guidelines specifying when state ownership, or mixed public-private ownership, should prevail. The government may want to retain shares in a privatised company to ensure that the company is not fully controlled by foreign investor or prevent other investors from theoretically targeting the company for takeover or pursue business policies inconsistent with national priorities. A simple transfer of ownership rights to the private sector alone may not bring about the desired benefits of improvement in prices and service quality. Significant complementary action may be needed, such as government-led initiatives involving the overall macroeconomic policy framework, and, with selling a monopoly firm, there is the need for complementary regulatory and competition policies. Industries in which firms are not natural monopolise should be opened to competition.

Price and exchange rate stability and cyclical macroeconomic factors are in general very important to the success of a privatisation programme. The important point here is that, in developing countries such as those of the Caribbean and Sub-Saharan Africa where privatisation is a more policy measure the macroeconomic framework is critical to success as well the privatisation sequencing. These must be consistent with the phasing of the macroeconomic reform measures. It is difficult, for instance, to sell state assets in an economic environment of an overvalued exchange rate.

Preparing for Privatisation

Before embarking on privatisation, government should be clear as to the guiding principles and rationales underlying the privatisation programme, and these principles should be made known widely, and require balancing trade-offs between public, private and mixed ownership. For individual candidates for privatisation, there should be a good business case, underlined by value for money. Prior to privatisation, preparatory steps of the company, or the industry in which the SOE operates may be needed to prepare for the actual privatisation transactions. Getting the company ready for privatisation is one of the most important requirements and involves addressing issues like corporate governance, meeting the stock market requirements for listing, putting in place an optimal capital structure (capital restructuring), removal of non-commercial objectives, such as public, or universal services obligation and unbundling the monopoly component from the competitive component. It may cover legal changes, pre-privatisation industry/company restructuring, and addressing employee issues and stakeholder relation concerns.

Sequencing the delivery of the privatisation is an especially important consideration at the beginning of the divestiture exercise. Sequencing relates to developing objectives and priorities, including measures to build support; preparation of a privatisation strategy; selection of enterprises to be privatised; enacting the legislation which may be required, and the choice of method to be used. Getting the company ready for privatisation is a very important requirement and involves; addressing issues like corporate governance and meeting the stock market requirements for listing; putting in place an optimal capital structure/capital restructuring, as with the NCB transaction, and removing non-commercial objectives, such as public or universal services obligation.

Legal and Institutional Policy Framework

Privatisation is a complex procedure and, for it to be successful, a transparent and credible institutional framework will be required. There will be a multiplicity of stakeholders. Therefore, it is important to clarify their respective roles and responsibilities. Preferably, a professional entity operating at arm's length from the political policymaking process should be charged to steer the execution of the transaction, supported by a regulatory body charged with assuming regulatory responsibility in the infrastructure industries. Privatisation involves distribution of scarce benefits. There should be high level political support, preferably at the level of the president or prime minister.

Legal Framework

A government may consider one of two approaches to the legislative framework: the introduction of a privatisation specific framework legislation (privatisation-based legislation), or legislation related to each transaction (transaction-based legislation). With privatisation framework legislation, one unifying privatisation law, or a set of laws are put into place. The purpose of privatisation-based legislation is to:

1. state the broad privatisation policy and objectives and the governing principles;

2. specify the institutional structure, and
3. in some cases, the legislation may also specify the privatisation modalities and provide for sale of shares to employees, such as through an Employee Share Option Plan (ESOP).

Sometimes, the country's constitution may need to be modified to allow for privatisation of a particular SOE, as in Germany, regarding the privatisation of the telecoms sector. In other cases, countries may resort to transaction-based legislation. In other words, there is no overarching law for the privatisation programme, but a privatisation bill is passed for each transaction. In Japan, legal authorisation is needed for each transaction. In Jamaica, no authorisation was needed as most companies to be privatised were limited liability businesses operating under the national companies act (The Companies Act) and all that was needed was notification in Parliament as to the companies or list of companies earmarked for privatisation.

This was sufficient for transparency and to indicate government's priority, and helped to simplify the privatisation procedure, avoided the need for specific parliamentary approval through legislation and helped to depoliticise the privatisation decision-making around the transaction process. In most countries, other legislation may affect the privatisation process, such as the public procurement law and procedures, the securities law (in the case of public offering), and the insolvency and bankruptcy law.

Whether or not parliamentary approval is needed varies according to the respective laws and regulations of each country. Simplified procedures help to speed up the privatisation process. It is best to embed the privatisation in a legislative process as this improves transparency and predictability of the process and, therefore, even some governments with the option of requiring only a simple approval from parliament choose to pass a privatisation law, setting out the agreed policies and modalities of privatisation. Where legislation is not required, the main issue that governments have to address revolve around the privatisation strategy to be adopted, the level of restructuring that is needed and in the sequencing of the programme.

Institutional Framework

The multiplicity of actors involved in the privatisation process, each with their own vested interest, dictate that there should be a well-organised institutional framework. Without a clearly defined institutional framework and an allocation of a clear set of responsibilities, obtaining decisions at the different levels on the various privatisation-related issues becomes a problem and can significantly slow down the execution of the privatisation transaction and programme. Political actors often want the process to be speeded up, yet they are often the main cause of delays. Too often, one hears a Privatisation Authority reporting that they are waiting for the privatisation item to be placed on the Cabinet agenda. Preferably, the institutional framework should be structured as part of a hierarchy of responsibilities. At the top of the hierarchy should be a cabinet level decision-making committee, or council (Council of Ministers or Ministerial Subcommittee for Privatisation), with the Ministry of Finance, or the Cabinet Office serving as the secretariat. This is a body that provides policy direction and takes key privatisation transaction decisions, such as the approval of the shortlist of bidders and the preferred and reserve bidder.

At the next level, there should be a Privatisation Authority which should be a professionally staffed entity (preferable centralised), vested with the full authority of government to enter into contracts on behalf of government and with the responsibility for executing the privatisation programme and individual transactions. Examples are the Bureau of Public Enterprises in Nigeria and the Presidential Parastatal Reform Commission in Tanzania both of which were legislatively created, and the Jamaica Development Bank, which was designated by the Cabinet of Jamaica.

Once the privatisation decisions are made by the Council of Ministers, or Ministerial Subcommittee for Privatisation, the Privatisation Authority then follows through to ensure that the transactions are implemented transparently and efficiently, and according to the law, government's policy, and approved timeline. Regardless of how the privatisation is administered institutionally, the designated Privatisation Authority should play the central role in seeing through the privatisation from beginning to end. Its first task is to prepare the list of SOEs for sale.

Legal restructuring of the company may be required to separate the monopoly elements from competitive elements and establishing a regulatory authority. It may involve unbundling subsidiaries which are incongruent with the business being privatised and hence could complicate the transaction, especially when the subsidiaries are held jointly with another enterprise other than the potential purchaser and when the combined market share of the subsidiaries and the potential purchases give rise to antitrust concerns. It may simply be ownership restructuring, which is required involving the shifting of ownership rights from the line ministry to the privatisation authority assigned to carry out the privatisation transaction. Other factors to take into consideration involve the various due diligence exercises, covering technical, organisational, accounting, financial and tax, economic and regulatory, environment and social considerations. It may simply involve removing real estates or other items of public interest, not related to the core function of the business being privatised. Where necessary, the Privatisation Authority sees to the alteration of the structure such as ownership, financial and, or market structure. It also sees to the valuation of the assets for sale. The Privatisation Authority works closely with the other parties regarding the timing of the transaction; ensuring that changes that are needed are implemented, managing the public consultation(s), and securing support from stakeholders, acting as an intermediary between the SOE, the relevant decision-making bodies, the public, the industry players, and external advisors involved in the various stages of the transaction. The Privatisation Authority is also responsible for the recruitment of external advisors.

At the third level, as the case arises, Privatisation Enterprise Teams should be established by the Privatisation Authority. The Privatisation Enterprise Team is a specialised group of experts, drawn from the public and private sectors, with knowledge of the industry which forms part of a particular privatisation. The Privatisation Enterprise Team works with the Privatisation Authority and the External Advisors in seeing through the individual sale transaction.

In embarking on a privatisation programme, major new investments should be avoided once a decision has been taken to privatise, as these may not fit into the plans of the new investor and become stranded investment. Governments should not try to second guess the new investor. In developing countries, SOEs are often encumbered with a large portfolio of debt, and many have negative net worth. In most instances, private buyers do not wish to take on debt beyond genuine trade debt, even if the sale price is generously discounted. Governments may be in a better position to recover the debt. In Nigeria, for example, a separate company parked the non-trade related debt.

Another major problem is that of legacy labour liabilities, such as pension and severance costs. The new investor may not wish to take these on, hence the need for labour restructuring to establish the number of workers essential to the ongoing operation, and to establish the true pension obligations. In Nigeria's electricity privatisation, some six thousand 'ghost workers' were found on the payroll, including people who had died several years earlier, and their regular salaries were still being paid out. Some countries, like Oman and Pakistan, have legislation protecting workers or requiring the employment of a certain number of workers, or carrying unattractive severance packages. These should be negotiated prior to the closing of the sale so that price adjustment can be made. Severance costs are often financed by sales proceeds.

Legacy environmental problems will need to be addressed. SOEs are notorious for neglecting environment matters. The new investors will not want to take on such obligations and will want to see an environmental impact analysis in the case of polluting, or other activities which cause degradation of the environment.

In industries like telecommunications and electricity, market related matters will need to be considered. Here, the issue relates to the level of vertical and horizontal unbundling which may be needed. Restructuring may need to involve removing non-viable units, separation of competitive from non-competitive businesses, and identification and separation of peripheral assets such as real estate holdings, sport, and health complexes. These should be divested separately. A robust regulatory framework is essential for utilities and may have to be undertaken simultaneously with implementing the privatisation programme, although it is best to provide the regulatory framework before commencement of privatisation of the utility. There may be the need to provide for post-privatisation monitoring, especially for large transactions. In Jamaica, the regulatory frameworks were developed after the commencement of the divestiture programme with telecommunications electricity and the financial sector. Introducing a new regulatory framework, or anti-trust legislation, which involves new legislation, new organisation, and training of new people, is an exceptionally lengthy process. The regulatory agency and the competition authority need to be separate and independent from the rest of the machinery of government.

In some countries, it was felt that there was a need to develop a list of companies to be privatised. In Jamaica, the Seaga government felt that developing a plan and a list of SOEs for privatisation was too risky; instead, it adopted a case-by-case method and selected firms which were demonstrably profitable. Each completed transaction was billed as a success.

In countries where privatisation is new, it will be necessary to sell the idea nationally, separate from promoting each divestiture. The latter will involve market sounding, getting a feel of private investors' level of interest and concerns, considering these concerns – as Jamaica did in the toll road public/private partnership transaction. There will be the need to follow up with road shows to the local and regional markets, as well as overseas for large transactions to assess investors' appetite for the transaction. The government of Jamaica later backed up its privatisation programme with a policy statement on the privatisation procedure and policy and a list of SOEs earmarked for privatisation. In adopting partial privatisation instead of 100 per cent, as was the case of NCB, TOJ, and Jamaica Public Services Company Limited (JPSCo), the opportunity was also provided for the market to become more familiar with the industry or the company, and to deal with some of the information asymmetry problems that are often encountered when privatising industries or companies.

Jamaica's Macroeconomic Issues

The macroeconomic policy framework which the IMF and the World Bank designed for the government of Jamaica in 1981 provided the economic framework for privatisation with the following reform objectives:

- Reduction in the size of the public sector and the state's involvement in economic decision-making and resource allocation;
- Progressive reduction of external debt as a proportion of GDP, and reduction of dependence on external assistance for the financing of external and current account deficits;
- Increase in the levels of investment and productivity through private sector export-led development;
- Development and maintenance of an incentive structure and business climate conducive to improving long-term private sector investment, both local and foreign, and, through this

process, facilitate the transfer of ownership of critical industries to the private sector;

- Stabilisation of the macroeconomic environment, reduction of the fiscal deficit and restoration of GDP growth projected to average 3 per cent to 4 per cent per annum.

In terms of economic policies, the government also moved away from fixed exchange and interest rate policies and, in so doing, facilitated freer interplay between the forces of supply and demand in the allocation of resources throughout the economy. Ceilings were placed on public sector wage settlements as part of a package of maintaining a 7.0 per cent inflation target and tighter controls were placed on public expenditure, with a target of 2.0 per cent for the fiscal deficit. Consequently, the policy of subsidy pricing in the larger public enterprises was reversed, with public enterprise managers mandated to generate targeted surpluses. Initially, they were asked to cover their operating needs and meet 30 per cent of their capital needs.

In the early 1980s, the popular term used in relation to the sale of public assets in Jamaica was 'divestiture.' A steering committee, or enterprise privatisation transaction team, was created for each transaction, comprising the board and managers of the SOE slated for privatisation, private sector representatives, and officers from the Ministry of Finance and the Attorney General's Department. The enterprise teams were backed up by a transaction team, including officers from the National Investment Bank of Jamaica (NIBJ).

Initially, these transaction teams were equipped with a part-time staff, with the responsibility of assessing divestment proposals. It was not until 1983 that a more formal structure was introduced involving a full-time divestiture secretariat, based at the Jamaica National Investment Corporation (JNIC).[8] The secretariat functioned as the technical arm of the divestiture committee. Besides a small core staff, the secretariat relied mostly on overseas-based consulting firms and locally based international accounting firms, such as Price Waterhouse and KPMG for the technical evaluations, reviews of proposals and negotiations.

Methods of Privatisation

The size of the transaction and the absorptive capacity of the international market may influence the sale to be carried out and whether the privatisation should be executed in instalments. Sequencing the delivery of the privatisation is a very important consideration at the beginning of the divestiture exercise. Sequencing concerns a large SOE, or several SOEs already unbundled within the same industry. With a single SOE, the issue is whether the government should sell the shares in two or more instalments, necessitating more than one privatisation transaction. If the industry is already unbundled, sequencing relates to the order of putting the entities up for sale. Staging of the sale can build momentum and gain credibility among investors and the public to facilitate subsequent sales. Market requirements may also affect the pace of sequencing. The type of buyers is also important, such as industrial buyers versus financial buyers, with the latter most likely to be involved in a transaction with a shorter-term horizon than the industrial buyers. The existence of a privatisation master plan is appealing to some public officials, but the complexities and uncertainties of major transactions strongly suggest that the process cannot be planned in intricate detail.

The privatisation methods are usually guided by market conditions, and the government's objectives, as well as external factors. These include: objectives of the divestiture programme; the size of the enterprise to be divested; the level of development of a capital market in the country; the characteristics of potential entrepreneurs and investors; the level of fiscal pressures on the state; the importance of good management to the enterprise or industry; the extent to which efficiency and competition are desirable, and the level of state-holding desired, if any. These considerations will, in different ways, affect the method selected.

Popular privatisation methods include the following: [9]

- Commercialisation and Corporatisation;
- Auctions (mass);
- The sale of shares through the stock market: outright or partial sale, (IPOs or secondary offering), or capital raising;
- Trade sales by competition, or private treaty;
- Management Buyout;
- Private provision of public services, or Public Private Partnership (PPPs);
- Transfer of assets under leasing arrangements, contracting out of services and transfer through concessions;
- Liquidation;
- Financial privatisation, i.e., reducing subsidies and increasing, or introducing user charges. This latter method was used in

New Zealand involving the introduction of a charge to users of certain public services.

Each of these methods can also achieve different objectives.

Commercialisation or Corporatisation

Some countries begin the reform with the commercialisation and de-monopolisation of the SOEs. Where the SOEs are not incorporated, the government may need to proceed first via corporatisation as part of privatisation process. This involves the incorporation of departmental enterprises as limited liability companies and introducing commercial principles in their operations in addition to exposing the SOEs to market forces and hard budget constraints. In New Zealand and Australia in the 1980s in several cases, government resorted to corporatisation. However, corporatisation and commercialisation did not reduce the losses and financial reliance of SOEs on the government budget. In Jamaica, however, over 90 per cent of the SOEs earmarked for privatisation were limited liability companies,[10] and corporatisation was only needed in Jamaica in the case the case of the postal service and in a few other areas. This allowed the Jamaican government to move straight to the sale process of each SOE identified for privatisation.

Private sector principles can also be introduced to the SOEs through a Memorandum of Understanding (MOU), or a performance contract. A performance contract, or an MOU, usually has a short duration period of 3–5 years. The MOU is an agreement between the SOE and the portfolio Ministry, in which the two parties reach an understanding regarding objectives and targets (financial and physical) to be achieved. The MOU can be implemented without incorporation of the departmental enterprise. However, the agreement has no legal force and is therefore a weak form of commitment. Where MOUs are adopted regarding commercialising SOEs, a monitoring agency should be set up or appointed, and should be an external body to the sector ministry and the entity being monitored to provide for transparent accountability.

Public Auctions (Mass)

Public auctions were used in several of the Eastern and Central European countries, as they were found to be the most realistic means of rapidly privatising a substantial number of state-owned assets and services. Public auctions can take place as a simple priced-based auction process where price is the sole criteria for the sale. Public auctions as a privatisation method are more appropriate for small value transactions. Auctions of this type provide an open and competitive bidding platform, making privatisation highly transparent. A major drawback is the inability to impose conditions of sale. Auctions may take the form of an English auction, a Dutch auction, a first or discriminatory price auction, a second or uniform auction, or a pro rata auction.

The technique of auction is transparent, simple, and familiar, and cost effective. It avoids the complex problem of valuation, as the auction determines the price buyers are willing to pay (however, a valuation may be done to set a reserve price). It ensures that the property or activity is transferred to those who value it most, and it allows market prices rather than political considerations to guide the disposal process. In Jamaica, this option found limited use. The National Hotels Supplies Limited, however, was auctioned in 1987 for J$3 million.

INITIAL PUBLIC OFFER (IPO), OR SECONDARY OFFER AND CAPITAL RAISING

IPOs

The government may opt for an IPO, involving a 100 per cent outright sale or partial sale of less than 100 per cent. The IPO involves the following stages: pre-planning phase, planning phase, execution phase, and post listing phase. A direct sale of SOEs via the stock market has been one of the most important methods of privatisation in Jamaica and in many other countries. Sales by share offer allow for the state to substantially reduce the size of its operations. In addition to transferring ownership and raising funds, public offers often raise additional capital for an enterprise through the issue of new shares (capital raising) and this capital can be used to grow the company and repay external debt, etc. IPOs can be carried out in the domestic market, or the international market, or both. IPOs involve the offering of shares to retail and/or institutional investors. The shares may be offered on a fixed price method where the government decides on a price before the offering date. With institutional or foreign investors, governments often resort to book building. A fixed price method is popular with risk-averse participants, whereas government may be more willing to use book building to maximise issue proceeds. The choice of method should be dealt with on a case-by-case basis. Special arrangements, which allow for employees, customers, and small investors to acquire shares in a privatised company, such as through instalment payments and discounted prices, also allow for wider local public participation. A public offering, however, produces dispersed shareholdings which, in the absence of a well-functioning market for corporate control, can deprive the company of strong governance and/or strong technical and financial management expertise. With the sales of the shares of the Caribbean Cement Company of Jamaica in 1987, the outcome of the IPO transaction was defused ownership, with no strategic technical partner to deliver the expected efficiency gains. If the enterprise is large and the objective is to achieve wide share ownership, then share offerings involving setting aside a percentage of shares for employees and small investors may be appropriate. In Jamaica, the government had also placed a limitation of 7 per cent on the sale of Caribbean Cement Company shares in 1987, which could be taken up by anyone, or anyone connected buyer. This ownership restriction, however, depressed the price of the stock, resulting in pressures from the small shareholders for the restriction to be removed.

The Prospectus

The most important document for an IPO is the prospectus, which should be prepared by the financial advisor and transaction advisor in cooperation with the Privatisation Authority. The prospectus should provide information on the country's economy and governance, the industry, and its structure, the company, its physical and operating attributes, including a summary of the key financial and risks of the company. It should also cover the dividend policy, environmental issues, the regulatory regime, and economic issues relating to tariff, such as subsidies, employee restrictions, and the government plans for the company, e.g., whether there will be capital raising or secondary offer down the line and the anticipated time frame. The prospectus must cover the legal and listing requirements of the relevant stock markets. If there are restrictions applying to the nationality or the type of company which can participate in the acquisition, then these should be clearly stated. Restrictions are best limited and should only be included if they are strictly necessary to protect certain essential public interest and to facilitate competition such as cross-ownership restrictions. Sometimes, questions have been raised whether the sale of an SOE in one country to an SOE in another company constitutes privatisation.

Secondary Offering

A secondary offering is a public offering of stocks already listed. For example, it is typically used when companies are of such substantial size that the sale of the targeted percentage to investors could not be achieved in one transaction, or, more often, when a government wants to further reduce its stake in a company. Secondary offerings are less complex than IPOs. For example, setting the price may be less difficult as the shares have already traded on the market. A form of secondary offering is accelerated book building (ABB). Here, the government charges several financial intermediaries, typically investment banks, with the responsibility of placing tranches of shares of the already listed SOE with institutional investors. ABB reduces the preparation period and the execution window, allowing a minimisation of legal and related costs. It does not require the preparation of a prospectus, nor the creation and execution of an advertising campaign. It allows for differential market exposure. However, the price obtained may be at a discount relative to the public offering, but this is compensated by lower implementation costs and the speed of the method. In addition to the generic benefits of privatisation, listed companies may have to comply with codes of corporate governance as regard their structure, the role and independence of directors in decision-making, and other such features that provide confidence and protection to investors, and ultimately lead to a more transparent and efficient management. Retail investor participation serves to deepen the local capital market.

Capital Raising

A government may also seek to raise additional capital for the company. Here, the funds raised go to the company, rather than directly to the government. This is usually undertaken when it is felt that the capital cover is inadequate and there is a reluctance of the government, or its inability to put in extra cash. Capital raising can be combined with share offerings.

Advantages and Disadvantages of the Different Methods

The disadvantages of public offering/stock market sales are that they are very expensive and time consuming, result in a dispersed shareholdings structure and may not bring the desired technical and management expertise or foreign investment where this is needed. In other words, it may not produce a strategic technical or strategic financial partner which may be crucial for the success of the privatisation, especially in technology-driven industries or industries with large financial needs, like water, telecommunications, banking, and electricity. For example, the Jamaican government learnt from the experiences of selling the shares in the Caribbean Cement Company Limited in 1987 that there was no strategic technical partner to drive the technical improvement programme. Broad-based share ownership, therefore, may have to be weighed against the participation of a strategic technical investor to gain access to external markets, new technology, foreign capital, or modern management skills in order to reduce the commercial risk to general or institutional investors.

A public offer is more advantageous for large profitable SOEs, especially when additional capital is required, and the government intends to transfer full ownership to private investors. When there is a general share issue, shares are usually offered at a fixed price, or a tender for the price, or a combination of both. This process provides for more transparency and allows for a wider distribution of ownership if this is an objective. Large private placements on the stock market typically will need to be underwritten by one or more investment banking firms, of which one or more of these may also be a transaction advisor. Bolivia adopted a form of capitalisation during its privatisation in the 1990s, emphasising the particulars of capitalisation mechanism, in that the receipts from the sales of 50 per cent of the shares of the privatised companies were used to capitalise the companies and not paid over to the Treasury. The remaining 50 per cent of the shares were placed into a Pension Trust for the benefit of all Bolivians and the dividends distributed by the Trust, paid annually to the citizens. The word privatisation was very unpopular and was not used.[11] In Jamaica, because of the size of the NCB and TOJ transactions, phased sale of the shares was adopted, as this approach allowed for orderly disposal of the state's interest. In the initial TOJ transaction, Cable & Wireless became the lead investor/manager to provide technology, access to foreign capital and credit, and modern management skills.

Golden Shares

Where there are major national interest or national security issues, or where international or bilateral agreements are part of the industry arrangements, or the industry is one that it is sensitive, the state may seek to retain a 'golden share' with certain reserve rights powers. The term golden share was introduced by the British during their privatisation programme and refers to the retention by government of one non-voting share, which gives it certain specific rights, for example, to block a subsequent takeover, or other specified actions. New Zealand also adopted this approach and called the one share, the Kiwi Share, with retention of special rights to a single share. Using the golden share is not in line with the EU law. Where the private sector has concern about a government's commitment to complete the privatisation transaction, it is possible to park government shareholding into a Privatisation Trust and, through a Deed of Mandatory Privatisation, ensure contractually that the commitment given by government will be honoured. This was contemplated for the privatisation of the Sangster International Airport in Jamaica

Share Option Plans

The special arrangements which allow for employees and small investors to acquire shares in privatised companies, such as through instalment payments and discounted prices, also allow for wide public participation. Because of the possible extent of over-subscription, an allocation mechanism will be needed, as applied in the case of NCB, which provided for the smaller applicants to receive a greater proportion of shares applied for, compared to allocations to the larger applicants. A government may try to spread ownership to avoid concentration of power over time. Despite all the mechanisms employed, such as matching shares, bonus shares, ESOP shares, pricing discounts, and restriction of the amount any one shareholder can take, this usually is to no avail. In the Caribbean Cement Company sale, a limit was placed stating that no more than 7 per cent of the equity could be acquired by any one buyer. If the company is listed on the stock market limits on shareholding distort the future true price of the share, and the very small shareholders will be the ones lobbying to have the limit removed so that they can maximise the return on their investments through better price, triggering off ownership concentration.

Trade Sale

Trade sales can involve competitive bidding as an auction, or it may involve a sale to selected purchasers as a negotiated sale or via an unsolicited bid. A trade sale involves the direct sale of shares of the SOE or public assets to a buyer or a strategic investor a strategic financial investor. Strategic investors typically have similar operations to the company, which is put up for sale. When the private investor only takes up a minority stake in the privatised company, a substantial role in management will typically be demanded by the strategic investor and the important management participation conditions will need to be set out in a Shareholders Agreement or in a Technical or Management Services Agreement, separate from the Share Sale Agreement. A trade sale typically can be carried out with minimal legal, institutional, and financial restructuring and requires less effort, and involves less cost compared to an IPO. The privatisation transaction process may provide for later listing on the local stock exchange. Once a company is listed on the stock exchange, typically the Shareholders' Agreement falls away, as in most cases, such agreements would be inconsistent with the stock market listing requirements. A key specific requirement of a trade sale is the technical expertise and know-how, and the financial capacity that the strategic investor needs to bring to the table. In fact, the importance of a trade sale is the benefit of the experience and know-how, and new investments that are being brought to the company by the new partner. Most times, the strategic investors are larger size companies, with more resources and operations in the more developed markets. Even when there is good local management, foreign investors may come up with innovative ideas as regards efficient management methods and may introduce more effective staff renumeration schemes. On the other hand, a sale to a strategic investor may not bring in the strict governance regime that would be required from a listed company. A trade sale can be carried out through competitive bidding, selective bidding by a pre-determined set of buyers, or through an unsolicited offer.

Competitive Bidding

This more common and preferable as it is more transparent and allows for the market to set the price of the shares, or the assets, i.e., provides for securing the highest price at the best possible terms, therefore maximising sales proceeds and value for money to the government and the company. Trade sales and public offers can be combined in several ways. In many cases, the strategic investor comes on board first and the strategic investor then helps the privatised company to be listed on the stock market as an IPO. In most cases, the government sells an additional stake of its shares, thereby raising more funds, whilst the company benefits from the advantages of privatisation via a public offer. Sometimes, the strategic investor may use the IPO as an exit route for their initial investments. In a trade sale process, prospective buyers may place an offer for a specific company or set of assets, and, normally, the state sets out a specific time period within which prospective bidders must respond. Trade sale is the most appropriate method for disposing of ailing companies, as it allows for rapid disposal where there is an absence of a strong equity market, or appetite for companies of this nature. Competitive bids may take the form of simple price-based bidding, where price is the sole criterion for sale; or may involve other factors such as a business plan and evaluation of the bids based on a combination of factors and not just price, which may include an investment plan. The competitive process, which involves price and business plan /investment plan typically has phases. Phase one, the preparatory phase, involves financial, technical, economic/ regulatory and legal due diligence; provision of high-level information on the assets or company to be sold; preparation of a list of prospective buyers; preparation of a communication plan and execution timetable; consideration of competitive issues, and execution of a competitive analysis; market soundings; preparation of a data room (virtual data room (VDR) today); preparation of process letter of expression of interest and its notification; initial bidding instructions, and process of initial evaluation from interested parties.

Private Placement

With private placement, the transaction typically involves lower placement costs and may be more appropriate for small or medium-sized companies, or where the state owns a small minority interest in an enterprise, or where the public issue of shares is unattractive. It is more appropriate to use this method when there is only a few known potential bidders. It is of specific advantage when strong management infusion and new technology or foreign investment is important.

There is, however, the risk of underpricing, and there is political concerns related to clientism, favouritism, and corruption. Trade sale, in terms of integrity of the process, has the disadvantage of low transparency and is prone to accusations of corruption unless a very strict procurement process is established for conducting the negotiations and is adhered to by the government. Once prospective firms have been selected from the EOI stage, the process moves to phase two involving road shows; contact with prospective bidders; signing of non-disclosure agreement; opening of virtual data room (VDR); VDR question and answer sessions for prospective buyers; bidders carrying out due diligence; constant interaction with bidders, which may involve investor conferences; development of evaluation criteria for determining preferred bidder; determination of technical and financial criteria; the minimum pass mark for bidders' financial proposal to be considered, and preparation of Share Purchase Agreement (SPA) and Shareholders Agreement (SHA) if less than majority sale. There is a second round of Request for Proposal; including bidding instructions issued to shortlisted bidders, along with SHA and SPA and any other relevant legal documents; verification of due diligence of bidders, and an evaluation team established to assess responses from bidders responding to the RFP.

Once final bids are received, there is an evaluation of bids received, followed by a selection of preferred and reserved bidders, final contract negotiations, government decision on selected bidder and public announcement of the selected bidder. This is followed by a closure process involving contract signing and asset verification. In some instances, the government may request a 'best and final offer' from the remaining shortlisted bidders that have met the minimum technical requirement.

Trade Sale Through a Negotiated Sale

Under a negotiated sale, the government has the flexibility to negotiate with the selected buyers individually and to present a different set of conditions to each. It is best suited for cases where the universe of potential buyers is very small and well known, rendering a competitive process uneconomic. Like private placement, the main drawback is a lack of transparency. In order to mitigate the problem of lack of transparency, clear rules are required regarding the selection and negotiation process. The government should not change the process midstream.

Management Employee Buy-Out (MEBO) and Employee Buy-Out (MBO)

This involves employees (in the case of an EBO), or employee and management (in the case of an EMBO) buying out the company in which they work, and may involve a leveraged buyout, whereby part of the purchase price is debt financed and the loan is secured against the assets. It typically involves the sale of the enterprise through a new legal entity in which a significant, or majority, stake is sold to employees. This technique is more appropriate for labour-intensive small and medium-sized enterprises with low capital intensity. Leveraged buyouts run a high risk of failure, and their success depends on the motivation and competencies of the key actors and their ability to secure external financing. In Jamaica, in 1984, the oil refinery, PETROJAM, was divested through the route of a management buy-out. However, the oil refinery, which is capital-intensive, ran into problems, as the management team was required to come up with 70 per cent (US$68 million) of the value of the assets on signing the share sale agreement but they could not secure external financing and keep up with the instalment payments to the government, resulting in the National Investment Bank repossessing the company. EBOs sometimes have corporate governance weaknesses in that insiders may seek to pursue objectives such as job security at the expense of an increase in the value of the company. It can also result in restricted access to capital without the support of financial investors. It may not be easy to raise equity capital and, if the employees are a heterogeneous group in terms of skills, interests, and objectives, effective decision making may be hampered as a result of the need to reconcile conflicting objectives and interests.

Debt Equity Swap and Convertible Bonds

Governments sometimes adopt debt equity swaps as part of reducing its debt. Swaps can ease financial constraints and help improve a country's investment climate; however, care is needed to ensure that the deal is to the benefit of the country. In a debt for equity swap, the debt holder who wants to buy an enterprise swaps debt worth a fraction of its face value in the secondary market for equity, usually at a rate that is better than the secondary market price, but still below the face value. Swaps may be a way for heavily indebted countries to bring foreign investors, including commercial banks, into a transaction that might not go through without such participation.

As a country buys its debt back, it becomes a better credit risk, the secondary market discount on the debt drops and this reduces the incentive for an investor to engage in such a swap. Swaps of public debt for private equity may also raise the issue of inflation and government borrowing requirements. The Jamaican government adopted debt swap during implementing the privatisation programme and also purchased PeroCaribe debt from the government of Venezuela, for US$1.4 billion in 2015.

Convertible Bonds

A convertible bond gives the bondholder the option to exchange the bonds for a predetermined number of shares in the issuing company. It is a means of raising capital at a lower cost than that of an issue of ordinary bonds. The issue price and the nominal yield are set in advance, which presupposes an implicit share value. It is most suitable to dispose of minority blocks. It is a complex instrument and is not commonly used as a privatisation method. From the perspective of the seller, the disadvantages are that the investor decides when to exercise the conversion option. If the stock performs poorly, there will be no conversion, and an investor is stuck with the bonds' subpar returns and ultimately the government does not achieve its objective to reduce public sector ownership.

Employee Share Ownership Plans (ESOP)

ESOP is a mechanism adopted to facilitate wide share ownership. It is usually structured as a separate legal entity to which the company sells the shares. Employees are each allocated a number of shares which are held for them according to the terms of the ESOP. Funds required to purchase the shares for ESOP may come from different sources: employees' personal funds; employer contributions, or external sources. What distinguishes ESOP from other employee ownership programmes is that shares are paid for partly, or fully from future corporate earnings. If the ESOP is financed with borrowed money, to be repaid with employer contribution, it is called self-financed, leveraged ESOP.[12]

Management Contracts or Privatising Management

In the management contract form of divestment, a contractor takes responsibility for operation and management of a facility, service, or programme with the freedom to make day-to-day management decisions. The contractor is paid a management fee and may not be entitled to share in the profits, although the fee may be linked with profits or performance. Management contracts are more appropriate where the state seeks to revitalise loss-making undertakings. Where the enterprise continues to experience major operating losses, or where major capital investment is needed, conflict of interest often emerges. It can also lead to short-term profit maximisation against the long-term interest of the enterprise. Some of these problems can be solved by linking rewards with specific objectives or providing for a purchase option. The sugar holdings and the National Water Commission in Jamaica were first divested by this process.

Leases

General leases are also widely used as divestiture instruments. This method usually involves the leasing of a facility providing public services, with the lessee assuming responsibility for the operation and maintenance. The state retains ownership and policy control over the public services, while obtaining the benefits of private sector management and commercial operation. Leases can be of two broad types: operating leases and, financial or capital leases, or sale and lease-back.

An operating lease is a contract that involves periodic payments for the use of the equipment/assets, which remain in the ownership of the lessor and is usually for shorter periods.

It is up to the lessor to maintain the equipment during the life of the contract. An operating lease is treated like renting, with the payment considered as operational expenses and the asset being leased stays off the balance sheet of the lessee. A capital lease or finance lease is an agreement where the lessor agrees that the ownership of the assets will be transferred to the lessee when the lease period is over. It allows the lessee the choice of acquiring the assets at a lower price than the market value at the end of the lease, and the tenure is usually of longer-term duration. Under the lease arrangement, the lessor is required to provide the services and maintain the assets involved in delivering the services. Leasing may be an attractive option where it is politically difficult to sell outright a particular asset. For example, it is difficult to sell land associated with hydroelectricity or land associated with airports. Under the sale and leaseback arrangement, an SOE that owns fixed assets sells them to a private party and simultaneously executes an agreement to lease the property, or assets back for a period.

A lease enables the state to negotiate advantageous contractual conditions by encouraging competition among potential lessees. It overcomes several obstacles, such as legal barriers, underdeveloped capital markets, and problems of valuation. Its main disadvantage is that lessees have no incentive to maintain and improve the value of the leased assets beyond the level necessary for earning a satisfactory return on their investments during the life of the lease. This problem can, however, be mitigated by giving the lessee a stake in the residual value of the assets to be paid upon termination of the contract. With Jamaica, several earlier hotel privatisations in the early 1980s were carried out through leases. Jamaica also implemented a major land lease divestment programme, with the tenure of the lease typically lasting forty-nine years. When it is politically difficult to affect an outright property right sale, leasing may be the only option available to the government. Selling large tracts of lands, especially to foreign investors, can be politically sensitive, but leasing may help to overcome this problem. The weakness of the lease mechanism is that the banks may refuse to accept the lease as collateral for a loan, preferring collateral as outright title to the asset.

Contracting Out

In contracting-out of services, the state or municipality arranges for a private firm to perform specific services. This method has proven to be important in divesting municipal and social services. Contracts are awarded through competitive bids. There are practical issues in enforcing standards and meeting capital requirements. Extensive background checks are necessary, as well as the need to guard against bid rigging. The contract needs to carefully specify the performance criteria and the penalties for failure to perform. There should be an agency responsible for monitoring the contract, although this can be contracted out as well.

Public Private Partnership (PPP)

Under a traditional public sector procurement path, the government engages a contractor to construct a facility and upon completion the government pays the contractor and takes on the responsibility for operation and maintenance of the facility. Under a PPP path, the private sector service provider/contractor is not just responsible for the delivery of the facility but may undertake the financing and the ongoing operation and maintenance of the facility. Upon successful construction of the facility, the government will then pay the contractor a fixed annual amount. In a case where the project generates its own income during operation, for example, roads, ports, airports, and power plants, the government is not normally required to make payments to the contractor. Instead, the contractor is assigned the right to receive revenues from the operation and management of the project as part of a concession agreement. There are several variations of this model. In the Build-Own-Operate Transfer (BOOT) version, the state transfers development and operating rights for a fixed period, including the transfer of investment and the commercial and financial risks to the private investors. An important aspect of PPP, therefore, is the risk-sharing between the private and public sectors. Alternatively, there is the Build-Own-Operate (BOO) arrangement. Here, the private sector designs, finances, and constructs the facility on behalf of the government. Invariably, large investment sums are involved, and, in many instances, the concession or PPP contract is given for periods ranging from fifteen to fifty years to an investor or consortium of investors. These projects are highly leveraged, and the loan capability is based on the future revenues from the project. In the case of the BOT/BOOT mechanisms, investors, not only seek prices sufficient to recover costs and repay debts, but also to make reasonable returns on investments. There are various other forms of PPPs, including Design-Build-Operate-Maintain (DBOM), and Design-Build-Finance-Operate and Transfer (DBFOT). Increasingly, concessions have involved the private investor bringing in new capital. The private sector/ contractor does not receive any income before the commencement of the operation of the facility, hence there is a strong incentive to successfully complete the facility within the agreed project deadline. Three of the major new power stations in Jamaica adopted BOOT arrangement in the 1990s. The Highway 2000 East West Link also adopted the BOOT type arrangement.

Using PPP allows for implementation of major infrastructure projects which could not normally be funded by government, such as the highway projects in Jamaica. However, the usefulness of PPPs has to be assessed on a case-by-case basis. Important features are responsibility for demand risk and value for money in delivering the project. PPPs are complex transactions and normally require an appropriate legal and regulatory framework which provides for confidence and transparency to potential investors and enhances the efficiency of the tender, negotiations, and award of such contracts. Using a suite of technical and legal advisory services is recommended. The key is substantial preparation and design.

Privatisation sometimes involves a private financing initiative (PFI). This approach was often adopted in the UK, in which public and private firms formally work together to provide the service or infrastructure. It can also be adopted for low-cost housing, or urban development projects in which government agencies and private organisations, or non-governmental organisations work together informally to deliver services or provide infrastructure informally to deliver services or provide infrastructure.[13] All the above privatisation methods at one time or other was adopted by the Jamaican authorities with stock market floatation and trade sale the most widely adopted methods.

Risk Appraisal

Introducing the private sector in the delivery of infrastructure and/or services involves the determining who is responsible for the risks and the subsequent allocation of risks between the private investor and the government, and this requires an efficient allocation of risks in a commercially enforceable contract.

Note in PPP transactions, an important requirement is the equitable distribution of these risks. Risks should be distributed according to the party that controls the or is able to minimise the impact of the risk.

Table 10.1: Description of Major Project Risks

Risks	Descriptions
Development Risk	Risks that the project sponsors cannot develop the project.
Construction Risk	Risk that the project sponsors and operators cannot arrange the financing (debt and equity) to fund the capital cost.
Completion Risk	Risk that the project is not completed or not completed on time and within budget.
Operations Risk	Risk that the private operator cannot deliver the performance level during the operation phase of the project.
Demand Risk	Risk that the demand for service is overestimated.
Exchange rate Risk	Risks that variations in the exchange rate have a material impact on a company's financial position
Repatriation risk	Risk that the project company cannot transfer its profit to its foreign investors.
Legal & Regulatory Risk	Risk that changes in legal and regulatory regimes lead to a project becoming inoperable or materially affect the ability of the project company to discharge its obligations.
Force Majeure	Risks beyond the control of the project company (e.g., natural disasters, wars, etc.)
Political Risk	Risk of expropriation, arbitrary changes to contract, etc., resulting from changes made by the government.

Valuation of the Business or Assets designated for Privatisation

Government officials usually require a valuation of the business or the assets to be privatised for transparency reasons. Sometimes, government policy requires a 'reservation price' or a 'minimum price' and legally, or procedurally, a special government body must give assent to the 'sale price' or concur with the privatisation procedure. Valuation methods are based on an estimation of the market value, but it also involves a measure of subjectivity and interpretation. Valuation is also influenced by the method of divestiture adopted. The best valuation is provided by the market. Valuation is useful for setting a benchmark for the sale and ensuring a fair and above-board process. Any company, private or public, can be valued based on one of the following methods:

- Discounted Cash Flow Method (DCF). The Discounted Cash

Flow (DCF) method, which calculates the present value of the projected stream of future earnings is frequently used when SOEs are being sold as an ongoing business. A discount rate is applied to the future cash flow to derive the present value of the future cash-flows. The political risk is usually built into the Weighted Average Cost of Capital (WACC) through the impact of the political risk on equity and debt costs. Debt is subtracted to arrive at the value of the company's equity. This approach requires financial modelling and is very complex, with several variables of varying sensitivity requiring the use of sensitivity analysis techniques. This method is typically adopted when strategic investor or public offering type transactions are involved. This method depends on reliable cash flow forecasts, and particularly also on the choice of realistic discount factors. Privatisation exercises often occur in periods of macroeconomic austerity when governments keep money supply tight and interest rates high. If, in such circumstances, the cost of capital is measured by the average yield of treasury bills, or government paper, this could lead to excessively high discount rates, and, thus, to unrealistically low firm values.

- The use of financial information from comparable companies, or of trading multiples in the case of public companies. The approach involves the application of derived valuation multiples to the latest financial results and a comparison across companies/transactions. This is a useful estimate of market value based on public information but requires interpretation. Invariably, only a small number of truly comparable peer firms are typically available and used for public offerings, especially developing markets.
- An analysis of comparable transactions or precedent transactions to determine multiples paid in the past for the acquisition of similar companies. This method places value on a change of control situation and is developed from public information. Valuation of multiples require interpretation as no transaction is alike and public data may be limited and sensitive to market fluctuation.
- An adjustment of net assets. Here, an estimate of the market value of the assets (fixed and current) is made and then balance sheet

and off-balance sheet liabilities are subtracted. The limitation of this approach is that it does not consider future cash flows and buyers dislike it. Asset valuation is more practical for small loss-making enterprises that are to be disposed of on a piece-meal basis, rather than as an ongoing concern.

- A replacement value estimate of the cost to replace the company's assets if destroyed (fixed asset, start-up costs and current assets). Typically, a higher valuation than through other methods is arrived at, and buyers dislike it as it does not consider expected returns.
- An earnings trend (price earnings ratio or PE ratio). This approach requires market information which may not be readily available, especially in emerging and developing markets. This approach is more applicable to secondary offer cases.
- An approach based on dividend yields. The dividend yield is a financial ratio that shows the percentage of a company's shares price that it pays out as dividend each year. The dividend yield equals the annual dividend per share divided by the traded stock price. This method also requires public information.
- A combination of these methods.

Where a strategic investor is sought for the majority portion of shares, with smaller portions being offered to other private investors, two methods of valuation leading to two prices are sometimes used concurrently. Private investors acquiring the smaller portions would then, for example, be able to buy at a price related to the business's previous performance corrected by the average market yield, whereas investors would be invited to tender for majority portion. This mixed approach, incidentally, was the preferred method of privatisation in Czechoslovakia, and continued in the Czech Republic, which placed high importance on a broad distribution of share ownership in its model of 'people's capitalism.'[14]

There is no one single correct method of valuation, and more than one method is often used to derive a range of values for the estimation of the value of business to be privatised. In developing and emerging markets, for example, there is often no comparable entity operating in the same market to allow for a peer-based evaluation. If the ownership is part public and the company is listed on the stock market, then the stock market share price may be a good indicator. The valuation of SOEs is not precise science. Valuation is even more problematic in the case of an electricity or telecommunication company that has been unbundled with no history of unbundled businesses being involved in independent trading. In Jamaica, net present values of the future stream of income was the method principally used for the trade sale transactions.[15]

The government is always sensitive to being accused of under-pricing to connected persons or favourites, whereas over-pricing may result in no sale with transaction expenses having been incurred and criticisms to contend with from those hostiles to privatisation. Government officials often look at the amount of money invested over the years, i.e., the historical book value because they wish to at least recover the past outlays, and not at the earnings capability of the company which is what the new investor is interested in buying. What was spent in the past is of no interest to a new investor.

There is therefore a need for a careful pre-qualification of bidders for an entity up for sale based on a business plan, the experience of the bidder, qualification of the operating company, and the extent to which the sale would concentrate market power to the detriment of consumers.

Privatisation of Utilities and Infrastructure Monopolies

The privatisation of utilities (water, electricity, telecommunications, and airports) presents special problems, especially after the privatisation has been executed. The issues involved in the privatisation of utilities differ from the privatisation of firms in competitive markets. This is because market failure conditions exist and, in several instances, there is the inability to facilitate competition after privatisation. The structure of the industry for the post-privatisation life also becomes critical.

In an industry characterised by high infrastructural fixed sunk cost and other barriers to entry, relative to the size of the market, one firm, the natural monopolist will produce at the lowest cost. The total cost of producing the total output by one firm will be lower than the total cost of any two or more firms producing the entire output. There are two costs associated with the production of a good or service: fixed and marginal cost. Marginal cost does not vary with output; for example, the fuel cost in producing one megawatt of power. At the same time, fixed cost does not depend on output; fixed cost falls sharply as output increases. There are two conditions which give rise to natural monopoly: economies of scale and economies of scope.

Water, and other network industries such as telecommunications, electricity, and gas share many natural monopoly characteristics. Water is said to be the classic natural monopoly, and it is virtually impossible to introduce competition other than yardstick competition. Efficient pricing in the classical sense is difficult as, even if long-run marginal costs were adopted, break-even would be difficult to be achieved. Where industries are characterised by high fixed costs, there is a compelling case to restrict new entrants, as this leads to undesirable duplication of fixed costs, and it is therefore better to have one, or only a few firms in the industry. Those features have accounted for failure in the privatisation of the National Water Commission (NWC) to date. These features have also proved to be problematic in the UK water privatisation.

Common Privatisation and PPP issues

A number of common issues normally come up during implementation of the Privatisation and PPP transactions. In privatisation and PPP transactions, demand risks often arise. In such a case, a private investor may seek a guarantee from the government that, if demand falls below a certain level, the government will provide a sovereign guarantee to mitigate the risk. This was the case with the East West Toll Highway in Jamaica. In the case of electricity sector, Independent Power Producers (IPPs) are private electricity firms that own generating facilities and generate electric power for sale to the utility and end users. IPPs minimise risk through a 'take or pay' Power Purchase Agreement (PPA). Irrespective of the amount demanded, the government procurement agency is required to take the committed capacity. This becomes a contingent liability by the government where such PPAs exist. In a financial crisis, some countries may find themselves with a huge volume of PPAs, so with the sharp devaluation of the country's currency which sometimes follows, the government may find itself unable to pass on all the increased costs to consumers and may be required to step in to bail out the procurement agency. Inventors may also be concerned with exchange risk. If the exchange rate is fixed, say to the US dollar, and if the country practices sound fiscal and monetary policies, the risk is not as great. However, if the currency is a floating currency and if the fiscal policy and monetary policy are loose, this becomes a major problem, as investors will seek risk mitigation measures to protect their capital investments.

JAMAICA'S INITIAL PRIVATISATION PROGRAMME 1981–90

With the Manley administration of the 1970s, with its statist policies, the government significantly expanded the SOE sector and the size of government covering all sectors: education; housing; telecommunications; energy/electricity; transport; health; mining; agriculture; financial services; tourism, and manufacture and distribution/retail supply. With the expansion of the public sector, there was a concomitant reduction in the size of private sector investment. The Public Enterprise Division in the Ministry of Finance estimated the number of SOEs in 1980 to be about four hundred.[16] The SOEs not only grew in number and size but they became a drain on the public purse. The privatisation agenda of the IMF and World Bank, in 1984, the IMF demanded that Seaga government deliver on his pre-election promises of a major divestiture programme. Despite the problem of the large public enterprise sector and the poor service standards, it was the escalation in financial exposure, the burgeoning budget deficit, the inability of the government to sustain the loss-making operations among the SOEs and to meet their foreign exchange obligations that finally led to the move to privatisation. The administration's divestiture process in the 1980s did not provide for any central executing machinery.

The Seaga administration initially focussed its efforts on improving the profitability of the SOEs through a programme of price increases in 1984, resulting in an increase in the cost to consumers of several public services including water, electricity, and telephone. In addition, their borrowing requirements were restricted, reducing the government's debt exposure. The administration also focussed its efforts initially on getting the principal entities, which became candidates for divestment in a condition that would make them more attractive to investors. In 1981/82, twenty-one major public enterprises were identified for divestment, along with close monitoring of their performances pending privatisation. Their accounts were consolidated into an annual report and the returns laid annually in Parliament. Their capital expenditure and recurrent expenses were seen to be almost as large as that of central government.

Non-divestiture options were first pursued as an intermediate step towards privatisation, in order to improve the commercial value of the enterprises to be sold. The government's divestment preparation programme incorporated management changes and reform, improved systems of financial reporting, an increase in the pricing of utilities to reflect domestic cost, and elimination of subsidies and cross-subsidies. Enterprises were required to meet a targeted rate of return on capital, modernise their maintenance practices and restructure their corporate organisation. Financial restructuring was also carried out, allowing an enterprise saddled with accumulated debt to 'clean up' its balance sheet, as with the Caribbean Cement Company sale. Operational restructuring was also carried to upgrade the enterprises' physical capacity and technology.

With the non-divestiture measures adopted, there was a decline in the deficit position between 1980/81 and 1984/85, and 1985/86 operating surplus of the twenty-one major SOEs was achieved and maintained up to 1988/89. The result was not only improved viability of the public enterprises, but there was also a trend showing a greater percentage of their capital needs being financed by internally generated funds, increasing from 56.4 per cent in 1985/86 to 86.1 per cent in 1988/89, even in an environment where capital expenditure showed significant levels of increases.

Progress on privatisation was very slow during the period 1981–86. The first sale in 1981 was a relatively small company that brought in US$0.7 million and involved Versair In-flight Services Ltd, an airline food catering company, which also operated the restaurant facilities at the two international airports. This company was originally formed in 1977 and was sold to a consortium of GraceKennedy of Jamaica, Goddard of Barbados, and Marriott of the US. This was followed by the sale of Southern Processors Ltd in 1982 for US$1.0 million. The company had been nationalised in 1973. The next reform exercise involved Jamaica Omnibus Service Company Limited (JOS), the Kingston urban public passenger transport company, and involved franchising public transport services to several private package holders involving several mini-bus operators. JOS initially became an asset holding company, with the private operators contracted providing the public transport services. JOS was eventually wound up in the latter part of the 1990s.

Selection of Entities for Privatisation

With selecting entities the policy adopted by the government between in the period 1985–89, continued to follow a case-by-case approach, rather than the more established policy arrangement of setting out an ambitious list of privatisation entities with targeted revenues and dates for divestiture. This shows that different circumstances require different approaches.[17] The government of Edward Seaga felt that success would be measured against the list, and failure to achieve such targets could have led to unfavourable consequences. Each successful sale was therefore projected as a major success story to ensure that public support was created and maintained. No comprehensive privatisation policy statement was issued prior to 1990. Policy statements were confined to the promotion aspect of the sale transaction.

The major turning point in the privatisation programme did not come until 1985, when the government was left with little option but to expedite implementation of the structural adjustment programme, inclusive of the privatisation component. The selection of entities during this period was guided by three sets of considerations; first, the Seaga administration was eager to stimulate and expand the stock market. It was, therefore, important to offer fairly profitable and attractive companies, such as NCB, TOJ, and CCC to the market. Second, the government sought to attract foreign exchange to improve its reserves. The funds brought in by Cable & Wireless (C&W) to increase its equity to 20 per cent in TOJ in 1987 and the conversion of the hotel leases to outright sale after 1987 facilitated the attainment of this objective. Third, the administration sought to achieve the political objective of a share-holding democracy and, in so doing, reverse Manley's cooperative ownership and democratic socialism. With the flotation of the shares of NCB, TOJ, and CCC, the JSE experienced the largest expansion in its history.

National Commercial Bank (NCB)was selected as an early candidate for the following reasons: it was a consistently profitable firm and a market leader and therefore offered a relatively safe or risk-free investment opportunity, nationally recognised with a national network of branches. The specific aim of the NCB sale over and above national objectives was that the government wanted the sale to be a success, more from a political point of view rather than from an economic one. In the selection of telecommunications, the government concluded that one of the main reasons for the poor performance of the domestic telephone company was lack of capital, especially foreign exchange. JTC's capital budget was restricted by World Bank credit conditionalities, which limited the level of foreign exchange the public sector could raise to fund capital needs. The government was therefore influenced mainly by the need to have access to foreign exchange and technology and especially from the realisation that the industry was becoming more competitive and substantial amounts of new capital was needed. This reflected a reversal of an earlier decision taken by the Seaga administration not to divest any of the utilities.

Early Privatisation Transactions

One of the first major privatisation transactions involved Soap and Edible Products Limited (Seprod) in 1985. This transaction established the road map for future divestment by share sale. Seprod was a joint venture of the private sector farming interests through the Coconut Industry Board and the government. Price controls in the 1970s had severely depressed the financial performance of this company and its survival was mainly because of the trade protection it was afforded during the period. Price controls were removed in 1983, so profitability more than tripled. However, the dismantling of import licensing and the removal of trade protection made survival problematic for Seprod, as the company found it difficult to compete with imports from other CARICOM countries.

The value of Seprod shares amounted to J$16 million, while long-term debt amounted to J$39 million, placing the company at the time in a negative net worth position from a historical accounting perspective. The sale involved a private placement to institutional investors (mainly Seprod distributors), an issue of new shares to the same investors, a public offer through the JSE, and an offer of 1.5 million shares to employees under an ESOP. The sale of shares and the new issue went at J$2.50 per share. However, the employees' shares were discounted to J$1.50 per unit. This transaction via the local stock market represented the first new issue in sixteen years and was over-subscribed. The sale demonstrated the principle that divestment of shares through small local stock markets in a developing country was a viable proposition. In the first two years immediately following the sale, there was a substantial rise in the value of the shares on the stock market. Price controls were, however, returned in 1987 and, partly because of this, profitability declined. In fact, the government had reneged on its privatisation commitments. The privatisation involved some retrenchment, although the ESOP scheme transferred some capital gains to staff.

In 1982, the Ministry of Agriculture embarked on a programme of sale of idle lands. By 1990, over thirty-six thousand acres (in lots of three to ten acres) of seventy-seven thousand acres earmarked for sale were sold to small farmers at an average price of J$2,000 per acre. Agro-21 Corporation Limited (Agro-21), as part of the leasehold programme which was launched in 1984 (forty-nine-year lease), divested thirty-four properties involving 34,571 acres, in addition to divesting fourteen agro-enterprises and/or assets. The lease programme proved to be a failure for lack of investment and working capital by the new private sector owners. Part of the problem arose from the fact that the commercial banks refused to accept leasehold titles as collateral for loans. Three of the state-owned sugar factories, which ran into financial problems, were liquidated and, along with the remaining publicly owned sugar companies, were placed under external management contracts initially secured through a management contract with Tate and Lyle. However, this privatisation turned out to be a failure and was subsequently abandoned. Export marketing of sugar was transferred from the Sugar Industry Authority (SIA) to an independent company managed by the sugar producers. The government-owned National Sugar Company was also closed down and a subsidiary of SIA was established to run the remaining sugar factories.

Implementing the privatisation programme was fragmented. National Hotels and Properties (NHP), under the Ministry of Foreign Affairs and Tourism, undertook privatisation of state-owned hotel properties through its own divestment committee. Jamaica National Investment Corporation (JNIC) handled divestments in the industrial and financial sectors, while the Bank of Jamaica handled the Workers Bank's privatisation. NHP itself was a subsidiary of the Urban Development Corporation, with a controlling interest in seventeen hotels in Jamaica. In the first phase of the hotel divestiture, NHP retained ownership of eight properties but leased out the operation and management to local and overseas operators. This was important to the government to show to the IMF that it intended to implement a divestiture programme. Land divestment and the land lease programme were handled through the Ministry of Agriculture, with a separate divestiture agency, the Agro-21. The Factories Corporation of Jamaica handled the government-owned factory complexes. Franchising of the urban bus routes was handled by the Ministry of Public Utilities and Transport, with the Ministry of Local Government, and the local Parish Councils handling the contracting out of the markets, garbage collection, and public cleansing facilities.

The National Planning Agency (now the Planning Institute of Jamaica) carried a mandate, up to 1985 under the Minister of Finance and Planning, to design an appropriate privatisation model but no clear framework was provided.[18] In the selection process, the Agency sought to ensure that both profitable and unprofitable enterprises were put up for divestiture to avoid a situation where the state would be left with only unprofitable and possibly unsaleable companies. An international accounting firm, Touche Ross and Company, was contracted to design an appropriate privatisation model but failed to produce a single satisfactory model, resulting in the abandonment of this initiative.

Privatisation of Some Key SOEs

Privatisation was attempted or executed for most of the major SOEs. A summary is provided for some key industries/companies. This in addition to the six privitasation cases discussed later.

Privatisation of the Caribbean Cement Company (CCC)

The second major transaction was CCC the sole monopoly producer of cement in Jamaica. The main reason for selecting CCC as the next candidate was that the transaction was seen to be large enough as a follow-up public offer to NCB and would continue to contribute to the development of the stock market. Significant improvements were also being made to the company's financial and operating performances and the management of the company strongly supported the sale. Last, it was not a politically sensitive privatisation. An interesting feature of the CCC divestiture was the offer of subscription warrants, issued based on one warrant for every five shares held. The subscription price was J$2.30 per share (as against the actual price of J$2.00) representing the only form of new funds which went into the company following on the divestiture. All subscribers were required to take up the shares allotted to them before December 1988. The warrants were tradable on the stock market. The privatisation also involved the sale of some shares to a strategic foreign investor at a relatively high price. This strategic investor, Scancem, was expected to provide management expertise, technology, and export marketing knowledge; however, there was no management contract involved.

With the CCC transaction, no applicant could initially acquire more than 10 per cent of the issued share capital (raised from 7 per cent, as was the case with the NCB sale). The government also agreed that, in the event of under-subscription, the state's shares would carry non-voting status. However, a golden share was issued to the government of Jamaica, providing for veto rights in case of voluntary winding up of the company, the creation of additional capital, or the creation of any new class of shares of more than 10 per cent of the issued capital. As with NCB, stocks were reserved for employees amounting to 9 per cent of the total issued share capital, with provision for acquisition through a discount facility and an instalment payment scheme.

Based on an offer price of J$2.00, the same as the sale price to Scancem the capitalisation realised J$250 million, with a price-earnings ratio of 8.70 on prospective 1987 earnings. The offer was under-subscribed and only 72 per cent of the equity offered to the public was sold to roughly twenty-three thousand shareholders. At the time, it was the largest stock take-up on the local exchange. Over 99 per cent of employees became stockholders. The stock immediately traded at $1.90, indicating that the offer was overpriced. No doubt the various restrictions also presented disincentives to prospective purchasers. Despite the disappointment in this privatisation, significant increases in investments and expansion of operations took place after 1987. In 1989, twenty-three thousand tons of cement was exported to the Eastern Caribbean from total production of four hundred and eight thousand tons.

Water Industry and National Water Commission

In the case of the National Water Commission (NWC), contact management had been tried in 1983 and 1986 with limited success. In 1996, the NWC twinned with the Thames Water International

Consultancy, a UK company, to benefit from best water practices. Certain management support services were also purchased from Price Waterhouse, a local accounting firm of management consultant, between 1996 and 1997. A major drawback of the management contract system in Jamaica was the inadequate institutional capacity to monitor performance on a timely basis and ambiguous contractual terms. Price Waterhouse, because of the poor financial state of the NWC in 1994 and its operating instabilities, concluded that a private investor was likely to view a long-term lease as a high risk. The conclusion was that a lease concession was not implementable. In addition, NWC capital needs to rehabilitate and expand the national water system was estimated at J$40 billion in 2021 for four hundred thousand customer base, NWC supplied 190 million gallons of potable water each day to four hundred thousand registered accounts, representing about 2 million people across Jamaica. Non-revenue water is about 60 per cent and in addition there is a sizable non-payer category.

After several attempts at privatisation, and to attract private sector interest in the water sector ended without success, private firms initially were only prepared to consider management contract. More recently, however, there has been some success in that NWC, which previously decided on who would be licensed, no longer carries the responsibility of providing entry to the market. Water licence is now subject to competitive bidding and OUR now plays an increasing role in determining who qualifies to obtain a licence, as well as in regulating private water. The result is that other companies have been allowed to operate sewage disposal and delivery of services, and there are now sixteen service providers other than NWC delivering water and sewage disposal services by 2020. These companies mostly operate in particular towns.

In 2015, the government announced that it was moving towards privatisation of water once again, this time to involve placement of the company's share on the Jamaica Stock Market, with the government retaining controlling interest with 30 per cent to 49 per cent for public listing. Based on international and Caribbean experiences, they were doomed to failure, especially as there was no involvement of a strategic technical partner.

Railway Industry and JRC

Attempt were also made to privatise the Jamaica Railway Corporation, which had been converted into a public statutory corporation in 1960. By the 1980s, the railway had lost all its bulk traffic to road transport except for bauxite and alumina and the bauxite companies. Mining traffic accounted for 81 per cent of JRC's revenues in 1991; non-bauxite rail haulage 3 per cent, and passenger services 11 per cent. Having lost faith in the capability of JRC, the bauxite companies contracted with the corporation for the right to use the rail network to transport their own traffic. Rail could not compete with road transport, especially over the short distances which occur in Jamaica, except for bulk transport of bauxite and alumina. After 142 years of public rail service operation in Jamaica, except for alumina traffic, all the other services were discontinued after September 1992. There has been considerable nostalgia about the public rail service.

Over the years, the government has been encouraging revival of railway service and in 1994, a group of local private businesses led by the GraceKennedy group presented a proposal to government to acquire and operate the railway.[19] Nothing came of this initiative and, in 1996, NIBJ issued EOI for private participation. An overseas consortium, led by Rites of India expressed interest and this was followed up with a Memorandum of Understanding (MOU), signed between the government and Rites. The Rites consortium, however, was only prepared to enter into a management contract, whereas the government was looking for a lead foreign investor to divest part of the ownership.[20] Because of this disagreement as to the form the contract should take, very little progress was made beyond the MOU stage. Rites continued to show interest and subsequently joint ventured with CPCS Transcom Limited of Canada. A new proposal was submitted to NIBJ and, as a result, an MOU was signed in 2000. As soon as Rites discovered that the government was pursuing the major toll road development project which ran parallel to the railway route, the company lost interest and informed the government that it had to make a choice between toll road development and the major rail improvements, as the freight traffic, which much of the rail investments had been predicated on, would now have to be shared with the toll road operator.

With the short distances that characterise transport trips in Jamaica and the highly developed highway network which has been taking place, it is difficult to see how major rail investment can be justified.

Rail cannot meet competition from road transport in an environment like Jamaica, except for bulk mineral traffic. This is in addition to the small size of the system as when in full operation the network covered 212 miles. The bauxite/alumina network covers a distance of less than seventy miles of the entire network. Jamaica's rail terrain is extremely harsh, with steep gradients and several severe reverse curves occurring just outside May Pen and up into Williamsfield. These characteristics make for difficult operations and high maintenance costs. As a result of these considerations, JRC has continued in business as a landlord.

Workers Bank

Workers Saving and Loan Bank (WSLB) was incorporated out of the government-owned saving bank in 1973 and was listed on the JSE. The Bank of Jamaica was responsible for divesting WSLB. The transaction was initiated in September 1990 and in February 1991 Corporate Merchant Bank, led by Delroy Lindsay, a local entrepreneur, outbid a shortlisted group of investors, offering to acquire WSLB for J$45.0 million (US$5.5 Million) for its 119,452,220 units of shares. The privatised bank came into operation on May 15, 1991, and, immediately on starting business, implemented an aggressive advertising campaign, introducing a set of new products including credit cards, insurance services, financial planning services, and remittances services with the UK through Girod Bank. The bank also engaged in branch network expansion and introducing Saturday banking. One year after privatisation, May 1992, the authorised capital of the bank had been increased to J$150 million of 300 million shares at 50 cents. A total of 128,665,534 stock units were issued and fully paid up. An ESOP was also introduced in 1993, comprising 6.0 million shares for the general employees and 4.0 million shares for an executive share option plan. As of June 20, 1993, the share capital was J$142 million (US$S6 million). In the following two years after privatisation, earnings per share was reversed from negative to positive.[21]

Liberalisation of the economy and the lifting of exchange control played a part in the improvements in the financial sector. Two years, however, was too short to conclude that the privatised Workers Bank was a sustainable business, as the company experienced turbulent times after 1995. WSLB's assets were among those of several local privately owned banks and financial institutions that, during the financial meltdown of 1995/97, were acquired by the Financial Sector Adjustment Company (FINSAC), a government-owned company. WSLB was liquidated, and FINSAC eventually disposed of its assets.

Hotel Industry

In mid-1987, National Hotels and Properties (NHP) instituted a divestiture programme for the hotels through direct sales and, by 1990, eleven of the seventeen publicly held hotels that were previously leased were sold outright. They were offered for sale in US dollars although local purchasers were allowed to pay 50 per cent of the sale price in foreign exchange, while non-residents were permitted to meet 25 per cent of the sale price through debt equity swaps. By June1990, hotel sale proceeds had amounted to US$60 million. The government had discovered that there was a major disadvantage with the leasing programme, in that it provided investors with very little incentives for investment in the hotels. The hotel sales were pursued quietly and raised substantial sums of money, peaking at J$311 million in 1989.

Municipal Services

Local and municipal services had formed one of the earliest parts of the divestiture programme. Between 1986 and 1991, eighty municipal markets, most garbage collection services in nineteen zones of Kingston and fourteen rural zones were contracted out for periods of three years, under a competitive bidding system. The public cleansing departments of the municipal authorities were closed down and replaced by five regional public sector companies (designated Municipal Parks and Markets), established under UDC to manage the bidding, contracting, and monitoring arrangements.

Public Broadcasting

In 1997, through the Public Broadcasting Corporation of Jamaica Act, the Jamaica Broadcasting Corporation (JBC) which was created in the 1958 and which began public broadcasting in 1963 was divested. The entity had two national radio stations and several regional radio stations in addition to television broadcasting. The JBC divestment began first with the selling of the regional radio stations in the 1980s. The television and the two radio assets were sold to Radio Jamaica Limited for J$70 million. The majority holding in Radio Jamaica Ltd, had been divested by share sale after 1985. At the time of privatising JBC, the government created a new entity, the Public Broadcasting Corporation of Jamaica to continue to provide public broadcasting service.

National Shipping Line

Approximately 40 per cent of the shares in the national shipping line, Jamaica Merchant Marine was sold to a consortium, comprising GraceKennedy Limited and Jamaica Banana Producers Limited.

Race Track

The government also began privatisation of Caymanas Track Limited (CTL), a horse racing track in 2006. Caymanas Park itself was part of a sugar plantation and was, at one time, owned by a sugar estate operator. Alexander Hamilton. The ownership of the property changed many times over the years until it went into bankruptcy in the late 1980s, resulting in the government acquiring the property in 1989. In the 1980s, the industry comprised seventy-three off-track betting parlours, 110 racing pool outlets and 533 bookmakers, located island-wide and several horse trainers, owners, breeders, and jockeys. There were five hundred owners, and about forty breeders, generating revenues of over J$40 billion in 2006. In 2006, there was failed privatisation. Both groups of investors who met the closing date for the RFP in early 2005 featured significant physical changes and improvements to the property. One bid featured redevelopment of the 196-acre racetrack and a fifty thousand square foot entertainment complex, including theatres, club houses, restaurant, a fifty-room hotel, private boxes with communication links for beaming races, and entertainment to North America and other countries. The other bids featured a family fun centre, simulcast transmission, luxury boxes, a bingo hall, live concerts, gaming lounges and parking for two thousand vehicles.

The privatisation effort was relaunched by BBJ with a confidential information memorandum on May 12, 2015, as selected tendering. The RFP was sent to Caymanas Racing and Entertainment Ltd (CRE) and Supreme Ventures Limited (SVL), pretty much the initial set of investors which had showed interest when CTL was offered to the market in 2005. Supreme Ventures was deemed the preferred bidder. Terms of sale were finally agreed and, after prolonged negotiations, the facility was handed over to the lessee on March 7, 2017. It took the government twelve years, from 2004 to 2016, to privatise CTL. By 1990, six of the factories previously leased to private operators were sold outright, as well as eight other miscellaneous loss-making operations, including the Jamaica Dry Docks, the small ship repair facilities. In the mining sector, Jamaica Gypsum Ltd was divested.

Tables 10.2A and 10.2B list the transactions handled by NIBJ, Agro-21, Ministry of Agriculture (MOA), Factories Corporation, Ministry of Public Utilities and Transport (MPUT) and NHP over the period 1981–90. Between 1981 and 1990, privatisation brought in just under US$350 million. In several instances, the government retained a minority stake, a 'golden share' where the protection of national interest was a consideration. Debt equity swap schemes were also introduced in the 1980s as a mechanism to facilitate the divestment process. In the initial phases, the government prohibited the use of this instrument in the divestiture of hotels, and it was not until 1989 that the debt equity swap scheme was linked to the privatisation programme; this allowed for 25 per cent of the purchase price of the hotels to be met through debt equity purchase arrangements.

Table 10.2A: Privatisation, 1981–90 (Sales)

Name	Date	Purchaser	Per cent Equity	Sales J$	Sales US$
Versair	1981	Private – Joint	100	1.2	0.7
Southern Processors LTD	1982	N/K	100	n.a.	n.a.
Seprod Ltd – I	1985	Private-Domestic	100	30.0	5.4
Seprod Ltd – II	1985	Public (16.5m shares sold, 10.5m new)	55	9.8	1.8
Assets of Banana Company	1985	Private/Domestic	n.a.	n.a.	n.a.
Rural Ice & Cold Storage Ltd	1986	Private/Domestic	100	0.5	0.1
Hanover Spices Ltd	1986	Private/Domestic	100	0.1	0.0
Hellshire Fish Farm Ltd	1986	Private/Domestic	100	0.3	0.1
Zero Processing & Storage Ltd	1986	Private/Domestic	100	4.0	0.7

Name	Date	Purchaser	Per cent Equity	Sales J$	Sales US$
Jamaica Oxygen & Acetylene	1986	Private/ Foreign	47	2.0	0.4
NCB	1986	Public	100	88.7	16.1
CCC (10 per cent to Scancem)	1987	Private/Foreign	100	25.0	4.5
CCC	1987	Public	90	157.4	28.6
TOJ (To C&W)	1987	Private/Foreign	83	102.3	18.6
TOJ (To C&W)	1987	Private/Foreign	72	183.5	33.4
Royal Caribbean Hotel	1987	Private/Joint	100	15.4	2.8
Serge Island Dairies Ltd	1988	Private/Joint	30	1.8	0.3
TOJ – III	1988	Public	53	108.5	19.7
Fantasy Resort (Hotel)	1989	Private/Domestic	100	22.4	3.7
Inn On the Beach (Hotel)	1989	Private/Domestic	100	0.7	0.1
Wyndam Rose Hall (Hotel)	1989	Private/ Foreign	100	132.0	22.0
Eden II (Hotel)	1989	Private/Domestic	100	60.0	10.0
Jamaica – Jamaica (Hotel)	1989	Private/Domestic	100	96.0	16.0
TOJ (To C&W)	1989	Private /Foreign	40	231.8	38.6
W.I. Pulp & Paper Ltd	1989	Private /Joint	81	38.1	6.4
Jamaica Gypsum and Quarries	1989	Private / Domestic	100	4.0	0.7
Trelawny Beach Hotel	1990	Private/ Domestic	74	n.a.	n.a.
Hedonism II (Hotel)	1990	Private/Domestic	100	n.a.	n.a.
Montego Inn	1990	Private/Domestic	100	n.a.	n.a.
Land for Agriculture (35,000 acres to small farmers/30,000 acres for com. farmers	1985 –90	Private/Domestic	100	n.a.	n.a.
Total				**1315.5**	**230.7**

Table 10.2B: Privatisation, 1981–90

Name	Date	Purchaser	Per cent Equity owned	J $m	US $m
JOS	1984	Lease/domestic	na	na	Na
Jamaica Sugar Holdings	1985	MC – Foreign	100	Tate & Lyle paid J$7.2m/10Yrs	Na
Various Hotels	1982	Leases	na	1.7	0.9
Various Hotels	1983	Leases	na	9.1	4.8
Various Hotels	1984	Leases	na	24.0	6.1
Various Hotels	1985	Leases	na	50.1	9.0
Various Hotels	1986	Leases	na	46.9	12.0
Various Hotels	1987	Leases	na	66.1	12.0
Various Hotels	1988	Leases	na	75.9	13.8
Various Hotels	1989	Leases	na	74.9	12.3
Port Antonio Marina	1998	Lease/Domestic	na	0.0	0.0
Total				**348.7**	**67.6**

Source: Christopher Adam, William Cavendish, and Percy S. Mistry, *Adjusting Privatisation: Case Studies in Developing Countries* (London: Heinemann, 1994).

Between 1985 and 1991, most of the entities approved for divestment by Cabinet, along with several agricultural and development properties, were ivested through leases, IPO, employee share offers, sale of shares of unlisted entities and asset sales as private treaties.[22]

Carl Stone reported that between 1981 and 1990, over 201 entities were privatised via share and asset sales, leasing, contracting out, and concessions. Of this total, eighty were markets, thirty-three were public cleansing entities, fifty were farm holdings, fourteen were hotel properties, and twenty-four were corporate.[23] Most of the transactions were carried out over the relatively short period of 1986–90, an achievement which Carl Stone considered remarkable and attributed the success to the fact that the process was decentralised, as no single agency had the management capability to handle the workload over such a short period.

In the period 1981–91, fifty divestiture transactions were handled through NIBJ and NHP, generating an income of J$1.8 billion, or 4 per cent of GDP. Apparently, there were some macroeconomic benefits from the programme. The external current account, which ranged from around 11 per cent of GDP in 1980 to 1986, declined to 5.5 per cent in the period 1987 to 1989. The public sector deficit also fell to 5.5 per cent of GDP but widened in 1988 to 13.5 per cent. During the ten-year period of the Seaga administration in the 1980s, however, the external debt more than doubled, reaching US$3.9 billion or 180 per cent of GDP.

Mary Allen referred to the paucity of data in assessing the aggregate proceeds from privatisation over the period up to 1991, but noted that NIBJ, formerly JNIC, received privatisation proceeds amounting to J$1,256.4 million, NHP J$882.2, and that during the first phase the total was assessed at J$2,138.6 million, excluding annual lease payment inflows.[24] The number of privatisation transactions handled by the various divesture committees was assessed to be 260 between 1981 and 1989. During this period, the committees stressed divestment of equity in commercial enterprises based on commercial criteria after considering national interest, as well as the discontinuance of enterprises that were no longer commercially viable. The priority for sale was based on budgetary and social impact and employment linkages.

The Second Phase of Privatisation, 1990–2002

A Bank of Jamaica study in 1991 recorded 325 public enterprises, with 102 being joint stock companies. The analysis showed that the profitable ones generated a surplus of J$7,11.3 million, while the loss-makers showed a deficit of J$975.7 million. The budget support needed for the 1990/91 financial year amounted to J$539.0 million. The income of the twenty-one specially monitored enterprises amounted to J$7.5 billion. Overall, marginal improvements were made in the finances of the SOEs during the decade of the 1980s.[25]

On returning to power in early 1989, the Manley PNP administration declared that, in the future, the private sector would be the engine of production and that the privatisation programme would be accelerated. The state would withdraw its interest from such areas as manufacturing, tourism, commercial banking, the operation of utilities, agriculture, and distribution through divestiture, and concentrate its efforts on providing incentives, regulatory framework, and a conducive environment for private initiatives to prosper. No new public enterprises were to be created. The government's interest in privatisation stemmed from the urgent need to improve the fiscal performance of the economy and the efficiency of the productive sector. A new ministry, the Ministry of Development, Planning and Production, was created and given the responsibility for privatisation, the development of competition policies and legislation, and introducing appropriate regulatory policies and laws for the financial enterprises and public utilities. I joined this new ministry at its inception in 1989, as special advisor to Deputy Prime Minister Patterson, and desk officer in the ministry with responsibility for the privatisation programme and regulatory policies.

It was the worsening financial situation in 1989 that forced the new PNP administration to fully commit itself to the privatisation programme and to continue the privatisation of the Jamaica Telephone Company by selling the remaining shares in 1990 to C&W and, in so doing, giving C&W majority control in the monopoly utility. This unplanned shift from a predominantly public monopoly, first to a mixed enterprise and finally to a private monopoly was a cause for serious public concern. This monopoly structure, the exclusive franchise, and the absence of an independent regulator were to become major issues of national controversy in the 1990s

The responsibility for supervision of NIBJ was transferred to the portfolio of the Office of the Prime Minister (OPM) in December 1990, and all divestment operational and implementing functions were centralised within the Privatisation Division of NIBJ. The hotel privatisation initiatives, that were nearing completion, were, however allowed to continue on their separate track under the direction of the UDC. As early as late 1989, the reporting structure of the secretariat was integrated into the management structure of NIBJ, and the NIBJ board, in effect, became the Divestment Committee, with the Divestment/ Privatisation Division functioning as the board's secretariat. The assignment of privatisation to the Office of the Prime Minister reflected the importance ascribed to divestment as a fundamental policy instrument of the new administration.

Under the new structure, a Cabinet Privatisation Subcommittee, chaired by the prime minister, was established. This committee dealt with privatisation policy matters and approved and reviewed the entire divestment programme and the list of entities selected for divestment. NIBJ, as the central implementing agency, was responsible for gathering information, identifying, or removing practical barriers to completing individual transactions, assisting the enterprise management to prepare each entity for privatisation, and co-coordinating the sale negotiations. Its technical staff consisted of a small core group, and much of the development and analytical work was carried out by outside consultants.

For each privatisation transaction, an enterprise team was normally created, consisting of a member from the portfolio ministry, officials from the Ministry of Finance, the Attorney General's Department, NIBJ and professionals from the private sector. The structure provided not only for a more centralised approach, but it also offered a better opportunity for institutional co-ordination around NIBJ. Simultaneously, the enterprise team approach facilitated consensus building, wider participation, and commitment to the programme. Once the Cabinet approved the privatisation modality, a negotiating team was selected for the large transactions to conduct negotiations with private sector parties. The division of responsibility between NIBJ and the Cabinet facilitated flexibility and transparency in decision-making.

The government also formalised ESOP; for this exercise, an overseas consultant and two local firms were employed to develop the scheme and the related legislation. The team presented its report in 1992, followed by appropriate ESOP legislation. It provided for special tax concessions to employees and employers. The employer could claim tax deductions for contributions made to employees to purchase shares in their companies; employees were not required to pay taxes on up to 25 per cent of annual income used to buy such shares. Another major departure from the previous administration's approach involved the introduction of an officially approved list of companies to be privatised, and a phased programme with a time frame for the divestment of each firm, asset, or function. Listing of entities was not new for, when the PNP took office, there was a list of fifty-seven companies targeted for divestment. Ministry Paper 34 of 1991 carried a list of sixty assets, enterprises, and functions as candidates for privatisation.[26] The Ministry Paper did not, however, carry the selection criteria. The first meeting of the Cabinet Privatisation Committee deliberated on this policy and the following broad principles were adopted:

- Firstly, fixed assets, companies, and the hotels, which were in advanced stages of negotiation, were to be given the highest priority.

- Secondly, distressed assets were to be considered. Where the economic, financial, and administrative burdens were such that major costs were being incurred with very little benefit, every effort was to be made to dispose of these facilities, either as ongoing businesses or as fixed assets. Many government companies which had ceased operations fell into this category.
- Thirdly, companies and functions, which were no longer central to the new mission of the government, as with companies in manufacturing, agriculture, and distribution, were to be transferred to the private sector.
- Fourthly, for the first time, the utilities were to officially form a part of the privatisation programme. The major motivation here was to secure foreign capital to meet the investment requirements of the utilities and to attract foreign technology and management skills.

In addition, the following measures were later made a part of the policy:

- No direct financing or loan guarantee was to be provided.
- All appropriate regulatory issues were to be dealt with prior to or simultaneously with the privatisation.
- There were to be no new investments, other than for the ports, electricity, and water.
- Sales to other public enterprises were not to be treated as privatisation.
- No unsolicited offer was to be processed other than for small transactions.
- All aspects of the transaction, on completion, were to be in the public domain.
- All offers were to be open to local and foreign investors.

In the valuation of assets, the principle of economic valuations was again emphasised, and multiple valuation methods were required. The policy also called for arms-length relationships in effecting the transactions. Introducing objective evaluation criteria and arms-length relationships met the mounting criticism of the new administration that the distribution of some assets had been selective and made in the interest of favoured groups or on partisan grounds, with secrecy surrounding several transactions and criticism that assets were sold below market value. Strong pressures came from the middle class and from capitalist entrepreneurs, who were strategically placed to influence the process to proceed with the privatisation programme.

Most of the critical resources needed to sustain the privatisation programme came from USAID, and, in the case of the utilities, the World Bank and the IDB provided loan funds. USAID had, earlier in 1991, provided a grant of US$4.0 million to the NIBJ and to the hotel divestment programme, in addition to extending guarantee facilities to seven Jamaican banks to enable them to extend 50 per cent guarantee for eligible assets. There were two other USAID guarantee schemes, the Small Business Loan Portfolio, and the Jamaica Resources Mobilisation Facility Grant. IDB and the World Bank funded several studies and valuation exercises as well as providing financing for the engagement of local and overseas experts.

The 1993 Private Sector Development Adjustment Loan (PSDAL) provided major funding for the renewed programme to cover the period 1993–96, as well as providing the central direction for the privatisation agenda for the rest of the 1990s. The assets, entities, and functions listed for divestiture represented 50 per cent of the public enterprise sector, in terms of revenue. All the major loss-makers were included. The programme was expected to yield J$4 billion over the five-year period 1993–98, or 10 per cent of GDP. Electricity, water, sugar, Air Jamaica, Petrojam, the remaining NCB shares, and the railway were assigned the priority enterprises for divestiture.

For the first time, clear objectives for the overall programme were established as follows:

- to secure greater efficiency in the operations of enterprises through private ownership;
- to reduce the drain on government's fiscal resources caused by poorly performing SOEs;
- to optimise the use of the government's limited managerial resources;
- to secure access to foreign markets, technologies, and capital;
- to widen the base of ownership and to facilitate direct equity participation by a wide cross-section of the economy.

In more specific terms, the programme sought to reduce government's responsibility for major development roles in the productive sector; reduce public debt exposure; support the budgetary effort; contribute foreign exchange to meet IMF conditionalities; provide for more players in the market and promote competition to provide for a more competitive economy. While the prime minister, deputy prime minister and one or two technocrats were fully committed to the privatisation programme, anti-divestment sentiments by many supporters of the PNP and the bureaucracy who were emotionally committed to the idea of the state playing a leading role in the economy were very pronounced. Their support for the privatisation programme was more from loyalty to the leadership than from conviction. Support for privatisation of the utilities was even weaker. Divestment could reduce not only the role and importance of certain ministerial portfolios but also eventually could lead to elimination of ministries, as in New Zealand, where two ministries were eliminated.

Several middle-class professionals who had risen to senior positions in management and influence in the country under the period of statism were not prepared to see their positions of influence abolished through privatisation. Their support was rather tepid. Divestment of critical assets and companies also undermined party clientism, restricting the opportunity to provide benefits and privileges to preferred parties.[27]

The commitment made to the World Bank was for completion by 1996 of privatisation of all fifty-seven packages of assets, entities, and service functions that were identified for divestment. The priority enterprises to be divested were the sugar mills/estates, Air Jamaica, the rest of the shares of NCB, Petrojam, JPSCo, JRC and the Sangster International Airport. By 1995, over half of these were sold or leased. Since the programme was instituted in 1981, divestitures completed represented 10 per cent in agriculture; 39 per cent in manufacturing, and 51 per cent in services. Air Jamaica, NCB, the sugar estates/factories and JPSCo were completed and the loss-making operations of JRC were closed in the period up to 2001. A further twenty-seven entities were also added to the list.

The privatisation programme was continued by the PNP administration, even after the clientele relationship with the IMF was suspended in 1996. In several instances, the SOE, or state asset, was transferred to the private sector. However, the state was still required to continue providing financing as in the case following the privatisation of Air Jamaica, the sugar estates, and urban transport. In these instances, although the government was not the majority owners it ended up meeting theessential capital financing to ensure continued operation of the respective company

The privatisations transaction which took place over the period 1991–2001 are shown in table 10.3 below.

Table 10.3: Privatisation Transactions, 1991–2001

• **Dairy Industries:** The government of Jamaica sold its 5.5 per cent equity to the major partner, which held pre-emptive rights to the sale for J$71 million;
• **National Cassava Products:** this company was formed in 1974 and closed in 1992. The asset was sold to Sorn Hill Aggregates Ltd in 1993 for J$3.2 million;
• **West Indies Glass:** 64.5 per cent of publicly held shares were sold in 1991 for J$40 million;
• **RJR "B":** sold in 1991 for J$15 million;
• **Jamaica Frozen Foods:** assets sold in 1991 for J$8 million;
• **Mallards Beach Hotel**: assets sold in 1991for US$16 million;
• **Americana Hotel:** assets sold in 1991 for US$11 million;
• **Workers Savings and Loan Bank**: 75.4 per cent of publicly held shares sold for J$45 million;
• **Negril Cabins:** asset sold in 1991 for J$15 million;
• **Government Printing Office**: ESOP transaction in 1992 involving sale of equipment for J$350 000 and lease of building at estimated lease proceeds of J$37.3 million;
• **Caribbean Steel Co.:** publicly held shares sold in 1992 for J$15 million;
• **Cornwall Dairy:** assets of factory (land, buildings, and machinery) which was closed sold for J$9. 49 million;
• **Jamaica Soya Products:** 60 per cent publicly held shares sold for J$49.5 million in 1993;
• **Skyline Hotel:** assets sold in 1993 for J$100 million;
• **Caribbean Cement Co.:** 14 million publicly held shares sold in 1993 for J$168 million;
• **National Computer Centre:** sold to employees as part of ESOP in 1993;
• **Sugar Estates (Frome, Monymusk, Long Pond, and Bernard Lodge):** sale of factories and adjacent lands including leased cane lands sold in 1993 for J$1.36 billion;
• **Holiday Inn Hotel:** assets sold in 1994 for US$22 million;
• **Water Valley:** land sold in 1994 for J$14 million;
• **Grains Jamaica Ltd:** 52 per cent of publicly held shares sold in 1994 for J$33.92 million to Taylor Cross Inc.;

• **Eastern Banana Estates Ltd (EBEL)**: 39 per cent of publicly held shares sold for J$287 million in 1994;
• **Victoria Banana Estates Ltd:** 100 per cent of publicly held shares sold in 1994 for J$43 million. Share restructuring in 1990 led to the government reducing its equity from 77 per cent to 39 per cent. Commonwealth Development Corporation then converted part of its loans to equity; EBEL and Victoria Banana were merged and sold to Jamaica Banana Producers Ltd, a local firm, and Fyffe of the UK, with the government holding 5 per cent equity interest after the transactions.
• **Air Jamaica Ltd:** This transaction covered the sale of (70 per cent) shares and assets in 1993 for J$270.56 million plus US$18 .23 million. Handing over took place in 1994;
• **Trans-Jamaica Airlines:** majority share sold to Air Jamaica Acquisition Group in 1995, (became Air Jamaica Express) for J$20 million;
• **Tanners Ltd** : 17.55 per cent publicly held shares sold to joint venture partner with pre-emptive rights for J$494, 900 in 1993;
• **Police Garage:** maintenance services contracted out in1994;
• **Catering for Infirmaries:** contracting out of catering services in 1994;
• **Things Jamaica:** shares sold in 1996;
• **Cotton Polyester Textile Mills Ltd**: The Chinese government with a shareholding of 46 per cent and the government 54 per cent built this factory, closed for most of its life. This plant was leased;
• **Highgate Foods Ltd**: minority publicly held shares sold to joint venture partner with pre-emptive rights in 1996 for J$1.173 million;
• **Jamaica Grain & Cereals Ltd:** shares sold to joint venture partner with pre-emptive rights in 1996;
• Share sale of an asset in **Long Pond Poultry Assets** in 1996;
• Eleven additional items were brought on to the list in 1996;
• **Phase Three of Sugar privatisation:** this involved the leasing of sugar cane lands to cane farmers: Frome 1,778 hectares: Bernard Lodge 1,359 hectares, and Long Pond 3,243 hectares in 1996. Lease involved disposal of twenty-eight parcels with estimated lease proceeds of J$50 million;
• **Petrojam:** this was a transaction involving a sale of 70 per cent of shares in the oil refinery, 70 per cent of Petrojam Ethanol and Petronal Fermentery/Distillery, 49 per cent in of Petcom (petrol stations) and 100 per cent of three vessels owned by Petrojam Shipping Division to the management (Management Buy Out – MBO) in 1996. Although the agreement was signed, the group could never honour the financial terms, and the business remained with the government;
• **Sugar Estates/Factories** were returned to GOJ in 1998;
• **Petrojam Belize** consisting of cane lands, factory, and Santa Cruz Lodge sold in 1998 to the government of Belize for US$5 million;

• **Ariguanabo Textile Buildings** (closed for over ten years): part of complex leased to L'land Ice Company Inc of Texas for water purification operation in1998 for J$6.0 million; part of building a complex lease to Issons Sales and Service Ltd in 1998 for J$1.8 million;
• **Alstrom Building System Ltd;** sale of 10.5 million publicly held shares for J$23.8 million in 1999;
• **Caribbean Cement Company:** 181.3 million shares or 43 per cent of equity sold in 1998 for US$29.84 million;
• **Farm Machinery Complex:** land and building leased to Spring Plain Nursery and Garden in 2000 with lease proceeds of J$310 000;
• **Solar Salt Complex:** industrial complex leased to Industrial Chemical Company Ltd in 2001 for the production of salt for an estimated J$12 million;
Aqualipa : 70 per cent publicly held shares sold to Jamaica Broilers in 2001.

Continuation of the Privatisation Programme after 2009

The government continued the privatisation programme after 2009. Table 10.4 lists the transactions which took place between 2009 and 2022.

Table 10.4: Privatisation Transaction Summary, 2009–22

No.	Asset /Company	Purchaser	Date	Method of sale
1	Long Pond Estate	Everglade Farm Ltd	July 09	Sale and lease
2	Hampden Sugar Estate	Everglade Farm Ltd	July 09	Sale and lease
3	St. Thomas Sugar Factory	Golden Grove Sugar Ltd	July 09	Sale and lease
4	Cotton Polyester Factory Complex (21 areas)	Urban Development Corporation	Feb 10	Asset sale
5	Ariguanabo (14 acres and building)	New Era Homes Ltd	Mar 10	Asset sale
6	Montpellier Citrus Lands (524.76 acres)	Ramble Enterprise Ltd	May 10	Asset sale
7	Monymusk Sugar Estate	COMPLANT International Sugar Industry Ltd		Asset sale
8	Bernard Lodge Sugar Estate	COMPLANT International Sugar Industry Ltd	July 10	Asset sale

No.	Asset /Company	Purchaser	Date	Method of sale
9	Frome Sugar Estate	COMPLANT International Sugar Industry Ltd	July 10	Asset sale
10	Jamaica Pegasus Hotels Ltd (59 per cent)	Kevin Hendrickson	Dec. 10	Share sale
11	Cotton Polyester Factory Complex (3.2 areas)	Urban Development Corporation	Dec 10	Asset sale
12	Mavis Bank Coffee Factory	Ja Producers / Pan Jam Inv.	Oct 11	Asset sale
13	Bloody Bay Hotel Dev. Ltd	Village Resorts Ltd	Mar 13	Share sale
14	Wallenford Coffee Farm Company	AIC Int. Investment Ltd	Aug 13	Share sale
15	Windalco -Alumina operations	UC Rusal (Russians)	May 14	Share sale
16	Farm Machinery Centre	RYCO Jamaica Ltd	Jan 15	Asset sale
17	Kingston Container Terminal	King Freeport Terminal – owned by Terminal Link Ltd	April 15	PPP long term concession
18	Petcom	Phoenix Fuels & Associates Ltd	April 16	Asset sale and shares sale
19	Caymanas Track Ltd	Supreme Ventures / Supreme Ventures Racing and Entertainment Ltd	Feb 17	Long-term lease of property
20	KIW International	Jamaica Teas Ltd	Mar 17	Asset sale and share sale
21	Montpellier Citrus Lands (1,609.5 acres)	Jamaica Green Botanical Producers Co Ltd	Oct 16	Long-term lease
22	Montpellier Citrus Lands (acres)	Min. of National Security	Mar 18	Asset sale
23	Norman Manley International	GAP	Oct 18	PPP -long term concession
24	Wigton Wind Farm Ltd-Refinancing Debt	Amount owed to Petrocaribe Development	Dec 18	Debt swap

No.	Asset /Company	Purchaser	Date	Method of sale
25	Wigton Wind Farm Ltd-	100 per cent IPO Stock Exchange	May 19	Share sale
26	Fort Clarence	Guardsman Ltd	Sept 19	Dev lease
27	Silver Sands Lands Phase 1	Six individual investors	Nov 19	Residential land sale
28	German Shipyard Repairs	Kingston Dry Dock/ German Ship Repair	Mar 20	Property sale
29	Silver Sands Lands Phase 2	Nine Individual Investors	Oct 21	Silver Sands Lands Phase1
30	Greater Bernard Lodge (Phase 1) Residential	CEAC Solution, Kemtek Dev & Construct. & West Indies Homes	Feb 22	Residential land sale
31	Greater Bernard Lodge (Phase 2) light industrial	Kemtek Dev & Construct & Linyun Cloud	Feb 22	Industrial land sale
32	School Solar Energy	Roswall Institutional Sust Energy Ltd		PPP-long term concession

Source: Jamaica Development Bank

The major transactions were the sugar industry, the coffee industry, Windalco, Pegasus Hotel, and the Norman Manley International Airport. In three instances, the transactions involved transfers from one government agency to another, hence were not privatisation transactions. These involved the two transfers of the Cotton Polyester Factory Complex (24.2 acres) to the Urban Development Corporation and transferring Montpelier citrus lands to the Ministry of National Security. It would appear that some of the assets privatised earlier on were returned to government and were a part of the assets sold after 2009, such as the Farm Machinery Complex and the Ariguanabo Buildings.

Several of the assets were residuals of SOEs which had been liquidated. However, there was a cost to the government in having to provide security and maintenance over the years. With privatisation, these costs are no longer an issue.

Assessing the Impact of the Privatisation Programme

Mary Allen noted that overall public sector balances fell from minus J$1,653.5 million in financial year 1985/86 to minus J$526.34 million in financial year 1990/91.[28] This was largely because of improvements in the current balances of the SOEs, especially over the period of financial year 1986/87 to 1990/91 and particularly with the National Water Commission (NWC,) Jamaica Public Service Co. (JPSCo) and the Jamaica Telephone Company (JTC), a result of their cost-cutting programme. Privatisations proceeds over the period were estimated at J$1.81 billion. The period also saw a significant reduction in the level of credit allocated to the public sector, falling from J$2.39 billion in 1985 to J$1,43 billion in 1990, a decrease of 62.4 per cent. At the same time, credit to the private sector increased from J$2.41 billion in 1985 to J$7.34 billion in 1980, an increase of 300 per cent. Foreign exchange inflows from privatisation were estimated to amount to US$178.0 million, forming a significant proportion of foreign capital inflow. The privatisation inflows contributed significantly to Net International Reserves at the Bank of Jamaica.

Fifteen of the thirty-one companies listed on the Jamaica Stock Exchange in 1990 were totally or partially privatised SOEs, giving a boost to the stock market over the period 1985 to 1990. Trade in the privatised SOEs represented an increasing proportion of total volumes between 1985 and 1990.[29]

Results of the Privatisation Programmes

William Megginson and Natalie L. Sutter noted that researchers and analysts face many methodical problems in analysing the effects of privatisation, in particular data availability and consistency.[30] In addition, there may be fundamental differences in the economic environment in the pre- and post-divestment periods. Other problems arise when using accounting or financial data in determining the correct measure of operating performance; selection of an appropriate benchmark and statistical tests also present challenges. Two common approaches have been regularly adopted: comparing the performance of the SOE firms to privately owned firms, as has been done in the NCB and BNS cases as shown later, or comparing pre-privatisation (under SOE operation) and post- privatisation (under private management), or with a counterfactual.

Extensive empirical literature (mainly from the 1980s) comparing public and private enterprises in industrial market economies concluded generally, but not uniformly, that private firms exhibit higher productivity and better performances than public enterprises, particularly in competitive markets. Analysis of sixty-one privatised companies in eighteen countries (six developing and twelve developed) showed that, in at least two-thirds of the divestitures, there had been efficiency, profitability, and capital investment improvements in the post-divestment period.[31]

In Jamaica, privatisation has facilitated the development of Jamaica's embryonic stock market and has brought a wider section of society into the mainstream of productive investment. Results of surveys carried out by Data Resources showed that 59 per cent of respondents expressed the belief that the overall benefits to Jamaica from privatisation have been positive, especially in terms of employment creation, investments, and foreign exchange earnings. Respondents have been less clear as to the benefits to consumers.[32] Despite the positives outlined, there have been no definitive studies involving the use of counter-factual analysis in Jamaica to show that the productive efficiencies in the enterprises transferred from the public sector to the private sector improved.

Criticisms of the privatisation programme have been made regarding programme implementation. It was felt that the focus was too much on financial performance and inflows, instead of implementation efficiency measures, and not enough effort was paid to the efficiency of operations after privatisation. The initial Caribbean Cement Company sale is regarded by many to have been a failure, especially since the government assumed the debts before selling the shares. Petrojam selling a highly capital-intensive asset to a group of managers (Management Buy-Out) without the new owners being able to access to major sources of investments was ill-advised, and the government has had to repossess this firm. The sale of TOJ has been criticised by the media and the public for granting British C&W a forty-nine-year monopoly and a guaranteed rate of return of 17.5 per cent to 20 per cent on capital after tax and on revalued assets. The government should not have bundled domestic services with international services as a part of the privatisation restructuring package if the interest of consumers was its priority. The process provided for the large transnational investor the opportunity to exert considerable leverage over the government. This was compounded because the chairman of the reboundled company was the chairman of Jamintel, representing C&W London's interest whilst being the major advisor to the government on the privatisation transaction.

The ESOP Programme was, to some extent, motivated by government's desire to win the support of the trade unions and workers and had nothing to do with economic efficiency. The restraint on the levels of equity ownership, while socially desirable, did not enhance economic efficiency.

While Jamaica may have been successful with the privatisation of firms in competitive markets, its experience with the privatisation of utilities and regulated industries has not been exemplary. Privatisation of the sugar industry, and NWC and the initial privatisation of Air Jamaica were extremely difficult to execute and, by and large, have been disastrous in terms of the cost to the country. The Air Jamaica privatisation proved to be expensive to the Treasury in the post-privatisation era as in the pre-privatisation era. The taxpayers were saddled for years with responsibility for loan guarantees to meet the airline's capital requirements and direct funding of its losses. No study was ever conducted to support the argument that the wider economic benefits to the tourism sector outweighed the loss burden undertaken by the taxpayers. Operational losses of air Jamaica for the first year after privatisation (the initial privatisation) was over US$40 million. Jamaica also lost Category One aviation sector rating with the US, and it is claimed that the downgrading to Category Two contributed to most of these losses. Besides absorbing major debts of Air Jamaica in the earlier privatisation, the government had to provide loan guarantees to the order of US$54 million and continued to fund Air Jamaica, even after the company was under majority private management. This privatisation presented a major conflict of interest with the majority shareholder, a hotel operator. The private investor's interest was low hotel tariff to fill his hotel rooms as against higher fares, maximising returns to the minority investors.

Privatisation of the sugar industry and the public passenger company, JOS, has also been a costly affair to taxpayers. Private operation of the defunct railway is an illusion and is shaping up to be another JOS privatisation in the making.

Developing countries like Jamaica find themselves in weak negotiating positions when selling state assets that require large capital injection to foreign firms, as with electricity and telecommunications. These firms will seek to extract their 'pound of flesh' through unreasonable terms and conditions. Refusal of bidders to accept cross-guarantees to the private power providers in the electricity privatisation, or in seeking to extract a high price for this cross-guarantee, led to the breakdown of the negotiations in the first JPSCo privatisation attempt in 1995. Ownership issues in the water sector and economies of scale in capital investment have, until recently, deterred any serious privatisation initiatives. These issues have been intractable. Regarding the Port Authority, most of the port operation activities have, over the years, been in the hands of private operators, and only the development functions remained in the hands of the public sector.

Since competition is the best regulator, the Jamaican governments should have introduced competition through vertical or horizontal unbundling of those parts of entities which allow for new firms to enter the competitive markets. Where competition is not possible, as in sections of telecommunications transmission, and in electricity transmission and distribution, an appropriate regulatory regime should have been developed much earlier to regulate prices, quality, and new investments. The need for a well-defined regulatory framework is clearly demonstrated in the Jamaican experience as a precondition to successful privatisation of infrastructure and utility enterprises. Regulatory methods which are appropriate in one environment may differ in another. Developing regulatory regime requires considerable technical competence and practical experience and there is a need for each country to consider its regulatory endowment.[33] Privatisation will remain an attractive option once short-term political considerations can be overcome. The huge amount of financing required to provide the water services, electricity capacity, telecommunications services airports and the road infrastructure development needs cannot be financed with the parlous state of the Jamaican public budget.

One of the most important lessons learnt is that it is not only ownership that matters but structure as well. A structure which allows for competition should be the desirable goal. It is competition which provides the incentive for productive and allocative efficiency. Industries which are state-owned invariably offer little or no opportunity for competition, hence no market incentive for efficiency. Evidence also exists to show that the higher the level of political control the greater the level of inefficiency of public enterprises. Even with SOE operations, the lower the amount of political control the better the performances to operate efficiency. Among the twenty-six developing countries which the World Bank listed as carrying out privatisation programmes in the 1980 and 1990s, Jamaica has been highly ranked. The Futures Group in the 1990s described the Jamaican government then as being among the world's most committed to market-based reform. The programme has benefited several classes in the society: several professionals, small and medium-scale businesspeople, and first-time entrepreneurs have been given the opportunity to operate their own businesses. The traditional mercantile and real estate and trading interests have also acquired major shares in many of the companies and assets which have been sold.

Notes

1. Dennis Rondinelli and Max Iacono, *Policies, Institutions for Managing Privatisation International Experience* (Geneva: International Labour Organization, 1996)
2. David Newberry, *Privatisation, Restructuring, and Regulation of Network Industries* (Cambridge, and London: MIT Press, 2000).
3. Natural monopoly in an industry is one characterised by high infrastructural fixed sunk cost and other barriers to entry relative to the size of the market, one firm, the natural monopolist will produce at the lowest cost. The total cost of producing the total output by one firm will be lower than the total cost of any two or more firms producing the entire output. There are two conditions which give rise to natural monopoly, economies of scale and economies of scope.
4. Oliver Campbell White and Anita Bhatia, *Privatisation in Africa* (Washington, DC: World Bank, 1998).
5. Christopher Adams, William Cavendish, and Percy S. Mistry, *Adjusting Privatisation-Case Studies in Developing Countries* (London, Heinemann, 1992).
6. World Bank, *World Development Report* (Oxford: Oxford University Press, 1996).
7. J. Vickers and G. Yarrow, *Privatisation: An Economic Analysis* (Massachusetts and London: MIT Press, 1998).
8. Carol Jones, 'Privatisation: The Jamaica Experience,' Commonwealth Secretariat Conference on Privatisation in Developing Countries, Islamabad, Pakistan, March 1992.
9. Peter Jackson and Catherine M. Price, *Privatizing and Regulation: A Review of the Issues*, Longman Economic Series (London: Longman, 1994).
10. Vincent M. Lawrence, 'Post-Privatisation Issues: "The Jamaican

Experience,'" Paper Presented at the Post-Privatisation Conference in Latin America, Buenos Aries, Argentina, 1995. Lawrence was chairman of the National Privatisation Negotiating Team under PNP Administration.

11. Headley Brown, 'Planning and Management of the Privatisation Process: The Jamaican Experience 1981–1991,' Paper presented at Commonwealth Secretariat Conference on Privatisation in Developing Countries, Islamabad, Pakistan, 1991.
12. Gover Barja Daza and Manual Urguiolo (2003), *Capitalisation and Privatisation in Bolivia: An Approximation to an Evaluation* (Washington: Center for Global Development, 2003).
13. R. Jeffery Gate and Jamal Sagher, *Employee Stock Option Plans* (Washington: World Bank, 1995).
14. Rondileni and Iacono, *Policies, Institutions for Managing Privatisation International Experience.*
15. Cezley Sampson, 'Privatising Jamaica: Lessons from Small Developing Economies,' Paper delivered at Commonwealth Secretariat Conference, Botswana, 1997.
16. Lawrence, 'Post-Privatisation Issues.'
17. Mary M. Allen, 'Privatisation and Monetary Development in Jamaica: A Preliminary Assessment,' presented at the 23rd Annual Conference of Regional Programme of Monetary Studies, Belize City, Belize, November 24–28, 1991.
18. Charles Vuylstyke, Helen Nankani, Rebecca Candoy-Sekse, and Anne Ruiz Palmer, *Techniques of State-Owned Enterprises: Method of Privatisation* (Washington: World Bank, 1998).
19. S. Sterling, 'Jamaican Privatisation Process, Evolution, Management and Evaluation,' Commonwealth Secretariat Conference on Privatisation in Developing Countries, Islamabad, Pakistan, 1992.
20. Portland Group, *Rail Transport Regulatory Structure* (Kingston: JRC, 1995).
21. Rites, *Proposal for the Revitalisation of the Rail System* (Kinston: JRC, 1997)
22. Helen Chilupe, *Privatization in Reality: The Case of Jamaica*, report prepared under the Robert McNamara Fellowship Programme (Washington, DC: World Bank, 1993).
23. Allen, 'Privatisation and Monetary Development in Jamaica.'
24. Carl Stone, *Putting Enterprise to Work: A Study of Privatisation in Jamaica* (Kingston: National Investment Bank of Jamaica, 1992).
25. Allen, 'Privatisation and Monetary Development in Jamaica.'
26. C. Tyndale, *Survey of Public Enterprises* (Kingston: Bank of Jamaica, 1991).
27. Ibid.
28. Richard Bernal and Winsome Leslie, 'Privatisation in the English-speaking Caribbean: An Assessment,' in *Privatisation in Latin America and the Caribbean: North South Centre* (Miami: University of Miami, 1997).
29. Allen, 'Privatisation and Monetary Development in Jamaica.'
30. Ibid.

31. William Megginson and Natalie L. Sutter, 'Privatisation in Developing Countries: An International Review,' *Corporate Governance* 14, no. 4 (2006).
32. World Bank, *Property Rights and Enterprise Reform: World Development Report* (Oxford: Oxford University Press, 1996).
33. Data Resources Systems, (1995), op.cit.
34. Pablo Spiller and Cezley Sampson, 'Telecommunications Regulation in Jamaica,' in *Regulations, Institutions and Commitment: Comparative Studies of Telecommunications*, ed. Brian Levy and Pablo Spiller (Cambridge: Cambridge University Press, 1996).

CHAPTER ELEVEN

Conclusions and Lessons Learnt

MAIN CONCLUSIONS

In the period before independence in 1962, the government, through the public sector in Jamaica, provided a limited range of services to the wider population, focusing on education, public health, the maintenance of law and order, welfare, and national road building and maintenance. It was left up to the private sector to take on the responsibility for the provision of productive services and the utilities, including electricity, telephone, and urban transport, street lighting, and gas services in Kingston. At the same time, there was minimal interference by the government in the operation of private business except for the utilities, which were subject to public regulation. Through the 'ad hoc' rate boards appointed by the colonial governor.

This all changed starting in the decade of the 1970s, with the public sector taking on the responsibility of driving economic development, including ownership and operation of production and commercial enterprises. By the decade of the 1980s, the size of the public sector and the level of expenditure by the government had grown out of control to account for over 40 per cent of the GDP. The poor performance of the Jamaican economy after the 1970s was attributable to the overburdening of the public sector, which had operated at a level well beyond the size necessary to ensure sustained economic growth. If this hypothesis holds true, then the reduction of the public sector through privatisation and liquidation should have seen improvements in the economy over the future years.

What is important, however, is not just the size of the public sector but its effective management and control by the authorities. What is clear in Jamaica is that ownership matters both in theory and in practice. The experience is that portfolio ministers routinely intervene din the day-to-day operations of the companies and their interventions invariably carried political undertones, rather than focus on the setting of clear policies and objectives and on the monitoring of performances to ensure that the objectives are attained. The Jamaican experience demonstrates that it is not so much public ownership which works against efficiency and development, but the level of political and bureaucratic interferences by ministers and civil servants. Invariably, ministerial interference is not guided by economic efficiency consideration, but more often than not by seeking to distribute scarce benefits for political gain.

The reforms over the last three decades have acted as a catalyst for improved economic performance, in both the public and private sector. Commitment and ownership are also necessary for the continued successful implementation of the ongoing reform measures.

Since 1980, there has been a clear shift in the role of the private sector as a driving force in the economy, accompanied by a decrease in the number of employees and public entities, as well as a reduction in their operations. However, it is important to note that the public sector and public enterprises still maintain a significant presence and continue to be large and complex. Some activities, especially in the infrastructure and development areas, will probably continue to involve active public sector participation although selected areas can now be delivered by public-private partnership where the private sector takes on most of the commercial risks. One of the critical issues for the future will, therefore, be continued improved financial performances and rationalisation of the number of existing entities, several of which are virtually inactive and for which no valid case can be advanced for their continued existence.

There is still a major challenge to secure improved financial performances of the remaining SOEs to generate rates of return on capital employed, comparable to the private sector. Although the Port Authority, for example, may show large profits, when considered in terms of return on capital, the performance cannot be satisfactory. The challenge is to ensure control and accountability, especially in their financial reporting and in meeting their statutory obligations. Excessive controls, as observed in some of the current directions being pursued, can stifle entrepreneurship and undermine the fundamental principles of independence and autonomy that initially motivated the establishment of these enterprises outside the civil service structure. The original intent was to foster a sense of self-reliance and freedom from centralised bureaucracy, but overly restrictive measures can hinder this objective. Public enterprises are expected to operate with a high degree of managerial freedom if they are to be effective. At the same time, if controls are weak, or loose, as they were originally, the question of accountability to the taxpayers and why public enterprises are in the hands of the state arises.

With privatisation, SOEs like the Jamaica Public Service Company, National Commercial Bank, Caribbean Cement Company, Jamaica Telephone Company, and the Jamaica International Telephone Company were divested in the 1980/90 period. The government found it difficult to divest Air Jamaica, components of the sugar industry and urban transit, resulting in several failed attempts at privatisation during the period and even when these entities were passed over to the private sector, they continued to be financed from the public purse. All enterprises that are trading and commercial entities should be classified separately for monitoring and control purposes. Control could be addressed through a separate Public Enterprise Act for public trading enterprises. Countries like Ghana and Malawi have employed governance control through a public enterprise, or the State-Owned Enterprise Act.

With the reform of the public sector and public enterprises, there needs to be a coherent and well-articulated vision and strategy. The reform agenda cannot be imposed from external sources if it is to be sustainable and successful. There must be a high degree of local inputs and ownership, including at the level of the prime minister and the minister of finance. Of critical importance is the quality of the consultants recruited to support public sector reform and privatisation programmes with knowledge transfer to ensure continuity, as well as the alignment of incentives to support the long-term sustainability of the programmes. It is also important to consider that both the public and private sectors have important functions to fulfil in a mixed economy, which is what most economies are today; competing in some respects and cooperating in others, in such a manner that neither should frustrate the other. One can also expect the relative importance of each sector in contemporary mixed economies will continue to shift, with changing sector performances, changing ideas, and policies.

One of the important structural changes that the Jamaican economy has experienced is increasing the level of urbanisation alongside rural depopulation. As urbanisation increases the proportion of economic activities in the primary sector (agriculture, manufacturing, and mining) decreases; conversely, the share of the services sector (financial, tourism, and telecommunications) increases, accounting for over 65 per cent of economic activities by 1970. As society urbanises, the service sector increases and more of its activities become monetised, with major implications for the public sector, especially municipal public sector management. Until recently, management of major urban centres and municipal management were restricted largely to the experiences of the Kingston and St Andrew Corporation (KSAC) as outside of Kingston and St Andrew, until 1943 the population size above five thousand of the urbanising towns were few. Jamaica now has three urbanising towns with a population of over one hundred thousand and nine with a population of over twenty thousand, presenting major environmental problems from unplanned development, creating the need for improved urban planning and professional municipal public management.

The early population settlement and economic structure in Jamaica was a deterrent to developing self-sufficient towns. Jamaica cannot continue a policy of dependent urbanisation and development, or with a policy of 'infilling' as is now being pursued in Kingston. The 2023 earthquake, which devastated major parts of Turkey, should be a warning sign for Jamaica.

This vision for new Jamaican towns and cities of the future should be to move away from the colonial legacy, which historically shaped the growth of towns. Jamaica now needs to plan the development of its next two or three major urban centres to accommodate population sizes varying from one hundred and fifty thousand to two hundred and fifty thousand, over the next two decades, to avoid further unplanned urbanisation and environmental degradation, and a decline in the quality of life. The decline of agriculture has had a major impact on the parishes, being the main source of employment. The underperformance of the local agricultural sector has resulted in Jamaica becoming a net importer of food and a fall in the quality of people's diet, now partially supplied with imports mainly from the US. Jamaica's development policy must find a solution to the large tracts of fertile agricultural land that now lie idle and is threatened by unplanned development.

WHAT HAVE WE LEARNED?

Negatives of Jamaica's Privatisation

Despite undergoing significant structural adjustments since 1980, Jamaica has shown limited evidence of reaping the benefits of these changes. Privatisation efforts between 1980 and 2005 have resulted in one of the poorest economic performances within the Caribbean region during that period. As a result, many Jamaicans have shifted their focus towards pursuing future opportunities by migrating to North America rather than relying on the prospects offered by the domestic economy. Criticisms of the privatisation programme have been made concerning its implementation. It was widely believed that the emphasis placed on financial performance and inflows overshadowed the importance of implementing efficiency measures after privatisation. Insufficient attention was given to optimising operational efficiency. The sale of Telecommunications of Jamaica came under scrutiny from the media and the public. It was criticised for granting British C&W a forty-nine-year monopoly and a guaranteed rate of return, ranging from 17.5 per cent to 20 per cent on capital after tax and on revalued assets. The situation was further exacerbated because the chairman of the company also held the position of chairman of Jamintel, representing C&W London's interests, while simultaneously serving as a key advisor to the government of Jamaica on the privatisation transaction..

Privatisation of the sugar industry and the public passenger transport company were costly affairs to taxpayers. The sugar estates and factories encountered problems in the initial privatisation transactions and were returned to the government after two earlier attempts. The last sugar privatisations after 2009 again proved a failure and almost all the assets privatised have been returned to the government.

Imperial preferential trade arrangements gave colonial administrators and Jamaican politicians a false sense of security, which resulted in modernisation of the sugar industry being undertaken until it was too late. Jamaica failed to modernise its sugar and banana industries in the 1950s and again at the end of the 1970s, seeing the industry as an export business. The entire viability of Jamaica's agricultural sector has been destroyed over the last three decades with the termination of preferential trade agreements. The EU has now accepted that these preferential schemes which benefitted Jamaica and ACP countries in the post-war years are now untenable in the modern trading era and no longer need Jamaica and the Caribbean sugar and banana, hence the industry has become dispensable.

The economic fundamentals of the agricultural industry are such that without some element of trade protection, it makes no difference whether it is publicly, privately, or mixed owned. Jamaica could not achieve competitive sugar production after four hundred years. It is doubtful that a competitive industry could now be achieved because Jamaica has neither the research nor development infrastructure required for the efficient production of sugar and banana for the export market. Jamaica now has only two companies operating in the sugar industry and they have confined their operations to the production of rum and rum cream where there is some competitive advantages and niche marketing is possible. Interestingly, these two companies have been in the private sector since the days of slavery and were never privatised. The government now finds itself with large swathes of the most fertile lands in Jamaica without knowing what to do with these lands. The upshot seems to be unplanned property development, a repetition of Portmore, except that Portmore was marginal lands. Portmore was never designed as a new town. It was a Matalon/West Indies Home Construction project to build twelve thousand houses.

The earlier Air Jamaica privatisation proved to be expensive to the Treasury in the post-privatisation era as in the pre-privatisation era. The taxpayers were saddled for years with responsibility for loan guarantees to meet AJ's capital requirements and direct funding of the airline's losses. Besides absorbing major debts of Air Jamaica in the earlier privatisation, the government, in addition, had to provide loan guarantees to the order of US$54 million. This privatisation presented a major conflict of interest in the case of the majority shareholder, a hotel operator.

Developing countries, such as Jamaica, often face challenges in negotiations when selling state assets that require significant capital investments from foreign firms, as seen in the electricity and telecommunications sectors. In such situations, these firms may aim to secure advantageous terms and conditions for themselves. An important lesson learned from these experiences is that ownership alone is not sufficient; the structure of the arrangement is equally crucial. A structure that promotes competition should be the preferred objective. It is competition that fosters incentives for both productive and allocative efficiency.

Benefits of Jamaica's Privatisation

Fifteen of the thirty-one companies listed on the Jamaica Stock Exchange in 1990 were totally or partially privatised SOEs, giving a boost to the stock market between 1985 and 1990. Privatisation of NCB was therefore an important trendsetter, showing that small domestic stock markets can accommodate privatisation. Overall, privatisation facilitated the development of Jamaica's embryonic stock market and has brought a wider section of society into the mainstream of productive investment. Among the twenty-six developing countries which the World Bank listed as carrying out privatisation programmes in the 1980s and 1990s, Jamaica has been highly ranked.

Several of the privatised entities benefitted from significant inflows of capital and technology, such as the hotel and the telecommunication companies, and this has allowed for modernisation, higher levels of efficiency and higher quality products and services to the consumer. In the case of TOJ, prices for domestic telephone rates remained fixed after the 1987 privatisation until 1996, with the number of lines increasing twofold. Cellular phones and privatised operation have brought prices down to the level of availability to almost all Jamaicans.

The government and the Ministry of Finance have benefited from the flow of income, as well as domestic and foreign exchange which have been transferred to the Treasury. Loss-making enterprises have been removed as a burden to the national budget, with the effect of contributing to the reduction in the size of the budget deficit. The government has received foreign exchange inflows to allow it to meet crucial financial tests by the IMF as part of the objective of stabilising the foreign exchange rate. In the first ten years, over fifty companies were transferred to private ownership. Of the seventy entities and assets listed for divestment in Ministry Paper No. 34 in 1991, more than half were divested by 1995. Excluding the privatisation of land and municipal services, proceeds from divestment over the period 1981–95 amounted to US$275.5 million.[1]

There have not been sufficient detailed studies of pre-and post-privatisation periods in Jamaica to determine the comparative benefits and efficiencies over the two periods. However, international studies indicate that privatised industries in competitive markets do better in the post-privatisation period. With privatisation of monopolies, the result is nuanced. One of the few detailed studies undertaken to date in Jamaica showed that the performance of NCB during the post-privatisation five-year period in terms of real revenue growth, growth of assets, growth in deposits and market share was weaker than in the five years period prior to privatisation. In the pre-divestment period cost to revenue averaged 75 per cent, while in the post-divestment period the average was 79 per cent.[2] There, indication is that once a company is designated for privatisation, several forces come into play to incentivise improved performances.

On completion, the new PPP Highway 2000 Network was expected to bring significant economic benefits, such as reduced travel time, increased productivity to commercial users, and reduction of vehicle operating costs because of the provision of a better road surface. It was also expected to serve as a catalyst for economic development along the route and the main tourist areas bordering the route. Although resources from these schemes have assisted the government to increase the delivery of road infrastructure, the implications for the government's stock arises. According to an analysis by Nekiesha Spenser, deferred debt financing has increased the debt stock of the government of Jamaica. Jamaicans will eventually be responsible for servicing of the debt owed if Trans-Jamaican Highway cannot pay back its commercial loans.[3] While Jamaica may have been successful with the privatisation of firms in competitive markets, its experience with privatisation of utilities and regulated industries has not been exemplary. The government has found privatisation of the defunct rail system and water industry extremely difficult to execute and has yet to transfer those two sectors to the private operators.

General Lessons Learnt

- The privatisation of the larger infrastructure enterprises has proved far more difficult to execute. This directly results from the complex and often competing objectives, the need to satisfy competing and conflicting special interest groups and the sheer difficulty of privatising firms which traditionally were characterised as natural monopolies. The trade-offs among the various objectives and competing interest groups can be politically intractable. Invariably, the consumer benefits are at the lower end of the priorities. The desire for the new managers to maintain powers of influence and the opportunity for clientism can be powerful factors deterring privatising utilities.

- Privatisation affects the economic and social environment. The privatisation process helps to clarify and redefine the role of the state in areas of production and regulation. In areas of infrastructure privatisation, the role is shifted from the state being a producer to that of a regulator. By privatisation of firms and breaking up monopolies, competitive pressures are induced in the economy, and this should lead to greater productive efficiency. Competition based on economic pricing principles force firms to be more efficient, eliminate inefficiency and, in this process, offer competitive prices to the consumer and enhance consumer surplus and allocative efficiencies.
- By clarifying property rights and the rules of commercial contracts, the conditions for attracting investment and entrepreneurial initiatives are enhanced. Privatisation allows for introducing management technology and special management skills, which can lead to the development of new products and markets.
- In the Jamaican situation, there are several lessons for other developing countries: Privatisation must form a part of the macroeconomic and structural adjustment programme. Sequencing therefore becomes a critical problem.
- In changing from state controlled or state managed economies there is the need to establish the appropriate commercial infrastructure. The focus of the divestment effort should go beyond selling off state assets. Restrictive business practices and monopoly forms of operation will not go away overnight. There will be the need to introduce competition, anti-trust, and fair-trading laws to support the competitive process and enhance the rights of consumers.
- It was necessary for the government to remodel the civil service and public bodies sector as a major new initiative in 1990, incorporating incentives and practices from the private sector. In fact, 1990–2005 saw the execution of the largest institutional building programme in Jamaica in the public bodies and civil

service sector since Sir John Peter Grant's initiatives in the 1870s. It is in this period that the executive agency institutional form was introduced, totally transforming the delivery of public services, with users of public services considered as 'customers' as against being seen as burdensome taxpayers. Public bodies were given the authority to introduce accrual accounting and to charge user fees, incentivising efficiency of their operations.

- Privatisation is a revenue enhancing measure for the state's Treasury. Between 1981 and 1989, the revenue generated for sales and leases amounted to 31.26 per cent of GDP, Between 1990 and 1998, proceeds from privatisation amounted to J$5.25 billion, approximately 19.8 per cent of government revenues and 6.2 per cent of the GDP..
- Privatisation will only succeed if the various sectors in the society perceive individual benefits and if the process is transparent. In the case of the privatisation of NCB and Caribbean Cement Company public perception of success was important to subsequent privatisation, hence a trade-off between the best value for the shares and wider public participation may be necessary.
- Privatisation can occur in an environment of a thin domestic capital market. At the time, the privatisation programme was initiated, only thirty-four firms were listed on the stock market, with a small shareholder base. The Jamaican experiences show that the public can respond to new investment initiatives. Measures should be built into the process to encourage smaller investors. Underdeveloped capital markets in themselves are not major impediments to privatisation. A substantial portion of NCB shares was taken up by borrowed funds.
- The Jamaican early experiences highlight the importance of an appropriate strategy consistent with the domestic economic environment. The preferred approach by the World Bank and USAID called for the drawing up of a long list of entities which offered divestment potential. The case-by-case approach adopted by the JLP administration of the 1980s went against the grain. In the early stages, where the learning process is important and there is a need to develop the technical skills to execute the programme, long and ambitious lists can be counter-productive.

Success is going to be measured against this list. The selection of a critical number of enterprises and demonstrating that privatisation works may be preferable to a grand list initially.

- In the case of liberalisation and privatisation in the financial sector and privatisation of infrastructure and monopoly utilities, the development of an appropriate regulatory framework must be a precursor to privatisation. Liberalisation and privatisation were conducted in these sectors in Jamaica in the absence of an appropriate regulatory framework, and this has certainly contributed to high levels of failure in the financial sector and the exploitation by TOJ of its monopoly position in certain areas of operations. The government was too late in developing the regulatory regime for the financial sector and for the utilities. The view also is that the taxpayer should not have shouldered all the costs, as there were investors involved who were professionals, with some capability of assessing the risks involved in each investment.
- The Employee Share Ownership Programme was, to some extent, introduced to buy the support of the trade unions and workers and had nothing to do with economic efficiency. The restraint on the levels of equity ownership, while socially desirable again, did not enhance economic efficiency.
- Old company laws which do not clearly define property rights, accountability, and reporting responsibilities will require updating. These changes are necessary to protect less sophisticated investors who will be brought into the investment market. While Jamaica recognised the need for these changes, it was slow in its implementation, and most of the legal changes came long after introducing the programme.
- Foreign participation in the investment process must be carefully considered and planned. At the same time, the state will need to be practical and avoid confusing foreign direct investment with issues of sovereignty and nationalism. The areas that require large amounts of capital, access to technology and skilled management such as the utilities and the financial sector are the areas which are sensitive to the criticism of 'selling out to foreigners.' The sale of 80 per cent of TOJ to Cable and Wireless, and the response of the public coloured public

perception towards subsequent overseas private investment in electricity and the airports. The negative public reaction which has been demonstrated seemed more towards the method of sale, the monopoly rights which were granted, and the price-fixing formula. It is possible to structure joint venture deals with local private and overseas investors, which minimise the perceived negative impact of foreign direct investment.

- The institutional mechanism and the level of leadership provided are also critical to success. The diffusion of privatisation responsibilities over several ministries is ill-advised because it fosters duplication of effort and often results in unskilled persons effecting divestment. In a small developing country, a centralised institution as with the NIBJ is advisable. The prime minister must be directly involved and provide active leadership to the programme. Only the prime minister or a president with his over-riding authority can deal with ministers and ministries that see privatisation as a mechanism for the reduction of their power base and who operate to hinder the process.
- The privatisation process is long, especially for economies which developed sizeable public sector holdings. Even after three decades of privatisation, Jamaica still has a sizeable public sector. Public attitudes toward divestment will vary over time. Long-term commitment is therefore needed, and the temptation to extract political mileage when the public may seem disillusioned should be resisted.
- An important lesson for developing countries embarking on forms of infrastructure project development and implementation, without previous experience in the field, is that governments need to listen to the developers and investors and the financial market and be prepared to adjust the original design to accommodate financial and investor market needs. In the case of PPP, there is no better advice than exhaustive preparation.
- In addressing its economic problem, Jamaica has had to turn to the neoliberal economic policies of the IMF and World Bank since the 1980s and WTO trade liberalisation since 1995. These policies have had the most long-lasting effects on economic performance and the structure of the economy,

virtually dismantling the agrarian sector. The period 1990–2001 saw a steady decline in local food production year in year out, accompanied concurrently by a steady increase in food imports. The declines have been associated with an increase in acreage of idle land and increasing rural poverty.

- There have been several criticisms of IMF neoliberal economic policy and structural adjustment reform over the period 1980–2010. They were externally driven and half-heartedly implemented by successive Jamaican governments. Most notably, Joseph Stiglitz, a leading international economist who had spent time at the World Bank stated that the time frame prescribed by the IMF policies which tried to force resources to move from less productive sectors to more productive sectors was too short.[4] The IMF's one-size-fits-all approach to structural adjustment pointed to the absence of consideration of historical and local realities.
- The World Bank attributed some reasons for the failure of the economic adjustment before 2010 to excessive delays in addressing the fiscal balance, and the exchange rate, too much reliance on overseas financing, excessive tightening on public spending and credit, crippling public investments. The loans were overloaded with conditionalities, often peripheral to the industry where the privatisation is taking place. In terms of relationship with the IMF, the Bank relied on the Fund on questions of short-term economic management and stabilisation. There was, therefore, a gap in terms of medium-term considerations, and there were often inconsistencies between the Bank's programmes and those of the IMF. For example, imposing unprogrammed import duties conflicted with import liberalisation.
- In the development of a market economy, the creation of new market-oriented institutions becomes necessary. Political economy examines the interplay between institutions and human behaviour, highlighting how institutions influence choices and how human behaviour, in turn, leads to changes in institutional frameworks. The development of the competition policy and competition law in Jamaica is a classic example of the reshaping of a market economy by ascribing a wider role for the

private sector in the production and distribution of goods and services and in the allocation of economic resources. Private sector development and competition are inextricably linked in economic development, and competition plays a major role in improving allocative and productive efficiency.

- The Jamaican economy emerged in the 2000s as a small, technologically, and financially dependent one, with limited capacity to diversify production on its own. The country's debt to GDP over the period 1990–2002 averaged 117.6 per cent, peaking at 148.5 per cent in 2002, placing Jamaica among the most indebted countries in the world. Debt servicing in the beginning of the 2000s consumed 50 per cent of the recurrent budget, and interest payments was 16 per cent of GDP, leaving little for health, welfare, and education. This has been one of the root causes of Jamaica's poor GDP growth.
- Jamaica's major economic problem going into the future will be the debt problem. Jamaica addressed the problem by implementing a debt exchange programme between 2010 and 2013. This debt exchange was a condition of the IMF bailout of the economy. The programme provided debt service relief and, coupled with international financial support, it successfully reduced the debt burden and mitigated short-term liquidity risks. Certainly, the return to the IMF after 2009 contributed immensely to what seems to be the turnaround of the Jamaican economy. Growth in the economy, however, while positive, except for negative growth in the years 2012, 2017, 2019, was relatively small, typically under 1 per cent, with the best year being 2011 at 3.19 per cent. Growth in 2020 was minus 9.4 per cent because of the COVID-19 pandemic but rebounded to positive of 4.6 in 2021. Jamaica could resort to tax cuts for the first time in living memory.
- After forty years of unsuccessful attempts by the IMF to restructure the economy, important changes seem to have occurred at last. The IMF is now showcasing Jamaica as the example of a country that achieved macroeconomic stabilisation without political upheaval. This period however is too short to come to such optimistic concussion. The jury is still out.

Notes

1. Richard Bernal and Winsome Leslie, 'Privatization in the English-Speaking Caribbean: An Assessment,' Policy Papers on the Americas, Volume X, Study 7, University of Miami, Miami, 1997.
2. National Investment Bank of Jamaica, *Study on the Performance of the Privatized Companies, 1983–1990* (Kingston: NCB Group Limited, 1990).
3. Nekiesha Spenser, 'Financing Road Infrastructure,' Department of Government, UWI, 2006.
4. Joseph Stiglitz, *Globalisation and its Discontent* (New York: W.W. Norton & Company, 2003).

PART 4

Industry Liberalisation: Six Case Studies of Sector Privatisation

Privatisation of the Aviation Industry: Air Jamaica and the Two International Airports

BACKGROUND TO AVIATION SECTOR PRIVATISATION

The aviation industry in Jamaica in 1995 fell under the control of the Airports Authority of Jamaica (AAJ), which was established in 1974 as a statutory corporation. The AAJ owned and operated the two international airports: Sangster International in Montego Bay and Norman Manley International at Palisadoes, in Kingston. In addition, AAJ owned and operated the five domestic aerodromes: Boscobel in Ocho Rios (re-named the Ian Fleming International Airport), Tinson Pen in Kingston, Ken Jones in Port Antonio, as well as those in Negril and Mandeville. AAJ operated as a landlord, responsible for fire services and airport security matters. Security activities were contracted out to private sector firms.

Besides the airports, the government of Jamaica owned and operated Air Jamaica Limited, the national flag carrier and Trans-Jamaica Limited, the domestic airline. Figure 12.1 shows the location of the airports and aerodromes in Jamaica

The airlines contracted their ground handling services. The AAJ also concessioned out several services to the private sector, covering car hiring, catering, banking, and retailing, including duty-free retailing In 1994, AAJ's Kingston head office staff numbered 35, while Sangster employed 303 staff and Norman Manley 300. In addition, there were fifty-five staff members in the western and eastern divisions serving the aerodromes. Because of the financial demands made by the sector on the public purse, the two international airports and Air Jamaica were made a part of the privatisation programme that the PNP launched on returning to power in the 1990.

Figure 12.1: Current Location and Proposed International Airports and Aerodrome in Jamaica

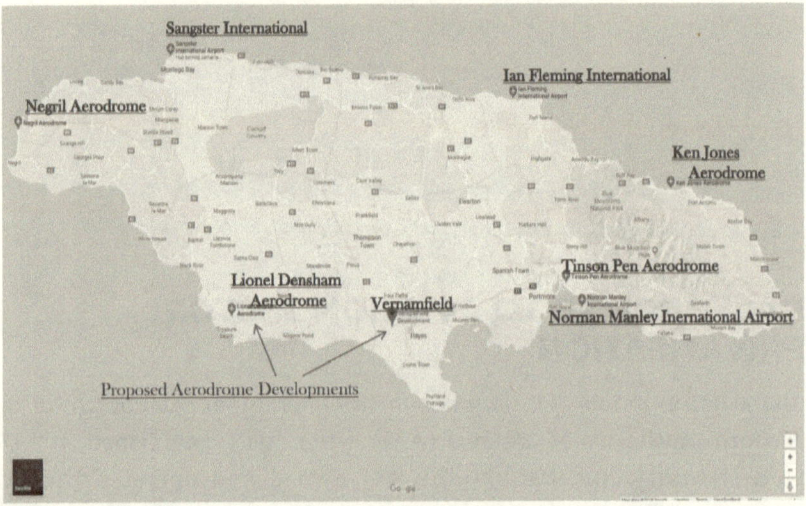

Source: Audley Deidrick, 'Jamaica's Airport PPP Experience,' presentation, Caribbean Workshop and Forum on Public Private Partnership for Debt Managers, Commonwealth Secretariat and DBJ, Kingston, Jamaica, June 2022.

The state also controlled the Civil Aviation Department (CAD), part of the Ministry of Public Utilities & Transport, providing air navigation services, air traffic control, communications, meteorology services, regulation of air safety, and regulation of airport activities. Plans were for Boscobel, ten miles out of Ocho Rio (now the Ian Fleming International Airport-IFLIA) to be developed into an international airport, providing services mainly to North America and the Caribbean. The Air Transport Licensing Board (ATLB), a statutory body, carried responsibility for the approval of air transport licences and permits and regulating prices relating to passenger and freight (excluding air navigation charges). International Aeradio Limited, another state-operated enterprise (SOE), formerly Aerotel, provided telecommunications services.

Airport charges were the subject of negotiation between the airports and the airlines; however, the agreed charges required the approval of the portfolio transport minister who carried responsibility for aviation policy and international air transport agreements, with the Ministry of Finance being responsible for customs, and the Ministry of National Security for immigration. The Ministry of Tourism handled matters related to the tourism industry and played a large part in the aviation industry's development, as tourism accounted for a major portion of air traffic.

Under extreme and continuing pressure from the huge external debt burden, Jamaica, like many Latin American countries in the 1980s, was pressured to seek market-based solutions, including the sale of national assets to generate funds for redeeming the national debt.[1]

As part of the restructuring of the aviation sector, the Portland Group of the UK was engaged by AAJ in 1994 to carry out a study on aviation sector regulation, funded by the IDB.[2] The restructuring provided for the unbundling of AAJ and the creation of two subsidiary companies: Norman Manley International Airport Limited and Sangster International Airport Limited, in readiness for their privatisation. Initially, the two companies were to operate independently of AAJ, with their own boards of directors.

The regulatory legislations governing the operation of air travel and airport operations were set out in the Airport Law (1969), the Civil Aviation Act (1996), and the Colonial Air Navigation Order of 1961. As a part of the airline industry restructuring, new legislation was put in place to corporatise the CAD and create an independent Civil Aviation Authority (CAA).[3] A decision was also made to proceed first with the privatisation of SIA and to focus on an initial physical improvement programme at NMIA, including the construction of a new air terminal building, new baggage handling facilities, and major rehabilitation of the airport runway, which had fallen into a deplorable condition. In addition to privatising the airports, the government was committed to privatising Air Jamaica, the national airline, as part of the conditions under the World Bank Structural Adjustment Loan Programme.

Privatising Air Jamaica

Unlike the airports, the characteristic of the airline industry is that it can be operated in competitive markets. Nevertheless, over the years governments have sought to impose a high degree of regulation on the industry, especially entry into the market on the principle that unrivalled competition would lead inevitably to rate wars, resulting in the lowering of safety standards and turmoil in the industry. The concern then was that a liberalised airline market would work against the interest of the consumers. Liberalisation and privatisation of the airline industry in the 1990s in the UK and the US, however, demonstrated that competitive outcomes could be achieved, and this was possible even in small airline markets, as long as it was relatively easy for new airline providers to enter and leave the market.

Historically, the case for regulation and public ownership of airlines was not based on the rationale that airlines were natural monopolies but on the argument that a deregulated industry and competition would lead to destructive outcomes in terms of quality of services, continuity, reliability, and safety, as well as presenting opportunities for discrimination against some groups of customers.[4] Regulation, however, more than anything, repressed innovation and protected inefficient firms, resulting in a misallocation of resources by throwing prices out of alignment with marginal costs. Deregulation did not produce the dire consequences previously predicted. The US action in liberalisation of the industry in the 1980s set off a wave of aviation sector deregulation and privatisation globally.

The global airline industry in the 1990s was characterised by extensive levels of state ownership, with the US being an exception. The US was one of the first countries to liberalise its airline market in 1978 and, despite the US's deregulation efforts, the world airline industry continued to be heavily regulated. In the US, the airlines historically were mostly owned by the private sector and were subject to public regulation by the United States Civil Aviation Board. In the UK and Europe, the situation was the reverse, with airlines being owned by the states. Privatisation of the airline industry was first initiated by the Thatcher government in the UK, leading to the privatisation of British Airways (BA) in 1986 through a public offer.

While, from a commercial point of view, only a few airlines can serve a route, the threat of competition may provide for competitive prices. In other words, the market at least can be made contestable.[5] The practice, however, had developed, whereby government-owned airlines were provided with huge subsidies to their national flag carrier, based on the view that a national airline was in the overall economic interest of the country. With weakened incentives for productive efficiencies, and with the existence of strong market power, the environment was provided to airline workers and unions to propagate highly restrictive work rules and to seek more than market rates for labour. One of the major problems, which worked to the disadvantage of the government in the Air Jamaica privatisation, was the restrictive work rules and the airline's elaborate and costly fringe benefit schemes.

In a cartelised market, most states act to set prices to protect the survival of their national airline. As well as regulating security, safety, noise, and service standards, there were high degrees of economic regulation, and this was so for Air Jamaica's traffic in both domestic and international markets. Economic regulation of scheduled international flights was, and still is governed by bilateral air service agreements between governments. This provided each government with the power to determine that one or more of a country's national airlines can operate services between both countries and into designated airports.

These agreements specify capacity limits for existing airlines, require airfares to be approved by each country, and regulate entry of new players to the airline market. National governments are therefore actively involved in the allocation of routes, fixing of airline fares, entry licensing of airlines, and regulating the use of their domestic airports. Airfares are also coordinated by the airline cartel: the International Air Transport Association (IATA). In most situations where bilateral arrangements exist, approvals from both governments are needed to effect changes to airfares, for new entrants to the industry, and for introducing additional services on existing routes.

Air transport as modern industry came about at the turn of the last century. It did not exist until after the Second World War, and its share of passenger transport traffic was negligible. It was during this War that its true potential as an economically viable mode of transportation came to be realised. Towards the end of the Second World War, around fifty-five governments met at what has become to be known as the Chicago Convention in late 1944 to set up the international regulatory framework, as it relates to international air transport rights that should be allocated among the nation signing the convention. At the time, fifty-four countries signed the agreement and since then over 190 countries have signed and have become members of the International Civil Aviation Organisation (ICAO). The convention established five basic principles called the five freedoms, which form the basis of air transport regulation except for the five freedoms, outlining a laissez faire approach in determining air transport tariff, which became unacceptable to most nations. At the Bermuda convention in 1946, bilateral arrangement replaced multilateral agreement where each pair of nation state were given allocation right to carry passenger between the two territories. Airlines that may carry traffic between two states must be airlines of either state or both. Each state was required to designate the airline or airline from each country, which it would allow to operate on a route between the two countries, with the only restriction being capacity on each route allowed.

The other important institution regarding regulation of the industry is that of the International Air Transport Association (IATA). This is an inter-airline (as opposed to an international) association which attempts to set fares to be charged between points on international routes. In the US, however, the Civil Aeronautics Board of 1938 was not granted the power to approve rate fixing agreements. The US government decided informally to recognise the rate fixing agreement of IATA, making IATA a powerful body in international aviation industry.[6] A characteristic of Caribbean air transport industry is that it is dominated by tourism, mainly North American originated, giving the US a powerful say in regional transport matters. With airports, the US regulatory authority sets conditions that must be met by each country's airport which is used as origin and destination points regarding US traffic.

Air Jamaica's Market in the 1980 and 1990s

Most of Jamaica's airline traffic has been between two countries: the US and the UK. Traffic to the UK can readily be routed through Miami; therefore, Air Jamaica encountered a fair degree of competition in one of its main markets. Governments like Jamaica's are continuously exposed to the lobby of powerful interest groups to provide and protect their interests, while there is often very weak lobby to protect the interests of airline customers. Airline regulation in Jamaica centred on tariff and security and, in the case of tariff, it was enforced to protect the national flag carrier, leading to higher market prices. This income redistribution practice resulted in consumers paying higher prices to Air Jamaica, the US and UK airlines. There were also powerful lobbies against the removal of regulations.

The government of Jamaica justified the national flag carrier on the grounds of externalities: the socio-economic benefits of national sovereignty, which it claimed, and to support the development of the tourist industry and the economy. As yet, no one has seriously placed a cost on these nebulous externalities. It has yet to be shown that the overseas airlines would fail to compete and take up the tourist and business traffic to and from Jamaica in the absence of a national flag carrier. Despite the existing restrictions caused by regulation, Air Jamaica faced higher levels of competition than normally prevailed in a cartelised market or in many other markets where two or more governments operate to restrict services. In its main market – Jamaica to the US, several US carriers may offer services into Kingston and Montego Bay, and in addition, there is intensive competition from charter services.

Development and Growth of Air Jamaica

Following independence in 1962, Jamaica entered an agreement with Trinidad and Tobago (British West Indian Airways) and the British government (British Overseas Airways Corporation) and formed a partnering agreement in August 1963 to provide for the first Jamaican airline. Air Jamaica Air Services Limited, owned by the government 51 per cent, BOAC 33 per cent, and BWIA 16 per cent. BWIA employees in Kingston were transferred to the new airline, with services beginning between Kingston and Miami and New York on May 1, 1996.

Without alerting its partners, the government established a new airline, Air Jamaica (1968), in partnership with Air Canada. The establishment of Air Jamaica (1968) followed from a feasibility study carried out in 1966, and the new airline began operation on April 1, 1969. It started operating as a joint venture, with the government holding 60 per cent of the equity and Air Canada the remaining 40 per cent, with Air Canada as the managing partner. The initial route network – Kingston and Montego Bay to New York and Miami – was operated by three McDonald Douglas aircraft and one DC-9-30 aircraft. The last-minute change of heart by the Jamaican government to pursue a more independent approach for Jamaican air services post-independence came as a major surprise to the Trinidad and Tobago (T&T) government and developed into a major diplomatic problem between Jamaica and, in particular, with the then Trinidad prime minister, Eric Williams. This rupture was to affect diplomatic relationships between the two countries for several years, already made tense by Jamaica's decision to secede from the West Indies Federation in 1961 prior to gaining Independence. For Eric Williams, Jamaica was not a country to be trusted regarding its words.

Early Growth and Financial Performance of Air Jamaica

In the 1970s, Air Jamaica proceeded to rapidly expand its route network, flying to thirteen destinations, mainly with used equipment, providing services into Chicago, Philadelphia, Toronto, Detroit, Puerto Rico, and Montreal besides the original Miami and New York routes. Long-haul services to Europe (London and Frankfurt) commenced on April 1, 1974. The annual number of passengers carried increased from 139,619 in 1969 to 674,000 in 1976 because of the expansion of the tourist traffic. A Boeing 727 aircraft was added to the fleet towards the end of the 1970s.[7]

While growth slowed in the 1980s, new routes to Baltimore and Atlanta in the US were nevertheless added. Route and fleet expansion in the 1980s was often not based on financial justification. In 1983, Air Jamaica commenced non-stop operation with a Boeing 747-100 from Kingston to London, with this flight continuing to Frankfurt. Later, an Air Airbus A300 aircraft was added to the fleet, flying non-stop from Kingston to John F. Kennedy International Airport in the US. In 1980, the government acquired Air Canada's 40 per cent equity holding, so Air Jamaica became a fully publicly owned enterprise.

Air Jamaica started operations from inception with a weak capital base. It had never corrected this problem over the years and, while it made a surplus before interest charges in the initial years, thereafter it made continuous losses and exposed the Jamaican government's treasury to continuing financial burden. In the twenty-two years of its operation up to 1992, it had run up steady losses most of the years. In thirty-two years of operation (1968–2000), Air Jamaica made annual losses, except for two years.[8]

By 1993, the company had a fleet of five A-300-Airbuses, and four Boeing 727-200 aircraft, which were fully owned or were bought under a capital lease programme from the manufacturers, or from international airlines. A service to Los Angeles was provided contractually to Jamaica Vacations Limited (JAMVAC). The Los Angeles route was extended in July 1989 to San Francisco through the leasing of an L1011 Tri-Star aircraft from Hawaiian Airlines. The airline also added services to Grand Cayman and Curaçao. A change in market conditions, however, made some of the North American routes uneconomic, forcing cutbacks in some routes in January 1990. Service to Tampa was discontinued in February 1990, and the service to Toronto, Canada, was replaced by a joint service operated by Air Canada under a commercial agreement from April 1990. In addition to regular and charter services, the company also operated cargo services, which significantly expanded with the acquisition of the two Airbus aircraft from Varig Airlines.

In the markets Air Jamaica operated in 1993, its main competitors are American and Continental Airlines, see table 12.1 below. The New York and Newark routes were the most competitive, coming from both American and Continental.

Table 12.1: Competitive Airlines on Air Jamaica Routes in the 1990

Air Jamaica Market Competition Routes	Direct Market Share	Competitors
Miami	65 %	American Airlines
New York/Newark	42 %	American and Continental
Atlanta	100 %	Nil
Philadelphia	100 %	Nil
Baltimore	100 %	Nil
To Jamaica	60 %	American and Continental

Source: Air Jamaica: Annual Report, March 1990.

In 1989, the government announced plans to privatise the airline, but it was not until May 1994 that the partial sell-off took place. From a financial perspective, Air Jamaica had performed poorly over the five years to 1992, with accumulated deficits of J$191 million in fiscal year 1989, J$321 million in fiscal year 1990, and J$304 million in fiscal year 1991. Losses mounted considerably from J$31.7 million in 1985 to an all-time high of J$118 million in 1991. Because of these losses, the government was required periodically to inject large sums into the airline's operation from its inception. Cash infusion in 1990 was J$286.7 million and for 1991 J$291.7 million. The company's finances showed it would not have retired more than 55 per cent of its current liabilities through liquidation of its current assets.

Table 12.2 below shows operating revenues for the period 1991 and 1992. The company carried a negative working capital for most of the period. The government had to guarantee loans amounting to several millions of dollars to cover lease payments for the company's fixed assets, which were primarily for aircraft and ground equipment.

Table 12.2: Air Jamaica Operating Revenues (J$000) 1990–91

Revenue Source	1991	1990	Change %
Passenger	903,973	891,942	1
Freight	85,310	68,750	19
Charter	74,155	11,502	85
Other	79,155	112,653	- 42
Total	1,143,062		5

Source: Air Jamaica Financial Report, March 1991

In 1993, the lease payments totalled J$136 million, primarily for aircraft. The projected lease payments for 1994 and 1995 were J$143 million and J$105 million, respectively. Additionally, there was a further estimate of J$700 million for the period from 1996 to 2000. Between 1990 and 1991, passenger traffic revenues increased by 1 per cent per cent, cargo traffic by 19 per cent, with charter services increasing by 85 per cent. The company showed an operating loss of US$11 million in 1993/94 financial year. In the 1990s, Air Jamaica experienced significant problems with US customs, arising out of the transportation of unmanifested cargo, mostly drugs, resulting in fines amounting to US$3 million in 1990. The company had considerable long-term liabilities. If Air Jamaica then was a privately owned company, it would have been insolvent and placed in receivership. A major problem with Air Jamaica's operations was that it could not integrate into a global or regional airline market arrangement that would have provided the airline with the opportunity to benefit from economies of scale in areas like aircraft procurement, as well as being able to benefit from a hub and spoke traffic structure. Table 12.3 shows the financial forecast of Air Jamaica for the financial year 1993/94.

The value of Air Jamaica, to a certain extent, depended on the level to which the government was prepared to maintain a high fare structure and, in so doing, transfer income from consumers to producers.

The higher the tariff levels the greater the potential profits to a privatised operator. The privatised operator also has a strong incentive to preserve the existing regulation.

Table 12.3: Air Jamaica's Financial Forecast 1993/94

Statistics	1993/94
US$ per mile	$0.14
Passenger Revenues US$000	158 440
Cargo	11,828
Charter	5,376
Incidentals	8,602
Total	184,247
Expenses (Salaries)	32,661
(Aircraft leases)	31,560
Total Expenses	195,881
Profit/Loss	- (11.634)

Source: NCB 1995

Air Jamaica Privatisation

In late 1989, the Jamaican government announced plans to privatise the fully state-owned Air Jamaica. In April 1990, invitations for expressions of interest were sent to British Airways, Air Canada, and Delta Airlines, but in all cases, the responses were negative. The government then held discussions with Dullum Company, a venture capital company based in Washington DC, on a proposal involving the International Finance Corporation, local private investors, and employees. Dullum eventually withdrew its offer in April 1991. Preliminary discussions then followed with Okado Group of Nigeria, also in 1991, and again the outcome was further disappointment as Okada decided not to pursue further participation in the divestiture. In June 1991, National Commercial Bank Group, the major local commercial bank and Cochrane Investments of Canada, made an offer to the government. Failure to arrive at an understanding between NCB and the government negotiating team on the basic principles for sale resulted in NCB withdrawing its offer. Austin Blades Finance, on behalf of the Austrian Airlines and Swissair also held discussions with the Jamaican government, without moving to the stage of a formal offer.

Having failed to secure a buyer, the government made a second privatisation attempt in October 1992. Invitations for 'Expressions of Interest' were again sent out to the Aviation Leasing Group in the US, Austin Blades, Marsio Aviation Enterprise (USA), NCB Group Limited, and S.G. Warburg and Company. Austin Blades wanted the government to treat with them exclusively (sole source), but this was refused. They then withdrew from the scene. Aviation Leasing Group submitted a proposal in December 1992 but refused to supply the negotiating team with the information requested, resulting in withdrawal of their offer. The only serious expression of interest came from the NCB Group in January 1993. NCB's proposal called for the government to assume responsibility for the full redundancy costs; coverage of existing guarantees; provision of a fifteen-year tax exemption on profits and dividends, provision of a special discount on fuel (at the level of ten US cents), suspension of part of the airport tax for five years, and for the government to bring in US$7 million in equity. Based on a valuation carried out by Avmark Airline Consultants, the market value of Air Jamaica was established by NCB at US$51.8 million in March 1993. This was further reduced to US$30 million because of losses sustained after 1993. Avmark also advised NCB that there were several serious shortcomings associated with the operations of the airline. The Airbus fleet was considered unsuitable for the route structure then in existence; certain provisions of workers' agreements, as they related to the flight crew and flight attendants carried serious cost implications, and the employees' attitude was inimical to achievement of a viable operation. The government considered the offer and recommended the conclusion of an agreement in mid-1993, subject to NCB meeting certain conditions. At the end of 1993, no firm understanding was reached and, as a result, the discussions were terminated in early 1994.

The World Bank, in its review of the Air Jamaica privatisation efforts in 1993, listed several reasons for their failure:

- Lack of formal privatisation process and procedures;
- No clear definition of terms of reference provided to the different actors of the government regarding their tasks;
- No prospectus or information memorandum was prepared presenting to investors the main features, situation at privatisation, and potential of the company;

- The valuation of the company which was carried out failed to fully recognise the value of the route rights;
- There was no air transport policy and a regulatory framework for the aviation sector; hence, it was not possible to explain to a private operator the regulatory rules such an operator would be required to follow; and
- The airline's management, as a group, was involved in the negotiations, creating conflicts of interest. The role of the managers of the company should have been to provide technical support to the process and the necessary information and not be directly involved in the negotiations.

The government had failed to set out clearly its policy on the proportion of the company's shares that it expected to retain. In order for the airline to benefit from national flag status, 51 per cent of equity had to be owned by Jamaican shareholders. The privatisation was constrained by the need to place control of the airline in national hands so as not to lose standing in bilateral negotiations. This has been a common problem with airline privatisation in Latin America and in developing countries. This was in sharp contrast to the constraints encountered in the privatisation of telecommunications. The requirement for a 51 per cent local shareholding seemed to have discouraged foreign investors.

The traffic rights, which accrued under the international agreements, while necessitating majority Jamaican ownership, did not call for the government as a shareholder. There was lack of clear leadership, and this was further complicated by the multiplicity of agencies which were involved in the negotiations: NIBJ, the Special Privatisation Committee, the management of Air Jamaica, the Ministry of Public Utilities and Transport and the Ministry of Finance, with no clarification of their respective roles. Air Jamaica also had, up to 1999, the right of first refusal to operate any new route granted to Jamaica, as well as the right to oppose the operation of a foreign carrier that could represent a threat to its position. This aspect of the agreement was never reassessed from a legal standpoint.

The period 1990–94 was an exercise of failed attempts to sell the airline, including an attempted merger with Trinidad and Tobago's British West Indian Airlines. In the divestiture of an airline like Air Jamaica, there were two options: restructuring the balance sheet of the company and selling the business, or the assets: the aircraft equipment and property and a set of privileges relating to route rights.[9] In a deregulated market, the value of the routes is virtually zero, as any airline has a right to enter. If regulation severely restricts market entry, then the routes will carry some value.

The Jamaican government could have liquidated the company and sold the physical assets of the airline, separate from the route rights. In fact, as Air Jamaica was bankrupt, with extensive liabilities in excess of assets, there was no airline as a going business to privatise. Most overseas airlines interested in the acquisition of Air Jamaica initially expressed interest only in the route rights. American Airlines was adamant there was no airline to sell. The asset-liability relationship of the airline was such that, if anything, the government needed to pay the private operator to take it over. In selling the routes, separate from the physical assets the cost to the government would have been much lower, as the routes carry attractive prices, and the pricing formula could have provided for the government to share in profits of the privatised airline if certain levels of traffic were achieved by the private operator.

The Third Attempt at the Privatisation of Air Jamaica

In January 1994, the new minister of finance, Dr Omar Davies, because of the size of Air Jamaica's impact on the fiscal budget, took a strong position on the airline's mounting financial cost to the Treasury, resulting in the minister announcing that the government would cease further financial support to Air Jamaica as of March 31, 1994. Price Waterhouse was then brought in to calculate the cost of liquidating Air Jamaica. The accounting firm's report submitted by the prime minister to the Jamaican Parliament had a liquidation cost of J$2.14 billion, as a worst case and J$1.4 billion as a best case, with the main difference being the treatment of the aircraft leases on termination.[10]

Certain members of the Cabinet continued to take the position that a national airline was strategic to the tourism industry and that national sovereignty was at stake, although no financial or economic data were ever provided to support this position. Airlines, like any operation, need to be treated as a business, eschewing considerations like national symbol or national sovereignty. Up to then, the operation of the airline was subordinated to the wider commercial objective. Despite this position of some of his cabinet colleagues, the minister of finance insisted the airline could not continue with business as usual. In early February 1994, he announced that Air Jamaica would be put up for privatisation a third time.

On this occasion, the negotiations were led by the minister for transport, Horace Clarke, instead of an enterprise negotiating team. Offers were received from two domestic interest groups: the Issa/Hart family led one group, which also included NCB and the Moo Young family (a well-known Jamaican entrepreneurial family, with major investments in the tourist industry). The other syndicate was led by Peter Rousseau from the Ciboney Hotel Group and included some Canadian investors who had previously served on the board of Air Jamaica when Air Canada was a shareholder. The first group offered to purchase only the routes and required that the government take over all the airline's liabilities. The Jamaican government rejected this proposal outright. The second group failed to provide evidence that they had the financing to complete the deal and the negotiations were terminated.

Later that year, another group led by Jamaican hotelier Gordon (Butch) Stewart and the Moo Young family, calling themselves the Air Jamaica Acquisition Group (AJAG), entered the picture at the last minute. In mid-1994, the consortium regrouped its principal investors to comprise the Appliance Traders Group (Stewart's trading company), the NCB Group, and the Moo Young family. An agreement was eventually struck with AJAG in May 1994, providing for a holding company, Air Jamaica Holdings, to take over the business of Air Jamaica.

The Sale Agreement

Details of the agreement are summarised as follows[11]:

- AJAG was to be allotted 70 per cent equity in the new company, with the government retaining 25 per cent (valued at US$9.375, or J$312 million) and the employees being allotted 5 per cent.
- The issued share capital of the new company was set at a nominal value of US$37.5 million and the agreement provided for AJAG to bring in US$26.25 million in new capital, paid in cash, while the government would be issued with J$500 million in deferred shares with conversion rights after two years.
- The government was required to take up all the redundancy costs for all eligible employees, as well as for any excess of current liability over current assets.

- The government was required to maintain the existing sovereign guarantees and, in consideration, received a fee of 1 per cent of the principal amount of such guaranteed sum.
- The agreement provided for an Employee Share Option Plan to be put in place within twelve months of takeover by AJAG.
- The divestiture agreement provided for the government to absorb debts from the old Air Jamaica Limited, amounting to J$1.42 billion and US$29.65 million.
- Appropriate tax incentive to be provided.
- AJAG, in demonstration of its intentions in completing the transaction, was required to put in place an escrow account amounting to US$1 million or the equivalent in Jamaican dollars on the signing of the agreement. In addition, within thirty days of signing, a further amount of J$33.3million was to be placed in the escrow account. Three days prior to the takeover date, the balance of US$24.25 million or the Jamaican dollar equivalent would be paid into the account.

The agreement was finally signed on November 1, 1994. PricewaterhouseCoopers had calculated that, had the company been liquidated at the end of September 1994, the government would have had to face an estimated cost of J$2.75 billion. It was then felt that divestment was the cheaper alternative to liquidation.

Problems of Operating under Private Majority Control

The problems of the national airline were numerous: over-paid airline crew; over-manned labour force with the workers practising very restrictive work rules; inappropriate fleet of aircraft for the route structure; poor fleet reliability; punitive leasing arrangements; old aircraft with high energy costs; fleet with utilisation levels at 70 per cent – lower than comparable US fleets; relatively low-traffic route densities, and excessive debt burden. Taken together, this did not augur well for the future of the privatised airline. One of the internal reports concluded that the problems of the national airline were so intractable as to defy managerial initiatives that could lead to commercial viability in the normal context. In addition, Air Jamaica had to face stiff competition from American Airlines on its US routes and from British Airways on its UK routes, two of the largest and most powerful airlines in the world. Both these airlines subsequently announced major cooperative arrangements. Air Jamaica's inability to network into the hub-and-spokes structure of the US aviation system, flying mainly point-to-point traffic, was its major operational and economic handicap. The linking of the airline with a hotelier presented serious conflicts of interest. While the other investors would want to maximise profits through higher airfares, the hotelier wanted to maximise tourist flows through lower airfares and higher hotel rates. Most importantly, operation of an airline requires sophisticated technical and international airline managerial capabilities, which the Stewart organisation did not have. In other words, a strategic technical partner was needed.

In the period of private operation under Butch Stewart, executive chairman of Air Jamaica Limited, there was another exercise of route expansion to some twenty-five locations, including Grenada, St Lucia, Grand Cayman, Curaçao, Barbados, Bonaire, Antigua, and Fort Lauderdale. Some of these destinations were the locations where Stewart's Sandals hotel chain had operations. While Air Jamaica was starved of capital by the private sector majority stakeholder, Sandals continued its hotel expansion in the Caribbean, with Sandals Grande, a 284-room hotel opening in St Lucia in the 1990s at a capital cost of EC$20 million.[12]

Between September 1994 and January 1996, Air Jamaica continued to operate at a loss. In this period, the airline operated non-stop services to London and Los Angeles, with a new fleet of Airbus A320 aircraft. The government had to revisit the agreement and write-off a significant portion of the liabilities of the privatised airline, in addition to providing sovereign guarantees to facilitate the acquisition of new aircraft in 1997. Overall, the total sum injected by the state into the new Air Jamaica amounted to US$169 million in loans and other assistance following privatisation. A loan in the amount of US$45 million to Air Jamaica from Conclear Limited in 2000 had to be guaranteed by the government. This is despite Minister Davies's earlier announcement that Air Jamaica would be subjected to hard budgets.

Subsequently, in July 2000, the government converted the US$169 million loan to equity, taking the government's equity to 45 per cent, in addition to an amount of preference shares to be determined at a future date. This seriously diluted the equity held by the private investors. The experience is that small airlines like Air Jamaica, mostly operating point-to-point aircraft movements, find it difficult to survive the competitive global aviation market environment without a high degree of government protection and large state subsidies. The government's actions continued to serve the operators' interest at the expense of the consumers and taxpayers.

The real question posed was whether the cost to the consumers and taxpayers was justified based on the wider interest of the tourist industry and externalities to the economy. Had the Jamaican government liquidated the old Air Jamaica and auctioned the assets and route rights, the net cost to the consumers and taxpayers would have been lower. In fact, Air Jamaica sold one of its prized assets, the airline slot at Heathrow Airport to a competitor, Virgin Atlantic Limited. With a fully privatised operator, the government would then have a strong interest in regulating the market to facilitate competition. Competition more likely would have produced much lower prices for consumers. The taxpayers would not have had to face continued subsidies to the privatised airline. The Jamaican airline privatisation experience showed that the operations of small national airlines carry heavy economic cost to the national budget. The claims that there were benefits from sovereignty and to the tourist industry and micro-economic benefits to the wider economy did not warrant this cost when essential social services, such as health and education, were being denied of critical funding.

Although there were improvements in operating performances shortly after privatisation to the Butch Stewart consortium, AJAG, this did not translate into financial viability. The private investors failed to bring in any real additional capital up to 2001 and, had it not been for the cross-subsidised benefits to their hotel operations, it is most unlikely that they would have continued to be involved in the business. In fact, it would seem that the hotelier used the airline to market his hotel operations. The government faced the unpalatable position of continued subsidisation of the privatised airline.

The situation of the government funding a partially privatised business proved untenable, requiring the AJAG consortium eventually, in December 2004, to return the airline to the government. With Air Jamaica once again falling under full state ownership and control, the government once again faced continued financial exposure from the continued losses of the airline. Between 2004 and 2007, Air Jamaica, once again under state control, continued to accumulate huge losses.

The Fourth Airline Privatisation

Privatisation was put on the table again in 2007 by the new Jamaica labour Party (JLP) administration. The new government was intent on removing an unsustainable venture resulting from the financial haemorrhage of the airline. In 2009, the International Finance Corporation, an affiliate of the World Bank, was appointed lead privatisation transaction advisor. The government received support from the Canadian International Development Agency, the US Treasury, and the US Trade and Development Agency. When privatisation was resurrected, Air Jamaica had made losses forty years out of forty-two years of operation. The JLP administration, now in power, had taken the position that there was no economic rationale for continued involvement in Air Jamaica, and the tourist industry could operate without a national flag carrier. The new government's priority was to remove Air Jamaica from the national budget as, by then, along with sugar and urban transport, they were proving to be the most expensive state operations, making the support of government unsustainable.

Expressions of Interest (EOI) were received from prospective bidders, five of which fulfilled the EOI requirement, and were technically evaluated, with four of the five bidders meeting the technical requirements. In the end, two of these bidders, Indigo Partners and Caribbean Airlines, submitted firm proposals. By deadline June 30, 2009, Indigo was selected as the preferred bidder; however, negotiations which had begun exclusively, after four months of talks broke down at the stage of finalising the deal, resulting in negotiations being terminated by mutual consent. Instead, the prime minister of Jamaica had approached the government of Trinidad and Tobago regarding a merger or acquisition by Caribbean Airlines. As a result, the Jamaican government successfully finalised an agreement with Caribbean Airlines.[13]

Under the terms of the agreement, the government of Trinidad and Tobago provided new investments of US$50 million to Caribbean Airlines to fund the acquisition. The government of Jamaica took 16 per cent equity in the new airline. It also retained ownership of all Air Jamaica's real estate and industrial assets. These were, in turn, leased to Caribbean Airlines. Air Jamaica's approximately one thousand employees were made redundant, and the government accepted liability to meet all the legacy labour and pension costs. Caribbean

Airlines acquired Air Jamaica's fleet and route rights as of May 1, 2010, and opened a new office in Kingston. On May 27, 2011, Jamaica's finance minister, Audley Shaw, and Trinidad and Tobago's finance minister, Winston Dookeran, signed the shareholders' agreement, giving the new airline access to all the routes formerly held by Air Jamaica. On July 1, 2011, all Air Jamaica and Caribbean Airlines flights began operating under Caribbean Airlines, with 'BW' IATA code. Air Jamaica ceased operations in 2015, bringing an end to one of Jamaica's most costly state adventures.[14]

Air Jamaica Express Limited, later Trans-Jamaica Airlines Limited until it was taken over by the Gordon 'Butch' Stewart Group in 1984, was controlled by Air Jamaica. When Air Jamaica was re-nationalised in 2004, responsibility for Air Jamaica Express Limited remained with Stewart's organisation. Trans-Jamaica Airlines once operated the domestic services and, in addition, flew on a few Caribbean routes: Cayman, Georgetown, Havana, Santiago, and Port-au-Prince. In the 1990s, routes were also operated to Belize City and Cancun, Mexico. After continued financial losses, the airline ceased operation in October 2005, and the IATA code JQ was assigned to Jetstar Airways.

The earlier privatisation of Air Jamaica was highly unsatisfactory, in much the same way as the privatisation of sugar which also went to mostly local investors and contrasted with the privatisation of telecommunication and electricity, which involved major strategic international technical investors. While global conditions in the early 1990s, when virtually all major airlines lost money, played a part in the earlier failure, the particular problem of a small airline which was not anchored into a global or regional network exacerbated matters. In all the earlier privatisation transactions, the government failed to achieve its objective. The operation of the airline under the earlier local private management fared no better than as a state-operated enterprise. Privatisation, in fact, did not get the airline out of the market, as was the case of Venezuela.[15]

One clear lesson learned from the Air Jamaica privatisation is that governments need to select private partners with greater capacity and commitment to financial underwriting and strong industry technical and managerial expertise. Airlines need large investments. There was the need for better planning by the government of the privatisation process. Hard-nosed decisions needed to have been taken on the valuation of the airline. The airline's privatisation should be guided by economic rationality rather than nebulous considerations like national pride, national symbolism, or potential benefits to the tourist industry. There is no available evidence to support the claim that the absence of a national flag carrier would have negatively affected tourism. With the Jamaican airline industry, the level of competition was such that there was no need for a new regulatory structure. At least government was sufficiently astute not to introduce any new regulatory requirements beyond those coming out of the bilateral agreement and international conventions.

PRIVATISATION OF AIRPORTS

Privatisation Structure for Sangster International and Norman Manley International Airports

In the 1990s, there was a growing recognition that airports were attractive commercial ventures, capable of managing their own financial obligations. In deciding to privatise the airports, Jamaica was following the path taken by the UK British Airports Authority, Kansai Airport in Japan, Zurich in Switzerland, Vienna International in Austria, and Toronto Terminal 3, in Canada.[16]

A primary issue was whether the government should restructure the airports for privatisation and provide for more competition having taken a decision in 1991 to include the airports in its overall privatisation programme and to restructure the industry before privatisation. The airports' operational activities were to be separated from the Airports Authority of Jamaica; further, the operating activities at the two international airports were to be vertically unbundled and two new companies created, one to own Norman Manley International Airport (NMIA Limited) and the other to own Sangster International Airport (SIA) Limited. There were two views, as was the case in the UK privatisation: one was to retain the international airport operating activities as one company and the other to take the route of separation and create two independent companies and privatise them separately. The decision favoured unbundling into two international airport companies and to execute two separate sale transactions, proceeding first with the privatisation of SIA.

There are several instances where international airports located close to each other are operated under common ownership, such as in New York, Paris, Berlin, and London, where Gatwick and Heathrow were privatised to a common ownership. There does not appear to be marked economies of scale to be gained in keeping the two airports under one ownership and management.[17] Professor Marshall Hall, a Jamaican government advisor, was of the view that the airports privatisation ought to have been conducted separately to facilitate competition. Increasing competition in a privatised airport, however, has implications for the sales proceeds to the Jamaica treasury. Increasing competition in the market reduces the potential scope to generate monopoly rent.

Airports provide two bundles of services: first is landing and take-off of aircraft and the handling of passengers; second, they provide increasingly for a wide range of commercial services for passengers, such as banking, restaurants, car hiring facilities, duty-free shops, parking, etc.; aircraft refuelling and provision of heating and air conditioning. The airport, however, does not itself provide many of the commercial services; these are franchised to private sector entities and, in return, the airport as landlord receives a franchised income. Revenues from the two groups of activities are of equal importance to the airport's total turnover. Even security and portering are subcontracted; hence, the airport staff probably represent less than 10 per cent of workers at the airport. Most of the services provided face limited or no competition. The airport receives higher franchise fees when it awards exclusive franchise such as duty-free liquor retailing. There was a growing view in Europe at the time that airports ought to be developed as major shopping centres. This makes the airport privatisation different from the privatisation of other infrastructure companies.

The primary services of airport are aviation-related: facilitating the landing of aircraft; airside operation and providing for the departure and arrival of passengers (landside operation). The retailing business also forms a part of landside operations, typically referred to as the terminal side. As a result of the two sets of operations, airports receive two broad sets of income: aviation income and retailing and real-estate income. A critical issue raised with privatising Jamaica's two international airports was whether unbundling would affect the proceeds from the sale of the assets versus providing for competition between the two airports which, ostensibly, was expected to benefit airport users. Even if ownership was divided, there would remain an element of residual market power requiring regulation, and thus a case for a new regulatory framework.

A second major issue was whether rate-based regulation for airports, as practised in the US, was more appropriate than price cap regulation, the new approach to incentive regulation, as was being developed in the UK. The basic idea of rate-of-return regulation is that the regulated firm is allowed a fair rate of return on its rate base, a measure of the firm's capital assets. The limitation of rate base regulation is the well-known overcapitalisation it engenders[18]; consequently, there is a tendency towards overinvestments. It also encourages price discrimination and, in some circumstances, the setting of marginal prices below marginal cost for those activities which require marginally more capital. Rate base regulation is said to be cost plus regulation and results in inefficiencies. The alternative to rate base regulation is incentive regulation involving RPI-X formula,[19] as was adopted in the UK airport privatisations and British Telecommunications privatisation.

A third issue was whether there should be a continuation of the single-till approach, a structure which historically has been used for fixing the charges at airports. David Starkie has argued that complementarities between airport retailing and property rent on one hand, and the number of aircraft landing and passengers passing through on the other provides the airport with an incentive to expand airside output.[20]

A fourth policy issue was whether the airside should be unbundled from landside with the government continuing ownership of the landside. The solicitor general argued that, because of national sovereignty issues, the landside could not be privatised.

Background to the Development of Sangster

Sangster Airport was conceived in 1936 and, in 1940, the runway was built, with the construction of the rest of the landside facilities completed in February 1947. The airport was originally named Montego Bay Airport, and it was an aerodrome. At the time, Montego Bay was a playground for celebrities and the rich and the premier holiday location within the Caribbean. Pan American Airways flew the first flight into the airport in 1949 and was the initial airport operator. The first terminal building was built on the north side of the property but was shifted to the southern side during an upgrading exercise, necessitated by the continuous growth of traffic. The terminal on the southern side was built and opened in July 1959, with a capacity to accommodate five hundred passengers per hour, with parking space for seven aircraft.

The airport, as it existed in 1995, had a single runway of eighty-seven hundred feet, a parallel taxiway with three direct taxiways connecting to the runway, with high-speed take off and holding bays at the west end. There were eight gates, and passengers had to walk from the terminal building to the aircraft at the parking positions. This was a major impediment during the rainy season. An expansion was carried out to the departure lounge in 1993, at a cost of US$10M, financed by a loan from the European Economic Community (EEC). The terminal building then was upgraded to handle 1,350 passengers per hour; however, the 1993 peak had reached two thousand passengers per hour.

Traffic and Financials

Table 12.4 below presents the passenger traffic history of Sangster International, with projections for the years 1996–2010. Traffic more than doubled from 576,403 passengers in 1965,[21] to 1.16 million passengers in 1995, and the projection was for passenger traffic to increase to 3.2 million over the period 1996–2010.

The ratio of airside to land revenues was 70:30. Landing and terminal fees, however, were relatively low compared to world standard. It was the practice to offer competitive rates to the airlines to attract visitors to the island.[22]

Table 12.4: Sangster International Airport Traffic History and Projection in 1996

Year	Passengers (Actuals)	Year	Passengers (Projections)
1985	576,403	1996	1,239,986
1986	718,922	1997	1,327,940
1987	748,848	1998	1,422,133
1988	711,439	1999	1,523,008
1989	760,248	2000	1,631,037
1990	841,921	2002	1870,629
1991	831,478	2005	2,297,593
1992	930,112	2008	2,822,009
1994	1,011,368	2010	3,236,554
1995	1,157,857		

Source: Cezley Sampson, 'Regulatory Framework in the Privatization of Airports: A Case Study of Jamaica,' paper delivered at Latin American Caribbean Privatization, January 1996.

The decision to modernise and expand Sangster International was taken by the PNP administration in 1990 because of the inadequacy of the facilities and with traffic growth doubling every decade. A United States Trade Development Agency grant provided for the funding of a feasibility study that was undertaken by Birk Hillman Zipperley. The consultant was required to provide a traffic projection in 1995 and table 12.5 shows the actual traffic for Sangster for the period 1985–95 and the projections from 1996 to 2010 (Conference in Lima, Peru.)

The study confirmed the need to expand the terminal facilities and proposed two options: a greenfield design project,[23] and an integrated terminal development, which would retain the best features of the greenfield design, and yet form an expansion of the then existing facilities, providing for flexibility, and a more cost-effective development. To ease the congestion at the two airports, the government also gave permission for outgoing immigration processing to be introduced based on 'nothing to declare' in December 1993. The Jamaican government's airport privatisation programme was also based on the assumption that, with private sector involvement, there would be greater benefits to the economy, as was the case in the UK.[24]

In the financial year 1993/94, the AAJ made a profit of J$38 million, on an income of J$492 million. The organisation carried bad debt provision of J$45 million in 1993/94 and accumulated provision of J$94 million, most chalked up by Air Jamaica, which refused to pay most of its outstanding airport charges. The revenues of Sangster were J$285 million with passenger traffic volume of 1,071,000. The overall AAJ traffic volume was 1,973,000 terminal passengers, and 40,900 commercial aircraft movements. Norman Manley, with half as much passenger traffic, had a higher direct or variable cost than Sangster. Although the AAJ was profitable, the profit level did not cover its capital financing. There was an outstanding loan of J$485 million, of which J$264 was unlent by the government.

In 1993, the AAJ increased its fees charged to the airlines, but the airlines refused to cooperate. That same year, the departure tax was US$12.50, of which US$5.00 was to be labelled Passenger Facility Charge (PFC) to be transferred from the government to SIA Limited. The increase was expected to add US$2.80, and US$3.40 respectively for a passenger round trip, a tiny amount in relation to the passenger travel cost. Plans were instituted to include the PFC in the passenger ticket cost. The Civil Aviation Department (CAD) had an income of J$48 million and an expenditure of J$36 million. The CAD's accounts were based on income and expenditure, with no balance sheet.

The feasibility study for a new terminal was commissioned by the government in 1991 and the report was submitted in March 1992. The study included a Passenger and Cargo Study, carried out by Aviation Planners Associated, Inc., and a financial and economic impact study carried out by Kenneth Leventhal and Company, both companies considered leaders in their field. The government accepted the consultants' proposals to proceed with expansion and privatisation of the Sangster airport. For the design of the project, Birk Hillman, and Company, aviation architects, engineers, and planners, was contracted at a cost of US$7.4 million to design the Sangster terminal building. In addition, Infrastructure Management Group (IMG), a leading aviation management consultant, was awarded a contract to carry out the management audit, while Ernst and Young was simultaneously engaged to assist with the development of a hypothetical financial statement for the new SIA Limited, with a view to separation of Sangster's accounting, financial information, and system from the AAJ.

The government was also able to secure financial assistance from the UK Overseas Development Association (ODA, now DFID) to engage economic and legal consultancy support to develop the aviation regulatory framework and the new legalisation for the restructured aviation sector. As noted earlier, the Portland Group was engaged as the economic regulatory consultant, while Gillian White was engaged as the legal consultant, both of the UK. Concurrent with the airport feasibility study, the NIBJ commissioned QDM Limited of the UK and Reason Foundation of the USA to examine the privatisation options. The government had earlier decided for fast-track development hence a decision to build first, and privatise later.

The Organisational Structure of the Privatisation

The structures for preparing the international airports for privatisation can be summarised as follows:

1. Vertical unbundling of landside terminal operations from airside operations and privatising the landside, leaving Sangster and Norman Manley airside with the AAJ, or another government agency;

2. Creating terminal companies at Sangster and Norman Manley, and providing for a management contract, or long-term lease contract for the landside;
3. Vesting and privatising the integrated airside and landside assets at Sangster and Norman Manley with the government retaining a golden share in the privatised entity; and
4. BOT (Build-Operate-Transfer) development for the new terminal facilities.

Airports can be privatised as vertically integrated entities, combining landside and terminal building and operations, or vertical separation into landside and airside. Vertical unbundling of the airport into landside and airside raises several issues. In the UK, at the time of privatisation of their airport operations, consideration was also given to vertical unbundling of the BAA for privatisation. However, issues such as coordination and coherent development of scarce land resources within the airport parameter ruled this out. International experiences at Birmingham Airport privatisation also showed that operational issues, such as ground control movements, fire and rescue services, security and fuel supply, and general maintenance, as well as financial and administrative services became unnecessarily complicated. Operational and capacity planning problems developed between Eurohub and the Birmingham International Airport. There are also airside investments, whether a government would in the future be ready and able to make such investments to meet the private sector investment schedule for the landside. With separation, it is also difficult to operate the 'single till' approach to airport pricing. It also makes it difficult to comply with the International Civil Aviation Organization (ICAO) recommendation for commercial revenues to make some contribution to the cost of aeronautical activities.

Vertical integration of landside assets (terminal building) and airside (runway land and operations) into one company at each airport for privatisation, on the other hand, presented considerable risks to the Jamaican government and did not guarantee private sector financing, which was a major goal. Vertical integration presented fewer risks to private investors. The boundary problem, which was substantial, would be avoided and the government could address the sovereignty concerns with a 'Golden Share' and by establishing an appropriate regulatory structure. Experiences at BAA privatisation in the UK shows that legislative complexity should not be the overriding reason for the choice of structure and that the sovereignty problem could be managed through long-term lease for the land.

The option of the BOT approach was to be accommodated in 1994 but could be considered for the privatisation of the Norman Manley transaction later. The government, however, decided on vertical unbundling; some reasons which led the government to taking this position were as follows:

- The government's financial advisers, Citibank, were of the view that the traffic forecasts were sufficiently strong to ensure debt coverage.
- The government stood to gain a higher capital gain once the expansion was completed.
- US Exim Bank indicated an interest in financing the project, and
- There were concerns that, if the terminal was built under BOT, the developer's primary concern would be short-term profit.

Added to these were the government's concerns about reducing public sector involvement in the development of airports and rescheduling of its debt at the Paris Club. The decision went for a design and build option and privatise later. The financial structure developed by Citibank, the financial advisor to the NIBJ, which was contracted in April 1992, estimated the new facility to cost US$104 million, which would mostly be the landside development.

Consideration was also being given at the time to a merger of the AAJ with the CAD; the latter entity was still operating as a civil service department, with considerable restrictions on its operations. The reason for such a merger was for the CAD to escape the civil service restrictions and, more so, to benefit from the AAJ compensation package, which was much higher than the civil service pay scale that applied to the CAD. With the plan to unbundle the two international airports from the AAJ, concerns developed among AAJ managers as to their future.

SIA Ltd was eventually incorporated to own the landside and to serve as the special purpose vehicle for construction of the new terminal building. The SIA, in due course, would own the 70 per cent private shareholding, with the balance held by the AAJH and the Accountant General on behalf of the government. Its main functions were to cover the as following:

- Take full responsibility for all landside planning and capital expenditure;
- Manage the airside under long-term contract from AAJ Holding Limited (say ten years and renewable);
- Receive all the revenues at Sangster, other than the airside income that would be collected by the SIA;
- Receive contract fees for the operation of the airside at Sangster; and
- Be responsible for airside operating costs.

AAJ Holding Limited was to be a wholly owned government company, and would:

- Own the freehold of both Sangster and Norman Manley properties.
- Manage the government's shareholdings in SIA Limited and NMIA Limited.
- Award and monitor management contracts or leases with SIA Limited for airside at Sangster, as well as for Norman Manley airside.
- Have responsibility for major airside planning, with SIA Limited and NMIA Limited.
- Be responsible for raising major airport airside capital investments, and
- Receive airside revenues (principally the equipment related to landing fees).

The AAJH was to carry no operational responsibility, and the AAJ was to be phased out. The CAD was to be corporatised as the Civil Aviation Authority (CAA). Its duties and powers would remain, more or less, identical except that it would assume responsibility for the domestic aerodromes. The merger of CAD with AAJ was to be shelved. It was also felt that a long-term lease would be more appropriate than a management contract in terms of commitment. Both SIA Limited and NMIA Limited were to be given aerodrome licenses.

The recommendation also was for economic regulation of the airports to be introduced as a new function and assigned to the Office of Utilities Regulation (OUR), separated from safety and technical regulation, which was to be carried out by the corporatised CAA. Economic regulation was to be unbundled from safety and technical regulation. This, however, was seen by some to present risk to the new investor.

One reason given for building and privatising was that a private consortium would encounter considerable delays in assembling the financing package, and there would be complexity and delays in drafting the legislation to facilitate privatisation of the vertically integrated airport, inclusive of the airside. The various external consultants, however, advised against privatisation of a vertical unbundled airport (vertical separation of landside from airside). The consultants felt that there were significant advantages to devolving operational and financial responsibility for the airside to the terminal company. Privatisation by long-term lease for the land (forty-nine years) was advanced as a solution to the concerns raised by the solicitor general that sensitive assets (the patrimony of the country) were to be sold to a foreign investor by the government.

The Proposed Financial Structure

The proposed financial structure advanced by Citibank is detailed as follows:

- Senior debt US$49 million.
- Subordinated debt (twelve-year loan with a two-year construction period) US$20 million. Investors in this tranche would have a subordinated claim on the net cash flow from the project (a violation of the senior debt coverage ratio would trigger a blockage of payment to the subordinated debt). At the time, the forecasted interest rate was London inter-bank offer rate (LIBOR) plus five hundred basis points, depending on market conditions at the time of issuing. This could be funded in hard currency or local currency. It was felt that the tourist sector would pick up most of this financing.
- Convertible bonds US$20 million. This was to be a thirteen-year private placement of debt convertible to equity after the fifth year. It was to be placed on the local market, mostly in the local currency to finance local cost. After five years, investors would have the right to change their bonds, including the capitalised unpaid interests for a number of shares in SIA Limited, or have the option to cash out as against taking equity.

A lead underwriter was to be appointed for placing the equity and convertible bonds. It was planned that existing employees at Sangster would participate in the form of the ESOP Share Option Participation Plan.

- Income from departure tax US$20 million: this portion of the financing was to be funded through an increase to the existing departure tax and introducing an airport passenger development charge (PFC). Passenger departure tax was then J$500 (approximately US$14 at the then rate of exchange) of which US$5 was being paid over to SIA Limited. This was to continue for three years.
- Total US$104 million: at the time the internal rate of return (after adjustment) for an investment of US$104 was approximately 16.5 per cent, which, when compared with averages cost of capital for the project (8.5 per cent) provided an attractive financial return for the equity investor.

In the proposed financial structure, the plan was for the senior debt to be placed with a multilateral, or bilateral funding institution, that the subordinated debt would be placed with offshore financial institutions, and the convertible bonds would be an instrument designed for the local market. The Ministry of Finance pledged a portion of the departure tax flows as the government's equity contribution, at a rate of US$5 per departing passenger. This was estimated to bring in US$7 million per year for three years.

In test marketing the package, a very favourable reception was received. However, US EXIM Bank which was interested in financing the senior debt took Jamaica off cover at the time the project was being presented for financing. At this point, Citibank came up with the option of establishing a Privatisation Trust. The structure, which was finally developed and accepted, called for the following:

- Creation of a subsidiary company, AAJ Holding Limited and allocation of the shares to be issued to the government to be held by a new company, AAJ Holdings Limited, fully owned by the government;
- An initial tranche of equity to be placed on the market, either as straight equity, or as convertible bonds, or a combination of both;

- The balance of the shares was to be parked in a new vehicle: Privatisation Trust, managed by privatisation trustees;
- As further equity was needed, additional shares were to be sold to the private sector from the Trust, and the government would benefit from any capital gains;
- While the shares remained in the Trust, they were disenfranchised and could not be voted by the government, thus effective control would pass to the private shareholder;
- In addition, provision was to be made for a Golden Share in the Article of Association of SIA Limited, which would give the power to veto any strategy that could halt or reverse the privatisation process (or Deed of Mandatory Privatisation). In addition, the government was to hold a reserve right share conferring special rights to the state requiring the majority shareholder to first obtain the government's approval before disposal of the whole or any material part of the assets, take any decision which would impinge on the sovereign rights of the government, or increase the shareholding of a single foreign investor beyond 25 per cent of the equity. Equity of 70 per cent was to be sold on the financial market, as well as to international investors on a phased basis.

While the Privatisation Trust concept was being developed, the Overseas Private Investment Corporation (OPIC) came on board and, as a result, the need for the involvement of the US Exim Bank was no longer critical. Both local and overseas investors were to be eligible to purchase shares which were to be offered to the public. In November 1993, the landside, or terminal facility of Sangster, was incorporated as a limited liability company (Sangster International Airterminal Limited). AAJ Holdings Limited was also incorporated. Initially, SIA Limited would operate within the framework of AAJ, with the chairman of AAJ being the chairman of SIA Limited. AAJ Holdings Limited and the accountant general were to own the government's 30 per cent equity in SIA Limited, with the 70 per cent held by the Privatisation Trust for the new private investors. SIA Limited was to be provided with a forty-nine-year lease for the land and a long-term licence to operate the airport. To avoid two management structures at the Sangster International Airport (for airside and landside) the management of the airside was to be contracted to SIA Limited. The government also agreed to introduce legislation providing for vesting of the lands from AAJ to SIA Limited and transferring responsibilities from AAJ to SIA Limited. The landside was to be ring-fenced to provide for clear separation of landside from airside. The legislation on vesting of the assets and functions and draft bill was presented to the government's Legislative Committee on March 29, 1996.

The Design of the New Terminal Facility

Birk Hillman was retained to complete the final design work for the new terminal at Sangster, and the consultant presented a three-level configuration, providing for separation of activities: ground floor, or level one was to provide segregated areas for airlines' service function and ramp facilities for baggage handling; level two was to provide facilities for passenger handling, such as security, checkpoint, ticketing and concessions for departures, while level three was to provide a sterile arrival collecting system from all gates to a new immigration hall. After exiting the immigration hall, a connecting bridge would link the arriving passengers to the rest of the arrival facilities: baggage claim and customs. There were to be twelve gates, with the existing terminal to be used for charter and domestic flights, and additional four gates, with passenger loading bridges.[25] The space being allotted to facilitate commercial concessions was ten thousand square feet, reflecting the modern trend of commercialising airports. It was estimated that the airport would earn some 25 per cent of revenues from the various concessions. The 'single till' method of pricing would reduce the airport charges paid by incoming landing aircraft and passengers.

Separation Issues – Vertical Unbundling of Landslide from Airside

In the vertically unbundled airport (airside separated from landside), a decision would have to be made about facilities for the fire and rescue services, as two separate fire and rescue service operations would create problems of communications, control, and finance. There was the need to allocate the responsibilities clearly to avoid the downgrading of the response time of the services. Should one organisation be given the responsibility to provide overall fire and rescue services for the airport, there would be the need to share costs. This could be done based on either call out or a flat fee of the shared services. Call out presented a problem, as it would put pressure on one entity to minimise call outs.

Airport security operations already involved multi-organisational responsibilities between airlines, the single airport operator, and the national police. Separation of responsibilities would further complicate security management. Issuing and control of airport passes would become a divided function, with the potential for gaps in security operations. The delivery of this service could be contracted out. The state's role would be to provide a tight system of regulation and monitoring to ensure that ICAO and domestic standards are met.

There was no set position whether the apron and fuel hydrant system should belong airside as against landside. It was deemed necessary that whoever carried responsibility for the apron and fuel system investments should also carry responsibility for operation of the fuel hydrant system, to avoid complication from divided charges.

When there is a separation of ownership, insurance liabilities need to be shared, and it would be necessary that the insurer is satisfied that the division of responsibilities does not increase the insurance risks. If management and ownership are both separate, then insurers are likely to perceive increased risk and impose higher insurance premiums. The legal doctrine of sovereign immunity may limit the governments' liability for injuries resulting from negligence in transportation operations. This, however, is not extended to the private enterprise. Without some protection from potential liability, airport privatisation can prove difficult to execute.[26]

Then there is the allocation of responsibility for airport policy and planning which, of course, should remain the responsibility of the government following privatisation. The long lead time for planning schedules, the limited availability of land, the public issues related to airport noise, and other environmental matters dictate that the state must maintain a critical role in planning of investment for airport infrastructure after privatisation. Once separation of operational roles is entertained, the regulator would need to be given reserve roles to intervene between the state and the appropriate operators of the airport service.

Managing and Regulating Airport Slots

Efficient use of capacity should be one of the main objectives of airport regulation. The effective use of the airport slots is central to efficient use of existing airport capacity. Several parameters need to be considered, and regulating airport slots can be a difficult issue.[27] In Jamaica, the allocation of slots is the responsibility of an airport scheduling committee, made up of representatives from the leading airlines and the AAJ. The committee allocates slots according to guidelines laid down by the International Air Transport Association (IATA), which provides a strong preference to 'godfather rights,' i.e., previous users of particular slots in an equivalent season receive preference.[28] This was very much a cartel process, for which the AAJ and the government avoided making changes.

In Europe, however, the EU had proposed that, in certain circumstances, up to 50 per cent of slots may be removed from existing users and made available to new entrants. Europe was looking at an alternative system of regulating slots. The demand for airport slots is also influenced by inter-governmental air services agreements, which often limit the number of airlines allowed to operate on a particular route and may also designate the airports in the respective country which particular airlines may use. Except for a few airports such as Heathrow, where peak period pricing prevailed, non-market mechanism was the procedure adopted.[29] Market period pricing would have been the best option for Jamaica to adopt to ensure economical use; however, this was not favoured by the airline cartel. With the UK, after privatisation, a company – Airport Co-ordination Limited, an association of the eight largest airlines and BAA – was established. The company employed an in-house coordinator to carry out the administrative allocation arrangements. In the US, the airlines scheduling committee plays a more advisory role and is not charged directly with the allocation of slots. Under the British Airports Act, if it is revealed that discriminatory practices were employed by Airport Co-ordination.

Aviation Sector Regulation

Historically, private airline services have been regulated in the US under the US Civil Aviation Act. With liberalisation after the 1970s, the airline market through the Airline Deregulation Act in 1978 the US government allowed the airlines considerable freedom in setting airline tariff. Jamaica, like the UK, also significantly reduced the regular requirements for the airlines other than safety and security matters.

With airports and airport services, regulation have been far more stringent at the privatisation British airports in the 1980s. The UK perused both privatisation and liberalisation at the same time, with tight economic regulation being applied to the major airports and which previously formed part of the British Airport Authority. Airport Authority in Jamaica in consultation with the airlines have been empowered with the authority to intervene and manage slot allocation.

As Norman International and Sangster International were seen not to be in competition, the decision taken by government, there was no need to include an obligation to promote competition following privatisation. There were, however, the suggestions that the two airports should have been privatised to separate owners to facilitate competition. Despite separate privatisation transaction, the privatised airports were eventually acquired by the same owner. Like the BAA, the Jamaican airports were to be subjected to price regulation, the reason being airports are natural monopolies for origin and destination traffic; their markets are inelastic; operating a monopoly in an inelastic market and to set your own prices constitute the perfect business scenario.[30]

The selection of option in privatising airports will depend on government's intention behind the privatisation: maximisation of revenues, wider share ownership, the desire for a quick sale, or the need for new capital and technology. Jamaican priority was for new capital and new technology to drive the expansion of the airport to meet the increasing demands of tourism. In going to the market, for the privatisation of the airport, the arrangement presented was for economic regulation to come under the authority of the multi-sector regulatory agency: the Office of Utilities Regulation, with security and safety regulation falling under the authority of the newly created Civil Aviation Authority (CAA). In this way, economic regulation would be separated from safety, technical, and environmental regulation. The OUR had been developed in response to privatisation of the utilities sector, and the reason was that this represented an opportunity for airport regulation to benefit from the wider regulatory experiences of the OUR. In addition, this would provide for a more cost-effective outcome, as against creating a new industry-specific, Civil Aviation Regulatory Authority.

Civil aviation in Jamaica, as in several colonial operations, commenced operations as a civil service department, responsible for airports, air traffic control (ATC) and regulation. The regulatory functions mainly related to safety and technical operation matters and ensuring compliance with international and bilateral aviation agreements and obligations. The US is unique in that sometimes airports are operated by airlines, as with the Montego Bay Airport being operated by Pan American Airways in the 1940s. However, problems present themselves when airports are directly linked with an airline.

Traffic growth over the years led to airports being profitable; hence, they were commercialised and corporatised, as was the case in Jamaica. Air Traffic Control (ATC) did not follow that pace of institutional development; hence, it remained a civil service department. The desire to corporatise ATC was in keeping with the trend toward commercialisation. There have, however, been very few instances of ATC privatisation.

The CAD was responsible for the provision of air traffic control services covering overflying within Jamaica, providing flight information within the region and terminal air traffic control at the airports. Ground movement of aircraft was controlled up to where the airline marshallers guided them to the gate. The CAD's air traffic control activities were monitored by regular inspection carried out under contract by the US FAA and UK CAA. The CAD also carried out regular aircrew and airport personnel licensing, registration of aircraft, aircraft operations, air worthiness of aircraft, and security. With the proposed privatisation, charges for landing, parking, and terminal fees were to be subject to economic regulations. These charges averaged US$6 per passenger in 1991. With the landside fees, these were to be liberalised and subject only to the competition legislation. At the time of the proposed changes, the aviation charges were negotiated between the airlines and the AAJ, subject to ministerial approval. The government also imposed an airport tax (US$11 per passenger), and part of this was earmarked as user fees and assigned to AAJ as part of the divestiture package. The portion assigned to AAJ was to be replaced by a passenger facility fee of US$5, with the income from Sangster going to the concessionaire.[31]

The ATLB carried responsibility for issues of route licenses and air charter permits. It had a small secretariat provided by the CAD; the board members were drawn from external bodies of the government and appointed by the minister of transport. The incumbent solicitor general served for years as the chairman.

Jamaican Airport Regulation

Historically, airports in the Caribbean have been regarded as public service. Under-pricing of airport charges has been a policy feature of many Caribbean governments. Low airport charges were an incentive to attract tourist traffic and expand each country's tourist industry. With the tight budgetary constraints which developed in the 1990s, Caribbean governments could not provide financing to meet the cost of airports and other infrastructure investment when needed; hence, they had to look to sourcing infrastructure financing from the private sector. In fact, in the privatisation of Sangster, the OPIC made it clear to the Jamaican government that a robust economic regulatory regime was a precondition for the investment commitment.

Security costs at the airports have been a major issue and have been high, relative to world standards, amounting to 21.5 per cent of total airport cost in fiscal year 1993. This was because, in the beginning of the 1990s, the US FAA and customs increased security requirements for Jamaica in response to the growth in illegal drugs and arms traffic. The increase reflected both procedures and technology.

There are several airport charges applicable at airports. In the 1990s, in the UK, various expenses related to aircraft hangars and cargo sheds, security charges, licenses for check-in desks, rental fees for accommodation and VIP lounges, concession fees, car parking charges, and ground handling charges, particularly those managed by airport operators like Manchester, were subjected to strict economic regulation. The International Air Transport Association (IATA) considers landing fees (levied for aircraft passengers on arrival or departure), passenger handling fees, and aircraft parking fees as being most critical to the airlines, requiring regulatory scrutiny. The separation resulted in two bundles from which the airports derived their revenues, and a two-pricing regime.

Departure tax is a general tax imposed by government; in the case of Jamaica, the US$12.50 then prevailing per departing passenger was excluded. An additional charge, passenger facility charge (PFC), was introduced in the US in the 1970s as a development fee to finance capital expansion. There are three ways in which the three critical charges may be determined: administratively, which was quite common at many small airports; rate of return, and a variant rate base regulation, popularly adopted in the US, and price cap, or revenue cap, often referred to as incentive regulation, introduced by the UK government in the 1980s.

Jamaica, like the British, chose price cap regulation. In the aviation industry, a price ceiling is adopted limiting airside charges to a fixed percentage below the retail price index, the efficiency factor subject to five-yearly review. With the Jamaican airport, the revenue yield variant was adopted with the output used being passenger mile Portland Group.[32]

The Passenger Service Charge (PFC)

The passenger service facility was central to the success of the airport privatisations and was based on US experiences, intending to provide the financing for the airport development and expansion with the US. It was introduced at a rate of up to US$3.0 per passenger. In Canada, it was as high as US$15.0 per passenger at the Vancouver Airport. The government of Jamaica accepted in principle the PFC to fund the expansion of the airport, and as a result, new guideline were issued starting with the PFC at US$5.0 per passenger separate from the departure tax, which wend to the ministry of finance as a tax.

The Privatisation Transaction

The various consultants from inception recommended privatisation of the vertically integrated airport. The government, however, opted for vertical separation (landside from airside) based on the advice of the solicitor general. It was, however, felt at the time that inclusion of the airside, as assets of SIA Limited, would cause complex and time-consuming legislative changes. The solicitor general was also of the view that, because of certain sovereign obligations, the airside should not be privatised. The prime minister's view was that, if the legislative changes had begun in 1993, it would have been completed by 1995. There was also the feeling that the privatisation of an airport was of greater interest to the public than power and telecommunications, striking at some emotional feelings related to the patrimony of the country. The government took the initial decision to go the route of vertically unbundling the airside from the landside, based on concerns that were raised about national security issues, regarding the airside being controlled by foreign investors. At the time, I was the chairman of the Airports Authority and the project director for the airport privatisation transaction. I took a different position from the solicitor general and advised vertical integration of airside and landside. Prime Minister Patterson held a meeting with Solicitor General Rattary and me, but the matter was not resolved. The prime minister left the matter to be determined by the market. When the project was eventually taken to the private investor market, the government came up against investor concerns in several areas:

- The industry structure of vertical unbundling into landside (terminal building) and airside (runway infrastructure) did not find favour with investors. Private investors contended that there was no advantage to be gained from unbundling, and vertical unbundling introduced too many major operational problems and risks, making it difficult to obtain financing in the private financial market.
- The ownership structure of the government holding 30 per cent equity was also seen to present additional risks to the potential private investors and bidders. Private investors saw no need for the government's continued participation in the ownership of the airport, especially where the government's expressed policy was to withdraw the state from commercial business and to reduce its financial exposure.
- Serious concerns were also expressed regarding the proposed regulatory framework, involving separation of economic regulation from technical regulation, with the OUR responsible for economic regulation, and the Civil Aviation Authority responsible for technical and safety regulation. Some argued, in imposition of safety and technical regulation, costs could be incurred. Hence, coordination would be required between the two, with the possibility of disagreements.
- The government also wanted to give the aviation regulators considerable discretion, while the private investors wanted limited discretion. The private investors feared regulatory expropriation with wide regulatory discretion.
- The financing structure did not find favour with potential private investors.

There was a further problem with the privatised Air Jamaica's poor payment history and the company's refusal at times to pay the various airport fees. Air Jamaica, at one point, owed the AAJ up to J$1 billion and because of this poor payment record, private investors in the Sangster Airport privatisation project sought sovereign guarantee, which the government was reluctant to provide.

After eleven years, the SIA privatisation project had not been concluded. In the meantime, the project cost escalated to US$140 million, although this included some landside capital expenditure which the government required to be carried out. With these developments, drastic changes had to be made to the project divestiture model.

The government finally agreed to return to the vertically integrated landside and airside model, as was originally proposed. This new industry structure provided for a single concession, eliminating all the uncertainties of vertical unbundling. The government also agreed for the private sector to take 100 per cent equity stake, instead of involving the government with participating at 30 per cent, subject to both appropriate economic and technical regulation by the Civil Aviation Authority. The government further agreed to a single regulator and, as a result, a new aviation sector legislation was enacted in 2002 transferring all regulatory powers over the airports to the Civil Aviation Authority, thus creating an industry-specific regulator, instead of involving the OUR, as a multi-sector regulator. Prior to this arrangement a memorandum of understanding was entered into with United Infrastructure Company/Airport Group International (UCI/AG) to evaluate the feasibility of the project. On conclusion of its investigation, the UIC/AIG issued a preliminary report in January 1997 and requested that consortium be granted further time to carry out its due diligence and submit a full proposal. The request was granted; however, the UIC/AIG proposal was unacceptable in many areas was rejected. The Airport Authority was also concerned with a sole source arrangement.

The government then approved a fully competitive and transparent bidding process and Expression of Interests (EOI) were issued in the latter half of 1998, followed up with road shows to identify private investors' concerns and level of interest. The new transaction structure approved by the government, and which was presented to the market, provided for a single industry regulator, integration of airside and landside and for 100 per cent privatisation (no limitation on ownership by a single investor), with a long-term lease for the airside. The final privatisation transaction advisory team to government consisted of UBS

Investment Bank as investment banker/financial advisor, assisted by its Caribbean-based CFAS Limited and Clifford Chance as legal advisor. However, Clifford Chance's involvement was later transferred to DLA Piper, an aviation marketing consultant as regulatory and economic advisor. In the final stage, the international financial institutions like the World Bank played minimal role.

The final round of bidding was launched in November 2000, and in April 2001, thirty-five firms responded to the EOI. Twelve of these eventually submitted applications for pre-qualification. The main criteria for identified by the privatisation team at the prequalification stage were as follows:

- Experience in the development management and operations of the airport.
- Ability to raise the funding to finance the expansion of the airport.
- Demonstrated technical capability and qualification of key personal and
- Experience in operating airport in an efficiency driven regulatory environment.

In April 2001, four firms were eventually short-listed to acquire Sangster Airport, with a consortium led by Vancouver Airport Corporation, with financing support from IFC selected as preferred strategic investor. The consortium comprised Vancouver Airport Services (Canada), Agunsa (Chile), Astrum (Israel), and Dragados (Spain). The transaction was completed towards the end of 2002, when the final sets of transaction documents were signed.

Under the revised agreement with Vancouver Airport Corporation – the international consortium and Montego Bay Jamaica Airports Limited – the AAJ retained ownership of the non-movable assets of the airport, owned prior to privatisation, and was required by the government to manage the concession agreement to ensure that the private operator fulfilled its contractual obligations. The private operator was provided with a long-term concession to run from 2003 to 2033. The private operator was required to pay a concession fee to AAJ and, at the end of the contract, was required to transfer the airport's assets acquired during the period of the concession back to the AAJ.

The Airport (Economic Regulation) Act was passed in 2002 and provided for the economic regulation of the international airports in Jamaica to be carried out by the Civil Aviation Authority, with responsibility for the setting of aeronautical charges under the Act. Section 6 (1) of the Act makes provision for introducing an airport improvement fee (AIF), which was implemented on February 15, 2003. The proceeds from the fee were to be placed in a separate Airport Expansion Fund, specially designated for each airport, and was to fund infrastructure development at each airport.

Post-Privatisation

In 2006, there was a change in ownership of the concessionaire. Abertis Infrastructure SA (formerly Dragnos) became 74.5 per cent shareholder, with Vantage Airport Group (formerly Vancouver Airport Services) 25.5 per cent. This consortium eventually sold its stake to the Mexican company, Grupo Aeroportuario del Pacifico (GAP). The GAP completed the acquisition of 100 per cent of the shares. The acquisition price for the concession, which had another eighteen years on the contract with the government, was not separately disclosed. The financing was 100 per cent of the acquisition via bridge loans, with external resources provided by Scotiabank Inverlat and BBVA Bancomer, with short- and long-term loans. There has been upgrading occasioned from the continuous growth in passenger traffic to the extent that, in 2007 it handled 3.7 million passengers. The SIA in 2007 had two terminals, one for international flights (F), and the other for domestic travel (C). Sangster handled passenger traffic of 3,633,998, with 40,764 aircraft movements in 2014.

MBJ Airports Limited also commissioned a new customs hall, arrivals lobby, and transportation centre in March 2007. Since then, further expansion and renovation projects, such as the relocation of the immigrations hall and duty-free mall, were completed in September 2008. This facility has increased the handling capacity to nine million passengers per annum. Relocation of the domestic terminal was also carried out.

Plans have been put in place to expand the airport to world-class standard. The new eastern concourse at Sangster (the result of phases 1A and 1B) was officially opened in December 2005. Phase Two was then due to commence towards the end of 2006; however, because the economic conditions were favourable and the tourist trade was increasing, Phase Two was brought forward to January 2006. In 2009, the arrival hall was extended to the south concourse, and the terminal building doubled to forty-seven thousand square feet, providing for more retail outlets There have been twelve additional loading bridges and gates, bringing the total to eighteen loading bridges. The new aircraft refuelling system and implementing new ground transportation improvements have also been provided.

From 2003 to 2015, Vantage held a technical services agreement with MBJ Airports Limited. Since 2015, the Concession is owned 74.5 per cent by GAP from Mexico and 2.5 per cent by Vantage from Canada. During this time, 2003–5 the concessionaire has invested US$200 million into the expansion of the Sangster Airport, including US$20 million runway rehabilitation and overlay, financed by shareholder loans and IFC loans designed to improve the passenger experience and increase non-aeronautical revenue, such as opening of the Caribbean's first ever walk-through World Duty-Free boutique.[33]

The SIA posted its best traffic in 2019, 4.7 million passenger traffic, with tourism contributing 95 per cent the traffic. The concession fee accounts for 45 per cent of SIA revenues and over US$200 million has been invested by the concessionaire. The Concessionaire now plan a runway expansion estimated to cost US$70 million and work is scheduled to be completed in 2023.[34]

Norman Manley International Airports Limited

Approval for the privatisation of Norman Manley Airport was given by Cabinet in November 1993. Norman Manley Airport was to be developed in three phases over five years, starting in 1995. Phase One involved the government providing US$7M in the 1995/1996 financial year to expand the customs hall by sixteen thousand square feet, installation of two baggage handling systems, upgrading of arrival and departure areas, and configuration of the transportation arrangements to improve traffic flow. Construction began November 1, 1995.

The second phase comprised improvements, mainly to the airside and involved expenditure of US$50 million, financed by the IDB (US$28 million) and Japanese Exim Bank (US$15.0 million), with the remaining US$7.0 million being met by the Airports Authority. Major life cycle rehabilitation of the runway and taxiway was needed. The refuelling hydrant system was to be upgraded, and the communications and air navigation systems modernised. As a part of the preparation for divestment Norman Manley's landside facilities were also to be prepared under Phase Two for privatisation, i.e., creation of a separate company to hold the landside assets of the airport. The third phase was to involve further expansion and the privatisation of landside.[35] Over the period since the decision to privatise the NMIA, over J$150 million has been spent on airside and landside facilities.

The principles which governed the privatisation and regulation of Sangster International Airport were to govern the privatisation and regulation of Norman Manley as well. Following the incorporation of SIA Limited as an airport terminal company, Norman Manley was similarly incorporated. After completing the programmed improvements, including a new passenger terminal and comprehensive overhauling of the runway, carried out towards the end of the 1990s, the government launched the privatisation of NMIA in December 2014. The government reissued an 'Expression of Interest' notice on March 30, 2015, with a submission deadline of April 17, 2015. At the time of privatisation, the NMIA was the subject of a management contract by a private operator.

The airport covers 224 hectares of land and is surrounded by the Kingston Harbour to the north and the Caribbean Sea to the east and south. The airport airside has a runway of 2,716 metres long with three high-speed exits that allow aircraft to leave the runway rapidly. The aircraft apron provides facilities to accommodate sixteen commercial airplanes. The passenger terminal building provides for ten thousand square metres of covered area with a total covered landside area of 39,881 square metres.

The three largest airlines operating from NMIA in 2016 were Jet Blue, 24 per cent; Caribbean Airlines, 23 per cent; American Airlines, 20 per cent, with others sharing about 5 per cent, except for West Jet with 3 per cent. The North American market accounted for 76 per cent of total scheduled seats, reflecting a concentration of Jamaicans in American cities such as New York, Miami, and Fort Lauderdale

Table 12.5: Passenger Airlines Serving NMIA

Caribbean Airlines	Caribbean Airlines
Aeraogaviota	Fly Jamaica
Cayman Airways	Insel Air
Caribbean Airlines which took over Air Jamaica	Inter-Caribbean Airways Formerly Air Turks and Caicos

Foreign Flag Airline	Foreign Flag Carriers
Air Canada	Delta Air Lines
American Airlines	Jet Blue Airways
British Airways	Spirit Airlines
Copa Airline	Westjet

Source: Norman Manley International Airport PPP Information Memorandum

The other main destinations are Toronto and London. Passenger traffic has been growing at 1.5 per cent with air cargo at 2.5 per cent over the period 1992–2016. Kingston benefits from a relatively small proportion of the tourists with Sangster International dominating this market. The volume of passenger traffic has increased from around 1.1 million in 1992 to just under 1.6 million in 2016. The forecast is for traffic to increase to 3.1 million by 2048. The NMIA's revenues increased from US$26.4 million in 2012 to US$37.3 million in 2016, split almost equally between aeronautical and non-aeronautical sources. The forecast capital need for the airport over a thirty-year period was US$77 million.[36]

International Finance Corporation was engaged by NIBJ as the transaction advisor along with LeighFisher as technical consultant, Ernst & Young as accounting and audit consultant and Gide Loyrette Nouel A.A.R.P (GLN), Patterson, Mair, Hamilton as legal advisor. An enterprise team was also established by the NIBJ, the agency responsible for the privatisation of the NMIA. In March 2015, tendering for the privatisation of the NMIA was initiated. However, the process was aborted as the privatisation structure was not well received by the investing market, hence this initiative was a case of re-tendering the new initiative. The timeline required the Request for Qualification on February 20, 2017, issue of Request for Proposal on May 1, 2017, submission of bids by November 2017 and transaction closing in August 2018. During the Sangster International privatisation exercise, the legal and regulatory framework was established, comprising the Civil Aviation Authority as the Airport Industry-Specific Regulator (Economic Regulation) Act and the Airport Authority Act. No changes were expected to the industry or regulatory or legal structure.

The winning bidder was expected to enter a long-term concession through a project with the AAJ, the grantor of the concession, and finance and completing a modernisation and expansion programme. The government was expected to meet a part of this cost of the expansion, which was expected to include a three-hundred metre runway extension along with additional capital works. The concessionaire was expected to pay an annual concession fee as a percentage of gross earning and pay the grantor an upfront concession fee of US$5 million and annual fees as a percentage of gross revenues.

The criteria for the selection of the winning bidder comprised technical capability and investment, operation capacity, demonstrated commercial capability, and a share of gross revenues as part of the concession fee. Following on the Expression of Interest notification, the RFP proposal was shared with five investors who were deemed pre-qualified proponents. They were:

1. Cedicor SA (Aeropuertos Argentina 2000 SA).
2. Zurich Airport International AG, and A-Port Chile SA.
3. Korea Airport Corporation Latin America, GK Capital Management Limited, and GraceKennedy Limited.
4. China Harbour Engineering Company Limited (CHEC)
5. A consortium of Ada International Limited and Corporación Aeroportuaria del Este SAS (Punta Cana International Airport), Jamaica Producers Group Limited and GBG Energy S de RL.

Two local companies, GraceKennedy Group and Jamaica Producers Group Limited, were part of two of the consortia shortlisted to participate.

From the group receiving the RFP three submitted a proposal. After the evaluation on October 10, the government announced that Grupo Aeroportuario del Pacifico S.A.B. De C.V. (GAP) was the preferred bidder for the NMIA concession. A twenty-five-year concession with an option to renew for a five-year agreement was executed between the PAC Kingston Airport Limited (PAC), a wholly owned subsidiary of GAP and the Airports Authority of Jamaica (AAJ). The transaction was finalised in October 2019 and will run until 2044. The NMIA also posted its best traffic in 2019, amounting to 1.8 million passenger traffic, with the majority being travellers visiting friends and relatives and business travellers making up 60 per cent of NMIA traffic in 2019. The current Master Plan: 2022 to 2025 projects an expenditure of US$31.0 million and a further US$134 million for the medium term up to 2030.[37]

Notes

1. Robert Grosse, 'A Privatisation Nightmare: Aerolineas Argentinas,' in *Privatising Monopolies: Lesson from Telecommunications and Transport in Latin America*, ed., Ravi Ramamurti (Baltimore: John Hopkins University Press, 1996), 203–220.
2. Portland Group, *Regulatory and Institutional Study for the Airport Sector in Jamaica: Diagnostic Review* (Kingston: AAJ and IADB, 1994).
3. The writer became chairman of the Board of AAJ in 1993 and was also made chairman of NMIA Limited and SIA Limited and project director for executing the physical improvements and the privatisation programme. I remained chairman up until the middle of 1999 when I was contracted by DFID and seconded to the Presidential Parastatal Reform Commission in Tanzania as Principal Privatization and Regulatory Consultant.
4. Alfred E. Kahn, *The Economics of Regulation: Principles and Institutions* (Cambridge and London: MIT Press, 1998).
5. M. E. Levine, 'US Deregulation: Evidence from 10 Years of Experience,' Revue International de Droit Economigue, March 1987.
6. Report of the Federal Commission, *Enquiry on Civil Aviation in the West Indies* (Trinidad and Tobago: Government Printing Office, 1960).
7. MPUT, 'Air Transport Sector Plan: Air Jamaica Five Year Plan, 1978–1982,' May 1978.
8. Sasekea Harris, 'Privatisation experience in Air Transport in Jamaica: The Case of Air Jamaica,' paper submitted for the Master of Science Degree in Government, University of the West Indies, 2017
9. P. Forsyth, 'Airlines and Airport: Privatisation, Competition and Regulation,' *Institute of Fiscal Studies* 5, no. 1 (February 1984): 61–75.
10. Government of Jamaica, Ministry Paper No. 35, 1994.
11. Ibid.
12. Sasekea Harris, 'Privatisation experience in Air Transport in Jamaica.'
13. IFC, 'Public Private Partnership Story, Jamaica, Air Jamaica,' *IFC Bulletin*, February 2011.
14. *Jamaica Gleaner*, July 21, 2010.
15. Janet Kelly, 'One Piece of a Large Puzzle: The Privatization of Vaasa,' in *Privatising Monopolies: Lessons from Telecommunications and Transport Sectors in Latin America*, ed., Ravi Ramamurti (Baltimore: John Hopkins Press, 1996), 241–277.
16. Airline Business, 'A Private Approach to Airport,' January 1993.
17. David Starkie, *Aviation Markets: Studies in Competition and Regulatory Reform Institute of Economic Association* (Hampshire: Ashgate Publishing Company, 2008).
18. H. Averch and Leland L. Johnson, 'Behaviour of the Firm under Regulatory Constraint,' *American Economic Review* 52, no. 5 (1962): 1052–69.
19. Stephen Littlechild, 'Regulation of British Telecommunications, Profitability,' Department of Industry, UK, 1983.

20. David Starkie, 'Reforming Airport Regulation,' *Journal of Transport Economics and Policy* 35, no. 1 (2001): 119–35.
21. Lamarre Valois, 'Jamaica Transportation Survey Report,' Ministry of Communications Works Government of Jamaica, Kingston, 1969.
22. Ellis Juan and Cezley Sampson, 'Airport in Jamaica: A Case Study in Airport Privatization through a Combination of PPI Mechanism (Wraparound),' in *Airport Infrastructure: The Emerging Role of the Private Sector, Recent Experiences*, ed. E. Juan, (Washington, DC: World Bank, 1995), 193–221.
23. Greenfield development refers to developing a system for a totally new environment and requires development from a clean slate – no legacy code around. It is an approach used when you're starting fresh and with no restrictions.
24. Alison Munro, *Government Policy as to Airport Privatization* (London, Department of Transport, 1993).
25. Birk Hillman Consultants, *Preliminary Design Report: Sangster International* (Kingston: AAJ, 1993).
26. A. Robert, 'Is Your Airport a Pot of Gold?' *Airport Magazine*, May 1992.
27. Cezley Sampson, 'Regulatory Framework in the Privatization of Airports: A Case Study of Jamaica,' paper delivered at the Latin American and Caribbean Conference on Privatisation, Lima, Peru, 1996.
28. Previous users received preference.
29. Ian Jones, Ivan Vieholt, and Phillip Marks, 'The Economic of Airport Slots,' *Fiscal Studies* 14, no. 4 (1993): 37–57.
30. Peter Forsyth, 'Airlines and Airports: Privatisation, Competition and Regulation' *Fiscal Studies* 5, no. 1 (1984): 61–75.
31. Juan and Sampson, 'Airport in Jamaica.'
32. Portland Group, *Regulatory and Institutional Study for the Airport Sector in Jamaica: Diagnostic Review* (Kingston: AAJ and IADB, 1994).
33. ICAO/MKIS/IATA/MBJ, 'Public Private Partnership (PPP): The Jamaican Case Study, Sangster International Airport,' 2015.
34. Audley Deidrick, 'Jamaica's Airport PPP Experience,' presentation at the Caribbean Workshop and Forum on Public Private Partnership for Debt Managers, Commonwealth Secretariat and DBJ, Kingston, Jamaica, June 2022.
35. Juan and Sampson, 'Airport in Jamaica.'
36. Kingston Norman Manley International Airport PPP Information Memorandum, Airport Authority of Jamaica and Development Bank of Jamaica in association with the IFC.
37. Deidrick, 'Jamaica's Airport PPP Experience.'

CHAPTER THIRTEEN

Development Liberalisation and Privatisation of the Jamaican Agrarian Economy: Sugar and Banana

HISTORICAL DEVELOPMENT OF THE SUGAR INDUSTRY

It was in new Guinea that sugar cane was first domesticated. From New Guinea cane spread westwards.[1] Sugar arrived in India possibly around 2000 BC. Sugar cultivation then spread to Persia and from there was taken to the Mediterranean by the Arabs. It was grown in Crete, Cyprus, and Sicily. From the Mediterranean, Spanish and Portuguese expansion carried the sugar cane southwards in the fourteenth century to Maderia and the Canary Islands, and here sugar evolved into a global industry. It was through the Portuguese in Maderia and the Canary Islands that the use of slave labour was introduced on a large scale and the division of labour between the enslaved and their absentee owners was perfected in the expansion of the sugar industry.

From the island of Gomera in the Canaries, Columbus and his sailors took cane cuttings during his third voyage to the New World Greater Antilles: Cuba, Puerto Rico, and Hispaniola. In 1509 when the first Spanish colonists arrived in Jamaica, they brought sugar cane with them.[2] The growing of sugar in Jamaica by the early settlers was mostly for domestic use. By the time the Spanish were forced out of Jamaica by the English in 1655, there were at least thirty small sugar plantations.

Soon after the English arrived in the West Indies, they grew sugar, first in St Kitts, Antigua, and Nevis and then Barbados in the 1620s. Although sugar was mainly grown as a smallholder crop, it ushered in the beginning of the plantation system. By 1655, Barbados became the main British territory in the West Indies for sugar production and the wealthiest of its colonies in the Americas. The island thrived as England's most important sugar colony, possessing some 358 sugar mills by 1683, producing four hundred hogshead of sugar.[3] Between 1625 and 1650, the English brought with them White indentured labourers from Europe to work on the plantations. During the reign of King Charles I, some thirty thousand indentured servants arrived in the Caribbean from Europe to serve as labourers in the growing of sugar. The experiment, however, proved unsuccessful, as the tropical climate and tropical diseases proved inhospitable for people accustomed to more temperate conditions.

Upon arriving in Jamaica, the English quickly shifted their focus to growing sugar because of the availability of larger land space. Against rising sugar prices in London, Jamaica expanded sugar production fivefold between 1700 and 1750 and would treble by 1774, replacing, Barbados as the leading English sugar growing island in the West Indies.[4]

Sugar plantations spread through the parish of Trelawny and then along the north coast through St James, and then southward along the Westmoreland plain. Along the North Coast, sugar spread east to St Mary and Portland and continued on to St Thomas. By 1740, there were four hundred sugar mills in Jamaica and, by 1768, Jamaica had 648 sugar estates producing 68,180 hogsheads[5] of sugar.[6] By 1786, the number of sugar estates on the island had increased to 850, making Jamaica not only the richest but the most valuable British overseas possession. Jamaica's inhabitants and absentee proprietors became some of the wealthiest people in the world. In 1774, the per capita wealth in England was around £42; in comparison, the per capita wealth of Jamaica's plantocracy was £100.[7]

The sugar industry enriched the White owners, mainly absentee investors, an emerging elite in Britain by the mid-eighteenth century. In fact, the description of a rich person in England was as 'rich as a West Indian planter.' The British colonies came to form the backbone of Great Britain as the leading capitalist nation.[8] Britain amassed great wealth from the sugar industry of Jamaica and the West Indies, and its income financed Britain's industrialisation and its emergence as one of the leading capitalists nations in the world. It achieved this status through the expropriation of profits from the sugar and slave trade that accompanied the plantation method of sugar production.

Not only did the West Indian economy provide large quantities of sugar for the British sugar refineries, but Jamaica and the Caribbean became important markets for the export of British goods. By the end of the seventeenth century, sugar had moved from being a luxury good for the elite in Europe to being an essential item in the diet of working-class people. This change in demand led to rapid expansion of sugar production in Jamaica, resulting in the island becoming the world's leading sugar exporter in the eighteenth century, before the island was overtaken by Brazil.

When Sugar Was Gold: 1750–1807

In the period 1750–1807, sugar was 'gold,' with the number of estates mushrooming from 430 in 1739 to 775 in 1775 and peaking at 859 in 1804, before declining to 320 in 1833.[9] Coincidentally, during the 125-year period between 1689 and 1815 known as the 'long eighteenth century,' Britain, with a population of under 10 million (less than half that of France), rose to the status of a world power. Britain rose from a commercial economy to an industrial one. Royals, landed barons, aristocrats, and parts of the rising bourgeoisie which formed the establishment, and which exercised political and economic control over society were the main beneficiaries of the expanding sugar industry and the rising British industrialisation.[10]

The number of sugar estates was highest during the period of the Atlantic trade. In 1754, about 11 per cent of the sixty White women who were listed as owning real estate in Spanish Town identified themselves as planters; among the well-known White women planters was Mary Eldridge.[11]

The Rise and Fall of the Plantation Economic System

Sugar production was perfected under the plantation economy that emerged as an efficient system for production and export of sugar as a commodity. The cultivation of sugar cane on plantations involved an integrated operation that encompassed various components. This included a factory system that entailed planting, reaping, and transporting canes to factories, managing the production of raw sugar primarily for export, utilising unpaid labour under a system of chattel slavery, and implementing methodologies for managing business and labour. Collectively, these components formed the plantation system of production.

The Plantation Economy was so named and criticised by a group of Caribbean economists: Lloyd Best,[12] George Beckford,[13] Norman Girvan and Cherita Girvan,[14] George Cumper,[15] and Clive Thomas,[16] who contended that it created economic and social dependency in Jamaica and the Caribbean; inefficient agriculture; high export prices; high foreign exchange cost, and technological stagnation in agriculture. In addition, the plantation economy created a rigid class-structured society, which disadvantaged the peasant class and favoured the small creole Whites or near Whites at the top of the hierarchical class structure.

It was the British who perfected the system of chattel slavery and the supply of cheap labour to Jamaica and their West Indian sugar plantations. The wealth from the trade in enslaved Africans triggered intensive rivalry among the British, French, Dutch, and Portuguese, resulting in Mercantilism, a policy aimed at restricting the trade in goods and chattel to its own colonies. The policy of mercantilism came to underpin maritime trade whereby only British ships could carry British manufactured goods and enslaved Africans to their West Indian territories, providing an assured market for sugar and other agricultural products for over 150 years. According to S. Mintz, Jamaica and the West Indian territories' mercantilism guaranteed Britain regular supplies of raw sugar for her sugar refineries in the UK while ensuring that the territories remained exclusive markets for British manufactured goods.[17]

Protectionism, which propped up the sugar industry, however, came up against the free trade movement and capitalism led by Adam Smith.[18] Not only was there a movement for free trade and the removal of protectionism, but there also emerged, at the same time, the movement for the abolition of the slave trade. Smith exposed the inefficiency of protectionism and the bankruptcy of the plantation system and highlighted the point that the plantation system only benefited a small, privileged and wealthy elite, while the rest of society suffered. The movement for the abolition of the slave trade which followed exposed the immorality of the trade in human beings. Abolition ended the transportation of enslaved people from Africa to Jamaica and other West Indian colonies after March 1808.

The abolition of the trade in enslaved Africans and the eventual abolition of the system of African enslavement in 1834 marked the beginning of the decline of the sugar industry, with the loss of the supply of free labour on which the plantations were dependent: The abolition of slavery was the defining moment in the fortunes of the Jamaican and West Indian plantation system and brought about the end of protectionism and mercantilism and the triumph of capitalism.[19] By the middle of the nineteenth century, Jamaican sugar became less competitive with high-volume producers like Brazil and Cuba, and production subsequently faltered.

These developments wrought havoc on the plantation system, as the Jamaican plantocracy could not convert the ex-enslaved into a wage labouring tenant class, similar to the ones established in the post-Civil War South of the US. On having gained their freedom, the newly freed Black Jamaicans fled in droves to the interior hillsides of Jamaica to establish free villages,[20] as their new communities.

The decline in sugar and other traditional agricultural products was dramatic. If we compare the three-year period 1830–34 just before emancipation with the three-year period 1846–48 immediately after the Emancipation Act, the scale of the impact on the economy was disastrous. The island exported less than half the sugar, rum, or ginger; less than one-third the coffee; less than one-tenth the molasses, and nearly two million pounds less of pimento, as shown in table 13.1

Table 13.1: The Decline of Agricultural Exports, 1830–48

Year Exported	Sugar Hogsheads	Rum Puncheons	Molasses Casks	Ginger Pounds	Pimento Pounds	Coffee Pounds
1830	100,205	35,025	154	1,748,800	5,560,620	22,256,950
1831	94,881	36,411	230	1,614,640	3,172,320	14,055,350
1832	98,686	33,685	799	2,355,560	4,024,800	19,815,010
Total	293,772	105,121	1,183	5,719,000	12,757,740	56,126,310
1846	36,223	14,395	76	1,462,600	2,997,060	6,047,150
1847	48,551	18,077	22	1,324,480	2,800,140	6,421,122
1848	42,212	20,191	2	320,340	5,231,908	5,684,941
Total	126,989	52,666	100	3,106,320	11,029,108	18,153,213
Diminution	166,783	52,455	1,083	2,802,180	1,628,532	38,983,097

Source: John Bigelow, 'Jamaica in 1850 Excerpts Form Economic Conditions, 1851.'

The Sugar Duties Equalisation Act of 1846 which liberalised the importation of sugar into the UK after 1854 and the expansion of the demand in Europe for beet sugar further aggravated the plight of the West Indian sugar planter, leading to a protracted period of economic decline at the end of 1890s. However, it was the expansion of demand for beet sugar in Europe after 1870s which provided competition for West Indian sugar. With the US introducing countervailing duties on beet sugar from Europe, there was a short respite in Jamaica's export sugar market. The US then granted special terms to Puerto Rico, the Philippines, and Cuba and sugar from these sources replaced West Indian sugar in the US markets.[21]

Between 1804 and 1854, the number of estates fell by 60 per cent, almost halved between 1844 and 1854. John Bigelow noted the sharp decline in export from an official report of the exports from the island, comparing production of Jamaica export crops in the three years prior to the Emancipation Act, with the exports for the three years preceding the month of October 1848; as summarised earlier in table 13.1.[22] The abandoned sugar works and plantations dislodged some thirty thousand labourers, putting two hundred thousand acres of land out of cultivation.

Table 13.2 below shows the decline in the number of sugar estates over the period 1663–1854.

Table 13.2: Rise and Decline of Sugar Plantations, 1663–1854

Year	No. of Sugar Estates in Jamaica
1663	57
1700	n.a.
1730	n.a.
1739	430
1748	NA
1768	651
1775	775
1789	710
1800	n.a.
1804	859
1815	n.a.
1828	n.a.
1832	653
1833	653
1834	646
1844	644
1848	504
1854	320

Source: James Robertson, *Map of Jamaica* (1804) and based on the survey 1709–99 published in 1804, Montpelier, James Blackwell and John Bigelow (1851), G. Eisner (1961), 'Jamaica 1830–1930.' Clinton Black,[23]

The number of estates had increased from 430 in 1739 to 775 in 1775 and peaked in 1804 at 859, declining thereafter, falling to 320 in 1833. John Bigelow stated that the decline was shattering for the economy and its people, with prices of estates falling to rock bottom: Fair Prospect estate, which used to yield five hundred hogsheads of sugar, and was valued at £40,000, was sold in 1841 for £4,000.[24] All over Jamaica, there was wide-scale abandonment of sugar plantations. By 1865, the number of sugar estates had declined to three hundred and continued to decline, so, by 1930, the number had fallen to thirty-nine. The average size of estates in cane was 187 acres in the 1860s; by 1930, the average size of estates in cane lands had increased to 661 acres, the result of amalgamation and centralisation and the creation of central factories. The several small factories and small estates which had existed in 1860 were replaced by larger factories and larger plantations, which made it possible for superior equipment to be employed. The post-war period, 1920–30, saw a recovery with the best years being 1922 and 1830, with 1.0 million cwt. each year, and the worst year being 1924 with 455,000 cwt.[25]

Sugar production in Jamaica declined from 39,400 tons in 1839 to 16,800 tons in 1880.[26] Clinton Black stated that the decline after the 1830s was devastating for the economy, with prices of estates falling to rock bottom. The record crop of 1805 was not repeated until 140 years later in 1945.[27]

Performance of Sugar Exports, 1814–1950

Export of sugar in the period 1814–36 experienced fluctuating decline between 1.77 million cwt. and 1.01 million cwt. The decline continued after 1809, fluctuating between 0.76 million cwt. in 1809 and 0.29 million cwt. in 1900. In 1903, exports fell to a low of 98,000 cwt.[28] In the period after the First World War, Europe, especially Germany, had developed and expanded beet sugar production. Germany capitalised on the new development and became the principal supplier of sugar to Britain by 1839, replacing Jamaica in the British market by 1880. In 1853, Britain imported 1.476 million tons of sugar, of which 14 per cent was from beet, 17 per cent from British cane sugar, and 69 per cent from foreign sugar. By 1980, British imports had increased to 3.278 million tons of this beet sugar.[29] The price of sugar again fell rapidly in 1873 and continued to fall until the end of the 1890s. Sugar production continued its downward movement and, in the period 1871–1901, sugar exports fell by about 43 per cent.

The West Indian planter class, their British absentee owners and their merchant supporters fought back to protect their interest during this period, with the planters' main success being able to secure compensation of £20 million for the abolition of slavery. The Imperial government in London had to take out a bond to finance the payments, amounting to some 5 per cent of GDP; almost 10 per cent of the population in the UK benefited from the compensation.

Donovan Stanbury noted that the latter half of the nineteenth century represented the darkest days for the Jamaica sugar industry.[30] With the depressed condition, the plantocracy resorted to intensive lobbying of Westminster, and this led to the establishment of the 1887 Royal Commission of Inquiry, which recommended that Brittan reintroduced protectionist measures, especially against European beet sugar to save the Jamaican and West Indian sugar industry.

Some trade protections were reintroduced in 1902, but they were not institutionalised until 1929. The West Indian Sugar Commission of Inquiry of 1929–30, which was established after the First World War recommended the reintroduction of a tariff and subsidy regime in Britain to protect West Indian sugar. Protection was to include purchasing at a price above the cost of production in the West Indies, backed by imposing non-reciprocal tariff to be applied against non-imperial sugar. The preferential price was to cover not only production cost but also freight, depreciation, and a profit margin. Besides trade protection in the UK market, the Sugar Manufacturer Association in Jamaica was granted monopoly rights to market all sugar consumed in Jamaica. These arrangements, while providing an assured market in Imperial Britain dis-incentivised the local sugar producers from modernising their agricultural and manufacturing methods and improving the efficiency and lowering the cost of production. In effect, a cost-plus pricing regime was introduced for sugar export with a guaranteed profit margin.

This trade protection, coupled with the First World War, wreaked havoc on European beet sugar production, while giving Jamaican and West Indian sugar a new lease on life. The period after the war was accompanied by an aggressive expansion of the industry, and sugar production increased from 55,596 tons in 1929 to 156,502 tons in 1941.[31] The 1929 Imperial Preference Act was carried forward into the Commonwealth Sugar Agreement of 1953, and these arrangements remained in place until the UK entered the European Common Market in 1973. Upon joining the EU, the preferential arrangements were transferred into Sugar Protocol of the Lomé Convention under which African, Caribbean and Pacific producers (ACP) could access the EEC market at preferential prices, as well as under a quota system. The preferential sugar arrangement gave a false security to West Indian politicians regarding the future of the industry and, in part, continued to work against improving the efficiency of the industry or in the diversification of agriculture. In 1950, sugar production was 271,582 tons; by 1959, production rose to 378,255 tons, with the decade of the 1960 representing the best years for the industry in terms of production and exports.

Performance of the Industry, 1945–69

Table 13.3 shows the production and export performance of the industry from 1945 to 1969 (in five-year intervals) for cane milled, raw sugar produced, and export tons.

Table 13.3: Sugar Production and Export in Tons, 1945–69

5-Year Periods	Sugar Cane Milled – 000	Raw Sugar Produced	Export
1945	1,325	152,000	118,000
1950	2,476	271,000	221,000
1955	3,565	396,000	289,000
1960	4,326	418,000	363,000
1965	4,721	515,000	484,000
1969	3,993	368,000	302,000

Source: Owen Jefferson, *Post-War Economic Development of Jamaica*

Output of sugar increased threefold from 1.32 million tons of cane milled in 1945 to 4.7 million tons milled in 1965. Part of the increase in sugar production was because of increased acreage into cultivation and improved management provided by Tate & Lyle and other transnationals.

Sugar production reached five hundred and fifteen thousand tons in 1965, while export of sugar reached four hundred and eighty-four thousand tons. The year 1965 marked the highest performance of the industry in terms of cane milled, sugar produced, and sugar exported. After 1965, decline again set in, with cane milled falling to 3.99 million tons, sugar produced to three hundred and sixty-eight thousand tons, and sugar exported to three hundred and two thousand tons respectively, in 1969. Despite the expansion in the 1960s, in 1969, production did not meet international export commitments. The year Jamaica gained independence, 1962, sugar production was nearly five hundred thousand tons, grown on some sixty thousand hectares of land, accounting for 22.53 per cent of export earnings, and was the largest employer of labour. The period saw a transformation of the industry through factory centralisation, resulting in the number of sugar factories declining from thirty-nine in 1930 to twenty-six in 1944, with an annual average output of 5,842 tons. In 1930, there were only three foreign-owned sugar factories and only six were incorporated as limited liability companies. By 1936, British multinational Tate & Lyle had acquired twenty-five farms and built Frome sugar factory, not only the largest on the island but the most modern, able to refine raw sugar into white sugar. Frome became the dominant producer on the island. This period saw, for the first time, infusion of foreign capital by the British multinational conglomerates into the industry.

With introducing new investors, new varieties of sugar cane, more modern methods of agricultural techniques for the first time were employed, involving wider use of chemical fertiliser, as well the employment of more modern factory production techniques. Between 1927 and 1943, yield increased from twenty-seven tons per acre to forty-three tons per acre.[32]

Despite the improvements made by the new foreign investors, the Jamaican planters remained moribund in archaic farming and production methods. Most Jamaican planters continued to operate with old technology, achieving low sugar recovery, poor factory utilisation, accompanied by low yield by the smallholder farmers, rendering Jamaica a very high-cost producer, when compared to other Caribbean producers, such as Cuba and the Dominican Republic.

Between 1954 and 1965, the cost of production in Jamaica increased from 69 per cent, while output rose by only 10 per cent; hence, despite rising production, several of the sugar businesses were loss makers in the 1960s. Over the period 1956–59, yield varied between 9.03 tons per acre and 10.86 tons per acre of raw sugar, well below the productivity levels of Cuba and the Latin American producers. In 1960, the industry regularly employed about twenty-three thousand workers during crop time, and thirteen thousand out-of-crop time, giving an estimated employment of about sixty thousand, with labour cost accounting for about 48 per cent of production cost, inclusive of growing cane.[33]

Although production expanded after the Second World War, sugar's contribution to GDP in 1953 had fallen to 9.1 per cent, declining further to 4.5 per cent in 1968 and, as a share of merchandise export, it fell from 46.5 per cent to 20.0 per cent. As a share of exports of goods and services the decline was from 31.5 per cent to 12.5 per cent. Sugar's contribution to the economy, in relative terms, declined sharply because of the rapid expansion of the bauxite and alumina, or mineral industry, and rise of tourism. Sugar, however, as a labour-intensive industry remained the largest employer of low-wage workers. For years, the Jamaican government refused to allow the industry to mechanise farming methods.[34] Dependence on manual labour to save jobs stymied the development of what had become elsewhere, a technology-driven industry after independence. The result was Jamaica's failure to significantly improve technology, both in the factory and in the field, preventing the creation of a more sustainable industry, and the generation of more jobs in the wider economy in the long term.

Although the industry rebounded, little of the benefits flowed to the sugar workers and the ordinary people of Jamaica. The result was widespread unrest, starting in the sugar belt area of the island, but spreading to other parts in 1938. The 1938 labour upheaval which started in the sugar belt, not only gave birth to the modern trade union movement in Jamaica, but it ushered in the two-party political system, culminating in adult suffrage in 1944, internal self-government and finally independence in 1962. There is no doubt the politics and social conditions of the sugar workers and their protestations played a major role in Jamaica obtaining self-government and political independence.

While Jamaica gained political independence, and there was a rising brown middle class, the economic conditions of Black Jamaicans, especially in the sugar belt areas, experienced marginal improvements. Jamaica's sugar business was recording repeated financial deficits by 1965. The newly independent government established the Mordecai

Commission of Inquiry in 1966 to examine the state of affairs of the sugar industry and recommend remedial measures.

Although sugar production had reached its zenith in 1965, the estates were chalking up losses. Monymusk Estates operated by the West Indies Sugar Company (WISCO), for instance, lost over US$4 million on cane farming operation between 1967 and 1970.[35] The unprofitable farming side of the cane business was perpetuated by the government's continued refusal to allow labour-saving methods in harvesting, as was being practised in Australian sugar farms, for fear of job losses. Then Prime Minister Hugh Shearer, a former union leader, felt such a move would carry major political and social ramifications. His administration was prepared to resist mechanisation in order to protect the employment of the large number of low-paid sugar workers, most of whom were aligned to the Bustamante Industrial Trade Union, an affiliate of the Jamaica Labour Party of which Shearer was leader. As a result of the continuing financial losses, Tate & Lyle in 1970 gave up the agricultural side of the industry, triggering public intervention for the first time in direct ownership and operation of sugar estates. The government stepped in and purchased Tate & Lyle's Frome and Monymusk estates, comprising sixty thousand acres in 1971 for US$8.1 million.

State Ownership in The Sugar Industry, 1960–72

The government was drawn into public ownership of the sugar business for the same motives as earlier governments had been drawn into public ownership of the urban bus transportation operation, and earlier still into public ownership of the railway, that of protecting the welfare of workers and avoiding massive socio-economic dislocation. Following its acquisition of the two operations, the government vertically unbundled the factory operations from the agricultural sugar lands and leased back the factory business to Tate & Lyle. Simultaneously, the administration also purchased the Bernard Lodge Sugar Estate and, along with the Frome and Monymusk lands, brought them under the control of a newly created state-owned enterprise, Frome Monymusk Land Company Limited (FMLCo).

Having acquired the sugar lands, the plan was to privatise these lands by subdivision at Frome, Monymusk, and Bernard Lodge estates into plots of one hundred to five hundred acres, and outright sale (transfer of title) to local farming communities so that local farmers would carry out the agricultural side of the sugar business. In this way, the government was vertically and horizontally unbundling the agricultural side of the industry, the component which was labour intensive, leaving Tate and Lye to operate the sugar factories which were the capital-intensive side and which were more profitable.

1972–80 Employee Buyout (EBO) Form of Privatisation: PNP Cooperatives

With a change of administration in 1972, a People's National Party (PNP) government took an entirely new approach regarding assets acquired from the private operators and opted for a form of employee buyout (EBO), with the operating entities being sugar cooperatives, and this lasted for six years between 1974 and 1980. The freehold arrangement planned by the previous Jamaica labour Party (JLP) government was replaced by leasehold, as this provided the government with some measure of continued control and freed the farmers from the upfront capital costs of acquiring the sugar lands.[36] The initial plan was to proceed with implementation of three blocks of lands, one on each of the three estates, expecting all the lands would be developed as sugar cooperatives on successful implementation of the three pilot projects. In the pilot projects, one thousand acres were to be subdivided into lots of thirty to forty acres with a requirement that these form a cooperative under FMLCo guidance. FMLCo would continue to own the lands on behalf of the government and facilitate the development of the cooperatives. It would also provide certain marketing and related functions, such as ploughing and use of mechanical tractors.

The project did not get off the ground for some six months, and it was through the driving force of the Social Action Centre, a Jesuit NGO, that the project was pushed through.[37] Finally, in May 1974, FMLCo pushed ahead with the three pilot cooperative projects, with a start date commencing with the 1974/75 crop season. However, there was further change in the project arrangements as instead of thirty- to forty-acre individual lots, the entire farm was to be organised as one production unit, with the workers being members of a single organising unit. The pilot projects were respectively Morelands in Monymusk, Barham in Frome, and Salt River in Bernard Lodge, comprising over six thousand acres of land, based on a forty-nine-year lease, involving five hundred worker/farmers.

The workers involved were made redundant and given between J$500 and J$2,000 in redundancy payment. With a high world market price for sugar in 1974, the first year of operation showed a profit. The success provided the basis for implementation of full programmes of cooperatives, resulting in some forty-five thousand acres, involving some five thousand sugar workers/farmers, controlling some 20 per cent of all sugar lands in Jamaica in 1975. Had the government proceeded with the original plan of subdividing the blocks of land into smaller parcels for sale, as the previous government had planned, possibly thousands of sugar workers would have been disenfranchised.

In 1976, the government created another state-owned enterprise, National Sugar Company Limited (NSC), to take control of the factories acquired from Tate & Lyle Limited and which were under FMLCo management. Between 1975 and 1985, the NSC acquired and operated eight of the factories on behalf of the government: WISCO's Tate & Lyle factories of Frome and Monymusk in 1975; Gray's Inn in St Mary in 1975; Bernard Lodge in 1976; Sevens Estate in 1977, and Long Pond, Duckenfield, Holland, and Innswood in 1978. Thus, by 1977, the government had acquired effective control of 65 per cent of the country's sugar processing capacity. The volume of cane and sugar per hectare, however, experienced a sharp decline as poor quality cane and agronomic practices, and obsolete machinery affected productivity, and the matter was made worse by poor and inefficient transportation. The industry also came under attack from smut and rust disease infestation and adverse weather. In addition, this was when shortage of foreign exchange reduced access to required input supplies, such as fertilisers and plant protection chemicals that were not available in the quantities required, or not available on a timely basis. These factors impacted investments and, consequently, on the modernisation of the industry and contributed to the decline in production after 1965.

During the six-year period that the cooperatives existed, they did little to improve the poor working conditions of workers and to expand sugar output. The period saw a sharp decline in production and exports. The cooperatives had inherited an industry that was in decline, with operations that were rundown and needing injection of new capital. The financial deficit chalked up before the cooperatives took over the sugar lands continued during each year of operation, with serious cash flow problems, while the debt continued to mount.[38]

During this period, the government made efforts to expand the export market for sugar through the 'Iran Sugar Deal.' However, this initiative faced an issue with the contract arrangement. It was structured as a simple CIF (cost insurance and freight) contract, when it should have been CIFO (cost insurance freight and unloading), meaning that the seller would be responsible for cost, insurance, and freight, while the buyer should have provided unloading berthing facilities upon the ship's notice of arrival at the port. In addition, the buyer should have been responsible for unloading the cargo within the time specified in the freighting contract and, if not, be responsible for demurrage charges or deterioration in the cargo, which may accrue from delays in unloading.

The privatisation of the of the state-acquired sugar lands as described above was an employee buyout. This involves the employees of an industry, or company obtaining majority control of the assets of a company, or industry, to which they were previously employed and creating a new corporate structure, concentrating management in a small group from a widely dispersed set of participating workers. EBO should provide job security. In an employee buyout, the workers are usually paid redundancy and other labour-related obligations due to them. This can either be used to finance the business, or for personal expenditure. With sugar, most of the redundancy payments were used for personal expenditure and not reinvested in the cooperatives.

A major problem of the EBO, and this also goes for the cooperative structure as well, was the existence of a conflict of interest in that, at one point, workers obtained weekly wages from the cooperatives, hence they had an interest in being unionised and securing higher pay. At the other end, they were participant owners in the cooperatives, where the rewards would be provided as dividends at the end of the year, a much more uncertain way of benefiting from their endeavours. During the period, some workers went on strike – against themselves – to demand higher wages and better conditions.

The cooperatives also had limited access to management skills, as the managers of the former Tate & Lyle operation did not join cooperatives. This would have made privatisation an employee management buyout (EMBO), and at least would have provided for some management expertise to be available to the cooperatives. In the absence of such expertise, the cooperative had to rely on the former managers of Tate &

Lyle, who had moved over to the Frome and Monymusk Land Company, and they had not bought into the cooperative structure. In fact, they were hostile to the entire scheme.

Donovan Stanberry raised the point that, with a vertically integrated industry of factory and farm, Tate & Lyle would have been able to use the more profitable factory business to cross-subsidise the loss-making field operation.[39] It was therefore unrealistic to have saddled the farmers with the cane lands without some form of support. However, with a cooperative of factory and farm, it is unlikely that the workers would have been able to find the capital or obtain access to capital which would have been needed for the capital-intensive factory operations, making the vertical integration of factory and sugar farming more disastrous. EBO works well where the business is labour intensive.

Stanberry also cited several other reasons for the failure of the 1970 cooperative venture as follows:

- Much of the lands meant for growing cane was marginal and in saline condition, not ideal for sugar farming.
- There was too much delay by the government in implementing the new arrangements; in fact, at some point, the government was in a state of inertia and, had it not been for the activism of the non-governmental organisation, the Social Action Council (SAC), in mobilising the workers, little progress would have been made. There was a noticeable gap between the government's policy pronouncement and implementation.
- There was over-staffing of the cooperatives by sugar workers. All workers involved in the cooperatives were guaranteed three days' work per week in the out of harvest time, whereas under Tate & Lyle's operation they would have been made redundant during this period.
- Under Tate & Lyle, the factory operated between Mondays and Fridays and avoided overtime. With the cooperatives, the workers insisted on weekend work at added cost to operations. The workers, while being participant-beneficiaries in the cooperatives, insisted on continuing being members of their trade union, demanding similar pay as obtained by non-cooperative estates.
- The board and managers of FMLCo were non-cooperative. The managers systematically undermined and frustrated the

operations of the cooperatives. The cooperatives relied on SIA, and FMLCo, a subsidiary of SIA for accounting, payments, human resource management and certain other administrative services.[40] The sugar workers were ordinary cane cutters, many with limited education; they were looked on as an underclass by the managers of FMLCo.

- There was lack of coherent implementation of a strategy and absence of preparation by the government of the members of the cooperatives for their new role.

These factors combined to work against long-term success. The cooperatives also had inherited obsolete practices, were overwhelmed with the problems and, by 1980, were insolvent and on the verge of bankruptcy. Many other factors, other than inefficient state management, contributed to the decline of sugar in the 1970s, including falling world price, falling yields, declining quality, labour unrest, and factory inefficiency.[41]

There were several other financial failures across a significant portion of the industry in the 1970s. With NSC taking over factory operations of Frome, Monymusk, and Bernard Lodge and several local privately owned sugar businesses, as well as the distilleries and shipping facilities, the government became the dominant player in the industry by 1979. Further state involvement did not result in any major new capital infusion in the industry in the 1970s.

Between 1975 and 1985, the NSC acquired Monymusk, Long Pond, and Innswood distilleries, sugar warehouses, and two shipping facilities in Clarendon and Westmoreland. With this acquisition, the government came to own twelve sugar factories and controlling interest in the Sugar Manufacturers Corporation of Jamaica and the Sugar Producers Association (JSPA). With the acquisition of Monymusk, Long Pond, and Innswood distilleries, it also came to own most of the distilleries, and their operations were transferred to a newly created SOE, National Rums Limited (NRL), a subsidiary of NSC, in 1979. Through NRL, the government came to control 49 per cent of the rum industry, with the other 51 per cent mostly being owned by Wray & Nephew Limited and Hamden Estates Limited. The rum interests formed the Spirits Pool Association (SPA), through which all Jamaican rum was marketed. The SPA then owned Caribbean Molasses Limited (CML), responsible for marketing Jamaican molasses. Almost all the operations the government had acquired were losing money in 1979. The cumulative losses for the NSC in 1980 was J$82 million.[42]

Table 13.4 below shows sugar production and export performances over the decade of 1970–80, the period of the sugar cooperatives. This was the period when Jamaica, as an independent country, was supposedly in control of the economy. Cane milled declined from 4.2 million tons in 1970 to 2.76 million tons in 1980 and, similarly, sugar outputs fell from 373,900 tons to 250,700 tons in 1980. Sugar exports at the same time fell from 298,000 tons to 131,800 tons in 1980.

Table 13.4: Sugar Production for Five-Year Period: 1970–80 PNP Cooperatives

Year	Cane Milled – 000 (tons)	Sugar Output (tons)	Export (tons)
1970	4,214	373,900	298,000
1975	3,581	366,400	258,400
1980	2,764	250,700	131,800

Source: Sugar Industry Authority of Jamaica – Sundry Years

Sugar Privatisation: Privatisation by Contract: 1980–

On the JLP returning to power in 1980 and regaining control of the sugar assets,[43] the cooperatives were dissolved in 1981.[44] In 1980, sugar cane fields occupied 25 per cent of the total land acreage under cultivation, employing forty thousand workers, or 18 per cent of the island's workforce, although employment was seasonal. Sugar acreage by 1984 had declined to forty thousand hectares. Farms over two hundred hectares held the overwhelming share of the land under cane, usually occupying the more fertile coastal plains. In 1986, Jamaica had to import sugar from Guatemala to meet its domestic demand and export quota obligation. In fact, Jamaica has consistently imported most of the refined sugar to meet the demand for the product needed in the food and beverage industries. There have been accusations that some of this duty-free sugar found its way into the regular market. Duty applies to sugar imported for the retail trade.

In 1985, it was clear that NSC was short of critical investments, and this led to the government approaching the World Bank for a loan to rehabilitate the industry's facilities, starting with Frome, Monymusk, and Bernard Lodge. The loan conditionalities required restructuring of the of government-owned sugar assets. In this respect, Jamaica Sugar Holding Limited (JSH) (another SOE) was created in 1985, and the operations of Frome and Monymusk were transferred from the NSC to the JSH, with the government assuming some J$200 million of the JSH's debt. The World Bank then provided US$40 million for the rehabilitation of the government's field and factory operations. The SCJ was closed down in 1985 to reduce government intervention in the industry. Responsibility for export marketing of sugar was transferred from the SIA to an independent company, managed by the sugar producers. Three of the state-owned factories that had run into financial problems were liquidated. By 1985, the number of factories in the industry had dwindled to twelve, supported by twenty-four thousand registered cane farmers, with the sizes varying from half an acre to fifteen hundred acres.

As a part of the World Bank Agricultural Structural Adjustment Agreements, the government was to be relieved of management of the sugar business and, as a result, Tate & Lyle, was invited back as the management contractor. The privatisation contract provided for incentive payments for output over one hundred and twenty thousand tons per annum and £850,000 termination cost, irrespective of the reasons for termination of the five-year contract. The Tate & Lyle management contract of 1985 did not last for long as, with a weak competitive industry position, the company's intervention made little difference. As a result, Tate & Lyle, United Fruit Company, and several of the other private operators exited the industry in Jamaica in the latter half of the 1980s.

As part of the reforms, the government also had to write off J$212.0 million of debt. The JSH, like the NSC before, was plagued with a weak financial base, losing J$102.7 million in 1988/89 and J$64.2 million in 1989/90, and had to rely heavily on borrowing from the SIA.[45] Some lands once used for cane cultivation were taken out of and put into alternative crops, mainly bananas, and winter vegetables, the latter for the US market. The lease programme also proved to be a failure for lack of investments and working capital by the new private sector owners. Part of the problem arose from the fact that the commercial banks refused to accept leasehold titles as collateral for loans.

In 1982, the Ministry of Agriculture also embarked on a programme of sale of idle lands, and by 1990, over thirty-six thousand acres (in lots of three to ten acres) of seventy-seven thousand acres earmarked for sale were sold to farmers at an average price of J$2,000 per acre. Agro 21 Limited, a state-owned company, as part of the leasehold programme which was launched in 1984 (lease contracts were for forty-nine years) divested thirty-four properties involving 34,571 acres, besides divesting fourteen agro-enterprises and/or assets.

Up to 1990, general privatisation of the industry was strongly resisted, and this was although the privately owned factories remained profitable, with high rates of capacity utilisation (90 per cent), in sharp contrast to the low levels of utilisation (40–65 per cent) in the state-owned plants. The political imperative of employment protection guaranteed that the 1985 reforms involving some private sector participation would run into difficulties.

The JSH lost US$12 million in the financial year, ended September 1991 on turnover of US$27.5 million. Petroleum Corporation of Jamaica (PCJ), and another state entity, Petronol/Bernard Lodge subsidiary, reported a loss of US$0.9 million on revenues of US$2.85 million and had an accumulated deficit of US$4.5 million. The NSC's Long Pond broke even on US$4.8 million revenues; however, it had an accumulated deficit of US$0.6 million. Table 13.5 shows the performance of the sugar industry over the period 1980–90.

Sugar cane milled fell from 2.76 million tons in 1980 to 2.57 million tons in 1990; factory production fell from 250,700 tons to 219,100 tons, with exports fluctuating between one hundred and fifty-one thousand tons and one hundred and thirty-one thousand tons over the same ten-year period.

Table 13.5: Sugar Production for Five-Year Periods, 1980–90

Year	Cane Milled – 000 (tons)	Sugar Output (tons)	Export (tons)
1980	2,764	250,700	131,800
1985	2,270	210,000	151,000
1990	2,572	219,100	147,100

Source: Sugar Industry Authority of Jamaica – Sundry Years

Sugar Privatisation in 1990 Onwards

By the end of the 1990s, the privately operated factories: Wray & Nephew's New Yarmouth and Appleton, Tropicana's Duckenfield and Hampden and Worthy Park accounted for 38 per cent of total national production. The state sector comprised the JSH, with 57.1 per cent of shares held by the accountant general and 42.9 per cent by the SIA. The JSH owned the two largest factories/estates. The inactive National Sugar Company held the shares in Long Pond, which was leased to and operated by independent private farmers. The other state factory/ estate, Petroleum Corporation of Jamaica's Bernard Lodge, should have been converted to ethanol production following its takeover in 1986. The PCJ did not go through with this plan and, after temporary closure, Bernard Lodge reverted to sugar production. Of the public sector holdings, the JSH accounted for 47 per cent of output, Long Pond 7 per cent, and Bernard Lodge 8 per cent.

Restructuring the Sugar Industry in Preparation Second Round of Privatisation

The World Bank conditionalities required liberalisation of agricultural importation and deregulation of the domestic marketing of sugar, subject to imposing a levy based on world market prices or a benchmark price. Domestic prices of raw and refined sugar were also deregulated.

To prepare for the 1990 round of privatisation, the government was required to restructure the industry. In the 1970s, state interventionist policies of the Sugar Industry Authority (SIA) were created as a statutory body by an amendment to the Sugar Industry Control Act of 1937 – an outcome of the Mordecai Commission of Inquiry, replacing the Sugar Control Board. The World Bank also insisted on a separate accounting of the proceeds of the sale coming from sugar and molasses which, up to then, was carried out by the SIA.

The Authority's main responsibilities were to regulate and control the industry, including the functions of arbitration, monitoring, planning, research and development, and marketing of sugar and molasses. Section 6 of the Act empowered the SIA to be the sole marketer of all sugar in Jamaica. The Authority has been funded by a charge, levied on each ton of sugar produced in Jamaica. The regulation stemmed from the peculiar structure of the industry, with several contending groups seeking to benefit from the price paid for sugar. The Authority adjudicated between the contending parties (farmers and manufacturers) in determining the price paid to farmers for their cane. In addition to determining the price, the Authority also handled the sale of Jamaican raw sugar and importation of raw sugar. The SIA had dramatically expanded its role in the industry, taking on a very wide and conflicting role in the 1970s, acquiring real estate and rolling stock, responsible for allocation of foreign exchange and functioning as the industry's banker. The Authority, in addition to its regulatory function, took on operational roles, funding the industry, creating operating subsidiaries, owning industry assets, providing extension services to independent farmers, and acting as the principal advisor to the Minister of Agriculture on industry matters. The Authority also handled the sale of Jamaican raw sugar and the importation of raw sugar. In this regard, it determined quota allocation. This ended in 1986, as the World Bank required this function to be removed from the SIA and handed over to a new company, Jamaica Cane Products Sale Limited (JCPS).

The SIA was reorganised to focus on its primary statutory regulatory role, monitoring, and quality control, with all its commercial functions being transferred to the JCPS, a company created and owned by the farmers and sugar manufacturers. The JCPS was created under joint ownership by the All-Island Jamaica Cane Farmers Association (AIJCFA) and the Sugar Manufacturers Association (SMCJ), which was incorporated in 1986. The JCPS was assigned the commercial duties associated with acquiring local sugar for Jamaica's export market, as well as the responsibility for importing raw sugar for local consumption. The JCPS took over these commercial functions, formerly executed by the SIA, and acted as its agent for the marketing of all sugar destined for the preferential export markets in the EU and the US. This was carried out through an agency agreement between the JCPS and the SIA. The Sugar Control Act was later amended in 1994 to facilitate most of these changes. The SIA also regulated domestic wholesale prices, as well as the price to cane farmers. The JPCS was a convenient vehicle to pool all sugar produced in Jamaica by all the factories and sell in bulk to British sugar refiners, as well as taking over responsibility for the importation of all sugar to Jamaica, selling mainly to the food manufacturing industry and retail distributers. The JCPS handled all the warehousing, shipping, and logistics. Jamaica Cane JCPS was incorporated in 1984.[46]

The JCPS made its margin from selling of imported sugar on the local market and on the price paid by Caribbean Molasse Limited, which purchased bulk molasses on behalf of all the distributors. The company sold sugar in the local market at a higher price than obtained in Europe. The profit from this was added to the export revenue to determine the declared price of sugar and ultimately the price paid to farmers. In this way, consumers of sugar in Jamaica were subsidising all the parties in the industry's local supply chain. The price paid for cane was based on the quality of cane delivered at the factory and was determined by testing through core sampling, carried out by testing infrastructure owned by the SIA, but based at the individual factory. The actual testing was carried out by the SIA.

The Second Round of Privatisation

In 1991, pressure from the World Bank resulted in withdrawal of the US$40 million earmarked to rehabilitate the industry. This led the government to include the sugar industry in the set of businesses approved for privatisation.[47] Besides the government absorbing J$200 million of Frome and Monymusk' s debt in 1985 before Tate and Lyle began its management contract, the four estates had accumulated a total debt of J$543.5 million. Monymusk experienced financial losses seven out of the previous eight years; Bernard Lodge accumulated losses all eight years. Frome was slightly better, accumulating losses in four of the previous eight years, while Long Pond accumulated losses in three of the previous eight years.[48]

An Enterprise Team was eventually created for the divestment in September 1992 and began preparatory work on privatisation of government-held sugar estates.[49] The financial pressure of the sugar and airline industry on the budget had become untenable, eventually leading to the government reluctantly accepting privatisation, in keeping with its commitments with the World Bank. A major reason for government reconsidering its position was the large indebtedness of the state-owned sugar operations. Between 1985 and 1992, the sugar SOEs, including Long Pond, accumulated J$3,441 million of debt.[50] Technically, the sugar companies were insolvent and poised to become a continuing major burden on the fiscal budget of the government.[51]

For the industry to survive, major overhauling was needed to modernise aged and obsolete equipment. One estimate was that

J$2,934.8 million was needed to bring the industry up to date.[52] Another estimate considered this conservative and estimated that J$5.852 million was needed.[53] It is against this background that then Prime Minister Patterson presented to Parliament Ministry Paper No. 34, with the decision to recommence privatisation of sugar in the early 1990s, despite the previous failed attempts through EBO/cooperative management, contract and lease arrangements.

The decision to privatise the industry, more than anything else in 1991, was driven by the desire to reduce the drain on fiscal resources and to improve efficiency through private operation and was one conditionality of the World Bank. The Bank insisted that the privatisation proceed because of the large fiscal drain on the central budget of government. Sugar, however, was one of the most politicised of the industries slated for privatisation, with the pricing of sugar products outside of the hands of the producers. Jamaica's export of sugar, as shown earlier, was sold through a non-reciprocal preferential trading system, mostly through European Union quotas, and at prices substantially higher than the prevailing world market prices in the 1990s.

After consultation with the industry, the NIBJ, in considering the market for privatised sugar assets, concluded that there was only a handful of potential buyers with the capacity and willingness to finance such a risky operation as sugar. The result was the government, from the start, was in a weak negotiating position, with low bids expected. Although the estates were valued by the Divestment Committee at J$3.1 billion, it was unexpected that this sum would be realised. Thus, the following was set out by the government as the guiding framework for the privatisation:

- There was to be broad-based ownership capable of ensuring improved labour productivity, improved factory efficiencies, and productivity sensitive to the need of the community.
- The proposed divestiture of the cane lands was to be broad-based, with a long-term lease arrangement, as opposed to the direct sale of the sugar lands.
- Redundancy entitlements were not to be tied to a worker's investment. It was agreed that redundancy matters would be addressed according to existing laws.
- There would be the need for a new regulatory framework.

- There was to be continued centralised marketing of sugar and centralised importation of sugar.

Advertisement inviting expressions of interest (EOI) were issued on June 7, 1993, for receipt of interest by close of September 4, 1993. Ten potential investor groups responded. At the end of the evaluation, exercise approval regarding negotiations was given by the government regarding two of the shortlisted bidders for the sugar estates, covering Frome, Monymusk, and Bernard Lodge Estates and Long Pond Sugar Company, successors of Long Pond Estate. Following on the consultations and clarifications of the following terms were arrived at:

1. Outright sale price for the factory and factory land at Monymusk, Frome, Bernard Lodge, and Long Pond at J$1.4 billion;
2. Lease income to the government for the lands associated with the transaction at J$25 million per annum, renewable every five years, with a lease tenure of forty-nine years;
3. The government to retain 24 per cent of the equity in the new special-purpose vehicle created to operate the privatised assets with 10 per cent share ownership retained for the workers, and 15 per cent for cane farmers, both to be held initially by the government, to be divested subsequently to both groups;
4. Thirty per cent to 60 per cent of the proceeds of new foreign exchange earnings from the preferential sugar quotas to be appropriated by the government over a five-year period;
5. The new investors were to bring on board J$1.3 billion of new capital over five years to rehabilitate the industry and to enable the production of three hundred thousand tons of raw sugar per annum to be produced from fifty thousand acres of sugar lands;
6. Technical know-how to be provided by Wray & Nephew Ltd, local owners of Appleton Estates and Tate & Lyle (international investor), partners in the bidding consortium;
7. There was to be involvement of financial investors: Manufacturers Merchant Bank, Island Life and Corporate Merchant Bank in the Long Pond Sugar Company Successors to ensure sound financial support;
8. Tate & Lyle, one of the consortium partners and previous holder of a management contract for the four estates was required to

release their claim of £850,000 from the government, ending the management contract prematurely, consequent on the divestment of Frome, Monymusk, and Bernard Lodge.

Besides selling the business below the privatisation valuation, the government had to write off a substantial portion of the debt and agree to a reduction in the workforce. Ministry Paper 34 showed that the government had to write off J$2.679 million of the J$3.441 million.[54] In particular, sugar imports (except brown sugar) were to be decontrolled and domestic prices allowed to be market driven. Steps were also taken to protect the industry from cheaper imported sugar, and this was implemented through an import tax regime and a minimum import entry price. Privatisation of sugar was to be carried out in three phases:

- In the first phase, the four publicly held factories were to be sold and the relevant farming land leased to new owners. This was accomplished in 1994, when the factories and 18,400 hectares of sugar lands were divested, with fifty-four hundred hectares to independent small farmers.
- In the second phase, the cane farms which were not allocated to the four factories were to be leased (in twenty-eight parcels over a forty-nine-year lease tenure) to local farmers in 1996, involving some fifteen thousand acres in some thirty-three parcels of land ranging in size from 76 to 550 acres. Full divestment of cane land was completed in 1998.
- The third phase involved the lease of non-cane lands. It was in this phase that a consortium acquired the three factories: Frome, Monymusk, and Bernard Lodge. Long Pond's sale was implemented through a management and employee share purchase plan and a new company, Trelawny Sugar Company Limited (TSC), was formed as the operating unit.

The consortium of investors for the factories comprised Jamaican rum and sugar companies: Wray & Nephew; a British sugar conglomerate, Booker Tate; financial partners, Manufacturers Investment Limited and National Commercial Bank, each of the parties taking 17 per cent of the equity, with government retaining a minority of 49 per cent, of which 25 per cent were reserved for the workers, small farmers, and the remaining 24 per cent to be divested later through an IPO. The financial backers were Island Life, Corporate Merchant Bank, and Pan Caribbean. The TSC was required to pay J$160 million. In the process, eighty-five hundred workers were made redundant in 1993, at a cost of over J$475 million, all funded by the government.

In the 1990s, the industry employed forty-one thousand workers in crop time and twenty-eight thousand during the out-of-season period. Additionally, some 653 housing lots were promised to be made available to workers in parcels ranging from thirty-five hundred to ten thousand square feet. Some of these proposals, however, were never carried through. The new owners operated the business under the corporate structure of the SCJ. Stanbury reported that the estimate was that the new owners invested about J$25 million after assuming control on December 29, 1993, part of which went into a major irrigation scheme at Monymusk.[55]

The Experiences of the Sugar Industry Under the 1990s Privatisation

During the period, export prices fell from £449 per ton in 1996 to £389 per ton in 1997, resulting in a corresponding drop in the price for sugar paid to the industry from J$20,564 per ton to J$17,190. At the same time, there was a revaluation of the Jamaican dollar from J$40:US$1 to J$32:US$1 over the period. The revaluation of the Jamaican dollar and the fall in export prices significantly affected the financial fortunes of the companies. Between 1993/94 and 1995/96, crop years there was an 8 per cent increase in production in the industry and a corresponding 28 per cent increase in production on the divested sugar lands, moving their share of the industry production from 60.5 per cent to 71.3 per cent.

The new owners operated the divested business for the crop years 1993/94 to 1997/98. The government, however, provided no new capital, as a minority partner, to match the majority shareholders.[56] The performance of the industry over the period 1990s is shown in table 13.6.

Cane production fluctuated over the period, increasing from 2.29 million tons in 1995 to 2.62 million tons in 1996, then falling to 2.41 million in 1997 and then rising to 2.56 million in 1998. Sugar production, however, increased from 211,500 tons in 1995 to 236,500 tons in 1997, before falling to 186,100 tons in 1998. Exports of sugar also increased from 144,880 tons in 1995 to 181,300 tons in 1996, before falling to

167,000 tons in 1998. Sugar production, which used to be carried out in some 775-sugar works in 1773 by 1999 (some 220 years later) came to be carried out by eight central factories. Land under cane cultivation fell from 59,936 hectares in 1973 to forty-two thousand hectares in 1999.

Table 13.6: Sugar Production for Periods, 1995–2000

Years	Cane Milled – 000 (tons)	Sugar Output (tons)	Sugar Export (tons)
1995	2,295	211,500	144,800
1996	2,624	237,900	181,300
1997	2,413	236,500	170,900
1998	2,560	186,100	167,500
1999	3,312	204,200	177,500
2000	2,025	203,000	168,897

Source: Sugar Industry Authority of Jamaica

The fall in sugar prices and the revaluation of the Jamaican dollar seem to be the reasons the private investors backed out of the deal after a few years of operation. The privatisation partners, however, had failed to bring sufficient capital to upgrade the run-down operations. The privatisation exercise was again a failure, and eventually the private members of the consortium returned their 51 per cent stake to the government. The privatised owners could never compete in the marketplace, despite the sugar trade preferences which were still in place in the EU market. With failed privatisation, the government reacquired Frome, Monymusk, and Bernard Lodge for J$1. Long Pond all but went bankrupt and, by 2000, the operation was again brought under public control.

As with Air Jamaica, the government had to inject large sums, even during the period of private management, to keep the operations alive. Subsequently, the government took back operations of the factories through the SCJ (Frome, Monymusk, and Bernard Lodge). The Duckenfield factory was owned by St Thomas Sugar Company Limited, while the Long Pond factory and Hampden Estates were owned by Trelawny Sugar Company Limited but operated by the SCJ Group. Hampden, on its return to the government, was closed as a factory, leaving only the distillery operational.

The World Bank reported in its Implementation Completion Report in 1996 that the privatisation was expected to be difficult because of the social and political sensitivity, and the large, unionised workforce. The bank also noted that, with skilful management and transparency, the privatisation process itself was carried out smoothly, and stated that it could be considered a case study of best practices.[57] Despite the comments of the World Bank, the privatisation discriminated in favour of local investors, with little effort being made at the time to attract new foreign investors with strong financial capabilities. The principal requirements for successful privatisation of the sugar industry were a significant number of new investments, mostly in foreign exchange, high-quality sugar management expertise, and the ability to transfer modern technology to the operations of the privatised companies. Private ownership and private property rights did not create a sustainable operation; market structure was just as important.

The involvement of the Jamaican commercial banks in direct investments in the sugar industry reflected another case of commercial banks deviating from their core business of deposit and retail banking into fields like agro-industry operation, an area in which they had no expertise and had little to contribute other than finance. As was expected in situations where the government had discriminated in favour of domestic groups, the local investors failed to provide the capital to ensure success and, as a result, the government found itself an involuntary owner once again of most of the sugar industry.

The Third Privatisation Exercise: 2005/09

Between 1998 and 2005, the government continued to operate the assets reacquired, subject to minor restructuring; however, the industry continued to rack up losses, putting serious pressures on the Treasury. This was coming when, through FINSAC, the Ministry of Finance had to plough billions of dollars into the financial sector to avoid the collapse of the economy. The losses being accumulated in the sugar industry, along with changes to EU sugar regime challenging the existing EU trade preferences led the then Minister of Finance Dr Omar Davies to intervene in 2005 and to insist that priority be given to privatisation of sugar and Air Jamaica so that the state could hand over the assets of these industries to the private sector to make the investments and relieve the government and the Treasury of the continuing cycle of funding losses from these two industries. In the period after 1996, the

PNP administration had severed its relationship with the IMF; hence, there was no external pressure to continue with privatisation.

With the intervention of the minister of finance, the minister of agriculture, Roger Clarke, established a high-powered privatisation team in 2005 to fast-track the divestiture of the state-owned sugar operations.[58] A Sugar Transformation Unit was created by the Ministry of Agriculture in 2006, and the mandate was given to the NIBJ to prepare the estates for divestment. The process included identifying all the sugar lands acquired by the government and ensuring that registered titles existed. The main assets which had inadvertently reverted to State ownership, and which were to be divested were:

- Monymusk, in the parish of Clarendon;
- Frome, in the parish of Westmoreland;
- Bernard Lodge, in the parish of St Catherine;
- Duckenfield, in the parish of St Thomas, and
- Long Pond and Hampden, in the parish of Trelawny.

The NIBJ and the Enterprise Team sought to pre-qualify investors with an announcement of the investment opportunity on May 15, 2006, for the financing, modernisation, operation, and management of the state-owned factories and related sugar cane lands. Advertisements were placed locally and overseas, inviting proposals for prequalification to bid. The Expressions of Interest (EOI) required interested investors to pre-qualify for selection to receive an Information Memorandum and the Request for Proposals, which was issued by the Development Bank of Jamaica (DBJ). The DBJ replaced the NIBJ in 2006 after the two institutions were merged earlier. The final privatisation transaction exercise for the publicly owned sugar assets started in May 2006 and was concluded on July 30, 2010. The process started with offering assets as if they were one package. There were several cancellations and repetitions of the process. The necessary detailed market soundings had not been carried out by the vendor to determine the appetite of the investor community for the sugar assets, whether they should have been unbundled in smaller packages, and the conditions to acquire these assets. When the government finally unbundled the assets into separate individual packages, the transaction went much more smoothly thereafter.

The policy directive handed down by the government to the Enterprise Team was as follows:

- Create an economically sustainable private sector-led industry through privatisation of the sugar SOEs' assets;
- Improve the economic diversification, social resilience, and the environment, and
- Maintain progress towards macroeconomic stability.

The intended date for the receipt of documents was June 15, 2006; however, this was later extended to June 30, 2006. On receipt of the EOIs and on evaluation, four investor groups were pre-qualified to bid for the assets offered as of June 30, 2006. They were:

- Dhamphur Sugar Mills (India),
- J Wray & Nephew (Jamaica),
- Energen Development (Jamaica), and
- Angostura (Trinidad).

Following the short-listing and the closing date for submission of proposal documentation, the DBJ decided to suspend the existing exercise and to recommence the whole privatisation process, with the objective this time of widening the field, hoping to reach a wider investor pool. As a result of the change, an extensive media communication programme was launched, covering the *Financial Times, The New York Times, Sugar Journal,* as well as the local press: *The Gleaner, The Jamaica Observer,* and *The Sunday Herald.* The deadline date for submission of interest along with pre-qualification documents was set for December 22, 2006. Only one additional investor group pre-qualified from this exercise: Coimex of Brazil.

The DBJ was still receiving expressions of interest after the proposed closing date to pre-qualify bids, and they were deemed compelling enough to warrant a reopening of the exercise once again. Cabinet therefore approved the reopening of the prequalification process, with a final deadline for the submission of prequalification documentation set for June 29, 2007, an extension of a maximum of two months. By this time, the JLP administration had returned to power, led by Bruce Golding. Golding was not prepared to contend with the losses of the industry and accorded high priority to the divestiture. This gave impetus to the privatisation as, by then, the accumulated losses were J$35.5 billion.[59]

Eventually, there were eight investor groups pre-qualifying from the former PNP-led administration to receive the bid packages. Following the reopening and evaluation of five proposals which were received on this occasion, one was disqualified and returned because it was received after the deadline. Four proposals were finally evaluated by the Enterprise Team, and three investor groups were taken to the next phase of the privatisation exercise. They were Stirling Partners from the Bahamas, Infinity Bio-Energy from Brazil, and Flo-Sun Incorporated from the US.

The Information Memorandum was issued on December 14, 2007; the pre-qualified bidders were advised of its availability and the deadlines for submission of their technical and financial bid proposals. All investor groups purchased the bid documents and submitted the relevant proposal to meet the bid closing date. The requirement for the investor groups was to acquire 75 per cent of the equity of the entire portfolio of six government assets and produce ethanol, besides sugar, with the government to retaining 25 per cent of the equity of the special purpose vehicle created to operate the assets.

The Brazilian investor group Infinity Bio Energy was assessed as the preferred bidder, and the Cabinet gave approval to the DBJ to close the transaction by June 27, 2008, with a handing over date by September 30, 2008; however, negotiations did not begin until March 11, 2008. Even although heads of agreement had been reached with Infinity Bio Energy Limited after an extensive period of negotiations and despite numerous accommodations and time extensions, the investors failed to meet some conditions. Most important was mobilisation of the capital to carry through with the privatisation of all six sugar factories and two distilleries; as a result, the negotiations were terminated on January 30, 2009. Infinity Bio Energy cited difficulties in mobilising the capital because of the 2008 financial crisis. By the end of December 2008, the government had already paid off the seventy-five hundred workers made redundant, costing the government J$1.9 million.

Following failure to conclude the sale of the sugar assets, Prime Minister Golding authorised the DBJ to continue with the privatisation proceedings with all interested parties; however, on this occasion, interested investors were to be given the opportunity to bid for all or some assets. The Information Memorandum was updated and modified to reflect these changes and include Petrojam Ethanol Limited among the assets to be divested. With these adjustments, re-advertisement notices were issued to the media over the period from Friday, February

13 to Wednesday, February 18, 2009. The eight discrete packages offered on this occasion were as follows:

1. Package 1: The Monymusk Sugar Factory and Estate
2. Package 2: Frome Sugar Factory and Estate
3. Package 3: Bernard Lodge Sugar Factory and Estate
4. Package 4: St Thomas Sugar Factory and Estate
5. Package 5: Long Pond Sugar Factory and Estate
6. Package 6: Hampden Distillery and Estate
7. Package 7 : Great houses and great house lands at the various estates
8. Package 8: Petrojam Ethanol Limited

These assets which were offered for privatisation were eventually handled under three rounds: one for Petrojam Ethanol Limited; one for Trelawny Sugar Company involving the sale of the Long Pond factory, factory compound and the Hampden distillery and lease of great houses, sugar cane lands and non-sugar cane lands, and the third for Frome, Monymusk, and Bernard Lodge Sugar Estates. After repeating the full bidding process, the three packages were offered to Fred M. Jones Estate Limited/Seprod Limited, Everglades Farms Limited, and Complant International Sugar Company Limited.

St Thomas Sugar Estate

Regarding Petrojam Ethanol Limited's assets at the deadline of March 13, 2009, EOIs were received, ranging from particular parcels of lands at each estate to proposals requesting the entire packages (all the sugarcane industry assets, including Petrojam Ethanol Limited). Following evaluation of these EOIs, four interested investors were short listed to receive the Request for Proposal and bid documents. They were: Energen Development Ltd.; Eridania Suisse (SA); Everglades Farms, and Fred M. Jones Estate Limited/Seprod Limited. On the receipt of a proposal from these investor groups, DBJ held further consultation and, based on the consultations and clarifications which were completed on July 3, 2009, Seprod/Fred M. Jones Limited was selected as the preferred bidder for the St Thomas Sugar Estate. The privatisation was for outright sale of sugar factory and lands, encompassing the factory compound, and lease of sugar estate lands and non-sugar cane lands for a seventy-five years.

Again, after consultation and clarifications, Everglades Farms Limited was selected as the preferred bidder and negotiations concluded on July 16, 2009, for the sale of the Trelawny Sugar Company involving sale of the Long Pond factory, factory compound and the Hampden distillery and lease of great houses, sugar cane lands and non-sugar cane lands for seventy-five years. Eight EOIs were received at the deadline date of May 26, 2010, for Frome, Monymusk, and Bernard Lodge Sugar Estates; however, Cari-Med Limited and Theodora Holdings Limited withdrew their interest. Of the six remaining investors, four submitted proposals by July 2, 2010, the deadline date. Evaluation was carried out on July 6, 2010, on the proposals received from Everglades Farms Ltd, Energen Development Ltd, Integrated Agriculture and Energy LLC, and Complant International Sugar Company Limited.

After further consultation and clarifications Complant International Sugar Company Limited, a Chinese investor., was selected as the preferred bidder and negotiations successfully concluded with Complant to acquire Frome, Monymusk, and Bernard Lodge Sugar Estates. Cabinet gave the approval on July 12, 2010, for the JDB and the privatisation transaction team to commence negotiations with Complant. Negotiations begun in the week of July 12, 2010, and concluded involving an outright sale of sugar factory and the lands encompassing the factory compound, and lease of sugar estate lands and non-sugar cane lands for seventy-five years. Signing of the Agreement took place on July 30, 2010.

In 2012, the minister of agriculture reported to Parliament that the government had to absorb J$35.58 billion of sugar debt which had accumulated since 1999 when the state assumed responsibility for Frome, Monymusk, and Bernard Lodge operations. The *Gleaner* of November 9, 2021, reported that most of the privatised assets taken over had run into financial difficulties and some investors had returned the privatised asset once again to the government.[60] The detail of the privatisation arrangements for each estate in 2009 and developments since are summarised below.

Pan Caribbean Sugar Company Limited/Complant

The SHA was executed between Complant and the government for the three privatised factories: Frome, Monymusk, and Bernard Lodge estates on June 30, 2010. The factories and the land within the factory compound went by direct sale (transfer of title) for US$9 million. In addition, Complant acquired thirty thousand hectares of sugar lands by leasehold at a rate of US$35 per hectare with a lease tenure of fifty years.

The Frome Sugar factory is in Georges Plain, Westmoreland, six miles from Savanna-la-mar, the parish capital. Frome was constructed in 1930 and most of the original equipment was replaced over a period. The estate lands at Frome were leased from the Frome Monymusk Land Company Limited, a company wholly owned by the government of Jamaica. At the time, the sugar estate had 12,844 acres (5,200 hectares) of cane lands, 98 per cent of which were fully planted in cane.

Bernard Lodge came to be owned by the Sugar Company of Jamaica Limited, which had been incorporated in 1993 by a consortium of companies and was subsequently acquired by the government in 1998. The SCJ also operated a sugar factory and an ethanol fermentary and a distillery.

The Monymusk Experience

The government operated the business between 1999 and 2010 until it was divested to the PSCS. Complant, the Chinese investors, established Pan Caribbean Sugar Company Limited (PCSC) as the special-purpose vehicle to operate the privatised sugar business acquired from the government. Complant made a commitment to invest US$127 million in field and factory operations as part of a rehabilitation programme. In addition, the Chinese made a commitment to carry out feasibility studies regarding building a new sugar refinery to process two hundred thousand tons of raw or brown sugar to white sugar and to start the production of ethanol at an estimated US$221 million. At the point of takeover, the three factories could not produce two hundred thousand tons of raw sugar. Sugar production on this scale would have required significant expansion in cane production, well beyond the existing level at takeover. The PCSC's SHA provided for the suspension of duties on a wide variety of goods of production inputs and machinery.

An estimated J$2.38 billion was spent in the Monymusk Sugar Development Area, covering rehabilitation of cane roads, construction of some eighty-eight houses; 230 farmers obtained subsidised loans. In addition, two agro-parks were built, comprising two thousand acres, as well as financing of twenty-eight small projects, valued at J$322 million. Overall, the government spent J$9.3 billion on the several sugar development areas around the island.[61]

Frome and Monymusk were the two largest sugar production fatalities on the island. There was access to eighteen thousand hectares of irrigated flat lands, with accompanying good annual rainfall around Bernard Lodge and Monymusk that could have accommodated expansion of sugar cane production.

Complant, on takeover, contracted the SCJ to handle the crop on the three estates for 2010/11. Ministry paper 20/12 of March 2012 reported that J$6.3 billion had been invested, inclusive of investment to expand 949 hectares of new cane lands, mostly carried out in 2010/11 when the SCJ operated the business on contract. In addition, the PCSC obtained a permit to build co-generation power facilities at Frome and Monymusk, with the excess power beyond the needs of the sugar factories to be sold to the JPSCo grid. Complant assumed operational control in August 2011. The PCSC only retained a percentage of the complement of workers used by the SCJ to operate the plant and adopted a model whereby it carried out several services previously contracted out to the community. With the duty-free concession allowed the company, it could bring in equipment, such as tractors and haulage trucks from China, and carry out the operation at a much lower cost.

Sugar cane production at Monymusk estate declined from 231,575 tons in 2012 to 85,599 tons in 2015, reflecting serious neglect and lack of knowledge of sugar cane production and the operation of a vertically integrated sugar business. In contrast, independent farmers increased their cane production from 65,739 tons in 2012 to 167,842 tons in 2015. Overall, sugar production, which was 26,329 tons in 2012, declined to 19,775 in 2015 and, by 2020, had fallen to 11,168 tons. The Monymusk factory recovery index (FRI) declined from 91.85 in 2011 to 70.67 in 2018. For Frome, the FRI varied between eighty-one and seventy-four, respectively. Relationship between the Chinese management and the community and the independent small farmers can be described as strained, manifesting itself in regular cane fires in the out-of-crop period.

With these developments, the PCSC registered operating difficulties with the Ministry of Agriculture in April 2016, maintaining that these had forced them to discontinue operating the Monymusk factory for the crop year 2016/17. Despite the reported US$200 million investment to date, the company continued to chalk up losses. Having withdrawn from the JCPC marketing arrangement, the PCSC was obtaining a lower price for its sugar, when compared to the other factories that had remained with the JCPC. The company reported that the equity injected on acquisition was US$60 million; the rest was short-term debt finance; the losses had severely eroded its equity. Listed on the Hong Kong Stock market, Complant's only option to avoid bankruptcy was to close the Monymusk plant for the 2016/17 crop year. This required the government's intervention once again to rescue the situation and temporarily minimise the social and economic cost to the community. The intervention was estimated to cost the government J$250 million. Since 2018, the Monymusk factory has been shuttered. All cane reaped by independent farmers have since been transshipped to neighbouring Worthy Park Sugar Factor in St Catherine for processing. In 2019, the PCSC formally returned the Monymusk-leased lands to the government, amounting to eighteen thousand hectares, mothballing the factory. The PCSC, however, continues to operate the Frome factory, where sugar cane farming cost is lower, as it is rain fed.[62] Squatter settlements are now taking place on the Vere Plains on lands that were formerly in sugar cane and owned by the SCJH. Significant acreages are now being transformed into housing estates, especially in the Clarendon and St Catherine areas; in other areas lands are idle, and in ruination.

Golden Grove Sugar Company in St Thomas

The St Thomas Sugar Company in the eastern part of Jamaica was privatised to Fred M. Jones Limited and Seprod Limited on July 16, 2009, resulting in creating Golden Grove Sugar Company Limited (GGSC) as the special purpose vehicle to carry on the business for the consortium. The sugar factory and some 10.5 hectares of factory land were bought for US$500,000. The cane lands were leased at a rate of US$53 per hectare per annum, with a lease tenure of fifty years, renewable for a further twenty-five years.

The GGSC set about rehabilitation of the factory and expansion of cane production. The company reported investments of J$3 million by 2015, including expansion of 284 hectares of new cane lands. Production increased from 12,587 tons in 2010 to a record of 19,403 tons in 2014. The GGSC diversified its market and installed new packaging and bagging equipment to supply the domestic and regional markets in order to avoid dependence on the European export market. With this development, the GGSC persisted and obtained its own export licence from the SIA to market its sugar locally and in the export market in 2012. The GGSC, through the consortium partner, Seprod Limited, made their first export shipment of branded sugar, amounting to 125 tons to Barbados in 2016, followed later by shipments to Trinidad and Tobago and other Caribbean islands.

The company, however, suffered massive losses from inception, reporting in the *Gleaner* in July 2015 that it had accumulated a working capital deficit of J$1.3 billion, following losses of J$922 billion for the 2013 and 2104 crop years. With the level of losses, Seprod questioned the continued operation of the GGSC and decided in 2019 to withdraw from the sugar business. The GGSC had also planned to enter the co-generation market, but this was not to be. It continued its cane growing operation, withdrawing from the sugar production business, using the cane produced as animal feed for Seprod-owned Serge Island Dairy. The closure of the factory resulted in the loss of 150 manufacturing jobs, accompanied by a further loss of 540 cane-farming jobs. The failure of the sugar business in St Thomas followed on failure in banana by Eastern Banana Estate Limited, which also closed permanently in 2008. The closures brought disastrous social and economic consequences to an area which had depended on sugar for over four hundred years and banana for 250 years, signalling the end of plantation and estate sugar and banana production in St Thomas.[63]

Everglades Farms Limited

Everglades Farms Limited acquired the assets of Trelawny Sugar Company, comprising Long Pond Sugar Factory, the Hampden Sugar Factory and Distillery, great houses, and 38.8 hectares of factory lands. The assets were sold outright at a price of US$1.5 million in June 2010. The Long Pond Factory was in operation, but Hamden was closed. Some eight thousand hectares of cane lands were also leased to the company at the rate of US$40 per hectare per annum. The lease payment, however, was deferred for three years beginning in July 2012. The tenure of the lease was fifty years, with an option for renewal for an additional twenty-five years. One requirement of the SHA was for 60 per cent of the leased sugar lands acquired on transfer day to be brought back into sugar cane production within ten years. The Everglades Company was backed by the Hussey family, owners of the Terra Nova Hotel in Kingston/St Andrew.

Following low production in 2010, Everglades closed production in the 2010/11 crop year. Some of US$20 million was reportedly spent on refurbishing the factory, rehabilitating the distillery at Hamden and planting 426 hectares of new sugar lands. As a result of the investments and rehabilitation, the factory operations recommenced in crop year 2011/12. Production of sugar increased from 3,984 tons in 2012 to 11,724 tons in 2014. Despite the investments, the operation continued to chalk up losses and, as a result, in 2015 the owners notified the government that, because of mounting debt since commencement of operations, the factory would be shuttered in 2016. The company pointed to the loss of the guaranteed high prices and assured market in the UK as contributing to the losses. Much of the investment was made with short-term loans. The new JLP administration had just returned to power in March 2016 and operated the Long Pond Factory for three months of the crop year. The factory has not opened since 2016, and Everglades Farms returned some eight thousand hectares of land to the government in 2019, except for two hundred hectares around the factory. Again, unplanned housing developments surfaced for some of the very fertile Long Pond agricultural lands. However, the Hampden Distillery after US$1.5 million rehabilitation continues to operate profitably.

The Long-Standing Private Operators

In 2010, Worthy Park and Appleton Estates (New Yarmouth estate was subsumed in Appleton) operations were the sugar interests remaining in private hands in the sugar and rum business in Jamaica after 2010. These two businesses were never acquired by the government at any time.

Appleton Estate in St Elizabeth (near Black River) was founded in 1655 by the Dickinson brothers and has been in continuous production for over 470 years. Production of the famous Appleton rum dates back to 1749. Like most sugar estates, ownership changed several times until business was acquired by J. Wray & Nephew Limited in 1912. This company later became a subsidiary of Lascelles Demercado Limited, which, in recent years, was taken over by Angostura Holdings of Trinidad and Tobago, and finally by the Campari Group of Italy in 2012.

J. Wray & Nephew Limited acquired New Yarmouth estates in Clarendon over time and, through a lease, also acquired Holland

Estate lands in St Elizabeth. New Yarmouth estate discontinued sugar production in 1994, with the cane produced at the estate transhipped to Appleton sugar factory for processing into sugar, but the company continued with the distillery. Holland Estate was acquired by the government in the 1970s, and the cane lands was leased to Wray & Nephew Limited.

At the time of the last privatisation in 2009, the company was producing 31,625 tons of sugar, or 25 per cent of Jamaica's production. The capacity of the factory's production facilities can produce fifty thousand tons of sugar per annum (around 60 per cent of installed capacity performance). Since 2014, production of sugar continues to average thirty thousand tons per year. Its operation was disrupted in 2015 because of environmental problems. On resumption in the 2016/17 crop year, it could not reach the production levels previously achieved in earlier years, with production in 2017 at 18,926 tons and 10,925 tons in 2019. In 2018, the company returned the leased Holland Estate lands to the government. In 2020, the new owners, the Campari Group, closed the factory, being mainly interested in rum production. Continuation with sugar production would have resulted in major losses. The company divested the cane farming side, via leasing of the lands to a group of independent cane farmers, and the cane is transhipped to the Frome factory in Westmorland for processing. The closure of the Appleton sugar factory by some of the most experienced sugar managers in the business after 450 continuous years of operation shows that sugar production is not for novices.

Worthy Park Sugar Estate is situated in one of the most fertile valleys in Jamaica, at Lluidas Vale in St Catherine and has been in continuous production since 1670, starting with the Price family.[64] The little town of Lluidas Vale was at one point owned by the Clarke family until the 1970s when the Manley administration took action to transfer ownership of the village. The sugar lands were originally acquired by patent, a gift from the British Crown. Sugar production begun in 1770 when sugar was king. Throughout history, the estate's ownership has passed through the hands of only three families. The current owner, the Clarke family, creole White, has had ownership for over three hundred years. This is a sugar property experienced the history of slavery, slave village, indentured East Indian workers, absentee ownership, and trade liberalisation in the 1850s, the long period of mercantile trade, non-reciprocal preferential trade protection, and seem to have been able the withstand a second period of trade liberalisation which started in 2009.

The factory is comparatively small, with an installed capacity to process two hundred and seventy-five thousand tons of sugar cane each year. Despite its small size, it has constantly been one of the most efficient sugar operations in Jamaica, both in terms of yields of sugar from field operations and from the factory in terms of conversion of cane to sugar. In 2009, the estate produced 21,675 tons of sugar, or 17.5 per cent of the island's production. Sugar production remained at around this level of twenty-one thousand tons over the next four years, then climbing to 27,650 tons in 2014 and has remained around twenty-two thousand tons since 2020. The factory has taken in cane resulting from the closure of Long Pond, Monymusk, and Appleton sugar estates. Although it tried to acquire the Innswood sugar lands for cane production, this was denied by the authorities, and today these lands lay fallow. Even the three hundred acres of lands which it acquired from Caymanas Estate on lease is now threatened with urban development. So much for the efficacy of the bureaucracy. In 2005, the estate diversified into the rum distillery, resuming a tradition dating from 1741 and which was discontinued in 1962. The company has also diversified into production of sugar for the domestic market by investing in modern bagging and packaging facilities and can now exploit the regional market. Prices in the retail domestic market are more lucrative than export to the European and US markets. Worthy Park is one of the few sugar businesses which has shown positive results from new investments in terms of increased production, increased efficiencies, and profitability. The company invests significantly in research to improve efficiency in the field and factory and remains competitive. In 2018, Wisynco, a local manufacturing and distribution company owned by the Mahfood family, acquired majority shares in Worthy Park Estates. This was accompanied by a distribution and marketing arrangement in which the Wisynco Group assumed responsibility for the distribution and marketing of all Worthy Park products (Sugar and Rum) in Jamaica.

Further Liberalisation and Regulatory Changes in the Sugar Industry After 2009

Since 2009, with further liberalisation of the industry, there have been further changes in the sugar regulatory framework. The Ministry of

Agriculture, as part of the sugar reform, decided that, with privatisation, the producers should market their output, hence the role played by the JCPS was no longer needed and, in the 2018/19 crop year, the company was disbanded. At the time, the JPCS was literally bankrupt, not able to pay some manufacturers the declared price for sugar in 2018.

The PCSC, one of the new producers, demanded and obtained his own agency agreement from the SIA to market its sugar, followed by the GGSC in 2015. This left Worthy Park and Appleton, the two private producers, as Everglades had closed its factory in 2106. In 2020, both companies obtained their own licence and agreement for the marketing of their sugar from the SIA. With the disbandment of the JCPS, some mechanism was needed to take over the responsibility of adjudicating between manufacturers and farmers on the price to be paid to farmers for cane supplied to the factories. The solution was a Sugar Prices Committee, comprising representatives of the sugar farmers and marketing agents/manufacturers.

The operations of the SIA were then reduced by some 50 per cent. Each company is now licenced by the SIA and has an agency agreement, allowing the companies to handle the marketing of their own sugar overseas, as there is no quota to be distributed by the SIA and the government among the manufacturers. A new development on the local domestic marketing has been mandatory packaging and labelling requirements for domestic brown sugar. The quality of local sugar in the market has improved significantly even though the price is higher. Major investments have been made in the packaging of brown sugar and its branding.

The SIA no longer provides extension services; these have been transferred to the All-Island Jamaica Cane Farmers Association. With these changes, the cess paid by manufacturers has been drastically reduced (at the insistence of the manufacturers). The result is that the SIA's budget was reduced from J$505 million in 2018 to J$250 million for the two years ending 2020, resulting in the closure of the SIA's Kingston office and concentration of its activities at its Mandeville office, the home of the SIA's research infrastructure and 50 per cent of staff being made redundant. The SIA has been right-sized to accommodate liberalisation; it now plays the role of regulator, which was its main statutory responsibility.

Performance of the Industry Since Privatisation in 2009

Table 13.7 below shows the six sugar operations in 2014, along with the 29,705 hectares of land leased to the various companies on privatisation, and the amount of sugar produced by each factory in 2014.

Table 13.7: Sugar Factories with Estate Acreage and Production, 2013/14

Factory	Hectares	Production Metric Tons
Frome – Westmoreland	8,008	38,603
Monymusk – Clarendon	7,298	23,091
Appleton – St Elizabeth (always privately owned)	5,268	33,890
Worthy Park – St Catherine (always privately owned)	3,503	27,650
Everglades – Trelawny	2,367	11,724
Golden Grove – St Thomas	3,262	19,403
Total	**29,705**	**154,361**

Source: Sugar Annual Report (2015) USDA Foreign Agricultural Service

With further closure after 2018, some 50 per cent of sugar factory capacity in Jamaica was closed permanently. Ultimately, only two operations, both privately owned, remained in sugar production in 2020.

Table 13.8 shows the industry production and export performance over the period 2000 to 2020, considering the last privatisation exercise in 2009. Sugar cane production fell in the period from 2.025 million tons in 2000 to 1.9 million tons in 2010. It increased to 2.1 million tons following the complete privatisation in 2009, increasing further to 2.1 million tons in 2011. With the closures, cane milled has been on a sharp decline, reaching 509,000 tons in 2020. Sugar production in 2000 was 203,000 tons and fell to 124,600 tons in 2003. It rebounded in 2004 to 181,400 tons, but since then has been on sharp decline, reaching 49,000 tons in 2020.

The only year that production registered an increase was shortly after the last round of privatisation when, in 2011, sugar production registered one hundred and fifty thousand tons. Sugar export fared even worse, declining first from 168,878 tons in 2000 to 128,550 tons in

2003 and then progressively declining to 11,594 tons in 2020. In 2020, no sugar was exported to the UK. In crop year 2014/15, Jamaica exported eighty-three thousand tons of sugar, valued at US$60 million, with seventy thousand going to the European Union and thirteen thousand tons going to the US.

Table 13.8: Sugar Production for Periods, 2000–20

Years	Cane Milled – 000 (tons)	Sugar Output (tons)	Sugar Export (tons)
2000	2,025	203,000	168,897
2001	2,231	199,000	156,907
2002	1,965	170,000	138,145
2003	1,775	124,600	128,540
2004	1,993	181,400	159,908
2009	1,900	123,000	120,000
2010	1,900	120,000	93,000
2011	2,100	150,000	
2016	1,127	79,300	38,044
2017	1,131	81,100	34,967
2018	1,028	76,700	39,900
2019	744	56,500	22,824
2020	519	41,700	11,954

Source: Sugar Industry Authority of Jamaica – Sundry Years

Local demand for raw sugar in 2014/15 ran at fifty-one thousand tons, met from local production. For the crop year 2013/14 exports was eighty thousand tons.[65]

Local consumption of raw sugar in 2020/2021 was thirty-five thousand tons, and sixty thousand tons of refined sugar, making ninety-five thousand tons, reflecting a decrease of 16 per cent over the previous year's total of one hundred and fourteen thousand tons. Most of the refined sugar is used in the food industry. In addition, one hundred thousand tons of molasses and five thousand tons of raw sugar is utilised in spirits production.[66] The factories in operation in 2019 were Appleton, operated by Campari, Worthy Park, and Monymusk.

Worthy Park, a four-generation private sector operation, with 2,825 hectares of cane lands could produce 22,319 MT of raw sugar compared with Frome which, when in government hands for several years since 1970s and with much greater cane lands, produced less raw sugar.

Despite liberalisation and the fact that sugar is a highly traded commodity,[67] about 40 million tons of sugar was traded in 2005, representing 30 per cent of world production; however, most of the international sugar trading was still carried out under special arrangements: long-term contracts and bilateral agreements. It is quantities of sugar exceeding the amounts from these arrangements which end up in the world market. In effect, according to Richardson, the world market is where excess sugar is dumped, susceptible to high levels of price volatility; this is the market Jamaica was expected to compete in after 2009.

Based on past performances, Jamaica would not have been able to survive in the world market for sugar in its five-hundred-year history without trade preferences. Mercantilism facilitated its expansion when sugar was gold. The unilateral decision by Imperial Britain to liberalise sugar trading through the 1846 wrought havoc on the Jamaican economy after 1850, with disastrous consequences for its people. This was not in the interest of Europeans who, by then, were major producers of beet sugar and, as a result the Brussels Convention of 1902 brought back trade protection for sugar.

Sugar by 1950 no longer played the strategic role it once played in global trade and the Common Agricultural Policy (CAP) of the EU (1950) protected European beet sugar, not West Indian cane sugar. Colonies could piggyback on measures designed for European agricultural producers. The reality is that as an independent nation, Jamaica is no longer strategic on the global horizon and has become dispensable.

Although sugar experienced a major decline in its overall contribution, falling to less than 2 per cent of GDP in 2020, it remains one of the largest employers of low-paid workers. In several parishes, it remains the principal livelihood for rural families. The sugar industry has, over the years, formed the most important sub-sector in agriculture, accounting in the 1990s for 16 to 18 per cent of agricultural employment. In terms of foreign exchange, sugar in the 1990s earned US$100 million, generating 54 per cent of agricultural exports and 7.4 per cent of merchandise exports.

Several factors account for the dramatic decline of Jamaican sugar production and export. They include loss of trade preferences, especially in the European and UK markets; intensified foreign competition; poor levels of productivity; low efficiency and high costs of operation; massive overheads at the factories and plantations; lack of reinvestment; insufficient automation, particularly in the harvesting operations, and reduced quality of cane.

The situation in 2020 is far from what the government expected in 2010, and the government operated Long Pond in the 2016/17 crop year. With the cessation of the Long Pond factory in crop year 2016 and Monymusk in 2018, the government was reluctantly back into direct operation of the sugar business, providing subsidies to independent cane farmers to transport their cane to factories outside of their areas. The Ministry of Agriculture noted that, between April 2016 and March 2020, an estimated J$806 million was provided by the government to meet the cost of this intervention. The government cleared all the debts and absorbed all the operational losses after receiving the factories back from the ill-fated 1990 privatisation for one cent and J$4 billion in debt. The total losses accumulated by the industry up to 2020 has been estimated at J$30 billion.[68]

In divesting the sugar lands, the government leased, rather than outright sale; however, it made no contingency plans what should become of these lands should they be returned to the government on failure of the divestiture. Experience indicated that this was a distinct possibility. Some twenty-nine thousand hectares of lands have been returned by the privatised owners, including Bernard Lodge and Monymusk lands by the PCSC, and including eight thousand hectares of Everglades Farms lands in Trelawny. Some of these lands are now being sold to developers. The government now plans to use some 4,677 acres of the most fertile lands in Jamaica, near Bernard Lodge, already outfitted with irrigation, for urban expansion, making the greater metropolitan area of Kingston and St Andrew more inhospitable, when vast tracts of lands suitable for township development already lay idle in the Mammee Bay area of St Ann which is a tourism growth point.

The government of Jamaica with much fanfare, announced in 2020 the leasing of three thousand acres of Innswood land to billionaire banker Michael Lee Chin for a major high-tech mango orchard and a range of vegetable projects, but so far nothing has come of this project. There have been complaints from farmers in the Bernard Lodge area of them being pushed off their lands in 2021 to facilitate housing development. Small farmers once again seem to face the fight to obtain arable lands, as they did when sugar collapsed in the 1830s and when the sugar planters were compensated with £20 million pounds and the freed African Jamaicans received not a 'willy penny.'

It was the loss of the EU preferential prices triggered privatisation in 2005. It was common knowledge that Jamaica was one of the highest sugar producers, yielding sugar at US one cent above its cost of production in 2005. With a 39 per cent reduction in prices, and with EU prices on the way to approaching world market standard, the economic fundamentals of the Jamaican sugar industry were such that, whether private or public, there was little chance of the industry remaining anywhere near its former level. The writing was already on the wall for everyone to see from as early as 1965.

The nostalgia of ' king sugar' seems to have blinded everyone, just as the nostalgia of railway service has been mesmerising the authorities in recent times. An industry or business can only survive in the liberalised world if it has competitive advantages to exploit. Jamaica's sugar has no competitive advantages. The sugar industry is going through a shake out, on a scale even greater than at the time of the abolition of the slave trade and slavery and the end of mercantilism.

One requirement of the EU funding was diversification, especially of agriculture. The Ministry of Agriculture had identified crops such as papaya under drip irrigation, ackee, orchard crops, including soursop, mango, guava, coconut, citrus, limes, vegetables and, in the livestock area, goat and beef cattle production, as suitable alternatives. The EU provided industry restructuring funds amounting to Euro 1.3 billion to be split between eighteen ACP countries, set against estimated export earning losses of Euros 2.5 billion. In 2020 the EU, for example, provided Euros 145.6 million, or J$2.1 billion in grant resources to support seventeen programmes and projects in Jamaica.[69]

These global and hemispheric liberalisation processes, which were started in the 1990s, have resulted in further opening of the Jamaican domestic market to imports of agricultural produce from industrialised countries like the US. This now presents formidable challenges for a small country like Jamaica, with a relatively weak and uncompetitive agricultural sector. The EU accepts liberalisation of the sugar trade which the World Bank had been advocating since 1979. The World Bank Report on the Caribbean Region stated that the Bank saw no future in export agriculture for Jamaica and the Caribbean islands, and only a limited future for the agriculture industry.[70] The report further stated that, not only were historic preferences in the EU sugar protocol likely to be eroded, but that they had been poorly utilised by the Jamaican and Caribbean people. While the WTO argued that the convention was illegal, the World Bank argued they were ineffectual.[71] As far as the World Bank was concerned, the sugar industry in the Caribbean had been in terminal decline since the 1970s, and the respective governments had failed to reform the industry to increase exports or diversify their countries' agricultural base.

There was no sugar exported from Jamaica to the UK in 2020, but the country has continued to export sugar to the US; however, the volumes are in much smaller quantities, being 5,856 tons in 2020. US's importance as a purchaser of Jamaican sugar resurfaced in 2005 and, by 2019, the US was taking most of Jamaica's sugar, albeit in tiny quantities, with virtually no export to the EU. The total export of sixty-five hundred tons in 2020 marked a dramatic change from the years when sugar accounted for most Jamaica's export earnings and, in fact, sugar ended up as a major export agriculture crop. Most of the sugar cane now produced goes for molasses and rum production and the domestic market.

THE DEVELOPMENT AND PRIVATISATION OF THE BANANA INDUSTRY

Its Historical Development after 1870

The banana industry came to dominate economic activity in Jamaica and rural life after the 1870s and, as with sugar, rail transport played an integral role in the rapid expansion of the industry. Banana production, however, is said to have existed in Jamaica well before 1835. In 1516, the commodity, like sugar was taken from the Canary Islands to Hispaniola this time by Spanish missionaries, and from there found its way to Jamaica via Martinique from where the first variety *Gros Michel* is said to have come.

Banana, a quick growing crop that can be ready for reaping within a year, also had another advantage over sugar; it can be grown on hillside lands and can be harvested throughout the year. As Jamaica's soil conditions and heavy rainfall in certain parishes were suitable for banana cultivation, it took off readily. Besides Gros Michel, other varieties were later introduced.

In 1879, there was only one estate near Port Antonio described as a banana plantation; however, by the 1880s, there were more than one hundred banana plantations owned by shippers, merchants, and some former sugar planters. Small holders cumulatively cultivated approximately thirty-five hundred acres, and the middle sector (farms varying from twenty acres to several hundred acres) farmed sixteen thousand seven hundred acres.[72]

Lorenzo Baker and the Boston Fruit Company became the most important property owners in Jamaica to grow bananas beginning in the banana growing parishes, of St Mary, St Catherine, and St Thomas.[73] The company directly cultivated a portion of the lands in its ownership and leased the rest to tenant farmers. Baker soon faced increased competition, especially from the Keith and Lindo families who were engaged in a thriving fruit trade from Costa Rica to New York. In 1879, Baker became the agent for a newly formed shipping company that enabled him to expand his transportation of bananas. Banana, as an estate crop, saw the number of estates increasing from 113 in 1893 to 455 by 1910. By 1902, Baker controlled almost the entire island's banana export trade.

The Boston Fruit Company, started with $200,000 and two ships in 1887; by 1896, the company was shipping more than four million bunches of bananas, six million coconuts and large quantities of pimento, coffee, and cocoa from Jamaica. The company at one stage employed two thousand people, owned fifty thousand acres, twelve steamers, and had purchased Jamaica's railway from the government.[74]

Jamaica became the first commercial producer and exporter of banana in the Americas. The Gros Michel variety dominated the Jamaican banana industry and world trade for well over one hundred years. The specific characteristics which gave it certain advantages were its attractive colour and appearance, heavy symmetrical bunches, which allowed unpacked transportation, long and slender fruit, five times as long as broad. The Gros Michel, however, carried certain disadvantages in that the height of the plant made it vulnerable to strong winds; it had a lower planting density and relatively lower yield per acre. The Gros Michel eventually succumbed to the Panama disease and was replaced by the Cavendish subgroup (Robusta and Lacatan) after the Second World War.

The *Robusta* variety was introduced from Guatemala and planted in south Manchester in 1909, while the *Lacatan* variety was introduced from Trinidad and planted at the Hope Experimental Station. The Valery variety closely resembles the Robusta but is more resistant to wind; however, it was attacked by black sigatoka disease and nematodes (root rot). Other Cavendish varieties introduced during the resurgence of the banana industry in the late 1980s and early 1990s were the *Grand Naine* and the *Williams Hybrid*, referred to as Giant Cavendish cultivars. The Cavendish varieties are resistant to the Panama disease.[75] The Banana Board has been developing some 150 varieties at the Banana Breeding and Research Station at Bodles, St Catherine since the 1990s, to find higher yields and wind-resistant cultivars; however, to date, the new varieties have not been wholly accepted by farmers because of fruit quality, especially the taste.

The banana export industry in Jamaica dates back to 1866, with large-scale farming first taking place in the parish of Portland. Most small holders were already experienced in production and marketing when the first North American traders began purchasing the fruit in the 1890s. Black Jamaican women also played a crucial role in the industry, transporting bananas on the estates during reaping days and operating as middle brokers (higglers) in the domestic cash economy. Regular export of bananas began in 1901 when Sir Edward Jones Imperial Direct Steam Line employed the United Fruit Company and later bought out by them. Some 650 tons of bananas were being shipped to the UK by 1900.

Portland, St Mary, and St Thomas were the parishes which were the pioneers in expanding banana cultivation, with St Mary becoming the chief parish for banana cultivation at one stage. Acreage under production reached eighty thousand acres by 1929, spread over the parishes of St Mary (fifteen thousand), St Catherine (twelve thousand), Portland (nine thousand), St Thomas (eight thousand), and St James (five thousand). In 1902, four parishes (St Mary, Portland, St Thomas, and St Catherine), accounted for 80 per cent of banana export production. The Rio Cobre irrigation scheme in 1890 expanded production in St Catherine.[76] Banana was grown in all parishes, including St Andrew and Kingston, even if it was a backyard or home garden. The development of the banana industry transformed Port Maria and Annotto Bay, both banana shipping ports near the rail line, from sleepy settlements into thriving urban centres. At one stage, the population of Annotto Bay exceeded twelve thousand residents.

The industry in 1880 was exporting only three hundred and thirty thousand stems, but rapidly increased to 97 million stems by 1895. By 1890, bananas had replaced sugar as Jamaica's principal export. Production rose from 5 million stems in 1897 to an average of 20 million stems a year in the 1920s and 1930s, representing over half of exports. Banana acreage expanded from around ten thousand acres in 1891 to seventy-three thousand acres in 1934. The average size of the banana estate increased from 75 acres in 1893 to 120 acres in 1920.[77]

The growing of bananas, especially in Portland and, to some extent, St Mary in the 1880s–90s, became a small holder economic activity. More than 90 per cent of land holdings in Portland, then the largest producer of bananas, was on farms of less than ten acres.[78] In the latter part of the nineteenth century, the growing of bananas was strongly associated with 'blackness,' sufficiently strong to discourage many of the white plantocracy from cultivating it for export, even when the sugar industry was dying. By 1890, the Boston Fruit Company purchased nearly four-fifths of the bananas exported, mostly from small growers.[79]

To support the industry after a major hurricane in 1912, the government, in response to local representation, established a network of Cooperative Loan Banks across the island for facilitating loans to small holders. The Western St Mary Cooperative Loan Bank was one of the largest lenders and, under the management of the Rev. A.A. Barclay, assisted by W.B. Cummings, the Cooperative advanced most of the loan money to purchase Pembroke Hall and Donnington in the Bagnolds district of St Mary. Six properties with 4,417 acres were gained for £59,000, subdivided into lots of five to fifty acres and sold to 450 farmers.

In 1922, the assessment for taxation on the first two properties increased from £9,000 to £30,000, and the area under cultivation was ten times what it was before the properties were purchased. The outcome of this initiative was that this area eventually became one of the most productive banana growing areas in Jamaica and continued to do so until the demise of the export industry in 1997.[80] Initiatives like these enabled Jamaican smallholders to become independent people with secure livelihoods, unlike sugar workers who were never lifted out of poverty and continue to live on the margins even today.

Small holder growers of export banana faced many challenges when trying to sell their highly perishable fruits to brokers and shippers, determined to maximise profits and minimise risks. Unlike most other crops, bananas need to meet very strict standards for export, so they need to be handled and transported with extreme care. The fruit also must be transported expeditiously to meet stringent shipping deadlines, at least within two days of reaping, as delays beyond this period seriously affect the quality.

To ensure quality fruits reach destination markets, shipping agents would notify growers of when and where they could sell their bananas, and this allowed farmers two to three days to harvest their fruits and take them to the buying stations. These agents were critical to the operation of the industry, as they decided on quality and pricing. Bananas that were harvested prematurely or were bruised or damaged were subject to rejection, as was common when they were transported by road in the 1880s. In seeking to manage their risks, shipping companies developed quality standards, which the farmers had to meet to avoid their fruits being rejected. Banana cultivation and export are susceptible to heavy rains and storms and a crop can be almost destroyed by hurricane. Hurricanes struck the island in 1874, 1880, 1886, 1889, and 1903, and have been more frequent in recent years. In addition to hurricane, there have been frequent blowdowns, or localised windstorms, causing severe pre-harvest losses. Although a banana crop is usually wiped out from the hurricane, the fields can recover quickly, allowing for harvesting of the fruits within six months. Sugarcane has the advantage in that it can withstand the major effects of both hurricanes, storms, and drought, with major challenges being flooding and blocked roads.

Banana and the Developments of the Transport System

The traditional mode of transport, prior to the linking of the railway from Kingston to Montego Bay in the west and Port Antonio in the east, was by road using pack animals, or animal-drawn carts. This form of transport caused considerable damage to the bananas, with high rates of rejection, limiting the scope of the industry. The risks related to transportation was on the grower. Cultivators usually wrapped their fruits in dry banana leaves before placing them on a cart. Drivers sometimes had to travel thirty to forty miles by road before reaching the buying station. Roads were shabby and, in rainy season, sometimes impassable. Railway, with the advantage of speed, efficiency, fewer damages during the journey and lower transport costs, quickly became the mode of choice for transport in the industry. By 1938, rail transported 60 per cent of the island's bananas and provided over 80 per cent of railway revenues.[81]

There is a correlation between the economies of scale of the banana industry achieved in the period after 1900 and the extension of the railway over the same period. The extension of the railway not only opened the interior areas of Jamaica to cultivation of bananas at just the right time, but it also benefited other domestic export crops, facilitating diversification of the island's agrarian economy. The rise of the banana trade during the second half of the nineteenth century also changed production and trade patterns on the island.

It was the banana industry that drove the railway expansion across the island. Changes in government's policies in the 1950s, regarding banana transportation, first came to impact negatively on the railway revenues. Instead of shipments to buying stations, wharves, or rail stations, bananas were taken first to boxing plants, many of which were on the plantations, away from the rail line. The shift of banana transport from the railway came to be one of the major downfalls of the railway. By the end of the 1960s, only about three thousand tons were transported by rail. Both the Port Antonio and Frankfield lines, which relied heavily on bananas, citrus, and sugar cane, saw revenues on both lines devastated. The shipment of bananas by railway transport ceased in 1968 and, by 1972, the railway ceased to be the principal carrier for agricultural crops; had it not been for the bauxite industry, the railway service would have collapsed at this point.[82]

Development of the Industry after 1900

The core of the labour force on these newly established banana plantations was comprised mostly indentured East Indians and Black Jamaicans. Between 1899 and 1906, approximately twenty-seven hundred South Asian men and women had been recruited to work on the banana estates. The government provided the health care for the indentured workers, creating a problem with the Black Jamaican day workers who did not get this benefit. Banana plantations, along with sugar, therefore played an important role in absorbing East Indian indentured labour into the Jamaican agrarian economy.

Between 1897 and 1903, small settler acreage declined in both absolute terms, and as a percentage of total land in banana plantation, with the drop steepest in St Mary, Portland, and St Thomas. St Catherine's banana production, however, more than tripled. During the first decade of the twentieth century, small holdings in St Mary, Portland, and St Thomas stagnated after increasing over three decades, with farmers switching to other export crops like coffee and cocoa and ground provisions.

The backward integration and consolidation pursued by the United Fruit Company and other transnationals enabled them to control the industry as part of a cartel in 1902, and a deal with Elder Dempster Company of the UK effectively gave United Fruit Company control over exports from Jamaica to Britain. They not only came to control export from Jamaica to the US and Britain, but they also controlled sources of supply from Latin America, so they came to control multiple sources of supply and distribution in the markets.

With less good land available for banana, and with stagnant prices and increasing rates of rejection of their fruits at the buying stations, the Jamaican small holders at the beginning of the twentieth century was pushed into insolvency. Cultivators responded forcefully to their growing marginalisation and violent altercations broke out between the smallholders and the buying agents. The Colonial government, while seeming pleased with the expansion by the transnationals of banana estates, raised concerns about deforestation caused by small farmers using more hillside forestry areas in order to expand their acreages. Social pressures, however, forced the colonial administration to give more consideration to the smallholders after 1920 by providing agricultural extension services.

In 1895, Henry Blake, shortly after his arrival in Jamaica (as governor) introduced legislation providing for the sale of small parcels of crown lands, as part of an effort to promote stable small-scale cultivation and to stabilise the rural communities. The same year the Jamaican Agricultural Society (JAS) was formed to uplift the small settlers with better agricultural practices and, by the early part of the first decade of the twentieth century there were three thousand members. Faced with the stranglehold of the transnational cartelisation of the banana market in the 1920s, the colonial government subsidised the creation of small-scale growers' cooperatives and banana research stations in Jamaican and Trinidad. The objective was to promote disease-resistant varieties, such as Lacatan and Robusta and, in so doing, create more opportunities for small holders.

In 1927, a cooperative organisation, the Jamaica Banana Producers Association (JBPA) was conceptualised, and it gained support from a broad cross section of farmers. By 1929, the JBPA began buying banana directly from farmers for shipping to the UK at preferential prices. By coming together, banana farmers could act as one body and protect their independence and prevent large companies like the United Fruit Company from assuming complete control of the trade. With the help of the government, within a few years, the JBPA was handling a substantial portion of the trade and running its own shipping line. The transnational banana companies, especially the United Fruit Company, saw the control they had over the industry threatened and mounted a frontal attack, insisting they would only relent if the cooperative status of the JBPA was withdrawn. Around the same time, a hurricane in 1933 dealt a severe blow to the farmers, wiping out 50 per cent of their crop and, at the same time, they had to face price undercutting in the overseas market from the transnational companies.

The JBPA could not match the prices of the transnationals and was on the verge of bankruptcy. As a result, they were forced to register as a limited liability company in 1936, operating as a private trading company, but still largely owned by the farmers. In return, the transnational companies agreed to donate 1 US cent for each banana exported as a bunch to a fund to support rural development.

Both United Fruit Company and Standard Fruit participated in the financing of the fund, which was used to set up Jamaica Welfare Limited in 1937. Jamaica Welfare engaged itself in self-help projects: adult literacy, cooperative housing, village sports, craft production, and home economics. It was taken over eventually by the government and has been transformed into the Social Development Commission.

Jamaica's main protected market in the years after the Second World War was the UK, benefiting from the Commonwealth Trade Preference Agreement. The agreement protected bananas from Jamaica and other Caribbean islands (especially the Windward Islands) against competition from Latin America bananas into the UK market, which was then restricted to four thousand tons per annum. Growers in the Windwards, like Jamaica, were mainly smallholders and faced the same competition from the transnational shippers.

The Expansion of the Banana Industry, 1939–69

Table 13.9 shows the expansion of the industry from 1939 to 1969, with volumes in export tons increasing from 1900, reaching 361.2 million tons exported in 1937. However, with the 1939 hurricane, exports fell to 5.8 million. In 1940, exports again expanded to 14.7 million tons.[83] Between 1890 and 1940, banana held the top spot as an agricultural export, accounting for 50 per cent of the nation's export earnings. The industry steadily expanded after 1920, peaking with exports of 361,200 tons in 1937. The following year 1938, there was a decline to 351,700 tons, and a further decline to 251,600 tons in 1939. By 1943, export tonnage had fallen to one hundred and twenty thousand. The industry suffered from hurricanes in 1903, 1904, 1915, 1916, 1817, 1939, and 1944, as well as from diseases – Panama disease in the 1930s and leaf spot in 1940.[84] Table 13.9 below shows volumes and values of banana exports 1939–69.

Table 13.9: Expansion of Banana Selected Years Exports, 1939–69

Years	Stems (millions)	Tons	Export Value J$ Million
1939	23.8	320,000	5.8
1946	5.9	78,000	2.2
1949	6.6	88,000	4.6
1951	3.7	49,000	2,6
1954	11.6	155,000	10.6
1960	10.2	136,000	9.6
1965	15.1	200,000	12.6
1967	14,9	192,000	13.6
1969		151,000	12.6

Owen Jefferson, *The Post War Economic Development of Jamaica*.

Banana expansion benefited from the Ottawa Agreement of 1932, which provided imperial preference to shipment of bananas from the West Indies. A Tripartite Agreement between JBPA United Fruit Company and Standard Fruit Company resulted in JBPA shipping all its bananas from Jamaica to the UK, so Jumana and the West Indies share of shipment to the UK market increased at the expense of the decline to the US market.

The Canadian market began receipt of increased shipments from Jamaica also after 1936 supplied by United Fruit and Standard Fruit companies. In 1941, United Fruit Company exercised its right to cancel the 1936 Agreement because of War. In the 1940s, Panama disease broke out in Jamaica, seriously affecting production and exports. With the Second World War, and the resulting difficulties of ocean shipments, exports to the UK were temporarily suspended. As a result of the conditions during the war years, two important events occurred. Firstly, a Banana Committee was established as an advisory board to the British representative who directed the buying and selling of bananas in the domestic market and, secondly the All-Island Banana Growers Association (AIBGA) was formed at the initiative of R.F. Williams. The purpose of the AIBGA was to give growers an influential voice in the management of their industry. Other stalwarts of the industry in this period were Jamaican Charles Johnson, father of the current chairman of Jamaica Producers Group, Ralph Burke who was instrumental with A.C. Goffe and Cecil Goffe and other in establishing the AIBGA.

Exports however fell from 23.0 million stem in 1938 to 4 million stems in 1944. The period the 1941 and 1944 also experienced hurricane wreaking havoc on production. By 1951, after the War, export was resumed with 49,990 tons exported that year. The industry recovered following the major 1951 hurricane, which had virtually wiped out the 1952 crop. In 1953, acreage increased from sixty-two thousand in 1951 to ninety thousand in 1953. In 1950, bananas accounted for 14.3 per cent of visible export, increasing to 18.7 per cent in 1953. Prices were depressed during the period 1953–63, resulting in banana accounting for only 7.7 per cent of visible trade in 1968.

In 1952, the British government terminated the special buying arrangement and return the industry to private operators. The colonial administration established the Banana Board as a statutory body under the Banana Board Law, No. 24 of 1953, with the sole right to buy bananas for export to overseas markets. The Board was charged with regulating the purchase, sale, exportation, and marketing of bananas, promoting the interests and efficiency of the industry, and assisting in its development. The Board contracted with the JBPA and United Fruit Company for the buying of bananas from the growers, their transport to the UK and for the marketing in the UK market.

Bananas and the Birth of the Tourist Industry

Jamaica's tourism industry started in the late 1890s, with the coming of visitors to Portland on banana boats owned by the United Fruit Company. By then Lorenzo Baker, was head of United Fruit Company and is credited with bringing the first tourists to Port Antonio, then the hub of the banana trade. The boats were fitted out to carry Americans to the warm Caribbean destination during frigid winter months. The tourist trade gradually took off, riding on the back of the banana industry. A.C. Goffe transformed the 597-acre Windsor Estate in St Ann's Bay into a luxury hotel with Buick cars and horses available for riding. The Windsor opened in 1953, one of the country's largest hotels and along with the Titchfield Hotel in Portland attracted international stars such as Errol Flynn, Joe Louis, and Nelson Rockefeller. As banana continued to dominate Jamaica's economy, and investors, the rich and famous, and others continued to flock to the island upper income residential homes developed around Coral Gardens in Montego Bay.

Post-War Developments

In the period 1954–60 banana exports level remained relatively stable until 1961 when high prices triggered an increase in export tonnage. In 1963, the industry shifted from the *Gros Michel* variety to the more durable Lacatan. Between 1960 and 1971, Jamaica was exporting, on average, about one hundred and fifty thousand tons to the UK. Between 1970 and 1982, exports fell from 133,100 tons to 22,000 tons. Although major efforts were made by the government and farmers, production decline continued in the 1980s, with 1984's export amounting to only 11,100 tons, one of the worst of the century.[85] The Banana Board also assumed responsibility for the Banana Insurance Fund in 1965. After 1965, production and exports fluctuated widely because of the various hazards, especially from frequent hurricanes and storms. Hurricanes Flora in 1965, Carmen in 1974, Allen in 1984, and Gilbert in 1988 wrought havoc on production and the financial situation of farmers.

Restructuring in the 1970s and Privatisation in the 1980s

Government intervention in the Banana Industry started in the 1930 and was institutionalised in 1953, with the creation of the Banana Board by the Colonial government and continued up to 1984 when all banana production activities were divested from the Board. The marketing function of the Board was terminated and financial support to the Board ceased. Between 1984 and 2010, the government's direct role in banana production was discontinued. Direct support recommenced in 2010 when with direct support to the Banana Board with a budget support of J$48.2 million and an EU grant of J$18.3 million.

In the 1970s, the market requirements for bananas changed from bunches to boxes. As a result, the Banana Board introduced centralised boxing plants throughout Jamaica in 1975. The boxing plants replaced the many district buying stations, resulting in farmers having to travel longer distances to sell their produce, thus incurring higher post-harvest damage and losses because of longer processing times. Rejection rates at the boxing plants increased and prices were low, leading to some farmers abandoning their farms.

In the 1970s, the Banana Board introduced several 'mother farms' – that were financed directly by government loans. These large farms were established with the primary objectives of increasing production, boosting the income of the Banana Board and addressing the rapidly rising cost of its operation. The farms established included Spring Gardens, Lower Leyton, and Golden Vale in Portland, and Spring Field in St Thomas. The government then established the Banana Company of Jamaica Limited in 1979 and transferred the marketing functions of the Banana Board to this new company, which became the sole exporter of bananas.. The reforms proved to be a failure, with the state farms and the Banana Company of Jamaica incurring continuous losses, resulting in the entire industry coming under scrutiny.

Besides frequent hurricanes and heavy storms, the industry suffered several setbacks, including diseases because of poor agronomic practices; absence of irrigation; too many small farmers working lots of under forty-nine acres, often on hillside plots which could not deliver economies of scale; absence of large estates which could deliver economies of scale; high transportation cost from farms to packing plants, from packing plant to ports and from the island ports to the UK.

In the UK market, after the 1960, the Caribbean had to face competition from Côte d'Ivoire, Suriname, and the Dominican Republic. In 1967, the Caribbean held 97 per cent of the UK market; by 1972, this had fallen to 72 per cent. Jamaica also had to share the UK market with the Winward Islands Banana Growers Association. Globally, the island could not compete with bananas from Central and South America.

Lands were provided to banana growers in the 1970 on forty-nine-year leasehold arrangements. Produce was sold to Banana Export Company (BECO), a limited liability company owned by small and large growers. The growers received income directly from BECO from the sale of the bananas each week and shared in dividends. The Banana Company of Jamaica, however, ceased operation in 1984 and was eventually wound up, and the state farms, the boxing plants, and the Research Department of the Banana Board were closed.

The Export Performance of the Industry, 1965–75

Table 13.10 shows the declining trend of Jamaica's banana exports over the decade 1965–75.

Table 13.10: Export Tonnage, 1965–75

	1965	1966	1967	1968	1969
Export Tons from JA	189,000	200,300	187,000	153,200	149,200
Total UK Imports	353,200	331,000	322,200	318,800	329,100
JA bananas as % of UK imports	53.5	60.5	58.3	48.1	45.3

	1970	1971	1972	1973	1974	1975
Export Tons from JA	133,100	125,900	127,000	107,700	71,300	70,200
Total UK Imports	306,900	315,600	289,300	287,300	278,100	279,400
JA bananas as % of UK imports	43.4	39.9	43..9	37.5	25.6	25.1

Source: Marjorie A. Stair, 'Banana Board,' 2013.

Banana export declined from one hundred and eighty-nine thousand tons in 1965 to seventy thousand tons in 1975. Jamaica's share of the UK banana market fell by more than half, from 53.5 per cent to 25.1 per cent. As part of 1980s reforms, the boxing plants and the Banana Board's farms were privatised and the Banana Export Company (BECO); a grower's organisation was formed to take over responsibilities for export marketing and licensing of growers. The BECO employed the Jamaica Marketing Co. Limited (JAMCO), a state-owned company based in London to handle the overseas marketing and shipping of bananas. With these changes, the Banana Board relinquished all its responsibilities for supplying planting material, leaf spot control, and extension services to the BECO. The Banana Board between 1979 and 2008 performed a minor regulatory function.

The BECO purchased bananas from growers and shipped through JP Shipping, selling the export volume through the state-owned Jamaica Marketing Company (JAMCO), based in London. JAMCO was established by the Jamaican government in 1970 to supervise the marketing of all commodities in the UK market. Bananas were ripened and marketed by JBPA and Elders & Fyfe. JAMCO, chaired by John Pringle, was effective in obtaining high prices for Jamaican bananas. I also served on both JAMCO's and BECO's boards and was chairman of Eastern Banana Estate Limited (EBEL) in the 1990s.

The privatisation of the banana industry and the establishment and eventual dominance of the Banana Export Company Limited significantly reduced the role of the Banana Board after the 1980s. This control became even more pronounced when BECO became the implementing agency of the European Banana Support Programme in its initial years. One major achievement of the BECO years was the significant upgrading of the Port Antonio port in 1993 to accept larger boats. Shipping of bananas in the heyday of the Banana Board was done from ports in Kingston, Montego Bay, Lucea, Bowden, and Oracabessa.

The Banana Industry after Restructuring Privatisation in the 1990s

Privatisation in the banana industry took place as land lease method: twenty-five years in the first instance, with an option for a further twenty-four years. Rental was agreed at 5.5 per cent of the value of the land, ranging from J$500 to J$3,000 per acre, giving an annual rental value of J$378,120 per annum. The banana industry after the 1990s came to be centred on three large-scale estates, with two of the newly created companies operating under one group: Jamaica Producers Group. In the restructuring of the sugar industry in the early 1980s, Gray's Inn sugar factory was closed, along with three other sugar factories. The land associated with the Gray's Inn factory amounted to two thousand acres and formed a part of St Mary Banana Estate Limited. NIBJ elicited proposals from investors for the acquisition of the property for agricultural use. In 1987, the Jamaica Banana Producers Association

(JBPA) consortium submitted a proposal outlining a plan to convert the two-thousand-acre-property to the growing and exporting of bananas.

Jamaica Producers Group became the largest shareholder in St Mary Banana Estate Limited and also held a major stake in Eastern Banana Estates Ltd. The government, as the major shareholder, and Fyffes (a UK distributor) also held a stake in Eastern Banana Estates. Victoria Banana Company Limited was solely owned by the government. JPG, a vertically integrated company, held joint ventures with Dole, an American banana company in the UK to market bananas, holding about 15 per cent of the UK market which was supplied by ACP, Latin America, and EU sources.

The consortium at St Mary Banana Estate Limited was led by JBPA and included the Commonwealth Development Corporation (CDC) of the UK with 35 per cent stake, International Finance Corporation (associated with the World Bank) 15 per cent, and JBPA, with 50 per cent. Board membership was respectively JBPA, CDC, and IFC, with the chairman coming from JBPA and being the managing technical partner. By 1992, the estate produced twenty-six thousand tons of bananas for export, representing 34 per cent of banana exports. f. JBPA had also in 1986 acquired the neighbouring Agualta Vale property and exported 1,457 tons from this property in 1987.

St Mary Banana Estate Limited diversified into the growing of mangoes, papayas, coconut, and fresh vegetable. The parent company changed its name in 1992 to Jamaica Producers Group, reflecting the more diverse nature of its business. It had acquired a facility in the UK to produce freshly squeezed citrus juice as well.[86] The Group has since sold its banana business in the UK to Dole Fruit Company of the US and has no more interest in exporting bananas to the UK. It has also moved its it snack business from the UK to the Dominican Republic.

The government privatised part of the sugar lands in St Thomas to another consortium, creating Eastern Banana Estate Limited (EBEL). In this venture, the consortium comprised JBPA, CDC, and the government of Jamaica, with the government owning 35 per cent, JBPA 50 per cent, and CDC 15 per cent.

EBEL exported twenty-nine thousand tons or 38 per cent of total banana exports in 1992. The EBEL agreement in 1992 also called for the government to divest most of its interest in the company, with JBPA and CDC having the pre-emptive rights to take up its share. The CDC's interest in St Mary was subsequently sold to JP after CDC insisted that JP sell bananas on the open market in the UK. CDC's 30 per cent interest in Eastern Banana Estate Limited was sold to Fyfe's of the UK. Fyfe later sold its interest in EBEL to JP. The farm was then leased to Duckenfield Estate to grow sugar cane; however, Duckenfield subsequently closed its sugar factory and exited the sugar cane growing business. The government later reduced its interest in EBEL to 5 per cent.[87] Eastern Banana Estate Limited was closed after hurricane Dean in 2007. Victoria Banana Estate Limited, fully owned by the government ran up massive losses and was closed after the government and the Israelis ended their commercial relationship.

St Mary Banana Estate Limited continues to produce bananas. However, production is carried out mainly for the local market (both green and ripe bananas) and to supply the local chip factory, which also exports. St Mary, through JP, also exports small quantities of ripe bananas to the US. The company has diversified into plantain, pineapple, sweet potatoes, and limited agro-forestry. External factors, mainly the termination of long held trade preference agreements and frequent hurricanes have impacted negatively on production. One outcome of liberalisation is that the large supermarkets in the UK became the dominant purchaser of bananas and they insisted on buying from the cheapest sources.

For several years small farmers from the banana growing parishes relied on income from the export of bananas, first to the US and then to the UK, which provided a guaranteed preferential market. Shipments to the UK started in 1901and, from then, Jamaica became the main supplier of the fruit to Britain until problems were encountered, following Britain's entry to the European Union.

From the vantage point of the small settler/small holder community, the period between 1870 and 1900 is of major significance. This period provided the first opportunity for small holders to gain access to land and to participate meaningfully in the export trade, particularly the expanding North Atlantic market. Up to then economic exploitation and marginalisation of African Jamaicans was still part of their lived experiences. Banana provided the main opportunity for small settlers to independently forge their livelihood away from the sugar plantation system.[88]

From its inception, bananas were cultivated as a cash crop by small farmers, as well as for export. The inter-cropping of bananas and coffee was of particular importance because coffee required shade and banana provided the constant cash flow and, as the old saying goes – you 'knot yuh socks' with the coffee – i.e., coffee provided income for savings and re-investment, hence creating very secure livelihoods for farmers. With a combination of other export crops: coffee, pimento, and ginger, as well as ground provisions, small settlers came to produce most of the food for both the local and export markets after 1880. Despite this, the Colonial government's support and policies continued to favour the plantocracy.

The Banana Trade Preferences and the WTO Intervention

The banana industry, like sugar over the years had benefited from imperial preference in 1900, followed Commonwealth preference in the 1930s, which continued up to 1963, providing a secure market for Jamaican and Windward Islands banana exports. In 1967, Jamaica and the Windward Islands entered a market sharing agreement regarding the UK market with Jamaica benefiting from 52 per cent share of the UK market and the Windward with 42 per cent. When Britain entered the EU, banana exports from Jamaica and other ACP countries were provided with duty-free access to the EU of up to eight hundred and seventy thousand tons per year up to 1993. Exports above this level attracted a tariff. Non-ACP bananas were also allocated a collective quota of 2 million tons. Special prices per ton were also set for the import of both ACP and non-ACP bananas entering the EU market, with lower prices for ACP bananas. With the restructuring of the Common Agricultural Policy in 1992, the EU created a single market regime for bananas after 1993, harmonising the import polices of the UK and the EU. These reforms were largely aimed at reducing agricultural surpluses and controlling the budget cost by reducing the level of CAP price and sustaining a competitive agricultural market.

Jamaica had been benefitting from the EU Banana Support Programmes (BSP) of 1999, aimed at improving the competitiveness of the country's industry. The three large estates and the larger growers reduced their cost of production, declining by 30 per cent over the period 1997–2000, and by 20 per cent over the period 1997–2001. The smaller growers accounted for about 14 per cent of the bananas exported in 2001. The larger growers and the estates, before the changes to the EU banana regime, could produce profitably at the EU tariff quota rate of

75 euros per ton; however, the smaller growers had difficulty, so many exited the industry.

The original trade preference system to ACP countries was under the Lomé Convention and later the Cotonou Agreement. The original regime was challenged by Latin American producers and the US, representing its banana transnationals and after a series of rulings, in the late 1970s the WTO dispute resolution body ruled that the EU banana regime was in breach of the GATT and GATS Agreement, mainly because of the discriminatory practice of setting aside a set quota for ACP countries (including Jamaica and Windwards), and the allocation of licences which permitted discrimination against third-party countries. With the end of banana trade preferences to Jamaica and the rest of the West Indies after 2000, the death of the industry, like sugar, was only a matter of time. Between 1995 and 2000, Jamaica on average exported sixty-five thousand tons at an average value of US$38 million per annum.

In April 2001, the US and some Latin American producers finally agreed a EU proposal; the first phase was to be implemented between July 2001 and January 2002. The EU reform centred on replacement of agricultural price support (subsidies) with direct aid payment to farmers affected by price cuts, although direct aid payment became conditional on compliance with environmental provisions, among other things. Further reforms were implemented coming out of the Doha Round of Multinational Trade Liberalisation launched in 2001. In 2003, a single payment scheme was introduced to replace the direct aid payment to farmers. In the new system, the EU removed banana import quotas and replaced them with preferential tariffs on non-ACP exports.

The Cotonou Agreement was rolled over into the Partnership Agreement, which linked the ACP-EU with over one hundred partner countries, which was to expire in 2020. In April 2020, the ACP Group of States became the Organisation of African, Caribbean and Pacific States (OACPS) and a new agreement was being finalised for implementation. The new arrangement specified a movement away from country-specific quota allocation to one allocation for all ACP members. This has had the effect of making it difficult for small Caribbean exporters to take advantage of the overall quota and, with the change in the allocation of import licenses, effectively reduced the incentive to buy bananas from Jamaica and traditional ACP suppliers.

Box 13.1: Experience of a Smallholder/Grower in Jamaica

This is the experience of a banana exporting small farmer with thirteen acres, operating in St James from 1989 to 1997 and the challenges faced.

Despite the support of the Western Banana Development Company – a private company owned by the Agricultural Credit Bank, the Jamaica Producers Group and a couple of other shareholders – at the end of the 1980s, some conditionalities of the IDB Agricultural Sector Loan resulted in the removal, almost overnight, of subsidies on fertilisers, land preparation and on agricultural loans. Farmers were suddenly forced to face extremely higher prices for all agricultural inputs, and market interest rates for agricultural loans were introduced. The problem was compounded, at the time, by a shortage of the supply of plastics – used for banana sleeves (export quality bananas was not possible without protective sleeves) and tunnel pads used for packing in boxes. There was also a shortage of phosphate fertilisers, pushing up the cost even further than NPK fertiliser from which subsidies had been removed.

Compounding these problems, in May 1994 all the rivers in St James overflowed their banks, affecting many banana farmers. As the General Manager of WESTBAN, I calculated the costs of providing assistance for affected farmers and found that input costs for exports had increased by 57 per cent, whereas the export price had increased by less than 20 per cent over the same period.

Fortunately for the St James banana farmers, there was a profitable domestic market with less stringent quality requirements, so many of us simply discontinued exporting. It meant there was no need for banana sleeves and tunnel pads; leaf spot control spraying costs were reduced, as we did not have to maintain as many sprayings' cycles. The domestic market was mainly the tourist/hotel market for ripe bananas, strong local demand for green bananas and three banana chips factories (two in St James and one in Westmoreland) purchasing green bananas for processing. This was during the period when developments in the financial sector necessitated the intervention of FINSAC, and farmers were exposed to very high rates from the commercial banks.

Suffice it to also say that, in the initial stages of the implementation of the European Banana Support Programme, virtually no assistance was provided to the banana farmers in Western Jamaica. It is on record, through evaluation of the programme, that approximately 65 per cent or more of the funding to support banana production under that programme went to the few large producers, since they controlled most of the exports.

The Economic Partnership Agreement (EPA) comprising a Free Trade Agreement (FTA) between the CARIFORUM countries (CARICOM countries and the Dominican Republic) and the EU as well as technical and financial cooperation arrangements took over from all previous agreements.

The EPA is the successor agreement to the trade component of the current Cotonou Agreement, which provided one-way preferential tariffs and technical and financial cooperation arrangements for the CARIFORUM countries. The Cotonou Agreement was legitimised by the WTO based on a waiver of its Most Favoured Nation (MFN) clause until the end of 2007. CARIFORUM signed the Economic Partnership Agreement (EPA) with the European Union in October 2008.

The EPA is a WTO-compatible trading arrangement that allows for duty-free and quota-free access to most of CARIFORUM's goods and services. This new regime allows the EC to continue granting preferential access to ACP bananas without fear of being challenged by MFN suppliers. The EPA allows for trade between the EC and CARIFORUM with no WTO waiver, which was due to expire in December 2008 and the EC indicated that it would not be renewed. Provisional application of the Agreement began on January 1, 2008, with formal signing in October of the same year.

On December 15, 2010, finally a landmark agreement between the European Union and the Latin American banana producing countries was signed. The agreement is summarised as follows:

- The EU will cut its MFN import tariff on bananas in eight stages, from the current rate of €176/ton to €114/ton in 2017 at the earliest.
- The tariff will be reduced to €148/ton, a cut of €28/ton once all parties sign the deal.
- Latin American banana producing countries will demand no further cuts in the framework of the Doha WTO round of talks and settle several legal disputes pending against the EU at the WTO, some dating back as far as 1993.
- The EU will freeze its cuts for up to two years if the WTO /Doha talks on agriculture are not concluded by the end of 2013.
- The EU is required to 'bind' its tariff once WTO members certify the new tariff regime.
- The EU has settled its dispute with the US.
- ACP bananas will still be able to be exported to Europe duty and quota free.

This agreement further reduced the margin of preference in the market for ACP banana exports, despite the Economic Partnership Agreement. Notwithstanding, the EPA, the EC is still obliged to rebind its banana tariff, which will also still be subjected to the market access disciplines in the multilateral process. The advantages offered by the signing of the EPA have not prevented the significant erosion of preferences in Jamaica's favoured export market. Only the Dominican Republic in the Caribbean seems to have benefited from the EPA, with significant increases in exports to Europe. Since EPA, almost all Caribbean exporters have experienced a decline in shipments to Europe.

After 2000, the domestic market for local consumption (supermarkets and the tourist trade) expanded and, with better prices, this contributed to the viability of the industry. In the domestic market, both ripe and green bananas are marketed, with ripe bananas carrying a higher price. Green bananas have been sold to the processing industry since 1965 for manufacturing banana chips. A small amount of banana and plantain chips from Jamaica entered the export market from as early as 1964; however, the export quantities remain small.[89] The domestic market for bananas has always been strong; however, to date no studies have been carried out to determine its potential. STATIN/PIOJ reports on domestic food crop production since 2011 have not been covering bananas for the domestic market.

The Banana Export Company's exports effectively ended after Hurricane Dean in 2007, and its operation was wound up on March 31, 2010, the government having closed the Banana Trading Company Limited, the major input supplier to the industry, in December 2009. By 2008, St Mary had 65 hectares in banana, compared to 6,070 hectares in 1965. St Catherine, which had 3,642 hectares in 1965, fell to 83 hectares in 2008, while Portland which had 3,642 hectares fell to 388 hectares in 2008.

Consequences of the New EU WTO – Banana Regime

Table 13.11 shows the volume of bananas exported since the changes to the EU banana regime. Between 2000 and 2004, banana export volumes experienced a steady decline from 42,045 MT in 2000, to 28,657 MT in 2004, with export value falling from US$22.9 million in 2000 to US$12.8 million in 2004. The industry is now centred on a few growers. St Mary Banana Estate, Tulloch Estate in St Catherine, and some medium-sized farms in St Mary continue to produce for the hospitality market, domestic supermarkets, and small volumes for export. Some 90 per cent of the farms are four hectares and below and these farms also grow other crops. Farms of twenty hectares and below now account for forty-three of total cultivated banana farms.[90]

Table 13.11: Export Banana Production by Volume and Value, 2000–2004

Years	Tons	By Value US$ million
2000	42,045	22,896
2001	43,052	18,271
2002	39,986	17,556
2003	39,936	18,844
2004	28,657	12,814

Source: *PIOJ Social and Economic Survey* – Sundry Years

The production and export structures developed in Jamaica and other Caribbean countries under conditions of trade protection afforded by the European Union and the US, government regulation and government assistance, have been radically changed because of the WTO (Uruguay Round) trade liberalisation and the Caricom External Tariff in the 1990s.

Between 2014 and 2016, Jamaica tried to re-enter the EU/UK market under the CARIFORUM/EU Economic Partnership Agreement (EPA); however, this was unsuccessful as UK market prices had plunged and Jamaica's cost of production was uncompetitive. Since then, there has been minimal export to the UK. Jamaican production cost in 1997 was about 40 per cent higher than Ecuador and Costa Rica, about 50 per cent higher than Colombia, about 25 per cent lower than the Windward Islands, and 40 per cent below Martinique at US$680 per MT. More recently, there have been more stringent requirements for export certification which are now standard practice, designed to ensure environmental, economic, and social sustainability. Jamaican and British Caribbean farmers cultivating on small hillside lots cannot achieve economies of scale and produce at lower cost to compete with Latin American banana producers.[91]

The major Caribbean banana producers today have been the Dominican Republic, Suriname, and Belize, while St Lucia and Dominica, Caricom exporters have been struggling to remain in the export industry. This is because of their inability to achieve significant economies of scale, erosion of preferential access to the EU and UK markets and inability to compete with bananas from Latin America and competition from former ACP countries of Cameroon, Cote d'Ivoire, Dominican Republic, and Belize.

The problems faced by Jamaica and the Windward Islands' banana producers are both short-term and long-term, and they cover fluctuations in production, due to frequent hurricanes and storms, diseases, insecure land tenure, drastic changes in international trade policy and export rules, praedial larceny and relatively high production cost from the inability to achieve economies of scale.

Table 13.12 below shows the competitive position of Jamaica and Caribbean banana producers relative to Latin American transnational dollar producers. In almost all areas, Jamaica and the Caribbean banana producers are at a competitive disadvantage.

Table 13.12: Comparative Competitive Position of Jamaica and Caribbean Banana Producers

Jamaica and Windward Islands Smallholders		Latin America Plantations
Cultivated area	Land hilly or mountainously limited availability	Large plains and ready land availability
Soil conditions	Relatively poor soil and low yields up to 10 MT per acre	Rich soil high yield 18–24 MT per acre
Farm Ownership	Mostly independent small holders	Large estates integrated with US transnationals (Dole and Chiquita)
Labour cost and working conditions	High wage rates and reasonable social conditions	Low wage rates and low social conditions of workers
Farm input cost	Unit cost high because of diseconomies of scale and varying soil types	Economies of scale; low input cost
Transportation	Smaller volumes of higher shipping cost	High volume and lower shipping cost

Source: Oral Telphia and Okeleke Nzeogwu, 'Case Study of Jamaican Banana Export Farmers: Threats, Opportunities and Survival,' *Journal of Applied Business and Economics* (2009).

Disadvantages include land mostly on hilly terrain versus large plains; relatively poor soil versus rich soil; production mostly on small lots versus large integrated estates; high cost of wages and high unit production costs versus low wage rates and low unit production costs, benefiting from economies of scale. Dollar bananas also benefit from lower per unit shipping costs because of the higher shipment volumes.

Unlike sugar, there has been little opportunity to obtain cost reduction in the banana industry from further amalgamation of operations. Between 1990 and 2003, the supply of ACP bananas to the EU fell from 10 per cent to 4 per cent. In 2009, the preferential trade agreement from which the industry had benefitted since 1936 and had become dependent for seventy-three years finally ended. The focus of the industry since 2010 has been on the local market and encouraging increased domestic consumption. Banana production for export began its decline at the time of the infestation outbreak of the black sigatoka disease in 1996.

Like sugar, banana has had a profound impact on settlement development in Jamaica and, like sugar, the industry has shaped internal migration, impacted urbanisation, and played a profound role in shaping the hierarchical structure of the class system in Jamaica. Whereas sugar plantations from the seventeenth century onwards were integral to the creation and maintenance of socio-economic hierarchal structure, with a small group of Whites (White supremacy) at the top and the mass of the Black Jamaicans (Black inferiority) at the bottom, banana played a signal role in granting independence and freedom to Black Jamaicans, allowing them to expand the number of free villages all over the island. The industry no longer sees a future for exports of fresh banana and has been focusing on developing the domestic market and expanding the value chain on the island. The banana industry could produce about fifty-five thousand tons of fruit in 2015. In 2015, the government offered the industry infrastructural support and planting materials that were valued at J$53.5 million to help in its recovery and competitiveness. Most of the funds came through the European Union and the Banana Export Expansion Programme. The Dominican Republic seems to be the only Caribbean country to meet the competition from Latin-America and the Philippines, earning US$228.9 million from banana export in 2021.

> Banana came when the freed Black Jamaicans from the sugar plantations were struggling to escape the continued yoke of white supremacy and, since banana cultivation afforded small holder cultivation on hillside lands with minimum capital expenditure and infrastructure, banana can be said to be responsible for the development and expansion of the small settler/free village structure which has dominated the rural Jamaica horizon after the 1870s. Regrettably, both banana and sugar seem to have had a long innings and they are now at the dawn of playing a very minor role of what is left of five hundred years of Jamaican's agrarian economy.

The Post-Independence Experiences of Epsom and Annotto Bay, St Mary

The sharp decline of the banana and sugar industry around the areas of Annotto Bay, St Mary after 1995 is summarised in Box 13.2

Box 13.2: The Post-Independence Experiences of St Mary

In Tony Weis's qualitative survey of small farmers in and around the Annotto Bay area in 2006, he concluded that the social and economic problems of the Annotto Bay region epitomised the current agrarian crisis in Jamaica with the inequities closely mirroring those of Jamaica. Around Annotto Bay today, 96 per cent of landholders (and 80 per cent of the landless) control only 38 per cent of the land in the parish, much of which is steep hillside land, not very friendly to modern agriculture techniques. In contrast, 1 per cent of landholders control 53 per cent of the land.[92] Annotto Bay, at the peak on the banana industry, was the third largest town in Jamaica with a population of over twelve thousand; it was a leading sugar plantation centre, and latterly the leading banana centre. Despite a precarious existence from 1850 to 1950, rural small settlers came to form the foundation of life in Annotto Bay and St Mary. With the slow disappearance of small holdings, small sugar and banana farmers, and sugar workers around the area since 1980, the town has been dwindling, reflecting the malaise of rural Jamaica.

In the early 1980s, the Gray's Inn Central Factory shuttered its doors. St Mary Banana Estate, one of the largest banana plantations on the island, came to the rescue in the 1980s by replacing sugar lands with banana on the coastal plains. Banana farming came to dominate Annotto Bay's economic environment for the two decades 1980–2000, providing most of the wage labour employment in the area.

Estate sugar and banana, and small holder sugar and banana have now been discontinued around Annotto Bay. These lands, which once thrived from sugar cane, cattle pen keeping, and latterly banana farming, now lie empty, despite attempts to introduce alternative crops such as pineapple, sweat pepper, and papaya. With the demise also of smallholder farming, occasioned by globalisation and economic liberalisation, Annotto Bay and the surrounding villages now experience high levels of unemployment, increasing poverty and violence. With high levels of out-migration overseas and to the fast-growing urban centres of Jamaica, Annotto Bay and the once thriving rural smallholdings and villages of Epsom, Enfield, Fort Stewart, and Dover Road, and other surrounding villages, are now in terminal decline. Rural Jamaica now relies largely on large-scale remittances from the migrating rural settlers to Canada, the UK, and the US, which now underpin the survival of the once free villages; otherwise, these villages would now form part of our historic relics.

Rising agro-imports have taken a serious toll on Annotto Bay's small farmer's livelihood. The social and economic structure of St Mary has also been undergoing rapid transformation. The small settler Black Jamaicans who populated the area after emancipation are disappearing, either from the harsh realities of competition, or from out-migration. All over rural Jamaica, citizens have abandoned, or are abandoning living on steep hillsides. Much of lands in these areas are being returned to forest. Liberalisation has meant that markets like the Coronation Market in Kingston, and parish capital markets are now flooded with cheap competitive agricultural products from the US, Latin America, and China.

With large out-migratory flows from Annotto Bay the social safety valve for the area has been out-migration to the US and Canada, and locally to Kingston. The remittance dependency mentality is one of the dominant factors working against young villagers taking up agriculture in the Annotto Bay Area.

Notes

1. L.C. Polopolus, 'World Sugar Markets and Entangled Government Programmes,' in *Sugar and Related Sweetener Markets: International Perspective*, ed. A. Schmitz and T. Speen (Wallingford, UK: CABI Publishing, 2002), 7–9.
2. B. Richardson, *Sugar: Refined Power in a Global Regime* (London: Palgrave Macmillan, 2009).
3. Polopolus, 'World Sugar Markets and Entangled Government Programmes.'
4. Matthew Parker, *The Sugar Barons* (London: Windell Books, 2012).
5. A large barrel
6. E. Williams, *Capitalism and Slavery* (Durham, NC: University of North Carolina Press, 1944).
7. Parker, *The Sugar Barons.*
8. Williams, *Capitalism and Slavery.*
9. Robertson Map of Jamaica (1804), 'Survey 1709–1799,' Montpelier, James Blackwell.

10. Duncan Weldon, *Two Hundred Years of Muddling Through: The Surprising Story of Britain's Economy from the Industrial Revolution to COVID-19* (London: Little Brown Book Group, 2021).
11. Christine Walker, *Jamaican Ladies: Female Slave Holders and the Creation of Britain Atlantic Empire* (Durham, NC: University of North Carolina Press, 2002).
12. Lloyd Best, 'Outlines of a Model of Pure Plantation Economy,' *Social and Economic Studies* 17, no. 3 (1968): 283–326.
13. George Beckford, *Persistent Poverty: Underdevelopment in Plantation Economies of Third World* (Oxford: Oxford University Press, 1972).
14. Norman Girvan and Cherita Girvan, 'The Development of Dependent Economics in the Caribbean and Latin America: Review and Comparison,' *Social and Economic Studies* 22, no. 1 (1973): 1–33.
15. George Cumper, 'Dependence, Development and the Sociology of Economic Thought,' *Social and Economic Studies* 23, no. 3 (1974): 465–82.
16. Clive Thomas, *Dependence and Transformation: The Economies of the Transition to Socialism* (New York: Monthly Press Review, 1974).
17. Mintz, S., (1985), op.cit.
18. Adam Smith, *An Enquiry into the Wealth of the Nation* (London. Statham and T. Cadell, 1776).
19. Donovan Stanberry, *How Trade Liberalization Affects a Sugar-Dependent Community in Jamacia, Global Action and Local Impact* (London: Palgrave Macmillan, 2022).
20. In addition to the free villages established with the support of the protestant church, some of the settlements were squatter settlements or settlements of freed Black Jamaicans who were able to buy land with their own resources.
21. Gisela Eisner, *Jamaica 1830–1930: A Study in Economic Growth* (Manchester: Manchester University Press, 1961).
22. John Bigelow, *Jamaica in 1850: The Effects of Sixteen Years of Freedom on a Slave Economy* (New York and London: George P. Putman, 1851).
23. Clinton Black, *History of Jamaica* (London and Glasgow: Colins Clear Type Press, 1958).
24. Bigelow, *Jamaica in 1850.*
25. Ibid.
26. Eric Williams, *British Historians and the West Indies* (London: A & B Publishers, 1964).
27. Clinton Black, *History of Jamaica* (London and Glasgow: Colins Clear Type Press, 1958).
28. Eisner, *Jamaica 1830–1930.*
29. Richardson, *Sugar: Refined Power in a Global Regime.*
30. Stanberry, *How Trade Liberalization Affects a Sugar-Dependent Community in Jamacia.*
31. M. Harrison, *King Sugar Jamaica, The Caribbean, and the World Sugar Industry* (New York: New York University Press, 2001).

32. C.H Feuer, *Jamaica and the Sugar Workers Cooperatives, the Politics of Reform* (Burlington, VT: Westview Press, 1984).
33. Owen Jefferson, *Post War Economic Development of Jamaica* (London: Unwin Brothers Limited, 1972).
34. Ibid.
35. H. Levy, 'The Social Action Centre Story 1958–1998,' in *Spitting in the Winds: Lessons in Empowerment from The Caribbean*, ed. S.F. Brown (Kingston: Ian Randle Publishers in association with the Commonwealth Foundation, 2000).
36. MOA, 'Development of Frome/Monymusk/Bernard Lodge Lands,' 1972.
37. Monica Frolander-Ulf and Frank Lindenfield, *A New Earth: The Jamaican Sugar Workers Cooperatives, 1975–1981* (Lanham, MD: University Press of America, 1984).
38. Carl Stone, 'The Sugar Cooperatives 1974–1980,' in *Plantation Economy, Land Reform and the Peasantry in Historical Perspectives: 1838–1980*, ed. Claus Stolberg and Swithin Wilmot (Kingston: Friedrich Ebert Stiftung, 1992)
39. Stanberry, *How Trade Liberalization Affects a Sugar-Dependent Community in Jamacia.*
40. M.A. Crichlow, *Negotiating Caribbean Freedom: and the Sate of Development* (Lanham, MD: Lexington Books, 2005).
41. Belinda, Coote, 'Sugar the Case of Jamaica' *IDS Bulletin*, Institute of Development, 19, no. 2, (1985): 54–58
42. Stanberry, *How Trade Liberalization Affects a Sugar-Dependent Community in Jamacia.*
43. Derick Heaven, 'Report to the English-Speaking Caribbean Fourth Sugar Meeting 1994,' presentation to Sugar Industry Authority, Kingston.
44. A. Brown, A., and Helen McBain (1993), 'Studies in Caribbean Public Enterprises,,' Vol. 1, IDS, 1993.
45. Derick Heaven, 'Sugar Industry in Jamaica,' presentation to the Diplomatic Corp in Jamaica, Kingston, 2004.
46. Heaven, *Report to the English-Speaking Caribbean Fourth Sugar Meeting 1994.*
47. Government of Jamaica, Ministry Paper, (1991), Government of Jamaica..
48. NIBJ Report, 1994.
49. Government of Jamaica, Ministry Paper 34, 1994,
50. Ibid.
51. Diaram Ramjeesingh, 'The Impact of Failed Privatisation on a Developing Country: A Cases Study of the Sugar Company of Jamaica,' in *IDEAZ* 1 and 2 (2004).
52. Ibid.
53. R. Clarke, 'Sugar Industry Under Scrutiny,' *New World*, Inter Press Service, 2001.
54. Government of Jamaica, Ministry Paper, 1994.

55. Stanberry, *How Trade Liberalization Affects a Sugar-Dependent Community in Jamacia.*
56. Ibid.
57. World Bank, *Implementation Completion Report, Jamaica* (Washington: World Bank, 1996).
58. I was made a member of the of the PNP Divestiture Team.
59. Government of Jamaica, Ministry Paper 20, December 2012.
60. *The Gleaner*, November 9, 2021.
61. Stanberry, *How Trade Liberalization Affects a Sugar-Dependent Community in Jamacia.*
62. Ibid.
63. Ibid.
64. W. Craton and J. Walvin, *A Jamaican Plantation: The History of Worthy Park 1670–1970* (Toronto: University Press of Toronto, 1970).
65. Courtland Grant and Margie Bauer, *Jamaica and Sugar Annual Report 2011* (Washington, DC: USDA, 2011).
66. Rasheeda (April 2021) USD, 'Gain and Global Agricultural Information Network.
67. B. Richardson, *Sugar* (Cambridge: Polity Press, 2015).
68. Stanberry, *How Trade Liberalization Affects a Sugar-Dependent Community in Jamacia.*
69. Planning Institute of Jamaica, *Economic and Social Survey 2020* (Kingston: PIOJ, 2020).
70. World Bank, *Time to Choose: Caribbean Development in the 21st Century* (Washington, DC: World Bank, 2005).
71. Ben Richardson and Pamela Ellen Ngwenya (2013), op. cit. (NOT PREVIOUSLY MENTIONED)
72. John Soluri, 'Bananas Before Plantation: Smallholders, Shippers, and Colonial Policy in Jamaica, 1870–1910,' *Iberoamerica* 1, no. 23 (2006): 143–59.
73. D.W. Rodriquez, *An Outline of the Economic History of Production and Trade with Respected to Jamaica* (Kingston: Government Printer, 1955).
74. Marjorie A. Stair, 'Banana Board – Sixty Years,' Kingston, 2013, pamphlet by Banana Board on its 60th Anniversary.
75. Marjorie Stair, 'Banana Board Notes on the History of the Jamaican Banana Industry,' meeting notes, 2022.
76. Theodore Sealy, Clinton Black, and Richard Hart, 'A History of the Banana Industry with Special Reference to the Part Played by Jamaica Banana Producers Association Limited,' Kingston, 1984.
77. Ibid.
78. Wilson Randolph Bartlett, 'Lorenzo Baker and the Development of the Banana Trade between Jamaica and the US 1881–1890,' (PhD Thesis, American University, 1977).
79. Edger M. Beacon, *New Jamaica* (New York: Walbridge, 1890).

80. C.A. Wilson, 'Men of Vision – Series of Biographical Sketches of Men Who Have Made Their Mark upon Our Time,' *The Gleaner*, 1939.
81. Railway Departmental Report, 1903.
82. Veront Satchel and Cezley Sampson, 'Rise and Fall of the Railway in Jamaica,' *Journal of Transport History* X, no. 1 (2003): 2–21.
83. Theodore Sealy, Clinton Black, and Richard Hart, 'A History of the Banana Industry.'
84. Marjorie A. Stair, 'Banana Board – Sixty Years.'
85. Ibid.
86. Helen Chilupe, *Privatization in Reality: The Case of Jamaica*, report prepared under the Robert McNamara Fellowship Programme (Washington, DC: World Bank, 1993).
87. In the period 1993/1996 the writer served as Chairman chairman of EBEL.
88. John Soluri, 'Bananas Before Plantation: Smallholders, Shippers, and Colonial Policy in Jamaica, 1870–1910,' *Iberoamerica* 6, no. 23 (2006): 143–59.
89. Elizabeth Morgan, 'Banana Export: The Demise of the Green Gold,' WTO update, August 23, 2021.
90. Brandon Gaille, 'The Jamaican Banana Statistics and Trends,' 2018. Brandon Gaille Marketing Advice.
91. Oral Telphia and Nzeogwu, 'Case Study of Jamaican Banana Export – Farmers Threats, Opportunities and Survival,' *Journal of Applied Business Economics* (2010): 1–11.
92. Tony Weis, 'The Rise, Fall and Future of the Jamaica Peasantry,' Journal of Peasant Studies 33, no. 1 (2006): 61–88.

CHAPTER FOURTEEN

Reforming, Privatising, and Liberalising the Telecommunications Industry

SPONSORED BY

FLOW

BACKGROUND TO PRIVATISATION OF TELECOMMUNICATIONS IN JAMAICA

The Jamaican experience in introducing competition in the telecommunications sector has confirmed the conclusion reached by researchers that introducing competition in the sector since the 1980s not only leads to improved performance over monopoly provision of services but also results in lower prices, wider choice of services, wider access, and faster expansion in capacity.[1]

Telecommunications was the first of the utility industries to have undergone reform and privatisation, not only in Jamaica, but in most countries in the world, following major technological changes experienced in the industry in the 1980s. It was the breakup of American Telephone and Telegraph (AT&T) in 1982, followed by the reforms of British Telecom (BT) in the UK in 1983, as well as in Chile, that pioneered new developments setting these changes in motion. Deregulation of telecommunications started in Chile in 1982, with introducing a new market framework for telecommunications, based on the market principle.[2] Jamaica was one of the early reformers, when the country began instituting structural reforms in 1985 by merging the domestic and international telecommunications businesses, creating Telecommunications of Jamaica Limited (TOJ) in order to facilitate the privatisation. M. Lodge and L. Stirton pointed out that, following Jamaica's telecommunications privatisation, the World Bank has used the Jamaican example as a guideline on how to promote private investments in the sector.[3]

Early Historical Development of Telecommunications in Jamaica

Much of the developments in telecommunications in Jamaica and the Caribbean has centred on the operations of Cable and Wireless Limited (C&W) (a subsidiary of Cable & Wireless UK), which until 2001, was the main player in the industry in Jamaica and the Caribbean. Telephone services were first introduced to Jamaica in 1883, when fifty lines were installed in Kingston by West India and Columbia Electric Company (CEL). CEL was later renamed West Indies Telegraph and Telephone Company (WITEC). In 1893, the Telephone Law was enacted, and this law remained as the main instrument guiding the development and operations of the industry until 2000. In October 1892, the Jamaica Telephone Company was incorporated by private investors to provide telephone services in Kingston. In 1925, the JTC acquired WITEC and obtained a forty-year licence for the Kingston and St Andrew Corporation (KSAC) area. The licence gave the government the right to acquire the company at the end of the licence period, at a price to be agreed on by the company and, if the parties could not agree, the takeover price was to reflect revalued assets of the company. The company, or any twelve ratepayers, could file for rate reviews by a Rate Board, a three-member ad hoc group appointed by the colonial governor in council. The company was allowed an 8 per cent return on rate base. Any deficiency (returns below 7 per cent) over a particular period or surplus (above 9 per cent) would be carried forward into an Excess and Deficiency Account to be kept for future rate adjustments.

Besides the JTC 1925 licences, several companies operated telephone services in the rural areas of Jamaica; however, in 1939 the colonial government, through the post office, nationalised the rural services, while the Kingston service remained privately operated by the JTC. In 1945, one year after universal suffrage, the government privatised the telephone business of the post office to JTC and, granted the company a licence for the rest of the island (excluding the KSAC), with an expiry date of January 1967, or to expire with the KSAC licence, whichever date was later. The system of rate determination continued to be that of the Rate Board, although the board, however, lacked permanent staff and institutional memory and instead used external consultants paid by the company to carry out its work. Controversy developed following an application in 1953 for a rate increase, and the JTC refused to the pay the external consultants, disagreeing with the method of rate determination adopted, resulting in government having to pay the cost.[4]

In 1958, the JTC was further awarded a Special (Wireless) Licence under the 1958 Radio and Telegraph Control Act, to be followed in 1962, with the award of two further special licences: the (Telegraph) Licence and the Telex and Teleprinter Licence. During the process of development the JTC came to be controlled by Telephone & Trust General (T&GT), a UK based company. The company's shares were issued on the London Stock Exchange and T&GT came to take a controlling interest of 50.2 per cent of the JTC's stocks. The rate Board granted rate increases over the years 1952, 1956, 1957, 1958, and 1960. Up to the 1960s, the JTC was left alone by the government to get on with its business except for periodic intervention by the Rate Board in setting rate. The period coincided with sustained growth, with the number of lines increasing from 1,437 in 1950 to 41,152 in 1962 achieving an accounting rate of return of 5 per cent to 7 per cent.[5] In an environment of low inflation, low real interest rate, and a less assertive government the regulatory arrangement worked reasonably well.

The Second Period of Regulatory Development and Private Ownership Change

The accommodative environment all changed after independence in 1962. With independence, there was increasing demand for services, and the new government in 1962 declined to grant further rate increases, requesting expansion in services to meet the increasing demand. The company, however, refused to carry out expansion, requesting rate increases to compensate for previous revenue deficiencies, as allowed in the 1954 licence. Eventually, negotiation between the government and the company broke down in 1963. By 1966, the government had created the Public Utilities Commission and the British shareholder of the JTC; Telephone and General Trust (T&GT) sold its majority stake in the JTC to Continental Telephone Company of Canada (CTCC). This marked the end of the colonial era. Negotiations ensued between the government and the private parties between 1963 and 1966. During this period, a new licence was granted in 1965, amended in 1966 to accommodate the Public Utilities Commission (PUC) Act which, in 1966, provided for a utilities regulator to regulate the telephone and electricity industries.[6]

The PUC became operational in 1966, and, in addition, the existing licences were amended (valid for twenty-five years), replacing the original All-Island Telephone Licence, what had been granted under the 1893 Telephone Act; while the Special (Wireless) Telephony Licence and the Special (Telegraph) Licence Special (Telex and Teleprinter) Licence were awarded under the Radio and Telegraph Control Act of 1958.

Several material changes were made to the 1966 amended licence as follows:

- It required T&GT to reduce its shareholdings from 50.5 per cent to 20 per cent.
- The term was shortened to twenty-five years, and not forty years as before, but renewable for a further ten years, starting in 1967.
- The excess shares were to be offered to local Jamaicans through the Jamaica Stock Exchange as part of the government's policy of promoting local ownership.
- No single shareholder was to be allowed to hold more than 20 per cent of the TJC's equity.
- T&GT, with 50.5 per cent Jamaica was given six years to dispose of the excess stocks and reduce its shareholding to 20 per cent.
- Instead of a fixed rate of return on rate base, the new licence only provided for a 'fair' rate of return, with the rate base to be determined by the PUC. Determination of the rate base in subsequent years proved to be a testing matter; for example, there was the question as to whether works-in-progress was to be treated as part of the rate base.

With introducing the PUC rate, hearings became public, and parties other than the government and the company could participate in the proceedings. The company's case for an increase was presented by lawyers and investment bankers, often from overseas. With the new arrangement, relationships between TG&T and the government, and between T&GT and the PUC became very adversarial. TG&T as under the Rate Board system of regulation refused to invest and expand services without first being awarded rate increases. The result was stagnation in the number of main lines in the 1960s with the number of lines increasing marginally by 1967 over the level in 1962. Loans to the JTC from TG&T fell from J$1.2 million in 1963 to J$0.8 million in 1966.[7] Part of the refusal to invest stemmed from uncertainties associated with the licences that were due to expire. In Jamaica, the convention had developed accommodating licence renewal, but this was never offered to TG&T.

Acquisition of Jamaica Telephone Services by Continental Holdings of Canada

T&GT decided to sell out and exit the industry in Jamaica but could not find local buyers to purchase the excess 30.2 per cent equity holdings, a requirement of the government. In the end, a new private party entered the scene: Continental Holdings Limited (CHL) of Montreal, Canada, a reputable telephone investor with an interest in Barbados and the Bahamas, and who agreed to acquire T&GT's interest in the JTC. The government gave its approval in 1967.[8] The minister at the time was Robert Lightbourne. The CHL sought the government's permission to retain the excess shares of 20 per cent minimum for three years, ending January 1971. The agreement which was eventually reached between TG&T, the CHL, and the government allowed the CHL to acquire all of TG&T shares in the JTC. In addition, the CHL agreed on the following:

- to undertake at any time chosen by it, in consultation with the government, during the next five years to refinance the US$11.5 million fifteen-year World Bank Loan, based on interest of 1 per cent above Jamaica New York prime rate existing at the time for twenty-five years, with an annual Sinking Fund of 2 per cent of principal, and otherwise upon the usual terms applicable to a long-term financing for telephone utilities.
- The CHL undertook to lend the JTC, as and when required by the JTC, sums of money up to US$5 million at the rate of one 0.5 per cent above the New York bank rate existing at the time, subordinated to the existing World Bank loan. Such loan to be redeemed from the sale of additional shares of the JTC, where such issue of shares being held by the CHC, or otherwise by bank, or other loans from other sources. The timing of the offer of shares was to be sufficiently flexible to avoid conflict with other share offerings in Jamaica.
- The CHL would cause the JTC to purchase materials and equipment from any of its affiliated companies, except that these were to take place on a commercially competitive basis, and that it would not take, or accept any commission, or discount

regarding any purchase by, or for the telephone company and it would direct that purchases in the best interest of the JTC.

- The CHL would reduce its share ownership in the JTC to 20 per cent level as required by the license by January 1, 1971, provided however that the government considered it necessary that it should divest itself of the shares beyond January 1, 1971. The shares to be sold would be offered at the then current market rate.
- The CHL would expedite the present development programme so that, instead of being completed in the five years required by the licence, it would be completed in three to three-and-a-half years. The CHL also agreed to provide the financing to enable the JTC to undertake certain other important projects, besides the programme agreed on in the licence.
- The CHL agreed to undertake the studies to determine the investment and rates that would be required to change the present metering system to a flat rate. The result of these studies to be made available to the PUC to determine the desirability of implementing the findings.
- The CHL would undertake to expand programmes to train technicians, both locally and in the company's plants in the US.
- The CHL agreed not to agree with the JTC to supply management services at a fee. This stipulation, however, was not to preclude the CHL from supplying and charging for consultants and special services to the JTC, so long as such services were supplied, and charged for in conformity with paragraph 37 of the All-Island Telephone licences, 1966.
- The CHL agreed to give full support to the local AT&T factory.

The expansion programme required £5 million capital investments over five years; however, the CHL agreed to increase and finance the expansion programme to the level of £6.575 million within three and a half years. With the new agreement, the government greeted the CHL's involvement in the JTC and Jamaica with enthusiasm. The company, shortly after takeover, increased its investment commitment to from J$25 million to J$45.2 million because of the poor quality and underinvestment over the years. The CHL, however, seems to have overestimated the JTC's equipment, as evidenced by the price it paid for the shares and the valuation of its investment.[9]

The Period of Regulatory Change, 1967–75

The period of the CHL and the JTC's operation in 1966–75 under the PUC was controversial with conflicts between the PUC and the JTC. In 1968, the JTC embarked on the new development programme, changing its forecast of investment and revenue needs. The JTC, under CHL ownership, made its first rate application to the PUC in 1969. However, the hearing was protracted and continued well into 1970, only for the PUC to reject the application outright, stating that it needed to revise the whole tariff structure, rather than going ahead with just piecemeal increases. As a result of these developments, the company suspended its expansion activities in July 1971 and, at the same time, applied formally for a rate increase of 17 per cent. The PUC responded with an increase of 15 per cent, effective December 1971. The JTC followed this up with another application for an increased rate of 52 per cent in April 1972 and, on this occasion, the PUC granted an increase of 35 per cent in September 1972. During this time, the price of JTC shares on the local stock market fell to J$0.28, well below the price of J$1.13 per share that the CTC had paid per share.[10] In its August 1972 annual report, the PUC stated that future rate increases would be contingent on improvements by the JTC in the quality of services, and not just with the level of investments made by the company. The report further stated that the licence condition stipulated a 'permitted rate of return' and that this was not an absolute entitlement.

By this time, the PNP had taken over control of government in 1972 and was in sympathy with the CTC's position in seeking rate increases. The result was a meeting between the prime minister with the PUC chairman, Dr Marshall Hall, and its Board. The prime minister failed to influence the PUC's original decision. In fact, Dr Hall clarified that the PUC was not to be dictated to in its decision on rate adjudication, which infuriated the Prime Minister Manley, whereupon in March 1973 the Jamaican government imposed a 12.5 per cent stamp duty on international and domestic calls and subsequently transferred the proceeds to the JTC as a direct subsidy, to enable the company to proceed with the investment programme. In return, the CTC transferred 10 per cent of the JTC's outstanding stocks to the government of Jamaica. The PUC strongly objected to imposing the stamp duty and communicated its position on the matter in a letter to Eric Bell, minister of public utilities, in December 1972, informing the minister that the stamp duty was an infringement of the law, because it was decided on without public participation.

With the new financing from the stamp duty, the JTC commenced a new investment programme in June 1973. However, much of the investment went replacing technically and physically obsolete equipment without adding to an expansion of the network. The government subsequently amended the licence to provide for a minimum return equivalent 'to the high point in the immediately preceding year of gross redemption yield of the last external long-term loan bonds of the government in the United Kingdom.' As part of the financing from the stamp duty, the government acquired equity in the JTC in 1973, reflecting the PNP's ambition for state ownership in the utilities. In fact, soon after the PNP came to power, a meeting was held on March 30, 1972, with the JTC and the minister of public utilities, Eric Bell, and, in the meeting, the company indicated it would not object to equity participation by the state.

The PUC again objected the company's stocks being transferred to the state because it diluted the ownership of the minority shareholders' shares. In April 1974, the JTC requested another rate increase, this time of 81 per cent and, in July 1974, the PUC allowed an increase of 53 per cent. This was to be the last increase the PUC handed down regarding telephone rates.

The advent of the American-style quasi-judicial rate of a return form of regulation marked another major regulatory turning point in Jamaica, substantially changing the way the utility industry (telephone and electricity) was regulated. The PUC was an independent body, with its own permanent staff, with the mandate to regulate all aspects of the telephone and electricity companies' operations. It had power similar to the Public Utility Commissions in the US; but not only did it have less experience, it did not have the precedents and administrative rules guiding US regulators. As a result, the PUC faced immense regulatory challenges during its existence. The JTC now faced a traditional 'rate of return' mechanism for determining its tariff without an explicit minimum, as was the situation in under the Rate Board system.

This was a period after the oil price shock of 1972 and the commencement of a sharp slide in the Jamaican dollar against the US dollar. Despite substantial increases in inflation (prices doubled between 1969 and 1971), no rate increases were granted during the eleven-year period of 1960–71. The same was true of the railway rate, and much the same for electricity rates, reflecting the political pressures on an independent government in responding to the needs of the voting population.

The conflicts between the PUC and the JTC revolved around the definition of the rate base, the accounting procedures, how depreciation should be treated, the cost of capital, what were reasonable costs, transfer pricing practised by the CHL, and the procurement procedures.[11] Further, in the 1972 rate hearings, the Jamaican Tax and Ratepayers Association presented evidence against the JTC, and again in 1974, this time joined by the Jamaica Hotel and Tourist Association. Following the PUC decision, the Tax and Rate Payers Association filed an appeal to the Supreme Court. The JTC also followed with an appeal to the Supreme Court as well. On this occasion, the Court denied the JTC's appeal, despite its earlier decision when it heard an appeal in 1956 and had reversed the Rate Board's decision that had blocked the JTC from recouping a shortfall on its profits. JTC had given a commitment to undertake a major development programme to be financed by the CTC; instead, the JTC sought rate increases to finance the investment programme. This was a major problem for the PUC, and the Commission refused to grant such increases as was the earlier case under the Rate Board with TG&T. Interestingly, in 1969 and 1973, the JTC issued new stocks to fulfil its financial and to reduce its holding in favour of local investors. However, Jamaicans failed to fully take up the offer and CTC, having underwritten both issues, ended up with 68 per cent of the outstanding shares rather than the 50 per cent it had initially acquired.

Public Ownership of JTC

The result was that the CTC, like TG&T earlier. was willing to sell its interest in the JTC to the government or anyone in 1975 and exit Jamaica. Nationalisation of the JTC was less of an ideological stance and more a complication of the licensing arrangement. During the period 1970–75, the JTC's profits had stagnated, barely sufficient to cover real depreciation of assets (1970 being the only profitable year).[12] The company was not sufficiently profitable to attract new capital, hence the CTC indicating as early as 1971 to Minister Bell that it welcomed government investment in the JTC. The first step was taken in 1973 with the government's acquisition of 10 per cent of the JTC. In fact, the CTC took advantage of the PNP's policy of public ownership of utilities and negotiated a sale to the government in September 1975. The government then acquired most of the remaining equity from the local private sector, allowing it to increase its holding to approximately 95 per cent of the JTC's stocks by the end of 1975.

In 1976, following the takeover of the JTC in 1975, the government transferred regulatory responsibility for the JTC to the minister of public utilities.[13] The PUC Act remained on the books and was not removed until 1995, when the new regulatory arrangement was brought into place. The government pricing policy between 1975 and 1980 under state ownership did not change, and the company's financial future remained precarious.

The period of 1890 to 1970 a period of private ownership and public regulation was of significance in that private investors were not prepared to put equity or borrowed capital into the utilities operation to expand growing demand. Instead, the private investors CHL, CTC, TG&T at different times insisted that the regulator or government provide rate increases before any investment to meet goring demand. Private investors were not prepared to take on the investment requirements in a developing country. It is this more than anything else which drove to public ownership of the telephone company, rather than political or any other economic reasons.

Early Development of International Services

Domestic telephony and international telecommunications in Jamaica historically developed on two different tracks: a domestic track outlined above and an international track as set out below before they were eventually brought together under one operation. After the laying in 1868 of the Florida-Havana cable, which connected Europe and the US with Cuba, two companies were formed with the objective of establishing submarine telegraph communications from Cuba through Jamaica, firstly to Colon, Panama, and secondly to Georgetown, Guyana, via the chain of islands bordering the east of the Caribbean Sea. The West Indies and Panama Telegraph Company was formed in 1869. The result was that international telephone services came to Jamaica in the 1870s with the expansion of the undersea cable from Florida to Holland Bay in Jamaica by the West India and Panama

Telegraph Company (WIPT). The formation of a merged company, came to be known as Cable and Wireless Limited, a UK government-owned company, and this company came to acquire all the shares of Eastern and Associated Telegraph Companies and the Marconi Company, in exchange for shares in the merged company.

The period that followed the emergence of Cable and Wireless Limited saw a great deal of reorganisation of the basic structure of the company, and vast progress was made in integrating the two great systems of overseas telecommunications: the submarine cable and the beam wireless. In 1932, Cable and Wireless Limited took over the WITP, with responsibility for operating all the international telecommunications systems.[14] The West Indies subsidiaries, including the Jamaica branch, all became part of Cable and Wireless Limited in 1938, operating the international services between Jamaica and the rest of the world.[15] In 1973, the general manager was Trevor Minott, a Jamaican engineer, with Horace Barber, the government's financial secretary, as chairman, and with Eric Sharpe, chairman of Cable and Wireless UK, also being a member of the board.

C&WL inherited the network in 1938, operating the international telecommunications service for Jamaica until 1971 when JAMINTEL was formed, reflecting a consortium of government 51 per cent and C&W UK Ltd of 49 per cent. The government was then given the option of increasing its equity stake to 75 per cent over the next fifteen years and to purchase the remainder of the stocks by 1988. The original authorised share capital of the company was J$15.0 million. In the decade that followed, telecommunications cable went ashore on virtually every territory in the Caribbean, involving a system of overlapping companies, creating a most untidy and unwieldy situation of telecommunications ownership. C&W inherited the situation in 1938 when it took over the competing companies and systems of international telecommunications.[16]

In 1961, a joint venture was formed, comprising Jamaica's Post Office's international telecommunications business with the international activities of C&W West Indies Limited, creating C&W Limited, previously owned by the British government. C&W West Indies, prior to 1961, did not require a licence to operate.[17] There was a difference in the relationship between C&W Jamaica and the Jamaican government when compared to the JTC, in that C&W was an imperial operation, so Jamaica's relations with C&W was on a government-to-government basis, while the JTC had been privately owned until nationalisation. JAMINTEL, unlike the JTC, was not regulated by the Public Utilities Commission in the 1960s.

International telecommunications, prior to the 1960s, was of little public concern, seeing that only a few wealthy citizens had telephone service. C&W, however, had seen the need for several new innovations, in particular investment in a new earth station and in the development of satellite communications. Cable and Wireless Jamaica (C&WJ) obtained its first licence in 1961, and this licence was amended in 1968 in several ways and extended for a further period of twenty years. JAMINTEL inherited the special licences granted under the Radio and Telegraph Control Act of 1958. They were specific to a particular technology, and these external telecommunications licences were due to expire in 1987.

The 1968 amended C&WJ licence included the right of the government to terminate the licence at will. With termination C&W was required to sell all its assets to the government at an agreed price, set by an arbitrator. The licence also provided for the company to earn a fair rate of return, rather than a specified rate of return.

The main features of the agreement are summarised below:

- JAMINTEL to take over C&WJ's wireless international telecommunications business and its licence, which was to expire in 1988.
- C&W would contribute building, land, and equipment, worth approximately US$4 million.
- C&W would lend US$8 million to JAMINTEL (repayable in seven years, with three years' grace, at 8 per cent interest) to buy C& W's remaining assets and provide working capital.
- The government's contribution of US$4 million (or J$3.4 million) would be provided through the use of a loan from C&W. This loan was to be repaid through a loan from C&W. The loan was through the use of up to three-fifth of the government's annual receipts from JAMINTEL's dividends, without charge of interest.
- Annual dividend was to not to exceed 15 per cent of equity.
- JAMINTEL was to be managed by Jamaican personnel.
- The government had the option of further acquiring JAMINTEL's assets at book value, according to a specified formula of up to 60

per cent by 1981; 75 per cent by 1986 and up to 100 per cent by 1988.

The participation of government as a majority shareholder in JAMINTEL in 1962 reflected the JLP government's policy of Jamaicanisation of key foreign-owned industries. The government had the option of wider public participation on the Jamaica Stock Exchange, and this option could have been pursued. This decision may have been influenced by the failure of the JTC's local stock floatation in 1969.

Restructuring and Nationalisation of JTC's Domestic Services in 1972–75

The government of 1972 had taken on its socialist stance of intervention in the productive sector of the economy, and the result during the period 1972–75 telecommunications, electricity, and urban transport which had developed, essentially under private ownership, came under public ownership. JTC shares were acquired, first with an allocation of 10 per cent of its stocks to the state in 1972, followed by the state majority takeover in 1975. By then, the state had acquired 95 per cent of JTC shares, including shares of held by the public that were listed on the stock market, with about 5 per cent remaining, owned by several small shareholders, who had refused to sell their shares to the government upon nationalisation.

Development in the Telecommunications Which Eroded Its Natural Monopoly Condition

In 1970, the JTC and JAMINTEL, respectively, shared international call revenues based on a 30 per cent:70 per cent split. JTC unilaterally after the merger changed this in 1984 to a 60 per cent:40 per cent split. Following the merger in 1987, there was a further change in the sharing of revenues, resulting in a ratio of 68 per cent for the JTC and 32 per cent for JAMINTEL. This, more or less, reflected the expropriation of C&WL's interests in JAMINTEL. Whereas international revenues in 1978 accounted for 20 per cent of the JTC's total revenues, by 1991 international revenues came to account for as much as 80 per cent of JTC's total revenues resulting in extensive cross-subsidisation of the unprofitable domestic business from the international business, reflecting another opportunistic action by government. By then, the state was majority owner in both companies, and there was no reserved rights clause requiring agreement by both parties on changes to the revenue-sharing formula.

One of the first technological interventions was the introduction of direct dialling 1977. Direct dialling had a major positive impact on the revenues of both the JTC and JAMINTEL and the foreign exchange earnings of the country. International direct dialling to Canada and the US commenced in 1978 and, with this change, dramatic growth in the demand for international telecommunications took place. Between 1979 and 1985, JAMINTEL's profitability increased significantly, due mainly to the introduction of international direct dialling, and this did not taper off until 1985/86, following price increases in 1984. In 1985, there were only 141,500 telephone lines (all fixed lines) in operation in Jamaica. Expansion had been taking place, however slowly, at the rate of about five thousand lines per annum under public ownership. The supply and the state's financing could not keep pace with demand which existed.

Besides increases in overall size of the market, the growth in international telecommunications also reflected increases in total revenue per line. Callers were not only making longer calls, there were also increases in international rates of 50 per cent in 1979/80, and again in 1984, reflecting the government's policy which required selected public enterprises, like the JTC to recover their operating costs and contribute to the financing of their capital needs. The JTC used price increases to improve its financial performance in 1984.[18] JAMINTEL's after-tax returns on fixed assets in 1982 exceeded 10 per cent. The increase in international telecommunications in the 1980s provided a windfall to both companies, allowing them to improve their performances, even as real prices fell. The improved profitability also relieved the pressures for rate increases. For a developing country like Jamaica, net hard currency revenues from international calls became an important source of foreign exchange in the 1980s, as shown in table 14.1. Jamaica earned US$222.2 million from international telecommunication revenues, whilst Trinidad and Tobago earned US$149 million at the same time Jamaica earned US$106.6 million from the US because of the settlement rate system with Jamaica's settlement payment as a percentage of telecom income being 47.9 per cent compared to Trinidad and Tobago at 29.2 per cent. Jamaica's teledensity (ownership of phones per 100) in 1995 was 11.58, compared to Trinidad and Tobago at 16.8.

Table 14.1: Revenues from Settlement Rate Income for Selected Latin American and Caribbean Countries

	Per capita income US$	Revenues in US$m 1993	US payments as settlement US$m 1993	Settlement payment as a % telecom income	1995 Teledensity per 100 persons
Jamaica	1553	222.4	106.6	47.9	11.58
Trinidad & Tobago	3587	149	43.5	29.2	16.04
Ecuador	1476	179.0	67.0	37.6	7.05
Nicaragua	431	60.6	22.6	37.3	2.08

Source; ITU/WTDC (November 1995), Pressures for Reform of International Accounting Rate System and ITU (May 1996), Americas Telecommunications Profile.'

In 1993, Jamaica's per capita income was US$1,553 compared to Trinidad and Tobago at US$3,587. In all cases with the US, the surplus exceeded 20 per cent of telecommunications revenue, whilst with Jamaica, the overall surplus with all countries exceeded 80 per cent of telecommunications revenues by 1995.[19] The US not only had the largest consumer' market, but the US outgoing calls also lasted much longer than incoming calls for cultural reasons. In addition, the large immigrant community in the US accentuated the imbalance in revenues.

This Bonanza Did Not Last into the 1990s

Another new technological development in the 1980s was Call Back as a delivery system. A typical call from the US in the 1980s cost US$0.25 per minute. Call Back resulted in the loss of revenue to the local incumbent telephone company. Call Back grew to be the equivalent of 4 per cent of US international outgrowing traffic worldwide. The typical call back technology relied on uncompleted call signalling and involved customers in foreign countries who subscribed to the service, dialling a US telephone number and after a certain number of rings, hanging up. The US call back company, through its computer, then initiates the call in the opposite direction to the foreign telephone number. When the foreign caller answers, he or she receives a US dial tone from the switchboard at the reseller's US location, and the customer can then place a call to the US or other foreign destinations. There were several versions in making call back and the ITU declared most legal, except for call bombardment and answer suppression which were declared illegal. Pressure, however, from TOJ led the Jamaican government to declaring call back illegal, as it reduced TOJ, income sometimes.

Between 1985 and 1995, US carriers paid US$25 Billion in settlement charges to overseas carriers. The annual charges escalated from US$2 billion in 1985 to US$4 billion in 1995. In order to correct the US revenue imbalance, the US Federal Communications Commission (FCC) in 1996 took unilateral action directing US carriers to reduce the high settlement benchmark rates paid to foreign carriers.[20] International benchmark rates declined progressively from US$1.25 per minute in 1985 to US$0.85 per minute in 1993. With developed countries, the US benchmark rate eventually fell to US$0.23 and 0.39 cents, and for all counties from US$0.60 and US$0.39. Introducing a dual benchmark rate recognised the implicit condition that international telecommunications cost were now distance sensitive.

Performance of the Telecommunications Companies Before Privatisation

The high levels of profitability of both companies in the 1980s formed one of the attractive features which augured well for their privatisation. The introduction in the 1980s of value-added and enhanced services, new technological developments in the 1980s the telecommunications industry became multi-product driven, with the boundaries between computer and telecommunications increasingly being blurred. Telecommunications services became tradable economic activity, amongst the fastest growth area in international trade and an important source of foreign exchange for small developing countries like Jamaica. Much of this income from international calls provided to TOJ, not only to modernise its network in the 1980s but to subsidise domestic callers.

While the JTC was profitable, it had been only marginally so. Its rate of connection below eleven persons per one hundred was less than desirable, with substantial unmet demand. With the reform programme which Prime Minister Seaga had implemented in the 1980s, there had been some improvements; however, this satisfied only 63 per cent of recorded demand, and the average waiting time to be connected was as high as 156 weeks (three years).[21]

JAMINTEL, which provided international telephone services, telex services, telegraph services, leased circuits, facsimile services, international data access, and circuits for satellite television, had a record of reasonably good profitability and had declared dividends every year of its operation, except 1977. With the JTC's poor record regarding its rate of connecting customers, the level of teledensity had reached only 3.55 per one hundred, compared with developing countries' average of five telephones per one hundred residents, reportedly this was one of the most inefficiently managed utilities.[22] In the 1970s, the communications sector, of which telecommunications formed a part, accounted for only 1.2 per cent of GDP.[23]

Privatisation of the Telecommunications Industry

The merger of the JTC and JAMINTEL started in 1985 and was approved in 1987. The new company TOJ, which was the outcome of the merger, was especially created for the privatisation vehicle and was incorporated on May 19, 1987, with an authorised share capital of J$1billion. It acquired JAMINTEL's equity via a share swap in June 1987 and purchased all JTC's shares with its own equity (following independent valuation of both companies' businesses). Despite the earlier commitment Prime Minister Seaga had made not to privatise the telecommunications industry, within two years he was to reverse this decision. Several developments had taken place or were taking place in the industry which led to the prime minister's change of mind.[24] First, he believed that privatisation had to begin with profitable businesses (demonstration effect); telecommunications was a profitable business and had a chance of being successfully listed on the Jamaica Stock Exchange.

Second, the government could not provide the finances needed to meet the rapidly increasing capital outlay required to meet consumer demands in the 1970s/80s. The prime minister believed that expanding telecommunications was critical to encouraging foreign investments. He also believed that the company's performance could be improved by accessing modern technology, finance, and foreign exchange. The JTC had not been able, in the first half of the 1980s, to modernise its facilities and expand at the rate required of the economy. The company had to rely on the ability and creditworthiness of the Jamaican government, and this had placed serious constraints on obtaining new financing for the JTC. JAMINTEL however, through its link with a technical partner, Cable & Wireless UK, could readily access finance, technology, and foreign exchange.

Third, both the JTC and JAMINTEL were two of the largest public enterprises (PEs) that were included in the list of twenty-one selected enterprises, with their capital expenditure plans subject to restraint under IMF loan restrictions. Privatisation, Mr Seaga concluded, would release the two companies from the arbitrary decisions of the government and the IMF. Conveniently, the JAMINTEL partnership agreement between the government and C&W was coming up for renewal, giving the government the opportunity to restructure the telecommunications sector. In addition, the IMF, the World Bank, USAID, and the Heritage Foundation were putting severe pressures on the government to fulfil the promises that had been made about creating a market-led economy and reducing the size of the budget deficit. The IMF's view was that a sizeable portion of the public sector financial activities was being carried off-budget and that the associated level of public sector investment being undertaken by the PEs rivalled central government's investment programme and required more accountability. In the 1985/86 fiscal year, the aggregate expenditure of the Specially Selected PEs totalled US$1 billion, exceeding the entire expenditure of central government that year, being US$835 million.[25] Debt servicing in the 1980s reached 65 per cent of the national budget and 150 per cent of GDP, severely restricting investments in the utilities, as the government had to provide guarantees to the loans of companies like the JTC, which lacked the capability of financing their own investments. Hence Adam, Cavendish, and Mistry stated that the telephony companies found their capital expenditure plans subject to being vetoed by the IMF.[26] The requirements for increased monitoring of selected PEs led to the enactment of the Public Bodies Management and Accountability Act as, up to then, the government had no legal instruments to monitor the PEs.[27] The Public Enterprise Division was established at the Ministry of Finance to carry out monitoring of the PEs in the 1980s and provide annual reports of the Selected Public Enterprises for Parliament each year.

Fourth, Mr Seaga also saw telecommunications as central to an export-led economic revival. In his budget speech, as finance minister and prime minister in 1988, he projected US$450 million to come from the first phase of his privatisation programme.[28] In fact, the privatisation of telecommunications, National Commercial Bank (NCB), Caribbean Cement Company, and Soap and Edible Products (Seprod) Limited eventually yielded J$626.1 million which, to put the total in perspective, represented 37.6 per cent of total privatisation receipts up to 1989, and 3 per cent of GDP.[29]

More than anything else, however, it was the World Bank and the IMF's structural adjustment loan programmes, which imposed privatisation as conditionalities, and which led to the divestiture of companies like National Commercial Bank and the TOJ. Here, it could be argued that it was more pragmatism which triggered privatisation rather than ideology.

To prepare for privatisation of the telecommunications companies, Mayer Matalon, the chairman of the Jamaica Telephone Company, and deputy chairman of JAMINTEL, and a leading Jamaican entrepreneur, convinced the government to create a holding company to facilitate the privatisation. Matalon was also an advisor to the prime minister and ambassador-at-large to the Jamaican government, while carrying out responsibility for the handling of most of the negotiations, along with Jamaica's financial secretary, Shirley Tyndall.

The merger of the JTC and JAMINTEL was implemented with the transfers being carried out through a vesting legislation of the assets and liabilities of the two companies to TOJ: Vesting of the JTC and JAMINTEL Act of 1995. Following the merger, Mayer Matalon, the outgoing chairman of the JTC, became the new chairman of TOJ. The government acquired a controlling interest in the JTC at the initial phases of the restructuring on July 23, 1987, and on May 19, 1987. TOJ acquired JAMINTEL's equity via a share swap in June 1987. This was on the basis of an external valuation by the investment banking transaction advisor. TOJ also acquired all JTC's shares. The total number of employees taken over in 1987 by TOJ amounted to 2,629, with 2,369 being former JTC employees.

Normally, a regulatory regime is developed to accommodate the privatisation of utilities; however, in this case both parties agreed to the new regulatory structure to follow privatisation, as the PUC, which previously regulated the JTC, had been put into abeyance in 1975. Deputy Prime Minister P.J. Patterson, also felt the PUC model of US quasi-judicial rate-of-return regulation of the 1970s would not have been appropriate for the newly privatised company.

The government, however, had given a commitment to pass the legislation immediately following the consummation of the merger.

A simple regulatory structure was put in place involving ministerial regulation, entitling both the JTC and JAMINTEL to 17.5 per cent and not more than 20 per cent in consolidated shareholders' equity at the end of each financial year. Such rate increase as TOJ might wish to make needed only the approval of the portfolio minister for telecommunications. Should the minister refuse to do so, the matter would go to arbitration, with a requirement for the minister, in consultation with TOJ, to appoint a current or former Jamaican Supreme Court judge as the arbitrator.

In effect, the licence granted to TOJ was extraordinary (albeit a government-controlled company at the beginning of the partnership), in that TOJ was granted risk-free monopoly position in the newly emerging telecommunications industry, with a required rate of return on investment. Normally, the regulatory regime has as its main objective the protection of consumers from the rent-seeking power of the utility. However, in this case, the primary objective was that of the need to entice C&W to make the investments in Jamaica, and hence guarantee the security of C&W's investment.[30]

Conditions of the Sale and the New Licence

The exclusive licence granted to TOJ covered the following key points.[31]

- A twenty-five-year licence renewable for a further twenty-five years, as the original licence, apart from the renewal provision, unless 2.5 years prior to the end of the licence, the minister of public utilities and transport notified TOJ that the government intended to acquire the telecommunications undertakings of either the JTC or JAMINTEL. In these circumstances, the government must revoke the telecommunications licence of the other firm and acquire all the assets as well. In the event of such a decision, it was stipulated that the acquisition must be at a fair market value, as determined by independent valuation.
- The licence could also be revoked if the portfolio minister determined that the licensee had failed to comply with its terms (including carrying out the prearranged capital development programme, estimated at J$1.9 billion) after a reasonable opportunity had been given to the licensee to remedy this failure.

- In the event of revocation, the licensee had a two-year period in which to sell its telephone undertaking. However, if it failed to do this, then within twelve months of the end of the two-year period, the government must buy the assets at a fair market price.
- Any such government acquisition had to occur under a prescribed regime, whereby it may elect to pay cash, or up to 95 per cent in promissory notes, denominated either in US dollars, or UK pounds, payable by half-yearly instalments of principal and interest, over a fifteen-year period, bearing interest rate at 2 per cent above London Interbank Offered Rate (LIBOR) for equivalent sized deposits.
- The company would also provide representation at the International Telephone Union.
- The company was required, under section 15 of the 1987 All Island Telephone Licence, to furnish and maintain an efficient and modern telephone integrated network.
- The government also agreed to modernise the laws relating to telecommunications by introducing a new Telecommunications Act, to replace the 1893 Telephones Act, which would then be revoked, and to update the Radio and Telegraph Act of 1958.

The JTC was granted a monopoly over domestic (both local and toll) telephone services, while JAMINTEL was granted a monopoly over all international calls. When TOJ wanted to introduce cellular services, it contended that the licence provided it with a monopoly over all telecommunications services, including cellular and, furthermore, that it had performed several investments in cellular development, a position supported by the minister of public utilities. Although the law then clearly specified 'wired communications' the licence on the other hand was silent about it. However, TOJ's interpretation was that it had a monopoly over all telecommunications services, at least those that were so commonly called.

The licence represented another major regulatory turning point in the regulation of the telecommunication industry, requiring the government to maintain the profitability levels of the company at their pre-merger levels. This was unique. While TOJ could not increase average real prices, as its profitability was close to the upper level of the permissible profit range, in principle, it was free to change the tariff structure. It, therefore, had an incentive to increase prices of the inelastic (domestic) services. The minister of public utilities and the company seemed to have struck a private deal to keep the sensitive domestic prices stable, so domestic prices did not change until 1984, focusing on increases in this period on the international service. In this way, the government avoided antagonising its middle-class political base. Had it encouraged competition in international service this would have been at the cost of the subsidies, as the international communication was the main financier of the subsidy in the 1980s. The cost of the cross-subsidy was that of maintaining the strong monopoly.

The 1988 licence created a simple mechanism for price adjustments and for dispute resolution. The government had a short time to answer to a request for a rate increase. If there was a disagreement, then the matter could be taken to arbitration and the arbitrator would have been required to set rates subject to the fixed rate of return, as specified in the licence. Unlike the PUC regime, there was no requirement for public hearings or consultation with the public. TOJ also had the right to appeal to the Supreme Court for any violation of the licence by the government, emphasising a regulatory regime based on contract, rather than on legislation.

Jamaican courts have had a long history of independence and protecting property rights, giving TOJ some reassurance in safeguarding the regulatory process. The licence also stipulated that the rate of return was to be based on the rate base, rather than the convention adopted in the US, that of shareholder's equity. If the rate of return turned out to be higher than C&W's opportunity cost of capital, then C&W had in incentive to increase its participation in TOJ, as well as for TOJ to finance its investment through retained earnings, rather than through long-term loans. TOJ also had a monopoly over the sale of domestic terminal equipment, a carryover from the previous licence.

In the implementation of the privatisation package, the government encountered several problems, and, in one particular instance, the company's trade unions contested the ownership of the assets, besides requesting that, on the date of the merger, each employee was entitled to a redundancy compensation package. With a simple transfer, there was an obligation to pay stamp duties and the two companies' debts would be subjected to renegotiation. This prevented the government from going through the merger as a simple transaction, requiring a Vesting Legislation to effect the transfer of assets, including the transfer of the workers and their labour obligations to the newly created company, TOJ. If the company had to pay stamp duties and redundancy for over two thousand workers, the cost to the parties would have been prohibitive.

The amount of shares issued at each tranche and on each date, along with the cost per share, and the receipts in Jamaican dollars and US dollar equivalent are shown in table 14.2 below. In the first tranche following the restructuring, C&W UK Limited acquired 9.411 per cent, with the government holding 82.711 per cent. In the second tranche, again reflecting the restructuring arrangements C&W London increased its stake to 20.002 per cent. In the third tranche on October 2, 1987, the government sold C&W London a further 20 per cent stake, giving C&WL 39.001 per cent.

Table 14.2: TOJ Privatisation of Share Capital (J$)

	Start	21 July 1987	2 October 1987	28 Sept 1988	13 June 1989	16 Nov. 1990
At the start, number of shares owned						
The government	798,718,828	696,381,990	512,902,030	368,402,030	193,265,300	Zero
C&W	90,799,952	193,136,800	376,616,760	376,616,760	569.753,490	763,018,790
Public	76,164,868	76,164,868	76,164,868	126,500,000	202,664,858	202,664,858
As a percentage						
The government	82.711	72.111	53.111	40.000	20.0	Zero
C&W	9.402	20.002	39.001	39.001	59.001	79.001
Public	7.880	7.988	7,988	20.99	20.099	20.99

Source: Pablo Spiller and Cezley Sampson, 'Regulating Telecommunications in Jamaica.'

Two per cent of the outstanding stock of 21.1 million was reserved for employees, while fifty-one thousand residential customers were granted priority for up to 1,750 shares each. There were major changes to the exchange rate over the period.[32]

Value of the Shares J$ million and US Dollars:

- 23/07/87 the government sells 102,336,848 shares at J$1 per share =J$102.3 million/US$18.56
- 02/10/87 the government sells 183,479 960 shares at J$1 per share =J$183.5 million/US$33.66
- 28/09/88 the government sells 126,500,000 shares at J$0.88 per share =J$108.5 million/US$19.69
- 13/07/89 the government sells 195,136,730 shares at J$1,20 per share=J$231.8 million/US$40.17
- 16/11/90 the government sells 193,265.300 shares at J$1.74 per share=J$336.18 million US$46.44

Total = J$962.2 million US$158.52

The employees purchasing through the ESOP scheme could freely resell only those shares that were priority shares. Discounted shares could be transferred within two years only to eligible employees, while free shares were not transferable during the first two years. Under the scheme, unsold employee shares were retained in a pool to be sold to eligible employees after close of the application list. Almost all shares reserved for the employees were taken up either at first or on the second round. The largest shareholder was Joseph M. Matalon, son of Mayer Matalon, with 0.5 per cent shareholding (TOJ 1991 Annual Report). After excluding dividend during the 2.5 years, the government received US$155 million.

On September 28, 1988, the government floated several shares on the Stock Exchange, and, with the success of the offer, the public holdings increased to 20.99 per cent. At this point, the Jamaican state and local private sector held 61 per cent, or majority. Edward Seaga, at this point, declared this was as far as he intended to divest the telecommunications industry to foreigners and this, he claimed with a 'golden share,' perpetually would have secured local majority control.

The local public offer of 1.26 million shares was also unusual regarding the underwriting arrangements. There was a consortium of fourteen financial intermediaries as underwriters; however, these were the same firms (institutional investors) from whom the government was expecting substantial demands. This was potentially an incentive-incompatible contract, in that it was in the collective interest of the underwriters to let the offer fail and then pick up what was good stock cheaply thereafter. To circumvent this outcome, the government insisted that, as a condition for underwriting the issue, each institution involved had to apply for half the shares which they were underwriting. These were called 'Provisional Placed Shares' so that, as a condition, minimum demand of 52.7 million was guaranteed from the underwriters of the issue. These applications for Provisional Placed Shares, which could not be withdrawn, had to be accompanied by a post-dated cheque for the full transaction.

In this way, the government camouflaged its concerns by presenting this regulation as a method of credit checking. The government thus made sure that the issue would not be manipulated by a powerful group of financial institutions. In the end, the public issue was mildly under-subscribed. A total of 11,114 applicants applied for 152,379,450 shares, triggering the share allocation rule which, while acting as usual in favour of the smaller applicants, did not have a steeply declining schedule. The effect was that there was a modest premium on the issue of J$0.02 per share, well below the normal premium on private share issues. Although the government sold the shares at a price well below what it received from C&W, the evidence suggests that, not only had it accurately priced the public issue but also that it had received a good deal on its earlier sales. A total of J$108,500,000 was received from the local TOJ Jamaica Stock Exchange transaction.[33] The offer on the stock market was the third time in as many years that the Jamaican government had engaged in public offering of stocks for the privatisation programme, the others being the National Commercial Banak and the Caribbean Cement Company.

The objective of the public offer was to secure widespread ownership, including allowing employees of the company to have preferential access to the shares. One of the most difficult issues was to determine the share price for the public offering. The NCB stock was oversubscribed 170 per cent, and the stocks traded at 67 per cent premium the day following the public offering. In comparison, the CCC stocks were under-subscribed by about 30 per cent and traded at a discount of 20 per cent the day following the offering. With TOJ, caution was the name of the game, and the stocks were offered at J$.0.88 per share, a discount of twelve cents below the par value of the shares.[34]

When the PNP took office in 1989, it faced a forced sale in divesting a further 20 per cent stake to C&WL, bringing C&WL's share stake to 59.001 per cent, or majority control. The two tranches of 20 per cent each were made to C&WL by a private treaty between the government and C&W (offering none of these shares to the Jamaican public). On the sale of the last tranche of 20 per cent, the government faced a situation where five days were left for the government to meet one of the IMF's critical conditionality tests: that of the net asset reserve. With five days to go, there was no foreseeable solution in which the shortfall in foreign currency could be raised. After contacts between Matalon and the financial secretary, Shirley Tyndall, arrangement was made for C&W London to post US$50 million in Bank of Jamaica's account by the Friday, understanding that, once the IMF test requirement was met, on the Monday morning the funds would be withdrawn immediately, and the government would later divest the last tranche of 20 per cent to C&W London.

The government, because of the IMF's conditionality, was forced to complete the remaining privatisation of the 40 per cent government holdings. This was inimical to its values, reneging on commitments given to the Jamaican public, including the Jamaican diaspora, that the shares would be offered transparently on the Jamaica Stock Exchange. With the last 20 per cent tranche, C&W already had gained majority control and was not enthusiastic about acquiring the tranche of 20 per cent. Enter Mayer Matalan again and, with his close personal ties with government and C&W London, he arranged the sale of the remaining 20 per cent to C&WL.[35]

The PNP, when in opposition, had been very critical in 1987 of the first sale of TOJ shares to the private sector, declaring that the policy would be reversed on the re-election of a PNP government.[36] Here again, we see that pragmatism more so than ideology dictated the course of events.

Neither administration understood nor came to terms with the complex issues surrounding the privatisation of telecommunications, nor the rapid technological developments that were taking place within the sector. The privatisation was largely treated as if the industry was in a non-competitive market, ignoring the opportunity for introducing any form of competition. In 1989, the whole privatisation of the telecommunications industry became very public, attracting considerable negative public and media commentaries. The controversy developed first with the public and later between the government and C&W, especially around the exclusivity clauses of the licences and agreement. In fact, a coalition of local forces (media, the public, and some public officials) developed, opposing the privatisation to C&WL. The government might well have extracted a higher price for the shares, seeing that it was transferring majority control to C&WL.

C&WL acquired 20 per cent of the equity in November 1990, taking its stake to 79.01 per cent, leaving the government with zero shares, and the public 21.99 per cent. Some fifteen thousand local investors from a resident population of 2.5 million applied for the shares during the public offering. The total value of the TOJ privatisation transaction was J$962.2 million and, converted to US dollar the value of the transaction amounted to US$158.52 million, one of the largest of the Jamaican privatisation transactions, hence the level of public interest.

A Different Path

With the re-bundling of international telecommunications services with domestic services, creating an administrative monopoly, Jamaica was taking a different path from the path taken by other Latin American and Caribbean countries. This was also unlike the US, where deregulation of telecommunications led to the breakup of the monopoly Bell companies, and the separation of international telecommunications under AT&T from domestic telephone services. The US policies provided for introducing competition in international business and introduction of competition in various aspects of services outside of voice telephony such as value addended and enhanced services. Similarly, Mexico, Venezuela, and Argentina, countries that restructured and privatised their telecommunications industry avoided creating a single administrative monopoly from combining local and international services under one operator.

In Mexico, Telemex was given an exclusive licence for international services for only seven years, and no exclusivity in domestic services, value-added services, yellow pages, and cellular service. Regarding Venezuela's CANTV, the company received a licence to operate switched telephone services for nine years, stipulating that public telephone, value-added services, and mobile cellular services were to be open immediately to competition. Argentina's ENTEL, upon privatisation, received exclusivity only to operate local basic services for five years following privatisation, and with a requirement that value added and international telephone services be opened immediately to competition. The UK, in 1984, also incorporated structural changes to the industry, in that telephony business was first separated from the post office. Prior to the privatisation, telecommunications in the UK was the monopoly, the responsibility of the post office; a state-owned monopoly. British Telecommunications (BT) became a public limited liability company in April 1984. As a part of the reforms, the UK government created a duopoly structure by allowing for one additional telecommunications company: Mercury Communications Limited, to compete with BT. In addition, the British government also awarded two mobile licences: Celnet, 60 per cent British Telecom owned, and Racal-Vodaphone.[37]

Mercury was created as a consortium, led interestingly by C&WL, the parent company of JOJ, which also had recently been privatised. Mercury obtained its licence in 1982. BT was privatised intact, with 51 per cent of its shares sold through the London Stock Exchange. BT became the first of the UK public utilities to be privatised by the Margaret Thatcher conservative government when 50.2 per cent of the company's equity were offered for sale in November 1984 at 130 pence per share, payable in three instalments. The offer was heavily oversubscribed, proving that a market existed for the shares of privatised state assets on the stock exchange.

The new UK industry regime provided for competition and public regulation and marked a radical departure from earlier experiences of operating the telecommunications industry. It was in 1980 that Sir Keith Joseph, the UK's secretary of state for industry, announced his government's policy to end the telecommunications monopoly by introducing competition and providing for some measure of liberalisation. The British Telecommunications Act was legislated in 1981. The government initially proposed the US-style rate-of- return regulation; however, Professor Alan Walters, the prime minister's economic advisor, argued against this, commenting that it would create poor incentives for innovation and for efficiency-enhancing behaviour. Further, he opined that the US approach was bureaucratic, with its quasi-judicial procedures and, instead, proposed an output-related profits levy. In his 1983 report, Beesley also considered the Walters scheme unsatisfactory and recommended instead a local tariff reduction scheme, which became popularly known as pre-cap, or RPI-X.[38] The formula required BT to set tariffs, such that the price index for a basket of its services increased by no more than the rate of general price inflation, minus 'X' per cent annually, with 'X' being a technological variable.

Controversy over the Telecommunications Industry Privatisation

Dr Carlton Davis, Jamaica's cabinet secretary, in an address at a workshop at Manchester University in June 2003, stated that the privatisation of Jamaica's telecommunications industry between 1987 and 1990 was, arguably, one of the most complex and, *ex post facto*, controversial efforts undertaken by Jamaica, following one hundred years in which the industry see-sawed between foreign capital, domestic private capital, and state ownership. Further this was an industry in which the international network was separately owned from the domestic network.[39]

Strong public criticisms developed from the early 1990s over the low price of the shares to C&WL, the closed nature of the offerings to that entity, especially during the last two sales transactions, and failing to provide for competition in the market, including access to connect to the transmission network by third parties. The entire TOJ privatisation over the period 1987–90 reflected a lack of planning, a lack of establishing clear objectives, a lack of transparency, and a failure to balance the long-term and wider interest of the society with that of the producers, and short-term gains.[40]

The 1893 Telephone Act also was not only silent, regarding customer equipment and international services, it never expected the new technologies of fibre optic transmission, cellular service, and digital data transmission. TOJ, however, had a first right of refusal to most domestic and international services and this gave the company a virtual monopoly over all telecommunications in Jamaica, excluding cable, radio, and television broadcasting. The Radio and Telegraphic Control Act precluded the company from owning and operating radio and television broadcasting services.

In honouring the commitment to provide a new Telecommunications Act, following privatisation in 1987, a new draft Telecommunications Bill and licence were presented by the Hon Robert Pickersgill, the portfolio minister, in 1991. Minister Pickersgill admitted he had invited the company's legal officer to prepare the draft legislation and licence.[41]

The draft presented provided for strengthening of the monopoly control, while the Attorney General expressed concern that the draft unduly favoured TOJ's interest. Pressures from other areas of Government eventually prevented this draft from being tabled in Parliament. The draft resurfaced again and was presented to Parliament in 1993 but was subsequently withdrawn after strong public protest and criticism by an active public and a vigilant media.

On June 15, 1992, *Insight Magazine*, a now defunct Jamaican newsletter, carried an article reporting that a major study carried out by Oxford University in 1992 on the privatisation of TOJ described it as being extraordinary and 'near reckless,' going further to state that it was a case of regulatory neglect. The magazine criticised the low priority the JLP government had given to the regulatory framework and commented, further, that developing countries like Jamaica were stampeding into privatisation under pressure from the IMF, without regard for market regulation and competition policies. In the opinion of the *Insight* article, the government had failed to break up the monopoly structure when this was possible and provide the necessary competition policy and law. It further maintained that there was a need for the government to balance private interest and public interest in privatisation. The article accused the government of treating the privatisation as a fire sale.

In the *Sunday Gleaner* of November 28, 1993, the editorial report drew attention to what it described as the 'blame game' between the JLP and the PNP who was responsible for the debacle. The article pointed out that it was the JLP that granted the extraordinary and reckless licence in 1988, under the 1893 Telephone Act, even though, at the time the licence was granted, C&WL was a minority shareholder in TOJ (20 per cent). It further emphasised the point that the government retained majority control of the company and also highlighted the point that, following further divestment of 13 per cent to Jamaican shareholders on the Stock Exchange there were to be no more divestiture and control would have remained in the hands of Jamaicans.

The article further pointed out that Mayer Matalon, the chairman of TOJ and advisor to the government, had also informed the prime minister that he had found a US buyer for a sale by private treaty for a further stake in the company. Seaga's reported response was that he had no intention of relinquishing the ownership of TOJ's shares to foreign control (letter from Seaga dated January 1988).

In the view of the article, the situation had changed in 1989, after a change of the government, and when Michael Manley, the new prime minister, sold the remaining shares to C&W, transferring majority ownership to a foreign private operator, he reversed a policy of not relinquishing majority control to foreign hands. Having transferred majority control to C&WL, the article reported Manley had also written a letter (the famous side letter) to Matalon, chairman of TOJ, giving a commitment to make such amendments to the 1893 Telephone Act as may be necessary to make sure that TOJ could enjoy exclusive telecommunications rights in, from, and through Jamaica, for twenty-five years, with an option for a further extension for twenty-four years. It was this letter, the article stated, that had allowed TOJ to claim there was an intention to widen the 1988 licence under the 1892 Act, to include services other than basic telephony. The article further claimed that Seaga's position was that, in a new legislation, there was no intention at the time to give TOJ rights beyond those already guaranteed in the 1988 licence.

It is important to note that the 1980s was a period of tremendous technological changes which destroyed a natural monopoly utility market structure. The industry was changing from simple voice telephony, and it is almost certain that neither Seaga nor Manley fully understood the impact that digital technology and fibre optics were having, blurring the lines between voice telephony, satellite broadcasting, computing, and mobile telephony. The fact of the matter is that, whether a state-owned utility or a private utility, this did not absolve the government from not introducing the right regulatory framework to ensure that the privatisation and regulatory structure balanced consumers' interest with private interest.

Dawn Ritch, a local *Gleaner* columnist, waged a crusade on the matter and, on October 31, 1993, in an article in which she reported that Mayer Matalan, chairman of TOJ, had stated that Deputy Prime Minister Patterson had made an announcement stating that the government was to replace the Public Utility Commission of 1966 with a new regulatory body. This, she commented, would amount to contravention of the 1988 Telephone Licence. Rich reported Matalon had stated that the privatisation agreement, as it stood, delegated the determination of rates to portfolio Minister Robert Pickersgill and, in the view of the TOJ, there was no role for another government agency.

Ritch further stated that she had met with Matalon and Pickersgill and that Matalon claimed that a new legislation was promised by Seaga. According to Matalon, she noted, the new legislation was expected to effectively create a monopoly, in fact entrusting the future development of the industry in the hands of TOJ, and that the new draft legislation which was being developed would provide for all likely future means of transmission to be controlled by TOJ. Ritch rightly pointed out in her article that TOJ had an exclusive licence for transmission, based on paired wire cable even it was stretched to include fibre optics. There was no way this could be treated legally to include a microwave, cellular mobile, and satellite technology, she commented. Rich further reported that she had spoken to Seaga, and the former prime minister's response was that he could not remember signing such a letter.

In fact, the reference to this letter being written by Seaga was an error, and it also referred to the famous 'side letter' Manley had written, addressed to Matalon. Rich reported she had also spoken to Manley, and he had promised to make the letter public, which he did. Rich further noted that, in her discussion with Manley, the former prime minister had stated that it was never his intention when he wrote this letter to extend the TOJ's rights beyond what was in the 1988 licence to include telecommunications in the fields, like data processing or other communications to operate business, nor to communicate in the fields like news and entertainment.

Alexander Rowe, in a *Jamaica Observer* article of December 22, 1993 reported that TOJ's lawyer, Trevor Patterson, had stated in an earlier *Sunday Gleaner* article that there was a letter to Minister David Coore from the company in which he (Trevor Patterson) had proposed that the licences be divided as follows: exclusive services, non-exclusive services, and exempt services, with exclusive services to include those normally provided by a national carrier: cellular radio, mobile radio telephone, associated cable systems and telex, facsimile, electronic mail, packet switching, and data transmission associated with cable systems. In effect, Rowe claimed here that Patterson was extending the exclusive services from switched telephony via paired wireline to mobile service, which the 1893 Telephone Law could not have expected. Cellular, radio telephony and mobile radio telephony were advanced technology-driven systems, and there was nothing basic about them. To have included voice and data transmission over cable system would have been to restrict development of cable TV.

When TOJ offered mobile services, it did not have the required permit under the existing licence. It was reported in the *Gleaner* that the minister of public utilities and mining, Robert Pickersgill, had given permission to TOJ to offer cellular service, pending TOJ's application for such a licence. This was reported in a November 1993 issue of the *Gleaner* to be the case, as stated by the public relations manager of TOJ. At a Public Accounts Committee, the permanent secretary in the Ministry of Public Utilities and Transport had also reported that TOJ was operating cellular service without a licence.

Eventually, an updated version of the draft Telecommunications Bill surfaced in 1994 as a public document from Minister Pickersgill's ministry. Only Dawn Rich's *Gleaner* report on November 14, 1993, stated that TOJ had a major hand in the legislative drafting of the bill. Ritch further reported in her November 14 article that she had in her possession a document from Minister Pickersgill whereby he had, in November 1993, requested Cabinet's approval of the new draft bill, facilitating the widening of TOJs exclusive licence, so that it would cover modern means of delivery of voice telephony service, and provision of all means of telecommunication services, which a modern telephone service supplier may provide. The bill further revealed that it had been the original understanding, when the current All Island Telephone Licence was negotiated, that as soon as the Telephone Act was modernised, TOJ's licence would be adjusted accordingly. Further, the widening of the licence had also been made a condition of the company's implementation of the current major capital development programme, which was intended to radically increase the availability of voice telephony service throughout Jamaica over the next ten years. Rich also reported that the minister claimed that this new Telecommunications Bill, when enacted, would repeal the 1893 Telephone Act. In addition, it would allow for the honouring of the original understanding given previously.

In the draft 1994 Telephone Telecommunications Bill, telecommunications was described as a system for the conveyance through the agency of electronic, magnetic, electromagnetic, electrical, or other appropriate energy, of messages as speech, music, and other sounds, or visual images, or signals serving for the impartation (between persons or things) of any matter, other than as sounds, or visual images, or signals for actuation, or control of machinery or apparatus. The claim by TOJ of services which a modern telephone service supplier may provide under exclusivity was certainly not borne out by the privatisation actions of the Latin American countries, the US, or the UK.

The question Ritch posed in her article was that, since Seaga had said he had given no such understanding to any TOJ official, and Manley claimed it was never his intention in the side letter to extend TOJ's licence beyond telephone services, to cover the wider fields of telecommunications, then on what basis was Pickersgill claiming that an understanding had been given?

In another article in the Insight magazine of November 16, 1993, Barry Brown stated that Matalon's apparent role in the affairs of TOJ raised doubts about the transparency of the privatisation of TOJ, with Matalon being chairmen of TOJ, when it was owned by Continental, and remained in that position when the company was divested to C&WL. Brown also pointed out that it should be recalled that Eric Bell had relinquished his ministerial responsibility for the JTC prior to this transaction because he disagreed with the terms of the acquisition which were being negotiated by Matalon and Pat Rousseau. Brown further reported that, under the JLP regime before and after the C&WL's share purchase, there was no change in the chairmanship of the JTC, or in the new entity of TOJ and that, with the change of government in 1989 Matalon continued unperturbed as chairman, even after some PNP insiders had felt he should have been replaced. Brown raised the question which side of the table Matalon represented in the negotiations during the tranche of 20 per cent in 1989, and in the tranche of 20 per cent in 1990. Brown wanted to know if he was representing C&W.

Max Lambie in a *Gleaner* article, as early as October 1991, stated that one advantage given to TOJ with the regulatory model was that, by a simple act of revaluing its assets, even aged and obsolete plants at current inflated values, this could have led to an increase in the company's income and that this was a very liberal provision, when compared with what was then allowed by the US Federal Utilities Commission. Lambie felt a formula which would have required revaluation at historical cost for high technology equipment would have been a more equitable formula, reflecting what the rate of exchange was. A valuation on current cost simply meant that, between 1991 and 1993, TOJ would have been able to increase asset valuation by over 40 per cent, triggering rate increase, possibly adding 35 per cent increase to its profits.

With these developments, in November 1993, the Gleaner followed up with an article reporting that Minister Pickersgill had assured the public that the country could rest assured that the exclusivity of any new TOJ licence would not extend beyond those services provided by a modern telephone service supplier. Further, the government was mindful of the licensees' interest and the public interest in the rapid development of telecommunications technology.

On this occasion, Minister Pickersgill specifically stated that the draft 1994 Bill would exclude from its purview television and broadcasting systems and certain radio services regulated under the Radio and Telegraph Act. In addition, the draft licence, which was in circulation, was prepared by TOJ and submitted to the ministry for consideration and did not represent the ministry's position on any new licence. His ministry, he said, had yet to make a recommendation to Cabinet on the matter.

This reflected the first instance in which the minister had backtracked on earlier statements which purported to give the impression that all forms of telecommunications, in, out and throughout Jamaica would be the exclusive purview of TOJ. In fact, portfolio responsibility for regulating radio and television services did not rest with the minister of public utilities, but with the minister of communications and the Broadcasting Commission, another agency which regulated content, as against economic regulation.

The *Gleaner* carried a TOJ supplement of two full pages on November 28, 1993, restating the arrangements which represented part of TOJ's formation, rebutting many of the criticisms which were being made against the company, and restating what it maintained had been promised by the government. The supplement also confirmed that the draft licence, which was in circulation had been prepared by TOJ, at the request of the government, and that the government had also requested the company to state the services which it considered were to be exclusive in the new licence. One of the major criticisms by the various commentators was that the government was providing C&WL with a risk-free monopoly position in the fast-changing telecommunications sector, with a guaranteed rate of return on its investment for fifty years.

Post-Privatisation Performance of the Telecommunications Sector

It has not been possible to disaggregate telecommunications from the wider communications industry. Communications had contributed 1.2 per cent in 1974 to total GDP, had risen considerably after 1974 and, in 2005, communications services contributed 7.1 per cent to total GDP. The contribution ratio increased at an annual average of 3.1 per cent over the entire period.[42]

There were some positive developments following the TOJ privatisation. The domestic rate in real terms (1996) was less than what it was in 1966. The company had digitised the entire network, making the Jamaican telecommunications system one of the most modern in Latin America and the Caribbean. In addition, a cellular service, albeit with obsolete technology, was introduced by TOJ in 1994. Privatisation resulted in improvements in terms of capacity expansion, access, profitability, and efficiency, when compared to the period under public ownership and management.

The major reasons for privatisation are that firms in private ownership and management are expected to be more efficiently managed and to display better financial and operating performances. Second, in Jamaica's case, privatisation was expected to reduce the need for public financing of the sector, although this was not the case in the airline and sugar privatisation, where the state was still burdened with financing of the sectors after privatisation.

L. Taylor evaluated the pre-privatisation (1981–85) and post-privatisation (1992–96) periods and reported that, over the first five years, the number of lines rose from 119,224 to 144,160.[43] In comparison, over the post-privatisation five-year period, the number of lines increased from 241,876 to 488,538. Both net profits per line and return on assets were higher in the post-privatisation period, compared with the pre-privatisation period. Table 14.3 below shows the pre- and post-privatisation performances as it related to capacity.

Cellular service did not exist before 1990 and TOJ was just one player. In fixed lines (stations and extensions) the number went from 119,224 in 1981 to 144,160 in 1985, with annual growth rates between 3.2 per cent and 5.4 per cent. In the period 1992–96, fixed lines grew from 241,860 to 488,586, with annual growth rates between 17.8 and 21.1 per cent. All-industry fixed lines numbered 506,544 in 2002.[44]

Table 14.3: Capacity Post- and Pre-Divestment

	Pre-Divestment (JTC and JAMINTEL – 1981–85)					Post-Divestment TOJ – 1992–96				
	1981	1982	1983	1984	1985	1992	1993	1994	1995	1996
No. of tel stations in service	119,224	132,517	136,776	136,778	144,160	241,876	292,956	342,255	411,777	488,586
Increase		6,503	6,790	4,261	7,382	49,776	51,080	52,269	66,552	76,761
Growth %		5.5	5.4	3.2	5.4	25.9	21.1	17.8	19.3	18.6

Table 14.4 below, at current dollar values, shows progressive improvements in nominal revenues, from J$143.6 million to J$385.7 million in the pre-divestment period, an increase of 168.6 per cent over the five years. When adjusted for inflation, the annual growth rate for revenues increased in the pre-divestment period from 13.4 per cent in 1982 to 49.1 per cent in 1987. In the post-divestment period, nominal revenues showed an increase from J$708.9 in 1992 to J$ 1,041.4 in 1996. The growth rate (adjusting for inflation) for the period from 1981 to 1985 varied widely between 2.8 per cent and 20.9 per cent; similarly, in the period 1992–96, the annual growth rate varied between -3.9 per cent and 27.4 per cent.

Table 14.4: Total Revenues Post- and Pre-Divestment

	Pre-Divestment (JTC and JAMINTEL – 1981–85)					Post-Divestment TOJ – 1992–96				
	1981	1982	1983	1984	1985	1992	1993	1994	1995	1996
Revenues current prices	136.6	152.7	183.2	258.6	385.7	2521.5	3890.3	5549.4	7754.9	9750.8
Growth rate %		13.4	20.0	41.2	49.1	106.1	54.3	42.6	39.7	25.7
Revenues constant prices	321.5	343.1	352.8	379.6	458.9	708.9	903.3	939.9	1083.4	1041.4
Growth rate %		6.7	2.8	7.6	20.9	0.2	27.4	4.1	15.3	-3.9

During the pre-divestment period, the Jamaican dollar exchange rate declined from US$1 to J$1.78 in 1981 to J$5.8 in 1985. However, in the post-divestment period the exchange rate deterioration was more marked, declining from J$12.22 to US$1 at the end of 1991 to J$37.26 to US$1 at the end of 1996. Much of the growth, at current prices was due to inflation. The increases in revenues in the pre-divestment period was 42.7 per cent compared to 46.9 per cent in the post-divestment period. Despite the inflationary pressures, there was a marginal increase in revenues in the post-divestment period.

Table 14.5 below provides a picture of the level of capital invested in the business over the pre- and post-divestment periods. In nominal terms, capital expenditure in the pre-divestment period (the period of state ownership) increased from JS$31.6 million in 1981 to J$127.5 million in 1985, a fourfold increase. In the period 1992–96, capital expenditure at current prices increased from J$1.44 billion to in 1992 to J$5.18 billion in 1996, a tremendous increase. When adjusted for inflation, the annual growth rate showed a movement from 0.5 per cent in 1982, to 22.9 per cent in 1983, then to 57.2 per cent in 1984, and then a decline of -4.7 per cent in 1985. In the post-divestment period, the growth rates were -29.3 per cent in 1992, increasing to 26.3 per cent in 1993, falling to -4.1 per cent in 1994, then rising to 20.7 per cent in 1985, and declining to -6.6 per cent in 1996. There was considerable volatility in the levels of investment over the period. There was however an overall increase in capital expenditure, despite the level of inflation.

Table 14.5: Capital Expenditure J$ million Post- and Pre-Divestment

Pre-Divestment (JTC and JAMINTEL) – 1981–85						Post- Divestment TOJ – 1992–96				
	1981	1982	1983	1984	1985	1992	1993	1994	1995	1996
Capital Expend Current prices	31.6	36.7	52.6	108.5	127.5	1443	2207	2900	4245	5185
Growth Rate per cent		16.1	43.3	106.3	17.5	45.5	52.9	31.4	46.4	22.1
Cap Exp constant prices	82.1	82.5	101.3	159.2	151.7	404.7	512.4	491.2	593.0	553.8
Growth Rate		0.5	22.9	57.2	-4.7	-29.3	26.3	-4.1	20.7	-6.6

Table 14.6 below further shows the profitability picture. The data show operating profit, net profit, net profit margin, earning per share (EPS), and return on asset for the two periods. Inflation adjusted showed operating profits increasing from J$129.4 in 1981 to J$174.9 million in 1985. In the post-divestment period, operating profits (inflation adjusted) increased from J$275.6 million in 1992 to J$485.2 million in 1995.

Table 14.6: Profitability Post- and Pre-Divestment

Pre-Divestment (JTC and JAMINTEL – 1981–85)						Post-Divestment TOJ – 1992–96				
	1981	1982	1983	1984	1985	1992	1993	1994	1995	1996
Nominal Operating Profits J$ m	49.8	55.8	70.1	98.8	147.0	980.4	17,771.0	22,76.0	34,73.0	
inflation adjusted J$ m	129.4	125.4	135.0	145.0	174.9	275.6	411.2	385.5	485.2	
Net profit million J$	19.1	30.9	34.4	56.5	53.5	420.4	993.9	1,149.1	1,692.0	1,890.0
Increase %		61.8	11.3	64.2	-5.3	45.8	136.4	15.6	47.2	11.7
Inflation adjusted %	49.6	69.4	66.3	82.3	63.7	118.2	230.8	194.6	236.4	201.9
Net profit margin %	14.2	20.2	18.8	21.8	13.9	16.7	25.5	20.7	21.8	19.4
Earnings per share cents	31.83	51.50	57.33	94.7	89.1	43.5	51.46	59.50	87.60	97.86
Return on assets %	4.9	7.3	5.2	5.9	4.1	4.0	8.3	6.6	7.7	6.3
CPI Index base 1988		38.5	51.5	68.1	84.4	355.7	430.7	590.4	715.8	936.3

Earnings Per Share (EPS) for 1984–96 restated for comparative (there was a one-for-one bonus issue in 1993/94)

All tables reflect adjustments for inflation, using CPI as shown in table 14.6

Source: Lenworth Taylor, 'Privatisation in Jamaica and the Case of Telecommunications of Jamaica Limited.'

The net profit margin remained relatively stable but was higher in the post-divestment period when compared with the pre-divestment period. Similarly, earnings per share and return on assets were higher in the latter period. The average earnings per share (EPS) for pre-divestment was 64.8 cents, while the average EPS for post-divestment was 68 cents. Being a capital-intensive industry, return on assets would be expected to compare to other capital-intensive industries being small and ranging between 4.0 per cent and 8.3 per cent over the two periods.

The data show operating profit, net profit, net profit margin, earning per share (share (EPS), and return on assets for the two periods. Inflation adjusted showed operating profits increasing from J$129.4 in 1981 to J$174.9 million in 1985. In the post-divestment period, operating profits (inflation adjusted) increased from J$275.6 million in 1992 to J$485.2 million in 1995. The net profit margin remained relatively stable but was higher in the post-divestment period, when compared with the pre-divestment period. Similarly, earnings per share and return on assets were higher in the latter period. The average earning per share (EPS) for pre-divestment was 64.8 cents, while the average EPS for post-divestment was 68 cents. Being a capital-intensive industry, return on assets would be expected to compare to other capital-intensive industries being small and ranging between 4.0 per cent and 8.3 per cent over the two periods.

Profitability of the companies was high following privatisation, but well within the prescribed range. It was not possible to determine how much of the progress was because of privatisation per se and, while there may be other contributory factors perhaps privatisation, despite the negatives as it related to the simple regulatory mechanism adopted, did help in the long run, especially in easing the public debt burden and in the accessibility of additional lines. For thorough comparison, counter-factual analysis would be needed.

In the period 1995/96 the fourteen Selected PEs (reduced from twenty-one to fourteen) capital expenditure was J$10.0 billion, whereas TOJ's capital expenditure was J$5.18 billion, representing 50 per cent of the total selected PEs capital expenditure. In contrast, JAMINTEL and JTC's capital expenditure in 1985 was J$128 million, or 12.6 per cent of the Selected PEs capital expenditure. In the period TOJ introduced toll-free and pay 800 service, voyageur internet services, in touch voice mail, and world talk prepaid calling cards, which could be used for local and international calls.

The conclusion is that, regarding overall post-privatisation, the period under private ownership and management resulted in marked improvements. The CWL also became more involved in the management of the company following privatisation by seconding management from the parent company in the UK. If the company had remained under public ownership, the level of investments would most likely not have materialised, owing to the IMF restrictions. In fact, the government's Treasury benefited from the sale proceeds, reducing the government's borrowing levels.

In the period following the public issue, TOJ's share price remained stable, with trading fluctuating between J$0.70 and J$0.95. This would seem to show that the TOJ sale missed out on the period when the JSE experienced rapid expansion in share prices: the first half of 1989. Following the public offer, TOJ share price lagged well behind the JSE Index. In 1998, the company was rebranded Cable and Wireless Jamaica Limited (C&WJ).

The government's overriding objective in privatising TOJ was to establish the conditions whereby the JTC could receive a major infusion of new capital. However, its over-concern with this objective led the company to ignore other important aspects of privatisation, for example, the need to provide an environment for efficiency-enhancing behaviour of the privatised TOJ. The government not only failed to consider pro-competition policies for the industry at privatisation in the second half of the 1980s, as was being considered by other governments in the 1980s, but it locked itself in a long-lasting arrangement by the granting of the fifty-year exclusive monopoly licence arrangement. While the simple regulatory regime which was established minimised the cost of regulation, on the negative side there was the inefficiencies of rate of return regulation which was adopted, resulting in TOJ not having sufficient incentives for efficiency improvements. It was the inadequacy of the rate of return regulation which led the UK to disregard adopting a rate of return regulation at privatisation.

The Winds of Change and Attempts to Introduce Competition Post-1995

Deputy Prime Minister Patterson and Attorney General Carl Rattray were opposed to the extension of TOJ's monopoly beyond what was legally already provided for in the licence. From as early as 1990, Minister Patterson had also expressed strong reservations against reintroducing the American-style rate of return, quasi-judicial utility regulatory structure. As minister of finance, planning and development, through the Economic and Production Council (a subcommittee of Cabinet), he established a committee and gave it authority to examine the institutional options in competition and utility regulation, and the policies which would be needed to bring about a more liberal framework. More specifically, the Committee was required to develop and present policies in the following covering: competition or antitrust, consumer protection, regulation of utilities and regulatory reform of the financial sector.

British Treasury economist Anthony Meyrick and I we were engaged over the period February 1991, to study and report on matters relating to utilities regulation. Separately, the governor of the Bank of Jamaica, as chairman of the Committee on the Financial Sector, had submitted to the Production Council, a report on the financial sector and banking reform and regulation, and had drafted legislation amending the Bank of Jamaica Act. With competition policies, with the support of two USAID-contracted consultants and myself, two reports and a Parliamentary Paper on competition policies were produced and submitted to the Production Council. The Council had authorised the drafting of the Fair Competition legislation.[45]

The Meyrick and Sampson Report examined the four utilities: electricity and power, water, postal services, and telecommunications and regarding telecommunications concluded that, despite the 1987 licence restrictions, vast improvements could be made to regulating the industry. The areas specially identified were regulation of quality and standards of services, scrutiny of efficiency of the industry operators through periodic management audits and provision for incentive regulation.

The report noted that there was an opportunity for competition in areas of telecommunications activities, which no longer carried natural monopoly elements. It also noted that, in terms of regulatory institution and control, the government should establish an Office of Utility Regulation, managed by a director general, and supervised by a small board appointed by the prime minister.

In terms of responsibilities, the report specified the following functions:

- Gathering information about customer requirements and long-term cost levels;

- Coordinating other aspects of regulation with other relevant agencies regarding areas of health and environmental standards;
- Adjudicating on consumer disputes;
- Investigating the scope for competition in utility industries;
- Advising the government on broad policies relating to utility regulation which should be pursued;
- Commissioning periodic efficiency audits;
- Regulating prices and setting service standards and service targets.

Regarding pricing formula, the report strongly recommended incentive regulation, using the formula RPI-X, modified to Jamaica's needs, and advised strongly against the US-style cost plus regulation, embodying rate of return formula; Patterson's Submission to the Economic and Production Council, dated December 5, 1991.[46]

In putting the report together, consultation was sought with affected parties. With the post office, the postmaster general supported the conversion of the post office from a ministry department to a public corporation. With the Ministry of Public Utilities, the ministry supported the general direction of the report; however, with the Ministry of Energy and Mining, the ministry was in favour of the pricing formula of RPI-X and a licensing arrangement providing for regulatory contract. JPSCo supported the establishment of an independent OUR, subject to its decision being appealed to the courts, as well as the principle of RPI-X.

The report specifically stated that, regarding the telephone licence and, despite what was exclusive, the government should arrive at an agreement with TOJ as to the areas which should be subject to competition after a decent interval for any such exclusivity based on mutual interest. The recommendation was made in view of the rapid technological changes taking place in the industry and that there was room for the parties to agree on introducing competition in cellular telephony, data transmission, and personal radio and new and other fringe technologies. The recommendations were approved by the Production Council.

Presaging Introduction of Competition in the Industry

A number of external forces were also at work in the industry, bringing about further radical changes in how the industry was to operate. In the 1990, the GATT, which largely dealt with tariff agreements, turned its attention to service trade, including telecommunication services. With the WTO in 1995 free trade principle of GATT applied to Trade in Services (GATS) resulting in a multinational trading platform embracing transborder data flows in much the same way as GATT embraced international trade in goods.

By 1990, international trade in services was estimated to have grown to 17 per cent of global trade, driven by liberalisation and deregulation. In fact, service trade had been expanding faster than trade in goods.[47] Telecommunications service was part of this rapidly expanding trade in services. By 1990, over 50 per cent of FDI were related to investments in the services industries and FDI in telecommunications service was expanding at one of the fastest rates.

Jamaica and Dominica, Grenada, Trinidad and Tobago and Antigua and Barbuda signed the GATS in 1998.[48] The current liberalisation of Telecommunications entered the shores of Jamaica and the Caribbean in the early 1990s. The high international call charges also came to be seen as a barrier to the expansion of export services. Competitive international telephone charges came to be seen as critical to the expansion of Jamaica's tourist and financial services, data entry and call centre business, and the IT industry.

Efforts to introduce competition were first initiated by the Fair-Trading Commission (FTC). The FTC challenged TOJ's monopoly in areas not explicitly covered by legislation and by the licences. In 1993, the FTC secured a voluntary agreement with C&WJ to liberalise the consumer equipment market. Following from an action in 1994 by the FTC and from Infochannel, an internet service provider (ISP), C&WJ, and the FTC agreed on several areas and these were set out in a charter on competition. The opening of the market in internet at the time was significant, not only because of the growth of data traffic but also because of the emergence of 'voice over the internet protocol' technology which facilitated the provision of call back services, through which the telephone users could bypass C&W's international gateway and connect to the domestic system.[49]

The government then went about developing a WTO Telecommunications Liberalisation Framework Agreement and this followed from a seminar I attended in the US in 1995, organised by INFRADEV. Following on this visit, technical support was obtained from INFRADEV in the drafting of a telecommunications liberalisation framework, taking into consideration WTO and GATS requirements for liberalisation of telecommunications. The INFRADEV-supported telecommunications liberalisation framework was also adopted by the Economic and Production Council.

Arising from the adoption of the INFRADEV Telecommunications Framework Document Minister Pickersgill invited the CEO of Cable and Wireless Jamaica Limited[50] and me to an informal meeting at his home and informed us we needed to resolve the impasse between TOJ and the government. After four hours of discussion, we agreed that C&WJ would be allowed to continue its monopoly for another ten years. After this, the market would be open to competition and liberalised, according to WTO/GAT mandate.

Prime Minister Patterson, in the meantime, had established a small committee comprising Minister Pickersgill, Attorney General David Coore, and myself, chaired by the cabinet secretary, which was mandated to develop a Telecommunications Policy document. I was charged with putting the initial document together, incorporating the INFRADEV telecommunications framework principles.

Key provisions of the Telecommunications Policy Framework document[51] are set out below:

- That the incumbent telephone company could maintain its exclusive franchise arrangements for basic telephony in keeping with the existing agreements.
- Enhanced services: Voice Activation Detection (VADS) and Value-Added Network (VANS) were to be the subject of competition. The incumbent telephone company, under supervision of the new utility regulator, would be required to allow interconnection for enhanced services at access charges and would accommodate universal services obligation.
- There was to be a new utility regulator, the Office of Utilities Regulation and, within this office, there was to be a deputy director general with responsibility for telecommunications regulation, with clear levels of accountability to Parliament.
- Universal services for basic telephony were to form a strategic aspect of the telecommunications policy.
- The government was to use its best endeavours to foster the development and use of telecommunications technology at

a higher level of service appropriate to meet social objectives for certain public fields such as education, health and national security.

The basic principles outlined in the Telecommunication Policy Framework document provided for access to the incumbent's network on terms and conditions which were non-discriminatory, phased liberalisation of mobile and VADS, arbitration of interconnection disputes, the establishment of an independent regulator and an appropriate structure for the allocation and management of the radio spectrum.

Franklin Anthony Brown commented that, for the first time in 1996, the government adopted a telecommunications policy, not only committing itself to introducing competition but also to liberalising the telecommunications industry, since exclusivity was the linchpin of the privatisation arrangement.[52] In that same year, 1996, the National Industrial Policy: A Framework for Development[53] was adopted by the government. The policy emphasised the importance of telecommunications to the country's economic development and, in particular, the importance of data processing and call centre operations as primary candidates for export growth and employment creation.

These developments signalled for the first time TOJ, C&W and the government's commitment to having in place a policy for a liberalised telecommunications industry. In 1997, Jamaica also collaborated with its CARICOM partners to agree on a common negotiating strategy with C&WL subsidiaries in the region. C&WL monopoly came from the US carriers which had been paying out some US$5.7 billion per year to overseas operators under the existing accounting settlement rate protocol, also came under opposition in 1997.[54] Telecommunication foreign earnings had grown to be third largest foreign exchange earner.[55] The FCC regarding Jamaica, a middle-income country, drastically reduced the settlement rates, from US$0.57 to US$0.19 per minute by January 2001.[56]

TOJ and C&WL challenged the FCC Order in the US and eventually lost at the US Court of Appeal.[57] The FCC order threatened to undermine the financial basis of the post-privatisation regime which had involved the incumbent cross-subsidising and expanding the unprofitable domestic services from the international services.[58] C&W also started legal action against the government, arguing that a private monopoly company was in the best public interest.

Prime Minister Patterson took the view that, if the changes needed were to be given the merited importance, a new leader at MPUT was needed to replace the incumbent minister of public utilities. The prime minister in 1998 chose Philip Paulwell, former executive director of the Fair-Trading Commission (FTC), a competition-oriented lawyer, as the new minister with responsibility for telecommunications. Paulwell also provided a more pro-competitive leadership and was not only well-informed on legal and technical development matters in telecommunications, but was determined to liberalise the industry, backed by the solid support of Prime Minister Patterson.[59] The newly appointed minister immediately took a more pro-competitive stance towards TOJ.

By the early 1990s, it was possible to facilitate competition in the telecommunications sector under three arrangements: facilities-based entry, resale entry, and mixed entry. This latter approach is sometimes described as entry through unbundled network services. Facilities-based competition creates conditions for effective competition, reduces the demand for regulatory intervention and pressures the incumbent to upgrade services. Resale, however, offers the easiest and quickest way to introduce effective competition. It provides for low-cost entry and efficient use of scarce resources in existing infrastructure. In addition, it creates opportunities for small investors to service niche markets without having to provide outlay for heavy capital investments in infrastructure.

In 1998, Minister Paulwell, by this time head of the Ministry of Commerce Science and Technology with responsibility for telecommunications, issued an updated version of the 1996 Telecommunications Policy and Regulatory document. In the updated 1998 Telecommunications Policy document, the Ministry declared the government's commitment to liberalising mobile services (including wireless in the loop), and other value-added services, and to introducing institutional reforms in the sector. In principle, the ministry's policies built on the commitments given earlier in the WTO Telecommunications Policy Framework and the 1996 Telecommunications Policy Framework document.[60]

Areas which Minister Paulwell specifically earmarked for liberalisation were mobile services (including wireless in the loop), and other VADS, to be accompanied by institutional reforms in the sector. He followed this up in 1998 by granting five Very Small Aperture

Technology (VSAT) licences to ISP operator under the Radio and Telegraph Control Act. Some of the ISP operators had been offering call-back telephone services, bypassing C&W's international gateway. The company found that the international call-back system was frustrating its administrative monopoly rights.

Up to then, TOJ had resisted all attempts by the government to issue competitive mobile licences. C&WJ at first attempted to prevent the use of call-back by disconnecting providers of call-back service and later contested the minister's decision to issue the five licences because the decision breached the exclusivity conditions in the licence. C&WJ initiated proceedings against the operators which were offering VIOP services, and proceedings seeking to annul the minister's decision on the award of the licences. These actions, however, were unsuccessful; as a result, C&WJ abandoned its action at the Supreme Court.[61] The company also claimed its monopoly was in the public interest.

By 1998, C&WL, more so than its local subsidiary, realised that technology, international trade liberalisation protocols and international regulatory developments had come to significantly reduce the opportunity to benefit from the monopoly on domestic voice telephony. C&WL executives in London concluded that the larger international data transmission market offered more profitable opportunities than the traditional voice telephony business. With changes in the very top levels of management in both London and Jamaica, and with decision-making on policy matters increasingly being centralised in London, the local company offered less resistance to the government's efforts to introduce a more competitive telecommunications market. C&W had been lobbying for regulatory barriers to be reduced in the US market where C&WL had less than 1 per cent of market share; hence, the small Jamaican and Caribbean markets became expendable.

G. Myers made an assessment and concluded that relinquishing the monopoly provided C&WL with the opportunity to reduce the company's obligation in unprofitable services.[62]

September 1998 also marked another critical juncture in the reform process.[63] C&WJ finally came to an agreement with the government to phase out the company's exclusivity, as set out in the 1987 licence and agreement. This made Jamaica the first English-speaking Caribbean country, and one of the first developing countries in the world, to embark on a process of full liberalisation of the telecommunications market.

The agreement between C&WJ and the government brought an end to the various court cases and legal disputes over interpreting the 1987 licence. In addition, it provided a timeline for the promulgation of the new Telecommunications Act, which was promised way back in 1988, the full liberalisation of the industry and introducing a new licencing regime. In this agreement, C&WJ undertook, in 1999, to surrender its five licences granted under the 1987 agreement and its rights of exclusivity for all forms of telecommunications to, from and through Jamaica, in consideration for the government adopting new legislation reflecting an understanding reached in a draft instrument, previously approved by TOJ. The government agreed to surrender its sovereign rights to set new policies for the telecommunications sector over a transitional period. Both parties agreed to the withdrawal of all litigations and claims relating to the twenty-five-year exclusivity dispute.

The agreement was to be implemented in three phases, starting in 1999, as follows:

- Under phase one, private operators were invited to bid for two mobile phone licences, one to utilise GSM technology and the other to use CDMA technology. The licences were auctioned, and the minister eventually issued the two licences. During the first phase, the minister was also empowered to issue cellular, reseller (data, internet, and international voice), and free trade zone service and carrier licences. Two mobile operators, Digicel Limited and MiPhone Limited obtained licences and began operation in competition with C&WJ. The Spectrum Carrier and Service Provider licences were auctioned to the two new mobile carriers: Mossel (trading as Digicel) and Cellular One (Caribbean), a subsidiary of AT&T of the US. The respective auctions for the spectrum rights netted US$47.5 million for the government.
- During phase 2, the minister's powers were extended to grant licences to include domestic carrier and service provider licences for voice facilities, resale of the incumbent switched domestic voice facilities, as well as voice-over-the-internet access, and facilities for subscriber television operator internet licences for licensed cable operators. Several of these licences

were issued. Subsequently, a licence for fixed switched voice service was awarded to a competitor to C&WJ. This new company, Flow International, provided converged services, involving high-speed digital internet, cable television, and land line voice telephony.

- In the final phase, three years after passaging the Telecommunications Act, all market segments were to be liberalised, including the market for international facilities-based operators. Because of this development, in 2004, the government awarded licences to two international cable operators to lay new submarine cable networks to Jamaica. One of the successful applicants, Columbus Communication, operating under the FLOW brand, also entered the market offering converged services, involving high-speed digital internet, cable television, and land line voice telephony, and became a significant competitor to C&WJ.
- The statutory provisions underpinning liberalisation were eventually incorporated in the 2000 Telecommunications Act.

In analysing the 1999 agreement, the following points are of significance. The 2000 Telecommunications Act reserved the power to the sector minister to issue general instructions to the OUR. This clause existed in the Financial Services Commission Act but was never invoked to limit regulatory independence. The reading of the Privy Council judgement later in the matter was that the minister's attempt to instruct the OUR what could be done in the mobile market was specific and not general direction and ran contrary to the authority afforded by the regulator in the statute.

- This power given to the minister to issue licences without a recommendation from the OUR provided an opportunity for political intervention into regulatory affairs and created tensions between the portfolio ministry and the regulator, eventually resulting in a court action by Digicel against the OUR and the OUR against the minister.[64]
- The minister reserved the power to determine the types of, and number of licences, rather than the regulator. This reduced regulatory independence and provided an opportunity for political intervention.

- The agreement provided for the triggering of several compensation claims. If the laws passed by the sovereign Parliament were inconsistent with the Policy Drafting Instrument (PDI), or if the courts or the regulator handed down decisions inconsistent with the PDI, then it would have been possible to trigger compensation claims. Theoretically, the government of Jamaica constitutionally has no control over Parliament but, notwithstanding, for a short period agreed to bind a future administration and the regulator to the agreement set out in the PDI.

The Telecommunications Act came into being in 2000 and, with its enactment, the OUR as an independent regulator took over responsibility for telecommunications regulation. As provided in the agreement, C&W was issued a new licence under the 2000 Telecommunications Act, shoring up, for a limited period, C&WJ's right to exclusivity. In *R vs OUR*, [65] the Supreme Court upheld the OUR's decision to allow the disconnection by C&W of the applicant company, which was engaging in bypass operation in contravention of Section 51 of the Telecommunications Act.

However, in 2003 a Jamaican Court of Appeal decision quashed those provisions of the Act which provided for phased transition to liberalisation on the grounds of constitutional protection of free speech, after a challenge by Infochannel, a communications provider which, prior to the Telecommunications Act, had voice over internet communications services.[66] By 2004, Jamaica had two land line carriers, besides three cellular carriers and over twenty internet services providers. C&WJ ceased to be the dominant cellular player, with the Jamaican market moving away from the duopoly for voice telephony to a more competitive one.

In the liberalisation agreement, the government provided for catering to universal services. The concept of universal service referred originally to a telephone being in every home in one country and was based on the notion of telephone being an essential service which should not be denied to any citizen, merely because of cost.

Universal service and universal access have undergone major changes in definition in Jamaica, and no longer focus on voice telephony (lines at home and public pay phones) and instead focus on internet access, reflecting the growing importance placed on information technology and the role it plays in development, not just in the economic sense, but also in social areas, such as health care, education, and in the provision of legal and other social services. It is for this reason that the government established the Universal Service Fund, financed by a levy on the industry players, to be used by C&WJ as part of the reform agreement, requiring the installation of internet terminals at main post offices, selected schools across Jamaica, and at public parish libraries.

The cost of internet service was a major factor militating against expansion. The uptake expanded from fifty-two thousand in 2005 to ninety-four thousand in 2005. The cost of dial-up service for twenty hours per month was about US$0.40 in Jamaica in 2005. Internet charges were very high in Jamaica compared with developed countries; however, with the expansion of broadband and the recent introduction of Flow International as a competitive carrier to C&WJ costs have trended down.

The main challenge facing the Jamaican telecommunications sector post-liberalisation is that of fixed and mobile and mobile-to-mobile interconnection. Interconnection refers to the physical and logical linking of public electronic networks to communicate to users of the same, or another undertaking. Non-discriminatory access is basic and a prerequisite for effective competition. Contribution of terminal revenues to overall revenues is higher for mobile operators than for fixed line operators and often influences decisions to invest. Mobile operators will protect high mobile termination charges. Under the 2000 Telecommunications Act, the OUR has handed down several decisions to reduce both mobile and fixed termination charges, the most recent of which was issued in 2022.

Enforcement of operator's obligation requires effective and speedy dispute resolution mechanisms. Multiple actors and overlapping responsibilities, as found in Jamaica, serve only to complicate this problem. Part of the problem is that the regulatory process cycle lagged market development in the early stages of the liberalisation exercise.

The first major initiative in arriving at a common policy agenda with C&WL and its sub-subsidiaries on liberalisation of the respective national telecommunications markets resulted from a meeting of CARICOM Ministers of Telecommunications at the end of the 1997. This was followed up in 2003 by a Heads of Government conference directing the CARICOM Secretariat to develop a CARICOM Connectivity

Agenda, providing a framework for individual members to assess, plan, and execute national strategies.

Regulatory Commitment

In the original 1993 World Bank Country Study on telecommunications by Pablo Spiller and Cezley Sampson, the authors developed the argument that there were three requirements for effective regulation (regulatory commitment), written restraints on discretionary action; restraint hindering reversal, or amendment of the overall regulatory regime, and institutions safeguarding these restraints. From this research the authors developed the theory of regulatory endowment, stating that it is a country's regulatory endowment which determines the quality and effectiveness of regulation.[68] The study was funded by the Policy Research Department of the World Bank and was initiated by the author through an approach to the World Bank. For comparison, four other country studies were undertaken and published, edited by Brian Levy and Pablo Spiller.[69]

Both the Jamaican and the UK privatisation relied heavily on licences: contract regulation as against simply primary legislation, with the objective of constraining regulatory description. A regulatory structure based on contract theoretically provides more safeguards to the investor than one simply based on legislation. It will not be seen by foreign investors to curb administrative discretion and political opportunism, since the party in power can unilaterally change the law. Regulation based purely on legislation suffers inherent weakness in safeguarding requirements. It is unstable, thus alternative institutions are needed to provide the stability required for credible regulation that honours regulatory commitment.

The OUR, which was eventually established in 1997 as a multisector regulator two years after the passing of the Act, carried the responsibility to regulate telecommunications, electricity, water, and transport.[70] In the period 1987–97, the minister of public utilities exercised responsibility for regulating the privatised JTC as well as the electricity utility. Ministerial responsibly for telecommunications and electricity regulation did not change with introducing the OUR Act in 1995, and the establishment of the OUR in 1997. During the period 1997–2000, the OUR was relegated to an advisory role in the Ministry of Public Utilities, as TOJ resisted all attempts by the OUR to play a more proactive role.

TOJ refused to provide the OUR with information unless the request was expressly authorised by the minister. In fact, it had taken the government thirteen years, from 1987 to 2000, to replace the 1892 Telephone Act, as promised in the privatisation agreement. Regulatory decision-making was in the hands of the sector minister from 1976, with the suspension of the PUC. Unlike the UK, the utilities were not privatised with passaging up-to-date primary legislation, specifying the general framework for regulation, and with the requirement that the utilities supplying the services specified must obtain a licence. The intention, however, was that enabling legislation would have been enacted to replace the existing industry Acts. The first of the industry Acts was not implemented until 2000 when the Telecommunications Act was passed. Efforts by the Ministry of Public Utilities from 1993 to introduce telecommunications industry legislation were mired in controversy. Prime Minister Patterson, who was dissatisfied with the situation, was forced to act and, instead, amended the OUR Act in 2000 to clarify and specify the role of the OUR as the regulator of the industries under its purview, with telecommunications being one of the specified industries. With introducing the amendments to the OUR Act in 2000 and the 1892 Telephone Act, the institutional landscape for telecommunications regulation drastically changed.

The main regulative instruments in Jamaica in 1995 now governing the telecommunications sector were as follows:

- OUR Act, 1995 (amended 2000);
- The Broadcasting and Rediffusion Act, 1949; (amended 1961, 1986, and 2001);
- The Radio and Telegraph Control Act 1958 (amended 1970);
- The Consumer Affairs Commission Act (2005);
- The Post Office Act;
- The Telecommunications Act of 2000;
- The Telecommunications Act 2015.

Several agencies are involved in policy formulation and regulation of telecommunications in Jamaica, and this is despite the original intention to establish a multi-sector structure. The key actors in the telecommunications sector are:

- The sector minister;
- The multi-sector Office of Utilities Regulation, established in 1997;

- The economy-wide Fair-Trading Commission (1993);
- The Spectrum Management Authority (2001);
- The Universal Access Fund;
- The Telecommunications Appeal Tribunal;
- The economy-wide Consumer Affairs Commission (CAC) which was established in 2006 as a statutory body to act as a consumer advocacy agent, relying mostly on consultation to resolve disputes between consumers and suppliers. The CAC, however, has the authority to initiate actions.

Despite the Telecommunications Act of 2000, there was a still absence of clarity regarding the regulation of interconnection charges. This led to a series of court cases between the OUR and Digicel, and the OUR and the portfolio minister.[70] The minister gave a directive that the OUR should not intervene in the mobile (cellular) market by setting rates, tariff, or price caps on the interconnection and retail charges made by any mobile competitor. The OUR's challenge was that the direction was not general, as permitted under Section 6 of the Act, but was specific and went beyond general policy direction.

The case was about the extent of the respective powers of the portfolio minister and the OUR. On April 9, 2002, the minister issued a declaration directing the OUR not to intervene in interconnection matters between C&WJ and the mobile operators. The OUR's position was that the minister in question had no such power to issue this declaration and issued a 'Determination Notice' on May 22, 2002, regarding interconnection charges. Mossel Jamaica Limited (trading as Digicel) challenged the OUR's decision, with the other parties being OUR, C&WL and Centennial Jamaica Limited. Judgment, as a judicial review, was first given by Judge Dukharam on December 15, 2003, and, in his decision, the direction of the minister in question was within the minister's powers and that OUR's determination contravened the minister's direction and, consequently, was unlawful.

The OUR took the matter to the matter to the Court of Appeal over the period November 19, 2009, and January 21, 2010, arguing that the direction was outside the minister's powers and invalid; therefore, the OUR was under no obligation to comply with the direction. OUR's determination fell within its powers and was lawfully made. The minister did not seek to waive the judgment of the Court of Appeal, but Centennial and Digicel sought to reverse the Court's findings. Further,

C&WL raised a new issue that the direction was 'Regulation' and ought to have been gazetted, and no such publication took place. On the latter matter, the ruling was that it was too late for this point to be raised.

Based on the 2000 Telecommunications Act, OUR was given the powers to regulate utility rates. With telecommunications interconnection of service, this provided for entrants to the market with the fixed line service, regarding which C&WJ initially carried monopoly control. Digicel's position was that the OUR had to comply with the minister's direction. The Court of Appeal's findings was that the minister's direction was ultra vires and OUR was under no obligation to accede. Digicel then took the matter to the Privy Council in London from the Court of Appeal in Jamaica[71]; the Privy Council dismissed the appeal.

Additionally, there was the need to clarify the roles and interfaces between the FTC and the OUR regarding competition matters within the telecommunications sector and the roles of the CAC, the FTC and the OUR. This is regarding consumer protection, as well as setting out the mechanism for formal coordination between the respective agencies. In 2000, the OUR regulated only wholesale fixed wire service prices, as retail prices were below the price cap. With mobile, following the methodology of 'caller pays,' only mobile termination charges were subject to regulation.

In a case heard in the Supreme Court September 27 and 28, 2006, January 5, 2011, and January 28, 2006, the issue surrounded whether C&WJ owned the copyright and all related rights in its customer base directory: Cable and Wireless Jamaica Limited being claimant and Mossel Jamaica Limited and Oceanica Jamaica Limited, affected parties. C&WJ maintained it owned these rights, being responsible for the first telephone directory made available to the public in 1927 and published each year. The data base was created in 1992. Mossel Jamaica Limited and Oceanica Jamaica Limited challenged C&WL's claim to these copyrights, especially following liberalisation in 2000. The Courts found that the data and customer base, in their present form, contained factual customer information and were not an original intellectual creation; they did not attract copyright protection.[72]

C&WL took the matter to the Court of Appeal seeking to reverse the ruling of the Supreme Court and the matter was heard in October 2011, December 2013, and April 2014. The Court of Appeal held that C&WL had failed to show that their compilation of customer and directory base listing was a literary work constituting an intellectual creation and confirmed the decision of the Court of Appeal; it stated further that C&WL's claim was not in keeping with the spirit of the 2000 Telecommunications Act promoting fair and open competition and promoting the interest of customers.[73]

Post-Liberalisation Performances of the Industry

Following liberalisation of the industry in 2000, a review was made to access service quality, universal service, prices, and cross-subsidies, rural-urban availability, and development. An important development was that rural farmer could use mobile phones to determine market prices, and for day-to-day communication. Table 14.7 below shows that investments in telecommunications grew from J$11.05 billion in 1995 to J$12.4 billion in 2005.

Table 14.7: Investments in the Telecommunications Sector 1995–2005

Year	Gross Investment Million J$	Mobile Investment Million J$	Land Line Fixed Investment Million J$	Broadband Investment Million J$
1995	11,050	1,250	9,550	250
1996	12,107	1,550	10,257	300
1997	12,118	1,750	9968	400
1998	12,126	2,200	9,426	500
1999	12,182	2,650	8,932	600
2000	12,197	3,650	7,847	750
2001	12,245	4,200	7,245	800
2002	12,269	4,750	6,669	850
2003	12,289	4,950	6,389	950
2004	12,276	5,150	5,976	1150
2005	12,376	4,950	5,578	1,850

Source: Constructed from information from MCST and C&W Annual Reports

These technologies have facilitated the breakup of the monopoly industry structure which prevailed for most of the previous fifty years and encouraged a wider role for private capital.

The measurement used to determine access is teledensity, the number of lines per capita. The number of lines, mobile sets, and teledensity have shown remarkable uptake in Jamaica since liberalisation in 2000. Table 14.8 shows that the growth on main lines was unspectacular over the period 1976–88, the period of state ownership and monopoly operation, as shown earlier, with the monopoly state company, JTC, unable to meet demand and with customers having to wait over eighteen months to obtain connection.

Table 14.8: Growth in Telecommunications, 1994–2020

Year	Customer Base (000) line	Mobile equipment (000)	Land line customers (000)	Broad Band customers (000)
1976			50.0	
1981			55.0	
1988			85.2	
1994	234.1	26.1	208	48
1995	291.3	40,3	251	52
1996	361.4	55.4	306	56
1997	439.3	71.3	368	59
1998	507.7	91.7	416	61
1999	611.9	117.9	494	63
2000	963.8	249.8	507	64
2001	1,151	640.4	511	68
2002	1,625	1,190	435	70
2003	1,934	1,483	451	72
2004	2,264	1,841	423	78
2005	3,090	2,700	390	92
2008	3,025	2,723	316	104
2010	3,465	3,181	284	118
2012	2,967	2,714	253	123
2015	3,389	3,005	254	163
2018	3,454	3,107	347	293
2020	3309	2,873	436	385

Source: Computed from information from MCST and C&W Annual Reports and https://our.org.jm/about-us/annual-reports.

During the period of the TOJ private monopoly, 1976–94, land lines despite the difficulty of obtaining services increased from seventy-six thousand to two hundred and eight thousand, increasing further to five hundred and seven thousand in 2000. During the period of liberalisation, competition, and multi-operator industry (2000–20) land lines actually declined from a peak of 501,000 in 2001 to 254,000 in 2015. Since 2015, land lines experienced a resurgence, driven by the need for internet connection.

Mobile phone which came on the scene in 1994 made relatively little progress until 2000, increasing from 26,100 in 1994 to 249,800 in 2000. In the initial period of liberalisation, 2000 to 2010, mobile phone increased from 249,800 to 3.18 million and has more or less stabilised since 2020. Mobile teledensity now exceeds one hundred, a mobile phone for every citizen in Jamaica. In the period after 2000, the number of mobile cellular subscriptions in Jamaica grew at an average annual rate of 9.98 per cent.[74]

Although the number of telephones is now more than the total population, available data reflect multiple ownership, and the actual access to telephones is more like 70 per cent, as many homeowners in rural areas did not have cellular sets in 2005. Perhaps, once cellular service reaches a village, most of the villagers have access.

Cellular has moved telecommunications from a luxury, used only by wealthy middle class in the few urban areas with fixed land lines to a basic service that both middle and lower classes use as their primary or only telephone service. The services now cover the entire island, well into the remote rural areas, and the cost has been brought to levels where access is affordable to low-income and the rural population. Teledensity per capita in Jamaica has been shown to be extremely high, by comparison with developing countries and even world industry standards.[75]

Between 2000 and 2005, the volume of calls measured in call per minute as shown in table 14.9 also exploded, with domestic business volume increasing from 143.9 million minutes to 1.26 billion minutes, reflecting the dramatic growth in the cellular market. The growth in the incoming and outgoing international business immediate post liberalisation has been much slower than the increase in domestic calls.

Table 14.9: Telecommunications Traffic, 1997–2005

Year	Domestic Interconnect (Million minutes)	International Outgoing (Million minutes)	International Incoming (Million minutes)
1997		60.7	345.3
1998		61.5	351.4
1999		64.4	347.4
2000	143.9	73.9	328.5
2001	965.1	95.6	413.8
2002	1,190.2	130.0	349.6
2003	1288.5	127.6	487.9
2004	1298.6	115.9	391.7
2005	1264.7	104.4	590.8

Source: Constructed from information from MCST and C&W Annual Reports

The World Bank Report on Institutions, Performance, and the Financing of Infrastructure considers the Jamaican growth to be a spectacular growth.[76] Growth has definitely resulted from liberalisation and competition, as well as new technologies which have significantly brought operating cost down and have made the service more accessible to the mass market. With introducing new technologies such as mobile broad band the take-up of internet service has also expanded rapidly.

The government has, since 2015, updated the 2000 Telecommunications Act. Although the intention was to craft an Information, Communication and Technology Act to reflect the convergence of telecommunications and information technology, the new Act is more an update of the 2000 Telecommunications Act and is already woefully out of date. It does not address the rapidly converging technologies and issues such as the interface between ICT and broadcasting and traditional telecommunications and big data analytics, artificial intelligence, and block chain technology.

Integrated regulatory framework, legislation, and rules, it would appear, are being developed without cross-sector communication between the agencies responsible for infrastructure development, ICT deployment and policy, cybersecurity, and industrial development. In today's world, more than ever, given the synergies and overlapping roles and responsibilities, there is a need for an integrated legislative framework that is conducive to the development of the Jamaican economy.

The Updated Act gives the portfolio minister a greater role in the sector, i.e., the minister may now give specific directions to the OUR and not just the general direction of policy. Clearly, this is out of step with the best international practice, thereby providing more opportunities for political opportunism and undermining the integrity and independence of Jamaica's regulatory regime, which could have a negative effect on foreign investment. Even the definition of some terms like broadcasting services contradicts today's technological development.

The changes also brought the regulation of the postal services under the new Act. The inclusion here seems to be a last-minute change, and clearly has not been carefully considered. Issues such as letter mail and universal service obligation were not adequately addressed. The post office today faces serious competition with the private sector operators in parcel delivery services business. In fact, parcel delivery services globally have developed be one of the most comitative market. In anything, protection should only be considered for letter mail and documents of a certain weight. In fact, in the UK as of January 1 Royal Mail lost its 350-year monopoly and the British postal market became fully open to competition.

The previous minister had been trying to unbundle telecommunications regulation from regulating the other utilities (water and electricity) and had commissioned a study to this effect. However, nothing came of this study and, had the government taken this step, it would have been another tragic mistake by the government.

Telecommunications and GDP

Figure 14.1 shows the contribution of communications services, inclusive of telecommunications to GDP. In 1974, communication services, inclusive of telecommunications, contributed 1.2 per cent to total GDP. In 2005 the services' contribution increased sharply to 7.1 per cent of total GDP, representing the year with the highest contribution. The contribution of communication services ratio increased at an annual average of 3.1 per cent over the entire period.

Figure 14.1: Contribution of Communication Services GDP to Total GDP 1974–2005 (%)

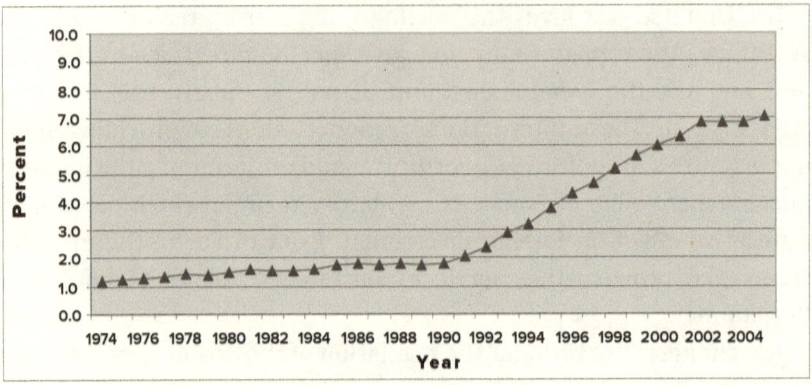

Source: Calculations, STATIN's National Income and Product Accounts, various years.

Figure 14.2: Growth Trend in the Contribution of Communication Services to GDP: 1974–2005 (Indices)

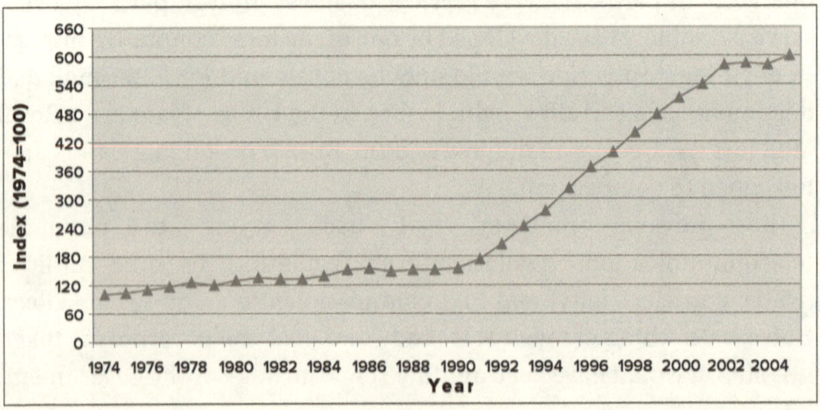

Source: Calculations, STATIN's National Income and Product Accounts – Sundry Years

Telecommunications and Employment

Data on employment were obtained from STATIN's Employment and Earnings in Large Establishments Report.[77] Between 1986 and 2006, the number of persons employed in communications services grew from 2,975 to 3,417, representing an overall growth of 15 per cent over that period. The contribution to total employment was very small and declined from 0.4 per cent to 0.3 per cent in 1986 and 2006, respectively.

Figure 14.3 shows the contribution ratios over the period, while figure 14.4 shows the growth trend in the contribution ratios. Despite this slight growth, the contribution to total employment declined over the period. The number of employees in the sector fell because the incumbent C&WJ and the new ISPs operated with only core staff. Both groups contracted out a wide range of services to small entrepreneurs, creating a new market for telecommunications subcontractors. Efficiencies in the sector meant that higher volumes were achieved with less manpower, enhancing labour productivity.

Figure 14.3: Contribution of Communication Services Employment to Total Employment: 1986–2006 (%)

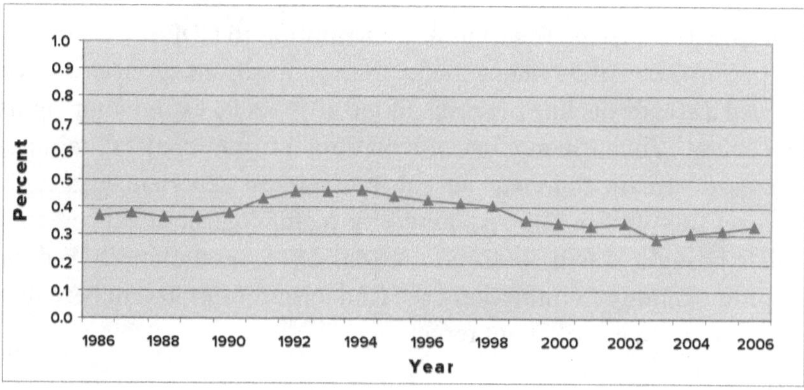

Source: Calculations, STATIN's Employment, Earnings and Hours Worked in Large Establishments reports – Sundry Years

Figure 14.4: Growth Trend in the Contribution of Communication Services Employment: 1986–2006 (Indices)

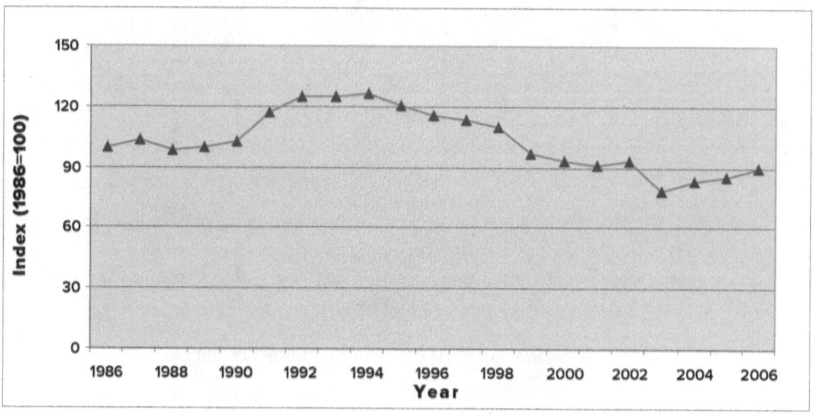

Source: Calculations, STATIN's Employment, Earnings and Hours Worked in Large Establishments reports – Sundry Years

For Jamaica and the rest of the Caribbean, the history of telecommunications, until the end of the 1990s, was one of monopoly service provision, either fully or partially privately owned. In some Caribbean countries, the domestic and international operations were separated, as with Jamaica and Barbados. The move towards introducing competition, which Jamaica initiated in the 1990s in what were previously franchised monopolies, is now being replicated throughout the Caribbean. This was not surprising as, up to the 1980s, telecommunication services were provided mostly by monopolies throughout the world.

Telecommunications Trade in Services Exports

Despite the strong growth in its contribution to GDP, the sector did not perform well in services exports. Communications services exports showed a steady decline over the period 1994–2005 as shown in figure 14.5 below. While the number of incoming international call minutes increased rapidly, the cost per call per minute experienced a rapid decline. This was mainly explained by technological advancements, which brought down international call rates and the US Federal Communications Commission's (FCC) decision to unilaterally reduce the international settlement rates.

Figure 14.5: Contribution of Communication Services Exports to Total Services Exports: 1994–2005 (%)

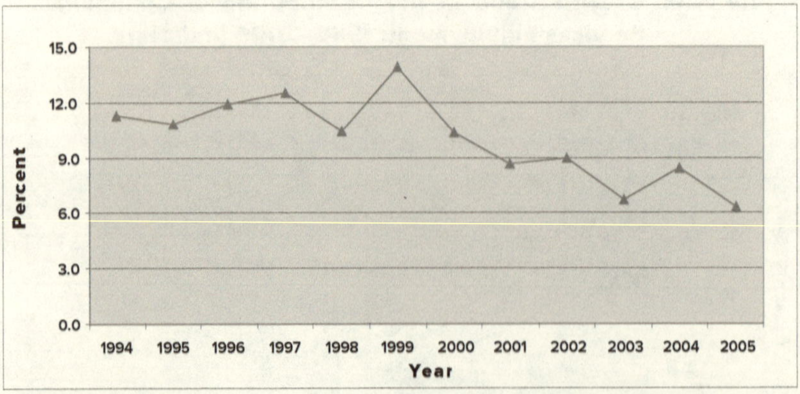

Source: Author's calculations, IMF Balance of Payments Statistics Online.

In 1994, communications services contributed 11.3 per cent to total services exports, but this fell to 6.4 per cent in 2005, its lowest contribution over the entire period. The highest contribution was achieved in 1999 (13.9 per cent). Between 1986 and 2005, the contribution ratio decreased by 11 per cent. This is partially explained because, prior to 1997, before the technological changes in the industry, the settlement rate was over US$1.50 per minute, compared to US$0.19 per minute after 1999. Although there was an exponential growth in calling activities, this growth did not make up for the decline in prices for international calls.

Telecommunications and Investments

Information and communications technologies (ICT) have increased the scope and importance of telecommunications transactions in Jamaica, as shown in table 14.10 below. There have been major investment flows into the sector, especially after 2001. In fact, the year 2001 represented the highest FDI inflows into Jamaica (US$112.5M), approximately 18.3 per cent of total FDI inflows. After 2001, FDI inflows fell considerably to US$55M in 2005, representing only 8.1 per cent of total FDI inflows.

Investments in fixed and mobile line entities have been tailing off, while investments in broadband grew, reflecting the recent demand for high-speed internet services. This could be partly because C&WJ had already built out a major part of its fixed line and mobile network by 2004, or that the industry reacted negatively to the issues over interconnection and settlement by slowing the pace of expansion.

Table 14.10: Foreign Direct Investment in Information and Communications US$, 2001–5

Foreign Direct Investment Inflows (US$M): 2001–5				
Years	Information Technology/ Communication	Growth Index (Index (2001=100)	% Contribution	Contribution Index (2001=100)
2001	112.5	100.0	18.3%	100
2002	52.3	46.5	10.9%	60
2003	105.7	94.0	14.7	80
2004	17.9	15.9	3.0%	16
2005	55.0	48.9	8.1%	44

Source: Calculations from IMF Balance of Payments Statistics Online.

Privatisation of telecommunications in Jamaica, despite the early market constraints and inability initially to liberalise the market has yielded favourable results in terms of investments and network expansion.[78] The Stern Report on Jamaica's Telecommunications System acknowledged the significant growth since liberalisation in mobile service in 2000, together with the increased volumes in international incoming calls as key drivers of the industry and economic growth.[79]

Notes

1. Roger Noll, 'Telecommunications Reform in Developing Countries,' SIEPA Paper, Stanford University, 2000.
2. Bjorn Wallenius and Peter Stern, 'Implementing Reforms in the Telecommunications Sector: Lessons from Experience,' in *Implementing Reform in the Telecommunications Sector*, ed. Peter Stern, (Washington: World Bank, 1994).
3. Gamal Ahmed, 'Regulation and Commitment in Developing of the Telecommunications in Chile,' Policy Research Working Paper, World Bank, Washington, 1994.
4. M. Lodge and L. Stirton, 'Globalization and Regulatory Autonomy in Small Developing States: The Case of Jamaican Telecommunications Reform,' *New Political Economy* 7 (2002).
5. R.A. Swaby, 'Some Problems of Public Utility Regulation by a Statutory Board in Jamaica: The Case of the Jamaica Omnibus Company,' *Social and Economic Studies* 23, no. 2 (1974): 242–63.
6. World Bank, *Current Economic Position and Prospects* (Washington: World Bank, 1974).
7. Cezley Sampson and Audley Harris, 'Rate Regulation in Telecommunications Sector in Jamaica,' Mona Institute of Business, June 1992.
8. Pablo Spiller, Pablo and Cezley Sampson (1996), 'Telecommunications Regulation in Jamaica,,' in *Regulations, Institutions and Commitment: Comparative Studies in Telecommunications*, ed. Brian Levy, Brian and Pablo Spiller, (Cambridge:, USA, Cambridge University Press, 1996).
9. Ministry Paper No. 15, The Jamaica Telephone Company, Government of Jamaica, 1967.
10. Spiller and Sampson, 'Telecommunications Regulation in Jamaica.'
11. Ibid.
12. R.A. Swaby, 'The Rationale for State Ownership of Public Utilities in Jamaica,' *Economic and Social Studies* 30, no. 1 (1981): 75–107.
13. Spiller and Sampson, 'Telecommunications Regulation in Jamaica.'
14. At the time I was a at the Advisory and Monitoring Unit, the advisory body to the minister took the position that there was no necessity for a government body to be regulating another government body hence the recommendation was for the PUC operation to be discontinued.

15. K.G. Baglehole, 'A Century of Service,' Cable and Wireless Limited 1868–1969, London, Cable and Wireless Limited, 1969.
16. *Daily Gleaner*, 'JAMINTEL What It Is and What It Does, the Genesis and Growth of JAMINTEL,' Saturday, May 2, 1981.
17. *Gleaner* Supplement, Saturday, May 2, 1981.
18. H. Barty-King, *Girdle Round the Earth: The Story of Cable & Wireless and its Predecessors to Mark the Group's Golden Jubilee* (London: Heinemann, 1979).
19. Spiller and Sampson, 'Telecommunications Regulation in Jamaica.'
20. Cezley Sampson, 'Liberalization of Trade in Telecommunications Services and the Implications of GATS/WTO for Developing Countries,' *Intermedia* 24, no. 5 (1996), London, International Institute of Communication.
21. Cezley Sampson, *For Richer for Poorer: The Impact of Telecommunications Settlement Rate Reform on Developing Countries* (London: Pathos, 1999).
22. TOJ Limited, 'Offer of Sale,' the Accountant General, Kingston, 1988.
23. Christopher Adams, William Cavendish, and Percy Mistry, *Adjusting Privatisation: Case Studies from Developing Countries* (London; Portsmouth; and Kingston: James Curry, Heinemann, and Ian Randle Publishers, 1992).
24. Constructed from information from MCST and C&W Annual Reports.
25. Lindsay Stirton and Martin Lodge, 'Rethinking Institutional Endowment in Jamaica: Misguided Theory, Prophecy or Doom or Explanation for Regulatory Change,' *SSRN Electronic Journal*, 10.2139/ssrn.610161, 2000.
26. Gladstone Hutcheson, 'Public Enterprise (Selected) Financial Relationship with Government of Jamaica: Political Economy, Budgetary Impact and Fiscal Risk,' departmental paper, Lafyette College, Pennsylvania, 2000.
27. Adams, Cavendish, and Mistry, *Adjusting Privatisation.*
28. Financial Secretary, 'Presentation at the Ministry of Finance/Public Enterprise Division Workshop on the Public Bodies Management and Accountability Act,' Kingston, 2003.
29. E. Stephens and J. Sterling, 'The Political Economy of Structural Adjustment: The Seaga Government in Jamaica,' paper presented at the 14th Annual Conference of Caribbean Studies Association, Barbados, 1989.
30. Adams, Cavendish, and Mistry, *Adjusting Privatisation.*
31. Ibid.
32. Telecommunications of Jamaica, 'Telecommunications of Jamaica, Sale of Shares,' Ministry Paper No. 78, 1990.
33. The exchange rate in 1987 and 1958 US$1 equals J$5.51 and in the 1990, US$1 equals 5.77. The major slide of the Jamaican dollar started in 1991, according to the Bank of Jamaica.
34. Adams, Cavendish, and Mistry, *Adjusting Privatisation.*
35. Alvin Wint, 'Pioneering Telephone Privatization in Jamaica,' in *Privatizing Monopolies: Lessons from Telecommunications and Transport Sectors in Latin America*, ed. Ravi Ramamuriti (Baltimore: John Hopkins Press, 1996).

36. Patricia K. McCormick, 'Telecommunications Divestment: An Erosion of Democracy in the Caribbean,' *Gazette: The International Journal of Communications Study* 59, no. 2 (1997): 91–104.
37. Spiller and Sampson, 'Telecommunications Regulation in Jamaica.'
38. Pablo Spiller and Ingo Vogelsang, 'United Kingdom: A Pacesetter in Regulatory Incentives,' in *Regulations, Institutions and Commitment: Comparatives Studies in Telecommunications* (Cambridge, MA: Cambridge University Press, 1996): 79–120.
39. Stephen Littlechild, *Regulation of British Telecommunications' Profitability* (London: HMSO, 1985).
40. Carlton Davies, 'Refocusing the Jamaican Sate: Privatization and Regulation of Key Utilities,' Joint Workshop CAAR/CRC and Aston University Business School, University of Manchester, England, June 2003.
41. M. Lodge and Lindsey Stirton, 'Embedding Regulatory Autonomy in Caribbean Telecommunications,' *Annals of Public and Cooperative Economics* 73, no. 4 (2002), https://doi.org/10.1111/1467-8292.00210.
42. Hopeton Dunn, *Globalization, Communications, and Caribbean Identity* (Kingston: Ian Randle Publishers, 1995).
43. STATIN's National Income and Product Accounts, various years.
44. Lenworth Taylor, 'Privatization in Jamaica and the Case of Telecommunications of Jamaica Caribbean,' *Journal of Public Sector Management*, Vol. 2, no. 1 (2000): 3–32.
45. Davies, 'Refocusing the Jamaican Sate: Privatization and Regulation of Key Utilities.'
46. Anthony Meyrick and Cezley Sampson (1991), 'Proposal for the Regulation of Public Utilities in Jamaica,' Ministry of Finance, Development and Planning, Kingston, 1991.
47. P.J. Patterson, 'Economic and Production Council Submission,' Kingston, December 1991.
48. Oxford University, *GATT to WTO* (Oxford: Oxford University Press, 1985).
49. Indiana D. Minto, 'Policy and Regulation in the Caribbean Communications Industry,' in *Public Administration and Policy in the Caribbean* (Boca Raton, FL: CRC Press, 2016), 358–378.
50. TOJ itself did not recognise the importance of domain name and willingly gave UWI rights to UWI domain name free of cost.
51. The CEO of TOJ, Mr Miller, was the husband of Portia Simpson. Not only was she a minister in the PNP government at the time but she went on to become prime minister.
52. Cezley Sampson, 'Telecommunications Policy and Regulatory Framework,' 2006.
53. Franklin Anthony Brown, 'Telecommunications Liberalization in Jamaica,' *International Journal of Regulation and Governance* 2, no. 2 (2003).
54. Government of Jamaica, 'National Industrial Policy: A Framework for Development,' Kingston, 1996.

55. James Deane, 'For Richer or Poorer? Impact of International Telecommunications Rate Reform on Developing Countries,' Panos Special Briefing Series, 1998.
56. Cezley Sampson, 'Liberalization of Trade in Telecommunications Services and Application of GATS/WTO for Developing Countries,' *Intermedia* 24, no. 5 (1996).
57. FCC, 'Policy Statement Accounting Rate Reform,' Washington, 1996.
58. C&WJ V. FCC and the USA, 344 US. App. D.C. 261; 166F .3d 1224.
59. M. Lodge and L. Stirton, 'Globalization and Regulatory Autonomy in Small Developing States: The Case of Jamaican Telecommunications Reform,' *New Political Economy* 7, (November 2002): 415–433.
60. Davies, 'Refocusing the Jamaican Sate: Privatization and Regulation of Key Utilities.'
61. Ministry of Commerce, Science and Technology, 'Telecommunications Policy: A Framework,' 1998.
62. *Infochannel Ltd v. C&W Jamaica Ltd*, Suit E014 (1999); and *Infochannel Ltd Vs Cable and Wireless* S.C/C. A 99/2000 (20.12.2000) and *Ministry of Commerce and Technology vs C&WJ*, Suit M089/98.
63. G. Myers, 'Squaring the Circle: Rebalancing Tariffs, While Promoting Universal Access,' in *The Internet Upheaval: Raising Questions, Seeking Answers in Communications Policy*, ed. Ingo Vogelsang and Benjamin Campaigne (Cambridge, MA: MIT Press, 2000).
64. Brown, 'Telecommunications Liberalization in Jamaica.'
65. Minister Paulwell issued instructions to the OUR not to intervene in setting interconnection charges. OUR claimed that the minister's directive amounted to a specific instruction, breaching the conditions of the OUR Act which limited the minister's powers to issuing general policy directives.
66. *R vs Office of Utility Regulation. World Telnet International Ltd*, Suit 81/2000.
67. *Infochannel v Ministry of Industry, Commerce and Technology, Office of Utility Regulation and Cable and Wireless Jamaica Ltd*, M.135/2001. The Court applied the 'hard look' doctrine. Courts will not be deferential to judgment of policymakers but will seek to investigate in detail whether the basis of their judgment was correct.
68. Spiller and Sampson, 'Telecommunications Regulation in Jamaica.'
69. Brian Levy and Pablo Spiller, *Institutions and Commitment, Comparative Studies of Telecommunications* (Cambridge, MA: Cambridge University Press, 1996).
70. The OUR became functional through the intervention of Ambassador Bernal (the Jamaican ambassador in Washington) and myself. We were able to persuade Dr Winston Hay, a Jamaican working with the World Bank and residing in the US, to return to take up the position. In setting up the institonal arrangement, I arranged for Prime Minister Patterson to appoint Earl Richard in an interim position for six months to physically establish the organization.

71. *Mossel (Jamaica) Ltd. vs. OUR and the C&WJ.*
72. No. 0079 of 2009, *Mossell Jamaica Limited (TA/Digicel) vs OUR C&WJ and Centennial Jamaica Limited.*
73. Case No 2005CD-002, *Cable and Wireless Jamaica Limited, vs Mossel Jamaica Limited and Oceanica Jamaica Limited.*
74. Case JMCA CIV 15 Appeal no 16/2011.
75. WORLD DATA ATLAS https://knoema.com/atlas/Jamaica/Number-of-mobile-cellular-subscriptionshttps:// Retrieved 12-2247.
76. Abas Kumar Jha, 'Institutions, Performance and Financing of Infrastructure Services in the Caribbean,' World Bank Working Paper No. 58, Washington, DC, 2005.
77. Ibid.
78. The employment, earnings and hours worked in large establishments report was published in 1988. It provides statistics on the number of employees, salaries, wages, and hours worked in establishments employing ten or more persons.
79. Patricia McCormick, 'The Political Economy of Telecommunications Divestment in Jamaica and Trinidad & Tobago' (PhD Thesis, Michigan Department of Telecommunications, Michigan State University, 1995).
80. Peter Stern, *Review of the Legal, Institutional and Regulatory Framework for the Telecommunications Sector and Recommendations for Reform* (Kingston: MCST, 2004).

CHAPTER FIFTEEN

Developments and Liberalisation of the Financial Sector

SECTION ONE

Development of the Financial Sector in Jamaica

Jamaica had acquired a well-developed commercial banking system by 1961, comprising six banks: Bank of Nova Scotia, Barclays Bank DCO, Canadian Imperial Bank of Commerce, Bank of London & Montreal, First National City Bank of New York, and Jamaica Citizens Bank. Deposits amounted to £58 million and advances to £37 million.[1] All six banks were subsidiaries of British, Canadian, or US-based financial institutions.[2]

One of the earliest banking legislations to be introduced in Jamaica was the 1904 Bank Notes Law. Before the establishment of the Bank of Jamaica (BOJ), Jamaica operated a Board of Commissioners of Currency, established under the Currency Notes Law of 1939. The Board had statutory authority for the issuing of government currency notes. Prior to the establishment of the Currency Board, commercial banks issued their own notes under the Bank Notes Law of 1904 which gave these notes legal tender.[3] By 1958, commercial banks had discontinued issuing their own notes. For Jamaica and most Caribbean countries, the early post-independence period was typified by the introduction of indigenous autonomous monetary authorities and Central Banks. In addition, three important developments emerged in the post-independence period. These were the employment of nationals in the middle and upper levels of management of financial institutions, the localisation of ownership of the foreign financial institutions through shareholdings by local individuals and firms and nationalisation.

Post-independence also saw the emergence of indigenous financial institutions, owned, and managed by local entrepreneurs.

By the time the BOJ began operation in 1961, Jamaica had been experiencing a credit boom; hence, policies were needed to limit credit expansion and increase imports, without discouraging inflows of investment capital. Policy implementation was largely executed through regular meetings of the BOJ and the bankers' committee. With the establishment of the BOJ Act 1961, provision was made for the BOJ to regulate the banking sector in Jamaica. In order to operate banking businesses, parties had to obtain a banking license from the Ministry of Finance and, in addition, had to make a commitment to fulfil minimum capital requirements, provide certain information to the Inspector of Banks, maintain reserves ratio at BOJ, and also maintain a specific minimum ratio of liquid assets to deposit liabilities. Regarding the management of the currency, on commencement of its operations, the BOJ continued with the policy of automatic exchange with sterling, and this arrangement continued up to August 1966, when the Banking Law was amended accordingly to accommodate a new arrangement. The BOJ was also concerned with maintaining an external equilibrium of the currency as a result of fluctuation in bank rate in the UK.

In 1963, the Jamaican exchange rate was on par with that of the UK, and this created an outflow of funds from Jamaica, resulting in a serious depletion of foreign exchange reserves. The situation worsened in 1964, when the UK adopted a restrictive monetary policy, leading to an increase in the UK bank rate. The BOJ then increased the Jamaican bank rate to discourage capital outflows. In 1966, the UK bank rate went up to 7 per cent and, as a result, the Jamaican rate was increased from 5 per cent to 5.5 per cent, and the outward commission rate was increased from three eights to one-half per cent. Sterling was devalued in 1967 and this was followed by a devaluation of the Jamaican dollar as well, with an accompanying increase of the Jamaican bank rate to 6 per cent.

The medium-term financial market was virtually non-existent before the 1960s. Commercial banks met business financing demand mostly through short-term overdraft. This opened the way for the government's intervention to fill this gap through the creation of Jamaica Development Bank (JDB) in 1969. This was followed by the establishment of the Jamaica Investment Fund (1970) and Jamaica

Mortgage Bank (1972). Like its counterparts in the other English-speaking Caribbean countries, Jamaica's financial system evolved mainly to facilitate international trade, which began with British colonialism. At the outset, the British financial system was transplanted into the Caribbean to service plantation economic activities, initially for sugar exports and later for other primary export products, such as bananas, rice, and other agricultural commodities. British financial institutions provided various financial services, including loans, deposits, lines of credit, export credit, and other business-oriented facilities. In order to provide financial services for multinational firms from their respective countries which established businesses in the Caribbean region, Canadian and American banks began operations in the Caribbean after the Second World War to support the activities of American and Canadian firms doing business in the region.

Some of the early banks were Canadian Bank Indies Limited (Sterling Bank) 1927; Canadian Imperial Bank of Commerce 1920 (incorporated in October 1975); Bank of London and Montreal, 1959 (incorporated in November 1980); Bank of Surrey Limited, which became Bank of London and Montreal in 1970; Citizens and Southern in 1967 (later Jamaica Citizen Bank); First National City Bank 1960 (City Bank); First Jamaican National Bank 1971 (gave up retail banking in 1978); BNS incorporated in 1966; Royal Bank of Canada (incorporated in 1971); and Canadian Imperial Bank International (incorporated into the Bank of Commerce in 1975). The government converted the Post Office Saving Bank in the 1970s into the Workers Savings and Loan Bank and listed part of its shares on the Jamaica Stock Exchange (JSE). The commercial banks that came into operation in the 1980s were First National Bank 1981, following the purchase of the branch of First National Bank of Chicago; Bank of Credit and Commerce, April 1982; Girod Bank 1984 renamed Century National in 1986; and Eagle Commercial Bank, 1988.

Jamaica's financial services[4] sector was not helpful to the country's economic performance in pre-independence days, as it should have been, in that the foreign-owned financial institutions that were dominated by commercial banks and insurance companies financed mainly commerce and, to a lesser extent housing, while diverting considerable amounts of Jamaican savings into investments abroad. The sector's contribution to total GDP in 1974 was only 1 per cent. It was not until after liberalisation in the 1980s that the sector saw rapid expansion.

After the 1960s, some Canadian and US institutions sold their local interest to the government, while other institutions terminated their local business activities. From the mid-1970s, many Caribbean countries, following the policy guidelines of the multilateral financial institutions, bilateral institutions, and donor agencies, implemented stabilisation and structural adjustment programmes which were geared towards free market liberalisation and reduced government regulation.

With the state-led development policies of the PNP administration after 1972, there was increased state ownership of the country's financial sector. Workers Savings and Loan Bank was created in 1973 from the Post Office saving and loan operations with 49 per cent state ownership. This was followed by acquisition of Barclays International, the first major financial institution to be nationalised. Upon nationalisation, the company was renamed National Commercial Bank. With the arrival of the Edward Seaga–led JLP administration in 1980, there was a significant policy shift, resulting in the introduction of a market-oriented approach, requiring the domestic and foreign private sector to lead the growth process.

By 1976, Jamaica's financial sector had grown to include nine commercial banks, operating a network of 165 branches island wide, six merchant banks, eight trust companies, nine finance houses, seven building societies, 103 credit unions, thirteen life insurance companies, Jamaica Development Bank, Jamaica Mortgage Bank, and a government's Savings Bank.[5] The number of credit unions had actually increased to 130 by 1966, but because of consolidation, the number progressively declined over the years to eighty in 1980. Building Societies date back to 1800, while the People's Cooperative Banks date back to 1900 and credit unions to 1941. The Jamaica Stock Exchange (JSE) was established in 1968; however, the market for stocks hardly existed prior to 1968, seeing that most of the companies were either foreign or family-owned.[6]

The Economic Environment in the Structure of the Banking and Financial Sector, 1962–85

Prior to the introduction of the financial sector reform and liberalisation programme in 1983, the banking and financial sectors in Jamaica had emerged as highly segmented markets, with specialised entities operating in each market segment. Over the years, savings in Jamaica was institutionally based, and banks had to compete with the non-bank sector for customers' deposits, covering insurance companies, building societies, and a network of credit unions. Post-independence Jamaica, as in many spheres of economic life, brought several changes to the banking sector. First of these changes involved Finance Minister Seaga's 1960s localisation policy, requiring financial institutions to be registered locally as joint ventures in partnership with local equity capital. Secondly, up to 1962, the Jamaican dollar was on par with the UK pound (sterling), with the result that monetary policy up to then was shaped mainly by the market behaviour of sterling. The financial system also made it easy for the Jamaican currency to be converted into sterling. Significant changes in the international financial system resulted after the oil shocks of 1971, which placed severe pressure on the Jamaican reserves and currency and, as a result, the country entered into its first Standby Credit Arrangement in 1973 with the IMF for US$26.5 million. This was accompanied by devaluation and alignment of the Jamaican currency with the US dollar instead of sterling. The exchange rate after the first set of devaluation was US$1.00=J$1.78.[7]

The third major influence, which came about after 1972, was increased financial intermediation through the establishment of new institutions. The JLP administration had earlier created the Jamaica Development Bank (JDB). With the coming into being of the PNP administration in 1972, the Jamaican Credit Insurance Scheme was established in September of 1972.

Under the PNP administration in the 1970s, the commercial banks took on a development role, that of mobilising capital for development financing, mostly through loan syndication and co-financing. Most commercial banks after 1970 also shed their passive role (merely operating as intermediaries) to become direct investors. Many became important shareholders, especially in hotels, agriculture, and in the real estate sectors. In so doing, they challenged the well-held view that commercial banking should only operate as deposit and loan institutions, with minimum market risk exposure, a model pursued in UK and Canada for years.[8]

In 1981, the government vertically separated the Jamaica Development Bank into two development banks: the Agricultural Credit Bank (ACB) and the Jamaica Development Bank (JDB). The former was created to serve the agriculture and JDB the industrial sector. It also established the National Investment Bank of Jamaica (NIBJ) in 1974, the National Housing Trust (NHT) in 1974, and the Caribbean Housing Finance Corporation (CHFC) in 1976.

The government again intervened in the financial sector in 1981 with the creation of the Jamaica Export Credit Insurance Company (JECIC), as a subsidiary of Bank of Jamaica. The JECIC was later converted into the Import/Export Bank with the mandate to manage government's lines of export credit financing. Trafalgar Development Bank, a private development bank came into operation in the 1980s.

The non-banking sector remained relatively small prior to 1961. By 1970, the sector had seen marked expansion. Between 1950 and 1968, the number of commercial bank accounts grew from two hundred and seventy-seven thousand to five hundred and forty thousand. The distributive trade in the 1960s came to account for 22.9 per cent of loans, 18.9 per cent of personal finance, 29.9 per cent manufacturing finance, and 5.5 per cent for agricultural financing. Table 15.1 shows that in 1970 there were six commercial banks in Jamaica with 132 branches (with J$330.4 million in loans). In addition, there were three trust companies, sixteen building societies, 127 credit unions, twenty life insurance companies, and one development bank, alongside the 265 branches of the Government Savings Bank.

By 1986, the number in the commercial banking sector had expanded to ten, operating 170 branches in Jamaica with a loan portfolio of J$3.8 billion. At the same time, the number of merchant banks amounted to eight, trust companies to eight, building societies to eight, life insurance companies to ten, credit unions to ninety-one, development banks to three, and finance houses to eight. In 1980, the credit card system was introduced and expanded rapidly covering foreign currency credit cards.

The expansion of the financial sector was accompanied by increased competition. There were also several mergers and acquisitions. Between 1971 and 1981, the size of insurance companies, credit unions, trust companies, building societies, and finance houses sharply expanded; however, because of the mergers and consolidation, each sector experienced reduction in terms of the actual numbers of institutions by 1986. The merchant banks grew out of the need to provide medium-term financing for the business sector, and they became very active in the money market in the 1980s. Even with the expansion of the near-bank business, commercial banks still experienced rapid expansion in both numbers and in their asset base. Several of the other institutions, particularly insurance companies and major local conglomerate companies, entered the banking market by establishing merchant banks, or acquiring equity in commercial banks.

Table 15.1: Evolution of the Banking and Financial System, 1961–90

	1961	1966	1971	1976	1981	1986	1990
Number of commercial banks	6	6	6	9	8	10	11
Number of commercial bank branches	69	71	131	175	179	155	170
Deposit J$ million	-	161.5	406.1	804.8	2,102.61	6,203.5	12,097.5
Loans J$ million		135.1	330.4	702.0	1,495.1	3,821.9	8,997.1
Number of Merchant Banks	-	-	3	6	6	8	21
Number of Trust companies		4	6	8	10	8	3
Number of Building Societies	7	13	16	7	10	8	5
Number of Finance Houses	-	-	-	9	10	8	5
Number of Credit Unions	110	130	127	203	96	91	80
Number of Life insurance Companies	16	20	20	13	13	10	10
Number of Development banks	1	1	1	1	2	3	3

Source: Gail Lue Lim, 'Jamaica's Financial System: Its Historical Development.'

After 1985, several aspects of the financial sector were liberalised through the removal of several of the restrictions that protected banks from competition, unleashing increased competition, with added exposure to international financial market risks. During the period of liberalisation, for the first-time banks were given the freedom to establish their own interest and exchange rate policies and to make investment decisions related to production and exports.

Jamaica's external debt, which was US$349 million, or 17 per cent of GDP in 1973 increased to US$1,209 in 1980, or 46 per cent of GDP. At the same time, the international reserves declined from a surplus of

US$37 million to a deficit of US$532 million. Unemployment was fairly, high during the period and, in October 1980, reached 26 per cent.[9] In the period up to 1980, the exchange rate moved unfavourably against the Jamaican dollar, and this was despite the assistance provided by the IMF in 1977. The Michael Manley redistributionist economic policies, sharply rising oil prices, depressed commodity markets, mounting debt service, and severe flight of capital and professional skills all combined with a highly unstable and violence-charged political climate to bring an end to the PNP administration at the 1980 elections.

Although there was restoration of economic growth over the period 1980–85, it was very weak. Investment and consumption levels were sustained by the considerable inflows of external borrowing.[10] The fiscal deficit, as a percentage of GDP, had declined markedly between 1984 and 1985, from 16.5 per cent to 7.8 per cent. The World Bank had, in 1985, approved a structural adjustment loan linked to a public investment programme that would have reduced public fixed capital formation in 1985/87 period to 8 per cent of GDP, from a level of 19 per cent in the early 1980s and would continue with a series of austerity measures (exchange rate adjustment, credit contraction, and reduced public spending).

By 1985, just under a quarter of government's debt had been financed by short-term bills, with commercial banks taking up 64 per cent of the offers. Both the World Bank and the IDB considered the credit subsidies and interest rate differential operated by the development banking sector to be distortionary, resulting in misallocation of resources and providing rent for the fortunate beneficiaries and mandated the removal of these policies.

History of Commercial Banking in Jamaica

The first commercial bank to be established in Jamaica was the Bank of Jamaica in 1836. This was not the same institution as the government-owned Bank of Jamaica. This was followed by the Colonial Bank in May 1837, the Planters Bank in 1839, and the London and Colonial (incorporated with Barclays International in 1925). Barclays Bank has had a long history in Jamaica with its early beginnings dating back to the June 6, 1836, when, under Royal Charter, its predecessor, the Colonial Bank, was established with a capital of £20,000 for the purpose of carrying on the business of commercial banking in Jamaica and the other British West Indian Colonies.[11] The Colonial Bank opened its doors to business May 15, 1837, on Harbour Street, the centre of the business district of Kingston. Colonial Bank became the Government Bank in 1864. Both these early banks were closely associated with the financing of the planter class. Colombia Bank was incorporated with Barclays Bank in London in 1925 and, in 1936, it was merged with the Anglo-Egyptian Bank Limited and National Bank of South Africa limited to become Barclays Bank (Dominion, Colonial and Overseas) Limited. Between 1925 and independence in 1962, Barclays Bank expanded from seven branches to cover an island-wide network of twenty-eight branches and several agencies and sub-agencies throughout all fourteen parish capitals and major towns. Kathleen Monteith's study of Barclays Bank DCO in Jamaica and the West Indies is a useful addition to the historical role played by Barclays in the colonial era.[12] The system of banking which developed after 1880 was one of branch banking starting with the Bank of Nova Scotia in 1889, following the establishment of the BNS. Two other Canadian Banks began business in Jamaica: Royal Bank of Canada in 1911 and Bank of Commerce in 1920.[13]

As part of preparing Jamaicans to take on a more important role in banking management, Barclays DCO, had established the first banking training school in Jamaica in 1962, and this entity inoculated much of the Barclays culture to the trainees. Barclays experienced another name change in 1954 to that of Barclays Bank (DCO) disguising its imperial brand image. This name was later changed in 1971 to Barclays Bank International Limited, this time discarding its imperial image. In 1975, the bank registered as a local company to meet the localisation requirements earlier mandated by then minister of finance, Edward

Seaga. Two years later, the bank was nationalised by Prime Minister Manley, being part of democratic socialist policy to control the 'commanding heights' of the economy. The bank was renamed National Commercial Bank Jamaica Limited (NCB).

National Commercial Bank (NCB)

Early in 1977, the PNP administration, as part of its policy to acquire maximum local ownership in the financial and banking sectors, announced its interest in acquiring one large and two small commercial banks. This announcement was viewed with great apprehension by the banking community. In the years 1968–77, Barclays International had experienced losses. Therefore, it was not surprising that when the Jamaican government offered in 1977 to acquire the company there was no resistance from London. The government also acquired Bank of Montreal, one of the smaller banks and, in 1978, merged this newly acquired firm with the re-named National Commercial Bank. At that time, NCB was experiencing fairly difficult economic conditions. It was the period when the crawling peg exchange rate was introduced, and the maximum surtax rate on income was increased to 80 per cent. The government had also introduced a new incomes policy, limiting pay increase to 15 per cent per annum. Inflation rate ran at double digit levels, with foreign exchange earnings were on the decline. The management of NCB had to face the apprehension and uncertainty of depositors about state ownership of the bank. The management felt that the confidence of depositors was of great importance, given the fact that in banking this is critical for successful operation. Despite these unfavourable conditions, the management was able to retain the confidence of the investing public, both at home and overseas.

One major change after state operation was that the expatriate managing director was replaced by Donald Banks, a Jamaican. NCB also retained management and staff it inherited and ensured that much of the tradition and culture of the old Barclay's was retained. With localisation of management, all decisions came to be made in Jamaica. Soon after nationalization, Don Banks created an executive management committee which he called the 'Prayer Group,' and this committee took responsibility for most of the policy and strategic decisions of the bank.

Banks provided continuity from the early 1970s up to privatisation. A strong, and highly respected paternalistic leader, he left the bank in

1992. His leadership style over the years had been participative, with an emphasis on sharing control and encouraging openness from his management team. As a result, he fostered strong loyalties around him. Most members of the team were appointed since he became the CEO, and he played a direct role in their career development. Banks achieved high levels of professionalism and financial discipline of NCB's management and staff, and there was absence of perceived political intervention by the Manley administration in the day-to-day affairs of the bank. Although some initial moves were made at political intervention, this was strongly resisted. Banks had joined the staff of Barclays Bank, DCO in 1952 direct from school. It was his feeling that the PNP administration was conscious of the public scrutiny of the bank and was anxious for a success story, and so did not entertain political interference in the bank's operations. By and large, the bank's management was given a fairly free hand on operational matters and banking policies, despite the fact that there were several political appointees to the Board. Unlike most of the other state enterprises NCB was never a financial burden on the public treasury. It paid corporate taxes at the same rate as its competitors. Privatisation therefore was not expected to have a significant impact on the government's fiscal balance.

Historically, like all the foreign-owned banks, NCB had been criticised for the export of capital through their repatriation of dividends and the export of locally mobilised funds for overseas investments. The banking community, being mostly foreign-owned, was also criticised for hindering economic development through investment policies, which reinforced mono-culture and trading activities. The banks were accused of promoting over-development of the consumption sector in their lending policies through disproportionate loans to traders and consumers. Much of this changed after nationalisation in the 1970s.

NCB had a fairly attractive history in terms of operational and financial performance, with relatively strong performance during the ten-year period of state ownership. By 1978, NCB's assets had grown to J$345 million, or 22.5 per cent of the total banking community's assets and, by the end of 1985 its asset had risen to J$2.25 billion, or 35 per cent of the commercial bank assets. Similarly, its share of commercial bank lending increased from 27.8 per cent in 1978 to 41.2 per cent in 1985, with pre-tax profit increasing from J$0.6 million in 1978 to J$26.7 million in 1987. The three largest banks in 1987 accounted for 71 per cent.[14]

During the period of state ownership, NCB reversed the traditional lending pattern. It saw its mandate after nationalisation as a financial institution dedicated to commercial and industrial development of the Jamaican economy. The company's lending to agriculture and tourism fully reflected this policy. In fact, in 1978 when there was excess liquidity in the banking system, due to the rapid expansion of credit and other banks were refusing to take consumers' savings, NCB decided as a matter of policy that it would not refuse to take the savings of Jamaican people and that it would seek out new and non-traditional routes to channel these funds. NCB was also an innovator, being the first bank to introduce credit cards in Jamaica and was the among the first to computerise its banking operations. Following nationalisation, the company developed an extensive network of community and national public relations programmes, which targeted areas of health, culture, community development, sports, and education. With its wide network of branches and agencies, it was well placed to take this personal approach to the selling of its services right across Jamaica, even into the deep rural areas of the country.

The first three years after state ownership saw NCB seeking to change its image from one servicing the White and coloured upper-class in Jamaica to one that was more multicultural, serving all classes in the country. The slogans: *We're your friends,' 'easy to talk to'* and 'we *understand* 'were used widely in press, radio, and TV advertisements to reinforce this new relationship. These words were backed up with visual images of smiling Jamaican faces representing the various ethnic mixes. Advertising themes, such as 'we *put the green in our nation,'* and if *you are a farmer who tills the land, a businessman, a worker, and a friend* ... with strong national anthem-like music and images featuring Jamaicans of all races with happy smiling faces, reinforced the image of NCB as a nation builder. The Bank consistently sent messages in its advertisement to the population encouraging nationalism and patriotism. Solidity and conservatism had clearly been the company's mantra inherited from the Barclays days.

There several major changes in personnel policies after nationalisation. The bank accelerated the pace at which Jamaicans were moved into position of responsibility and authority. Prior to nationalisation the bank's training school met most of its training needs. The company intensified training for all levels of staff in an effort to improve overall service and efficiency. The major strategic change in staff training involved a move away from technical skills training to a stronger focus on management development. Graduate training programmes were made available for all staff with first degrees. Some were trained locally. Others were sent on short-term executive courses, or on technical bank training courses overseas and at The University of the West Indies (UWI). For practical training, some were sent to different branches of Barclay's in the United Kingdom and to other countries in the Caribbean. A select group of managers was sent to the Manchester Business School in the UK, and the Department of Management Studies, UWI, as well as to international training programmes on bank management in Stockholm, Sweden. Overseas training, however, was only offered to those with senior management potential. Employees were provided with opportunities to learn all aspects of the bank's operations by rotating between departments and branches. In the period of state ownership and up to the early 1980s NCB managers had a fairly free hand under state ownership. They used this to shift the business from traditional short-term high-yield investments into expansion of lower-yield longer-gestation investments. When privatisation was announced the managers,' concern was that the new private investors would be more interested in short-term profit performance, and this was expected to bring about further changes to the structure of the investment portfolio.

The Period of State Ownership under JLP Administration

In 1982, the JLP administration sought to direct the private sector to focus on the production and export sectors. NCB moved in step with the government's policy and provided not only finance but business advice to the productive sectors and to small businesses. In 1981, medium-term financing was provided to residential, commercial, and agricultural sectors. Technical and financial advice was provided by a highly trained specialist staff group. NCB placed immense importance on face-to-face relationships with its clients, as part of its strategy in maintaining strong customer loyalty. Over the years, it also placed emphasis on good communication with its staff. The chairman of the Jamaica Bankers Association, in a public speech made in 1982, commented that NCB had gone through a period of scrutiny and soul searching by the public and emerged with flying colours. The bank, as a state-operated enterprise, had become fully accepted by all sectors of the Jamaican society.

In post-independence Jamaica, education levels and culture were changing, and employment patterns had to respond to these changes. Originally, new recruits by NCB were school leavers and young graduates. Fast turnover among young people forced the bank to recruit from a wider field, including highly qualified professionals. Most of the smaller banks did not provide any training opportunities for their staff and relied on NCB and Bank of Nova Scotia (BNS) to supply the market with a pool of trained clerical, technical, and management staff for the industry.

Table 15.2 shows the expansion of the NCB group and the company's diversification after 1985.

Table 15.2: NCB Group Subsidiaries after 1985

Activity	• NCB Limited • Commercial banking and the main subsidiary • NCB Investments • Diversified holdings and joint ventures in real estate, tourism, agriculture
Subsidiaries	• Resorts Limited • NCB Hotel Limited and Mammee Bay Club
Associated Companies	• Caribbean Home Insurance Company Ltd. • Ciboney Hotel Developers Ltd. • NCB Trust & Merchant Bank.
Merchant Banking	• West Indies Trust Co. Ltd. • Investment management and Management of NCB Pension Fund • Data Cap Processors (Export data entry) • Carp Corporation Self-administered health and pension schemes for corporateClients. (Medial coverage for employees). • NCB Insurance Services Ltd. (4 per cent saving plan linked to insurance policies) Noxid Ltd. • Group Computer Data Services

Source: Data provided by NCB Head Office

In the period up to 1980, the staff training school offered an average of thirty to thirty-five courses per annum, mainly in technical areas. In the post-divestment period, the range of courses more than doubled. A total of 1,646 staff members were trained on 329 courses between 1982 and 1986. By 1986, NCB had expanded to involve thirty-three branches, six agencies, five service centres with total assets of J$236 million, and with six million shares issued. The growth rate of employment in the commercial bank during the period of state control ranged between 6 per cent and 11 per cent per annum; this declined since privatisation. In 1987, the group employed 1,643 workers and, by 1992, the number had grown to 2,010 workers. The newer investment companies and their managers had come on the scene with highly specialised training; they were more innovative and responsive to change. This was reflected in NCB's hiring policy and practice. Over the years, the tradition and culture of the bank reflected much of its colonial heritage, and in 1990 despite the name change, there were fond memories and strong loyalties on the part of the older employees to Barclays image. These developments resulted in conflicts and tensions between the old guard; the conservative bank managers with over twenty years' experience in the company and the younger, energetic group with newer entrepreneurial skills. The traditional approach to management was not expected to serve NCB well in a dynamic and uncertain competitive environment, where trial and error would be more the order of the day. The changes in organisational structure resulted in increased labour turnover among the younger staff. The highly bureaucratic structure of the organisation also created gaps and time lags between putting forward good ideas and the incorporation of these ideas into management action.

Just prior to privatisation in 1986, the company was restructured and NCB Bank Group Limited was created as a holding company to own the shares of NCB: the commercial bank and its other subsidiaries and investments. This action provided for vertical separation as the commercial deposit-taking business was unbundled from the company's other commercial interests. By then, NCB had acquired investments in hotels, agriculture, and real estate. The restructuring also laid the foundation for the diversification of the company's business.[15] The new investment areas accounted for increased levels of employment: The level of female employees grew at a much faster rate than that of male employees. Earnings were no longer based on gender or marital status and, following privatisation, they reflected more objective criteria, such as performance on the job. Although wage differentials between female and male employees were removed; female employees, however, continued to move more slowly to higher positions in the company. In the period up to 1985, there were three female deputy general managers. The female employees felt local ownership made no significant changes to their position. The growth of NCB just up to first sale of share and the period up to 1989 is shown in table 15.3.

Table 15.3: NCB Financial Performance, 1982–89 (J$ million)

	1982	1983	1984	1985	1986	1987	1988	1989
Turnover	121.8	183.7	265.7	407.5	508.1	536.4	628.1	732.0
Pre-tax Profits	16.7	26.4	34.8	38.4	36.0	52.0	76.9	108.1
Taxation	7.6	12.1	19.0	20.1	18.5	25.3	34.4	43.1
Post- Tax Profit	9.1	14.3	15.8	18.3	17.5	26.7	42.5	65.0
Total Assets	1,101.0	1,373.0	1,815.0	2,250.0	2,735.0	3,247.0	3,728.0	5,029.0
Deposit	869.0	1,127.0	1,500.0	1,880.0	2,193.0	2,602.0	2,847.0	3511.0
Advance	617.0	822.0	987.0	1,128.0	1,452.0	1,794.0	2,046.0	2,859.0
No of shares (millions)	10	10.0	10.0	10.0	10.0	60,0	60.0	60.0
PE Ratio	n/a	n/a	n/a	n/a	12.67	8.41	5.56	4.68
Earnings per share	0.91	1.43	1.58	1.83	0.39	0.44	0.71	1.08
Gross profit margin	13.71	14.39	1 3.09	9.42	7.18	9.67	12.25	14.76
Closing stock price	n/a	n/a	n/a	n/a	4.94	3.7	3.95	5.05

Source: Christopher Adams, William Cavendish, and Percy Mistry, *Adjusting Privatisation: Case Studies from, Developing Countries*.

NCB continued to show profitability up to privatisation and thereafter. In 1982, it showed a post-tax profit of J$9.1 million and, at the time of the first tranche of share sale, post-tax profits had increased to J$13.5 million in 1985. After-tax profits went up by 34.49 per cent in 1982, 57.39 per cent in 1983, 10.32 per cent in 1984, 15.48 in 1986 and -3.37 per cent in 1986. Throughout the period, NCB operated in a competitive environment and was not provided with any special protection due to its status as a state-owned enterprise. Its main financial concern was that it was operating in breach of banking regulation owing to the fact that it had failed to meet its capitalisation requirements. It was therefore important that the government correct this breach before going to the market. In the period of public ownership, the bank had operated politically neutral. It was joint market leader with BNS, a nationally recognised brand with a substantial rural branch network. Importantly, NCB handled the salary cheques for the government.

Beginning in the early 1980s with the commencement of liberalisation of the Jamaican economy, NCB faced a more competitive environment, and for the first time, its managers were called upon to make decisions on interest rates, exchange rates and banking hours. They also had to make decisions related to investments, often in areas outside the group's competence. While the head office group, which was composed of professionals with deep and abiding commitment to NCB, the younger supervisory and technical managers in the new companies were more interested in career development. They were impatient with tradition and were not likely to remain with NCB if growth opportunities were limited.

Privatising NCB – Marketing the Privatisation Transaction

The first serious steps to privatise NCB was taken when the government transferred its shares held by the accountant general (the government's trustee) to the NIBJ. Responsibility for managing the transaction was delegated to the NIBJ. Some J$20 million of new capital was injected by the NIBJ to strengthen NCB's balance sheet and to correct its regulatory breach in exchange for an equal number of NCB's share. The result was that the equity increased from ten million in 1986 to sixty million 1987. The overall transaction proceeds were projected to raise J$100 million–J$190 million, mostly by public share offerings on the Jamaica Stock Exchange. Despite the weak regulatory framework, the authorities instituted privatisation and liberalisation of the financial sector, commencing with the privatisation of NCB in 1986.[16] In December 1986, the government sold 51 per cent of its equity through a public offering for J$90.6 million, or US$16.5 million (exchange rate of J$5.59 to U$1), and was by far the largest public offering on the Jamaican stock market then. This formed the first phase of the transaction. The assessment of the government of the IPO was that it was a spectacular success and showed that a developing country with a relatively low level of per capita income was able to mobilise domestic savings from the wider population, channel these funds through a small, undeveloped stock market, and shift control of a major state-owned enterprise to the shareholding public. According to Leeds, privatisation in developing countries in the 1980s was a new phenomenon and the roster of successful transactions was few.[17]

The second phase was implemented in 1991 under the PNP administration, through the sale of six million shares to Eagle Marchant Bank, the trustee for the Employees Share Option Scheme (ESOS), increasing the employees' equity ownership from 3.0 per cent to 10.5 per cent, then the single largest shareholder group. The government, as part of its policy, had declared that the remaining shares, amounting to 39 per cent of the stock, would be disposed of in 1992 by public issue. However, the government reversed its decision and concluded a private treaty sale with Jamaica M & N Investment Ltd, a syndicate owned jointly by Jamaica Mutual Life Assurance Society and Jamaica National Building Society for J$526 million.[18] Prior to the full privatisation, there were twenty-five shareholders. At the time of the final privatisation, Minister of Finance P.J. Patterson stated that the two financial companies: Jamaica Mutual Life with one hundred thousand life policyholders and Jamaica National with three hundred thousand savings and mortgage holders, allowed the government to achieve its objective of providing for a broad-based structure of ownership with over four hundred thousand shareholders.[19]

The privatisation of NCB marked the first major such activity in Jamaica and the significance is that it was carried out through an Initial Private Offer (IPO) on the embryonic Jamaica Stock Exchange and not as a trade sale to a strategic partner, which was more the conventional route followed by developing countries at the time. The major issue was whether a small stock market in a small developing country had the financial depth to accommodate IPO and retail privatisation.

Why NCB Was Selected for the First Major Initial Private Offer (IPO)

As a commercial business, NCB was a strong candidate for privatisation in keeping with Seaga's main objective to spread ownership as wide as possible and to begin the process of democratising ownership and reversing statism. The privatisation was taking place against the background of strong opposition from PNP Leader Michael Manley who claimed the sale of state assets would lead to re-concentration of asset ownership and pledged to reverse the arrangement and re-nationalise the bank on returning to power. Then Prime Minister Seaga was mindful of the fact that the overall success of the government's privatisation programme rested on the successful privatisation of NCB. This political reality conditioned the NCB sale and forced Seaga to opt for a privatisation methodology that would ensure the widest possible share ownership. He advanced the idea of democratisation of ownership by bringing large numbers of small investors to the equity market for the first time. With its restructuring in 1985 into a conglomerate group, National Commercial Bank Group became the largest financial operation in Jamaica, with combined assets of J$2.7 billion and with customer deposit of J4$.1 billion (US$490 million).[20]

As the sale had to be seen as a political success, economic factors came to be less important. Public finance consideration was therefore not included as a privatisation objective. Seaga felt that wide-scale share ownership would thwart any future re-nationalisation ambitions of a future PNP administration. It was also anticipated that a large share-owning base would serve as an attractive recruiting base for the JLP at the next elections. This aspect of the privatisation strategy was so important that the offer documents eventually provided for a special separate document called the 'Attitude of the People's National Party' which stated that:

> The President of the People's National Party has made a number of statements opposing the divestment of NCB Group, as have other members of the party. The attention of applicants is drawn to this statement which included suggestions that public control would be re-established over NCB Group. In a later statement, the President of the People's National Party has stated that he would not oppose the sale of up to 49 per cent of the issues share capital provided that the resulting shareholding is widespread.

The Objectives of the NCB Privatisation

Seaga established a limited number of clear privatisation objectives to the NIBJ:

a. To expand the local capital market, specifically expand the Jamaica Stock Exchange by about 10 per cent. Jamaica did not suffer from a shortage of domestic savings; therefore, the opportunity existed to encourage private companies to go to the market to raise capital via equity financing. A successful privatisation through the stock exchange was expected to carry a demonstration effect.

b. Prime Minister Seaga was concerned that, although NCB was not a drain on the government's coffers, the government would always be the ultimate guarantor of NCB's liabilities and more importantly he did not believe the government should be involved in the business of commercial banking. He expected the sale of NCB would remove the state from its active role in commercial banking.

c. It was also expected that privatisation of NCB would cause a more efficiently operated commercial bank.

Early Privatisation Policy and Structures

A report submitted to the Jamaican Cabinet in 1986 listed the following objectives of the overall privatisation programme:

- to improve the efficiency of the economy by placing more productive capacity under private control (the traditional economic reason for privatisation);
- to develop the local capital market and stimulate the involvement of many citizens in the free market system.
- to encourage more private investment and reduce the crowding-out effects of state ownership.
- to reduce exposure to the fiscal deficit; and
- to increase foreign exchange in cases where foreign investors would be permitted to participate.

The NIBJ was authorised to put on the market 36.6 million ordinary shares of the group, amounting to 51 per cent of the group's issued share capital, leaving 49 per cent in the government's hands. In addressing concerns raised that the government might, in the future, intervene opportunistically in the company's operation, Seaga made a binding agreement, whereby the remaining 49 per cent of the equity would not be sold before at least six months after the initial tranche of sale, and that the 49 per cent would not carry any future voting rights, while under state ownership. In addition, the government agreed to terminate its power to appoint directors to the board post-privatisation.

The Transaction Team

In 1986, a Privatisation Enterprise Team was created at the NIBJ to spearhead the bank privatisation transaction. The involvement of M.N. Rothschild in the privatisation team arose out of a chance encounter at a USAID conference in Washington D.C. in February 1986 by Richard Downer, an accountant from Price Waterhouse Coopers (PWC) Jamaica, who was advisor to Seaga. This encounter led to the engagement of Rothschild as Privatisation Transaction Advisor. In 1983, Downer had taken leave of absence from PWC to become executive director of the Bureau of Public Management in the Office of the Prime Minister, working closely with Seaga. By 1986, Downer had returned to PWC, but continued to advise Seaga, who eventually selected him to lead the NIBJ Jamaican Privatisation Transaction Team

At the February 1986 USAID-sponsored privatisation conference in Washington, Downer also met John Redwood, an M.N. Rothschild merchant banker and Oliver Letwin, who had just joined Rothschild. Redwood had been Margaret Thatcher's principal privatisation advisor in the early 1980s. In March 1986, Downer again met with Redwood and Letwin in London, and an understanding was reached in engaging Rothschild as the Investment Banking Advisor for the transaction. In fact, the creation of the Enterprise Team for the NCB transaction was a Rothschild's idea. The composition of the team eventually included mostly private sector players: attorneys, accountants, investment bankers; along with the government's political advisors.

Since the transaction in 1986, Redwood became a member of Parliament in the UK for the Conservative Party and was knighted as Sir John Redwood. Oliver Letwin also became a Conservative member of Parliament, and a minister in the Cabinet Office in the UK and also was knighted and is now Sir Oliver Letwin. I worked with Letwin on the Tanzanian telecommunications privatisation in the latter part of the 1970s. The Rothschild investment banking firm had been involved in several UK privatisation transactions; Rothschild advised on the privatisation methodology that was to be adopted for NCB's public share offering, or IPOs, similar to what Rothschild had carried out earlier in some of the UK privatisations, particularly the British Telecom and British Gas privatisation. Another key partner of the team was an up-and-coming Jamaican lawyer; Trevor Patterson, then a partner at the country's largest corporate law firm, Myers Fletcher & Gordon.[21]

Preparation for the public offering commenced in August 1986, and the timetable for the sale was short and was expected to be executed in a twelve-week period, as follows:

- Late September — Ministerial decision to privatise
- Early October — Drafting of all documents
- October 23 — Review meetings
- October 27 — Advertising starts
- October 29 — Pricing decision
- November 7 — Prospectus issued
- December 3 — Application list closes
- December 23 — Dealing commences

On November 8, 1986, the prospectus was ready, and about one hundred and seventy thousand copies were distributed island-wide. The NCB sale transaction represented the first substantial sale of assets by the government of Jamaica and the first to involve a public share offering on the local stock exchange. The transaction was therefore highly visible. The offer itself was twice as large as any previous stock offering in Jamaica. Eventually, NCB's management and the Seaga administration came to an agreement on the privatisation strategy, and, throughout the divestment, the managers and staff played an active and supportive role.[22] The promotion of the share sale was unique in that it was necessary to promote not only the company's shares but also the stock market, which was new to most potential Jamaican share purchasers. The bank's management and its advertising policy played a key role in marketing and promoting the transaction. Copies of the prospectus were distributed throughout the country through four registered stockbrokers, the post offices, and supermarkets; it was also reproduced in the national press. The publicity campaign leading up to the sale included television, radio, and press advertisements, press conferences, public meetings, and special briefings to key interest groups. The Jamaica Information Service (JIS) was also brought in and assisted in coordinating the publicity and marketing campaign. As the unions were sceptical, a series of special briefings were targeted at this group. Internally, Don Banks brought the entire staff behind the sale and secured this support by reserving a special share scheme for employee participation. Every effort was made to ensure that the public was targeted and that the sale would not be taken up by a handful of large and wealthy shareholders and institutional investors.

The First Sale Transaction and Its Terms

To secure the widest possible share participation, in the initial stages the government limited share ownership in NCB (also for the privatisation of the Cement Company). This restrictive condition of 7.5 per cent cap on any individual shareholder; however, this was later removed, both in respect of Caribbean Cement Company and the bank. Limitations on the percentage shareholdings, while having the desirable social objective of minimising the concentration of economic power in small economies, operates to distort share prices. Interestingly, it was the small shareholders who later lobbied the government to have this restriction removed. The critical share offer conditions were embedded in the bank's Memorandum of Association with the proviso that they could only be amended, removed, suspended, or altered if there was a unanimous agreement at a shareholder meeting at which at least 90 per cent of shareholders were present in person, or by proxy. This effectively made the provisions almost impossible to be removed or altered by the government.

The first sale transaction offered 51 per cent of the bank's group shares to the public during the last quarter of 1986. The other features of the sale are outlined below and involved putting on the market 26,683,560 shares out of 30,600,000 to the public. The remainder, 3,916,440 shares, or 6.5 per cent of outstanding stock were to be sold to the company's employees. At the time of the sale, the stock was not listed on the Jamaica Stock Exchange, but an application had been made for listing. The Memorandum and Articles of Association of the company were amended to require that any shareholder who had an interest in voting shares exceeding 5 per cent of the total be required to notify the company within five days, failing which the shareholder would lose voting rights in all shares for one year. In addition, any person with a shareholding of 5 per cent or more was required to give notice to the company's management of any additional purchase of stocks.

Other features of the offer are set out below:

- 26,683,560 shares out of 30,600,00 were offered to the public; an amount of 3,916,440 shares or 6.53 per cent of the outstanding stock were to be sold employees. Application was only accepted for a minimum of fifty shares.

- Participation in the offer was limited to Jamaican citizens, or companies incorporated in Jamaica and controlled by Jamaican citizens.
- Individual shareholdings were restricted to 7.5 per cent of the total outstanding stocks for any one shareholder. Voting rights would be suspended for all shares in the event of a shareholder exceeding this limit until the excess had been sold.
- The offer was conditional on application being received for eighteen million shares or more.
- The 49 per cent interest to be held in the Bank by the government (these shares were held by the NIBJ) could not be voted after the public offer was completed. Any subsequent purchase of shares by the government or any other statutory body would be subject to the same restrictions and limitations as for other shareholders.
- The price of the stock was quoted at J$2.95 per share.
- The Memorandum of Association prohibited the parent company, National Commercial Bank Group, from selling its shares in the NCB subsidiary or disposing of bank assets where such a sale would adversely affect the banking business and asset of the bank, where such a sale would adversely affect the banking business of the bank unless authorised by 90 per cent of the voting shares at a general meeting.
- Any alteration of the above restrictions would have to be voted on and resolved by 90 per cent of the voting shares in the company. The NIBJ team also came up with a share allocation scheme, designed to meet the government's objective of broad share ownership.

The whole objective of the share allocation was to bring as many small investors as possible into the market. The share allocation scheme is set out in the table 15.4.

The government also provided an employee share purchase scheme, so the largest group of shareholders after privatisation was the NCB employees, with about 12.5 per cent of the voting shares after the offering.

Table 15.4: NCB Share Allocation Scheme

No. of Shares requested	Number of Shares allocated	
1,000–1,500	1,000 plus 85.0% of additional	500
1,500–2,000	1,425 plus 70.0% of additional	500
2,000–3,000	1,775 plus 45.0% of additional	1,000
3,000–4,000	2,225 plus 35.0% of additional	1,000
4,000–5,000	2,575 plus 25.0% of additional	1,000
5,000–7,500	2,875 plus 20.0% of additional	2,500
7,5000–10,000	3,325 plus 12.5% of additional	2,500
10,000–50,000	3,638 plus 9.0% of additional	40,000
50,000–100,000	7,238 plus 9.0% of additional	50,000
100,000 and above	11,739 plus 8.5% of the remainder applied for	

Source: Leeds, 'Privatisation of NCB: A Case Study.'

Table 15.5 set out the Employee Share Option Scheme, which was introduced to secure increased participation of employees. The scheme was extremely attractive and was one of the first introduced in Jamaica.

Table 15.5: NCB Employee Share Option Scheme

Share	Minimum purchase and multiple purchase	Price
20 free shares	20	free
350 matching shares	50: 25 free and 25 purchased	One fee for each share purchased at offer price
850 discounted shares	50	10 % discount on offer price
850 priority shares, 2,070 in total	50	

Source: Adam et al., 129.

The government also provided a financing arrangement for employees to acquire shares in the divestiture. The plan provided the following features:

- The company made a loan of J$10 million (US$1.82 million) to the trustees of the Employee Share Scheme (ESS) to enable the take up of the entire block of shares offered under the scheme with the shares as collateral to the loan. Employees were then required to pay the trustees either in cash or by an easy payment plan of salary deductions over a two-year period. If the employees did not take up shares, the trustees would be required to pay for these shares at a discount agreed between the government and the trustees.

- Unallocated shares could be sold to any employee within one month after the close of applications, each employee being restricted to the purchase of fifty thousand shares from the unallocated pool. All shares in the plan were issued in the name of the trustees, and restrictions were placed on their transfer. Free shares were not tradable within two years, while the discounted shares were tradable only to other eligible employees. Any other shares were freely tradable, except those free shares acquired from the unallocated pool. All rights attached to the shares were vested in, and exercisable by the employees to whom the shares actually belonged. The employee concession was considered to be very liberal.
- The structure of the offer was such that if an investor applied for fifteen hundred shares, he or she would receive 95 per cent of the total requested, while an investor applying for one hundred thousand would receive only 12.7 per cent of the total requested.

The offer was considered a major success in terms of public take up. Over thirty thousand Jamaican citizens and institutions subscribed for shares, resulting in the offer being oversubscribed by 170 per cent, and hence a weighting formula was affected as presented in table 15.6.

Given the resultant price of J$2.95 per share, the allocations are summarised in the table 15.6. An employee purchasing free and matching shares for an outlay of J$516.25 ended up owning an asset of J$1,091.50, providing a capital gain of 111.00 per cent. Over 98 per cent of bank employees participated in the scheme, and this eventually made them the largest single block of shareholders. The cost to the government for the free and discounted shares in the ESS was estimated at J$1.2 million.

Table 15.6: Comparative Cost: ESS vs Normal Share (J$)

Share	ESS Cost J$	Normal Cost J$	ESS/Normal %	Effective Share price J$	Financial Gain
20 Free	0.00	59.00	0.0	0.0	59.00
350 matching	56.25	1091.50	47.3	1.40	516.25
850 Discounted	2,773.00	3,599.00	77.05	2.27	250.75
850 Priority	5280.50	6,106.50	86.5	2.55	0.00
Total 2070					826.00

Source: Adam et al.

Pricing the Offer

The pricing of the shares was one of the most controversial to be faced by the privatisation team. Pricing shares in a developing country market is extremely problematic. First of all, there are considerable uncertainties surrounding the estimation of demand for the large volume which was being placed on the market, secondly there was concern about the government's credibility, i.e., living up to its commitment post-privatisation. After making a comparison between NCB and its main competitor, BNS, the price of J$2.95 was fixed. This represented a price/earnings ratio of 7:6, based on earnings per share of J$0.39, and compared to a ratio of 14:0 for BNS and an average of 9:3 for the other major commercial banks. Within a few days of trading, the stocks rose to J$4.94, a 67.5 per cent increase on opening price. Based on this performance there was public criticism by some members of the media and the public that the sale was a give-away, as it was felt the price could have been set at J$3.5. The government of Jamaica received J$88.7 million from the sales proceeds; J$78.7 million from the public share issue and J$10.0 million from the ESS.

Privatisation of NCB was a decision of national importance and, in terms of public perception at the national level, it provided a good start for the Seaga administration. The inclusion of the employee share scheme and the discounted share offer were two of the most important strategic elements accounting for the over-subscription. As a mechanism to win support, it was highly effective as far as the public and bank employees were concerned. It was felt that support from the unions and members of the staff association contributed later to deepening employee identification with the company and hence provided for improved worker motivation.[23]

The strong demand for the NCB shares immediately post-privatisation seemed to have tempered, hence, the share price in June 1990 fell below the share price in December 1987. NCB's post-privatisation financial performance seemed to have later affected its attractions on the stock exchange. The table 15.7 below shows the performance of NCB share price on the JSE immediately post-privatisation.

Table 15.7: NCB Share Price Performance on the JSE, 1986–90

Date	NCB Share Price J$	Number of NCB Shareholders
Sale of shares	2.95	30,000
December 1986	4.94	30,606
December 1987	3.70	31,200
December 1988	3.95	29,790
December 1989	5.05	30,309
June 1990	4.55	30,451

Source: Adam et al., 12.

The Second Sale Transaction

In the second part of the sale transaction, I was very much a part of the transaction team, working out of Deputy Prime Minister Patterson's office. The second sale transaction was carried out in March 1991 through a private placement to NCB Trust and Merchant Bank, the trustees of the employee share scheme placement provided for the employees to acquire a further 6.4 million shares or 10 per cent of the equity. The government effectively reduced its non-voting shares from 29,395,420 to 23,395,420. The employees could take up shares in the offer, and this brought the trustees' holdings to 12.5 million, approximately 21.5 per cent of the equity interest. With a further 2.86 million shares held by senior managers and the West Indies Trust Company, an NCB subsidiary, the employees effectively came to control over 25 per cent of the group's equity.

The government's initial intention at the time was that the remaining 23.3 million shares, amounting to 39 per cent of the equity, would be sold in two equal tranches through public offerings, the first tranche being earmarked for shareholders other than employees and two million to be reserved for sale to Jamaicans overseas, especially those living in the UK. Initial marketing of the shares was even carried out in the UK and a promise was made to the UK Jamaican diaspora that a portion of the equity would be exclusively for them.

The Third and Last Sale Tranche of 39 Per Cent

A survey by Carl Stone in November 1990 showed that support for the NCB divestment had increased from 25 per cent to 52 per cent among lower-income Jamaicans and from 24 per cent to 58 per cent for PNP voters. Support for the middle and upper classes also increased from 80 per cent to 92 per cent over the period 1987–90.[24] This provided a sound background to continue in the divestment of the remaining NCB shares. The official launch of the sale of the final block of shares was planned for March 1992, and a team spearheaded by the NIBJ and a group of underwriters was assembled to market the shares. Advisors from PWC, lawyers from the UK, accountants, and public relations experts were all engaged to promote the sale. Problems with the public offer started in February 1992 when Insurance Company of the West Indies Limited (ICWI), an original underwriter, reduced its commitment from J$100 million to J$50 million. At one stage, it appeared that ICWI and its subsidiary, Jamaica Citizens Bank, contemplated a direct takeover of NCB with sympathetic support from the NCB management. The Manley administration attempted to dispose of the remaining shares by tender to institutions which the PNP administration, at the time, felt had lost out during the initial sale and were unsuccessful as the great proportion of the offers came in at prices below the prevailing prices of NCB shares on the JSE. The government believed there was collusion between the institutions.

The final disposal of the government's 39 per cent equity interest in NCB was carried out in 1992. This was implemented through a private deal and was in sharp contrast to the transparent and highly publicised first disposal by the JLP administration in 1987. In 1988, the JLP administration had announced its intention to dispose of the remaining shares. This then set off a battle in the financial sector between groups wanting to gain control of the banking group. In 1991, Parliament enacted legislation that altered the Memorandum and Articles to remove the 7.5 per cent ceiling on holdings by any single individual or group, as this restriction had come to seriously affect the market price of the shares as, from a commercial perspective, it affected the returns to shareholders.

The two other major institutional shareholders in 1991 were Life of Jamaica, part of the Insurance Company of the West Indies Group and the Eagle Group of Companies, two financial organisations that operated subsidiaries in life insurance, banking, and merchant banking. Both companies had earlier made moves to acquire a controlling interest in NCB in late 1991. Following Prime Minister Manley's announcement of the intention to the public on January 12, 1992, to sell the remaining shares, Eagle Group disposed of the five million shares it had acquired to the NCB subsidiary, West Indies Trust Company. The ultimate purchasers, however, turned out to be the ICWI Group. Eagle could sell its shares at the top of the market. NCB shares had peaked at J$36.00 in December 1991. With the sale of the shares acquired by Eagle, the share price fell sharply thereafter.

Jamaica M & N Investments Ltd, a syndicate of Mutual Life Assurance Society, then the largest life insurance company in Jamaica, and Jamaica National Building Society (JNBS), then the second largest building society in the island, entered the picture and made a counterproposal to the PNP administration. By this time, the share prices were in a continuous slide and most of the original underwriters had withdrawn their commitment. The government then was badly in need of foreign exchange, and the Mutual and Jamaica National syndicate could include a foreign exchange component in its offer package. The ICWI Group could not fund a foreign exchange component and so lost their competitive edge.

The options of the government at the time were to sell shares worth J$250 million to the ICWI Group, which would give that group controlling interest, with ICWI underwriting the remaining shares; or sell the entire block to the Mutual & Jamaica National syndicate, which had planned to carry out the purchase through an investment fund in the near future. This was in order to reduce the concentration of voting power by the syndicate which would lead to an increase in its ownership interest from 3 per cent to 42 per cent or postpone the sale and raise J$500 million needed for the national budget through a Treasury Bill offer.

On February 27, 1992, the government accepted the Mutual and National syndicate offer of J$526 million. It argued that the offer price of J$22.50 per share minimised the market risk for both the state and existing shareholders. An open market operation to raise J$500 million would have triggered higher interest rates, with consequent budgeting costs implication later in the year and would have led to a crowding out of the private sector for funds in the local financial market. Alternatively, the government could have chosen to further reduce public sector operations to compensate for the shortfall expected from the divestment proceeds.

Terms and Conditions of Final Sale Involving 39 Per Cent

The final terms of sale to Mutual and National Investments Limited (MNI) stipulated that the J$526 million be paid as follows: J$249.4 million to be paid on signing, and J$200 million on or before April 30, 1992, free of interest. The purchasers were entitled to 39 per cent of the voting rights. The MNI agreed with the NIBJ that, within six months of the agreement, they would offer, or procure the NCB offer for sale, by a public offering in Jamaica and/or the UK not less than eleven point seven million shares in NCB, if the offer was made an open-ended trust; or not less than five million shares in NCB if the company made a direct offer to the public, whether such shares formed part of the existing shares or constituted a new issue of shares in NCB.

There were severe criticisms by the media and some members of the public of how the PNP administration privatised the remaining NCB shares. Between November 1991 and January 1992, NCB shares lost a considerable proportion of their value. Delay in effecting the divestment after the 1991 announcement contributed to intensive speculation and the decline of the share value. It was felt that the government was not sensitive to the market behaviour of share prices. With more careful planning, some argued the government could have obtained a more attractive price. NCB management and employees were very dissatisfied, in that their involvement was negligible, compared with the JLP administration's first divestiture. Management and staff felt that there was a lack of transparency, and that the PNP administration gave no consideration to the employees' future. Staff complained that most of their information relating to the transaction came from the media, instead of from internal sources as in the earlier divestiture. On acquisition of the second tranche of shares by M &N Investment, the decision was also taken to merge the two banks within the new group.

Merger between NCB and Mutual Security Bank Limited

At an extraordinary general meeting on July 27 ,1992, NCB offered three bonus shares for each existing share and also introduced a stock split by converting the J$1.00 shares into units of J$0.50. This led to concern that M & N Investments was planning to reduce the proportion of shares they were required to resell to the public. The government, however, insisted that the divestment agreement called for eight point 3.0 per cent of the shares to be resold and that, under the stock split, the syndicate was required to resell sixty-four million, and not the 11.7 million, which would have been the case before the stock split.

At the time of the sale, Jamaica National and Mutual Life each had a controlling interest in two other financial subsidiaries. The chairman of Jamaica National was also the chairman of Trafalgar Development Bank. A Mutual Life subsidiary, Mutual Security Bank (MSB), was the third largest commercial bank in Jamaica, and this gave the consortium a 48 per cent market share in the commercial banking market. Shortly after the stock split, Mutual and Jamaica National notified the government that they wanted to create a strong financial entity by merging the two commercial bank subsidiaries. Since MSB, the 80 per cent–owned subsidiary of the syndicate was a publicly listed company, the merger had to be carried out under stock exchange rules. In 1993, NCB obtained permission to acquire all the rest of the shares in Mutual Security Bank and provided for the merger of the two commercial banks within the group.

The offer made by NCB for MSB called for a share swap of four NCB shares for every three MSB shares. No cash payment was contemplated. Serious public concern was also expressed about the merger, as it was feared that it would create a single bank controlling 48 per cent of the commercial banking sector, providing for further concentration of economic power and reduction of competition. The merger of the two commercial banks eventually resulted in one entity holding 48 per cent of the total assets of the commercial banking sector, 47 per cent of the loan advances, and 48 per cent of the daily foreign exchange transactions.

In giving approval for the merger in June 1993, the then Prime Minister P.J. Patterson insisted on the following conditions:

- Prior to the takeover, NCB was required to make a renounceable rights issue of ten million ordinary shares.
- This meant that NCB was required to give existing shareholders the right to purchase the shares, which M & N Investments could not take up.

No later than December 31, 1993, NCB was to make a public issue of at least thirty million shares, some of which were to be earmarked for an employee share plan for the staff of MSB, Mutual Life, and Jamaica National Building Society. M & N Investments was not to participate as an underwriter in either the rights issue or the public issue. It appeared from the agreement that M & N Investments was under no contractual obligation to resell the sixty-four million NCB shares to the public. The government's failure to enforce the agreement then left Mutual Life and Jamaica National with effective control of NCB. In essence, one connected group could now dictate policy in the bank, a dramatic departure from the original position of the JLP administration, which had sought to limit individual or connected ownership to no more than 7.5 per cent.

Post-Divestment

Post-divestment revenue efficiency showed a change from J$341,000 per employee in 1987 to J$306,000 in 1992. The level of employment had been expanding faster than the rate of increase in revenues. Over the pre-divestment period, real loans per employee per annum averaged J$980,500, compared to an annual average of J$980,800 in the post-divestment period. Real deposits per employee reflected an annual average of J$1,497,800 during the period of state control, compared to an annual average of J$1,478,500 in the post-divestment period. There had therefore been no significant change in productivity over the two periods. Profits per employee were, however, higher at BNS than at NCB. The general conclusion, therefore, is that private ownership of NCB did not improve labour productivity up to 1992. However, improvement is a long-term process, and maybe it was too early then to judge the real effects of ownership change on efficiency.

To reduce staff turnover, the company adopted a new strategy following privatisation and expanded recruitment to include mature personnel and applicants with qualifications other than matriculation, as well as those with university degrees. It was felt that these recruits would have been more receptive to a slower rate of promotion and less likely to leave the company. The group also had to draw from a much wider skills base in order to meet the technical requirements of the newer investments areas such as tourism and agriculture. The bank expanded the range of entry points into the company and new recruits after 1990 entered at almost every level other than division head, which was then reserved for people coming through the system. Significant changes took place in the company's promotion and compensation policies following privatisation. More objective systems of assessment were introduced for evaluating individual performance, with profit sharing and certain components of salary increases linked to the results of performance appraisals. More opportunities were provided for horizontal movement of staff from departments within the commercial bank and between companies in the group. The parent company discontinued its practice of secondment of staff to each company. Each company was made responsible for employing its own staff, and this provided for more decentralised control over human resources.

During the pre-privatisation period of 1981–86, real revenue had increased at an annual average of 21 per cent compared to 2.1 per cent between 1987 and 1992, the period of partial ownership and full management by the private sector. The real rate of growth of NCB revenues decreased following the company being fully privatised. This could not be explained by the overall performance of the financial sector, as the sector had grown faster in real terms over the post-divestment period than it did during the pre-divestment period.

There was a significant post-divestment growth in assets, increasing from J$3.142 million to J$14.884 million in 1992 (or by 463 per cent). In real terms, however, growth in the pre-divestment period averaged 10 per cent, compared to an average of 4 per cent in the post-divestment period. In real terms, the annual growth in loans averaged 9.9 per cent in the pre-divestment period, compared to an annual decline of 4.2 per cent in the post-divestment period. Following privatisation, NCB experienced a significant decline in the real rate of loan advances. This could be explained by the higher rates of investment in non-banking activities. The higher liquid assets ratio and cash reserve ratio in the post-divestment period also affected loan advances.

NIBJ Analysis

The data for this analysis came from the NIBJ.[25] Table 15.8 shows the profit performance. During the post-investment period, profits performed better when adjusted for inflation. The profit to revenue index (profit as a per cent of revenue) shows management's ability to control expenses. In the pre-divestment period, the index declined from 14.4 per cent to 7.2 per cent, compared the post-divestment period the ratio improved from 14.6 per cent in 1989, before falling to 12.5 per cent in 1990. If the average is taken for each of the two periods there was no improved performance in profit growth.

Table 15.8: Profit Performance Pre-Divestment (1983–86) and Post Divestment (1987–90)

	1983	1984	1985	1986	1987	1988	1989	1990
Earnings Before tax J$000	26,425	34,774	38,394	36,023	51,991	76,931	108,059	108,059
Net Profit J$000	14,337	15,817	18,265	17,462	26,694	42,544	64,999	94,728
CPI index	50.2	66.0	81.9	91.1	96,2	104.1	212.5	147.4
Return on equity %	32.1	27.1	24.9	11.9	21.5	22.5	18.23	26.9
Profit to revenue %	14.4	13.1	9.4	7.2	9.7	12.3	14.8	12.5
Adjusted profit before tax J$000	52,639	52,688	47,879	39,542	54,045	73,901	88,937	95,358
Before tax Profit growth %		31.6	10.2	-6.2	44.3	48.0	40.5	30.0
Adj. before tax profit growth %		0.09	-11.0	-15.7	36,7	36.7	20.4	7.22
Cost of revenue %	71.65	72.0	76.52	80.17	78.18	73.34	70.67	71.24

NIBJ (1991), 'Study of the Performance of NCB (1982–1990).'

Cost to income measures management's ability to control overheads. In the pre-divestment period, the average was 76.23 per cent, compared to 73.36 per cent in the post-divestment period. The difference is not statistically significant, although the direction shows improvement. The average annual return on equity during the pre-divestment period was 24 per cent, compared to 26.8 per cent in the post-divestment period, again not statistically significant.

Table 15.9 shows investment performances over the pre- and post-divestment periods. In September 1983, NCB had investments in subsidiaries valued at J$2.34 million. No acquisitions were made over the next two years but, at the end of the 1985/86 fiscal year, the book value of investments in subsidiaries stood at J$59.6 million, an increase of J$57.3 million. This was mainly because of the establishment of two new companies: NCB Investments Limited and NCB Data Company Limited. By September 1990, investments had increased to J$85.2 million, including investments in associated companies.

Table 15.9: Investment and Expansion Performances Pre-Divestment (1983–86) and Post-Divestment (1987–90)

	1983	1984	1985	1986	1987	1988	1989	1990
Investment in subsidiaries J$000	2,346	2,346	2,346	59,526	61,122	66,624	77,127	85,242
Other operating income /total income %	17.6	22,2	14.6	13.0	16.4	16.9	21.4	15.8
CPI index	50.2	66.0	81.9	91.1	96.2	104.1	121.5	147.4
Capital expenditure J$000	1,699	8,657	17,781	28,718	32,069	26,637	56.056	90,446
Capital expenditure adjusted J$000	3,384	13,117	20,490	31,524	33,336	25,558	6.137	61,374
Growth in Adj cap exp %		287.6	56.2	53.9	5.8	-23.2	80.3	33.0
Growth in actual capital expend		5,409.5	93.8	71.1	14.7	-16.9	110.4	61.4

NB Figures have been adjusted using the Consumer Price Index CPI base year and month was taken as at January 1988.

Source: NIBJ, 'Study of the Performance of NCB (1982–1990).'

After divestment, through NCB Investments Limited, NCB established a presence in many sectors of the economy: tourism, real estate (including ownership of shopping malls), and agriculture, among others. NCB acquired the Wyndham Hotel in Kingston and Singles Hotel on the north coast. The company became involved in life insurance though NCB Insurance Services Limited, which marketed the Omni Life Insurance policy. Table 15.10 shows the stock price performance over the two periods. From an offer price of JS2.95, the stock closed at J$4.94 at first day close, a gain of 67.4 per cent. On September 30, 1990, the stock closed at J$.3.09, a decline of 37.4 per cent on the initial listing price.

Table 15.10: Stock Price Performance Pre-Divestment (1983–86) and Post-Divestment (1987–90)

	1983	1984	1985	1986	1987	1988	1989	1990
End of year Stock price $					4.50	3.30	6.25	3.09
Earnings per share $	1.43	1.58	0.46	0.39	0.51	0.71	1.08	1.58
Dividends per share $		0.80	0.52		0.38	0.33	0.35	0.39
PE multiple					8.8	4.64	1.58	2.06
Stock price to BPS					1.89	1.21	1.86	0.59

Source: NIBJ, 'Study of the Performance of NCB (1982–1990).'

Earnings per share at the end of the fiscal year ending September 30, 1983, was J$1.43; following this, it climbed to J$1.58 in 1984, but subsequently dropped to J$0.46 upon the expansion of the number of shares outstanding from ten million to sixty million. By September 1991, it climbed to J$1.58. Earnings per share showed a steady increase in both the pre- and post-divestment period. The book value per share showed the accounting value of each unit of the company's stock. Following the listing of NCB stock in 1986, the ratio of stock price to book value per share fell in most years, up to September 1990. In September 1987, the multiple stood at 1.89, but by September 30 the multiple had fallen to 0.59, suggesting that the private management could not convince the investing public that the future value of the company would exceed its current accounting value. NCB share price substantially underperformed its main rival, BNS, which had higher profit and asset growth. The NCB sale clearly demonstrated the conflicting role of the state as a promoter and arbiter of the sale on the one hand, where the government wished to encourage as many applications as possible, and on the other hand, it had an obligation also to the specialist and knowledgeable investors. These specialist investors would normally have accurate information concerning the risks of equity investments and, ideally, some idea of how to form judgements about promotional material that the government had been producing.

The Performance of Financial Sector, 1980–2005

Tables 15.11 and 15.12 show the growth in the number of financial institutions and the growth in their asset base over the period 1980–2005.

Table 15.11: The Jamaican Financial System: Number of Institutions, 1980–2005

Year	Commercial Banks	FIA Institutions	Building Societies	Insurance Companies	Credit Unions	Development Banks
1980	10	8	4	n/a	n/a	n/a
1990	11	26	6	n/a	n/a	n/a
1995	11	35	25	10	80	3
1998	9	18	13	29	66	4
2000	6	11	5	25	61	2
2001	6	11	4	25	58	2
2002	6	10	4	22	56	2
2003	6	7	4	21f	52	2
2004	6	5	6	20f	50	2
2005	6		6	20f	48	

P – preliminary R : Revised F: Licensed and registered under FSC year ending March 31

Sources: BOJ and FSC

Source Planning Institute of Jamaica, Bank of Jamaica and FSC

The total assets base of the twenty-one merchant banks in 1990 amounted to J$4.5 billion, or 16.3 per cent of the asset base. Their numbers increased in 1995 to twenty-five; their asset base also increased to J$17.3 billion, while their share declined to 8.7 per cent.

In 2001, the number had fallen to thirteen. Their based declined to J$15.9 billion, with their share of the asset base falling further to 4.4 per cent. In 2006, their number fell further to nine, with the asset base increasing to J$44.8 billion and their share of asset base increasing to 6.4 per cent. This sector experienced probably one of the most rapid expansions in the period immediately following liberalisation, but contracted after the financial crisis and with introducing improved financial sector regulation.

Table 15.12: Financial Institution: Number, Asset Base, and Percentage of Asset Base

Institutions	1990	1995	2001	
Commercial Banks	11	11	6	6
No Assets ($)m	17,328	121,325	239,087	429,969
% of assets	62.5 %	61.1%	68.0%	61.7%
Non-Banks (assets)	10,469	77,271	112,745	267,946
	37.7%	38.9%	32.0%	38.3%
Merchants Banks	(21) 4,527	(25) 17,334	(13) 15,932	(9) 44,863
% of assets	16.3%	8.7%	4.4%	6.4
Building Societies	(6) 3,058	(32) 29,084	(5) 50,448	(4) 106,219
% of assets	11.0%	14.6%	14.3%	15.2%
Credit Unions	(80) 812	(82) 4,098	(66) 17,279	(47) 38,528
% of assets	2.9%	2.1%	4.9%	5.4%
Life insurance Companies	(10) 2,072	(12) 26,755	(7) 29,386 (b)	(6) 78.335.9c
% of assets	7.5%	13.5%	8.4%	11.3%
Total assets	27,797	198,596	351,832	697,915
	100%	100%	100%	100%
% of GDP	86.5 %	100.6%	100.8%	

Invariably, the merchant banks were linked to a commercial bank or part of a Conglomerate Group. The six building societies, at the end of 1990, had total assets of J$3.0 billion in with 11 per cent of the asset base. Their numbers increased to thirty-two in 1995, and their asset base increased to 14.6 per cent. By 2001, their numbers had contracted to five but, with consolidation, their share of the asset base only fell slightly to 14.3 per cent The eighty credit unions in 1990 had an asset base of J$0.81 billion; however, their numbers increased to eighty-two in 1995, and their asset base increased to J$4.1 billion in. In 2001, their numbers declined to 66.0 per cent, and their asset base increased to J$17.2 billion, with the asset base share expanding to 4.9 per cent. In 2006, their numbers declined further to forty-seven, with an asset base of J$38.5 billion and with their share of asset base increasing to 5.4 per cent.

The ten life insurance companies in 1990 had total assets of J$2.07 billion, with their share of the asset base mounting to 7.5 per cent. In 1995, their numbers increased to twelve, their asset base increased to J$26.7 billion, and the share of asset base increased to 13.5 per cent. In 2001, their numbers fell to seven, and their asset base increased to J$29.33 billion and their share of the asset base fell to 8.4 per cent. In 2006, their number fell slightly to six, with an asset base of J$78.3 billion and with an increased share of 11.3 per cent.

The JMB, which financed housing development, had assets of J$849.2 million on December 31, 1990. The ACB lent through People's Cooperative (PC) Banks, or through commercial banks. There was one private development bank, Trafalgar Development Bank, with assets of J$172.2 million 1990. In 1990, there were 107 People's Cooperative Banks. The PC Banks was established in 1905 to serve rural smallholders. Table 15.13 below shows the list of commercial banks in 1990 and the size of their asset base with the total amounting to J$17.3 billion.

BNS at J$4.9 billion and NCB J$4.8 billion accounted for over 50 per cent of the asset base. Commercial banks in 1990 numbered eleven, with an asset base of J$17.3 billion, and their share of the asset base at 62.5 per cent. In 2006, their numbers remained at six, with an asset base of J$430.0 billion, but their share of asset base declined to 61.7 per cent.

Table 15.13: List of Commercial Banks in Jamaica in 1990

Commercial Banks	Assets 31 Dec. 1990 J$ million	Commencement of Operation
All commercial Banks	17,309.2	Together, the 11 commercial banks operated a network of 165 branches
Bank of Nova Scotia	4,986.4	Locally incorporated 1966, 70% foreign owned
Mutual Security Bank	2,354.4	Locally incorporated 1971, originally RBC, Acquired by Mutual Life Insurance in 1985
Jamaica Citizens Bank	1,176.1	Established in 1967, originally 60% Citizen & Southern 100% Jamaican since 1980
Canadian Imperial Bank of Commerce	1,094.3	Up to 1975 CIBC of Canada renamed CIBC Jamaica in 1980
National Commercial Bank Ltd	4,817.0	Partly state owned since 1977, previously Barclays International. Government. divested 51% in 1986
Citi-Bank, N. A	388.9	Owned 100% by Citibank USA, incorporated in the US
First Jamaica National Bank	55.1	Began operations 1981 by purchase of First National Bank for Chicago interest
Workers Savings & Loan Bank	710.2	Evolved out of Govt. Saving Bank goes back to 1870. Incorporated in 1973, partially owned by the government
Bank of Credit & Commerce International Overseas	416.9	Began operation 1981 following purchase by First National of Chicago
Century National Bank	935.5	Began operation 1984 previously Girod Bank renamed Century 1986
Eagle Commercial Bank	392.7	Began operation 1988 by Paul Chen Young

Source: Gail Lue Lim, 'Jamaica's Financial System: Its Historical Development.'

SECTION B

The Background to the Liberalisation of the Financial Sector

In 1985, Jamaica attempted to move from direct to indirect instruments of monetary control for the first time. Prior to this, the system of monetary control had involved: global credit ceiling, directing credit operations through sector-specific refinance windows, operated by the Bank of Jamaica (BOJ) and activity-specific credit ceilings; a statutory saving deposit floor rate; and a maximum mortgage lending rate. Interest subsidies were determined not only through refinance operations but also through specialised agencies: a non-renumerated cash reserve ratio (which differed between commercial banks and non-bank financial institutions) and a non-cash liquid asset requirement. This system of monetary control existed with rigid restrictions on both current and capital account transactions and a fixed exchange rate through to 1983. Problems of large fiscal deficits as much as 16 per cent of GDP over the period 1981–85 were aggravated by a failure to adjust foreign exchange shortfall arising from a marked contraction in the bauxite/alumina industry, the country's major export earnings source. The period of the 1980s was one of substantial external borrowing by the government, the result of which was increased tightening of exchange controls and increased controls over money supply by the BOJ.

Under a very restrictive monetary policy over the period 1984–85, the BOJ relied heavily on the statutory reserve ratio, as well as the liquid assets ratio. By April 1985, the liquid assets ratio reached 48 per cent inclusive of treasury bills. This ratio was used both to control credit and to finance the public sector deficit. Including the treasury bills in the reserve ratio distorted the interest rate structure, as financial institutions imposed penalty interest rates on the private sector to make up for lower yielding treasury bill rates. Initially, these measures resulted in a reduction in the distortion of public and private sector interest rates, reduced the gap between deposits and loan rates, which at times had been as high as 20 per cent when compared to 5 per cent in North America, and provided for additional liquidity in the banking system.

The programme of financial sector reform and market liberalisation which was outlined in 1985 was aimed at gradually liberalisation of interest rates, removal of interest distortions, and utilisation of indirect instruments of monetary control. Credit ceilings were reintroduced in 1989 in response to mounting exchange rate pressure and credit expansion but were abandoned again in 1992.

Despite monetary tightening, the official exchange rate became overvalued and, by 1982–93, a parallel foreign exchange market had become a reality. Jamaica had been experimenting since 1975 with several exchange rate systems, commencing with a dual exchanges rate in 1977, followed by crawling-peg rate system, parallel rate and official rate, and an auction system, with the rate eventually unified in 1983 when a competitive auction system was introduced, allowing for the exchange rate to float through to September 1985, when BOJ intervened to revalue the Jamaican dollar. After operating these different exchange rate systems, the Jamaican dollar was finally floated in 1992. Introducing a competitive price foreign exchange auction was accompanied by dismantling of import controls. In the period of restriction, commercial banks circumvented the system over credit ceilings control by shifting loans and deposits to non-bank affiliates.[26]

The mediocre performance of the economy during the remainder of the 1990s was attributable, in part, to the dilemma in which the sector found itself for much of the decade. C. Kirkpatrick and D. Tenant,[27] D. Tennant and C. Kirton,[28] and C. Kirton and M. Leiba-Barnes[29] identified the characteristics of the period. These included the existence of strong financial repression; severe credit controls and high reserve requirements; preferential interest rates and central bank re-discount financing to priority sectors; elevated level of government involvement in financial institutions; dominance of commercial banks, and bureaucratic controls on entry into the sector.

Considerable progress had been made in stabilising the economy up to the mid-1990s. Fiscal position strengthened, with primary surplus reaching 13 per cent of GDP and overall public sector position shifting into remaining surplus position up to 1995/96. There was an improvement in the international reserves and a decline in the ratio of public debt to GDP reduced to 103 per cent. However, Gordon concluded that the financial market liberalisation was not accompanied by a strengthening of the supervisory capacity of the monetary regulatory authorities.[30]

The government accepted an institutionalist approach to financial market regulation with commercial banks in practice being regulated under the 1960 Bank of Jamaica Act, [31] while regulation of the insurance companies came under the Office of the superintendent of insurance in 1971. At that time, the near banks were not guided by a clear regulatory regime. Regulation of near banks was also introduced with an amendment to the Banking Law in the 1970, providing the BOJ with authority to supervise the non-bank financial institutions, as well as to regulate exchange controls. Regulation and supervision with different supervisory agencies for the other sectors were also not seen as a major problem. Market instability in the financial sector had not been a major concern until after 1990s.

The late 1980s and early 1990s saw the rapid growth of domestic entrepreneurs and their entry into the sector, accelerating its growth. Unfortunately, much of the investment supported by the savings that they mobilised was directed into investments in businesses and assets of questionable assistance to national growth. A notable feature was the use of holding companies as the focal point of conglomerate institutional structure. Some conglomerate financial institutions under common ownership included commercial banks, building societies, finance houses, merchant banks, unit trusts, insurance companies (life and general) brokerage firms and even offshore affiliates. While these new developments were emerging, there was no appropriate statutory regulatory framework to deal with them. Several of the new institutions that were taking deposits fell outside the supervisory remit of BOJ, such as development banks, investment and merchant banks, credit unions, mutual funds, and trust houses, as well as insurance companies. Credit unions, under the law, originated in the 1800s and were self-regulatory. The Building Societies Act dated from 1897 and was inappropriate for a modern financial system. In other cases, laws were not amended coherently, while, sometimes, legislation was entirely absent. Some statutes were counterproductive and inimical to desirable initiative and growth.

In 1992, the BOJ extended its responsibility to cover the supervision of building societies and those industrial and provident societies engaged in deposit taking and lending. Building societies had mushroomed in numbers from six to thirty within five years, and most of the societies were classified as proprietorship, or non-traditional, as against the mutual, or traditional group. There was very little public regulation in terms of transparency, prudence, and good management. To protect their market share, the commercial banks diversified their business, resulting in tremendous growth in the number and types of non-bank activities. The system of supervision was uncoordinated and uneven. At the time, the critical players were the Bank of Jamaica, the superintendent of insurance, and the Securities Commission, and they operated independently of each other. The outcome of this development was scrambled merchandising, and the blurring of distinction between the different segments of the financial system.[32] Besides new institutions, a whole range of new financial instruments entered the market during the 1990s, with large-scale investment manifesting itself in disintermediation and reduction in franchise value of traditional commercial banking. Additionally, there was no clear definition of capital adequacy requirements for these institutions. Limits on financial exposure to related parties were inadequate. Problems of interlocking directorates existed; for example, there were board members simultaneously serving on the boards of a bank and industrial companies, which were clients of the same bank. The authority of the Inspectorate of the Bank of Jamaica to address the regulatory concerns of the sector was severely limited. It is of note that there were legal constraints which restricted the Central Bank from issuing 'cease and desist' orders.[33] Almost any commercial firm or connected individual could enter the near-bank segment, and many did. The period also saw the emergence of many financial conglomerates led by commercial banks, seeking to maximise the possibilities of regulatory arbitrage which occurred because of different cash reserve requirements, as well as different levels of supervision. Some conglomerates, besides operating a range of financial institutions, were also involved in non-financial businesses such as hotels, agricultural enterprises, and transport operations.[34] Small conglomerates came to operate commercial banking, insurance, building society, and merchant banking activities, as well as to diversify from core banking and finance activities, and entered such fields as the property market, agro-industry, and the tourism sector.

Conglomerates also had interlocking boards of directors, common management structures, and personnel, and were involved in extensive intra-group business. These conglomerates were involved in significant business expansions beyond their traditional core businesses. They were aggressively involved in innovative financial activities as well as the acquisition of a substantial number of real sector projects. Some argue that these financial conglomerates were engaged in financial activities categorised as imprudent; in addition, there were often activities related to 'round tripping' geared towards meeting the specific requirements of the regulatory institutions.[35]

With the interlocking nature of the conglomerates, serious risks of contagion existed, thus negatively impacting the stability of the entire financial sector. During the period, growth in private sector credit which had reached 70 per cent in 1993 declined markedly to approximately 25 per cent by 1996. Additionally, there was a sharp increase in non-performing loans from 7.4 per cent in 1994 to 28.9 per cent in 1997. Conglomerates also experienced problems of illiquidity, mainly resulting from increased incidents of related-party loans that occurred between insurance companies and commercial banks with which they were associated. Part of the illiquidity problem resulted from long-term investments that were supported with short-term savings. Problems of insolvency then became an emerging issue with the deterioration in the capital base of the banking sector.[36] The overall result was a phenomenal growth of the financial sector during the first half of the 1990s. Between 1993 and 1996, the financial sector grew by 114 per cent in nominal terms. The prices of real estate, in which financial institutions had made large investments, showed significant increases. Given these developments, the asset/liability mismatch of many financial institutions became highly skewed, as they used short-term deposits to purchase long-term real estate investments.

The crisis period emerged when life insurance companies started experiencing serious illiquidity problems, which were compounded by a downturn in the equity and real estate markets, which negatively impacted their affiliated commercial banks. As such, depositors became apprehensive about the capability of the local banking sector and started a withdrawal of funds from domestic banks that were perceived as weak and deposits to foreign banks, which were viewed as more stable. During the period, margins narrowed, mainly due to increased competition. Many financial sector firms that had operated for years in a culture where decisions on interest rates and exchange rates were made by the government had no staff who were trained and experienced in risk assessment; these institutions exposed themselves to risky transactions, as they competed aggressively for the limited business opportunities. A range of new financial instruments were introduced, many of them for the first time in Jamaica; these were often off-balance-sheet and defied traditional classification. An example of such a product is an equity linked insurance policy, which is primarily geared towards wealth creation, whilst providing hedges against inflation. It could be considered either as an insurance product or classified as security. In several cases, insurance companies owned or controlled banks or *vice versa*, which often led to the banking arm providing loans imprudently to the insurance arm. Insurance companies also became involved in the real estate market. The competition in diversified markets led to low overall returns on investments, high surrender rates because of the deposit-like nature of the new insurance products, elevated levels of commission on new businesses, little or no incentives for new businesses, high levels of administrative expenses, highly leveraged operations and difficulties in meeting solvency standards.[37]

The period experienced low to negative real interest rates on savings deposits, which negatively impacted savings mobilisation and also reduced the pool of funds available for loans and advances from the sector. Inefficiencies existed in the sector, with large interest rate spreads, oligopolistic market conditions in the commercial banking sector, and excessive administrative expenses. Financial repression created the conditions for a dualistic financial sector, resulting in the growth of informal financial markets including money lending and 'partner,' which is the Jamaican variant of the rotating savings and credit association.[38]

The traditional experiences of bank regulation in Jamaica prior to 1990 focused on direct controls over interest rates, exchange rate, fees, business hours, and restrictions on lines of business. In deregulating the financial sector, the government failed to introduce prudential regulation focussing on capital, or 'own fund' of these financial institutions and on introducing deposit insurance. Financial market regulation, like other forms of regulation, was necessary and needed to correct market failure. With the financial sector, market failure arises from the difficulty of financial institutions to credibly demonstrate their level of risks to their clients. In the absence of appropriate prudential regulation immediately after relaxation of the traditional controls, most of the financial institutions took on more risks than was prudent; hence, the financial sector crises of 1997 and eventual failure immediately thereafter. Failing to introduce the appropriate financial sector policies resulted in the need for FINSAC's intervention to avoid systemic failure, and this proved to be extremely expensive, with the government having to meet the costs well beyond 2002.

The Financial Sector Reforms: Liberalisation and Re-Regulation

Jamaica was starved of foreign exchange after 1989 from the international financial institutions and in particular the IADB had been very critical of the government's fiscal policies, insisting on the removal of capital and foreign exchange controls in return for faster disbursing of further trade and finance loans. The government, as part of World Bank structural adjustment and IMF stabilisation programmes, had initiated a financial sector reform, beginning in 1985.[39] The structural adjustment policy prevailed during the 1990s. There have been some significant changes in the industry, including significant developments in technology and the regulatory framework, which have impacted the financial services sector, forcing it to adapt to such changes.

The reform of the financial sector after 1989 provided for the liberalisation of interest rates, floating of the exchange rate, removal of restrictions on investments and entry to each market segment. With liberalisation, several new players entered the financial industry, and the result was that no single firm dominated any segment of the market. As market segments were small, firms seeking to expand were forced to enter new markets, resulting in individual firms operating in a multiplicity of market segments. This development is often referred to as 'scrambled merchandising' and gave rise to the domestic conglomerate financial firms. The degree of competition was, therefore, not as great as it appeared from the rise in numbers.[40] Liberalisation, which was part of the IMF market-oriented policies, brought increasing competition after widening the group of non-bank financial intermediaries, including merchant banks, money market brokers, securities dealers, pension funds management companies, money transfer operators, and specialised exchange dealers, all operating in the formal financial sector. Additionally, the financial services sector also experienced the growth of unregulated financial institutions, such as investment clubs, Ponzi schemes, money lenders, and rotating savings and credit arrangements.

One of the major stated objectives of Jamaica's financial sector reform programme was to facilitate the development of a more independent monetary policy, which was expected to be less subordinated to the financing of the fiscal deficits. According to the Bank of Jamaica (2004)[41]:

> The objective of the programme was to disentangle the effects of the dominance of fiscal policy on monetary policy. In the past, the Central Bank had accommodated large public sector deficits. However, this often undermined the ability to pursue its primary role of influencing money and credit, consistent with the achievement of moderate inflation and stable exchange rate movements.

Changes in monetary policies followed a general review in 1985. One of the main results of the review was that measures were introduced to improve the efficiency of financial intermediation, as well as to improve control of the Bank of Jamaica over monetary and credit aggregates. Policy changes were also initiated in banking supervision and prudential regulation, beginning in 1989. The modification of rules regarding capital adequacy, lending limits, loan classification, and penalties for infringing banking codes were addressed in a series of new banking and financial sector legislations. Additionally, Securities and Exchange legislation was introduced in 1993 to improve prudential standards in the securities market. In the post-liberalisation period, there were marked changes in the Jamaican financial sector, characterised by rapid expansion in assets and considerable increases in the operations of both banks and non-bank financial intermediaries (NBFIs). As of 1997, commercial banks owned 50 per cent of total assets of the entire financial sector, with the top three largest banks accounting for 75 per cent.[42] The number of NBFIs rose from eight in 1985 to twenty-five in 1993, with total assets almost doubling during the period. See table 15.13 (Appendix A).

Jamaica's Financial Sector Crisis

The financial sector crisis emerged immediately after 1996 and has been subjected to detailed analysis, by C. Kirkpatrick and D. Tenant,[43] R. Stennett, P. Batchelor, and C. Foga,[44] and C. Kirton and M. Leiba-Barnes.[45] These studies explore Jamaica's financial sector crisis from both macro and micro perspectives. Macroeconomic instability, especially when characterised by macroeconomic dislocation, can make it difficult for borrowers to repay debts in full and on time. During the early 1990s, there was declining real GDP growth in Jamaica, which became negative by 1996. This macroeconomic instability impacted negatively on the performance of firms and households. Businesses which borrowed from financial institutions experienced difficulties in debt servicing, which impaired solvency of the lenders. In addition, high inflation rates led to an overblown financial sector. However, when inflation was brought under control in the mid-1990s, the rate of growth of financial institutions' asset prices declined, impacting assets which were also used as loan collateral. As real interest rates on loans increased, the capacity of borrowers to service their loans became significantly impaired, thus increasing the levels of non-performing loans. The Latin American experience is relevant in explaining the development which took place in the Jamaican economy, R. Hausmann and L. Rojas-Suarez have argued that, in Latin American economies:

> The higher interest rates made it more difficult for domestic borrowers to service their debts to the banking system and the contraction in bank credit triggered the decline in money supply, putting further pressure on borrowers and therefore banks. On top of all this, the adverse external shock may itself have caused a decline in the quality of bank assets.[46]

Another macroeconomic explanation which has been put forward is that the financial sector was fairly loosely regulated, as many of these regulatory institutions were not adequately staffed, nor did they have the appropriate corporate structure to deal with the sophisticated operations of the new institutions and the market realities which they were mandated to supervise. G. Bonnick has argued that even the Bank Inspection Department of the Bank of Jamaica did not have the capacity to regulate the increasing complexity of the groups in which the banks and other deposit-taking institutions were located.[47] With some of these financial institutions, they could frequently use legal loopholes to accept funds from the public, as well as businesses as deposits, or for investment. Capital adequacy criteria which were used by the various authorities were frequently not followed. It was only after the financial sector crisis that the regulatory institutions introduced Basel risk-rated criteria[48] for capital adequacy analysis.

The growth of financial conglomerates also created many problems, including those related to non-transparency, possibilities for contagion, self-dealing or non-arm's-length behaviour and capital inadequacy, due to round tripping. As indicated before, the legislative and supervisory framework was not equipped to deal with the activities of conglomerates and the new market realities. Additionally, there were problems of information asymmetry. Importantly, there were no legal regulations which facilitated the exchange of information among supervisory authorities. Bonnick further argued that the laws traditionally were skewed towards preserving the secrecy of customer relations with each institution so institutions did not share information.[49] Bonnick also pointed out that, frequently, customers were simultaneously indebted to several financial institutions. Further many financial institutions could not obtain adequate documentation on collateral, so many borrowers could access more credit than could have been justified by their income position. A serious problem which emerged was the absence of a credit rating bureau. In other words, it was the macroeconomic policies of the government which created the crisis.[50]

Some economists have posited the view that the financial sector's problems were typically macroeconomic in nature. The management of many financial institutions shared this view and rarely considered themselves to be culpable in contributing to the crisis. Not unexpectedly, those who functioned as managers of the financial sector cited mainly macroeconomic reasons as explanations for the crisis.

In terms of microeconomic explanations, several have been identified in the Jamaican experience. There were links between poor financial sector regulations and poor management of financial institutions. If financial institutions are not properly regulated, their management can operate loosely, creating serious problems for the institution, the sector, and the wider economy. Persaud has argued that important microeconomic problems which impacted the operations of failed financial institutions in Jamaica were management, and absence of or failure to comply with proper internal control procedures. It is useful here to quote Persaud in some depth.[51]

> The troubled banks showed a high incidence of fraud and irregularities indicating weak control mechanisms. Loan documentation was often not perfected and, in some cases, titles to properties used in collateral could not be found. In effect a practice has developed in the sector to have borrowers sign documentation

which was then not registered with the relevant governmental agencies, nor were required stamp duties paid. The result was that lender's interests were sometimes not protected in law.

Several banks and non-banks involved in a significant amount of non-core business, especially non-financial and real sector activity, did not have the expertise in these non-core businesses, requiring managers to perform duties outside of their core competencies. Many boards of directors of financial institutions were dominated by persons without the training and experience in the management of financial institutions. Persaud also argued that there was failure to exercise due diligence and care by the board of directors of these institutions in several instances. Gladstone Bonnick extends this discussion further by indicating where foreign owned and controlled institutions operating in the same environment and using indigenous managers did not experience the same problems.[52] There was a higher incidence of fraud and irregularities in indigenous institutions, indicative of a weakness in the control environment.

Alongside poor lending practices, financial institutions were also engaged in questionable accounting practices. Property values were inflated by using market values as the basis for such valuation. Profits may also have been inflated by using the 180-day period (non-payment of principal or interest) as the period after which a loan loss reserve had to be established. However, following the introduction of the Basle Agreement, which required loan loss provisions after ninety days; this development impacted negatively on commercial banks' profitability. In addition, many commercial banks used overdraft facilities to provide finance for heavily indebted, under-capitalised businesses. As the regulations changed, these large overdrafts had to be converted into loans with fixed repayment obligations. This development had negative effects on the operations of many of the companies which were borrowing from financial institutions, since they were now faced with debt obligations.

Indigenous banks which experienced problems have argued that government policy, based on moral suasion, required that loans be offered at preferential interest rates to selected development-oriented sectors. This was explained as part of these institutions' contribution to the national development effort. The indigenous banks argued that such activity contributed to their involvement in certain risky venture capital-type projects, which sometimes were transformed into non-performing loans, thus impairing the efficiency of their operations.

Bonnick, the first executive chairman of FINSAC, cited the main causes for the failure of the financial sector came from too many banks and insurance companies, poor credit management, diversification into non-banking areas, poor portfolio management, and flaws in the investment mindset of domestic entrepreneurs in the sector.[53] While the domestic financial institutions were involved in direct investment, often undertaken at the encouragement of the government, the overseas-owned counterpart (Citibank, Bank of Nova Scotia, and Canadian Imperial Bank of Commerce) stuck to their traditional conservative lending path, including holding a high percentage of their deposits in government paper. In terms of macroeconomics, James W. Dean argued that during the latter part of the 1980s the Bank of Jamaica had adopted a policy of borrowing US dollars and other foreign currencies abroad, buying Jamaica dollars domestically at current exchange rate, lending these to importers and others as suppliers' credits, finally collecting repayment from these suppliers in Jamaican dollars after thirty to ninety days.[54] With a depreciating exchange rate, the BOJ was left with losses, since its foreign currency borrowing on behalf of the private sector suppliers translated into greatly increased Jamaican dollar costs once loans became due. When the Jamaican dollar appreciated, the outcome was the reverse, in that the BOJ made a profit. Given the deprecating Jamaican dollar, the BOJ had an interest in financial market liberalisation. By 1990, Jamaica was running a loose fiscal policy. Moreover, the overall macroeconomy was verging on instability in that the fiscal deficit had reached record heights and was rising further because of bailout efforts stemming from the 1988 hurricanes, but more fundamentally because external indebtedness was being transferred into internal indebtedness. In addition, Jamaica had been carrying massive outstanding debt, debt service payments, and fiscal deficits. In Jamaica, monetary policy had historically been subordinated to fiscal policy with the BOJ subordinated to the Ministry of Finance. The BOJ had pursued the practice of purchasing government debt and issuing deposits to the government and in return; these later became part of monetary base.

As the fiscal deficit expanded, so too did the money supply. This was compounded by the massive bilateral and multilateral borrowing of the

Seaga's administration during the 1980s and the resource transfer after the 1988 hurricane, which in the absence of being sterilised added to the monetary base. Inflation rate jumped from 8.5 per cent in 1988 to 17.5 per cent in 1988. Despite nominal depreciation, the Jamaican currency was still overvalued in real terms. This set of conditions was on top of Jamaica's commercial banks and insurance companies' high levels of under-capitalisation, being under-supervised and under-regulated, as outlined earlier. Regulation governing entry and capitalisation of merchant banks and credit unions, and regulations regarding cross-lending between banks and merchant banks, was weak, partly because directors could not be held liable for bad debts. Deposit insurance did not exist. In summary, the government had extremely limited powers over the regulation of the financial institutions in the economy. In an overvalued currency, the financial collapse was not surprising.

When deregulation of interest rates and capital control commenced in 1990, the initial consequence was a sharp depreciation of the Jamaica currency. This then fuelled inflation and led to further depreciation. The BOJ was forced to respond with sharp increases in interest rates in order to attract short-term capital from abroad and to arrest the spiralling inflation, which by 1991 had reached the unpresented level of 80 per cent. In order to fund its rapidly expanding deficit, the BOJ issued ever-increasing amounts of treasury bills, which only sustained the high rate of inflation. The Jamaican dollar went on further sharp slide. Commercial banks were still burdened with a 25 per cent primary (cash) reserve requirement, as well as a secondary requirement to hold 22–28 per cent of their assets in treasury bills. Treasury bill rates climbed to 40 per cent, forming a lucrative business for the banks, so banks became overly casual about the rest of their portfolio, extending uncollateralised loans. There was a failure on the banks in their loan recollection and as the arrears became public, the outcome was a quality flight by depositors who moved their money to the larger of local banks and the foreign banks. With severe monetary contraction, several banks soon ran into financial trouble. After failures in 1994 and 1996 of two small merchant banks, and a medium commercial bank, and with the insurance companies facing liquidity problems, the government intervened by establishing the Financial Sector Adjustment Company, which committed some J$6.3 billion package of rescue and the fast-track Bill for tighter regulation of the industry.

Developments Following the Financial Sector Crisis

The first indigenous financial institution to experience serious problems was Blaise Trust and Merchant Bank Limited. On December 18, 1994, the minister of finance, Omar Davies, assumed temporary management of Blaise. Soon after, Century National Bank experienced similar problems. This was not the first time Jamaica experienced bank failure Jamaica has recorded a history of bank failures since the nineteenth century. There were three previous cases of local bank failures, with first in 1846 when the Planters Bank failed, further difficulties followed with the Bank of Jamaica (no relation to the current Bank of Jamaica) in the 1850s. However, it was eventually acquired by Colonial Bank in 1964. In 1864, London and Colonial was established, but it ceased operation in 1865. In 1926, the Bank of British West Indies Limited was established by a New Zealander, Robert Sterling, but this bank only operated for two months before it was closed.

The government quickly introduced legislation to strengthen the regulatory framework of the sector. Two new institutions: the Financial Institution Services (FIS) and the Financial Sector Adjustment Company (FINSAC) Ltd facilitated the resuscitation of problem-plagued financial institutions and to restructure and reorganise the sector. Established in January 1997, the objectives of FINSAC are listed as follows[55]:

a. To protect the investment of policyholders, depositors, and pensioners.

b. To restore liquidity and solvency to distressed institutions.

c. To strengthen the fiscal management capabilities of intervened institutions.

d. To improve the efficiency of the sector in mobilising and allocating financial resources.

e. To create an attractive environment for investors to recapitalise financial institutions.

f. To minimise moral hazard and promote prudential behaviour.

g. To promote strong corporate governance, managerial ability, and shareholder oversight.

h. To strengthen the sector through the establishment of appropriate institutional frameworks and regulatory structures.

Initially, FINSAC's operations were to be financed by the following sources:

a. Domestic borrowing through the sale of long-term local registered stock.

b. Issue of FINSAC notes guaranteed by the government.

c. Sale of proceeds from liquidation of assets and recoveries against non-performing loans purchased including final sale of rehabilitating institutions.

d. The government funding of any shortfall at the end of its operations.

FINSAC identified three strategies for its activities: intervention, rehabilitation, and divestment.[56] The stated objective of the government was that FINSAC was to operate for a period not exceeding seven years, and the institution was not to own assets normally held by a financial institution. FINSAC was expected to provide capital injections to protect depositors, pensioners, and those insured by institutions in the financial sector. As *quid pro quo* for its capital injection, FINSAC would obtain from the intervened financial institutions a combination of representation on the board of directors, equity participation in the institution of a minimum of 25 per cent and other assets, which included non-performing loans. Following this intervention, FINSAC owned deposit liabilities of the intervened institutions, while simultaneously depositing matching funds in replacement accounts as a solvent financial institution through which depositors could have access to their deposits. Table 15.14 shows the failed Banks acquired by the government in the period 1990–98. During this period, FINSAC intervened in the following bank

As such, FINSAC had equity and/or board membership in four out of commercial banks, five out of twelve insurance companies and two merchant banks.[57] Almost all of these financial institutions which experienced problems were locally owned and managed, raising whether the problem was generic to local ownership and management.

In addition, FINSAC intervened in several non-banking institutions, including:

a. Island Life Insurance Company

b. Jamaica Mutual Life Assurance Society

c. Life of Jamaica
d. Victoria Mutual Building Society
e. Crown Eagle Life Insurance Company
f. Dyoll Life Insurance Company
g. First Life Insurance Company

The resolution of the financial sector crisis came at considerable cost to the Jamaica taxpayers. A part of the development was involuntary re-acquisition of NCB Group by government. Following the fiscal crisis in 1997, NCB, like most of the other financial entities which came to be owned and controlled by local investors, had to seek the government's support in order to avoid collapse.

Table 15.14: Failed Jamaican Banks Acquired by the Government, 1990–98

Type of Failures	Name of Bank	Date of Failure
Bankruptcy/ Assignment of deposit liabilities, licence surrendered	Buck Securities Merchant Bankers	September 1998
Temporary Management Assignment of deposit liabilities Bankruptcy Court appointed liquidator	Caldon Finance Merchant Bank	February 1998 March 1998 September 1998
Assignment of deposit liabilities, Government -enforced surrendered licence	Fidelity Finance Merchant Bank	March 1998
Purchased by the government **Financial Assistance** **Merger**	Eagle Merchant Bank LTD	March 1997 November 1997 Date of announcement of merger September 1998 April 1999
Bankruptcy/ Closure	Blaise Trust and Merchant Bank	December 1994

Type of Failures	Name of Bank	Date of Failure
Assignment of Deposit Liabilities Licence surrendered	Intercontinental Merchant Bank	November 1998
Closure **Closure**	Century National Bank Ltd Century National Trust and Merchant Bank	July 1996 July 1966
Recapitalisation purchase of non-performing loans	National Commercial Bank	February 1997
Purchase of non-performing loans	NCB Trust and Merchant Bank	March 1998
Financial assistance merger	Corporate Merchant Bank	1998 April 19998
Purchased by the government **Merger**	Eagle Merchant Bank	March 1997 April 1999
Recapitalisation **Purchase of NPL** **Merger**	Citizens Bank Ltd	September 1977 April 1999
Merger	Citizens Merchant Bank	April 1999
Purchase of Loan Portfolio **Merger**	Island Life Merchant Bank	December 1998 April 1999
Merger **Purchase of NPL**	Island Victoria Bank	July 1998 April 199
Financial Assistance **Temporary Management by MOF** **Merger**	Workers Saving & Loan Bank	February and March 1998 April 199
Recapitalisation **Liquidity support**	Billy Craig Finance and Merchant Bank	January 1998 June 1998
Assignment of Deposit Liabilities **Licence Surrendered**	Partner Merchant Bank	April 1998
Assignment of Deposit Liabilities **Licence Surrendered**	Caribbean Trust & Merchant Bank	September 1998
Purchase of NPL	Horizon Merchant Bank	June 1998

Source: Jennifer Daley, 'Examining Bank Failures in Developing Countries: Lesson from Jamaica,' *ISER*, UWI, Mona, 2007.

Government intervention involved injection of J$19.5 billion (US$350 million), consisting of J$13.5 billion of central bank advances, J$4.67 billion of the FINSAC's bonds, and J$1.3 billion of purchases of shares and assets. The net effect of this intervention was that the state came to re-acquire majority equity interest in the NCB Group. The various holdings translated into 67 per cent equity interest in the Bank, and this gave FINSAC de facto control.

FINSAC came to acquire such non-banking investments as hotels, real estate, and agro-business and divested most of these, including the Wyndham Kingston Hotel.

Mutual Life, Life of Jamaica, and several of the other financial institutions with investments in NCB group also ran into financial problems and were acquired, or major share interests were acquired by FINSAC. In March 2002, FINSAC privatised its 75 per cent interest in the new NCB banking subsidiary to Advance Investment Council (AIC) Limited for US$217 million. Some of the real estate in the group in 2001 comprised the Bay West Shopping Centre in Montego Bay, St Jago Shopping Centre in Spanish Town, as well as eight of the lots in Sunshine Village in Negril. The non-banking business, such as the hotels and the real estate, were divested separately in individual packages. An interesting development was the dominance of Caribbean investors, Trinidad, Barbados, and the Bahamas as the new owners and operators of the divested financial businesses in Jamaica.

Regulatory Developments and Changes in the Financial Sector

The regulatory structure which existed prior to the 1990s relied on self-regulation and was very inadequate. The first move by the Jamaican government to modernise the legal and regulatory framework of the financial sector was not taken until 1991. This new policy approach culminated in the amendments to the 1960 Bank of Jamaica Act in 1991; the Act was further amended in 1994, 1995, 2001, and 2002. This Act clarified the multiple responsibilities of the BOJ and increased its supervisory authority over commercial banks. Bank and specified non-bank supervision responsibilities came under the Department of Supervision of Banks and Financial Institutions within the Bank of Jamaica.

Changes in the Financial Sector's Contribution to the National Economy

The sector's contribution to total GDP grew from 1.0 per cent in 1974 to a peak of 6 per cent in 1994 and then declined to 4.3 per cent in 2005, figure 15.1 and figure 15. 2. This growth was partially associated with an increasing number of financial institutions which grew rapidly from twenty-two in the 1980s to 187 in 1996, table 15.14: Appendix A. The annual growth rate of the share of GDP of the financing services sector increased from 2 per cent in 1975, with growth peaking at 6.3 per cent in 1994. This was followed by a decline in the contribution of financial services GDP to total GDP beginning 1996 through to 1998, reflecting the impact of a financial sector crisis which saw the collapse of several commercial banks and non-bank financial intermediaries.

Figure 15.1: Contribution of Financing Services GDP to Total GDP: 1974–2005 (%)

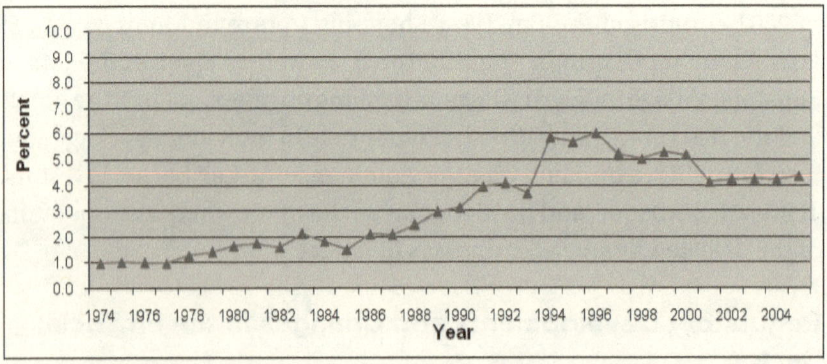

Source: Calculations from STATIN's National Income and Product Accounts – Sundry Years.

Figure 15.2: Growth Trend in the Contribution of Financing Services GDP: 1974–2005 (indices)

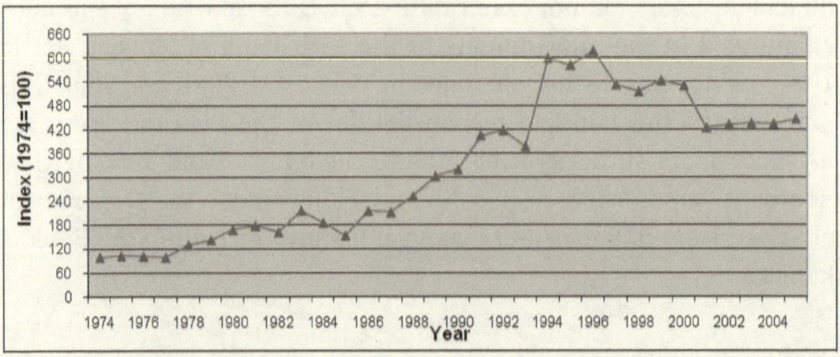

Source: calculations from STATIN's National Income and Product Accounts – Sundry Years.

Since 1998, there has been steady consolidation and increased output performance in the financial sector. At the end of March 2002, there were one hundred financial institutions, down from 187 in 1996. Of this amount in 2002, six were commercial banks, four were building societies, twenty-two were insurance companies, fifty-sixty were credit unions, two were development banks, and the rest were institutions registered under the Financial Institutions Act (FIA). In 2006, there were six commercial banks, five FIA institutions, four building societies, nineteen insurance companies, forty-seven credit unions, and two development banks, table 15.15: Appendix A.

Share of Employment

In the decade preceding the financial sector crisis, employment growth was robust in the financial sector; employment grew annually at 4.3 per cent. Inevitably though, the contraction of economic output adversely impacted the employment situation. In 1996, there were overall losses of employment in the economy amounting to thirteen thousand, while the job losses in the financial sector amounted to 653.[59] The Employment, Earnings, and Hours Worked in Large Establishments Report was first published in 1988.[60] Following the crisis, financial sector employment continued to decline steadily moving from a high of 11,636 in 1995 to its second lowest level in more than a decade of 9,581 in 2006. This represented an annual decline of 1.4 per cent over that period. In terms of contribution, Figure 15.3 shows that the contribution ratios have been declining steadily, moving from a high of 1.2 per cent in 1994 to less than 1.0 per cent in 2006.

Figure 15.3: Contribution of Financing Services Employment to Total Employment: 1986–2006 (%)

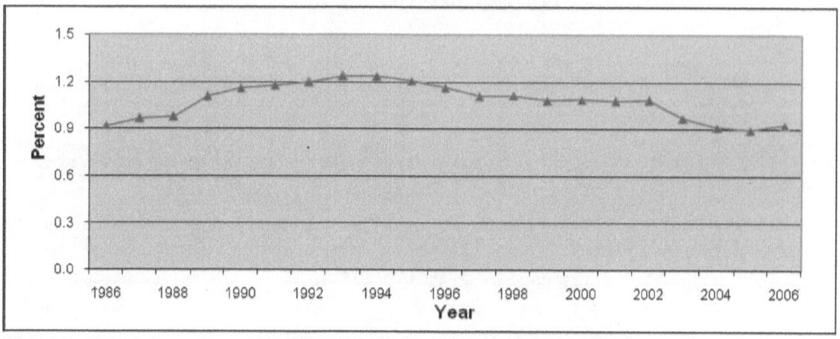

Source: Calculations from STATIN's Employment, Earnings, and Hours Worked in Large Establishments reports – Sundry Years.

Figure 15.4 shows that there has been a steady decline in the sector's contribution to employment, since 1996. This is expected, since the consolidation of many financial institutions would have significantly reduced the employment rate and furthermore, technological advancements have eliminated several jobs.

Figure 15.4: Growth Trend in the Contribution of Financing Services Employment: 1986–2006 (indices)

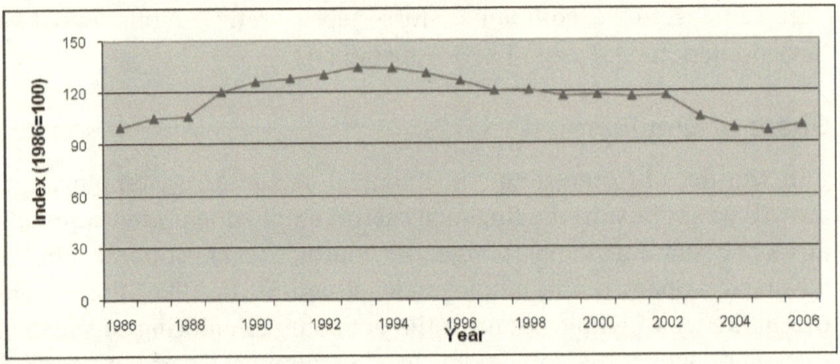

Source: Calculations from STATIN's Employ, Earnings & Hours Worked in Large Establish reports – Sundry Years.

Share in Exports

Figure 15.5 shows that there has been a relatively robust growth in financial services' contribution to services exports. The sectors contribution to total services exports grew from 0.3 per cent in 1994 to its peak position of 2.2 per cent in 2005.

Figure 15.5: Contribution of Financing Services Exports to Total Exports: 1994–2005 (%)

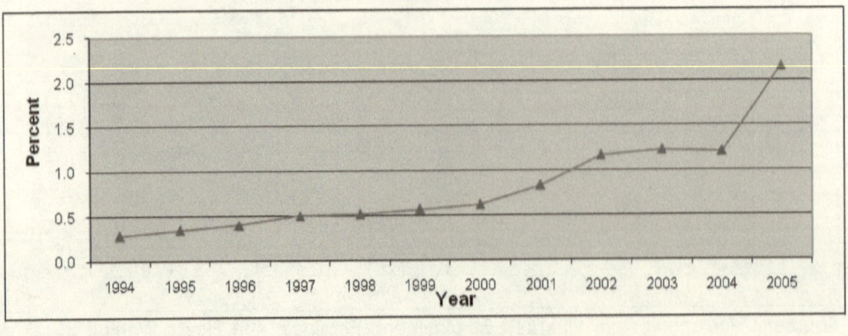

Source: Author's calculations, IMF Balance of Payments Statistics Online.

Despite the robust growth in financial services, when compared to other sectors such as tourism, financial services exports are still at the embryonic stage of development.

Notwithstanding the slowdown in the economy, following the financial sector crisis in 1996, figure 15.6 shows an improved growth trend in the contribution of financial services to total services exports. Exports grew from US$4.3 million in 1994 to US$50.36 million in 2005, representing an annual growth of 26.5 per cent over the period.

Figure 15.6: Growth Trend in the Contribution of Financing Services Exports: 1994–2005 (indices)

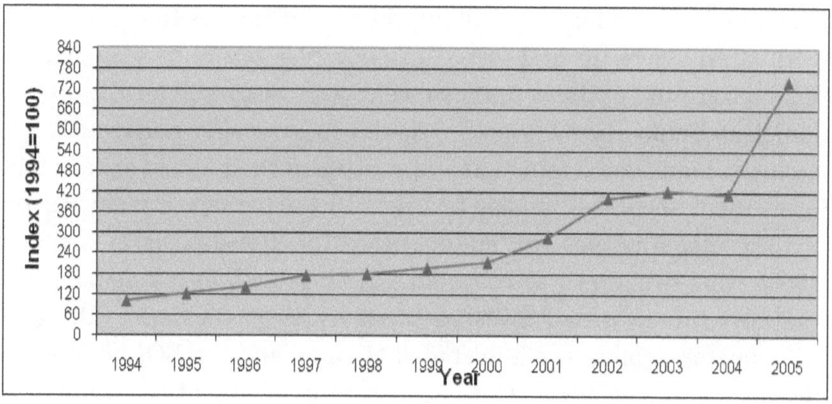

Source: Author's calculations, IMF Balance of Payments Statistics Online.

Share in Foreign Direct Investment Inflows

Because of significant data constraints, it is difficult to estimate the amount of foreign direct investment (FDI) flowing to the financial sector. However, with liberalisation and privatisation of the services sector, greater inflows of FDI have stimulated large investments in the financial services sector. Although no published data exist, the strong presence of regional financial firms in the Jamaican financial market after 1996 provides evidence of this increased level of FDI.

One of the most significant changes resulting from the 1996 financial sector crisis is that the remaining commercial banks are almost all controlled by foreign owners from Trinidad and Tobago, Barbados, and Canada. Foreign owners are much less likely to allow their Jamaican managers to take excessive and imprudent credit risks as was done in past years. In addition, competition within the sector is much more limited, due to the amalgamation of several institutions following the collapse of the sector. Many foreign-owned subsidiary banks such as BNS were unaffected by the crisis and achieved increased market share afterwards. BNS operated under strict credit underwriting standards, controls, and procedures, which were established by the Canadian head office.

The decline in domestic ownership has been a cause of concern in some quarters, fearing that the overseas owners may not respond to local development needs. The concern is that limited local flexibility may inhibit the ability of small or growing businesses to secure loans with attractive terms and rates. This, however, has to be seen against the background of the country's recent poor history of local banking. Jamaican banks currently hold a significantly smaller portion of their assets in loans and a much greater portion of their assets in cash and investment securities. It may be argued logically that a main reason for the disparity was the fall-out from the fiscal crisis of the late 1990s. This situation was compounded by growth in the demand for the government-issued investment securities in the 1990s. Through its monetary policy, the Ministry of Finance and the BOJ provided a lucrative and safe alternative to business lending by issuing low-risk and relatively high-yielding securities in the market as an inflationary management strategy; banks were able to invest in these securities, earning an attractive spread rather than undertake lending activity.

At the same time, the soundness of the financial services sector is important for the stability of the financial system and, ultimately, of the whole economy. Prudential considerations thus add a unique dimension to the subject of liberalisation of trade in financial services. This dimension is recognised, for example, in the provisions on financial services in the WTO's General Agreement on Trade in Services, which affirms that commitments to liberalise trade in financial services do not negate the right of governments to enact and maintain prudential measures designed to ensure the stability and integrity of the financial system, or to protect investors, depositors, and insurance policyholders. The prudential dimension underlines the importance of close cooperation between trade and finance officials in any negotiations on trade in financial services.

Despite the many disadvantages in financial liberalisation over time, the local financial sector increased its resilience, adapting itself itself and functions effectively in a changed situation. Ten years after the financial sector crisis, perhaps the country is now showing signs of recovery through increased employment and exports of financial sector services.

APPENDIX A

Table 15.15: The Jamaica Financial System: Number of Institutions, 1980–2000

Institutions	1980's	1990	1995	1996	1997	1998r	1999	2000	2001	2002	2003	2004	2005	2006
Commercial banks	10	11	11	11	11	9	6	6	6	6	6	6	6	6
FIA Institutions	8	26	30	30	25	18	14	11	11	10	7	5	5	5
Building Societies	4	6	25	25	13	9	5	5	4	4	4	4	4	4
Insurance Companies	n/a	n/a	10	29	29	29	25	25	25	22f	21f	20f	20f	19f
Credit Unions	n/a	n/a	80	88	73	66	65	61	58	56	52	50	48r	47p
Development Banks	n/a	n/a	3	4	4	4	4	2	2	2	2	2	2	2

P - preliminary
R - revised
F -licensed and registered under the FSC financial year ending March 31.

Source: Bank of Jamaica

APPENDIX B

Table 15.16: Jamaica's Financial System 1990, 1995, 2001, and 2006

Institutions				1995			2001			2006		
	No	Assets ($m)	% Assets	No.	Assets	% Assets	No. (a)	Assets	% Assets	No.	Assets	% Assets
Com. Banks	11	17328	62.3	11	121325	61.1	6	239087	68	6	429,969	61,6
Non-Banks		10469	37.7		77271	38.9		112745	32		267,946	38.4
Merchant Banks	21	4527	16.3	25	17334	8.7	13	15632	4.4	9	44,863	6.6
Building Societies	6	3058	11	32	29084	14.6	5	50448	14.3	4	106,219	14.8
Credit Unions	80	812	2.9	82	4098	2.1	66	17279	4.9	47	38,528	5.4
Life Insurance Companies	10	2072	7.5	12	26755	13.5	7	29386 (b)	8.4	6	78335.9 c	11.6
Total assets		27797	100		198596	100		351832	100		697,915	100

A) number of institutions refers to 1999, B) total asset at end of 2000 C) Total assets at end of 2005Source: Extracted from World Bank (2003:86), BOJ and FSC

Table 15.17: Selected Key Indicators of Financial Sector Performance, 1996–2005

	1996 DEC	1997 DEC	1998 DEC	1999 DEC	2000 DEC	2001 DEC	2002 DEC	2003 DEC	2004 DEC	2005 DEC
Real GDP _Financial sector(J$M)	13551.1	11577	11069.3	11774.5	11581.3	9388.8	9690.1	9981.5	10039.6	10463.1
Contribution to real GDP (%)	6.0	5.2	5.0	5.3	5.2	4.1	4.2	4.2	4.2	4.3
Growth Rate (%)	N/A	-14.6	-4.4	6.4	-1.6	-18.9	3.2	3.0	0.6	4.2
Average employment (000)	11.2	10.5	10.6	10.2	10.2	10.2	10.4	10.2	9.6	9.5
Total assets (J$M)	186,788	196,031	220,977	246,803	274,362	307,640	352,452	430,348	481,988	510,102
Total deposits(J$M)	129,863	147,118	154,371	164,329	188,829	204,908	230,584	256,491	298,418	322,481
Total loans(J$M)	75,016	73,534	52,900	54,305	58,752	69,587	97,719	129,168	149,501	177,288
Capital base (J$M)	8,155	4,971	8,789	21,662	23,867	27,416	30,112	34,725	40,757	48,927
Past due loans	11,196	22,004	14,163	6,940	5,619	4,732	4,505	4,688	4,487	5,131
Loan arrears/Total loans (%)	14.4	27.2	22.7	12.8	9.6	6.8	4.6	3.5	3.0	0.0
Capital base to total assets (%)	4.3	2.5	4	9.1	8.9	9.1	8.9	8.3	0.1	0.1
Loan Arrears: Capital base + provisions (%)	103.3	176.5	77.7	25.6	18.5	14.3	12.8	11.8	0.1	0.1
Pre-tax profit margin (%)	7.2	-16.1	-1.6	9.7	16	16.9	21.5	25.3	0.2	0.3

NB a) Balance Sheet data reported in the table relates to Commercial Banks, Licensees under the FIA, and Building Societies; b) Data for 1999 was not available at the time of writing

Sources: Planning Institute of Jamaica and Bank of Jamaica

Comments on the Financial Sector Privatisation Transactions

The significant transfer of wealth to employees which accompanied privatisation resulted in the policy being favourably accepted. The higher concentration of ownership which emerged since 1993, however, changed the balance of power away from the employees. This change had a crucial impact on the choice of future investments after 1993. Adams et al. concluded that, on balance, the government decided that the goal of broadening share ownership and the demonstration effect through a successful transaction were more important than the requirement of revenue maximisation, hence, the low price at offerings.[61] This represented a price-earnings ratio of approximately 7.6 NCB share, against a BNS price-earnings ratio of 14 per share, and an average of 9 for the other major commercial banks. In view of the strength of demand for the shares, the price skyrocketed opening day to reflect an increase of 67 per cent. Revenue maximisation/and efficiency were subordinated to political ends.

Notes

1. Commonwealth Economic Committee, *Commonwealth Development and Its Financing: Jamaica* (London: HMSO, 1964).
2. First National City Bank was the first United States Bank operation to be established in Jamaica, commencing operations in 1960, with a branch in Kingston.
3. Gail Lue Lim, *Jamaica's Financial System: Its Historical Development* (Kingston: Bank of Jamaica, 1991).
4. Financial services refer to services provided by depository institutions in Jamaica as well as Bank of Jamaica.
5. Lue Lim, *Jamaica's Financial System: Its Historical Development.*
6. Pauline Batchlor, Camile Foga, Gail Sue Lim and Novelette Panton, 'The Evolution of the Financial Sector in Jamaica 1970–1996,' in *The Financial Evolution of the Caribbean Community 1970–1996*, ed. Laurence Clarke and Donna Danns (St Augustine, Trinidad: Caribbean Centre for Monetary Studies Zenith Services Ltd, 1997), 299–352.
7. 1973 J$1.00 = US$1.00 – replaces Sterling as intervention currency, 1978 US1.00 = J$ 1.75; 1979 US$ 1.00 =J$1.78; 1984 US$1.00 = Range J$3.25 to J$4.75.
8. P. Chen Young, 'Financial Policy and the Banking Sector,' paper presented at the ISER, 1992.
9. Inter-American Development Bank, *Jamaica: Social Economic Report* (Washington, DC: IADB, 1990).

10. The outlays of between 1969 and 1989 was estimated at US$4.04 billion and the external debt increased to US$4.6 billion, exceeding the annual output in goods and services.
11. *Gleaner* Supplement, 'NCB 1977–1978, Fifth Anniversary,' Kingston, Jamaica, 1978.
12. Kathleen E.A. Monteith, 'Financing Agriculture and Trade: Barclays (DCO) in the West Indies 1926–1945,' in *The History of West Indian Enterprise and Entrepreneurship in Jamaica*, ed. Barry Higman and Kathleen E. A. Monteith (Mona: University of the West Indies Press, 2010).
13. Jenifer Daley, *Examining Bank Failure in Developing Countries: Lesson from Jamaica* (UWI, Mona: ISES, 2007).
14. NCB Annual Accounts, sundry years.
15. National Commercial Bank, Annual Report, 1986.
16. Roger Leeds, 'Privatisation of the National Commercial Bank of Jamaica: A Case Study,' John F. Kennedy School of Government, Harvard University, Cambridge, 1987.
17. Ibid.
18. US$1.00 = J$5.59 April 1987.
19. Money Index, March 3, 1992.
20. NIBJ, *Study on the Performance of the Privatised Companies, 1983–1990* (Kingston: NIBJ, 1991).
21. Leeds, 'Privatisation of the National Commercial Bank of Jamaica: A Case Study.'
22. The writer later came to work with Dr Letwin in the Tanzania Telecom privatisation in 1999/2001. Letwin and Redwood later became conservative members of Parliament in the UK. Both were to serve as ministers of the government of Jamaica in the UK, and Letwin and Redwood were knighted after serving as cabinet minister in David Cameron's administration. Patterson went on to become a leading partner in his own law practice in Jamaica.
23. KPMG, Peat Marwick & Partners, *Study of the Performance of Privatised Companies* (Kingston: National Investment Bank of Jamaica, 1992).
24. Cezley Sampson, 'Privatising Banking Services,' in *Management and Privatisation: Lessons Industry and Public Services*, ed. J. Prokopenko (Geneva: ILO Publication, 1990), Series No. 32.
25. NIBJ, *Study on the Performance of the Privatised Companies, 1983–1990.*
26. David Marsden, *Financial Sector Reform in Jamaica during 1985–1992: Possible Lessons for the Caribbean* (Washington, DC: IMF, 1995).
27. C. Kirkpatrick and D. Tennant, 'Responding to the Financial Crisis: The Case of Jamaica,' *World Development Report* 30, no. 11 (2002): 1939–50, DOI:10.1016/S0305-750X(02)00116-X.
28. D. Tennant and C. Kirton, 'Assessing the Impact of Financial Instability: The Jamaican Case Study,' *Nordic Journal of Latin American and Caribbean Studies* 36, no. 1 (2006): 9–36, doi.org/10.16993/ibero.181.
29. C. Kirton and M. Leiba-Barnes, 'Financial Sector Crisis in the 1990s:

Macro- and Micro-Economic Roots,' symposium on the Crisis of the Jamaican Financial Sector, University of the West Indies, Kingston, Jamaica, November 27, 1999.

30. Peter John Gordon, 'The Jamaican Economy Recent Developments and Prospects,' *Souls* (Fall 2001): 22–31.
31. Lue Lim, *Jamaica's Financial System: Its Historical Development.*
32. Bank of Jamaica, *Report of the Financial Subcommittee to the Economic and Production Council* (subcommittee of Cabinet) (Kingston: Cabinet Office, 1995).
33. Cezley Sampson, 'Post-War Structural Adjustments, Liberalisation, Public Enterprise Reforms and Privatisation: The Case of Jamaica,' department paper, Department of Government, University of the West Indies, Mona, 2007.
34. P.M. Green, 'Preserving the integrity of the Jamaican Financial System: The Challenges,' paper prepared for the Central Bank responsibility for financial stability workshop, Kingston, 1999.
35. Ibid.
36. Kirkpatrick and Tennant, 'Responding to the Financial Crisis: The Case of Jamaica.'
37. C. Malcolm, 'Outline Proposal for an Integrated CARICOM Financial Sector,' Annual Conference of the Caribbean Association of Indigenous Banks Inc., Caribbean Association of Indigenous Banks, Guyana, 2007.
38. Kirton, Clairmont (1996), 'Rotating Savings and Credit Associations in Jamaica: Some Empirical findings on Partner,' Social and Economic Studies, Vol.45.
39. Cezley Sampson, 'Post-War Structural Adjustments, Liberalisation, Public Enterprise Reforms and Privatisation: The Case of Jamaica.'
40. Cezley Sampson, 'Privatisation of National Commercial Bank Group,' department paper, MIOB, The University of the West Indies, Mona, 1996.
41. Bank of Jamaica, 2004.
42. R. Stennett, P. Batchelor, and C. Foga, 'Stabilisation and the Jamaican Commercial Banking Sector (1991–1997),' *Social and Economic Studies* 48, nos. 1/2 (1999): 345–77.
43. Ibid.
44. Stennett, Batchelor, and Foga, 'Stabilisation and the Jamaican Commercial Banking Sector (1991–1997).'
45. Kirton, Clairmont (1996), 'Rotating Savings and Credit Associations in Jamaica: Some Empirical findings on Partner.'
46. R. Hausmann and L. Rojas-Suarez, *Banking Crises in Latin America* (Washington: Inter-American Development Bank, 1996).
47. Gladstone Bonnick, 'Storm in a Teacup: Crisis in Jamaica's Financial Sector,' paper presented at the Thirtieth Annual Conference of Caribbean Centre for Monetary Studies Conference, October 1998.
48. The Basel III accord increased the minimum Basel III capital requirements

for banks from 2 per cent in Basel II to 4.5 per cent of common equity, as a percentage of the bank's risk-weighted assets. There is also an extra 2.5 per cent buffer capital requirement that brings the total minimum requirement to 7 per cent in order to be Basel compliant.

49. Ibid.
50. Paul Chen-Young, 'With All Good Intentions: The Collapse of Jamaica's Domestic Financial Sector,' Policy Paper on the Americas Volume IX, Study 12, Centre for Strategic and International Studies, Washington DC, 2003.
51. Welbourn Persaud, *Jamaica Meltdown: Indigenous Financial Sector Crash 1996* (new York: iUniverse, 2006).
52. Bonnick, 'Storm in a Teacup: Crisis in Jamaica's Financial Sector.'
53. Ibid.
54. James W. Dean, 'Can Financial Liberalization Come to Soon? Jamaica in the 1990s,' *Social and Economic Studies* 47, no. 4 (1998): 47–59.
55. FINSAC, *Annual Report* (Kingston: FINSAC, 1998).
56. Ibid.
57. Omar Davies, 'Public Sector Response to the Problems of the Financial Sector,' Ministry Paper No. 13/98.
58. Bank of Jamaica, *Bank of Jamaica: The First 40 Years 1961–2000* (Kingston: BOJ, 2004).
59. STATIN's Employment and Earnings in Large Establishments Reports.
60. It provides statistics on the number of employees, salaries, wages, and hours worked in establishments employing ten or more persons provided the only source of data on employment in financial services..
61. Christopher Adams, William Cavendish and Percy Mistry, *Adjusting Privatisation: Case Studies from Developing Countries* (London, Heinemann,1992)

CHAPTER SIXTEEN

Electricity Industry Development, Privatisation of JPSCo, and Industry Regulatory Reform

SPONSORED BY

FESCO

THE EARLY YEARS OF ELECTRICITY DEVELOPMENT

Jamaica's electric utility history presents an interesting case to review institutional structures from the several regulatory regimes, industry structures, and ownership structures that have prevailed over the last ten decades. Electricity supply in Jamaica goes back to the 1892, when the Jamaica Electric Light Company Limited (JELC), with a licence secured under the Electric Lighting Act of 1892, constructed a small coal-fired steam-driven plant, equipped with a 'Perkin Parker' engine. The JELC was located at the corner of Gold Street and Harbour Street in Kingston and remained a generating site for decades.

Electricity came to Jamaica thirteen years after Thomas Edison's electric lamp was introduced. The first town to receive electricity was Black River in the parish of St Elizabeth which was supplied to the Lynden brothers. The electricity supply at the time comprised arc lamps utilising carbon electrodes. The JELC was subsequently acquired in 1898 by Jamaica Electric Light and Power Company (JEL&P).[1] Another electricity firm, West India Electric Company (WIEC), established offices in 1897 at 151 Orange Street, Kingston, and operated a mule-driven tramcar. It later obtained a licence to produce electricity to replace animal power. The WIEC built one of the first hydro plants in the world on the Rio Cobre, near the Bog Walk Gorge, to supply electricity to the tramway urban transport system in the old capital, Spanish Town, and lower sections of St Andrew.

A severe earthquake struck the city of Kingston in 1907, ruining much of the property of JEL&P. The owners operated JEL&P up to 1923, when the newly formed Montreal-based Jamaica Public Service Company Limited (JPSCo) came into being that year and purchased the assets of WIEC, including the tramway system. It expanded the power capacity by installing a coal-burning power plant at Gold Street in Kingston. While the financing for JPSCo came from Canada, the US firm, Stone, and Webster Inc, provided management expertise.[2] Stone and Webster eventually came to own 20 per cent of JPSCo stocks. At the time of acquisition in 1925, the total connected customers amounted to 3,958, comprising the wealthy elites in lower St Andrew.

Between 1931 and 1947, several companies were awarded electricity licences in different parts of Jamaica. Over time, JPSCo acquired several of these operators and their licences, purchasing the last of the small power companies, a Savanna-la-Mar firm, in 1966. JPSCo became the sole supplier of electricity for public sale. Following negotiations to expand the power capacity to meet the needs of the economy, JPSCo was given an all-island franchise under a new twenty-five-year licence in 1966. JPSCo's customers increased from 3,958 in 1925 to 203,600 in 1960.[3]

JPSCo found itself, from the several acquisitions, with over 26 licences for different areas, often with different standards. Most of these had to be renewed annually, and the uncertainty created by the annual renewals made it difficult for the company to obtain long-term financing. This was unlike the Jamaica Telephone Company (JTC) which operated under a single forty-year licence granted in 1925. As a condition of a World Bank loan in 1966, the government converted these licences into a twenty-year exclusive licence for the entire island (the All-Island Licence). Arising out of a decision, the frequency was standardised in the late 1960s at fifty cycles per second (c/s) with the voltage supplied to residences at 110/220 volts. Other voltages mainly, 440 volts, were available for industrial use. The rates paid by consumers were also standardised.

Characteristics of the Electricity Industry in the 1960s and 1970s

In 1959, the installed capacity of JPSCo was 146,000 kW, with sales mainly going to manufacturing and commercial users and with residential users accounting for less than 20 per cent. The 1960 census showed that only 22 per cent of Jamaicans had electricity. In the 1960s and 1970s, the market for electricity in Jamaica was segmented into public service electricity and private electricity, with the bauxite companies, the Cement Company, and the sugar industry generating the bulk of electricity (self-generators) produced by the private sector. Public service electricity was further segmented into residential, commercial, industrial, and municipal street lighting. Electricity sales by 1972 amounted to 947,336 MWh of which 30 per cent was sale to residential consumers, 46 per cent to commercial and small industrial consumers, and 14 per cent to large industrial consumers. Net generation in 1972 was 1.107 million MWh and systems loss were 13.6 per cent, reflecting theft by consumers through illegal connections, as well as transmission and distribution technical lines losses. These losses have had a significant impact on both the overall electricity rates and the profitability of the company. The operating revenues for 1972 was J$20.8 million.

The inadequacy of the electrical generating capacity led the JPSCo and the government to negotiate external funding in 1966 to meet the increasing demand. This was provided through a government guaranteed World Bank loan of US$22 million and expanded power generation, transmission, and distribution capacities. Other forms of external funding were raised to meet the cost of installing larger and more modern generating stations at Old Harbour, Hunts Bay, White River, Roaring River, Rio Bueno, and Maggoty. The main generating points of Hunts Bay and Old Harbour were equipped with steam turbines, while White River, Roaring River, Rio Bueno, and Maggoty were equipped with small hydro-electric plants. From as early as the 1960s, approximately 95 per cent of generating capacity was heavy fuel based. Several small diesel units were also installed in various parts of the island. With completion of this programme, installed capacity exceeded peak demand, providing a comfortable reserve margin. During the mid-1970s, however, the condition and efficiency of the plants were allowed to deteriorate to where, by 1978, disruption in the power supply became a daily experience, resulting in significant problems for manufacturing companies and householders. Many wealthy customers and industries installed their own backup diesel-powered standby plants to avoid the consequences of the constant failure of the JPSCo system.

Private Ownership and Public Regulation of Electricity

The JPSCo utility, like telephone and urban public transport under private ownership, was initially regulated by 'ad hoc' rate board system. The rate board had the disadvantages of structural information asymmetry.[4] In the period of rate board regulation, the company operated with little or no government interferences and was allowed 8 per cent real return on capital, a satisfactory return in an environment of low inflation. The regulatory structure comprised long-term licences (or contracts), with the right to appeal to the courts, providing an avenue to the private investor to challenge government's opportunistic actions.

In the 1970s, electricity rates were frozen by legislation. The accusation by the government was that JPSCo was financing development capital through increased rates, rather than equity or loan capital. With this development, the relationship between the JPSCo and government became more problematical after independence in 1962. This set of protracted disputes between the parties culminated in the government enacting the Electricity Development Act and the Electricity Authority in 1958, giving it the power to generate its own electricity and to interconnect with JPSCo's transmission grid. The bauxite companies could take advantage of the Electricity Development Act and self-suppled their own generation needs. Coincidentally, these problems arose just at the time the JPSCo licence was coming up for renewal in 1966.

With raising expectations from independence, the government sought expansion of services to meet increasing demand, however the debenture holders of JPSCo responded by arguing that the company's financing arrangement precluded it from carrying out expansion, unless its electricity rates were increased. The government in the 1960s took the position that rate increases which JPSCo had applied for, like the increases requested by JTC, the telephone company, was not the right environment to undertake licence renewal. After protracted negotiations, JPSCo accepted a new exclusive All Island Licence in 1966, giving it exclusive right over electricity transmission, distribution, and retail supply. Most importantly, exclusivity was not granted for electricity generation. JPSCo also bound itself to be regulated by the PUC Act and the newly created Public Utilities Commission (PUC). Raphael Swaby commented that the creation of the PUC was a radical and fundamental new regulatory policy innovation, at a time, especially when the country was embarking on self-government.[5] The creation of the PUC signalled the intention of the government to exercise a more stringent regulatory control over the privately owned utilities, based on north American precedents, combining the power of the Federal Power Commission and the Security and Exchange Commission, in a manner subject to interpretation against a large body of American precedents.

Although the newly awarded licence did not provide for a rate increase, the government agreed to provide a guarantee to a loan, being offered by the World Bank, to enable JPSCo to finance an agreed expansion programme. At the time of the granting of the new licence in June 1966, Stone and Webster was the largest shareholder in JPSCo. The company, for the first time shortly after 1966 listed on the JSE, along with its listing on the London Stock Exchange, and made most of its board members Jamaican citizens, which was a requirement of the new licence.

The PUC Act also gave the portfolio minster the authority to licence enterprises to generate and supply electricity for public use. At the same time, the Electricity Development Act gave the government through the portfolio minister the authority to own, operate, and develop electricity. It was the Electricity Development Act that the government used through the minister to acquire shares in JPSCo between 1971 and 1974. Further, in order to expand the use of electricity from the low levels existing in the rural areas, the government established the Rural Electrification Programme Limited (REP) in 1975, a programme funded by the Inter-American Development Bank (IADB).

In the period of the PUC regulation of JPSCo, like with the JTC in the telephone sector, major problems were encountered in ratemaking. The PUC system followed a quasi-judicial North American public hearing procedure, which were not features of English and Commonwealth jurisprudence, requiring the PUC to rely on North American precedents.

In its responsibility for rate regulation, the PUC adopted a formula for rate changes that would afford the company a reasonable return on equity (as against a fixed return under the rate board system), based on original cost of the company's equipment (for such purposes, cost as far back as 1953 was recognised.) JPSCo made the first application to the PUC in 1969, and the hearing lasted until 1970. Major disagreement developed between JPSCo and the Commission during the hearings regarding the definition of the rate base, the accounting procedure, the defemination of the cost of capital, what was 'fair' rates of return, and the procurement practices of JPSCo. Whereas the US utilities, under ROR price fixing were required to show their assets at historical cost, ignoring all revaluation, JPSCo's management periodically revalued the company's assets at current replacement cost, allowing the company to inflate the values of its equity to support higher dividend payments. Plants were shown not at original 1953 (book value) and assets which were absolute, or written-off, were still carried on the books. At the same time, JPSCo was paying Stone and Webster 20 per cent of cost of capital projects regarding the Old Harbour power plant for commissioning fees.

The methodology adopted in ROR ratemaking usually states as follows: (original cost depreciation) X-rate of return + (operating and maintenance expenses). Costs are usually taken as historical; however, in the US, costs were taken on a prospective bias. Tariffs are derived by determining the revenue requirement of the regulated business, and then allowing responsibility for paying the cost of defined classes of customers (residential, commercial, and industrial), based on cost of actually providing the service to each class. At the Federal level in the US, the regulator FERC is only required to set rates that is 'just and reasonable,' with the outcome that the courts were left to determine what was meant by just and reasonable. Rate of return regulation encourages over investment 'gold plating'[6] and induces firms to settle for inefficient capital/labour ratio, as the more capital the firm uses, the more it is allowed to earn higher profits. Using historic cost also cannot account for rising inflation in periods of increasing cost trends. The process is also administratively burdensome and costly. At the same time, there is the problem of regulatory lag.[7]

The rate-on-rate base of Jamaica was 8.4 per cent, against 7.4 per cent submitted in the application and the rate of return on equity was 13.5 per cent, with JPSCo claiming it needed 13 per cent to 16 per cent return on equity. Galdstone E. Mills commented that the PUC regulatory rate-making process was turbulent, characterised by lengthy and adversarial rate hearings.[8] The World Bank in its review of the process, concluded that American style quasi-judicial, cost of return regulation was inappropriate for Jamaica, and that the system was a failure. Jamaica lacked the other institutions needed to make such a system work.[9] The US had developed rules of administrative process, affording substantial guidance; Jamaica had no such checks and balances.

Regulation of JPSCo During Public Ownership under the PNP

Only two days after the PNP had won the election, a second-rate application was made on March 1, 1972. JPSCo was successful in its request, obtaining a 29.5 per cent rate increase, effective May 1, 1972. These increases were in sharp contrast to the 1960s when, under private ownership, JPSCo could not secure rate increases through the Rate Board. Soon after the government acquired equity interest in JPSCo, a rate increase was granted for the first time in several years.[10] In order to cope with the adverse financial impact from the rapid escalation in oil price in 1974 on JPSCo, as well as the negative impact from the decline in the exchange rate, automatic monthly adjustments were introduced to the form of a fuel clause, being passed on to consumers in their monthly bills.[11] With the automatic increases from the fuel clause, consumers experienced sharp increases in electricity tariffs in Jamaican dollars.

In February 1974, JPSCo, under state ownership, made an application requesting the fuel clause adjustment to be calculated after thirty days, instead of the then requirement of sixty days.[12] From the early 1950s fuel cost has always had a major impact on rates. Prior to 1970, the fuel charge was not significant and varied between J$0.06 cents per kWh in 1972 and J$4.36 per kWh in 1974. With the oil price increase in 1974, JPSCo's operating expenditure went up from J$3.7 million to J$23.1 million, and fuel accounted for most of this increase. Rising inflation and devaluation triggered another rate application in May 1974. This application was also successful, and a 39 per cent increase was awarded. This was followed by another 42 per cent rate increase in December 1975, plus an additional cost-of-service adjustment of 1 per cent per month, effective January 1976. In March 1977, the cost-of-service charge was rolled into the tariff. In September 1977, a cost-of-service charge of 1.5 per cent per month was re-introduced. The fuel charge component had been in operation since 1924.

Following from the various disputes with the overseas equity owners, the government decided in 1971 to purchase all the 20 per cent stocks of Stone and Webster and then followed this up by acquiring most of the outstanding shares from private investors, so it eventually ended up owning 99 per cent of the company's equity. The other private shareholders of JPSCo by 1974 were also more than willing to sell their shares when the PNP administration announced its decision to acquire the outstanding stocks remaining in private hands, which amounted to a form of regulatory expropriation.

Regulation of the privately owned vertically integrated utility in Jamaica not only proved to be difficult and adversarial, but regulation via the American-style utility commission arrangement was also a failure. With compulsory acquisition of the rest of the company's shares in 1974, the end of the first chapter of the company's history, that of eighty-two years of private ownership, ended.

Rationale for State Ownership of Monopoly Electric Utilities

Between 1974 and 2001, JPSCo was largely state-owned, also being the monopoly provider of electricity. Under the socialist ideology, several arguments were advanced to support state ownership of utilities in Jamaica. When the state acquired JPSCo, the view was that private ownership and pubic regulation through the PUC had failed and as a natural monopoly electricity as part of the commanding heights of the economy and an essential service which should be owned by the state. Ownership of electricity was deemed to be central to sovereignty of the country; therefore, it should be constituted as a national responsibility, with the central objective being that of economic development, rather than for commercial profit. Electricity should not be left to the 'hidden hands' of the market. With government ownership, it was possible to address the wider social and development objectives of society as the objectives of transnational firms lacked developmental vision, as shown inexperience in the sugar industry.

There was the belief that the state could succeed where markets appeared to fail. Further the Jamaican domestic capital market displayed a reluctance to invest in low-yield long-gestation investments, leading inevitable to foreign direct control; a return to economic dependency and colonisation. Adlith Brown pointed out that one argument in favour of public ownership is that it reflected largely the greater responsibility for accelerating economic development assumed by the state because of political independence.[13] Even the official international financial agencies: IMF, World Bank, and the main bilateral funding agencies equally accepted the position of a strategic role for the electric and other utilities in the process of economic development in the years of the 1950 and 1960s. In fact, many of the state-owned power projects were initiated and financed by these agencies.[14]

PNP's Administration Rate Making of JPSCo as an SOE

In 1974, the PNP administration offered a subsidy on electricity to ease the burden on the poor, in the wake of the rapid rise in oil prices. This subsidy was later discontinued, but the problem of financing electricity generation remained. The government could finance from central government revenues, calling on the general taxpayer, or cross-subsidisation, which involved subsidisation by the higher-income groups who actually used most of the electric service. There was no evidence of any significant level of cross-subsidisation in favour of the poor in the 1970s. Large commercial users in 1976 were paying less per kWh than residential consumers, who paid the highest rates.

The rate differences between the two groups were reported to reflect the higher distribution costs for residential consumers, as well as the lower unit cost for larger blocks of power. Between 1970 and 1975, the cost of electricity went up from 1.48 Jamaican cents per kWh to 6.70 cents per kWh for residential consumers. In 1975, industrial users paid 4.5 cents per kWh, lower than the rate paid by residential customers. In several other regimes in developing countries, industrial customers were required to cross-subsidise residential customers.

With JPSCo in 1975 under full public ownership, the aftermath of nationalisation, the PUC became redundant. Minister Eric Bell, who had established the Advisory and Monitoring Unit (AMU) within the Ministry, added responsibility for the AMU to advise the Minister on rate matters relating to JPSCo and other public utilities. The AMU listed the following considerations as the main criteria for rate fixing: social considerations; external economic costs and benefits; the inflationary potential of utility rate increases; the substitutability of the product and consumer resistance, and that a controlled utility, especially a government-owned monopoly providing an essential service, was not entitled to speculative profits at the expense of the consumer.[15]

With the regular increases in fuel cost, JPSCo was forced to go back to the minister in 1978 and the basic rate was increased by 15 per cent in June 1978. A month later, a 2 per cent cost-of-service adjustment was reintroduced because of further devaluation of the Jamaican dollar. In

1978, the JPSCo obtained a new licence, which allowed the company to revalue its assets annually. Consequently, a significant proportion of the company's capital reflected the capital reserve generated by the revaluation, rather than new government equity capital. The 1978 licence stipulated that the JPSCo was expected to generate sufficient revenues to meet its operating costs, besides 30 per cent of its capital needs.

Although the PUC Act remained on the books up to the passing of the multi-sector regulatory OUR Act in 1995, no commissioners were appointed after 1975 and hence the Commission remained dormant until it was abolished. During the period 1975–97, the power of rate regulation was transferred to the sector minister. At the same time, this minister protected investors' interests, carrying out shareholder monitoring, while controlling the monopoly power of the state-owned utility and protecting consumers' interests. The only independent source of addressing consumers' concerns against the bureaucracy of the state and the monopoly of utility was through the Office of the Utilities Ombudsman, and his authority was limited to conciliation, as he had no powers over the actions of the utilities or the portfolio minister.

In addition to providing for the portfolio minister to assume responsibility as the electricity industry regulator, several other fundamental changes to the licence were also made. The provision regarding shares being made available to citizens of Jamaica was removed. An 8 per cent return on rate base, which was part of an earlier licensing system, was removed. In fact, all the provisions relating to rate base and rate of return were removed and prices were no longer subjected to any limitations. Despite the removal of the 8 per cent rule, determination of rates, however, were guided by the 8 per cent return per annum on revalued asset principle, being a World Bank condition on its loans to the government for on lending to JPSCo.

The licence and the amendment after 1975, therefore, moved away from the American rate base system of rate making of quasi-judicial public hearings, and gave considerable flexibility, discretion, and authority to the portfolio minister. Although the AMU could review and advise on utility tariffs and investment, the final decision rested with the minister.

The basic problem of regulation during this period was that consumers became concerned that their interest was no longer taken into consideration, and this triggered regular public protests. The minister came to be seen to protect the interest of the investor at the expense of the consumers. Sharp conflicts were encountered between the minister's role as the representative of the owner/investor and the need for reasonable returns on public investment, and his role as representing the consumers' interest. Over this period, the electricity and telephone utilities could never operate as autonomous commercial firms, and effectively became an arm of government itself, with high levels of ministerial intervention in pricing, investments, employment, wage determination, and procurement. In much the same way as in the UK in the post-war years, the long-term commercial interest of the enterprises was subordinated for broader short-term political and macroeconomic objectives.

State ownership of the electricity utility and ministerial regulation between 1975 and 1997 did not resolve the problem of providing efficient utility services. The loss making, which resulted, was not only because of subsidy pricing policies but also because of poor management, poor maintenance of the system, and major dis-investment in the company. The pricing policy of the PNP administration, which required the utilities to meet only operating costs and to contribute 30 per cent of its capital needs, effectively reflected cross-subsidisation by taxpayers. No sooner did the PNP come to power that rate increases were granted to the publicly owned JPSCo, which had been denied to the privately owned JPSCo. Adlith Brown and Helen McBain stated that, even with the subsidy, there was still the need for frequent price increases.[16] It is of note that when the government acted as a regulator of the privately owned utility; it denied JPSCo of price increases in keeping with cost increases, arguing that the consumers could not pay for the increase. Sometimes increases were refused for political reasons, in that the increase would have had to be implemented when elections were due. However, when the government was the owner and responsible for the company's financial obligations, substantial price increases were granted to the utilities. The industry's monopoly in the market also facilitated trade union opportunism, in that the unions could secure wage increases which could not be justified by increases in productivity. For example, in 1976, wage increases awarded to JPSCo workers averaged 71 per cent, while urban transportation utility averaged 90 per cent.[17]

Deregulation of the Generation Market and Introduction of PPPs in the 1990s

The JLP administration, which succeeded the PNP for most of the 1980s, reversed the PNP's subsidy pricing policy under pressure from the multilateral lending agencies, requiring the utilities and other public enterprises to earn 8 per cent real return. With the sharp devaluation of the Jamaican dollar from J$1.78 to J$5.13 against the US dollar in 1984, electricity prices experienced two further sharp increases, first by 40 per cent in January 1984 and then 54 per cent in May that same year.[18]

Prime Minister Seaga's policy in the 1980s was also against the privatisation of JPSCo, and this was despite his decision to privatise the telephone company in 1985. The decision to allow the introduction of independent power producers (IPP) into the industry and to demonopolise the generation segment in early 1991 was based primarily on the need to secure capital for the development of the generation segment and relieve the government budget of the cost of financing JPSCo, rather than any belief in the inherent superiority of private capital and competitive markets. More than anything else, it had been the large sums of capital needed to meet the expansion and upgrading of JPSCo, which forced the PNP administration in the 1990s to accept deregulation of the generation business and a policy to privatise JPSCo.

Electricity capacity studies in early 1990 indicated that US$257 million of expenditure was needed over the five-year period up to 1997 to meet the capital investments needed to satisfy increased electricity demand and replacement of obsolete plants, as well as to ensure that the JPSCo did not become a bottleneck in the system, constraining future economic growth. The total estimated new capacity projected for JPSCo for the ten-year period to 2000 was 1,052 MW. In the first five years, the projection was for 440 MW, of which 230 MW, or 50 per cent was to meet requirements for replacements of old and obsolete plants. The overall capital projection was US$1 billion for the ten years.[19] With serious restrictions imposed by the Treasury and with a feeble financial structure, the option of the utilities competing in the private commercial market for capital was not seen as a practical one. A public share offer on the Jamaica Stock Exchange was also ruled out.

In 1991, the JPSCo electric grid system comprised a single vertically and horizontally integrated company, with 443 MW of installed capacity. Approximately, 68 per cent was steam powered; 25 per cent diesel/gas turbines, and 5 per cent (24 MW) hydro. Peak demand in 1990 was 325 MW, giving a reserve margin of 35 per cent. Private operators, mainly the mining and sugar companies, continued to self-generate electricity; their installed capacity of 265 MW was almost 50 per cent of JPSCo's installed capacity.[20] Small exchanges of power took place between JPSCo and the private Bauxite company's self-generating plants connected to the national grid. Generation cost accounted for approximately 70 per cent of system costs. Fuel, mostly heavy, accounted for 60 per cent of generation cost and was supplied to JPSCo under the San José Accord, a bilateral agreement between Jamaica, Mexico, and Venezuela. This Accord provided Jamaica commercial concessions on its fuel oil purchases and the agreement had been in place since the 1970s.[21]

The transmission system consisted in 1990 of 170 circuit miles (272 km) of 138 Kv lines and 445 circuit miles (712 km) of 69 Kv lines, while the primary distribution system comprised seven thousand miles (11,200 km) of distribution lines. REP had proven to be highly successful in connecting the rural community to the national grid, increasing the level of connection from one hundred and sixteen thousand in 1970 to three hundred and five thousand connected customers by 1990, a more socially acceptable level. For the year 1990, the level of access to electricity was estimated at 80 per cent compared to 20 per cent in 1960. In the 1970s, the historical growth in demand was 3.3 per cent, followed by 2.2 per cent growth to 1985 and increasing to 6.1 per cent by 1990.[22] This expansion in connection formed part of the national objectives of both successive administrations over the 1980s and 1990s.

Jamaica's per capita consumption of electricity in the 1990s was about 2,000 kWh per person, which was relatively high and can be attributed to the high use of energy in the alumina industry. In fact, over the period 1972–85, residential consumers reduced their household consumption from 2,483 kWh to 1,505 kWh. During the 1980s, there was adverse public reaction to frequent power failures, despite JPSCo spending major sums on power plant rehabilitation programmes in 1982–85. In addition to major repairs to the steam generating units, the rehabilitation programme included the installation of a slow-speed diesel unit capable of generating 40MW, at a heat rate of just over eight thousand BTU/kWh. With this equipment in place, by the end of 1985 significant improvements were experienced in the power supply, with a marked reduction in power failures and voltage fluctuations.

Electricity prices were held down for most of the period 1965–74 by both the JLP and PNP administrations, with the effect that JPSCo was forced to operate at a loss for a significant part of its life after Jamaica's independence in 1962. Although intended as part of a policy to redistribute income to the poor, the main beneficiaries from this subsidisation policy were the middle classes, the main users of electricity. For the period 1975–80, the financial performance of JPSCo was inconsistent, with profits in some years and losses in other years (majority years being loss). JPSCo, with its inadequate source of income, over-staffing and high wage rates had to rely on the government for almost all its capital expenditure needs during this period. With inadequate funds and under-maintenance in the system, efficiency fell sharply, accompanied by regular load shedding, frequent intermittent power outages, and irregular voltages. The utility's systems losses increased from 17 per cent to 22 per cent, and over 50 per cent of this was non-technical loss, mostly theft of electricity.

The failure of the publicly owned JPSCo was evidenced by the time customers had to wait to obtain new service connections. Regular power outages and escalating prices triggered a call from the public for private ownership in the early 1990s. With public complaints, a result of the poor performance of JPSCo, financial pressure on the central budget, pressure from the IMF and World Bank to privatise major state assets and unfavourable press reports, combined to pressure, first to liberalise the generation market and ultimately to abandon a policy of public ownership of the electric utility.

The period 1985–90 also experienced a tapering off of price increases, outside of the fuel clause adjustment, so the financial performance of JPSCo up to 1990 continued to present a poor state of affairs. A 37 per cent increase in the basic tariff granted in 1990 reflects long-run marginal cost. The previous tariff setting system, which was based on declining block structure did not reflect marginal cost and was abandoned, following a major tariff review in 1989.[23] Electricity prices for residential householders in 1990, after the increases, amounted to just under US¢14/kWh with bulk, or wholesale electricity rates of US¢7.5/kWh.

It was these forces that combined to pressure Prime Minister Patterson in the early 1990s to privatise JPSCo. However, state capitalism had provided major economic power to a group who, in the past, were disenfranchised from the halls of power, and this group (board members and advisors of the public enterprises) was not inclined to see this power disappear, without offering strong resistance. Some managers rewarded themselves with compensation packages which became an embarrassment to the administration in power, as was the case reported at the National Investment Bank of Jamaica in 2001, which led to the resignation of two senior public sector managers. There was public outcry against these developments. This decision and the method of privatisation of the electricity sector, following the controversy of privatising the telecommunications monopoly to a foreign owner in 1987, forced the government to give more attention to the industry structure in considering the electric utility deregulation and privatisation, resulting in a structure providing initially for de-monopolisation of the generation segment in early 1991 and ease of entry.

The policy change allowed for the initial purchase of 130 MW of new generating capacity from independent power producers (IPPs). The bilateral funding agencies: World Bank, Inter-American Development Bank and International Finance Corporation provided over US$200 million as credit to facilitate entry by the IPPs. Introducing IPPs into the system followed a course of competitive bids and twenty-year 'take or pay' contracts, backed by government's sovereign guarantees.[24]

Three private power plants came on stream over the period 1993–96: a twenty-year contract for a US$103 million 72 MW medium speed diesel plant, next door to the main JPSCo power station at Old Harbour, developed by Jamaica Energy Partners Limited (JEP), a locally registered company of Wartsila Power Development Inc., of the US; a twenty-year contract for US$144 million 60 MW low-speed diesel plant at Rockfort, Kingston, owned by Jamaica Private Power Ltd (JPPL), a joint venture of Mohawk Power Company, International Energy Finance Limited and US Energy Corporation, and a three-year contract for a US$30 million 42 MW turbine plant at Bogue, St James developed by Kenetech Energy System. Inc.[25] Kenetech later sold 99 per cent of its investments to another US-based investor, Quixx Corporation. All the contracts went to overseas syndicates, mostly American interests. The large auto-generators at the sugar factories, and the cement plant produced supplies over their own demand and were also allowed, for the first time, to contract with JPSCo grid for the supply of bulk, or wholesale electricity.

The Electricity Market Structure for Privatisation

With the removal of the monopoly for the generation business, Jamaica's electricity industry entered the first phase of competition, that of competition for market, ending the vertically integrated industry structure with one monopoly operator, moving away from full monopoly, marking a significant market liberalisation milestone. The market was organised around JPSCo as the single buyer, still a vertically integrated company. The JPSCo, however, retained the legal monopoly for transmission, distribution, retail supply, and despatch, whilst owning significant generating capacity. The IPPs were allowed to compete for additional long-term generation capacity with JPSCo. The IPPs, however, had to sell all their bulk power to JPSCo. This form of competition is known as 'competition in the market,' where selling agents (generating companies) compete to participate in the supply curve to meet electricity demand (the load curve) on a given day; offers from the various suppliers are accepted in order of increasing cost until there is enough energy accumulated to fulfil the load curve[26] and differs from '*competition for the market*.'

The variety of market structures emerging globally from the reform of the power sector in the 1980s can be categorised according to the increasing competition afforded in the market. Essentially, there are four market structures: monopoly, single buyer, wholesale competition and/or fully liberalised, or retail competition.[27] The monopoly electricity market involves no competition at all since the market comprises a single vertically integrated electricity utility (state or privately owned) at all levels of the supply chain within a country or region. With the single buyer, or purchasing agent model, a single bulk purchaser is designated to facilitate competition for additional long-term capacity. It is generally accompanied by monopoly for the distribution sectors and electricity services is provided to consumers under regulated terms. With a single buyer, the industry structure can remain as one vertically integrated company, or it can be unbundled into three businesses: generation, transmission, and distribution, or simply separation of generation from a vertically integrated transmission and distribution/ retail company. The greater the degree of unbundling, the easier it is to accommodate competition later and to regulate the natural monopoly transmission and distribution network. Opportunities for competition can be maximised at the generation and retail market levels.

With wholesale power market, distributors and large users can be allowed to purchase electricity directly from generators that they choose, either in a power market, or bilaterally, and to transmit the electricity under non-discriminatory open access arrangements over the power network to points of consumption (retail users). Independent power suppliers (firms that specialise in energy trading, but do not own or operate distribution network) can then be allowed to compete with the large customers or larger users. Retail competition, on the other hand, involves much more complex trading platforms and is normally designed to allow all end users of electricity (including residential consumers) to choose their suppliers with open access provided to the transmission and distribution network, allowing for the procurement of their supplies competitively at the wholesale level from generators and electricity suppliers. Wholesale and retail competition are usually accompanied by full vertical unbundling of the industry structure into generation, transmission, distribution, and retail businesses and horizontal unbundling of generation. With JPSCo, the view was that the size of the network was too small and that a higher level of unbundling would have been too complex for Jamaica, and it would also have been challenging for the consuming public to comprehend.

The de-monopolisation of the generation sector which had taken place was based on the principle that generation was no longer a natural monopoly and could be opened to at least entry competition. New technologies such as distributed power and combined cycle generation system, using gas turbine (with natural gas as the fuel) to produce the electricity and with system efficiency of 50–60 per cent changed the economics of electricity generation in the 1980s. It became possible to introduce much smaller plants of 40 MW generation size into the system in modular form. Transmission and distribution, however, remained as natural monopoly requiring public regulation.[28] The conventional vertically integrated monopoly industry and market structure remained, more or less, the same in most countries until th1978 when the US, under the Public Utility Regulatory Policy Act, mandated the entry of IPPs into the generation market. These changes in the US triggered their adoption in Jamaica.

Following the decision to encourage private financing of electricity supply in order to relieve the government of the burden of financing the sector's investment needs, several measures were also taken to remove some barriers which were seen to inhibit the flow of private capital into the generation sector.

The most critical of the problems were insufficient security to safeguard foreign direct investments, the limited size of the domestic financial market, the absence of a legislative framework for the evaluation of projects, and the absence of an independent regulator for the sector. To address the regulatory limitation, the government decided in 1991 to introduce a new regulatory structure into the sector; however, it took between 1991 and 1997 for the OUR Act to be enacted and for the OUR to be established, fashioned off the UK's regulatory institutional framework. Jamaica provided for a variation from the UK model in that the UK adopted industry-specific regulators, while Jamaica adopted a multisector body to regulate, especially electricity and telecommunication. Additionally, the government also offered to provide sovereign guarantees to partially address one of the main concerns of the investors.

The industry structure which emerged in Jamaica post-liberalisation therefore consisted of the state-owned vertically integrated JPSCo, acting as the single buyer, the IPPs, and auto-generators which were required to sell all their surplus capacity of bulk electricity to JPSCo under long-term power purchase agreement (PPA), backed by the government's sovereign guarantee.[29] The pricing formula for the IPP bulk power followed a two-part structure comprising an availability or capacity charge and energy charge. The availability charge was calculated to cover the IPP's capital expenditure and fixed expenses, while the energy charge was calculated to cover marginal or fuel cost.

With JPSCo, as the incumbent operator and single buyer this carried implications for transparency, as JPSCo was responsible for system despatch of the IPPs and its own power, giving rise to opportunistic behaviour by JPSCo in the dispatching process. The level of liberalisation introduced was very restrictive, as the IPPs could not wheel electricity over JPSCo's transmission system and to sell bulk power direct to large end users and, in return, pay a transmission access cost for the right to wheel electricity over the single buyer's transmission system to end users. JPSCo claimed its licence barred any third-party sale of electricity and even restricted an own-generator from wheeling electricity over JPSCo's network to an associate or subsidiary company operations. A higher market liberalisation involving the large end-user market would have increased competition in the electricity market; however, this was ruled out.

In developing the IPP transaction, the government had limited experiences to go by. Some five key decisions had to be addressed. First, the government could unbundle generation from transmission, and either using a transmission and distribution company, or a vertically separate transmission company, or the vertically integrated JPSCo as the single buyer. The government adopted the least disruptive industry arrangement and retained JPSCo, a vertically integrated company, as the single buyer.

Second, there was a requirement in the transaction agreement for the government to delegate authority to provide for a non-resident private commercial entity to make withdrawals from a World Bank loan regarding a letter of credit. The government eventually concluded that granting the authority was the only practical solution.

Third, the government was required to guarantee JPSCo's payment obligations to the IPP and provide for the continuance of the guarantee, should JPSCo be privatised. The government found it acceptable to continue the guaranteed requirement up to the time of any privatisation of JPSCo. The period after privatisation presented a problem. Eventually, it was agreed that a clause providing indemnification be included in any future sale agreement of JPSCo as a counter-guarantee of these obligations. IPP-type capital investment, however, carried little risk to the investor, and Jamaican taxpayers carried this risk through guarantees, which the government had to provide initially to attract such foreign investments. This is followed by the availability or capacity charge in the PPA but is no longer the case with the latter IPPs.

Fourth, the requirement was raised for the project company to pay penalties or liquidate damages to JPSCo for failure to supply at a rate equivalent to the economic cost of the loss of capacity. Such a clause made the cost of the likely penalty to be applied several times the value of the IPP. This requirement was removed, as none of the bidders was prepared to undertake this obligation.[30]

The fifth issue was the question of the price to be included in the PPA for the sale of bulk power from the IPPs to JPSCo. In the determination of bulk electricity tariff, government officials made the comparisons between JPSCo's costs of production for generating voltage against the charges requested by the IPPs for bulk electricity. With the two

IPPs (JPPL's plant at Rockfort's price at the time for bulk electricity amounted to US cents 7.10/kWh, while the charge for JEP was US¢ 8.35/kWh.), JPSCo reported generation production cost for bulk electricity of US¢7.3/kWh.[31] In making this comparison, the government failed to consider the fact that JPSCo's average unit cost, as stated was sunk cost with an arbitrary method of cost allocation, reflecting historical accounting, with almost fully depreciated assets and with highly subsidised capital. Much of the international financial investors' (IFIs) cost of financing to governments were at rates much lower than the rates in the private commercial financial markets. It was, therefore, inappropriate to adopt this method of accounting as the basis for cost comparison.

Under state ownership, most of JPSCo capital financing came from the World Bank and the IDB and carried rates of 6 per cent and 7 per cent, much lower than commercial market rates. In contrast, the IPPs's cost of debt financing varied at the time between 11 per cent and 13 per cent in the private financial market. When Jamaica went to the private bond market in the 1990s, it was required to pay interest rates of 11–13 per cent, reflecting its risk premium and international credit rating. The government's financing to JPSCo through the multilateral agencies was therefore provided at a difference of approximately 5–6 per cent. Additionally, over the years, JPSCo had declared virtually no dividend to the state; therefore, its equity cost (a subsidy) was zero, whereas the equity returns, considering Jamaica's risk profile, would have been in the order of 25 per cent.

It is the unit cost of production that JPSCo would have incurred for the same generation capacity at commercial market rates of interest that was relevant; the utilities avoided cost. In the US, as explained earlier, the standard procedure for such evaluation was the long-run average cost of new investment capacity, as constituted by the utility. The general principle applied by the US FEREC in 1980 required that the price the utility had to buy from a qualifying power production facility should reflect the utility's avoided costs (the avoided cost principle)[32] by purchasing from an independent supplier, compared to the best alternative available.[33] This determines the reservation price. In the US, the prospective utility tenders for a solicitation for a fixed amount of additional capacity and selects a winner through competitive bidding or negotiates with a pre-qualified pool of applicants. It was also incorrect to make the comparison with the World Bank's 8 per cent return target rate. The fixed assets would approximate both the debt and equity employed by the IPP and, because the cost of debt obtained by the government for JPSCo was usually lower than the cost of equity, the return on net fixed assets would have been significantly less than on equity returns.

The purchase price of electricity from the IPPs to JPSCo was structured as a two-part pricing arrangement, as indicated earlier, comprising a capacity charge (mostly the capital cost of constructing the plant) and an energy element (reflecting mostly the fuel charge). With Jamaica, the capacity charge carried a 'take or pay' condition, in that JPSCo must pay the capacity charge whether it takes the power or not, so long as the IPP can deliver. This clause is very common to PPAs. The energy element allows for 'cost pass-through,' provided the heat rate and other efficiency targets were met to reflect market changes in fuel price, or changes in the exchange rate, as both costs are beyond the direct control of the power supplier. This cost is automatically passed on by the IPP supplier to JPSCo and eventually by JPSCo to the consumer. The net effect is that there is no specific guaranteed rate of return; the level of efficiency therefore ultimately determines the supplier's rate of return over a given period. This, however, was projected to be between 20 per cent and 25 per cent of equity, which was typical for private power projects in the 1990s in developing countries.

The single buyer model, through long-term private power purchase contracts, allowed the Jamaican system to take the initial step toward a more competitive industry structure. The government, however, could have unbundled the generation business from the transmission and distribution businesses, with a transmission and distribution company becoming the single buyer, in addition to allowing for common carrier competition and liberalisation of the large-end user market. This bypass policy would have provided increased levels of competition that JPSCo would have had to contend with in the market, providing stronger incentive for efficiency.

Although the electricity network remains a natural monopoly, transportation of transmission and distribution voltages could have been opened to the market through non-discriminatory interconnection policies. It was the adoption of non-discriminatory termination and interconnection policies, with the JTC telecommunication transmission network, which eventually provided the increased levels of competition in the liberalised telecommunications market in Jamaica, and which had the impact of marked reduction on consumer prices and wider choice in terms of service quality and range of services in the period following 2001.

Restructuring JPSCo for Privatisation.

Having privatised JPSCo, with a single buyer market structure (competition for the addition of capacity) in 1991, the government under World Bank financing contracted Coopers and Lybrand of the UK[34] to consider the most appropriate structure to take JPSCo to the market, and to recommend the most appropriate regulatory arrangements for the industry. On the conclusion of their evaluation in 1993, Coopers and Lybrand recommended unbundling of the industry into two markets: a fully competitive generation sector and a monopoly segment, comprising transmission and distribution and retail supply, which was to continue to be the subject of tight regulation.

Coopers and Lybrand's concluded that a single operating company (Genco) should be formed which would own all JPSCo's existing generating plant, together with the proposed gas turbine at Hunts Bay, with the remaining assets grouped as a transmission and distribution company, responsible for transmission and distribution and supply on an all-island basis.[35] The rationale for the vertical separation of generation without horizontal unbundling of generation (multiple generators) was that liberalisation and entry into the generation market would have been sufficient to eliminate the future monopoly of a privatised generation company, as their projection was that 70 per cent of the generation, following liberalisation, would be supplied by IPPs and co-generators and this would be so, even if the incumbent generator could bid for incremental capacity.[36] Coopers and Lybrand also concluded that there were no overriding economic reasons for the transmission and distribution company to own any generating capacity. Coopers and Lybrand also accepted the establishment of the multisector Office of Utilities Regulation, modelled off that of the UK, seeing that Jamaica was a small economy. The creation of the 'Office' was essential for the success of the privatisation. To ensure the independence of the DGUR, the consultant also advised that he or she was to be appointed by the prime minister, after consultation with the leader of the opposition, and that future grounds for dismissal were to be strictly limited to cause: misbehaviour, incompetence, loss of mental faculty, or criminal incrimination. Concurrent with the Act creating the new regulator, the consultant also argued for early enactment of electricity industry-specific legislation to replace the 1892 Electricity Lighting Act. The new electricity industry legislation was also to provide for competitive and transparent procurement and independent evaluation of new capacity.

The Electricity Act, along with the Telephone Industry Acts would empower the independent OUR to license and fully regulate each sector and remove all requirements for ministerial licensing and regulation and limit the role of ministerial intervention to one of establishing broad industry policies. At a minimum, the role of the sector minister should be approval of the licence on the recommendation of the OUR. This arrangement would provide for transparency and eliminate the possibility of political opportunism by the minister. These recommendations followed pretty much those outlined by A. J. Meyrick and Cezley Sampson.[37]

In the new structure the OUR would also carry responsibility for approval of the least cost expansion plans prepared by the transmission and distribution company, approve the PPAs, monitor the competitive bidding process, monitor PPAs tariff levels, establish a tariff for retail electricity and monitor and enforce licence conditions. There is a fundamental difference where the least cost expansion plan is prepared by a vertically separated transmission and distribution company, as against one prepared by the vertically integrated JPSCo with substantial generation business, and which company would bid for new capacity. Where the vertically integrated company prepares the least cost expansion plan and is responsible for load dispatching (system operation) the integrity of the system is seriously compromised, as there would always be the IPPs' concern that JPSCo generators would be given priority in dispatching. In fact, this was a common complaint by the IPPs.

Inevitably, the total size of the system to be operated and maintained by the IPPs would have to be such that it provides for reserve margins for emergencies and peak demand, as well as other ancillary services for load balancing. The question of security of the system could be addressed in the power purchase contracts. In fact, there may be some advantage to having several operators at the generation end so that, in an instance of industrial dispute in one of the IPPs, island-wide disruption of electricity may be averted.

A transitional period was recommended and, during this period, both unbundled companies (Generation and Transmission & Distribution) were to have been established as separate and independent businesses to facilitate shadow operation prior to privatisation. External separation and vesting (transfer of assets, employees, and liabilities from JPSCo to the two new companies) was actually targeted for April 1994.

THE JPSCo, engaged its own consultant, Price Waterhouse Utility Economics and Financial Consultants Group of Washington, US, to comment on Coopers and Lybrand's recommendations. Price Waterhouse rejected Coopers & Lybrand's unbundling proposal),[38] stating that the market for generation in Jamaica was too thin to accommodate competition. Competitive generation at an electricity size of 400 MW was not considered by PW to be practical, as the market share would be small, and the resulting sizes will be well below the optimal size. Price Waterhouse also argued most of the shares of the existing JPSCo to be made available to a single strategic technical partner, with 51 per cent controlling rights and with the remaining stake to be offered to a broad-based public, preferring continued government equity participation, the justification being that the government's equity participation would enable it to ensure that its social objectives were considered. Price Waterhouse further argued that privatisation would be politically and administratively easier as a single entity, as planning synergies in the present integrated structure would be lost from unbundling, and the privatisation process would progress with much difficulty if the sale involved more than one unit. This form of analysis, however, adopted electricity economics, which were derived from conditions prior to the 1980s, ignoring the advent of new generating technologies and market arrangements that were well on the way to changing the economics of electricity generation markets. The bureaucrats and JPSCo management, not surprisingly, supported the PW conclusions, arguing that the precedent set for electricity industry restructuring which was recommended by C&L was derived from developed countries, with large energy markets, and where competition offered efficiency gains that more than offset the benefits of the loss of internalisation and additional transaction cost, that the small transmission and distribution company would not be attractive to potential investors and that the privately held generation companies could collude to hold the transmission and distribution company to ransom and endanger the security of the system. These claims were made, although there was no empirical evidence to support them.

The transition from public to private operation, PW argued, would require higher rates of return and consumer would be required to pay higher prices for electricity. The higher electricity rates, it was claimed, would cause the government having to face political problems with consumers in an environment where there was a pending election and that higher proceeds would flow from an unbundled asset. There would as be lower transaction cost, and that a monopoly was financially a more attractive package to take to the market, as it would have preserved economies of scale and integration in the industry, therefore there would be a faster sales process with sale of the integrated company to a single strategic investor. The government would, therefore, have difficulty explaining the lower expected sales proceeds to the electorate. The continuation with a single incumbent vertically integrated company by bureaucrat would create less disturbance to the status quo, minimising the level of disruption to management (a group which was fearful of the privatisation). These advantages, the officials argued, outweighed any disadvantage of exercising market power from a single integrated company.

The longer-term advantages of a competitive structure and the overall longer-term benefits to consumers were sacrificed in favour of the investor group and special interests, a perfect case of the industry being captured in favour of the bureaucrats.[39]

The government finally took the position that it was more important to offer an attractive package to the investor market as a monopoly, as well as to placate the management group, rather than adopting policies geared towards the benefit of the consumer. The political fear factor introduced was sufficient to make the politicians rethink their original position to unbundle.

Coopers and Lybrand had merely sought to introduce a supportive environment for entry of competition at the generation end and provide for open and non-discriminatory access to the transmission and distribution network, with the ultimate beneficiaries being the consumers of electricity. The arguments provided by the bureaucrats were based on historical notions of electricity economics and the political fear factor. The government was led eventually into accepting the short-term consideration of maximisation of sales price over an industry structure that would have introduced stronger incentives, delivered competitive prices and ultimately superior services to the consumer over the long term and repeated the mistake adopted in the telecommunications privatisation in 1985/87.

Bureaucrats and the managers of public enterprises who derive their power and prestige from state capitalism will resist efforts to unbundle state-owned enterprises and expose them to competition and argue either for the enterprise to continue as a state monopoly or be transferred as a private monopoly. It was these same arguments that the utility managers earlier in the UK proffered, and which led to the privatisation of the telecommunications industry in 1985 as a single vertically integrated monopoly, and which later imposed undeniable future cost to the Jamaican consumer. The British utility managers had also posted the same dire warnings about unbundling the England and Wales electricity system and the economic consequences of doing so during the UK electricity industry privatisation.[40]

Bolivia, with a lower per capita income compared to Jamaica and with a small electricity market of the same size as Jamaica, 600 MW, demonstrated in 1995 that a small system can be restructured into several competing firms, with no significant increased costs from loss of economies of scale or punitive levels of transaction costs. There was the suggestion that the re-powering of the Old Harbour and Hunts Bay plants should also take place under the framework of competitive bids. JPSCo's management rejected this suggestion and opposed competitive tendering for the re-powering work. In the end, the company was given the first option to re-power its aged plants in the system. They IPPs feared opportunistic and discriminatory behaviour by JPSCo.

The decision reflected a classic public choice theory case which states that the beneficiary interest groups, in capturing the decision-making process and being rational utility maximisers, will ensure that their special interest prevails over the wider public interests. The transfer pricing practices of the past utility monopoly operator and the abuse of market power by the foreign-owned utility operator in the period up to the 1970s seemed to have been totally forgotten. The decision also reflected the mistrust of the socialist disposed public officials towards competition and the market. The bureaucrats continued to feel that they could succeed where the market failed.

Much of JPSCo's life as an integrated monopoly after independence had been one of inefficient operation, prolonged periods of power outages and under-maintenance. The JPSCo's performance in terms of transmission and distribution line losses at levels actually increased from around 13 per cent in the 1960s to between 17 per cent and 20 per cent by the 1980s and compared unfavourably with figures of under 10–12 per cent in developed countries.[41] These losses resulted from illegal connections, unmetered use, theft, and weak transmission and distribution systems, which could be reduced significantly by good management practices. One of the main reasons retail electricity is so expensive in Jamaica is that the legal users have to pay for the 20–25 per cent of illegal users.

Jamaica's electricity tariff and line losses compared unfavourably with that of Bolivia in 1996. The average retail tariff in 1996 was US¢ 4.50/kWh in Trinidad and Tobago, albeit Trinidad and Tobago being an oil producing country.[42] However, with Bolivia, retail tariff was under US¢7.0 kWh, with line losses of under 12 per cent. Jamaica's failure to effect separation was therefore another case of a missed opportunity of introducing a more competitive and appropriate industry structure in the island's utilities before privatisation.

The Aborted Privatisation Transaction in 1995

Private sector participation in the electricity system in the early 1990s was supported by a World Bank loan 605/OC-JA (US$82 million) which was signed in 1991. Further financing was also provided by the World Bank for the rehabilitation of the company's infrastructure through a loan 738/OC-JA (US$57.5 million) and for further support to the process of privatisation of the sector in 1993. The latter loan was called the Private Sector Energy Development Programme; it was part of a US$110 million programme, which was financed by the IDB and the World Bank.

The government of Jamaica eventually began the privatisation of JPSCo in 1995 through the NIBJ and as a result a Special Divesitutre Enterprise Team (DET) was created for the management of the transaction. Once the decision was taken to privatise JPSCo as a vertically integrated company, an internal memorandum was issued by the NIBJ stating that the objectives of privatisation were to achieve a sale of at least 51 per cent of the company's ordinary shares; relieve the budget from the financial burden of upgrading and financing expansion of services; give the enterprise a higher capability to attract domestic and foreign direct investment; optimise returns from the sale; and secure the lowest price for electricity to consumers, consistent with available commercial financing and the establishment of the systems' reliability at its economically efficient level. As some of these objectives were conflicting, inevitably, the final decision-making would be fraught with difficulties. Advertisements for pre-qualification were issued nationally and internationally the week of July 23–29, 1995, and fourteen responses to the EOI were received. After the receipt of these proposals the DET pre-qualified five applicants. On November 6, 1995, all five applicants: Southern Service, Houston Industries, Enron Corporation, Duke Energy and one other, were supplied with copies of the RFP, with a deadline for January 5, 1996, for their responses. Applicants were advised that the selection of the successful bid was to be based on the attractiveness of the offer price for the shares; the attractiveness of the development plan; the level of commitment to Jamaica and commitment to establishing linkages with local industries; the technical and managerial competence of the bidder to operate electric utility; and the level of technology transfer and local staff development anticipated. At the close on January 5, 1996, only two proposals were received: one from Houston Industries Energy and the other from Southern Electric International, both in the US. In fact, these were the only two bidders that were visited after the pre-qualification to carry out vendor due diligence. Some of the pre-qualification conditions acted as a disincentive to the other investors.

After analysis by the DET, the proposals of the two short listed bidders were rejected because the offer price was too low, the required retail tariff was too high, the proposed dividend policy was unattractive, and there was an unwillingness of the parent companies of the two bidders to guarantee JPSCo's payment obligation to the IPPs. During the negotiating process which ensued, the government sought to obtain a counter-guarantee relating to the JPSCo's obligation, already guaranteed by the state in relation to the IPPs' capacity. Both bidders declined to provide the counter-guarantees. Both also stated that a counter-guarantee by their principals carried a price, which would either have to be passed through in the rate to consumers or deducted from the offer price. This requirement was seen by the government to be a deal breaker, as it felt that future IPP investors would continue to demand government sovereign guarantees. With this counter-guarantee, it would continue to bear much of the risks in an industry where, eventually, it would hold only a minority equity stake. The problem, however, was that the highly leveraged financing regime of the IPPs made these guarantees essential. Without a parent cross-guarantee of the bidding company, or the government's counter-guarantee, it would have been difficult to ensure competitive procurement of new capacity.

Both bidders' offer price for the shares was also lower than the reserve price. While the sale of a fully integrated company may have seemed comparatively more attractive in terms of privatisation income to government, there would always be complications in determining the value of the business. Investors were not interested in the current sunk cost of JPSCo. It was the future earning capacity of the ongoing business that was of interest, and this was assessed by taking the net present value of the future cash flows over a given period in determining the sale price. In the case of utilities, there are three critical elements to be addressed: the expected price, future demand, and the scale of future investment. Market valuation is difficult to achieve in developing countries like Jamaica, where capital markets are thin.[43]

Valuation becomes more important when there is only one bidder. In a competitive and transparent bid situation, the bid price is a good indicator of the market price. The price of the shares, based on discounted value, rests on a whole range of assumptions, most critical of which are the rate of growth of future demand and future tariff obtainable from the utility regulator. The bidders would have pursued a worst-case scenario, contemplating higher risks in their analysis, when compared to the assessment by government bureaucrats, particularly where there is a questionable track record of the regulatory system. These problems have always raised controversy in the privatisation valuation process in developing countries.

Investors in utilities in developing countries prefer to lock in a specific rate of return into the bidding contract in order to reduce exposure to risk of regulatory expropriation.[44] Of the three options available for tariff regulation: rate of return regulation, price cap and negotiated contract, price-cap regulation. After the 1980s, price cap was considered by regulators as the preferred option.

With JPSCo, C& L had recommended price cap regulation, as this was less costly and less time-consuming to operationalise than rate of return regulation and had the added advantage of providing incentives for more efficiency gains. A major advantage of price cap regulation from the point of view of the regulatory process was that the JPSCo price would be decoupled from its internal cost of production. There would, therefore, be less opportunity for JPSCo, as a vertically integrated utility, to influence its price.

Where the regulatory capacity is inadequate, or subject to political interference, a negotiated concession (regulation by contract) is preferred by a foreign investor, rather than relying on legislation and discretionary decision of a new regulator. With JPSCo, the uncertainties as to the establishment of the new regulatory regime certainly influenced the price proposals of the bidders.

Although the recommendation for a new regulatory structure was advanced as early as 1991, up to the time of going to the market in 1995 for the sale of JPSCo, an independent regulatory agency to replace the PUC had not been created. The potential JPSCo investors would inevitably perceive a high risk when there was no clear structure as to a new regulatory regime. In such an environment, investor would evaluate income flows under the worst-case scenario and submit a lower offer price than the government's reserve price. The government was eventually faced with the decision to accept one bid or reject both offers. There was never any enthusiasm by public officials to transfer JPSCo to the private sector. State capitalism was still preferred by many from this group because it offered them greater economic power and personal benefits than would accrue to them under private ownership and control. For Prime Minister Patterson, privatising JPSCo was selling the patrimony of the country. The short timetable which was set for the privatisation also appeared to have been inadequate to resolve the complex issues thrown up in the negotiations.

The privatisation process attempted in 1995 was pronounced by the World Bank to have been flawed, in that it lacked transparency. The Bank gave several reasons for the failed process as follows: the government did not beforehand (a) establish a comprehensive regulatory process; (b) spell out a minimum price (c) spell out the evolution weightings, or (d) allow firms enough time to study JPSCo and carry out their due diligence and prepare their bids (the bid period was just three months).[45] The government had also set out an arbitrary limit of five firms to be pre-qualified, as a way of reducing the work of the bid review. When two of the pre-qualified firms asked for a time extension, their request was rejected; as a result, only two bids were received, both from firms which could bid within the allotted time because they had already initiated contact with Jamaica before the privatisation programme had announced. The gross deviations from standard procedures likely contributed to the failure of the process. Bid opening was followed by ten months of discussions with the two bidders in which elements other than price were considered. Finally, when discussions had been completed satisfactorily, and a firm selected, word leaked out that the lower price bidder was being recommended as the winner. This resulted in an outcry from the political opposition and the press, and concerns that the privatisation could become an issue in the forthcoming elections, whereupon the government cancelled the privatisation. Again, there was a public outcry in the media about the decision to keep the vertically integrated monopoly structure after the experiences of the telecommunications privatisation, contrary to the recommendations of C&L. The decision to abort the JPSCo privatisation came with a penalty to the country, as this decision breached the conditions under the loan agreement with the World Bank for the privatisation of the JPSCo, resulting in the withdrawal of World Bank support for the Jamaican energy sector in the latter part of the 1990s.

JPSCo during the Period of Internal Management Performance Contract

Prime Minister Patterson announced in Parliament on October 22, 1995, that the government had discontinued with of JPSCo privatisation, the reasons being the offer prices were too low; the bidders' proposed retail prices were too high; that the bidders were reluctant to relieve the government of its IPP counter-guarantee commitments, and the dividend policy was unacceptable. Patterson also announced that the government would seek to re-list JPSCo shares on the JSE. For this to come about, there would have had to be at least a 20 per cent floatation of the company's equity. JPSCo's historical financial performance, combined with continued state control, certainly would not have provided the framework for a successful floatation of 20 per cent of the company's equity. The government was later forced to reconsider the policy of public floatation of JPSCo's equity, as there was concern about earlier failed instances where public offers on the JSE. It then sought to achieve efficiency improvements through a three-year internal management performance contract. An internal management performance contract sets out a procedure for establishing clearly specified objectives for the chief executive officer and the public enterprise, on the one hand, and the objectives of the sector minister and the ministry on the other hand. JPSCo was to continue to operate as a vertically integrated SOE, except that the relationship with the government was to be on a more arms-length basis. To facilitate transparency, the counterparty to the management contract was the privatisation agency, the NIBJ. While this arrangement had a significant advantage in terms of good governance arrangement, in that it provided for a neutral and more credible agent to monitor the agreement, the performance contract was flawed, seeing that it provided for annual targets. During implementation of the contract, any attempt to bring the company into compliance, based on the failures which were apparent in monthly reports, was met with protestations that the review was not complete and that the target would be met at the end of the period. In addition, the newly created OUR could support the NIBJ in providing much needed support in monitoring the performance of JPSCo regarding its 1978 licence.

Internal management contract and framework agreements appeared on the scene in the 1990s as a new approach to leveraging some incentives associated with private sector management. The application of private sector operating principles, with the chief executive officer having an arm's length relationship through an internal management performance contract, which became the new instrument for regulating JPSCo, reflected the new public management principles[46] and followed the model adopted in New Zealand for the delivery of several social and economic services.[47] Jamaica's situation, however, differed from New Zealand's, therefore the results achieved in New Zealand could not have been expected in Jamaica. Historically, New Zealand operated many of its utilities as departmental enterprises, i.e., they were not separated from the central civil service.

The JPSCo management performance contract provided for an average tariff mechanism to hold tariff constant in US dollar terms for three years to March 31, 2000, explicit financial and non-financial targets, regulated operating and performance standards, and for JPSCo to operate in a manner to enable it to finance its expansion over time and pay annual dividends to its shareholders. The chairman of

JPSCo then was Professor Gordon Shirley, head of the Department of Management Studies, UWI.

Unless these conditions are legislated with checks and balances, there will be a violation of these agreements if left solely to ministerial discretion. JPSCo continued to fall under the Public Accounts Act and detailed intervention in its management by the Ministry of Finance was inevitable.

Michael Kerf and Warrick Smith stated that wider use of management contract in response to growing problems of the traditional public enterprise model did help to provide insulation from short-term political influences.[48] In the vast majority of cases, however, performance agreements have had a poor record of sustaining reforms. Problems often stemmed from conflicting objectives, which the government was tempted to pursue under these arrangements. There is a growing realisation that combining within government the roles of owner, regulator, and operator is a poor institutional structure for attempting to operate on utilities. In most cases, governments will find it difficult to implement the range of internal and external disciplines on which the effectiveness of corporate entities depends.

Management Performance contract carries several weaknesses. In the first place, the workers, major players in the efficiency matrix, are not bound by the agreements. Second, it is difficult to enforce the obligations, especially those commitments made by the government. Third, the political bureaucracy is rarely prepared to apply the punitive penalties in the contract because of the connected relationship between politicians and public managers. The UK and other countries' attempt to develop an institutional framework which allowed for progressive improvements in efficiency by state capitalism, more than anything else, resulted in a failure to provide strong incentives to the industry and their boards. At another level, it has been a failure to recognise the fundamental principal and agent problem in public enterprises. It was unlikely, therefore, that Jamaica would have found the formula to resolve these problems any more than the UK or, for that matter, find a solution that would reduce the temptation to use utilities to serve political and macroeconomic ends.

Performances of JPSCo under the Internal Management Contract

Most of the improvements to the reliability of supply over the five-year period up to 1998/99, as shown in table 16.1 emerged because of the new capacity brought on by the IPPs. Without introducing the IPPs, JPSCo would not have been able to meet the increased demand and, most likely, its financial position would have presented an unhealthy picture. Sales growth in GWh averaged about 6.5 per cent per annum, over the period 1994/95–1998/99. For the four-year period up to 1997/98, JPSCo experienced after tax losses. The year 1998/99, however, showed a profit of US$12.1million, with a return on equity of 13.6 per cent and return on assets of 10 per cent. The most significant point, however, was the dramatic increase in bulk power purchases from IPPs after 1994/95, increasing from 4 per cent to 30 per cent in 1997/98 and declining to 23 per cent in 1998/99.

Table 16.1: Pre- and Post-Management Performance Contract Results (Revenues and Profitability)

	Pre-Post Performance Contract			Post-Performance Contract	
	1994/95	1995/96	1996/97	1997/98	1998/99
After Tax Profit (US$)	-7,013	-1,602	-45,537	-56,823	12,122
Dividend Paid (US$)	5.1	4.6	4.7	4.7	4.6
Return on Equity	-1.6 %	-0.2 %	-19.0%	-33.1%	13.6 %
Return on Assets	0.9 %	0.9 %	-7.1 %	-9.4%	10.1 %
Sales Turnover (US$)	228,797,146	241,648,452	287,531,307	292,814,893	311,260,230
Sales GWh	1,890	2,037	2,147	2,334	2,476
Proportion of IPPs Bulk Electricity Supplies (%)	4 %	20 %	24 %	30 %	23 %
% Increase (GWh)		7.4	5.4	8.7	6.1

Source: Annual Accounts of Jamaica Public Service Company

Ancile Brewster stated that, under the management contract phase, earnest attempts were made to achieve the benchmarks set, with a review of the outcomes to 2000 having showed that, except for operational efficiency, neither of the previous the government's objectives, nor those specific to the contract had been fulfilled. Financial losses ballooned in the first year of the contract, mainly because of the onetime write-off of overvalued plant and unrecoverable receivables.[49] Further JPSCo's operations were severely disrupted by the general confusion consequent on the privatisation announcement.

Moreover, a series of mechanical problems prevented the generating sets from delivering the normal electrical output. The government also lost the opportunity cost of the proceeds from divestment. In summary, the management contract failed to deliver most of the agreed objectives.

Table 16.2 sets out employment and productivity data during the management contract period. The number of employees in the generation sector fell from 390 to 310, a decline of 20 per cent. The number of employees in distribution and sales remained relatively stable over the pre-and post-performance management contract periods. The decline in the number of employees in generation begun during the pre-management performance contract period, therefore the improvement could not be attributed to the effect of the internal management performance contract. Total employees declined from 2,113 in 1994/95 to 2,039 in 1996/97.

The numbers of employees for each of the two post-management performance contract years were higher than the year preceding the introduction of the contract. Productivity (kWh generated per employee) started its decline also in the pre-performance management contract period and continued up to the first year of the changes. However, in the second year, the productivity level was higher than the level achieved in 1994/95. Customers per employee showed progressive improvements over the five-year period, rising from 176 to 216.

As shown in table 16.3, technical and non-technical losses from transmission and distribution networks showed marginal improvements in the two post-performance management contract years; however, at 16.9 per cent in 1998/99, it was still above the 13 per cent level recorded in the 1970s.

Table 16.2: Number of Employees/Labour Productivity and Number of Customers

Features	Pre-Performance Contract			Post-Performance Contract	
	1994/95	1995/96	1996/97	1997/98	1998/99
Number of Employees in Generation and Transmission	390	357	324	321	310
Number of Employees in Distribution and Sales of JPSCO	1,254	1.281	1,268	1,298	1,251
Employees in Central Administration of JPSCO	469	477	447	475	514
Total Number of Employees	2,113	2,085	2,039	2,094	2,075
KWh Generated per Employee	1,064,289	941,263	951,077	940.537	1,102,598
Number of Customers	371,755	390,367	404,984	430,364	448,783
Customers per Employee	176	187	199	206	216
Proportion of Household Connected Access (%)	53%	55%	57%	60%	62%
Amount of Bulk Electricity bought from IPPs (GWh)	693	851	645	488	85
Total Number of Household Connected	330,162	346,823	360,067	381,817	398,387

Source: Jamaica Public Service Company

Table 16.3: Energy Losses

Losses (%)	Pre-Performance Contract			Post-Performance Contract	
	94/95	95/96	96/87	97/98	98/99
Transmission Loss (%)			1.8	1.8	1.8
Distribution Loss (%)			9.1	8.8	8.7
TOTAL (%)			10.9	10.6	10.5
Technical Losses (%)			10.9	106	10.5
Non-Technical Loss (%)			6.7	6.5	6.4
TOTAL (%)	17.3	16.0	17.6	17.1	16.9

Note: 1 – Breakdown of energy losses prior to 1996/97 is not available.
Source: Jamaica Public Service Company

Technical line losses were relatively stable, varying from 10.5 per cent to 11 per cent, while non-technical losses varied from 6.4 per cent to 6.7 per cent. Access to electricity also experienced progressive increases over the five-year period. Access to electricity is very high in Jamaica compared with other developing countries, but it was substantially below the level of Mauritius, another small island economy. Jamaica, with a population of 2.6 million in 2000, had four hundred and sixty-five thousand connected customers, more than the one hundred and forty thousand connected customers in Uganda with a population of eighteen million.

JPSCo's retail sales price was US10.5¢/kWh for industrial users in 1994/95 and 13.6 cents for household consumers, as shown in table 16.4. Retail prices for both household and industrial consumers declined in 1995/96 respectively, reflecting a decline of 11 per cent and 12 per cent. In 1996/97, prices reflected marginal increases. Prices remained relatively stable for the two management contract years. When one accounts for inflation, consumers seem to have benefited from the relatively stable prices over the five-year period.

JPSCo's bulk purchase price from the IPPs was US 9.2¢/kWh in 1995/96, rising to eleven cents in 1996/97, before falling to nine cents in the two post-management contract years. These changes, however, seem to have reflected the cost escalators in the power purchase agreements. JPSCo's overall retail prices were very high, when taken at the international level. JPSCo and the IPPs, however, produced almost all their generated power from imported fuel oil and did not have access to natural gas and significant levels of hydro-sources, which have yielded important benefits to other developing countries such as Bolivia and Trinidad and Tobago. It would appear that, once a decision is taken to privatise, significant forces come into play, leading to appreciable improvements in performance. Once the pressures to privatise are relaxed, the forces for improved performances also seem to weaken.[50]

Table 16.4: Pre- and Post-Performance Management Contract Results – Bulk Power and Industrial and Consumer Retail Prices

Electricity	Pre-Performance Contract			
	1995/96		1996/97	
	Industrial	Household	Industrial	Household
US Cents per KWh JPSCO CO Retail Prices	9.2	12.1	10.6	13.6
Average Bulk Power Price JPSCO buys from IPPs US Cent Per KWh	8.0		11.0	

Electricity	Pre-Performance Contract			
	1997/98		1998/99	
	Industrial	Household	Industrial	Household
US Cents per KWh JPSCO CO Retail Prices	10.2	13.7	10.4	13.1
Average Bulk Power Price JPSCO buys from IPPs US Cent Per KWh	9.0		9.0	

Source: Jamaica Public Service Company

The Forces Which Triggered the Second Privatisation Process of JPSCo in 2001

Between 1999 and early 2001, the performance of the electricity supply system in Jamaica declined sharply with recurrence of regular outages, irregular voltages, and load shedding. Some problems were because of lower levels of equipment availability from the IPPs and problems with the aged JPSCo's plants which were due for replacement and for which no capital had been provided. The demand on the system in 2000 was 521 MW, increasing at a rate of 6.5 per cent per annum. Installed capacity was 656 MW, of which 25 per cent of capacity was provided by the four private producers, amounting to 156.6 MW. The lack of new investment by JPSCo under state ownership, especially in providing new generation capacity and consequent deterioration in the reserve margin, led directly to the nationwide blackout in 2001, when serious plant failure developed at one IPP plant. The government could not provide the foreign currency to meet the cost of the high maintenance bills and fund the cost of imported fuel. The state-owned JPSCo also failed to provide the indicative investment plans to the OUR, a requirement of the licence to form the basis of competitive bidding for new capacity. State-owned JPSCo was in no hurry to encourage further entry of new IPP generation capacity. The need for additional capacity in the period 1998–2002 (over and above the capacity of the three IPPs which came on stream between 1994 and 1996) was forecasted in the World Bank Report.[51]

That report emphasised that 50 per cent of the additional capacity would have been needed to replace the older units, which were expensive to operate and prone to sudden failure. Apart from two co-generators, which provided an additional capacity of 23 MW during 1998, no new capacity came on stream between 1994 and 2001. The result was that reserve margins fell to 21 per cent. With prolonged outages at one of the large power plants at Hunts Bay, and a major plant failure of one of the IPP companies, the reserve margin did not avoid the recurrence of major island-wide power outages in the latter part of 2000 and throughout 2001.

JPSCo's Annual Financial Report showed that the company's financial performance declined further in 1999/2000.[52] Operating and maintenance cost increased by 36 per cent, mainly from a 90 per cent increase in oil prices and 28 per cent increase in the price of IPP purchased power, while operating revenues increased by only 28 per cent. Operating revenues increased mainly from 48 per cent increase in fuel component of the tariff. The non-fuel component remained unchanged from 1991.

The country's financial situation, especially the balance of payment, also continued to deteriorate, so the national budget for the financial year 2000/01 showed a shortfall amounting to J$7.2 billion. Revenues from JPSCo sale was probably the last major enterprise that could make a substantial contribution to the deficit. Under these circumstances, the decision was again taken to privatise JPSCo through trade sale of 80 per cent of the government's equity to a strategic technical private partner. It was practical consideration rather than any policy agenda which shaped the government's decision to privatise JPSCo in 2001.

The Sale to of Majority Sales to Mirant of the US in 2001

With the need for over US$300 million of additional investments immediately for the 160 MW new capacity, as well as investment for technical improvements in plant efficiency, Patterson was left with no option but to sell JPSCo, despite vigorous opposition from the portfolio minister of mining and energy. The decision to privatise came from a recommendation made by the PIOJ, one agency falling under the control of the Ministry of Finance. Sale of JPSCo provided an opportunity to reduce the public debt by US$120 million and again a strategic investor was sought.

Because of the pressure to obtain additional financial resources, the government again dismissed the restructuring and unbundling option, despite the interest shown by some of the potential investors in acquiring only the generation facilities because the sale of a vertically integrated JPSCo was the best option to ensure even development of the power sector and adequate and reliable power supply of electricity. This decision again reflected a distrust of the market and a failure to take the consumers' interest fully into account.

Instead of a competitive international tender (this was ruled out because of the time constraints) the government settled for what was a negotiated sale. Invitations for EOI were issued to four selected companies, including the two previously short-listed for the first privatisation exercise in 1995. Houston Energy, one of the original bidders, responded by stating that they were no longer interested in the Caribbean. Two of the others receiving the expression of interest, Duke Power and Enron Corporation, expressed interest in acquiring only the generation facilities, as this was the new realities of the global electricity industry, specialisation of investment. The government was, therefore, left with a sole source arrangement (a single bidder) with Southern Energy Inc. of Atlanta, Georgia.

An unsolicited EOI was also submitted by JIEC/AES; however, this was ultimately rejected on the grounds that the proposal did not meet the established timetable. The upshot was that a single proposal was entertained and negotiated between the government and Southern Energy Inc. (later Mirant Corporation). The JPSCo privatisation was an IMF and World Bank conditionality; therefore, it could be argued that the government had little flexibility and that its negotiating position was significantly weakened by the knowledge that funds from the transaction were expected to meet IMF commitments.

On September 21, 2000, Prime Minister Patterson announced that the government had signed a memorandum of understanding for the sale of 80 per cent of the equity interest in JPSCo. The agreement provided for a new twenty-one-year licence, accompanied by a new tariff schedule (February 2001) with significant price increases, which obviously sought to redress the tariff freeze effected since 1997. The new tariff also incorporated several recommendations from Hagler Bailly Study,[53] which had sought to align prices with cost.

The Sale Agreement

The final sale agreement between the government and Mirant which was reached in March 2001 provided for the following:

- Southern Electric's Subsidiary, Mirant JPSCo (Barbados) SRL to acquire 80 per cent of JPSCo's shares for US$201 million and assume US$120 million of debt; the government to provide a counter guarantee for this debt for a further twelve months after closing.
- Southern to commit itself to US$500 million new investments in additional generating capacity over a decade after closing.
- The government's 19.9 per cent remaining equity interest to be entitled to annual dividends. (The public already held 0.01 per cent of JPSCo's shares).
- Mirant to make available up to 5 per cent of its voting stocks to employees and to begin action to re-list the company on the JSE immediately after the end of the first three years.
- The government to assume responsibility for J$9.9 billion of JPSCo's debt of which J$4.7 billion was directly on the government's books and the balance of J$5.2 billion on JPSCo's books but guaranteed by the government at average interest rate of 6.6 per cent.

- The company to be relieved from GCT tax (value added tax) and import duties on capital expenditure for the first ten years.
- The government's 19.9 per cent shareholding to give entitlement to three board members and the remaining six board members to come from the majority investor/strategic investor.
- In the first three years, neither party to be allowed to transfer any portion of its equity and for the government to be allowed to assume operation of the company if the buyer ceased to operate all, or any substantial portion of the electricity system and for the government to have 'rights of first refusal' regarding Mirant shares; of the 242 properties owned by JPSCo, only 106 to form a part of the deal. There was to be no redundancy in the short-term.
- A new twenty-one-year exclusive all-island electricity licence was awarded in March 2001 by the government, under the terms of the then existing licence, except that the existing licence terms did not provide for any guaranteed rate of return. Regarding the right to additional generation capacity, exclusivity was provided for up to three years after closing, thereafter (April 1, 2004) new generation capacity was to be acquired based on competitive tendering. The new owners were to be permitted to continue with the vertically integrated structure, with exclusive rights to the transmission, distribution, and all the retail market.
- The company, under the licence conditions, was to give an undertaking not to abuse its position of market power and for tariff to be regulated by the OUR. The two-part pricing structure was to remain, with the non-fuel component subject to review every five years and the fuel component to be recalculated each month based on an indexation formula.

It is not possible to state whether the outcome would have been better under a competitive bidding procedure; however, it is interesting to note that, in 1996, Houston Industries had offered US$160 million for 50 per cent of the shares of JPSCo, which would have been equivalent to US$251 million for the 80 per cent of JPSCo. Fernando Lecaros, an IDB consultant, concluded that:

> The matter of Mirant's credibility soon subject to questioning and there was the view in certain quarters of the public that GOJ had not carried out adequate due diligence review exercise of Mirant of

> Atlanta businesses, as distinct from Southern Energy of Georgia, as subsequent events showed. Mirant was a major supplier of energy in Washington D.C., and the US press report had been drawing attention to Mirant's failure to provide reliable electricity to that city.[54]

The Licence/Concession Issues Under Mirant

The 2001 All-Island Electricity Licence, more or less, provided the legal framework for contracting and regulating the now privatised Mirant majority owned JPSCo. The relevant industry sector laws, up to then, were still the 1892 Electricity Lighting Act, the 1958 Electricity Development Act and the 1995 (amended 2000) Office of Utilities Regulation Act. The 2000 amendment to the OUR Act transferred the regulatory decision-making from the sector minister to the OUR and also gave OUR powers to encourage competition in the provision of prescribed services, to promote and to encourage the development of modern electricity utility services, as well as to set the rates and technical standards for prescribed services, independent of the minister.

Licences were required for all segments of the electricity business: generation; transmission; distribution, and retail. On the face, only JPSCo seemed to have had the legal right to provide electricity to third party end-users at a charge. Licences were also required for generation but, following 2004, such licences were to be awarded on a non-exclusive basis. Government guarantees were explicitly excluded from future transaction involving IPPs. From the private sector investors' point of view, the licensing procedure did not carry any significance for existing IPP generation, where the principal instrument governing the economic return on generation investment was the PPA, which was entered into with JPSCo.

Again, on the face, exclusivity was granted to JPSCo as a twenty-year licence for transmission, distribution, and retail supply, ending 2021. The licence permitted self, or an auto-generators to self-supply their own needs, but excluded any third-party sales, including captive plants. A captive plant is one which contract to provide electricity to an end user and does not require connection to the utility's transmission system. Under the licence, there were some questions whether a self-generator could transmit electricity over the utility's transmission system to an owned end use point, away from the owned generation point and to pay a wheeling charge to JPSCo, even though no third-party sale was involved.

The government retained the policy of IPP procurement of additional generation capacity, but failed again to require JPSCo's generation business (a competitor in the generation market) to be vertically unbundled from its transmission business, or transmission and distribution/retail business and provide for non-discriminatory access. In other words, the government's implicit position was that co-ordination and systems operation in a vertically integrated structure (internalisation) was best for the industry, although IPP producers were supplying more than 30 per cent of bulk powers at lower generation cost than JPSCo. The government continued with a restrictive version of the single buyer model, where the JPSCo, the vertically integrated utility, or single buyer continued to be permitted to compete to secure new capacity with IPPs, but all independent providers must sell their bulk supply to the single buyer, i.e., JPSCo and all retail consumers must remain captive to JPSCo's transmission/distributor/retail supplier businesses.

The pure single buyer model in Jamaica has resulted in high-cost operation and inflated supply prices. International experiences have shown that this model results in high capital cost solution and hinders further development to a competitive energy market. In several Asian situations, the system broke down, requiring re-negotiation. The high 'take or pay' clauses that sometimes are associated with the model respond poorly when electricity demand falls short of projection.[55]

Under normal circumstances, prices should fall when demand falls. However, electricity price rose when demand fell, where the contract carried high take or pay clauses. High take or pay clauses may also hinder merit order or economic despatch. In proceeding to sell JPSCo as a vertically integrated company, the government replaced a public monopoly with a private monopoly, as all consumers were denied choice of supply. The opportunity to graduate to a wholesale electricity market phase at a later date was precluded under the exclusive franchise granted for the transmission and distribution market segments and failure to liberalise the large consumer end-user market.

Again, no changes were made to the procedure for the tendering for new generation, even though the licence provided for the competitive tendering process. JPSCo, as the vertically integrated company, continued to be integrally involved in the bid process while, at the same time, being allowed to be a bidder for additional generation capacity. The company continued to also set out arrangements for pre-qualification of prospective bidders and establishing the evaluation criteria for the bid selection. There was an inherent conflict of interest in JPSCo being a major player and the incumbent in the generation market also determining the requirements and making recommendations to the OUR for the tender process, albeit OUR carried the right of approval and, to that extent, it could influence the outcome. It appears to be optimistic to expect prospective suppliers to go to the expense of preparing an IPP bid knowing that they may compete against the buyer's own proposal.

JPSCo continued to be responsible, inter alia, for long-term forecasting of adequate generation capacity and developing the least cost expansion plan. By this requirement, JPSCo had to submit a statement of its long-term planning procedures to OUR. Although the process was subject to regulator's scrutiny and approval, this gave JPSCo an unfair advantage. On the face, the provisions of the licence did not promote impartiality. There may have been a tendency by JPSCo to over-forecast. It would have been more appropriate for an independent party to take over these functions in relation to the tender and forecasting process.

This is also addressed in the new 2015 Electricity Act. The licence also provided for the establishment of an industry-specific Appeals Tribunal to hear appeals from decisions of the OUR, comprising three members, a judge and one nominee each from JPSCo and OUR. No appeal tribunal had been previously established. Regarding competition matters, Mirant JPSCo was exempted from the provisions of the Fair Competition Act, 1993 one of the few companies in Jamaica to be so exempted. In awarding the licence the government succumbed to pressure from JPSCo and gave the exemption, strengthening JPSCo's monopoly position in the market. The Ministerial Order (dated February 26, 2001) declared as follows: ... *the Fair Competition Act shall not apply to the generation, transmission, distribution, and supply of electricity by the JPSCo.*[56]

All the other players in the industry were subject to the conditions of the Fair Competition Act, in terms of uncompetitive business practices and abuse of market power, yet they were required to compete with exempted JPSCo. JPSCo was prevented from unduly discriminating against other parties, or show undue preference to any person, including its affiliates regarding the sale or purchase of electricity. Additionally, JPSCo was also required to purchase electricity at the best effective price reasonably obtained, having regard to the sources available, contractual arrangements and the government's policy. The company's licence stated that it should not take any action, or otherwise conduct itself in a manner that was likely to restrict or distort competition in the procurement of generation capacity which would be an abuse of a dominant position as defined by the Fair Competition Act. Regarding exemption, there was no effective mechanism outlined to monitor or penalise these behaviours.

While the OUR was empowered to identify abuse of market power, the only enforcement mechanism was for revocation of the licence. The shortcomings of the licence and JPSCo's dominance in the market, along with the fact that the Fair Competition Commission's analytical competitive powers were seriously constrained, hindered the growth and competition in the generation of the electricity market. In other words, with the absence of the Fair-Trading Commission having a surveillance role, some terms of the licence could operate as a barrier to entry for newcomers into the generation capacity market.

Further, JPSCo carried the responsibility for moment-by-moment load dispatching of electricity from existing plants. The licence prescribed merit order despatch. Merit order means that plants with the least economic costs should purchase and be dispatched first, i.e., in ascending order of marginal cost of production. It was the JPSCo's responsibility to schedule and order the despatch of electricity in merit order to meet a load demand. Further, the licensee was required to provide the OUR with information that OUR requested pertaining to the merit order system.

Competitors would have been required to submit information relating to their operations and their production costs, in order for the JPSCo to rank their marginal costs. There was the potential for a conflict of interest and for the licensee utilising this information to its competitive advantage. This function in a competitive generation market is normally performed by an independent load despatch committee, made up of all the generators, or one made up of independent experts, or a combination. It is well understood that, in order to have effective market reform, it is imperative to have independence and transparency within the market.

The 2001 JPSCo licence required that changes should be negotiated between the JPSCo and the government, and for JPSCo and the OUR to agree on some changes. In view of the significant regulatory implications, it was important that the regulator be involved in some way in any negotiations for a revised licence.

It is not good industry practice for the OUR, as the regulator to be directly involved in the selection of new entrants to the market, particularly since the PPA of any successful tender must be approved by it. With the separation of generation business from the retail supply businesses, the problem of conflicts regarding procurement, least cost planning, and load despatching under a vertically integrated structure would not have arisen.

The government's decisions were made in the interest of short-term gains, providing revenues to the Treasury against the longer-term interest of moving to a competitive market and delivering more efficient services to consumers. Had the government provided for liberalisation of the large consumer market after a transitional period of, say, five years (possibly with user demand exceeding 1 MW) and for equal and non-discriminatory access to the natural monopoly segment of the industry, the longer-term consumers' interest would have been better served. In this way, an element of product market competition could have been introduced at the retail end of the market during the life of the current franchise.

There was no guaranteed mechanism provided to ensure that the level of investments JPSCo declared to commit during the first five years would be implemented. From international experiences, it is extremely difficult to enforce capital programmes in post-privatisation periods. A defining problem of the sector was the asymmetric power between the regulator (OUR) and the electricity company (JPSCo). An example of the relative bargaining power of each follow: if investment plans were agreed upon between OUR and JPSCo and such plans were not implemented, or did not comply with the licence conditions, OUR did not possess the authority to demand its implementation, or compliance, or to apply punitive measures.

Mirant paid the government US$201 million for the 80 per cent equity in JPSCo. Following the sale, the company invested an additional capacity of 140 MW. It is difficult to disaggregate the price paid for the 80 per cent holdings in JPSCo, but it is fair to say that, with the estimated purchase price of US$201 million and the investments in generation, transmission, and distribution over the six years and any dividends paid since 2002, Mirant did not make a killing.

Mirant's Bankruptcy in 2003

Mirant Corporation, based in Atlanta, US, acting through its 100 per cent owned subsidiary, Mirant JPSC (Barbados) SRL, a limited liability company, which had acquired 80 per cent of the voting stocks (ordinary shares) of JPSCo in 2001, became insolvent. In 2003, Mirant Corporation went into bankruptcy proceedings (Chapter 11 under United States Law) and eventually came out of Chapter 11 proceedings in the US in December 2005. Subsequently, Mirant informed the Jamaican government that it intended to divest its Caribbean holdings, inclusive of the 80 per cent equity in JPSCo. Mirant issued an information memorandum through the investment banking firm, JP Morgan, in September 2006, inviting prospective purchasers of its Caribbean investments. Mirant also stated that its preferred method of divestiture was to sell the 100 per cent equity holdings in Mirant Barbados; however, it would consider individual offers for the businesses in the respective Caribbean countries. Since then, the company has experienced several ownership changes.[57]

Performance of the Privatised JPSCo under Mirant

It is important to look at some of the pre-and post-privatisation experiences.[58] By 2006, the installed capacity of both the public grid and the self-generators in Jamaica was just under a 1,000 MW, of which over 60 per cent was owned by JPSCo. With a further 204 MW from IPPs the public grid amounted to 804 MW, and accounted for 80 per cent of installed capacity. The auto-generators, mainly bauxite companies owned 194 MW.[59] Of the 1,000 MW capacity only 41.1 MW or 4.12 per cent came from renewable energy. The rest reflected an imported oil-based system. Renewable energy accounted for 5.3 per cent of the public grid capacity.

JPSCo owned four thermal plants and eight mini hydro plants. The only modern unit in the JPSCo system was the 120 MW combined cycle gas turbine, which was installed at Bogue, St James, in 2003/4. This was a project developed by JPSCo under state ownership, and Mirant followed through with implementation after an acquisition of majority ownership in JPSCo in 2001.

The company also benefited from donor agency financing, and the government was required to waive the import duty on diesel fuel as a condition of Mirant's investment. With the company's plants, over 50 per cent were over thirty years old. Some plants in 2006 were as old as forty years, and Mirant had no plans to replace these old plants over the medium term. Table 16.5 below shows the evolution of electricity production over the period 1994–2005. The high growth rate in production in the latter part of the 1990s slowed during the five-year period of 2000–2005. JPSCo added only 140 MW of generation capacity, and this reflected the first addition of capacity since 1997.

Table 16.5: Evolution of Electricity Production, 1994–2005

	1994	1996	1997	1998	1999	2000	2001	2002	2003	2004	2005
GWh	2324	2557	2768	2949	3100	3302	3361	3525	3696	3,717	3,877
Growth per cent 2005	4.1	5.8	8.3	6.5	5.1	6.5	1.8	4.9	4.9	0.6	4.3

Source: JPSCo

The company's first step was a J$15 million installation of a twenty-five-megawatt gas turbine unit at JPSCo's power plant at Bogue in Montego Bay, followed by the 120 MW plant in 2003/4. This completed the expansion programme and brought the total installed capacity to approximately 680 MW. Reserve margin declined from 26 per cent in the period of state ownership to minus 8 per cent in 2003 and reached 2 per cent in 2004 with the Bogue addition.

Service quality is measured by systems average interruption frequency index (SAIFI), systems average duration index (SAIDI) and customer average interruption duration index (CAIDI). While service quality improved in the initial period just after privatisation, as measured by a reduction in system power interruptions and voltage fluctuations, by 2005 the situation had again deteriorated alarmingly, culminating in a major blackout in 2006 lasting several hours, and involving the entire island. The reduction in service standard was not just the result of inadequate reserve margin but also reduced expenditure in real terms by Mirant JPSCo after privatisation.

The power deficit problem was improved by the government initiative involving special arrangement with one of the IPPs to bring on board 49 MW of new capacity after 2006. One of the major problems of post-privatisation operations ensured that the privatised operator met its investment commitment given in the licence. Most importantly the system continued to rely on high-cost oil products with major implications for the foreign exchange bill. A key requirement of the privatising should have been a firm commitment by Mirant to bring in the investment that would have allowed for switching to cheaper fuel – natural gas. Mirant JPSCo had no incentive to expend major investment to reduce fuel cost, as this was an automatic cost pass through to the consumer.

Failure to modernise the generating capacity had major implications for fuel efficiency, as shown by the poor performance of JPSCo's plant regarding the heat rate. The heat rate in the pre-privatisation period improved marginally by about 2 per cent, compared to an overall increase of 21.8 per cent in the post-privatisation period; however, most of the improvements in net generation and the heat rate were due to improved performances by the IPPs. Mirant JPSCo's heat rate performance declined marginally in terms of net generation and heat rate, as shown in table 16.6.

Table 16.6: Production and Capacity Performance Pre- and Post-Privatisation Five-Year Periods

Year	Net Generation & Purchases (MWh)	Pre-Privatisation 1996-2000	Post-Privatisation 2001-2005	Year	Net Generation & Purchases (MWh)	Generating Capacity (MW)	System Heat Rate (k/kWh)
1996	2,450,973	678.7	13,452	2001	3,317,116	688.2	13,215
1997	2,583,901	686.9	13,060	2002	3,401,951* 2,687,447*	743.6	11,477
1998	2,820,481	656.2	12,694	2003	3,696,005	785.6	11,342
1999	2,981,074	662.7	12,951	2004	3,717,022	767.6	10,805
2000	3,158,812	668.7	13,173	2005	3,877,990	767.6	10,336

Source: Sampson, 2005, The Electricity Sector Energy Policy Review, JPSCo Reports & Economic & Social Survey PIOJ, 2001, 2006

**JPSCo changed their reporting fiscal year from March 31 to December 31 in 2002. therefore, the figures represent twelve months ending March 31 and 9 months ending December 31, respectively.*

Heat rate in the pre-privatisation period ranged between 13,452 and 12,694 kj/kWh, while for the post privatisation period heat rate fell from 13,215 to 10,336 kj/kWh. While the overall system was showing an improvement in heat rate, this was because of improvements from the IPPs.

The IPPs, for example, showed a marginal decline in heat rate, falling from 8,246 in 2002 to 8,170 kj/kWh in 2004. JPSCo's gas turbines had some of the highest heat rates. JPSCo's average heat rate in the post privatisation period was 11,257 kj/kWh. Heat rate in the pro-privatisation period ranged between 13,452 and 12,694 kj/kWh, while for the post-privatisation period heat rate fell from 13,215 to 10,336 kj/kWh. While the overall system was showing an improvement in heat rate, this was because of improvements from the IPPs. The IPPs, for example, showed a marginal decline in heat rate, falling from 8,246 in 2002 to 8,170 kj/kWh in 2004. JPSCo's gas turbines had some of the highest heat rates. JPSCo's average heat rate in the post- privatisation period was 11,257 kj/kWh.

According to Duane Andre Rowe, JPSCo's aged units had marked implications for operational efficiencies in that they incurred high maintenance cost and were less dependable, particularly regarding forced outages.[60]

The number of customers served during the pre-privatisation period increased by 23.3 per cent compared to 7.8 per cent during the post-privatisation period. By 2006, over 90 per cent of households in Jamaica had access to grid electricity. Over the two periods, access increased from 390,367 to 562,000. Increased access was due mainly to the state-operated Rural Electrification Programme and was not because of any initiatives by Mirant JPSCo. In the pre-privatisation, generation increased overall by 28.5 per cent compared to an overall increase of 16.0 per cent in the post-privatisation period.

System losses have been one of the most problematic for JPSCo to control. Between 1996 and 2002, system losses were about 17 per cent of net generation; however, in 2002, after privatisation system, losses went on the upward trajectory, reaching 23 per cent in 2007, and this was despite incentives incorporated in the tariff setting formula to reduce losses. In 1996, system losses amounted to 413,642 MWh, increasing to 537,227 MWh in 2000. Following privatisation, losses went up from 566,387 MWh in 2001 to 822,836 MWh. The sale of JPSCo to a private investor in 2001 coincided with increasing system losses.[61] Electricity loss is usually made up of technical and non-technical losses, and non-technical losses in Jamaica occurs mainly from theft and corruption.[62]

The Trinidad Regulated Industries Commission confirms that it is difficult to precisely state what proportion of system losses is technical as opposed to non-technical loss, and often this has to be determined by special studies. However, in a paper presented at a JPSCo seminar in Trinidad in 2003, technical loss for Jamaica was estimated at 9 per cent and non-technical loss at 9.5 per cent. The largest component amounted to 5.2 per cent, and this was caused by 'throw up,' wires thrown up and hooked on to the company's open, low-voltage, secondary conducting lines, and which are mostly visible. The other forms of theft arose from more sophisticated measures, such as metre bypass, resorted to mainly by large residential consumers, and some commercial end users. The overall technical and commercial losses were over 18 per cent and were exceptionally high, when compared to international standards. In Oman, system loss was about 15 per cent on restructuring of the industry in the early 2000s and, by 2018, had been reduced to under 9 per cent.

System loss in Jamaica for 2003 was estimated to be just under 700,000 kWh based on an estimated net generation of 3,696,000 MWh in 2003 and non-technical loss of 9.5 per cent; the commercial loss equates to 346,750 MWh of unpaid for energy. JPSCo estimated the cost of unpaid energy to be about US$38 million. Most of this cost was not a loss to JPSCo, as the greater proportion of this was recouped within the tariff setting formula and paid for by legal consumers. Trinidad and Tobago has been reducing its systems losses, while in Jamaica it has been increasing. Since 1999, the megawatt hours of unbilled electricity in Jamaica have increased by 40 per cent. This reinforces the point that the high cost of electricity in Jamaica is due more to 60 per cent legal customers having to pay for the electricity consumed by the 40 per cent illegal consumptions. Illegal consumption is at every level in the society, including ordinary household consumers (upper and lower class) and industrial and commercial operators like supermarkets.

In 2003, the cost of system loss in Trinidad and Tobago amounted to about US$6.3 million. This compared with the estimated JPSCo's systems loss in Jamaica at US$76.74 million for 2003. Trinidad and Tobago could reduce the overall system's loss from 12 per cent in the 1990s to 8.5 per cent in 2004. Trinidad's electricity overall system loss comprised about 6 per cent technical loss and about 2.5 per cent for commercial or non-technical losses. In Oman, even under state ownership, system losses fell from 17 per cent to under 9 per cent in the first ten-year period on the industry restructuring. The median value of losses for Latin America in 2001–6 ranged between 16.5 per cent and 16.9 per cent. JPSCo's range was between 16.5 per cent and 22.9 per cent.[63]

Regarding the financial side of the JPSCo, operating revenues totalled J$9,817,237 in 1995–96, showing an increase in 1997, but declined in 1998. There was an increase in 1999 and a further increase in 2000. This means that, except for 1998, the revenues increased annually. Operating expenses in 1996 stood at J$9,685,962. This increased after 1996 and decreased steadily thereafter. This can be a contribution from lower fuel prices. Capital expenditure for the period showed an increase in 1996, a decrease in 1997, a slight increase in 1998 and a reduction for both 1999 and 2000, reflecting the level of expansion undertaken by the company for the period.

In looking at the trend, not much expansion was carried out by state-owed JPSCo. The company's equity fluctuated over the period, while return on equity was negative, except for 2000. The company recorded net losses for three consecutive years: 1996, 1997, and 1998 and profits for 1999 and 2000. From the net loss experienced in 2000/2001, $922 million of this was what was termed an exceptional item associated with a one-off redundancy payment. Revenue for that year, to a large extent, was explained by a 45.1 per cent increase in fuel charge, which was passed directly to customers. Increase in fuel cost was attributable to increasing prices on the international oil market. Overall, operating and maintenance cost declined in real terms.

Equity increased steadily during the post privatisation period, while returns on equity showed negative per cent for three of the five years reported. A net loss was recorded in 2001, a net profit in 2002, and two consecutive years of losses followed in 2003 and 2004, with profitability returning in 2005, as shown in table 16.7 below.

The completion of the last phase of the 120 MW combined cycle plant at Bogue in September 2003 was one highlight of that year, as well as finalising new wage and benefits agreements with the four unions representing employees. These labour agreements resulted in higher wage bills for the company. Customers also saw an increase in their bills, with the devaluation of the Jamaican dollar a contributing factor.

Table 16.7: Comparison of JPSCo's Financial Performances Pre-and Post-Privatisation: Pre-Privatisation (JPSCo) and Post-Privatisation (JPSCo)

Year	Equity J$b	Rate of Return %	Year	Equity J$b	Rates of Return %
1996	18,451	-6.7	2001	15,426,	-10.5
1997	7,184	-0.35	2002	17,777	6.5 2.5
1998	5,078	0-40	2003	19,709	-4.3
1999	NA		2004	22,609***	-.63
2000	6,136	2.21	2005	24,782***	5.8

Source: JPSCO Reports & JPSCO Statistical Review 2003

* Reporting years changed from March 31 to December 31, 2002, therefore two figures are reported on.

*** Figures taken from JPSCo Reports and reflect only purchases of property, plant & equipment, and purchase of intangible assets.

Electricity Pricing 2001–6

Electricity pricing should provide an incentive for efficient production. Table 16.8 summarises the economic regulatory framework embedded in the 2001 All-Island Licence. Non-fuel rate in the pricing formula was regulated until March 31, 2004, according to the tariff regime effective February 1, 2001. The rate structure over the period 2001–6 is shown in table 16.8 below.

The electricity incentives are ultimately reflected in the tariff that the utility company can charge, and the cost it can recover. With JPSCo the licence stipulated electricity prices to carry the following components: a non-fuel rate, which functions as a 'price cap' element, to be adjusted: a monthly charge to reflect changes in exchange rate, and annually to reflect performance-based measures, as well as fluctuations in the (local and foreign) inflation rate and a fuel rate that is adjusted monthly to reflect fluctuations in fuel costs, and which can be classified as a 'pass through' element at a minimum level of fuel conversion efficiency.

Table 16.8: Summaries of OUR Price Regulations applied to JPSCo in 2001

June 2001–May 2004 Rates	Basis	Monthly Revisions	Annual Revisions
Non-fuel component: price cap	Feb. 2001 rates	Forex[1]	Forex (60 %) + inflation (40 %)
Fuel component: pass through	Actual expenditure	JPSCo fuel + purchase costs	
May 2004 Rate Review	**Basis**	**Monthly Revisions**	**Annual Revisions**
Non-fuel component	JPSCo non-fuel operating costs, depreciation, taxes, ROI[2]		
June 2004–May 2009	**Basis**	**Monthly Revisions**	**Annual Revisions**
Non-fuel component: price cap	May 2004 Rate Review results	Forex[1]	Forex (60%) + inflation (40%) + performance indices
Fuel component: pass through	Actual expenditure	JPSCO fuel + purchase costs	

Note: [1] Foreign. [2] Return on Investment

In the rate formula, the average price (rate) of electricity to final consumers in J$/kWh is capped at a certain level that varies over time as a function of the performance of the company. In order to determine this rate and its variation, the licence distinguishes several components that go into a determination of the rate, comprising the following: a non-fuel base rate; a fuel rate, and extraordinary costs related to the government-imposed obligation. The non-fuel rate is determined every five years, starting from 2004. Rates are also adjusted monthly by index, reflecting foreign exchange variation. The non-fuel base rates are based on the non-fuel revenue requirement necessary to recover non-fuel operating cost.

Depreciation (tightly regulated rate), income taxes and return on net investment in the regulated asset (the rate base) of JPSCo were sufficient to provide for the requirement of consumers and allow for new investments at competitive cost. The allowed rate of return to apply to the rate base was JPSCo's weighted average cost of capital (WACC). The WACC should balance the interests of both consumers and the investor, considering the risks to capital in similar business and based on the actual capital structure of the company. The non-fuel base rate's annual adjustment is at the heart of the price cap mechanism and adjusts for four factors. First, it adjusts the price cap for change in a mix of US and Jamaican inflation ^1 (reflecting in theory at least the proportion of these rates in the company's non-fuel expenses). Second, the X- Factor, considers the offset to inflation resulting from expected productivity improvement in the company, relative to productivity in the economy. Third, the Q-Factor, adjusts for price cap for performance incentives reflected in a set of targets for quality of service provided to consumers. Fourth, the Z-Factor, adjusts the price cap for special reasons not captured elsewhere including, inter alia, natural and unpredictable disasters such as hurricanes.

A case came up where JPSCo made a claim for loss of profits which, the company maintained, resulted from damages it suffered because of hurricane Ivan. The OUR, however, did not accept all the claims made as a result of Ivan. This combination combines the performance-based rate adjustment mechanism (PBRM). Institutionally, Jamaica has tried 'ad hoc' rate boards up to 1965, a colonial imposition and ministerial regulation, up to 1997, and since then the more independent multisector Office of Utilities Regulation. Table 16.9 below summarises the tariff structure as effective February 1, 2001 (using a rate of US$1 to J$44). Rate review was required every five years once the new rate was accepted, subject to annual modification according to performance indices, variations in inflation and the exchange rate.

The 2001 tariff structure took into consideration the recommendations of the Hagler Bailly Long Run Marginal Cost and Tariff Studies (1998), which showed production cost of bulk electricity to be US 5¢/kWh, along with high transmission and customer service costs. The high cost recognised the high level of inefficiencies from public ownership. Privatisation was expected to improve efficiencies and reduce costs.

Following the rate review in 2004, a new tariff structure was established, and this is set out in table 16.10. Compared to the rates prevailing before June 2004, customer charges showed a slight increase with residential customers, with increases also in the other categories.

Table 16.9: JPSCo Tariff Summary, February 2001

Rate Category		Customer Charge ($/mo.)	Energy Charge (¢/kWh) Standard	Demand Charge US$ /kVa per mo. Standard	Demand Charge Off- Peak 2200-0600	Demand Charge Partial Peak 0600-1800	Demand Charge On- Peak 1800-2200	Fuel Charge US¢/kWh Standard	Fuel Charge Off- Peak 2200-0600	Fuel Charge Partial Peak 0600-1800	Fuel Charge On- Peak 1800-2200
10	**Residential**										
	First 100kWh	1.13	8.1					5.6			
	Over 100kWh	1.13	11.5					5.6			
20	**General**	10.9	8.6					5.7			
40-LV	**Power**	32.5	1.3	14.0	0.56	6.0	7.4	5.6	4.9	5.9	7.3
40A-LV	**Power**	32.5	5.2	5.6				5.6			
40-MV	**Power**	32.5	1.2	13.7	0.56	5.9	7.3	5.6	4.9	5.9	7.3
50-LV	**Large Power**	42.0	0.96	15.9	0.56	6.8	8.4	5.6	4.9	5.9	7.3
50-MV	**Large Power**	42.0	0.93	15.9	0.56	6.8	8.4	5.6	4.9	5.9	7.3
60	**Streetlight**	8.2	Note b/					5.7			
60	**Metered Circuits**	8.2	8.2					5.6			

Note: a/ LV=Low Voltage, MV= Medium Voltage b/ A separate table applies to un-metered circuits ($/lamp per month according to lamp type). Source; IDB (2002) Jamaica energy Sector Study, Washington.

Table 16.10: JPSCo Tariff Summary, 2004

Demand Charge US$ /kVA per mth.							
Rate Category	**Customer Charge US$ / mth**	**Energy Charge US ¢/kWh**	**Standard**	**Off- Peak 2200-0600**	**Partial Peak 0600-1800**	**On Peak 1800-2200**	**Fuel Charge US ¢/kWh**
10 Residential **first 100 kWh** **Over 100kWh**	 1.1 1.1	 7.6 13/1					
General	2.46	11.1					
40 A-LV Power	34.4	6,97	4.52				
40-LV Power	34.4	2.83	11.59	0.48	5.05	6.46	
50-LV Large Power	34.4	2.55	10.43	0.43	5.44	5.82	

Note: A/LV =Low Voltage, MV = Medium Voltage.

Source: Fernando Lecaros (2005), 'Jamaica: Energy Sector Update,' IADB, Washington

The energy charge was increased in all categories by substantial amounts, except for lifeline customers. All demand charges showed a significant decrease, the result of the cost-of-service study which corrected errors in the previous regime. However, the most dramatic increase came from the fuel charge, which reflected the increases in global crude prices, which gradually increased by 50 per cent between the two reviews. Some of the above are classical information asymmetry problems associated with aspects of pricing regulation.[64] June 1, 2004, brought into operation a price cap mode and the performance-based system.[65]

Table 16.11 set out the average electricity prices for residential customers over the pre- and post-privatisation periods.

Table 16.11: Average Electricity Prices Residential Consumer Pre- and Post Privatisation

Pre-Privatisation, 1996–2000		Post -Privatisation, 2001–5	
Year	Average Pieces US cents/ kWh	Year	Average Pieces US cents/ kWh
1996	11.5	2001	16.0
1997	12.1	2002	18.0
1998	12.7	2003	19.0
1999	13.3	2004	21.0
2000	14.0	2005	23.0 (est.)

Sources: Marbek Resource Consultants Ltd (2005 Draft), 'Post – Implementation Impact Assessment Jamaica Demand-Side Management Demonstration Project,' World Bank, Washington, DC and JPSCo 2003 Annual-Operational Statistics Report.

These cause the fundamental difficulty that JPSCo will always have more information than the OUR about its overall production opportunities, the costs of services, the operating characteristics of its network, the effort it expends to keep costs low, the attributes of its customers' demand patterns, the quality of the services it provides, the costs of improving that quality, and the responsiveness of its customers to various tariff structures.

Over the period of public ownership, 1996–2000, prices for residential consumers increased from 11.5 US cents/kWh to 14.0 US cents/kWh, an increase of 2.5 US cents/kWh, representing an increase of 17.85 per cent, whereas, over the five-year period of Mirant's private operation, prices increased by US 9.0 cents/kWh, or an increase of 56.8 per cent. Although increases in oil prices accounted for a significant portion of the increases, there is no evidence to show that Mirant's private management help moderate price increases.

Average electricity prices charged by JPSCo in the US dollar term reflected an increase over the 1996–2000 periods. This ranged from 11.5 US cents per k/Wh in 1996 to 14 US cent per K/Wh in 2000. Further increases took place over the other period 2001-2005. It peaked further during 2001 with 16US cents per kWh to a high of 21.33 US cents in 2005. When one looks closer, before privatisation the increase was less with a maximum of 0.7 US cents, as opposed to the period after privatisation where the increase over 2001–2 was all of 2 US cents and 2003 saw an increase of 1 US cent, 2004 an increase of 1.1 US cent and 2005 an increase of 1.23US cents per kWh. In essence, and not surprisingly, consumers were paying significantly more for electricity under Mirant's majority ownership and management, post-privatisation.

Divestment of Mirant's 80 Per Cent Equity Interest in JPSCo to Marubeni Corporation of Japan in 2007

Mirant Corporation, the parent company, of Mirant Barbados Limited, the company which had acquired the 80 per cent interest in JPSCo, ran into financial problems in July 2003 and sought protection from its creditors under Chapter 11 of USA Bankruptcy Law. There was local criticism that had the government carried out a proper due diligence exercise it would have discovered that Mirant was encountering financial and operational problems then, and that the company had problems in meeting its regulatory obligations in Washington.

In April 2005, Mirant JPSCo (Barbados) SRL, the subsidiary holding the 80 per cent JPSCo's equity, notified the government of bankruptcy court proceedings in a Northern District Court of Texas, requiring restructuring of the company under Chapter 11 Bankruptcy proceedings. The restructuring required the transfer of ownership of existing Mirant's US and non-US assets to a new off-shore subsidiary, New Mirant and including existing Mirant's interest in JPSCo. Subsequently, the US Court approved the restructuring plan and Mirant sought consent from the government for the restructuring and transfer of the 80 per cent equity from Old Mirant to New Mirant. On the December 28, 2005, the government gave the consent to Mirant

JPSCo (Barbados) SLR, and the consent document was signed by the NIBJ on behalf of the government.

Following the new arrangement, information came to the government that New Mirant was interested only in the generation business and wished to enter into discussion with the government regarding restructuring JPSCo by unbundling the generation business for Transmission and Distribution/Retail; and disposing of the transmission and distribution business. Subsequent information in February 2006 confirmed this position, but it was later denied by the New Mirant.

On July 11, 2006, a public notice was received from Mirant setting out the company's intention to repurchase forty-three million common stocks of Mirant for US$1.25 billion, and to sell its international business, including its 80 per cent equity in the JPSCo, 39 per cent interest in Power Generation Company in Trinidad and Tobago (PowerGen), 25.5 per cent interest in Curaçao Utilities Company, and 55 per cent interest in Bahamas Power Company. Mirant planned to sell its interest in the Caribbean businesses comprising 1,050 MW, and which had been profitable (US$156 million EBITA)[66] in 2005 to finance the loss-making 14,161 MW US businesses.

Although Mirant had stated that tender offer for shares in the company's common stock would have taken place on August 21, 2006, it did not specify the type of auction process for the disposal of the Caribbean businesses, although the government understood that the sale of the shares would have been by Dutch auction. In a typical Dutch auction, the seller starts by listing the minimum price and number of items for sale. Bidders specify their bid price and quantity. All winning bidders pay the same price. Auctioneers begin with a high offer price, until some participants will accept the auctioneer's price or a predetermined minimum price.

Under the First Amended and Restated Shareholders Agreement, dated July 16, 2001, Article 10.2(b) between the third and tenth anniversary date, Mirant could not reduce its majority holding below 51 per cent without first obtaining consent from the government, the minority shareholder. It was clear that the government's privatisation policy for the electric utility called for a strategic technical energy investor to hold majority control in JPSCo during the initial years after privatisation. The government therefore had a window to negotiate new conditions, triggered by Mirant's desire to reduce its equity below 51 per cent before the end of the tenth anniversary date, a key condition of the shareholders' agreement. There was a clause which stated that the consent should not be unreasonably held but it only applied after seven years.

Besides obtaining consent from the government for the sale, it also had rights of first refusal; however, the government would be required to purchase the shares at the price offered by the competing third party purchaser. Further, the government could choose to agree to the sale and trigger the 'tag along' rights which gave the government the right to join with Mirant and sell its minority stake of 20 per cent for a price not less than 95 per cent of the price stated in the original notice to the government. If the named purchaser decided against purchasing the government's portion of the shares in JPSCo, Mirant could not proceed with the sale.

The government, however, faced a problem in that there was a hierarchy of companies higher up the chain, Mirant JPSCo (Barbados) SRL, falling under the umbrella of Mirant's global organisational structure through which the sale could have been affected. The consultant to the government's advice was to use the sale opportunity to correct some of the earlier deficiencies in the licences and shareholder agreement (SHA) by attaching conditions to the consent requiring best practices in the industry, or consent to the sale, subject to the generation business being sold as an unbundled transaction from the transmission and distribution business.

The Mirant 2005 restructuring involved the transfer of Mirant's share in JPSCo to a new company. The government needed to understand whether the information from Mirant referred to the New Mirant replacing Old Mirant as the parent company at the pinnacle of the hierarchy of the Mirant group of companies. If it was Mirant Barbados that was being sold, the right of first refusal did not apply. Similarly, the right to 'tag along' did not apply if the sale was higher up the chain.

After the minority shareholder's third anniversary date, the government also had the right to sell 5 per cent of the equity to employees (Article 11.1) or list the company's shares on the Jamaica Stock Market to the extent reasonably necessary to permit any registerable securities to be offered and sold on the stock market. The government had earlier announced its intention to sell its 19.1 per cent minority shareholding via the local JSE. JPSCo had also recently issued notes to the value of US$180 million to refinance certain maturing debt.

As special advisor to the prime minister, I was required to obtain the opinion of Acres Management Consultants of Canada, Cambridge Economic Planning and Associates, the firm that was then carrying out a Regulatory Impact Assessment[67] and a consultant, financed by the IDB[68] as to possible options and plan of action to be taken by the government.

Some of the critical shortfalls identified by the consultants in the Mirant–government of Jamaica agreement were as follows:

- Since JPSCo, being a vertically integrated company without even accounting separation, let alone management or business separation, OUR's ability to provide incentives to improve efficiency was extremely difficult and, at best, could cause only marginal improvement. JPSCo had completed the accounting and other changes involved in the separation recommended by C&L, but the government subsequently ordered that the arrangements be cancelled, and the departments put back together.
- There was no obligation for JPSCo to buy all bulk power outputs from the IPPs according to an agreed methodology designed to produce an economically efficient outcome.
- JPSCo, being one player in the generation market, was also responsible for preparing the least cost expansion plan (LCEP), as well as being responsible for managing the tender for new capacity, albeit under the supervision of the regulator. JPSCo was, in fact, responsible for procuring a new capacity. This created a conflict of interest when JPSCo was required to prepare the LCEP, given the potential interest in building future generation capacity. This conflict of interest had been cited as one reason it took so long to develop or revise the LCEP.
- OUR, as regulator, suffered from serious information asymmetry in terms of regulatory information, as a minimum the licence should have expressly specified accounting separation between the JPSCo's businesses of generation, and JPSCo's transmission, and distribution/retail businesses, as well as to provide for an accounting ring fence for JPSCo single buyer operations as systems operator/load dispatcher. There should have been

separate pricing, performance, and service standards for generation, as distinct from transmission and distribution/retail supply. Even if common ownership of generation and transmission was permitted, the business of generation should have been made operationally separate from transmission and distribution/retail supply. This would have minimised the scope for cross-subsidisation and any unfair discrimination.

- Generators in the single-buyer model were not exposed to the demand side market signal and could not respond to them, creating the need for constant regulatory interventions to secure efficiencies. There was no opportunity for competitive pressure to be applied on JPSCo from allowing large consumers direct access to competing supply sources.
- JPSCo, an owner of the bulk of the generating capacity, was also responsible for the moment-by-moment load dispatching of power in the grid, creating a conflict of interest. This led to complaints from IPP's of discrimination in the dispatching of their generation plants. There was a lack of transparency and independence in the load despatch or system operations.
- The licence did not allow the OUR as regulator to impose penalties to obtain corrective behaviour. The main enforcement mechanism available to the government was revocation of the licence. Under the licence, the government's step-in rights were limited to the security of future supplies. The government needed to broaden the step-in rights, to ensure that, in the event of a crisis, it had wider powers to step in and secure future and efficient supplies of electricity.
- There was no obligation to supply end users/customers under the exclusivity.
- The licence worked against renewable energy sources, micro-turbines, and other forms of distributed energy.
- Since, with the existing financial constraint on the government, there was room for negotiation with Mirant and the new purchaser, the advice to the government was to negotiate for new improved conditions with the new purchaser. At the time in 2007, the remaining exclusivity period for the transmission, distribution, and retail supply business had whittled away to just fourteen years.

There is no room under the existing economic policy framework to return JPSCo permanently to the public sector. Over the oncoming five years, at least US$600 million of new investment was needed to provide additional capacity and replace old infrastructure. The Country Strategy Agreement required that the government reduce its debt to GDP from 137 per cent over the medium term, hence, long-term borrowing to finance an electricity capital programme was not an option.

On December 28, 2005, the consent was given to Mirant JPSCo (Barbados) SLR, and the consent document was signed by NIBJ on behalf of the government. The Mirant 80 per cent equity interest sale was finalised with Marubeni Corporation and TAQA (Marubeni TAQUA Caribbean) in 2007. Marubeni purchased its 80 per cent stake from the Mirant Corporation, which had purchased the 80 per cent stake from the government in 2001. More precisely, Mirant sold its 80 per cent stake to Marubeni Caribbean Power Holdings (MCPH) Inc, a subsidiary of Marubeni Corporation of Japan. Marubeni later transferred 50 per cent of its shares to Korea East-West Power Company (EWP).

Marubeni Corporation of Japan bought the Caribbean business of Mirant for US$1.082 million, which included related debt of approximately US$350 million, power purchase obligations of US $153 million and estimated working capital. Net proceeds to Mirant for the Caribbean business was US$565 million after payment of JP Morgan's fees and related transaction costs of US$14 million. The Caribbean businesses comprised Mirant Barbados Holdings with 80 per cent equity in JPSCo, 55 per cent equity holdings in Grand Bahamas Power Company, 39 per cent holdings in PowerGen of Trinidad and Tobago, 25 per cent holdings in Curaçao Utilities Company, and a US$40 million convertible preferred equity interest in Aqualectra in Curaçao. The method of acquisition was not direct purchase of the 80 per cent equity in JPSCo, but it would appear to be a purchase of the shares of the Barbados Mirant Holdings, which previously held the interest in Mirant's Caribbean operations.

Based on the quality of this buyer, the government was more concerned with an investment and reform programme from Marubeni. The following were the main points of concern requiring Marubeni to:

a. significantly improve efficiencies, especially thermal efficiencies from the existing low levels of 24 per cent for the oil-fired steam plants and 26 per cent for the gas turbine plants;

b. ensure conversion from heavy fuel and automotive diesel, preferable to natural gas to reduce fuel cost;

c. expand and strengthen the transmission system to improve efficiency and system security, with expansion in generation capacity to 2015; transmission investments would be required to evacuate the additional power and meet some of the systems security concerns expressed in the Forensic Report by the Canadian consultants;

d. reduce the high levels of system losses from 23 per cent to more acceptable levels; approximately 15.8 per cent was built into the tariff-over this 15.8 per cent (the cost went to JPSCo profit-and-loss accounts);

e. provide for generating technology which would facilitate improvement to the environment and that JPSCo meet certain environmental standards, especially regarding greenhouse gas emission from any new power plant and any off loading/terminal and transportation facility;

f. an industry structure providing for more transparency, reduction of the problem of information asymmetry and, overall, a structure which would enhance the effectiveness of the regulatory process.

With the sale of JPSCo to Marubeni, the government could secure the following changes to the licence:

- Marubeni consented to transferring responsibility for preparing LCEP, addition of new generation capacity and the management and administration of the competitive bid process for new capacity to the OUR.
- Mirant-controlled JPSCo, after April 1, 2004, would no longer enjoy exclusivity in the new generation market, including re-powering and replacements; this, however, continued with Marubeni-controlled JPSCo.
- Marubeni Corporation was required to give the government a written undertaking to be bound by the terms of the guaranty, prior to transferring ownership, should New Mirant cannot sign the *Parent* guaranty.
- The management and administration of competitive procurement processes for the addition of new generating capacity was transferred from JPSCo to the OUR. Subsequently,

it was realised that the OUR would be conflicted, and a separate procurement unit was established to procure additional generating capacity.

- There was also an agreement with Marubeni to cooperate with the government and the OUR to facilitate the introduction of renewable energy, including hydro, wind, and biomass and distributed power, as targeted in the government's energy policy.
- The OUR should not be involved in planning, procurement, or the despatch of electricity supplies. If The OUR were to be involved in these activities, it would remove the office from its regulatory role. It should concentrate on setting standards, tariff and monitoring and enforcement of the rules. However, retaining the single buyer vertically integrated approach and improving the licence was at least a first step to remove the conflicts and provide for a more transparent and effective regulatory framework. For these, OUR needed qualitative strengthening in areas. Concomitant changes were also required in the Energy Ministry

Marubeni Majority-Controlled JPSCo Since 2007

In 2007, there were 581,828 customers of which 520,085 were residential consumers, or just under 90 per cent of total consumers, with annual growth of the total number of customers at 3.7 per cent between 2003 and 2007, whereas total consumption sales have been growing at 1.1 per cent. Residential consumers accounted for 34 per cent of energy sales, increasing at just under 1 per cent per annum, while system loss was 22.9 per cent of net generation; per capita consumption was 1.284 KWh per annum in 2008. Table 16.12 shows the industry structure in 2008 shortly after the acquisition by Marubeni.

The capacity of the self-generator does not include dedicated capacity. JPSCo connected grid was 816.45 MW in 2006, with a peak demand of 629 MW. The self-generators, including all the bauxite/alumina and sugar companies, had a capacity of 200MW of which 30 MW was sugar industry owned.[69] REP Limited, connected seventy-four thousand households with electricity between 1975 and 2009. As a result, 90 per cent of the rural areas in 2009 had grid-connected electricity, up from 60 per cent in the 1970s.

Table 16.12: Electricity Industry Structure, 2006/8

Company	Main Role	Generation installed	Transmission	Distribution	Retail	Despatch
JPSCo	Monopoly supplier to final users	623 MW	Monopoly over Transco	Monopoly over disco	Monopoly over retail supply	Has the despatch function
Jamaica Energy Partners (JEP)	IPP	124 MW	na	na	na	na
Jamaica Private Power Company (JPPC)	IPP	61MW	na	na	na	na
Wigton Wind Farm	IPP subsidiary of PCJ	20 Mw	na	na	na	na
Jamalco	Self-producer alumina cogeneration	Up to 11 MW to sell to the JPSCo grid	na	na	na	na
Jamaica Broilers	Self-producer alumina cogeneration	20 MW to sell to JPSCo	na	na	na	na

Source: Arbelaez, Jorge P and Natacha C. Marzolf (2011) 'Power Possibility: The Energy Sector in Jamaican,' Washington, DC, IDB.

In all of Jamaica, 92 per cent in 2008 had grid-connected electricity, up from 70.8 per cent in 1994. The rest used mostly kerosene. Since 2006, REP with the use of concessional funds has been facilitating regularisation of households in twelve selected inner-city areas. In addition, REP has been using renewable energy technologies to provide electricity to homes where the cost of extending the distribution grid would have been too high, such as areas where the lines would connect less than twenty houses per mile. This followed up on a programme initiated in 1998 equipping two villages and about forty-five homes with photovoltaic technology on a test basis using funds provided by the World Bank Demand Side Management Programme.

In 2008, JPSCo accounted for 69 per cent of generated power connected to the grid. In terms of share of grid generation breakdown, heavy fuel oil/steam and diesel dominate, delivering to the grid 71. per cent, with combined cycle gas turbine at 17.2 per cent, gas turbine at 6.6 per cent and renewables (small hydro and wind) at 3.9 per cent and 1.3 per cent capacity, respectively.

Developments in the Electricity Sector Since 2010

There have been fundamental changes to the electricity sector since 2010.[70] Several of the recommendations outlined in the various consultancy reports (identified earlier) have been implemented by the government, including the introduction of a new Electricity Act 2015, replacing the 1892 Electricity Lighting Act, the 1957 Electricity Development Act, and the Electricity Frequency Conversion Act, consolidating the main sections relating to electricity generation, transmission, distribution, supply, and despatch. New sets of licences were also issued in 2016, in keeping with the 2015 Electricity Act.

The main changes to the Electricity 2015 Act[71] provide for a greater role for the minister responsible for electricity (regulation by ministerial fiat), taking a regressive path back the regulatory framework of the mid-1990s. This leaves the way open for political opportunistic behaviour by the minister as there are no checks and balances provided in the Act regarding the minister's intervention. The following are the main changes:

- The Ministry of Science, Energy and Technology (MSET) is responsible for energy policy and planning, as well as safety regulation of the electricity sector. It does the planning through the Electricity Integrated Resource Planning Unit within the ministry.

- The New Act at last provides for the unbundling of the electricity sector into generation, transmission, distribution, despatch, and retail supply, and requires the parties providing electricity services to obtain a licence from the ministry not the regulator as is the more conventional international practice. All generation licences are non-exclusive and, regarding the other licences, they may be exclusive, or non-exclusive.
- The Act introduces a new entity, the Generation Procurement Entity (GPE) as an independent not-for-profit public entity, responsible for procurement of additional generation capacity.
- The Act introduces a single buyer, responsible for contracting for the additional generation capacity at the transmission level, and through net billing at the distribution end (distributed energy).
- The Act provides for a system operator responsible for the system operation function, and despatch of bulk power in the grid.

The electricity industry, under the new Act is now organised around the following:

- A single buyer model in which JPSCo acts as the single buyer (system operator), grid operator (transmission and distribution) and retail supplier;
- The Act provides for JPSCo to own generation capacity, which is not unbundled from its transmission and distribution business; (JPSCo, however, has incorporated a subsidiary for the new plant it is constructing at Old Harbour);
- JPSCo has the first rights to replace aged capacity at Old Harbour; its subsidiary, South Jamaica Power Company, is building a 190 MW base load plant at Old Harbour, using LNG as the fuel source. (JPSCo seems to anticipate unbundling and incorporating South Jamaica Power Company as a subsidiary for the additional capacity it is installing at Old Harbour);
- An independent IPP, NFE South Power Holding, is building a 194 MW plant at Old Harbour (Port Esquivel) and will also use LNG from a floating storage and re-gasification plant at Port Esquivel;

Currently, the independent power producers providing bulk power to the grid are:

- **Renewables IPPs:** Wigton Wind Farm Limited, which has been privatised; BMR Jamaica Wind Limited; WRB Enterprises (Content Solar) and Eight Rivers, building a 37 MW solar plant as well;
- **Conventional IPPs:** Jamaica Power Company; Jamaica Energy Partners Company, and West Kingston Power Partners. In addition, there are co-generators: JAMALCO/NFE is also building a 194 MW co-generation plant using LNG near Old Harbour. JPSCo has a power exchange agreement with Jamaica Alumina Company (Jamalco), allowing the company to sell excess capacity to JPSCo. The bauxite and alumina companies and the sugar companies provide generated power (cogenerators) for their own use and also sell surplus to the JPSCo grid;
- The OUR continues as a multisector regulator, with reduced regulatory responsibilities, mainly for regulation of services and economic regulation.

The Act retains the Government Electrical Regulator, responsible for the safe introduction of new works into the system and certification and registration of electricians. Customers were paying US cent 31.1 KWh, or J$22.6/KWh in 2019, (JPSCo 2014–2019.[72] Installed capacity in the system in 2019 is shown in the table 16.13 below.

Table 16.13: Ownership of Installed and New Capacity under Construction 2019

No	Owner	Capacity MW
1	JPSCo	640.0 (61% of Capacity)
2	JEP	124.2
3	WKPP	65.5
4	JPPC	61.3
5	Jamalco exchange agreement	11.0
6	Wigton Wind Farm	62.0
7	BRM Wind Farm	36.3
8	Content Solar	70.0

Source: JPSCo's Five year Business Plan 2019–2024

JPSCo now has increased its renewable capacity with a 3 MW wind plant, several small hydros, and a 20 MW solar plant. JPSCo has seen its dominant position in the generation sector declining from almost 100 per cent at the beginning of liberalisation in 1990 to under 70 per cent in 2010. Its share of generated power in 2020 has fallen to under 50 per cent. The increased entry confirms the theory that, once there is free entry to the market, the incumbent will always find it difficult to maintain its dominant position.

The fuel sector has also been liberalised and, with introducing LNG into the system in 2016 some 114 MW, heavy fuel oil and automotive diesel have been replaced as the main fuel source. New Fortress Energy supplies most of the LNG. Currently, wind provides 102 MW; small hydro 29 MW; solar 20 MW, total renewable 151 MW. Liquid fuel still provides 760 MW of installed capacity.

Role of the Regulators

The Act seems to fucus more on extending the role of the minister in regulating the industry, rather than providing a robust, transparent regulatory framework. Certainly, it does not follow the best international practices in its design. By introducing such a wide role for the minister, without checks and balances, the way is open for opportunistic political behaviour, and it is most likely that foreign investors will, from my experience in other jurisdiction, factor this as country and regulatory risks. While it is an international practice in some regimes for the minister to grant licences, the best international practice dictates that this should be the remit of the regulator. The regulator should be responsible for the review of licence applications, similar to the provision in the Telecommunications Act, and the minister should grant the licences on the recommendations of the regulator.

In the Telecommunications Act, the provision provides for licence applications to be made to the OUR. The provision sets out the basis for the OURs' assessment, including the important requirement of 'fit and proper,' and assessment of market power. This is the case in Oman, where the where the authorities are restructuring and privatising the electricity industry. The experience of the 1990s with telecommunications and the ostensible capture of the minister by the company should be a lesson for Jamaica and developing countries.

The Act should prescribe certain minimum standards, at least regarding the processes and conditions to be satisfied, prior to granting a licence. There is a need for transparency and to avoid 'sweetheart deals' or connected person deals. Parliament should question the difference between telecommunications and electricity industry acts and should seek to obtain satisfactory answers. The whole section on granting of licences is muddled and needs thorough review by technical specialists and not just lawyers, who rarely have the specialised technical expertise required for infrastructure legislative drafting.

One cannot understand why the minister should be involved in a highly technical matter as electricity code. This is certainly a matter for the regulator if it is to follow best international practice. Electricity code and transmission agreements require constant reviews. If anything, the role of the minister should be to approve the code.

The OUR, with a transparent and robust institutional framework, should carry out responsibility for: approval of the least cost expansion plans, irrespective of which agency prepares it; approve all the PPAs; carry out 'fit for purpose' evaluation; monitor the competitive bidding process; monitor PPAs tariff levels; establish tariff for electricity transmission and distribution as well as for retail electricity, and monitor and enforce licence conditions.

Going Forward Suggested Role of the Regulator

- Carries out analyses regarding requests for new licences, suspension, revocation, transfer, and assignment, including changes to licence conditions, and should be required to make recommendations to the minister. If the minister decides not to accept the recommendation of the OUR, he/she should be required to state reasons in writing.
- Sets all tariffs for the sector, including transmission interconnection tariff, according to a prescribed formula.
- Deals with dispute resolutions as it relates to parties operating in the industry.
- Enforces the legislation and licence breaches.
- Carries rule-making powers regarding the regulation of the industry. The regulator ought to have powers to make and modify rules, given the dynamics of the industry, to better regulate the industry and provide for transparency in the exercise of powers granted in the Act. This should by order be published in the *Jamaica Gazette* after consultation with the minister.

- Makes recommendations to the minister on energy and electricity policies and on the overall development of the industry, taking into consideration the economic development of the country and the interest of investors and consumer.

The 2015 Electricity Act should have made provisions for introducing electric vehicles, as well as making provision for regulating technical, safety and service quality standards in the EV charging market.

The Act should have provided for the broadening of experts serving on the Electricity Appeal Tribunal to cover professionals in law, engineering, finance and accounting, economics, and utility regulation. The Act should also have specifically stated that the minister carries the power to establish the electricity market structure, taking into consideration changes in technology and economic operation/market condition prevailing, or expected in the industry. This was one of the major weaknesses of the 1892 Electricity Lighting Act. Because of the rigidity of 1892 Act, it could not expect the changes in technology and the operation of the industry as it unfolded, especially after the 1980s.

The 2015 Electricity Act needs to address consumer protection matters in the provision of electricity services in Jamaica, and should clearly state the distribution of roles in consumer affairs matters with the Fair Competition Commission.

The Act should give the power to the OUR to deal with disputes before they go to the Electricity Appeal Tribunal to avoid the Tribunal having to deal with every dispute. It should be an appellate body only.

The Electrical Inspectorate could easily be brought within the remit of the OUR to address technical regulation. A separate Electrical Inspectorate is a colonial anachronism. The regulator should regulate economic, technical, and service standards. There is no separate Electrical Inspectorate in Oman, Nigeria, or the UK. This seems to be a carryover from colonial days.

The law now makes the single buyer a permanent feature of the industry. Once the industry graduates to bilateral trading, there will be no need for a single buyer. The OUR should be given the power to evaluate the state of the electricity market periodically, considering its capacity to accommodate more competition and to make recommendations to the minister as to the additional forms of competition which should be accommodated. JPSCo is expecting the government moving to a more competitive electricity market and industry structure, facilitating a new transparent framework and with a system operator independent of JPSCo business.[73]

There should be a relationship specified with the environmental regulator regarding environmental matters as it affects the electricity industry. In a note on the electricity sector in 2008, the World Bank[74] concluded that Jamaica had reached an advanced stage of private sector participation, built extensive regulatory capacity, and had implemented tough reforms, including cost reflective tariff; however, the World Bank further noted that there was still room for improvements. This was certainly possible in the structure, regulatory and operational arrangement.

The privatisation and regulation of the electricity industry has been the most intractable partly because the network sector remains a natural monopoly, whilst the generation and retail sectors have lost their natrum monopoly characteristic and can be subjected to competition.

Notes

1. E.C. William, 'Jamaica Public Service Company: A Short History of Its Origin and Development 1923-1978,' Kingston, Jamaica, undated.
2. Raphael A. Swaby, 'The Rationale for State Ownership of Public Utilities in Jamaica,' *Social and Economic Studies* 30, no. 1 (March 1981): 75–107.
3. William, 'Jamaica Public Service Company: A Short History of Its Origin and Development 1923-1978.'
4. Swaby, 'The Rationale for State Ownership of Public Utilities in Jamaica.'
5. Ibid.
6. Harvey Averch and Leyland Johnson, 'The Firm Under Regulatory Constraint,' *American Economic Review* 52, no. 5 (1962): 1052–69.
7. Michael Posner, 'Taxation by Regulation,' *Bell Journal of Economics and Management Sciences* 2, no. 1 (1971): 22–50.
8. Gladstone E. Mills, (1974), *'Public Policy and Private Enterprise in Commonwealth Caribbean,' Social and Economic Studies*, UWI, Vol.10, No. 2
9. Gladstone E. Mills, 'A Reader in Public Policy and Administration,' ISER, Mona, Jamaica, 1990.
10. World Bank, *Development Report: 1997: The State in a Changing World* (Oxford: Oxford University Press, 1997).
11. Cezley Sampson, *Jamaica Public Service Company Limited: Strategic Marketing Case*, (Cranfield, UK: Cranfield Case Clearing House, 1992), 16–22
12. Electricity prices had been separated into a two-part pricing formula, consisting of a fuel clause element and a rate base element,

13. Fuel clause was introduced in the rate structure to reflect changes in the price of fuel on the rates, separate and apart from the other operating costs as a result of the oil price increase in the early 1970s.
14. Adlith Brown, 'Issues in Public Enterprise,' *Social and Economic Studies* 30, no. 1 (March 1981): 1–16.
15. Edwin Jones, 'Role of the State in Public Enterprise,' *Social and Economic Studies* 30, no. 1 (March 1981): 17–44.
16. Dhiru Tanna the Economist in the AMU and I were responsible for these recommendations to Minister Bell.
17. Adlith Brown and Helen McBain, 'Studies in Caribbean Public Enterprise,' (Institute of Social and Economic Research, UWI, 1983), 80–105.
18. Adlith Brown, 'Issues in Public Enterprise.'
19. Sampson, 'Jamaica Public Service Company Limited.'
20. Earle Richards, 'Overview of Private Sector's Role in Jamaica Energy/ Power Sector,' Jamaica Public Service Company Abstract, Kingston, unpublished 1991.
21. World Bank, *Jamaica Energy Sector, Strategy and Investment Planning Study*, ESMAP, Vol. 1, Main Report (Washington, D.C.: World Bank, 1992).
22. In 1991, the Venezuelan President Andrez Perez extended the San Jose Accord to Michael Manley of Jamaica. Oil price payment was provided for delayed payments to go into a fund to be used for development projects. In 1991, fourteen thousand housing units were due to be constructed at Portmore, and J$7 billion was used to build ten thousand units out of the San Jose Development Fund. The San Jose Accord replaced the Javamex Agreement, which died in child birth and which called for joint projects in bauxite mining, alumina refining, and aluminium smelting.
23. The San Jose Accord was initiated in the 1970s and was replaced by the Petrocaribe Accord in 2005 which, provided cheaper supply of oil to Jamaica and participating Caribbean islands. Petrocaribe was signed between Prime Minister Patterson and President Chavez and replaced the middlemen in the supply arrangement. Jamaica has had a long relationship with Venezuela despite the hostilities of the US against the relationship. The relationship goes back to the days of Simon Bolivar. Bolivar spent time in exile in Jamaica. The Petro Caribe facility is now defunct. Jamaica reduced its Petrocaribe obligations in 2015 when it used J$2 billion on the international market to retire J$3 billion of Petrocaribe debt at a price of J$1.5 billion. Some of the outstanding payments were converted into 49 per cent shareholding in Jamaica oil refinery Petrojam in favour of government-owned PdV Venezuela. Eventually, Jamaica set aside PdV shareholding in Petrojam after PdV reneged on a project to help to expand the refinery from thirty-five bbls a day to fifty thousand bbls a day facility.
24. World Bank, *Jamaica Energy Sector, Strategy and Investment Planning Study*.

25. Types of rates evaluated by JPSCo: Straight Line Meter Rate involving a constant price per unit regardless of the volume used. It is the simplest rate formula and derives its name from the straight line that results when the total bill is plotted on a rectangular co-ordinate for various consumptions. Its advantage is its simplicity but does not provide a lower price for increased volume used. Sometimes it is referred to as postage stamp pricing. Block Meter Rate where specified prices per unit sold applies to specified blocks of use, with the price per unit generally decreasing for successive blocks. Modified Block Meter Rate is similar to the above, except that an exception is made to the first block. Instead of a specified price per unit consumed in the first block, the rate provides an initial charge which permits a specified number of units to be consumed. It allows for the first block to carry a subsidy to meet universal and social services obligation and is sometimes referred to as lifeline rate. The fuel charge takes into consideration that the utility has no control over fuel prices and hence should not be penalised for increases in fuel prices. The price provides for an increase or decrease above or below a certain base fuel price, with adjustment applying to the energy sold to the customer. In this way, the customer contributes to payment for fuel in excess of that on which the rate structure is based or conversely obtains a credit on the account if the fuel price drops below the base value. It avoids frequent base rate adjustments. The base rate covers that specified by the regulatory authority.
26. National Investment Bank of Jamaica, 'Privatisation of JPSCo: Issues Affecting the Privatisation of JPSCo,' Appendix 1, February 1995.
27. Basil Sutherland, *Financing Jamaica's Rockfort Independent Power Project: A Review of Experience for Future Projects* (Washington, DC: World Bank, 1998).
28. Jorge P. Arbelaez and Natacha C. Marzolf (2011), *Power Possibility: The Energy Sector in Jamaican* (Washington, DC: IADB, 2011).
29. S. Hunt and G. Shuttleworth, *Competition and Choice in Electricity* (New York: John Wiley, and Sons, 1996).
30. Besant Jones E., 'Reforming Electricity Markets in Developing Countries: What Have We learned?' Energy and Mining Sector Board, discussion Paper No. 19, Washington, DC, World Bank, 2006.
31. Cezley Sampson, *End of Monopoly: Competition in Electric Markets: Comparative Studies* (Saarbrüken, Germany: Lambert Academic Publishing, 2002).
32. Sutherland, *Financing Jamaica's Rockfort Independent Power Project.*
33. In the more recent IPPs, there are still provisions for payments of liquidated damages; however, this only comes into play where JPSCo is able to receive and the IPP is unable to supply.
34. National Investment Bank of Jamaica, (February 1995), op. cit.
35. The 'avoided cost' is the price the entity would have paid to produce the same power itself or purchase it from another source.

36. Paul Joskow, 'The Evolution of Independent Power Sector and Competitive Procurement of New Generating Capacity,' *Research in Law and Economics* 13 (1991): 63–100.
37. I was engaged by Coopers and Lybrand as the local members of the consultancy team.
38. Coopers and Lybrand, *Jamaica Power Sector Regulatory Framework and Privatization*, Phase Two Report, Kingston, Jamaica, Section 205, 1993.
39. An important development in the reform of electricity market is that once generation is liberalised, the market will correct itself if entry to the generation market is free. This experience was also borne out in the UK privatisation. The two duopoly electricity generators with 60 per cent generation capacity at liberalisation saw their market share fall to under 30 per cent in no time.
40. A.J. Meyrick and Cezley Sampson, 'Proposal for the Regulation of Public Utilities' in Jamaica,' Ministry of Finance, Planning and Development, Kingston, Jamaica, April 1991.
41. Price Waterhouse Utility Economics and Financial Consultancy Group, 'Options for Privatisation and Regulation of JPSCo,' Washington, 1994.
42. Sam Peltzman,'Towards a More General of Regulation,' *Journal of Law and Economics* 19 (August 1976).
43. George Stigler, 'The Theory of Economic Regulation,' *Bell Journal of Economics and Management Science* 2, no. 1 (spring 1971): 3–21.
44. Colin Robinson, '*Profit Discovery, Rate of Entry: The Case of Electricity in Regulating Utilities: Time for a Change*,' ed. M.E. Beesley, (London: Institute of Economic Affairs, Reading, 1996) No.44.
45. W. Glen, 'Private Sector in Electricity in Developing Countries, Supply and Demand,' Washington, International Finance Corporation, Working Paper, No. 15, 1991.
46. Jamaica Public Service, *Annual Report 1995–96* (Kingston: Jamaica Public Service, 1996).
47. UNCTAD, *Design, Implementation and Results of Privatisation Programmes: Review of National Experiences* (New York: UNCTAD, 1994). Cable and Wireless purchase of the telecommunications utility is 1985 is a case in point where the tariff formula locked in the rate of return at 17.5 per cent to 22 per cent on revalued assets, after tax.
48. World Bank, 'Implementation Completion Report for Energy Sector Deregulation and Privatisation Project'; Jamaica Energy Sector Study,' IDB, Washington, November 2002. See also Fernando Lecaros (2000).
49. C. Hoo, 'Public Administration and Public Policy: Intellectual Challenges for the 1990,' Australian *Journal of Public Administration* 48, no. 4 (1983): 346–58.
50. J. Boston, J. Martin, J. Pollot, and P. Walsh, *Public Management: The New Zealand Model* (Auckland: Oxford University Press, 1996).
51. Michael Kerf and Warrick Smith, 'Privatizing Africa's Infrastructure: Promise and Challenge,' World Bank Technical Paper, No. 337, Washington, DC, 1996.

52. Ancile Brewster, 'An Assessment of Electricity Sector Privatization in Trinidad & Tobago and Jamaica,' Master of Business Administration Degree Dissertation, University of Warwick, UK, March 2003.
53. Acres Management Consulting, *National Integrated Electricity Expansion Plan and Efficiency Study: Final Report*, vol. 1, 2007
54. World Bank, *Jamaica Energy Sector Report: Energy Sector Assistance Programme* (Washington DC: World Bank, 1990).
55. JPSCo, *Annual Financial Report* (Kingston: JPSCo, 2001).
56. Hagler Bailly, *JPSCo Long Run Marginal Cost Study 1997–98* (Kingston: JPSCo, 1998).
57. Fernando Lecaros, 'Energy Sector Study,' for the Inter-American Development Bank Finance and Infrastructure Division, Washington, November 2002.
58. Fiona Woolf and Jonathan Halpern (2001*), Integrating Independent Power Producers into Emerging Wholesale Power Markets* (Washington: World Bank, 2001).
59. Ministerial Order, 'The Fair Competition (the Jamaica Public Service Company Limited) (Exemption) Order,' February 26, 2001.
60. Dahlia Arlene Green, 'Divestment: The Case of JPSCo-Public VS Private Ownership' (Master's Thesis, Department of Government, UWI, Mona, 2007). Comparative Data taken from his report.
61. Ibid.
62. Acres Management Consulting, *National Integrated Electricity Expansion Plan and Efficiency Study.*
63. Duane Andre Rowe, 'Planning Towards a More Sustainable Future: Electricity Generation System in Jamaica' (MPhil Thesis, Wolfson College, University of Cambridge, August 2007).
64. Sampson, Cezley (2005), 'The Electricity Sector Energy Policy Review,' Government of Jamaica.
65. Michael Moss, 'System Losses and Transmission Experience,' OOCUR Seminar, Port of Spain, Trinidad, September 2003.
66. Jorge Perez Arbelaez and Natacha C. Marzolf, NAME OF BOOK (Washington: IDB, 2011).
67. There are some important comments on the tariff system, which came out of the IDB study, and these are summarised below.
    - High consumption consumers, in addition to cross-subsidising consumption of less than 100 kWh per month, also cross-subsiding the consumption of those stealing electricity. Currently about 10 per cent of electricity produced is non-revenue earning due to theft and other commercial losses. If commercial losses can be reduced (i.e., more illegal users connecting), then the over-burden of the cross-subsidy on high-consumption users may be reduced. There is evidence, however, that a significant portion of the theft is made by more affluent consumers.

- Non-fuel includes operating costs, such as salaries, maintenance, interest on other borrowings not associated with capital investments, rents, leases, and other costs which are determined to be incurred in connection with the business. In this respect, strategic or opportunistic behaviour on the part of the regulated enterprise cannot be discounted: for example, prior to the 2004 rate review, there was an incentive to inflate operational costs which would have contributed to the revenue requirement, only to be reduced once JPSCo entered price cap regulation mode. This required continuous monitoring by OUR to determine any sudden deviation from trend.
- Depreciation rates are regulated in the licence and appear to be reasonable; problems may, however, arise, for example, equipment that is not in normal use due to technical obsolescence could continue to be depreciated and contribute to the revenue requirement. This was one of the major problems which the PUC encountered during the 1960s.
- With respect to the return on investment (ROI), this is often a major point of contention during a regulatory review and Jamaica's previous experience under the PUC brings this out very clearly. It is based on (a) the 'Rate Base,' defined as the value of the net investment in the business, and (b) on the weighted average cost of capital (WACC). Precedents in US utility regulation evidence the difficulties with this approach. There is a strong incentive for JPSCo to undertake capital-intensive investments on which it will earn a return, as opposed to more labour- or fuel-intensive ones (the so-called 'Averch Johnson effect' of rate of return regulation.
- Calculating the WACC can be another point of disputation. A formula is not provided in the licence, and the calculation could involve any number of parameters which are open to discussion, such as: the risk less rate, a 'beta' value taken probably from a foreign market (US), country risk, the expected market return, and the cost of JPSCo debt. On all of these items a few per centage points could mean a substantial change in the ROI. Rate-making Mechanism (PBRM). The PBRM is an annual readjustment process provided for in the licence which involves an adjustment of the Non-Fuel Base Rate starting June 2004, according to an 'Electricity Pricing Index' (PCI) whose elements consist of (i) an inflation and devaluation measure ('I'), (ii) a productivity component ('X'), (iii) a quality-of-service element ('Q'), and (iv) a catchall component ('Z'), 'the allowed rate of price adjustment for special reasons not captured by the other elements of the formula'. The problems with the adjustment formula lie in X, Q, and Z:

  > 'X should reflect productivity gains and should be subtracted from the rate of inflation 'X' was set at zero in the 2004 review a relatively weak incentive. The utility can submit an investment plan for the next five years but in reality, fail to implement it.

The 'Q' factor is problematic.

- 'Z' involves allowed price adjustments which affect JPSCo's costs that are not due to its managerial decisions and are not captured by other elements of the price mechanism; this, in effect, opens the door for escaping the price cap regulation jacket. EBITA earning plus interest, taxes, and amortisation provide an indication of the company financial condition

68. Cambridge Economic Planning Associates, 'Comments on the Electricity Policy and Mirant,' Cambridge, UK, 2006.
69. Donald Hertzmark, *Jamaica Power Sector: Restructuring and Regulatory Issue and Option* (Washington: IADB, 2006).
70. Cezley Sampson, 'Challenges in Electricity Sector: Jamaica at the Crosswords,' presentation at the Geological Society Exhibition, UWI, November 26, 2006.
71. JAMPRO, 'Jamaica's Energy Sector,' Jamaica Trade and Investment, Kingston, 2021.
72. The Electricity Act 2015 Act 18. The Act Came into operation August 27, 2015, and require that the Act be reviewed by Parliament within five years of the appointed day, hence, the review was due in August 2020.
73. JPSCo, *Tariff Review Application: 2014–2019* (Kingston: JPSCo, 2019).
74. JPSCo *Five Year business Plan 2019–2024* (Kingston: JPSCo, 2019).
75. World Bank, *Jamaica Electricity Sector Note* (Washington, DC: World Bank, 2008).

CHAPTER SEVENTEEN

Privatisation of Public Passenger Transport and Public/Private Partnership in the Road Sector

SPONSORED BY

TRANSJAMAICAN HIGHWAY LTD

HISTORICAL BACKGROUND OF ROAD TRANSPORT IN KINGSTON

The need for organised public transport in the Kingston and St Andrew Corporate Area (KASC) was recognised as far back as 1876 and, as a result, a tramway system was introduced. The tramway served the centre of Kingston well while it existed and was initially owned and operated by Jamaica Streetcar Company, which was founded in 1876, starting with four miles and fifty-one chains of track, circling the central area of Kingston. In two years, the system was extended to Halfway Tree, and the following year it was extended along East Queen Street to Paradise Street. Eventually, the line was to extend to Papine, Hope Gardens, Constant Spring, and Rockfort Gardens.

The 1880s saw further extension along the Spanish Town Road, towards May Pen Cemetery on the west, and to Constant Spring, six miles north of the city centre, with a belt line going to Rae Town in the east, and the East Street Line running through commercial Kingston to the railway station, Kingston Public Hospital to Orange Street, and back again to Cross Roads over the same route. The final extension was Windward Road to the top of Kingston Harbour.[1]

On December 4, 1897, the West India Electric Company (WIEC), a company registered in Canada, purchased the initial horse tramway, and replaced the horse-drawn trams with electric trams. The WIEC was related to the Montreal Street Railway Company, which, it appears, supplied Kingston's first thirty electric trams. Kingston's first electric line ran from the tram depot on Orange Street to the foot of King Street in downtown Kingston. WIEC's trams did good business in bringing produce from rural areas surrounding Kingston to the city's markets, so extra cars were required on the Constant Spring and Hope Gardens route to meet this traffic. On May 25, 1923, the WIEC was taken over by another Canadian company, Jamaica Public Service Company (JPSCo), which then operated the public electricity network. JPSCo operated the tramway from 1923 to 1948.

Table 17.1 shows the development and expansion of the tramway over the period 1876–1948. JPSCo closed the Kingston tramway system on May 10, 1948, claiming that it could no longer compete with road transport and also could not afford to maintain the right-of-way or construct needed extensions. Because of public protest, the Rockfort Gardens line continued operation for a few more months, until in August 1948 when the electric tram service was permanently discontinued.[2]

Table 17.1: Development and Expansion of the Kingston Tramway

Year	Section	Distance – Miles	Accumulation / Miles	Owners
1876	Kingston Tramway	4.00	4.00	Jamaica Street Car Co
1878	Kingston Tramway Extension	8.40	12.40	Jamaica Street Car Co
1899	Rockfort–Papine Tramway	11.60	24.00	West India Electric Co
1923	Kingston Tramway Extension	2.00	26.00	Jamaica Public Service Co
1948	Tramway service closed			

Source: W.R. Long, 'Railways of Central America and the W I, Washington, DC, and Jamaica.'

An earlier colonial transport study, the Hammond Studies, highlighted the plight of the railway and tramway in competing with road transport and in meeting the transport needs of the country.[3] The tramway operating on the main streets served Kingston until the advent of petrol vehicles after the First World War, when the service failed to cope with competition from numerous unorganised small omnibus operators and taxis. Fernley concluded the tramway had fulfilled its useful life, and that an organised urban public transport service, involving the use of omnibuses, was needed. With the Second World War, nothing was done about these recommendations.[4]

The growth of the city of Kingston, in terms of physical expansion and size of the population, was facilitated immensely by the development and extension of the tramway. The Kingston metropolis grew from 68,952, shortly after the tramway came into operation in 1871 to 121,264 in 1921, almost a twofold increase. By 1943, when the tramway folded, Kingston had grown to 202,930. The combination of the tramway and the railway, after 1900, led to the rapid expansion of suburbia in lower St Andrew. The city's population growth took off after 1911, partly because of rural-urban migration into the city and the internal mobility provided by the tramway network in Kingston.

As indicated earlier, the city expanded from the John Goffe eighteenth-century grid into lower St Andrew, encompassing outlying villages, of Papine, Constant Spring, Half Way Tree, and Spanish Town Road. By 1913, a settlement hierarchy was well established between the residential neighbourhoods in Kingston, in that the farther one moved away from lower sections of the city the finer the residences.[5] After the First World War, a pattern of motor bus transport and motor taxi cabs emerged to cover the expanded city, providing ad hoc services and, complementing the tram system, which formed the backbone transport service. There was intense competition between road transport operators in Kingston, and this led to introducing regulations to control buses that were plying illegally all over the town. The tramway was a victim of this competition, as the authorities felt that, given the congestion caused with the tramway operating in the same road space with urban road transport, road transport had to be given preference; as a result, the tramway was phased out in 1948.[6,7]

By 1946, several transport problems including congestion and a chaotic set of services had surfaced, C.E. Rooke[8] drew on the earlier Fernley Report (1938) on Public Passenger Transport Services in the Corporate Area.[9] Importantly, the Fernley Study called for the enactment of a Public Passenger Transport Law, which was enacted in 1947 as the Public Passenger Transport Corporate Area Act of 1947, substantially revised in 1953, providing a framework for regulating private sector road transport operators under licence. Under the 1947 Act, the Public Passenger Transport Board (PPTB). Regulation of this service, however, fell under two entities: the Public Passenger Transport

Urban Area Control Boards and the Public Passenger Transport (Rural Area) Control Board regulating public passenger transport services in the two other large urban towns – Spanish Town and Montego Bay in 1969.

Arising out of the new regulatory structure, exclusive short-term licences were issued for Western Kingston and St Andrew in 1948 to a local Company, Magnet Bus Company Limited, and for central and eastern Kingston to Jamaica Utilities Limited led by J. J. Lindsay. These licences were subsequently revoked by the PPTB because of the poor service offered by both operators in 1953.

The Creation of Jamaica Omnibus Services Limited

In March 1953, the government tried to address the problem of delivering Kingston's transport needs by granting an exclusive licence to a consortium of British Electric Traction (BET) of Birmingham, United transport (Overseas) Limited, and Gerald MacCauley, a local operator representing Enterprise Services Limited, represented by Harry Dayes; Lascelles Panton and the Close Brothers; merchant bankers, without seeking competitive bids.

The transaction lacked transparency, however, after extensive debate in the House of Representative in 1953 the government through the PPTB awarded a fifty-year exclusive licence (with provision for renewal for another twenty years) to the consortium to provide public passenger transport services for the entire Corporate Area. A special-purpose vehicle was created by the consortium; Jamaica Omnibus Services Limited (JOS) for the delivery of the services with effect from December 1953 for the Kingston and St Andrew Corporate, with the Island Traffic Authority (ITA), created in 1947 under the Road Traffic Act to regulate movement of vehicles on the island roads.

The JOS was capitalised with four hundred and fifty thousand pounds sterling and two hundred and fifty thousand pounds of 6 per cent preference shares, convertible to ordinary stock in 1960. In 1960, bonus shares to the value of two hundred and fifty thousand pounds from Capital Reserve increasing the JOS share capital to six hundred thousand pounds.[10]

The company started operations that same year in 1953 with a seventy-bus fleet, operating on fifteen routes. By 1960, its fleet was increased to 181 buses, operating on twenty-two routes, doubling the route mileage. The company increased its fleet from 264 buses in 1964 to 315 buses in 1965 and then to 362 buses by 1967, and 413 buses by 1969. In 1967, the JOS could despatch 346 buses daily. By the end of 1973, the company's' capital stood at J$2.7 million, being 5.4 million shares at par value of fifty Jamaican cents, achieved by capitalisations of reserves, including revaluation of assets. Over the years, the route network extended to Border between the parishes of St Andrew and St Mary, Red Hills, Gordon Town, Jacks Hill, along the northern parts corridor; Bull Bay, Harbour View, and Palisadoes Airport in the east; Six Miles in the west, along the south coast corridor.

Acquisition of JOS by the State in the 1970s

The first application for rate increase by JOS in 1958 was turned down, as the Board, was not satisfied with the level of management fees (7.5 per cent (gross revenues) being charged by BET, and the straight-line accounting method used for depreciation, instead of reducing balance method. In fact, the Board refused to grant any increase between 1954 and 1968. In 1968, an interim increase was awarded of one penny for the first stage followed by another rate application in September 1969. However, the hearing was adjourned *sine die* without an award only to be reconstituted in 1970 to consider a fresh application. An interim increase was awarded, confirming the earlier one penny increase for the first stage, effective April 1970. The final award provided for JOS to earn 8.5 per cent return on uninflated capital estimated at the time to generate J$1.3million of which J$ 944,00 had been the interim increase (US$1 to J$0.77 cent in 1970). The increase was acceptable to the JOS; however, subsequent rate increase application in 1972 after an adversarial hearing was rejected. The Board accused the company of a series of malpractices in contravention of the licence.

Although the government had established the Public Utilities Commission (PUC) in 1966 to regulate the utilities, regulation of public passenger transport was not, however, brought within the remit of the PUC, and the fragmented regulatory structure and passenger transport regulation continued, without inadequate coordination among the ITA and the PPTB and the Rural Transport Board. Securing a route licence, where a route crossed areas of two jurisdictions was a nightmare, contributing to widespread operation of illegal operation. This led Gerald Mills to conclude that the regulatory system of the 1960s and 70s had failed to achieve the objective of providing orderly transport.[11]

The government not only became dissatisfied with the services offered, but with the profits being made by the JOS. From initial capital of J$900,000 the British investors had earned J$5.3 million in profits in eleven years of operation, and in addition could put away J$1.3 million in reserves, after paying J$1,830,092 in management fees whilst paying out dividends of J$854,000.[12] In 1966, several Jamaican citizens were also added to the list of the company's shareholders, part of the JLP 1960 localisation of ownership policy.

The privately owned JOS provided public passenger transport services from 1953 to 1974 and by 1968 had transported 147,141.098 passengers, covering 12,811,551 route miles employing 2,243 workers at its peak.[13]

The services provided by the JOS, nicknamed 'Jolly Joe,' during most of the 1960s was satisfactory. However, the services deteriorated after 1965 and had become progressively worse by 1968. With new demands from an increased population and route expansion into new areas, often with lower traffic density, the company had failed to inject new capital to expand the services. Commitments which it had given to provide additional buses in the early part of the 1970s were not met.

It was at this point that the government made an offer to become part owner, first by acquiring 12 per cent of the company's equity, and subsequently to increase this to 35 per cent. As no agreement could be reached, this led to an offer to acquire the entire stock of the company. Thereafter, the discussions became acrimonious, as the parties could not agree on the price. Under the terms of the licence, compensation was due, and the government was required to pay fair market value. The government took the position that the calculation should be based on the written down value of the rolling stock, while the company took the position that it should be based on the replacement value, which would give a price of approximately J$6.0 million, in effect the value should include goodwill, compared to J$4.8 million on written down value and tax adjustment.

After protracted negotiation the owners of the JOS agreed to accept a price based on the net value of the assets. Eventually the parties agreed to a price of J$3,510,000, or 65 cents per share. The UK shareholders were to be paid in pounds sterling before March 31, 1974.[14] When the government offered to purchase the shares of the company, some local investors declined to accept the offer and continued as a minority group.

In 1974, the government announced that the state would acquire the entire shareholdings of the JOS. At the time, the BET and UTC together held 86 per cent of the company's stock. Payment was eventually made from a UK twelve-year loan, bearing an interest of 1.25 per cent above the London Inter-Bank Offer (LIBOR) rate, and was estimated to average 9.5 per cent over the tenure of the loan. The government had to borrow the funds from overseas to compensate the BET and UTC in foreign currency. The nationalisation of the JOS in 1974 became part of an economy-wide policy of state control of key industries, such as telephone, electricity, and urban public bus transportation.[15]

Public Passenger Transport in Kingston after Nationalisation

Beginning in the 1960s a dual system of transport service delivery emerged in the Kingston Metropolitan Area (KMA), with the privately owned and regulated the JOS competing with the unlicensed minibus operators (robots or para-transit operators) and illegally operated taxis, providing unregulated services and interloping on the JOS's franchised routes. In fact, the state-owned JOS had acquiesced with the minibus operators for them to complement and feed into the JOS's franchised routes. Once the robots interloped in the market, however, they quickly became popular because of their flexibility, convenience, and speed. In addition, they filled the gaps left unserved by the licensed operator. As early as in the 1950s illegal minibuses ('robots'), and illegal taxi operators had appeared on the routes of the privately owned JOS, pirating a significant proportion of traffic on the company's franchise routes.

Following the nationalisation of the JOS, minibus robots mushroomed on the company's routes. A combination of the authority's failure to grant cost-related rate increases led to more pirating of its traffic by illegal minibus operators and taxis. Further, inadequate investments severely impacted the company's ability to meet the transport requirements of a large and growing Kingston metropolis. In fact, the 'robots,' on entering the market in the 1950s, were temporarily removed from the JOS routes; however, because of political pressure, this ban was later relaxed. Robots operated by running ahead of the JOS's buses to pick up waiting commuters. They failed to comply with most laws and regulations, such as providing public liability insurance coverage or providing vehicles which met the required standard of fitness for public service vehicle.[16]

Under state ownership, the JOS chalked up a massive deficit. The company had to meet its capital loan repayment to UK Credit Guarantee Department (CGD) whilst experiencing decline in ridership after 1968 at a rate of 1 per cent to 2 per cent per annum. Route mileage, however, increased from 432 miles to 587 miles, with the number of routes increasing from fifty-eight to seventy-five. This resulted from political pressure to expand the services into the peri-urban loss-making routes. In the same period, the number of buses increased from 384 to only 427.[17] Under state ownership, the JOS was pressured by political forces to spread its aging fleet without matching increase in fleet size whilst having to compete with some eleven hundred illegal minibus operators. The company had to acquire special uneconomic-sized buses to traverse the thinly populated peri-urban routes of Irish Town and Mavis Bank in the foothills of the Blue Mountains and Bull Bay, ten miles into rural St Andrew.

By 1982, the robots and the unregulated taxis had increased their share of the public passenger travel market from 50 per cent to 79.6 per cent, with the JOS's share falling from 50 per cent to just around 20 per cent of the market. The competition and additional financial burden not only led to loss of traffic, but to serious deterioration in the finances of JOS, resulting in a loss of J$11 million per year in the first years of the 1980s. In providing for the mini buses to legally enter the market, a further split in the transport market emerged, comprising the licensed minibuses and the unlicensed, with the unlicensed accounting for 19 per cent of the market.[18]

A sharing arrangement was arrived at, through which the JOS agreed with the minibus operators (under the umbrella of the Jamaica Minibus Association – JMA) for certain routes to be operated exclusively by minibuses, with the JOS operating certain routes free of pirating, and that on some routes both parties would provide the service. In fact, in 1977, the government awarded a group of Portmore minibus operators a franchise to provide public transport services on the commuter route between Portmore and Kingston.[19]

With the steady decline in the quality of service and mounting debt from persistent annual financial losses, the JOS became insolvent by 1983. The government replaced public ownership and operation in the urban transport sector by partial liberalisation of the urban transport market. New arrangements were put in place, and this provided for the auctioning of the bus routes by the MPUT to private package holders, as they came to be known. Bids were received from thirty-one organisations, of which nine were successful in being allocated routes; however, one holder was awarded two packages. The new operators were awarded a set of routes, bus terminals, and fare stages, in addition to being allotted buses from the old JOS fleet. The fares chargeable continued to be determined by the PPTB (Corporate Area).

Although many of the operators belonged to the JMA, they were never formally organised. In fact, in imposing regulations most of their competitive advantages disappeared. Faced with these realities, the government was forced, after ten years of operation of the new system, to curtail the services after 1983, accepting the reality of a largely minibus operated service, replacing the state-owned urban transport system. The JOS carrier responsibilities were suspended, with the company ceasing to provide direct public passenger services. The JOS itself was not liquidated but survived as an asset-holding company, retaining certain regulatory and management functions.

The government again made further changes in the mid-1980s to allow package holders to sub- franchise the actual delivery services by individual minibus operators. The consequence was the system was reduced to a one-man one-bus operation. As the package holders could not control the individual operators to follow predetermined schedules, the arrangement proved to be unworkable. The government had also failed to provide a rate structure that allowed recovery of long-run marginal cost faced with an uneconomic rate structure the operator could not obtain financing from the banks, so the government had to provide a subsidy besides having to take over responsibility for financing new busses required to deliver the required service. Several new buses were acquired and leased to the package holder; however, they failed to meet the conditions of the lease agreement, of providing a centrally managed and controlled urban bus system. The system of a one-man bus was short-lived and was replaced by a cooperative system in 1992.

In 1995, the government produced a new policy arrangement involving a new structure for the KMTR, requiring the vertical unbundling of the transport investment function from the service operation function and established Metropolitan Management Transport Holdings (MMTH), with responsibility for the investment function (acquisition of new busses and depot facilities), with the JOS continuing to be responsible for service delivery through concession to private operators.[20] These assets were to be leased or rented to the operators (public or private). In addition, the MMTH was assigned the responsibility of training the transport operators, including the operators of the Jamaica Union of Transport Cooperative Limited (JUTC), which was later granted the exclusive franchise for the KMTR. The MMTM was also responsible for human resource development.

The MMTM buses were acquired duty-free, as this was one way to allow for standardisation, providing the opportunity for bus owners to access preferential or development financing offered by the government. The relationship between the MMTH and the bus operators was contractual.

The cooperative model was introduced in 1995. Five zones were created: Spanish Town and Papine were awarded to Conurban Transit; Portmore and Northern region to National Transport Cooperative and Eastern region to Metropolitan Transport Service.

The life of the cooperatives was, however, short-lived and, in 1998, the government once again was forced to take over full ownership, control, and delivery of urban public passenger transport services in the KMTR, with the newly created publicly owned Jamaica Utility Transport Company (JUTC). This entity continued up to 2022 as the main provider of public transportation services in the KMTR. An advantage of the new arrangement was that it relieved the operators of the large upfront capital cost. Some 350 Mercedes buses were acquired under the arrangement in 1996, of which forty units were dedicated to the school bus service. For the first time articulated buses were introduced into the Jamaican bus system. The government also gave an undertaking that the regulator would base the bus fare on economic criteria and would allow a rate of return of 15 per cent on invested capital. Four years after introducing the system (1998), the government abrogated the arrangement and entered negotiations with the three licence holders; National Transport Cooperative Society (NTCS), Conurban Limited and Metro Limited, offering the three operators the opportunity for joint venture with the JUTC to provide public transport services in KSAC through a single monopoly public/private operator, in addition to compensation for the unexpired portion of tier licenses. The three operators rejected the offer and through arbitration, claimed a loss of profit for the period 1995–98 on the grounds that the government failed to introduce a cost-related fare structure in 1995 under the agreement. The arbitrator handed down a decision in favour of the operators, to the tune of J$4.2 billion, plus interest. The government refused to be bound by the decision of the arbitrators and subsequently took the matter to the courts because the arbitrator erred in the method used to compute the compensation. The net effect was that the system was returned to the government and in the period of the first full year of public operation in 2002, the JUTC lost J$1 billion.

Table 17.2 shows the different ownership structure for Urban Public Transport in Kingston over the period 1948–2022.

Table 17.2: Urban Transport Ownership Structure in Kingston 1948–2022

Year	Type of Contract	Public/ Private	Ownership
1948–53	Short-term Franchise	Private Sector	Magnet Bus Company and Jamaica Utilities
1953–74	Fifty-year Franchise	Private Sector	Jamaica Omnibus Company owned by British Electric Traction Company Ltd and United Transport Company of UK
1974–83	Exclusive Franchise	Public Sector	Jamaica Omnibus Company
	Sharing with Minibus via Association	Small Business Operators	JOS and Minibus Association Members
1983–92	Franchise to Package Holders	Private Sector	10 Package Holders but nine Operating Companies
1995–98	Cooperative	Private Sector	Members of Cooperatives – three cooperatives controlled the five zones created were created.
1998–2021	Exclusive Franchise	Public Sector	Jamaica Utility Transport Company (JUTC)

Source: Constructed from Alexander, Roy (1996), 'History and Background of Kingston Urban Passenger Transportation,' Transport Retreat Paper, Ministry of Transport.

Between 1948 and 2021, Jamaica tried public monopoly and private monopoly, with different mixes of private sector participation in between; however, a major problem in Jamaica is that, too often, the policymakers have allowed the achievement of technical and economic goals, that of efficient and reliable transport to be eclipsed by the larger social policy of income redistribution and support to the small business sector development, with perverse outcomes.[21]

To meet political considerations, governments have, over the years, failed to allow passenger fares to be adjusted to meet the long-run marginal cost of operation, to the detriment of the companies and the quality of the service to commuters.

The Outcomes of the Charges from Private Operation to Public, then Back to Private, and Finally Back to Public Operation

Initially, the private investors failed to bring in new capital to meet the need for public transport in the expanding urban space, resulting in nationalisation of the urban public transport service company. The railway situation was repeated in urban transport. The decline in the number of bus seats in the KMTR was because of the failure of the government and the regulator to grant rate increases on a timely basis.

There was no rate increase between 1960 and 1968, in much the same way as there was no rate increase for the railways for several years, so the company could not earn sufficient revenues to secure loan financing to cover operating costs and meet debt repayment, in order to address the country's growing transport needs. This left a vacuum in the market, which was readily filled by illegal minibus and taxi operators eroding the traffic of the omnibus company. Eventually, the public passenger transport entity, the JOS, became the third largest drain on the public purse behind Air Jamaica and the sugar sector. When the JOS took over the franchise in 1953, the population of Kingston and St Andrew was three hundred and fifty thousand inhabitants, and the boundaries served by the company was restricted. By 1960, the population of the KMTR had increased significantly, and by 1970, the population had doubled, accompanied by a rapid geographic expansion of the KMTR. At the same time, the KMA had expanded to 250 square miles, a far cry from the Goffe Grid of one square mile, when Kingston was first established in 1701.

Jamaica's liberalisation and privatisation of public passenger transport presents a classic case in which ownership was transferred from the public sector, but other factors which would have encouraged efficient operation, such as an effective regulatory structure and cost-based rate regulation were not put in place by the government. Although the Office of Utilities Regulation (OUR), which was established in 1995, carried the mandate to regulate public passenger transport services, this responsibility was never removed from the Transport Authority which had replaced the Urban Public Passenger Transport Board as sector regulator under the 1987 Transport Authority Act. The OUR itself was reluctant to take on the responsibility for transport regulation and remained an advisor in the determination of tariffs.

Population Growth and Its Relationship with Transport

Between 1943 and 1970, the population of the KMA area more than doubled, increasing from 202,000 in 1943 to 472,321 in 1970. The rate of growth was at its highest in the 1950s, averaging 3.2 per cent per annum between 1943 and 1960, as against the national average of 1.6 per cent. The population rate of growth fell to 2.6 per cent between 1960 and 1970 but remained higher than the national average, at 1.5 per cent per annum. This rate of growth was accompanied by excessive suburban expansion. It was during this period that outlying business centres and shopping malls appeared on the scene to serve the new suburbia which attracted a movement from the older parts of the city. The suburban phenomenon had emerged during the intercensal period 1921–43 and accelerated between 1943 and 1966.[22] In the period since 1990, there has been increased densities occasioned by infilling. Many houses which stood on individual lots were demolished and gated apartment complexes and town houses built instead, accommodating several times the previous population. The extension of the transportation route network played a major part in the development and extension of Kingston suburbia.

The development of settlement structures in Jamaica, both rural and urban, has been intimately intertwined with the growth of public transportation. The railway played an important role in transferring surplus labour from rural areas to Kingston and St Andrew, the main early urban centres. Both the tramway and the public bus network have, over time, been the main contributors to the expansion of Kingston from the Goffe square mile into the Liguanea Plain of lower St Andrew, and latterly into the interior hilly regions of the Blue Mountains in rural St Andrew.

It is also important to note that transportation solutions are not the only avenues to improving mobility in the urban space. Urban growth policies and community design should also be a part of the package of public policy regime that is adopted to reduce congestion and provide efficient public transport services. As seen in Kingston, the haphazard location and arrangement of urban activities and the lack of physical relationship between housing, jobs, and services generate unnecessary travel. Part of the transport problem therefore has to be addressed by non-transport solutions. The structure of the urban transport system is central to the effective operation and amenable social life of the urban space and must be given major consideration in the design of new settlements and new towns.

THE ROADS SECTOR

Historical Background to the Road Sector Private Participation

The road sector was the last of the major industries in Jamaica to be opened up to private participation, following on the initiatives in the early part of 1990s, involving the liberalisation of the telecommunications, financial, and electricity generation sectors through introducing three independent power producers in the early 1990s. Toll roads, however, preceded the 1845 private railway in Jamaica. Several toll roads were built in the eighteenth century. The Jamaican Assembly approved its first toll gate in 1749, when a toll ferry was built at the mouth of the Rio Cobre to link Kingston with Spanish Town. Shortly thereafter, the first toll road was built running from Pindas River in Clarendon to Old Harbour. By 1770, toll roads had become widespread in Jamaica, and one of the most important of such roads was the one linking the Rio Cobre Gorge by Mount Rosser with the north coast port of Ocho Rios, built in 1780s. Toll roads often evoked strong public reaction, even riots, with the charges often seen as burdensome, resulting in turnpikes being abolished in Jamaica in October 1863. The arrival of the railway in 1845 reduced the dependence on road for internal transportation. A major road building programme was started in the 1890s, and by the 1940s, the main roads were macadamised.

Toll roads were not new to Jamaica and initially were based on the UK Highway Law of 1692, allowing parishes in the UK to charge local citizens up to 2.5 per cent of the land and property income to finance road improvements. The UK government had authorised Turnpike Trust to levy tolls and issue bonds also to finance the building and operation of turnpike roads. The system of toll road spread and boomed across the industrialised cites in the UK and was popular up to the 1850s.

The Jamaican transport infrastructure in the seventeenth and eighteenth centuries was basic, and which developed primarily to the meet the demands of the sugar and coffee plantation estates and were originally built, following the path of least resistance: along the coastline, or along river valleys. The result was that, until the end of the twentieth century roads in Jamaica were narrow and winding, extending over treacherous mountains. The road system in eighteenth century Jamaica was bridle paths and wain roads, built for wagons and were often in appalling condition, unsuitable for hauling heavy loads of sugar to shipping ports. Oxen and mule-drawn wagons were sufficient to meet the transport needs of the residents of estate villages.[23] Even up to 1900, it was cheaper and more efficient to send goods within Jamaica by coastal vessels, rather than by inland road transport because of the inadequacy of the road system and the mountainous nature of the island.

To finance road construction and operation, colonial Jamaica adopted the UK Vestry system of local government administration and replaced the ad hoc arrangement for road financing through the Commissioners of Highways, 1681 Highways Act. The Vestry system in Jamaica lasted from 1664 to 1865. The Act required vestries to annually examine conditions of roads and bridges and to carry out their repair through levying of taxes, mainly through poll and property taxes and through raising loans. In 1706, the vestries were relieved of the responsibilities for roads and replaced by highway commissioners who assumed responsibility for road upkeep. Poll taxes was abolished after emancipation. In 1851, the various laws were consolidated into a new Act, establishing the new commissioners of highways and bridges for each parish with the power to levy. To raise road financing, the Vestry system was first replaced by Municipal Boards and subsequently by the Parochial Boards, with responsibly for the development maintenance of roads. However, they had limited powers to raise funds and the shortfalls had to be met by central government.[24] In 1858, the responsibility for maintaining roads was transferred from to central government under the provision of the Main Road Fund. The system of the Parochial Board lasted from 19986 to 1962. Responsibility for main roads continue to fall under central government. In 1980, measures, however, were taken by central government under the guise of centralisation and efficiency to diminish the powers of local government. With the return of the PNP in 1990, functions such as local road, which were transferred from local government were returned, providing for a measure of dedicated sources of funding, Municipal Corporation Act of 1990.

Just at the time the Porus to Montego Bay and the Bog Walk to Port Antonio railway lines were being built, the government embarked on an extensive road building programme. In 1870, the island had less than seventy miles of main roads. By 1893, this had increased to 980 miles and by the 1930s there were over 7,200 miles of roads, accessible to motor vehicles, of which 1,350 of which were paved.[25] The government started in the 1980s directly to invest increased sums for network road infrastructure, building two-lane single carriageways; most of this was financed by loans from the European Union, the IDB, and other international funding institutions. The section from Negril to Montego Bay, a distance of seventy-seven km was funded by Japan Bank for International Cooperation (JBIC), with the section from Montego Bay to Ocho Rios, a distance of 105 km being funded by the CDB and the IDB and the section from Ocho Rios to Port Antonio, distance of 101.5 km, funded by the European Union. The government also improved the road infrastructure network from Kingston to Bushy Park in Clarendon and from Bushy Park to Williamsfield, just outside Mandeville. While the road infrastructure investment of over US$300 million significantly improved the road network, the rapid growth of traffic meant that, by 2000, the improvements would not have catered for the increasing traffic.

Main road financing until 2000, when public partnership arrangement was introduced, was usually undertaken by the Central government through loans from multilateral and bilateral development and financial institutions. Institutions like the World Bank, IDB, and the CDB not only provided loan financing, but they also provided technical assistance and expert advice. Financing took the form of long-term loans, guarantees, or concessional funding. The main bilateral institutions included the Canadian International Development Agency

(CIDA), The United States Agency for International Development (USAID), and the European Development Bank (EDB).

The Jamaican government has also used deferred financing. Here, the private contractor mobilises the financial resources receiving no immediate payment from the government. When the project is completed, the contractor is then paid and government takes over ownership and any debt acquired during project execution. In the period 1997/1998 to 2003/2004, several road projects in Jamaica were financed by differed financing such as the Rural Road Development Programme: Morant Bay to Negril to Savanna-la-Mar and from the Cement Company facilities in Kingston to Harbour View roundabout; arterial roads Island-wide involving 268 km and the dualisation and Road Improvement programme in Montego Bay.

Deferred financing was used for road improvement projects in almost all the parishes; major local contractors were West Indies Home Contractors Limited; Surrey, Paving and Aggregates Limited, and Pavement and Structures Limited. Between April 1999 and June 2002, J$3.6 billion was spent on deferred road project financing (Ministry of Finance, April 13, 2004) with the largest being the Washington Boulevard/Mandela Highway project in Kingston.

Figure 17.1: Government/International Financial Institutions Road Improvements 1980s/90s

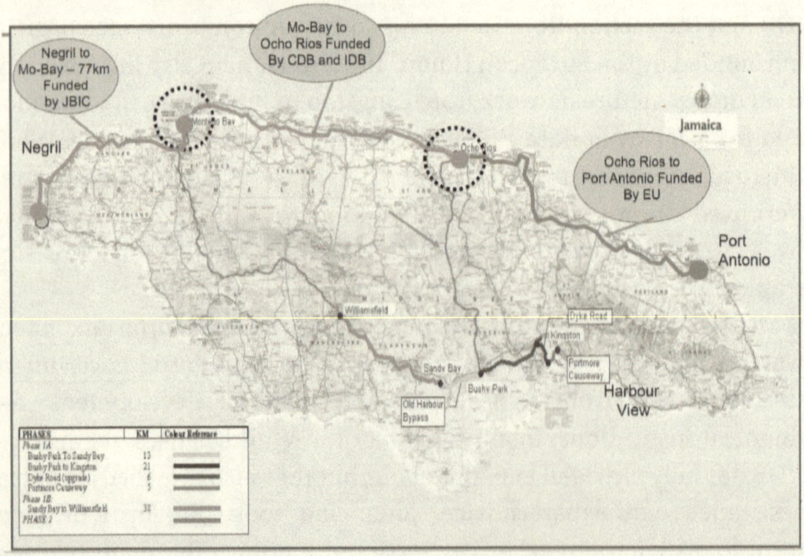

Source: Nicholson, George, (June 2022), 'Jamaica Highway PPP Experience' Presentation at Caribbean Development Bank and JDB Seminar in Kingston

Figure 17.1 shows the government/International Financial Institution Road Improvement projects in Jamaica over the 1980s and 1990s.

Bilateral and multilateral loans for road financing were also provided by the Kuwait Fund for Arab and Economic Development (KFAED), Saudi Fund for Development (SFD) and the CDB, USAID and the IDB. The CDB funded several road projects between 1971 and 2002, amounting to US$46.1 million; the IDB in the period 1973–2001 funded US$182.75 (part of the funds was used for hospital reconstruction); the KFAED in 2000–2001, US$25.9 million; the European Union in 1999 funded US$252.2 million. The Japan Bank for International Cooperation financed the North Coast Highway's Negril to Montego Bay leg; the IDB and the CDB financed the Montego Bay to Ocho Rios North Coast Highway leg with the European Union financing the St Ann's Bay to Port Antonio leg. The CIDA and USAID also provided small amounts as well.

Several bypasses to main towns were also constructed during the period. Spanish Town and St Ann's Bay bypass were funded by the World Bank; the Old Harbour bypass by the KFAED, government and Organization of Petroleum Exporting Countries; Melrose Hill bypass by Alcan and the Ministry of Works. In 2000, the island-wide main road network amounted to 4,794 km and the Parish Council/Farm Roads to 14,900 km.[26]

Road projects involve investments with slow amortisation and may not generate sufficient demand to make them self-financing through some type of user fee, or toll charges; hence, road construction in Jamaica over the years has mainly been financed through major participation by the public sector. In the 1990s, a number of countries, including France, Canada, Australia, and Argentina, resorted to private financing and concessions to private investors to build arterial roads. The driving forces were the rising traffic occasioned by motor transportation, and the difficulty governments were having to self-finance road construction or major bridge projects. In toll financing, the private sector is given a concession to construct and to operate arterial, or urban roads for a specified period.

Toll road concession typically requires a regulator to carry out monitoring and regulation after the road is built, to ensure that all parties comply with their contractual commitments. First generation road concessions experienced several problems, hence contract renegotiation also became essential for harmonious relationships. Historically, road authorities are typically irresponsible for:

- private sector participation in urban and or arterial road development by contracting out.
- planning and management of selected roads.
- the entire road network, or
- through donor financing for small infrastructure projects.

Modern private financing of roads was introduced in the UK in 1996 when the Department of Transport packaged parts of the UK's motorway network into several bundles and invited bids from the private sector for these packages to undertake the responsibility of the full road maintenance.[27]

In a second model, the road agency contracts out the entire network of roads and bridges and relieves itself of responsibility for maintenance. A third model typically involves donor finance support to construct and maintain arterial or urban roads. The government's Road agency becomes the contracting party and a road concessioning and regulatory agency monitors the ongoing performance of the parties to the contract. Some of the key factors that determine the structure of the financing are the average daily traffic volumes (arterial roads in Jamaica typically have ten thousand vehicles per day); rate of growth; government support, and level of grant financing, or guarantee. The country and the concession environment are also important. Demand is the crucial factor, and the private sector typically requires a government to guarantee payment should demand not meet an agreed contract level. Some road users also may not pay high toll rates just to reduce travel time and vehicle operating cost.

Toll Road Concessioning in Jamaica and Highway 2000

The island is divided by a central east to west mountain range, the highest section of which is in the east, tapering off to more level country in the west. As a result, the configuration of the system of main roads consisted originally of a belt line, running around the island, the greater portion being along the seacoast with loop lines on the plains of St Andrew, St Catherine, and St Elizabeth, and with three cross sections from south to north: one by way of Stony Hill, from Kingston to Annotto Bay; the second by way of Mount Rosser to the north coast, and the third from Savanna-la-Mar to Montego Bay. Three road networks cross a central range of hills at an elevation of about 1,350 feet, 1,800 feet, and 1,000 feet, respectively: Mandeville to the St Elizabeth plains; Stony Hill to St Mary via Junction, and Mount Rosser to St Ann. The original main road system passed through all the main ports and towns on the island. Besides the main roads, there is a parochial road system of approximately forty-five hundred miles, suitable for vehicular traffic.

Highway 2000

Highway 2000 was introduced as a millennium milestone for the government, which was to be an ongoing road project and, when completed, would link Kingston, the capital city, to the two major tourist destinations in Jamaica: Montego Bay and Ocho Rios through various parishes. A new route was later added, from Bushy Park in St Catherine, taking a Linstead/Bog walk route to Mammee Bay, just outside Ocho Rios. In the first phase of the Highway 2000 project, the East-West Highway involved an international tender in 2001. It was the largest project of the English-speaking Caribbean countries and, on completion, was the largest infrastructure project in the history of Jamaica.

The first phase was built by Bouygues Travaux Publics (BTP) of France. The second phase was originally also to have been built by BTP but ended up with China Harbour Engineering Company Limited (CHEC) in 2011, from an unsolicited proposal. Long-term funding was provided by regional commercial banks, multinational finance institutions, and the China Development Bank (CDB). A total of US$1.3 billion was committed to the East-West Highway and the North- South Link. The East-West Highway was completed in 2006 and the North-South Link in March 2016.

The Highway 2000 project was initially designed as a modern multi-laned tolled motorway, covering approximately 230 km. It was expected to significantly improve road transportation on the island, in much the same way the railway did in Jamaica in the 1880s and provide major solutions to the country's winding and unsafe road transportation network.

The East-West Highway project was conceived as a public-private-partnership and implemented as build-finance-operate-transfer (BFOT) thirty-five-year concession scheme, between the government, represented by National Road Construction Company (NROCC) and Trans Jamaican Highway (a private company) which was awarded the project following an international competitive tender process. Steer Davis Greave, the traffic consultant, in its traffic forecast to guide the investment, based their initial analysis on the KMA with a population of seven hundred thousand, with traffic forecasted to grow at 7.1 per cent per annum 2010.

The Highway 2000 project was the brainchild of Kingsley Thomas, then the managing director of Development Bank of Jamaica (DBJ) in the early 1990s. Major objectives were to reduce travel time and the level of accidents. Travel from Kingston to Montego Bay, on the old route, could take up to three and a half hours for motor car transport, and much longer for trucks having to climb Mount Rosser in St Catherine at a crawling pace.

When Thomas presented his idea of a toll road to finance road expansion in Jamaica to Prime Minister Patterson, it was summarily dismissed as a pipe dream, and he was told to concentrate on the development of the railways. Thomas and I had difficulty convincing the Jamaican authorities that, given the terrain of Jamaica, the rail transport system would never be a competitive and viable alternative to road transportation. With the existing rail system, even using the lowest flatbed trailer, it was not possible to transport containers through most of the many tunnels and, with the steep terrain, involving several severe curves. It would require expensive tunnelling to make rail a viable competitor. Jamaica, however, has had a nostalgic romance with the railway, and its resuscitation keeps being put back on the table by successive governments. Can someone please kill the rail?

When the road project was put to others, including then Finance Minister Omar Davies, the response was even more dismissive. Thomas was not daunted, however and, based on the experiences of Malaysia with toll roads, he went about researching the subject, including carrying out some initial project development. The project came in for some brutal criticisms by popular *Gleane*r columnist Dawn Ritch who had been a fierce critic of the telecommunications privatisation in 1985–87. Ritch, in a column in the *Sunday Gleaner* also dismissed the viability of the project, stating that it was another example of taxpayers' money being thrown away by the PNP in exuberant over enthusiasm, and that the PNP was in a mad rush to use Highway 2000 to provide jobs for political purposes.[28] She further maintained that, in the end, it was the Jamaican taxpayers who would have to pick up the pieces and carry the cost, eventually. In the Saturday *Gleaner* of May 9, 2001, the project was also strongly criticised for lack of information by the Jamaica Institute of Architects who expressed grave concern about the project's lack of transparency.[29]

Continuing the Dream

By the time the project was ready to go to tender with the East-West Highway, DBJ had spent US$20 million on design and development, all of which was later repaid by Bouygues, the winning bidder. In the development process, Thomas also arranged meetings in Montego Bay for Prime Minister Patterson to meet with President Chirac of France. France had been a major player of Public Private Partnership in road development, and Chirac who advised Patterson that since Jamaica had no experience with toll road construction, the best way forward was phasing of the project into smaller tranches, as it had initially been designed as a single project, hence the phasing approach was born. The project encompassed two inter-connected, grade separated dual carriageways of four to six lanes. Thomas also followed the meeting of the president of France with a meeting with the prime minister of Spain and Prime Minister Patterson. At the time, Spain was the major investor in the hotel sector in Jamaica. The prime minister of Spain gave his wholehearted support to the project. With the encouragement from the two European leaders, Patterson's became confident in the viability of the project and was able to convince most members of Cabinet to support the project.

Patterson concluded that, if successfully implemented, it would be a major boost to the Jamaican economy. Accordingly, he became an ardent promoter of highway development to where he was nicknamed the 'Prime Minister of Roads.' Even the multinational financial institutions, such as the IDB and World Bank, dismissed the idea as being too big, too risky and too ambitious.

Although the initial project development work was done by the DBJ, it soon became apparent that a specialised and dedicated agency was required, resulting in creating the National Road Operating and Construction Company Limited (NROOC) in February 2002, with a small and highly qualified staff, and with Thomas as its chairman.

Some of the leading international consulting firms were, at one stage or other, engaged by Thomas in trying to find solutions to the myriad problems thrown up by the project.

The list of consulting firms involved in the design and development work are shown below:

- USB Warburg .... Financial
- CHAS Limited .... Financial
- PWC .... Accounting and Finance
- Dehring, Bunting, and Golding (local) .... Financial
- Allan & Overy, UK (international) .... Legal
- Vaccianna & Whittingham (local) .... Legal
- Steer Davis Gleave .... Economic and Traffic
- Jentech Consultants Limited (local) .... Engineering
- Halcrow UK (international) .... Engineering
- Dessau Soprin (international) .... Engineering
- Hue Lyew Chin Engineering Ltd (local) .... Engineering
- Environmental Solutions Limited .... Environmental impact
- EnviroPlanners Limited .... Environmental impact
- CL Environment Limited .... Environmental impact

The alignment of the project is shown in figure 17.2 below.

Figure 17.2: Highway 2000 Proposed Alignment

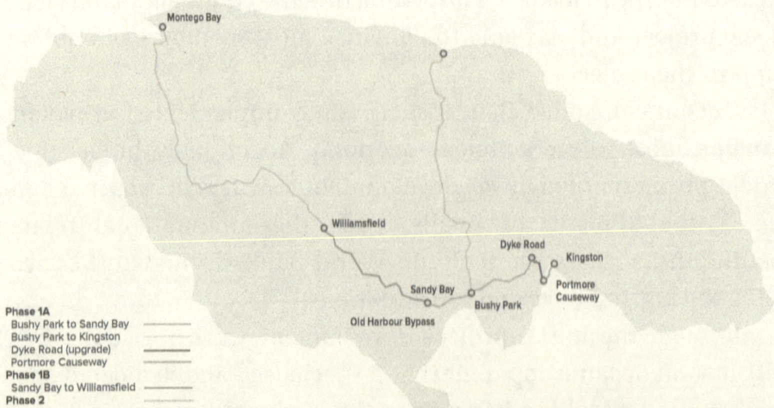

Source: Nekiesha Spenser, 'Financing Road Infrastructure,' Department of Government, UWI.

After ten months of intensive preparatory and design work, the project was ready to go to the market, inviting Expressions of Interest in October 1999. Phase 1a was to run from Kingston to Williamsfield, near Mandeville, and this provided for the construction of a tolled six lane bridge across the Portmore Causeway and improvements to Dyke Road. Phase 11 was to run from Williamsfield to Montego Bay, and from Bushy Park in St Catherine to Ocho Rios in St Ann. This network was designed to connect Kingston to Ocho Rios and then on to Montego Bay.

One of the overseas consultants, Dessau-Soprin's initial project cost was estimated at US$766.87 million, as shown in table 17.3 below. This was later revised up to a project cost of US$850 million. The occurrence of new issues and challenges meant that there had to be constant revision to project cost. With the route, the Bushy Park/Ocho Rios leg, a Linseed/Bog walk route to Ocho Rios was finally approved.

Table 17.3: The Initial Estimated Cost of Highway 2000

Section	Construction cost US$	Maintenance	Overall
Phase 1 Kingston Bushy Park–Bushy Park to Mandeville	235 million	2.75 million	237.75 million
Mandeville–Montego Bay and Old Harbour–Ocho Rios	523 million	6.12 million	529.12 million
Total	758 million	8.87 million	766.87 million

Source: Dessau-Soprin

Developing and Delivering the Project

In moving towards the adoption of toll concessions for urban and arterial roads in Jamaica, several studies were carried out in the early 1990s to examine the options of public-private partnership (PPP) arrangements, as this arrangement facilitates increased participation of the private sector; the private sector takes a greater share of the risks involved in the project execution. The difference between PPP and privatisation proper is that privatisation typically involves transfer of ownership of an existing facility, whereas, with PPP, the facility is yet to be built or major investment is required to an existing facility. The various PPP structures examined were as follows:

- Build-Own-Operate-Transfer (BOOT),
- Built-Transfer-Operate (BTO),
- Build-Operate-Transfer (BOT),
- Build-own -Operate (BOO), and
- Design–Build-Operate-Maintain (DBOM)

Under BOOT arrangements, the private consortium takes responsibility for designing, financing, and building the facility. The private investor qualifies as the temporary owner and operates the facility via a long-term concession, charging user fees to cover the cost (plus return on investment) of its operation before transferring ownership to the government, at no cost at the end of the concession.

In the BTO arrangement, the private sector designs, finances, and constructs the facility on behalf of the government. When construction is completed, the title is transferred to government, but the private sector secures a concession to operate the facility for a specified number of years until the cost of the project is recovered.

The BOT arrangement is similar to BTO, except that the title for the project is not transferred to government until the private contractor operates the facility for a specified period, after which all operations are transferred to the government at no cost. This approach allows the government to lessen its capital cost while realising a project when it cannot meet its financial obligation.

For BOO, this arrangement is more focussed on private sector participation. The private sector provides financing required and manages the facility as the owner. When the project is completed, a transfer to government is not a requirement. It allows the private investor to take full advantage of the return on investment.

None of these structures was found suitable for the Jamaican situation and a variation of build-operate-transfer (BOT), that of build-finance-operate-transfer (BFOT) was finally considered and found more suitable for Jamaican conditions. The developer was to carry primary responsibility for completing the design, constructing the network, arranging the financing, maintaining the network on completion, and collecting the toll fees, with the Road Agency retaining legal ownership of the network on behalf of government and with the toll concessioning agency responsible for regulatory oversight of the concession contract. Initial design would be determined by the Road Agency with the final design carried out with the developer. The whole suite of Highway 2000 projects initially was assigned as one concession.

The recovery of the private sector's cost is provided from the toll charges, which individual motorists are required to pay when using the road. In the agreement which was arrived at with developers/investors, the project also provided for the waiving of corporate taxes for twelve years and import duties on construction material. The Highway 2000 Project was the centrepiece of a menu of government projects, intended to provide a synergistic platform and catalyst for economic growth, job creation, and sustained development. The road projects identified by the Ministry of Transport were different, including bridges and a menu of several routes for development.

The first phase of the highway construction was undertaken as a Public Private Partnership (PPP) project between the National Road Operating and Construction Company Limited (NROCC), a wholly owned government company and French owned company; Bouygues Travaux Publics (BTP), This first phase of the project was eventually undertaken under the BFOT scheme. BTP was expected to complete the finance, build, and operate and, at the end of the 35-year concession, transfer the road assets to NROCC.

The Bidding Process

The government decided on competitive tender once the project features were determined. From the competitive bidding, eleven firms were pre-qualified. The main features of the bidding process are shown below:

- October 1999: The invitation to pre-qualify was dispatched to sixty-seven companies that had previously expressed an interest in the project. Seventeen companies eventually submitted detailed responses.
- December 1999: A meeting of the Bid Evaluation Committee identified four respondents as very strong candidates with a proven track record; three others were identified as strong, but with a less extensive track record.
- March 2000: The seven pre-qualified bidders were invited to attend a pre-bid conference in Kingston.

- From the seven firms, the pre-qualified four were subsequently invited to submit proposals for the first phase of the of Highway 2000 construction. The four firms were Bouygues Travaux Publics (BTP) of France, Concesiones de Infraestructuras de Transporte SA (CINTRA) of Spain, Dragados Group also of Spain and LTA Construction Limited of South Africa.
- These firms were invited to attend a bidders' conference; one group did not attend and was therefore disqualified. Two groups, Dragados and LTA, subsequently merged to form a new consortium. This left two participants in the competition – Bouygues and Dragados/LTA consortium.
- June to August 2000: The Request for Proposal package was released in phases and included the RFP, Route Alignment, Draft Concession Agreement, and the Information Memorandum.
- February 15, 2001: The bids were formally opened. The bid date was originally set for December 15, 2001, but was extended to February 15, 2002, to accommodate bidders' requests.
- February 2001: Bid evaluation and consultation with final round bidders. A consensus was arrived at between the sponsor and the final round bidders that the project should be sub-divided into phases and that a 'Best and Final Offer' (BAFO) round should be initiated.
- This was followed by meetings with investors on the technical and financing request for proposals after the release of the RFPs stage.
- May 3, 2001: The BAFO round was launched with a revised Request for Proposal and Data Book.
- May 18, 2001: The BAFO submissions were opened. Both bidders experienced challenges in structuring their financial package and were invited to a meeting in London over March 6 and 9, 2001 where it was accepted that the project, as structured, was too large for the market to accommodate and, after further discussion, the decision was taken to further subdivide it into smaller packages.
- May–June 2001: The BAFO submissions were evaluated, and a detailed report was submitted to the National Contracts Commission for consideration with a recommendation of the BTP as the preferred bidder.

- June 1, 2001: The BTP of France was declared the preferred bidder by the Cabinet of Jamaica.
- June to November 2001: Negotiation commenced involving finalisation of the Concession Agreement and the relevant implementation and facilitation agreements.
- November 21, 2001: Signing of the Concession Agreement and other agreements took place.

In the BAFO request, it was stated that bids would be evaluated against specified criteria as follows:

1. Optimum design construction, operation, and maintenance costs (lowest net present value of the sum of the construction costs and operation and maintenance expenditure over the tenure of the concession).
2. Optimal distribution of risk between guarantor and concessionaire.
3. Maximisation of the guarantor's share of net cash flow after operation and maintenance expenses and debt servicing were deducted from project revenues.
4. Ability to complete the project successfully within budget and timetable and capability of developing and managing the highway business.
5. Minimisation of the guarantor's financial contribution to the project and
6. Achieving financial closure in the shortest time before the end of 2001.

Bouygues, as part of implementing the project, incorporated a local company, Trans-Jamaican-Highway Limited, as the special purpose vehicle to complete the thirty-five-year concession with NROCC. The following agreements were executed:

a. Concession Agreement,

b. Implementation Agreement,

c. Shareholder Agreement,

d. Procured Debt Instrument, and

e. Guarantee Agreement.

It took five months from the declaration of the BTP as the winning bidder to achieve financial and commercial closure. The BTP was subsequently joined by Autoroutes du Sud la France SA (ASF), a subsidiary of Vinci and Société de Promotion et de Participation pour la Cooperation Economique (Proparco). There was an equity subscription later from the International Finance Cooperation (IFC) and from Proparco. The lenders also entered into a direct agreement with Trans Jamaican Highway (TJH), as the project development company, and included terms facilitating 'step-in rights,' without recourse to the government. These agreements covered loans from bond holders and from commercial banks. The Toll Road Act, which was necessary to cement the transaction, was given express treatment by government and was enacted in 2002, after the bids had been received, but before financial closure, and took less than four weeks to go through Parliament and to obtain the governor general's assent.

During the various negotiations, different bidders had different priorities, and it was found difficult to find a common ground suitable to all. Most bidders wanted traffic guarantees, i.e., for the government to guarantee some minimum levels of traffic/or revenues. This was rejected as from the government's position, the investor had to bear the demand risk. Eventually, both parties to the concession agreed to jointly post a letter of credit: Concessionaire US$15 million and NROCC US$10 million, to cover revenue shortfalls and cost overruns during construction. The levels were subsequently reduced when the BTP was designated the preferred bidder to US$6.75 and US$4.5 million, respectively. NROCC ultimately paid US$40.5 million for the additional feeder and take-off roads, realigning the Portmore Causeway pedestrian bridge, and relocation of the Spanish Town Toll Plaza.

The project required a competing road to be an alternate toll-free road. It was agreed that, if improvements were made to the competing road which negatively impacted the highway traffic volumes, then the operator was entitled to some compensation. It was also agreed that if the concessionaire's rate of return exceeded 16 per cent, then NROCC may participate in a share of the profits.

Final Structure of the Project and the First Phase Financing

The construction of the highway started in July 2002 and was eventually subdivided into phases as follows:

- Phase 1a, Kingston to Sandy Bay, including the Portmore Causeway and Dyke Road, (2006)
- Phase 1b, Sandy Bay, Clarendon to Williamsfield near to Mandeville (segment terminating at May Pen completed in 2012.
- 1c May Pen to Williamsfield (under construction scheduled for completion 2023).
- Phase 2a, Bushy Park, St Catherine to Ocho Rios, adjusted to Caymanas to Ocho Rios.
  a. Mount Rosser Bypass to Moneaque (completed 2014)
  b. Caymanas to Linstead (completed 2016)
  c. Moneaque to Ocho Rios (completed 2016.
  d. Phase 2b, Williamsfield to Montego Bay.

Figure 17.3: The New Highway Network North South Ocho Rios to Caymanas and East West Caymanas to Mandeville and on to Montego Bay

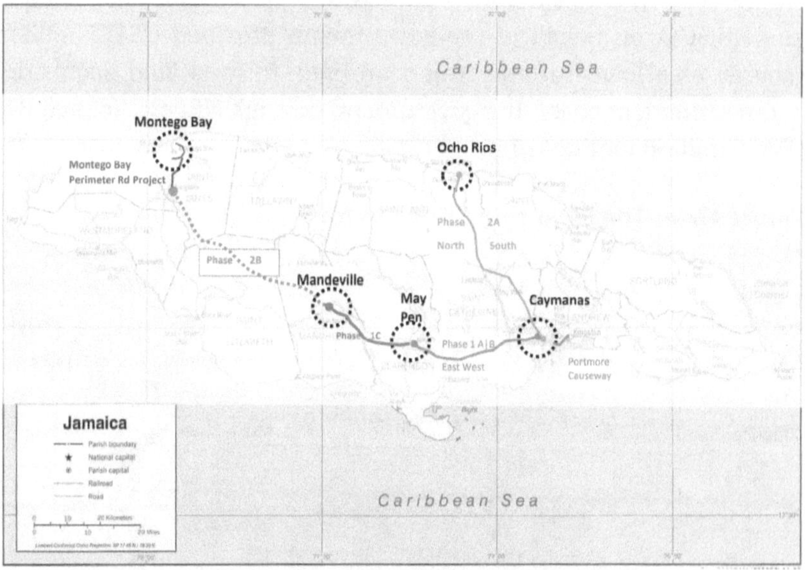

Source: Nicholson, George, (June 2022), 'Jamaica Highway PPP Experience' Presentation at Caribbean Development Bank and JDB Seminar in Kingston

Although it was decided that there should be further subdivision of the project into two broad phases, it was also decided that the winner of Phase 1 would be given the right of first refusal to carry out Phase 2. Hence, Bouygues of France was given this right. Subsequently, there were variation in the phasing. The overall design route embraced 233 km and is shown in figure 17.3, with the route running North South across the island to Ocho Rois from Spanish Town.

Financing Arrangement for Phase 1

Figure 17.4 shows the financing arrangement for Phase 1. The government and the developer agreed to jointly finance Phase 1 with the BTP responsible for providing financing for 69 per cent (US$225 million) and government's 31 per cent (US$27 million). The government went the route of infrastructure bonds and other debt, while the BTP took the route of financing through equity (US$27 million), as well as infrastructure bonds (US$198 million). Operation and maintenance cost were estimated to amount to 20 per cent of toll revenues.

The BTP successfully settled a US$130 million loan for Phase 1, which was financed by Royal Bank of Trinidad and Tobago (RBTT). This loan was provided as a bond and was to be repaid through toll fees. The NROCC, on behalf of the government, provided US$75 million, secured as a loan from an American bank to fund land acquisition and resettlement costs. The government, through NROCC, loaned BTP US$72 million for Phase 1a.

Figure 17.4: The Financing Structure for Phase 1

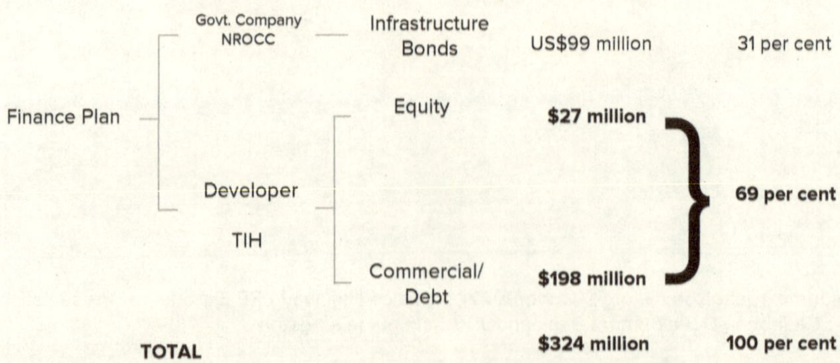

Source: NROCC/ Caribbean Development Bank

The subscribers were shown in the table 17.4 below. When the J$3.1 billion convertible bond at 4.5 per cent interest was floated on the Jamaican market, it was oversubscribed, with J$3.552 billion being raised, demonstrating that the local financial market had confidence in the project.

Table 17.4: Subscriber to the Local Convertible Bond Issue

Participants	Amount of Subscription Taken Up
National Insurance Fund	900.0
Life of Jamaica Limited	600.0
WIYCO (NCB Pension Fund)	700.0
Guardian Life	400.0
First Life	200.0
BNS	500.0
Total	3.1 billion

Source: *Sunday Gleaner* (May 5, 2002).

However, there was strong criticism by *Gleaner* columnist Dawn Ritch regarding the participation of the National Pension Fund in what she considered a very risky investment.

Five years after the thirty-five-year concession, the high financing cost, coupled with lower than forecast traffic level severely pressured the concessionaire and on the NROCC. This led the NROCC to borrow an additional US$75 million from Wachovia Bank in 2004, guaranteed by the government, to meet interest payments to its inflation-linked bondholder, and to write down earlier debt. A US$260 million loan was also secured from the Venezuelan government in July 2006. This loan was used to repay debt on the highway up to that date.

With the successful progress of the project NROCC, the TJH and the government made another pitch to the IDB and other institutional and financial organisations for refinancing of the commercial debts as new financing for completion of Phase 1. This time the project received a more receptive hearing; application for financing which was submitted was successfully concluded in February 2011. This financing package was considered for an eighteen-year limited recourse loan to the TJH from a syndicate of multilateral agencies led by the IDB and including the Europe Investment Bank (EIB) the IFC and Proparco (AFD). The total financing amounted to US$205.5 million: IFC 28.3 per cent including debt and equity; Europe Investment Bank 26.1 per cent debt only; IDB 26.1 per cent debt only; Proparco (AFD) 19.5 per cent debt and equity. Overall, the total financing was US$198.5 million debt and US$7 million equity. The proceeds were used to refinance the RBTT bond issues in 2001, as well as to refinance the expansion of the project towards May Pen, with construction of an additional 10 km four-lane segment.

Securitisation

Securitisation was necessary to address the commercial risks associated with the project. Parties involved in the securitisation arrangement and their roles are set out below:

- Originator – owner and 'generator' of the assets to be securitised. The originator in this case would be TJH, which has the entitlement to the asset, i.e., toll revenue.
- Servicer – services the assets to be securitised. In this case, where tolls are securitised, the servicer will collect and administer toll collection. For Highway 2000, this role is currently being done by Jamaica Infrastructure Operators (JIO).
- Investors – providers of the loan facility. Examples of investors in the securitisation market are private placement participants, pension funds, banks, mutual funds, hedge funds, insurance companies, central banks, international financial institutions, and corporates. The project contemplated that Venezuela's state development bank would have been the investor by providing US$80M of loan financing, although the investment could later be syndicated.
- Cash Administrator – provides banking and cash administration services for the investor.
- Table 17.5 below set out the distribution of risk allocation.

Table 17.5: Risk Allocation on the East-West Highway

	NROCC	Bouygues and consortium
Traffic		x
Revenue		x
Design and construction		Foreseeable
Access to lands	x	
Utility relocation	x	
Political risk	x	
Change of law	x	
Subordinated capital	x	
Standby equity	x	
Termination risks – guarantor	x	
Termination risk-developer	x	
Termination risk – no fault	x	
Outline design risk	x	

Source NROCC

Figure 17.5: Securitisation Funds Flow Diagram

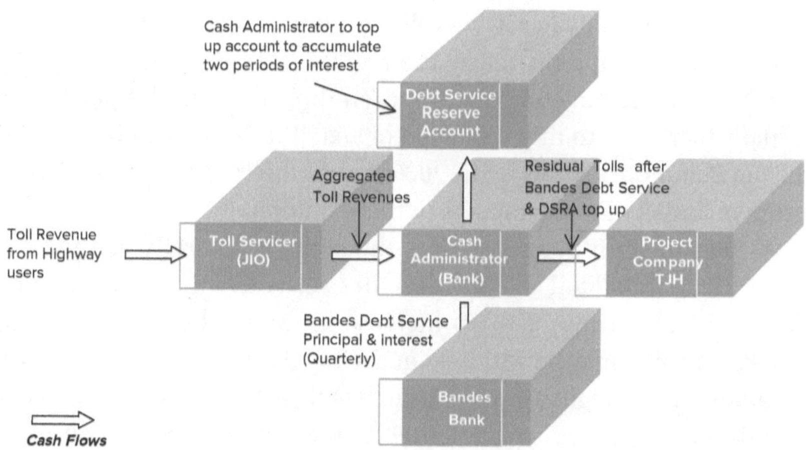

Source: Report Financing Proposal for Highway 2000 to the Republic of Venezuela

The securitisation fund flow is shown in figure 17.5. Toll revenues from users of the highway form the basis of the cash flows. The JHJ will receive the residual income after debt service and project costs.

Concession Agreement

The Concession Agreement, which was executed on November 21, 2001, between the NROCC and the TJH for a thirty-five-year term related only to Phase 1. Under the terms of the Concession Agreement, Trans Jamaican Highway Limited, the project company, had an incentive to undertake Phase 1B of the project (otherwise equity return would be capped at 8 per cent) with a right of first refusal to undertake Phase 2.

There was a proposed cap to the toll level in Jamaican dollars (in January 2001 values) of J$3.16/km for the Kingston-Williamsfield leg and J$45.1 for the Portmore Causeway. The tolls were indexed to US CPI and foreign exchange index. The project's tolling activity was supported by a regulatory framework (the 'regulation') which provided the power to the concessionaire to set tolls to maximise its revenues, subject to consultation with the guarantor. In the development stage of the project, the government engaged the services of Steer Davies Gleave to recommend parameters for the tolling regime. In view of the fact that the concession agreement required the concessionaire to take revenue or demand risk, the tolling regime accorded them significant flexibility in setting tolls, given that such levels were within a maximum (cap) limit set by the regulator. Traffic levels on the toll road on completion commenced at ten thousand vehicles per day but rapidly increased to fifty thousand or sixty thousand with the opening of the Portmore Causeway in 2006. Later, the traffic level moderated from macro-economic impacts in the economy.

As part of tariff determination, the concessionaire is permitted to set optimal initial toll levels within these caps and those optimal tolls. The regulator's consent to an increase in the level of tolls above the indexed ceiling may be withheld at the regulator's absolute discretion. In addition, the regulator may disallow any increases if such increases are deemed to be either attributable to an undue application of the toll indexation formula, discriminatory, or manifestly unreasonable, having regard to the efficiency and quality of service provided.

Land Acquisition

The concession agreement assigned responsibility to the guarantor to make available to the developer on a timely basis, all required land along the highway corridor to facilitate construction activity. The NROCC took all the action to ensure that all relevant land was acquired and turned over to the developer in conformance with the concession agreement.

Operation and Maintenance Agreement

A separate company, Jamaican Infrastructure Operator (JIO), was incorporated as the operator in September 2002, with the ASF and the BTP owning 51 per cent and 49 per cent, respectively. The construction contract was a lump sum contract for five years, under which the operator was to provide all services necessary for the project company to comply with its obligations related to the operation and maintenance and toll collection. The operator was required to perform its obligations under ISO 9000–2000 standards and good engineering and design practices.

Construction Contract

The BTP, through its local subsidiary, TJH, was the contractor for Phase 1 of Highway 2000, entering a Design and Construction contract on February 23, 2002. The contractor completed the design and carrying out construction of the road network identified in the Concession Agreement and obtained all necessary consents and permits. The contract was on a lump sum, turnkey, and fixed-term basis. Liquidated damages in the amount of US$20,000 per day applied against failure to complete any section of the highway (limited to 5 per cent of the contract price for that section). The contractor provided to the TJH a performance bond amounting to 8 per cent of the contract price.

Environmental Requirements

The developers were required to meet environmental standards prescribed by Jamaica's National Environmental Protection Agency (NEPA). The permitting process in Jamaica relies on environmental impact assessment (EIA) studies. The sponsors commissioned a Strategic Environmental Assessment (SEA) of the project to ensure support for the project by the country's environmental authorities.

The East-West Highway eventually involved 56.5 kilometre of four to six-lane grade separated tolled highways passing through several built-up areas, causing acquisition of 117 parcels of land (104 government-owned and 13 private) some forty-one residents were resettled (twelve small farmers, twenty-three squatters, and six tenanted individuals).

The contractor was also required to replant four kilometres of mangroves destroyed along the Portmore Causeway bridge. The community of informal small boat operators and fish sellers around Portmore, who had been squatting on land, also were relocated to more suitable environs. A total of eighty-one fishermen and twenty-three vendors were relocated and provided with boating, storage, vending, and other facilities at a permanent fishing complex, completed in 2009. Housing was also constructed for sixteen vulnerable residents who were squatting on the causeway beach and the new houses were handed over in 2011.

Conclusion of Phase 1a

Without the imagination and financial expertise of Kingsley Thomas and the dedicated, purposeful, skilled, and dogged leadership of Prime Minister Patterson, this project would not have got off the ground and proceed to completion. The hallmark of the project was meticulous preparation. When Bouygues's project manager was asked why the company was participating in the project in a country with no experience in toll road construction and operation, his response was because of the quality of the preparatory work that they had seen, Telephone interview with Kingsley Thomas.

Although traffic levels have fluctuated since project completion, the project demonstrated that citizens in small developing countries were prepared to pay for good highways. On completion of East West Highway by Bouygues, in 2006 traffic soared to fifty thousand or sixty thousand per day.

An important lesson for developing countries embarking on forms of infrastructure project development and implementation, without previous experience in the field, is that governments need to listen to the developer and investor and financial market and be prepared to adjust the original design to accommodate financial and investor market needs. The project was initially packaged as a 230 kilometre highway, but both bidders and financiers were of the view that, for a small developing country with no previous experience, that initial size was too much to accommodate in one step; hence, the initial project was not only phased, but the phasing was also constantly adjusted to accommodate new developments. In undertaking a project of this nature, governments should be mindful of limitations to their institutional endowment and capacity.

The North-South Link

With Phase 1 successfully completed by Bouygues, the government continued with Phase 2, the North-South link with the objective of bypassing Mount Rosser, the Bog Walk Gorge and Fern Gully, three points of severe restrictions on the road transport route to Ocho Rios. In March 2006, Cabinet gave the green light to the NROCC to proceed with the preparatory work. Successive governments since independence have all asked about finding a solution to improving traffic over this mountainous part of Jamaica. Major alignment studies were, in fact, carried out as far back as 1966.

The Bouygues concession contract had provided the TJH first right to pursue the construction of the North-South Link and, as a result, construction actually commenced July 15, 2007. At this point, major geological problems were encountered involving weak and unstable soil conditions not previously detected, resulting in a dispute between Bouygues and the government over which party was at fault. With the development of the dispute and no resolution, the project was suspended in July 2011. Following the suspension, various solutions were considered, but none was found acceptable to both parties. It became clear to the government that the conventional PPP model, involving the BOOT approach would not be commercially viable because of the escalation in the capital costs and the relatively low traffic volumes associated with this leg of the project to Ocho Rios.

During this period, China Harbour Engineering Company (CHEC) was on the final stage of another project in Jamaica, that of the Palisadoes Shoreline Protection and Rehabilitation and saw the development of the North-South Link as an opportunity worth pursuing. The CHEC had no experience in PPP road projects, but the company had previous experience in dealing with similar geotechnical problems and submitted an unsolicited bid to carry on the project to completion.

Having carried out its own geotechnical and traffic studies, the CHEC was of the view that the traffic volumes would be at higher levels than those projected by Steer Davies and that the geotechnical problem could be resolved. After several meetings with various government parties, the CHEC agreed on a new financing structure, not involving a PPP arrangement, but following the more conventional financing arrangement to complete the Mount Rosser bypass section of the project. A contract was duly signed on June 21, 2012, for the North-South Link to cover sixty-six kilometres of route miles and for the construction period to last three years, at a price of US$610 million and, in addition, the CHEC agreed to reimburse the US$120 million the government had spent on the Mount Rosser bypass up to then through a long-term instrument.

In the negotiations leading up to contract signing, the Caribbean Development Bank (CDB) agreed to provide long-term financing but explored the avenue of a government of Jamaica guarantee for their long-term loan, at which point the government refused to entertain sovereign guarantee to the project. The general conclusion by both parties was that toll revenue, especially in the earlier years, would not meet the financing cost of the project and ensure its financial viability. The CHEC requested that the government provide them with a certain number of adjacent lands over and above the requirement for the highway; such lands were to be used in future for commercial exploitation by the CHEC, in much the same way that lands were provided to the private investor during the Montego Bay phase of the railway project in the latter part of the nineteenth century. In the end, twelve hundred acres of government land along the highway route was provided to the CHEC but was subject to the government approving the various development projects and, if such lands were not developed within the specified timeframe, the undeveloped land would be returned. Part of the CHEC's commercial development plans called for the construction of some twenty-four hundred new hotel and residential rooms in St Ann.

The financing arrangement for the project, which was agreed with CDB was largely handled by CHEC and is shown below in figure 17.6. The agreement also specified that at no time must the number of Chinese workers exceed the number of Jamaicans. At the height of the construction, twelve hundred Jamaicans were employed and some seven hundred to nine hundred Chinese.

Figure 17.6: The Financing Structure of North-South Link

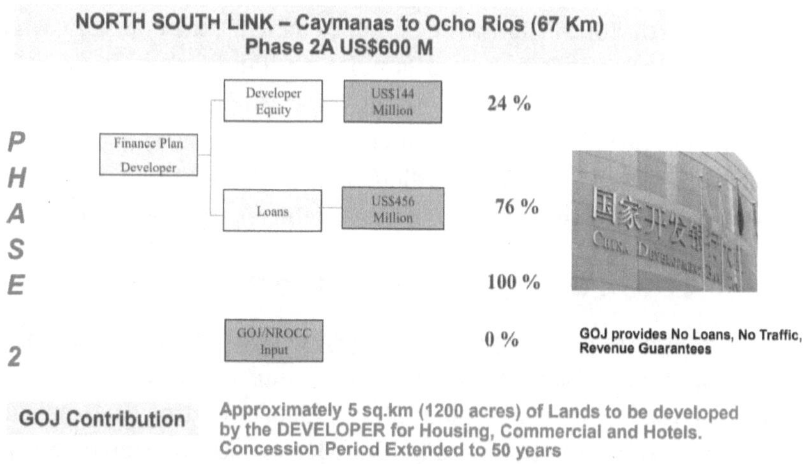

Enter the Contractor General

The procurement had proceeded relatively smoothly, only for the Contractor General (CG) to serve notice of his objection to the procurement, on the basis that the CHEC offer was unsolicited bid and *ultra vires*, regarding Jamaica's public procurement policy and that the proposal also was not financially viable. Following discussions with the Office of the Contractor General (OCG), the NROCC, the National Contracts Commission (NCC), the National Works Agency (NWA), and the government's legal officers, the NROCC allayed the concerns of the CG, including the allegation of possibility of corruption associated with sole sourcing, so the CG withdrew the objection; however, this delayed the project start for another six months.

As if the CG's intervention was not enough, a second major problem of concern was identified, this time from the National Environmental Protection Agency (NEPA). Besides major engineering concerns, the environmental issues presented new challenges. The contractor had to use a special mesh to prevent rubble and stones from falling off the hillside and onto the roadway. There was the need for forty-foot piles to be constructed to retain sections of the slope on Mount Rosser and stabilise the area.

Some 450 residents had to be relocated, along with the removal of 150 structures. These residents had to be compensated by the NROCC, over and above the payment of the land needed for the project. In excess of over fifteen million metres of material had to be moved, involving 1.5 million truck loads. Well into the project, NEPA issued a warning to the Jamaica North-South Highway Company (JNSHC), the company which the CHEC had incorporated in Jamaica to handle the construction, regarding run off and drainage into the sea at Mammee Bay. Some seven dams had to be constructed to remedy the problem. A major challenge was that the steep 8 per cent gradient section encountered over Mount Rosser posed challenges for some heavy vehicles traversing the route.

Benefits Expected from Highway 2000

On completion, the new road system was expected to bring significant benefits, such as reduced travel time, increased productivity to commercial users, and reduction of vehicle operating costs because of the provision of better road surface. It was also expected to serve as a catalyst for economic development along the route and the main tourist areas bordering the route. As well, the highway was expected to open the central and southern regions of the country to additional industrial and commercial activities, including expansion of tourism, agriculture and information technology.[30]

Phases 1 and 2 of the project were completed over seventeen years, 1999 to 2016, with the timeline for Phase 1 extending from 1999 to 2007 and Phase 2 from 2007 to 2016. The project brought in US$825 million of foreign direct investment (FDI) and substantially improved the image of Jamaica as a destination for implementing large construction projects. The project also spurred new economic activities in the KMA, and satellite towns like Old Harbour, May Pen and Ocho Rios, which are now the fastest growing urban centres in Jamaica. With these developments, there is the likelihood of reverse urbanisation, a shift of the population growth from urban areas like the Kingston Metropolitan Area (KMA) and Portmore to rural parishes, relieving the pressure on the KMA, Portmore, and Spanish Town.

Overall construction cost of both East-West and North-South Links is shown in table 17.6 below.

Table 17.6: Combined Construction Cost of the North-South and East-West Links

	Phase 1 Bouygues US$ million	Phase 2 CHEC	Indirect cost US$ million	Total Project cost US$ million
GOJ Equity in TJH	99.0	-		99.0
Admin interest & subsidy			183.7	163.7
Mt. Rosser bypass	-	120.0	-	120.0
Guarantors charge			40.5	40.5
Land purchase	-		43.6	
Total GOJ investment	99.0	120.0	267.8	486.8
Bouygues investor equity	27.0			27.0
CHEC investor equity	144.0			144.0
Project debt	198.0	456.0	-	654.0
Total private investment	225.0	600.0	-	825.0
Total Capital Cost	324.0	720.0	267.0	1,311.8

Source: B.S. Samuel and Albert Gillings, 'Jamaica Highway 2000 Case Study.'

NROCC financing amounts to a long-term bond at 3 per cent per annum over the first twenty years and 6 per cent per annum over the next thirty years, with cash payment forecasted to begin in 2032.

The Highway 2000 development will alter the hierarchy of town structures in Jamaica, in much the same way that the railway changed the hierarchy of town structures over the period 1850–1900. The project is not only expected to boost tourism but also to allow Kingston and Norman Manley International Airport to benefit more from Jamaica's tourist traffic. This is already showing up in the airport's traffic reports.

Although the traffic on the North-South Link since 2016 is below the level of being financially self-sustainable, the volumes have more than doubled in six years. The traffic volumes have progressively increased since 2016 up to early 2022, as shown in figure 17.7.

Figure 17.7: North-South Link Traffic Growth 2016 to 2022

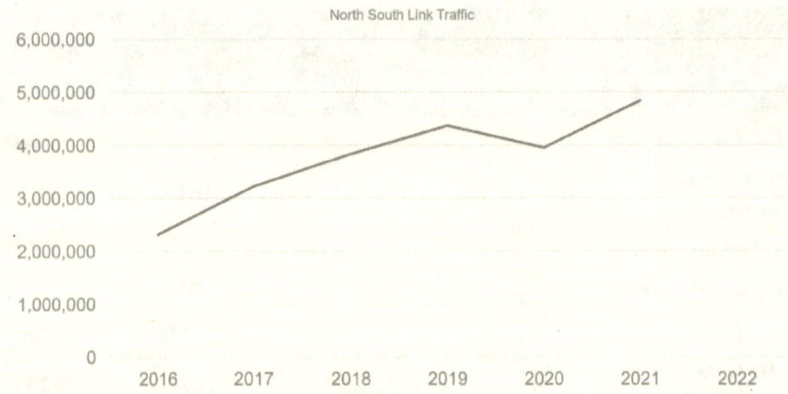

Source: Nicholson, George, (June 2022), 'Jamaica Highway PPP Experience' Presentation at Caribbean Development Bank and JDB Seminar in Kingston

The CHEC has stated that they are not in it for the short term; ten tears and they expect to see their returns on the project over the longer term. It is the CHEC view that traffic growth over the fifty-year period of the concession will make this project a financial success. The Chinese were given a fifty-year concession and as an incentive were provided with a substantial acres of land along or near the highway route.[31] The construction of the North West Highway was expected the cost almost double the East West Link, with only 20 per cent of the traffic. The position taken by the Chinese shows the different time horizon and commercial expectations, as most Western investments would expect to see significant return within the first ten years.

With the completion of the North-South Link, the NROCC and the TJH reached an agreement in 2019 to facilitate the exit of shareholders (Bouygues, Vinci and the MDBs) from the TJH. The company TJH was purchased by the NROCC using bridge loan, and the debt holders were repaid. The TJH, through an IPO, was then listed on the Jamaica Stock Exchange and the proceeds used to repay the bridge loan. The TJH simultaneously issued a bond to finance the highway debt.

Highway Projects involving CHEC in Jamaica

The government is implementing several other projects to complete the highway network in Jamaica. Most of these projects are being constructed by the CHEC and they cover the Kingston to St Thomas, on to Port Antonio leg, which began in 2022 and the May Pen to Mandeville leg. Most of the new highways are being developed as grade separated, dual multi-lane carriageways with four to six lanes. Table 17.7 sets out the list of highway improvement projects being executed, or already executed by CHEC. All these projects came about after 2000 and have transformed long distance travelling in Jamaica.

Table 17.7: Road Construction in Jamaica with CHEC involvement.

Road link	US$
North South Highway ending at Mammee Bay	730.0
Southeast	518.0
Montego Bay Bypass	220.0
May Pen/ Mandeville	188.0
Mandela Highway	64.0
Constant Spring widening Dualization	19.4
Barbican widening dualization	4.4
Total	**US$1,743.8**

The total amounted to just under US$1.74 billion. They include the Montego Bay Perimeter Road Project, primarily being designed as an alternate route to reduce traffic congestion in the city centre, as well as to provide additional capacity for the road network. It is being designed to include a bypass of Long Hill Road from Reading to Montpellier. Planned financing of this project is from the Treasury and construction is scheduled to start in financial year 2022/2023, retaining the CHEC as the contractor and seeking a concessionaire to operate the Montego Bay Perimeter Road on completion. The Ministry of Finance expects to float infrastructure bonds to secure financing to be repaid by toll charges.

The government is also planning completion of the North Coast Highway, a distance of the seventy-two kilometres and will involve mainly widening of the existing highway from Mammee Bay to Sea Castles, Montego Bay, with a bypass around Runaway Bay and Discovery

Bay. The project is being divided into two components: Phase 1 (brown field) segment, from Sea Castles to Mammee Bay to involve widening the road to four lanes, including auxiliary lanes and over pass, where necessary, a distance of fifty-nine kilometre, estimated at US$600 million; Phase 2, the Runaway Bay/Discovery Bay Bypass, involving construction of four lanes of twenty-three kilometre, with separated limited access, estimated to cost US$240 million.

Figure 17.8 below outlines the route structure. As there is no alternative route covering most of this segment of the highway, payment of toll fees by users will not be possible. Contracts have also been awarded for the Kingston to Morant Bay highway; however, like the Ocho Rios to Montego Bay leg, this project is not being developed as PPP, and the construction contract has been awarded to the CHEC.

Figure 17.8: Proposed Road Improvement: North Coast Highway Ocho Rio to Montego Bay

Source: Nicholson, George, (June 2022), 'Jamaica Highway PPP Experience' Presentation at Caribbean Development Bank and JDB Seminar in Kingston

The government of Jamaica took a decision to use alternative financing schemes for road infrastructure, because of the limited budgetary resources and the financial needs of the road sector. The irony of it all is that, when the project was finally completed, it was during the JLP administration of Prime Minister Holness. The JLP government, under Seaga, had strongly opposed the project but, on its opening, named the North-South Link the Seaga Highway. Interestingly, this was one of the first toll road construction and operation projects carried out by the CHEC. Since then, in July 2016, the CHEC entered into an agreement with the government for a US$64 million project to rehabilitate and widen the Mandela Highway, linking Kingston with Spanish Town via Ferry. This project has now been completed.

In October 2016, the government also signed another major road contract for US$384 million involving the construction of forty-three kilometre of roadway forming the Southern Coastal Highway Improvement Project, not tolled but financed by China Exim Bank. The reason for resorting to private sector financing, for what traditionally has been financed by the public sector through taxes and bilateral and multilateral financing, is the inability of the government to take on the direct financing of the large projects by the Treasury. Funds borrowed for the road projects were treated as off-budget when they were borrowed, but eventually the debt must be serviced, at which point they appear in the national budget as deferred financing.

Although resources from these schemes have assisted the government in increasing the delivery of road infrastructure, the implications for the stock of the government debt arises. According to an analysis by Nekiesha Spencer, deferred financing has increased the debt stock of the government of Jamaica.[32] The Minister of Finance, in the 2002 budget debate, for example, stated that in four years, the government disbursed J$8 billion through deferred financing, J$5 billion of which was included in the debt stock. Ministry Paper No. 20 further reported on March 31, 2004, that the debt stock had increased by J$3.83 billion because of deferred financing-related obligations; a total amount of J$1,577.87 million had been paid out in principal and J$ 1,100.46 million in interest, referring to Highway 2000 as being one of the major contributors.[33]

According to Ken Chaplin, Jamaicans will eventually service the debt owed if Trans Jamaican Highway cannot pay back its commercial loans.[34] Bouygues was given a thirty-five-year concession to charge tolls to the users of the highway. Portmore residents have, from time to time, complained about the high toll charges. However, Bouygues needs not only to recover its cost but must also make a return on its investment.

The East-West Link was constructed and implemented under conventional PPP arrangement, underwent the traditional procurement procedure involving an international competitive tender, and was financed by a mixture of commercial and international development banking funds. This was not so for the North-South Link, as this section was not commercially fundable; as a result, it required the Chinese government's financial support, in addition to Caribbean Development Bank financing, resulting in implications for the debt stock.

In more recent road construction projects, government has resorted to borrowing from the bilateral and international financial institutions, such as the Chinese Development Bank and China Exim Bank.

Rail Development as an Alternative

Recently there have been repeated government announcements of a Chinese interest. However, up to 2020, no project had matured. More recently, attempts have been made by the government to reactivate passenger transportation on the railway between Kingston, Spanish Town, and Old Harbour, and Spanish Town and Linstead, as well as a line linking Montego Bay to the interior, aimed at attracting tourists' traffic to the Appleton Estate. If these rail links are restored, there would be the question as to their commercial viability over the long term, especially in an environment of increased competition. Even when the railway had a monopoly on traffic during the Second World War, it made a loss. Almost all the studies Commonwealth Secretariat Investment and Rehabilitation Plan (1991), Jentech Study (1990), J. A. Young Study (1987), and the Wilbur-Smith Study (1993), present a bleak prospect for public rail transport in Jamaica.

Notes

1. Public Relations Department, KSAC (September 1961).
2. E.C. Williams, 'Jamaica Public Service Company Ltd: A Short History of its Origin & Development, 1923–1978,' unpublished manuscript by a JPSC Officer, Kingston, 1978.
3. Fredrick D. Hammond, *Report on Transport Problems in Jamaica* (London: Crown Agents, 1923).
4. A. Fernley, *Report on Provision of Public Passenger Transport Services in the Corporate Area* (London: Crown Agents, 1923).
5. Herbert George DeLisser, 'Twentieth Century Jamaica,' *Times*, 1913.
6. Carol Mae Morrissey, 'Ol' Time Tram" and the Tramway Era, 1876 to 1948,' *Jamaica Journal* 16, no. 4 (1983): 12–21.
7. H. Holgate, 'An Electric Tramway in the British West Indies,' *Cassier's Magazine*, 1898.
8. C.E. Rooke, *Report on Transportation Problem in Jamaica*, Government of Jamaica, 1946.
9. *Fernley Report on Public Passenger Transport Services in the Corporate Area, 1938.*

10. Eric O. Bell, Ministry Paper No. 12, 'Acquisition of Shares of Jamaica Omnibus Services Limited,' Ministry of Public Utilities and Transport, April 11, 1974.
11. Gerald E. Mills, 'Issues in Public Policy Administration in Commonwealth Caribbean,' *Social and Economic Studies* 23, no. 2. (1974).
12. Ministry Paper, No. 14, April 1984.
13. Nigel Harper, Fyzul Hassanali, Dennis Lewis, and Ruby Forsythe, A project presented to the Department of Government, UWI for the Diploma in Public Administration, 1969.
14. Eric O. Bell, Ministry Paper No. 12.
15. I joined the Ministry in 1976 as Transport Advisor and Special Advisor to Minister Eric Bell: Minister of Public Utilities and, in 1977, was made Chairman of JOS, serving until 1980. At the time of JOS nationalisation, the managing director of JOS J. Clymo, a White Englishman. He was eventually replaced by Allen Moore, a Jamaican. I was also made chairman of the Montego Bay Municipal Bus Company, which I was asked by Michael Manley to establish in 1976 within six weeks in anticipation of the announcement of the 1966 general elections which was to be made at Sam Sharpe Square in Montego Bay, and chairman of National Vehicle Corporation, the state-owned bus assembly plant, with Noel Grey as the first managing director of National Vehicle Corporation Limited and with Fitz McClymont as the first managing director of Montego Bay Municipal Bus Company Limited. This was all a part of transferring power from the creole White and upper-class Brown establishment to the new professional Black Jamaicans: from the 'great house to the cane field,' as Professor Rex Nettleford often put it.
16. Cezley Sampson, 'Paratransit Transport in Jamaica,' paper presented on Paratransit Transport Workshop at the Abbey Raymond, Paris, 1977.
17. Economic Production Council submission, 'Jamaica Omnibus Services Limited: Improvement of Fleet and Depot Facilities,' Ministry of Finance, No. 51, 1978.
18. Robert Cervero, 'Informal Transport in Developing Countries,' United Nations Centre for Human Settlements (HABITAT), Nairobi, 2000.
19. Economic Production Council submission, 'Jamaica Omnibus Services Limited: Improvement of Fleet and Depot Facilities.'
20. Cezley Sampson, Urban Transport Analysis and Policy Options: Kingston Metropolitan Region (Kingston: Metropolitan Transport Holdings Limited, 1997).
21. Robert Cervero, 'Informal Transport in Developing Countries.'
22. Ann Norton, Shanties and Skyscrapers: Growth of and Structure of Kingston (Kingston: Institute of Social and Economic Studies, 1978).
23. Edward Long, 'A History of Jamaca: General Survey of the Ancient and Modern Sate of the Island', Vol. 1–111 (1774), London, Lowndes in Fleet Street.

24. G. Collins, 'Actual and Potential Land Use in the Parish of St Catherine, Jamaica' (PhD Dissertation, Leeds University, 1965).
25. Patrick Bryan, *The Jamaican People 1880–1902: Class and Social Control* (Basingstoke and London: Macmillan, 1991).
26. Spencer Nekeisha, 'Road Financing Road Infrastructure in Jamaica,' Department of Economics, Mona, UWI, 2013.
27. Antonio Estache, Manual Romero, and John Strong, 'Toll Roads,' in *Privatization and Regulation of Transport Infrastructure: Guidelines for Policymakers and Regulators*, ed. Antonio Estache and Gines de Rus (Washington, DC, World Bank, 2000).
28. *Sunday Gleaner*, May 5, 2002.
29. *Saturday Gleaner*, May 9, 2001.
30. Aecom Consult Team, Synthesis for Public-Private Partnership Projects for Roads, Bridges & Tunnels from around the World – 1986–2004 (Washington DC: US Department of Transportation, 2005).
31. Ricardo D. Paredes, Privatization and Regulation: Challenges in Jamaica, Economic and Sector Development Series (Washington: IADB, 2003).
32. Dessau-Soprin International, 'Highway 2000 Project Preliminary Design Phase: Economic and Cost Benefit Analysis,' 2000.
33. Interview between Brian Samuel of the CDB and the manager of the CHEC in Jamaica.
34. Nekiesha Spencer, 'Financing Road Infrastructure,' Department of Government, UWI, 2006.
35. Ministry Paper No. 20, Government of Jamaica, 2002.
36. Ken Chaplin, 'Dark Side of Highway 2000 and Its Tolls,' *Jamaican Observer*, August 22, 2006.

Index

www.ingramcontent.com/pod-product-compliance
Lightning Source LLC
LaVergne TN
LVHW090252210926
848480LV00001B/4
* 9 7 8 9 7 6 8 2 8 6 8 7 1 *